Pershing's Crusaders

Pershing's Crusaders

THE AMERICAN

SOLDIER IN

WORLD WAR I

Richard S. Faulkner

 University Press of Kansas

© 2017 by the University Press of Kansas
All rights reserved

Published by the University Press of Kansas (Lawrence, Kansas 66045),
which was organized by the Kansas Board of Regents and is operated
and funded by Emporia State University, Fort Hays State University,
Kansas State University, Pittsburg State University, the University of
Kansas, and Wichita State University.

Library of Congress Cataloging-in-Publication Data

Names: Faulkner, Richard Shawn, author.
Title: Pershing's Crusaders : the American soldier in World War I /
    Richard S. Faulkner.
Description: Lawrence : University Press of Kansas, 2017. | Series:
    Modern war studies
Identifiers: LCCN 2016047599| ISBN 9780700623730 (cloth) |
    ISBN 9780700623747 (ebook)
Subjects: LCSH: World War, 1914–1918—Personal narratives,
    American. | Soldiers—United States—History—20th century. |
    United States—Armed Forces—Military life—History—20th
    century. | World War, 1914–1918—Campaigns—Western Front—
    Sources.
Classification: LCC D570.9 .F38 2017 | DDC 940.4/1273—dc23
LC record available at https://lccn.loc.gov/2016047599.

British Library Cataloguing-in-Publication Data is available.

Printed in the United States of America

10 9 8 7 6 5 4 3 2 1

To Bell Irvin Wiley
For Laura, Connor, Brenna, Shelby

CONTENTS

ACKNOWLEDGMENTS

To some extent, this book began on Christmas Day 1965, when my parents, Nan and Larry Faulkner, gave me a REMCO Doughboy playset. That playset, with its SPAD fighter plane, tank, armored car, cannon and five soldiers, sparked a lifelong fascination with the Great War. I thank my parents for encouraging my love of history and for this really fun toy. I am also indebted to a man I never met but wish that I could have: the late great Bell Irvin Wiley. His book *The Life of Johnny Reb* was the first work of serious history that I truly loved. In fact, I admired the book so much that as a young southerner I even put aside my ingrained antipathy for all things northern and read its successor, *The Life of Billy Yank*. Wiley's works opened for me that wide and imaginative world built around the question: "What was it like to have lived in the past?" It was his unfailing efforts to capture the experiences of the Civil War's soldiers that most inspired me to try to do the same for their Doughboy sons and grandsons.

This book has been over twenty years in the making, and it would not have been possible without the assistance of numerous talented colleagues and scholars. In two decades of squirreling away soldier accounts, documents, and records, I have racked up a number of personal and professional debts to those who have assisted me in this project. I am grateful to Emory Thomas, John Morrow, and Charles Sanders for their efforts to guide a headstrong army officer toward the scholarly exploration of history. Robert Doughty, Lee Wyatt, Gian Gentile, Ty Seidule, and the other members of the United States Military Academy Department of History offered mentorship, access to sources, and models of emulation for how to be a "practicing historian." For fourteen years I have had the privilege of serving with the talented members of the Department of Military History, United States Army Command and General Staff College at Fort Leavenworth. These comrades, most notably James Willbanks, Scott Stephenson, Maryln Pierce, John Suprin, Chris Gabel, Sue Rosell, and Sean Kalic, have offered me unflagging friendship, support, and advice on this work and my other endeavors.

I am grateful for the assistance of all of the dedicated librarians, archivists, and researchers who had a hand in this project. Timothy Nenninger and Mitch Yockelson offered me wise council and suggestions during numerous visits to the National Archives. The hard work and consideration of David Keough of the U.S. Army Military History Institute; Jonathan Casey of the National World War I Museum and Liberty Memorial; Mike Browne, Kathy Buker, and Elizabeth Merrifield of Fort Leavenworth Combined Arms Research Library; and Sandra Reddish and Robert Smith of the U.S. Army Cavalry Museum were essential in bringing this work to fruition. I must also thank Mike Briggs and the staff of the University Press of Kansas for their assistance, patience, and understanding in getting *Pershing's Crusaders* into print. Given the talents of all those listed above, any errors in this book are purely my own.

I have spent over thirty-three years in and around the U.S. Army, and my time in the company of soldiers has certainly influenced this work. It is my hope that being in combat far from home, coping with the inanity that is the natural purview of military service, and fighting and training while tired, cold, and wet have given me important insights into the lives of the dough-boys. I am grateful to all of those with whom I have served for their dedication to the Republic and for teaching me about war and soldiering.

I am most thankful for my wife, Laura, and my children: Connor, Brenna, and Shelby. Their unconditional love and support means everything to me. I am most appreciative of my wife. Laura has always been my best sounding board and editor and has endured endless proofreadings of drafts, my addiction to purchasing World War I letters and ephemera, and my obsession with this book.

ABBREVIATIONS

AEF GHQ	American Expeditionary Forces General Headquarters
Bde	Brigade
Bn	Battalion
CARL	Combined Arms Research Library, Fort Leavenworth, KS
Cav	Cavalry
CGSCSRP	Command and General Staff College Student Research Paper
Co	Company
Div	Division
DRL	Donovan Research Library, Fort Benning, GA
Emory	Robert W. Woodruff Library Special Collections, Emory University, GA
EN	Engineer
FA	Field Artillery
GO	General Orders
IG	Inspector General
IN	Infantry
MGB	Machine Gun Battalion
MDWW	*United States Medical Department in the World War*
MHIWWIS	U.S. Army Military History Institute World War I Veteran Survey
MP	Military Police
NARA	National Archives and Records Administration
NWWIM	National World War I Museum and Liberty Memorial, Kansas City, MO
PIO IN	Pioneer Infantry
QMC	Quartermaster Corps
Regt	Regiment
RG	Record Group
TN	Train
UGA	Hargrett Rare Book and Manuscript collection of the University of Georgia
USACM	United States Army Cavalry Museum, Fort Riley, KS

USAMHI   United States Army Military History Institute, Carlisle
         Barracks, PA
USMA   United States Military Academy Library Special Collections,
         West Point, NY

Pershing's Crusaders

1

Pershing's Crusaders
The American Soldiers of the Great War

Less than three weeks after the Armistice, infantry Captain Herman Ulmer pondered the difficulty of setting "down with any degree of accuracy a true and complete record of the events" of his weeks of fighting in the Argonne. He mused,

> One might succeed in producing a mere compendium of bald, bare facts,—after the fashion of a railroad time table—but it would require a book, volumes of books, to present the manifold and conflicting impressions which those events carried with them . . . Our impressions of those days are not settled. They are not formed as a mold, to remain unchanging forevermore. We are constantly extracting from those momentous times as we live them over in our memories, entirely new sensations, hitherto unaroused, or unnoticed in the multiplicity of our emotions. Our impressions of today are not the ones of yesterday, and it is probable that tomorrow will bring still newer ones. The recollections of that period inspire a myriad of thoughts, and we might write for years and years and never finish recording them all.

Ulmer neatly encapsulated the innate problem of using historical sources and the writing of history. The task of the historian is to sift through the "manifold and conflicting impressions" of those in the past in order to present a coherent vision or interpretation of historical events to those in the present. *Pershing's Crusaders* hopes to avoid being a "mere compendium of bald, bare facts" by recounting, as comprehensively, detailed, and vividly as possible the daily lives, experiences, and attitudes of the American soldier and Marine in the Great War.[1]

This book attempts to be a "travel guide" to the soldiers' experiences as well as an "anthropological" study of their world and their worldviews. As a "travel guide," it takes the reader on a journey that starts with the dough-boys' induction into the service and then moves through their training in the United States, their voyage to Europe, their training in France, their experiences in combat, and finally to their return home and demobilization. The "anthropological" aspects of the work examines what motivated the soldiers to serve and accept the verdict of the draft, their attitudes toward military service, what they thought about their allies and enemies, and the material realities of the troops' food, clothing, shelter, and weapons. It further explores the doughboys' sex lives, religion, medical care, morale, and discipline. The book is intended to give the reader an understanding of what it meant to serve as a doughboy in the Great War. *Pershing's Crusaders* seeks to make a human connection between the reader and the doughboys by giving them a deep and well-rounded appreciation of the soldiers' opinions and day-to-day existence in and out of battle.

The American soldiers of the Great War lived at a key point in the nation's history: the moment that the Republic emerged as a key player on the world's stage and embarked on its first large-scale foreign war. The war caught the doughboy generation with one foot planted in the nineteenth century with its assumptions of manhood and military glory and the other foot in the modernity of the industrializing and urbanizing twentieth century. In their time, they experienced a number of important "firsts" in American history. As such, they were the first Americans to endure modern high-tech mass warfare. In only nineteen months, the U.S. Army went from being a pitifully small constabulary force built on rifles, horses, and a few field and coastal artillery pieces to a four-million-man heavy weight possessing all the fiendish implements of mass killing. This process was far from smooth and pretty, and many a doughboy would suffer as the army painfully learned of the monumental changes to warfare that the Great War had initiated. In the process of learning, the American soldiers pioneered a modern American "way of war" focused on massive firepower and global power projection and sustainment.

World War I was the first time that large numbers of Americans came into intimate contact with foreign peoples and cultures. Prior to the war, foreign

travel for Americans was still largely confined to sailors, international businessmen, and a handful of relatively well-off tourists. Over the course of the
Great War more than two million Americans interacted with European civilization. These numbers dwarfed the number of soldiers who experienced far-
off societies in America's previous foreign wars. The American armies with
which Zachary Taylor and Winfield Scott invaded Mexico in 1846 and 1847
and the force that William Shafter took to Cuba in 1898 were less than half
the size of one of John Pershing's twenty-seven combat divisions. The total
number of soldiers serving in the Philippine War, the largest overseas deployment of American forces prior to World War I, was roughly equal to the
number of troops in one of Pershing's nine corps. As will be noted, it would
be wrong to argue that the Americans returned home from France with a
greater appreciation of multiculturalism. In fact, the doughboys' contact with
Europe and the Europeans served mostly to strengthen their faith in American exceptionalism and in the inherent superiority of American society over
all others. To a large extent the opinions of the returning doughboys helped
to set the stage for the rest of the assertive, confident, and bumptious "American Century" and shaped postwar American society. It is not too much of a
stretch to argue that the doughboys were the pioneers of the American sexual
revolution. Furthermore, in a departure from the self-affirming American
exceptionalism of their white comrades, African American doughboys returned home after having experienced a cultural model in France that offered
a counterpoint to Jim Crow America. In many ways, these black soldiers were
the vanguards of the civil rights movement.

The title of the book comes from a movie produced in 1918 by the War and
Navy Departments in conjunction with the Committee on Public Information (CPI). The movie itself is a rather typical piece of the CPI's propaganda
work, chronicling the dedication of the military, the hard work of the home
front, and the menace of the Germans. It is the movie's poster (reproduced
on the jacket cover) that is perhaps most revealing. On it, John J. Pershing on
horseback leads a mighty and resolute host of American soldiers into battle.
Although the poster is centered on Pershing, the American flag still occupies a
suitably prominent and appropriately patriotic place above him. In the background a ghostly cadre of crusader knights watches over their modern-day
doughboy counterparts as they embark upon their own holy and righteous
mission. To a very large extent, this poster captures how the doughboys saw

themselves and their war. Based upon their own views of the United States and influenced somewhat by the unbridled patriotism and fear-mongering of the CPI, most soldiers believed in the justness of the nation's cause and viewed themselves as crusaders who came to "make the world safe for democracy" by rescuing Europe from the threat of brutal German militarism. The doughboys were generally idealistic and ideological soldiers battling to protect hearth and home and to defend American principles and values.[2]

Although his name is prominent in the title, John J. Pershing, as well as his senior subordinates, makes only fleeting appearances in the pages of this book. It is striking how little Pershing is mentioned by his soldiers in their diaries and letters home. The few times that the author has seen him referenced by the troops were mostly in accounts of post-Armistice inspections and parades. This work focuses on the lives of the American Army's enlisted men and junior officers. As such, Pershing and the officers of the American Expeditionary Forces General Headquarters (AEF GHQ) appear onstage only when their policies and directives influenced the daily lives of the doughboy. It is important to focus on the "common" soldier of the Great War for several reasons. One is the changing realities of the battlefield itself. The size and scale of combat in World War I meant that senior officers could no longer directly influence fighting at the lower end of the tactical scale. As combat became more dispersed and decentralized, it was the soldiers and officers at the battalion level and below that increasingly decided how, and even if, their superior commander's orders were carried out. Second, as war shifted from being a matter of a few days of battle to weeks and months of combat, the individual soldier's morale, discipline, training, and physical condition grew in importance. Thus, understanding what motivated the doughboys to fight and the moral and physical realities of their world leads to a deeper appreciation of the AEF's challenges during the war. Last, the attitudes and opinions of the doughboys offer a greater understanding of American society at the turn of the twentieth century.

Pershing's Crusaders humbly follows the tradition of Bell Irvin Wiley in his classic studies *The Life of Johnny Reb* and *The Life of Billy Yank*, and of Don Rickey's *Forty Miles a Day on Beans and Hay*, Edward Coffman's *The Regulars*, and Lee Kennett's *G.I.: The American Soldier in World War II*. These insightful books have captured the details of the lives of American soldiers with unparalleled depth, breadth, and sensitivity. This work also builds upon the writings of Jennifer D. Keene, Chad Williams, Mark Meigs, Edward A. Gutiérrez, and other scholars of the American experience in the Great War. This book, however, seeks to present a more holistic and detailed exploration of the many facets of the doughboys' lives and attitudes than has been given in previous accounts.

Given the fact that over four million soldiers served in the American Army in World War I, it is no surprise that the doughboys had a variety of motivations for serving and a wide spectrum of opinion regarding military life, combat, their surroundings, and the people who they encountered during their time in uniform. Because of this multiplicity of personal experience, it is inaccurate to state that there was an "average doughboy." However, these varied masses of men did share certain commonalities of experience. After all, one of the goals of any military organization is to establish a great degree of uniformity in its ranks when it comes to things such as training, weapons, tactics, food, clothing, and shelter. The unchanging nature of war itself also created commonalities that united the doughboys. At its core, war has always been about killing, dying, fear, exertion, and privation. These realities were as well understood by an American soldier of World War I as they would have been by a Roman legionnaire of antiquity or as they would be by an infantryman of the twenty-first century. That being said, each war also has a subjective nature: the distinctive aspects of its time and place, such as technology and the period's societal realities, that make it unique from other conflicts in history. This work aims to illustrate how the doughboys experienced and understood both the objective and subjective realities of the Great War. When I use the understandably fraught terms "many doughboys," "a number of doughboys," or "most doughboys," it is only after I have seen comments on the subject in question reoccur time and time again in a wide variety of sources. Likewise, terms such as "some soldiers" or "a few soldiers" denote that similar comments of the topic in question arose in the sources, but were not, perhaps, the dominate opinion in the ranks.

To accomplish this holistic examination of the doughboys, *Pershing's Crusaders* rests upon materials drawn from a deep and varied array of primary sources. Wars in the era of mass literacy and growing military bureaucracies have produced a wealth of correspondence, firsthand accounts, and records that allow us to gain a deeper appreciation for the daily lives and experiences of the "average" soldier. The soldiers themselves were driven by a need to keep in tenuous touch with those back home and to record what they knew would most likely be the most momentous times of their lives. In conducting research for this work, I read over five thousand soldier letters and diaries, including over nine hundred letters that I had amassed in a personal collection that I hope will ultimately reside in the National World War I Museum in Kansas City, Missouri. The book also draws heavily upon soldier surveys, memoirs, unit histories, and unpublished manuscripts that detail soldiers' time in uniform and upon articles in military newspapers and journals such as *Stars and Stripes*. Many of these sources reside in the U.S. Army Military History Institute (USAMHI). In the 1970s, the USAMHI began sending surveys to World War I veterans to collect their personal accounts of the conflict. The quality of the answers to the surveys themselves vary greatly, ranging from detailed recounting of the veteran's service to terse and unenlightening responses to the queries. Although age and memory perhaps made some of the facts in the surveys problematic, the USAMHI also asked the veterans to send any of their letters, diaries, or other written accounts that they wished to donate to the institute. These additional sources, generally written during or soon after the war, were a treasure trove of material.

As armies grew larger over the nineteenth and twentieth centuries, their systems for training, supplying, and employing their soldiers became increasingly complex. This, in turn, created military bureaucracies that ran on an insatiable and varied diet of reports, studies, and investigations that kept the war machine lurching forward. The U.S. Army also sought to learn as much as possible from the conflict and scrutinized its wartime operations to prepare for future wars and further internal reforms. In addition to personal accounts, *Pershing's Crusaders* draws upon thousands of these official primary source materials to aid in drawing a nuanced portrait of the doughboys' world. The vast majority of these sources came from Record Group 120, "Records of the American Expeditionary Forces," and Record Group 165, "Records of the War Department General Staff," in the National Archives annex at College Park, Maryland. The work also uses staff studies, lectures, and student papers written in the Army War College, U.S. Army Command and General Staff College, and the U.S. Army Infantry School in the 1920s and 1930s.

To provide an immediacy and an intimacy that allow the work to make the key emotional human connection between the reader and the people of the past, as much as possible the book uses quotations from writings of the doughboys to make its points. To remain true to the past and its participants, all quotations have been left with their original spelling and punctuation, and the limited additions to the original passages were made only for added comprehension and clarity. It should be noted that the book's subtitle could more accurately be "the American Soldier *and Marine* in World War I" as I have used accounts from Marines throughout the work. Although there were subtle differences in the experiences of soldiers and Marines during the Great War, in all substantive areas the commonalities of their lives far exceeded these minor points of dissimilarity. Although I have sought to be as comprehensive as possible in discussing the doughboys' lives, as with any work of this scale there are bound to be omissions or subjects that deserve greater coverage. The work is limited to those Americans serving in France, Belgium, and Germany and does not discuss those fighting in Russia or Italy. Due to the uniqueness of their experience, the book also does not discuss the lives of pilots and aircrews. When I knew that other authors have covered some subjects in more depth than I could here, for example, in the experiences of American women in uniform, I deferred to them. I hope that any other omissions that have been made in this work will be filled in by other historians in the future.

2

"I Want You for the U.S. Army"
Motivations, Joining Up, and Conscription

The poster is the iconic image of the American participation in World War I. The rather irritable old man stares you down with a fixed and stern gaze and thrusts a finger in your chest. He is not here to make a plea or request but rather to make a direct and uncompromising demand. This Uncle Sam is not the benevolent late-twentieth- and early-twenty-first-century father figure willingly dispensing entitlements and largesse. This Uncle Sam is every archetypal teenager's quintessential "Old Man" pointedly asking his son, "What are you going to do with your life?" The redoubtable Uncle Sam in James Montgomery Flagg's poster is the best form of propaganda. It is simple in form and message and makes a direct appeal to the viewer's emotion: your nation is at war; we need men; it is your duty to serve and thus, "I want you for the U.S. Army."

In the spring of 1917 the nation needed Flagg's blunt poster for the simple reason that its Regular Army and National Guard contained only 8,990 officers and two hundred thousand enlisted men, and army planners estimated that the nation would need to commission an additional two hundred thousand officers and raise two to four million men to send a creditable force to France.[1] This fundamental problem raised a host of critical national, military, and personal questions. How could the nation raise and maintain such a massive military force without breaking the agricultural, industrial, social, and political underpinnings of the Republic, underpinnings that were vital to both the war effort and the well-being of the overall American society? How could the military select, train, and make the

[8]

best use of the human raw material the Republic provided within the limits imposed upon it by the government and people of the United States? Most importantly for this study and for the individual: Why are you serving? Why would you give up your personal freedom and agency to risk death and injury in a war half a world away from your home?

The answers to the first two questions were rather straightforward and mechanistic. Although there were a myriad of problems in mobilizing the nation for war, the expanding government and military bureaucracies, aided by legions of efficiency experts, economists, and other technocrats, were able to slowly and painfully drag the Republic into a war footing. The answers to the last two questions are far more interesting, are much harder to quantify, and are as old as war itself. War, at its essence, is about killing and dying. War demands that soldiers do what instinct, common sense, and peacetime moral and legal strictures tell them not to do: place themselves in mortal danger and kill their fellow man. Some of the ideas and desires that motivated the doughboys to face this ugly truth are basically the same that have influenced soldiers to serve since time immemorial. Other motivations, however, were deeply rooted in American culture and the social and political climate of the United States at the time.

George Orwell is reputed to have said, "If war does not kill you it is bound to make you think." Orwell was correct to highlight the role that combat plays in awakening in soldiers a questioning of their environment, but the fighter's process of thinking about war itself, and their individual place in it, begins long before the firing of the first shots. Why soldiers serve is a topic that has garnered much interest among historians, military men, and sociologists over the past seventy years. Among both historians and the public, World War I has been decisively overshadowed by the historical epics of the American Civil War and World War II. Although legions of historians have written on the motivations of the soldiers of those conflicts, few have studied the factors that inspired the doughboys. However, the findings of the scholars of the Civil War and World War II offer important insights into the general motives of soldiers in war as well as points of comparison in understanding the motives that encouraged the doughboys to serve.

In the past six decades, scholars of the American Civil War have created a thoughtful and nuanced interpretation of the factors that encouraged the conflict's soldiers to enlist and endure. In *Embattled Courage*, Gerald Linderman argued that the most powerful motivation for enticing most men to join the army was their deep-seated belief in courage and honor. Courage, an idea rooted in the values of the mid-nineteenth-century society from which the soldiers were drawn, simply, but uncompromisingly, meant "heroic action taken without fear." Linderman contended that men enlisted because the societies of both the North and the South put a high premium on individual courage and demanded men join the ranks to demonstrate their personal bravery and their related strength of character. The individual soldier's concept of honor naturally sprang from his commitment to courage. To have his peers accept his honor and reputation, the soldier had to always demonstrate the outward appearance of courage.[2]

Closely associated with the argument that courage and honor were motivations to enlistment was the idea of "manliness." As Reid Mitchell pointed out, "the very idea of man, soldier and citizen were inextricably linked. Remaining a civilian was thought unmanly; going to war a proof of manhood." Mitchell argued that serving in the war was a rite of passage that enabled the "Boys of '61" to be accepted in their communities as men entitled to the full privilege and responsibilities of patriarchal citizenship.[3]

Bell Irvin Wiley, the first great Civil War social historian, believed that most Civil War soldiers' reasons for enlisting were more prosaic than the high-minded ideas of "courage" and "manhood." While Wiley did not discount the importance of societal expectations of courage and manliness, he emphasized that the war brought an emotional release and excitement that encouraged men to join because it was the "prevailing vogue" and also out of a sense of adventure. Enlisting was thus mostly an escape from the monotony of farm and factory life.[4]

Linderman, Mitchell, and Wiley all down played the role of ideology and politics as a motivating factor in a soldier's decision to enlist. All three reduced the soldiers' ideological commitment to the rather vague belief in "union," "liberty and rights," or "the cause." Of the Union soldier, Wiley wrote, "One searches most letters and diaries in vain for soldiers' comments on why they were in the war and for what they were fighting." To Wiley, the soldiers of the Civil War were "as little concerned with ideological issues as were those of the 1940s." Ideology was simply something reserved for the goose-stepping lackeys of fascism and communism.[5]

In his aptly titled work *For Cause and Comrades*, James McPherson vigorously disagreed with this assessment. While not denying the importance of the other motivational factors propounded by Linderman, Mitchell, and Wiley, McPherson argued that a strong commitment to the political and social ideologies of their respective societies was what encouraged Civil War soldiers to join and stay in the ranks.[6] Contrary to Wiley's assertions, the Civil War soldier was never reticent to write on his view of what the war was about and on the other political and social issues of the day. To McPherson, the Civil War soldier was generally a "thinking bayonet" fully engaged and cognizant of the great issues of the day and willing to fight and die for his political and social beliefs.

The other great point of comparison for the doughboys' motivations is the experience of the World War II GI generation. During the Second World War, the new "science" of mass polling allowed researchers to gain a deeper appreciation of the thoughts and attitudes of the average soldier than had previously been possible. In their groundbreaking sociological study *The American Soldier*, Samuel Stouffer and seven other prominent sociologists and psychologists examined the overall motivations, opinions, and experiences of the American soldier in World War II. Their findings were based on an unprecedented survey of soldiers conducted by the U.S. Army Research Branch during the war. The surveys revealed that the desire to end the war and get on with their lives was the greatest personal motivation that encouraged the majority of American soldiers to join and stay in the ranks. Once in the army, the desire not to let down one's buddies was also intertwined with concepts of unit pride and masculinity to sustain soldiers in battle. Stouffer also found that "officers and enlisted men alike attached little importance to idealistic motives—patriotism and concerns about war aims." Despite this, however, he found that few American soldiers doubted that they were on the "right" side in the war.[7]

Stouffer and his colleagues' conclusions on the motivations of the GIs were generally echoed in the findings of the controversial historian S. L. A. Marshall. In his seminal work *Men against Fire*, Marshall claimed that, in the end, soldiers fought for their buddies and to gain and maintain the respect of their comrades. Although he did not totally discount the importance of soldiers fighting for a political or ideological cause (what he defined as a fundamental belief in the justice of the politics of the soldier's country and the length that the country goes to keep faith with its soldiers), he certainly placed these factors much lower on the individual's motivational scale. As Marshall noted, "lofty ideas and ideals we must have, if only to assure that men go forward. But it is unworthy of the profession of arms to base any policy upon exaggerated notions of a man's capacity to endure and sacrifice on behalf of ideas alone." To Marshall, it really did not matter why the soldier entered the service; the important part was what he did once he was in.[8]

Although the World War II GIs tended to downplay the influence of lofty ideas and overt patriotism in their desire and willingness to serve, it should be noted that their opinions were shaped by two decades of growing cynicism about America's role in the Great War. By 1941, many Americans had come to view the First World War as, at best, a failed experiment in misplaced idealism, or at worst, a deliberate plot by bankers and industrialists to make money at the cost of American lives. Much of the GIs' reticence to discuss political and ideological motivations perhaps rested on a desire to not be duped by the flag-waving hyperjingoism that had seemingly ensnared their fathers.

When examining the factors that encouraged the doughboys to volunteer or accept the verdict of the draft, it is clear that their attitudes and motivations were much closer to those of their Civil War fathers and grandfathers than to their GI sons. Although rapid industrialization and urbanization, the fruition of westward migration, and vast waves of immigration had profoundly changed the social, economic, and demographic realities of the nation since 1865, the espoused ideas and values of the men who filled the ranks of the Confederate and Union armies continued to resonate with those who went to war in 1917 and 1918. Given the relative closeness and importance of the conflict, it is not surprising that local communities and the popular press tended to make direct linkages between the "Boys of '61" and the "Boys of '17." The 69th Infantry, New York National Guard went so far as to issue a recruiting poster in the spring of 1917 that stated "Join the famous Irish regiment that fought in all the great battles of the Civil War from Bull Run to Appomattox." It is interesting to note that the public and the new soldiers themselves overlooked the veterans of the nation's most recent conflicts, the Spanish-American and the Philippine Wars, to find inspiration and validation in the service of those who fought in the Civil War.

In 1917, the Civil War was still a tangible and living event made flesh and blood by the surviving veterans of the struggle. As the soldiers of the Great War departed their towns for training camps and left training camps for

France, local communities paraded out their Civil War veterans to bless a new generation going off to fight a great crusade. These direct generational linkages at times proved quite amusing as northern soldiers found themselves in training camps in the Deep South. When invited to dinner in an Atlanta home while stationed at Camp Gordon, northerner Richard McBride was regaled by the matron of the house with the tales of life in the city under William Sherman's siege of 1864. Although she castigated the unlamented Sherman for his brutality, she did express hope that the "second 'Yankee' invasion would be more peaceful."[9]

For some doughboys, the Civil War provided a powerful incentive to serve. These men had grown up surrounded by the war's veterans and had listened to the stories of the conflict and of life in the army. For example, Leroy Bicknell enlisted in June 1917 to emulate his three uncles who had enlisted in the Union Army in 1861. The fact that two of the uncles died in action and the surviving uncle was severely wounded during the war did not seem to dampen Bicknell's desire to enlist. Likewise a soldier in the 314th Engineers volunteered because his father was a Civil War veteran and had instilled in him a "sense of duty" and patriotism to serve the Republic.[10]

In addition to these ties to family and national history, the factors that motivated the doughboys to serve were legion. Infantryman Martin Hogan acknowledged that "many and odd motives brought us together in those first days of the war . . . Some joined for drudging work at home, others because their friends had joined, but most of us volunteered unknowing why." He and his comrades were further impelled by a "sentiment to do America's service" and to measure themselves "fully up before the world." Hogan himself reflected the spirit of the age. In July 1917 he was an unmarried seventeen-year-old orphan who was footloose in the world. At a theater performance a National Guard recruiter asked that any man willing to serve the country step onto the stage and volunteer to do their duty. Hogan was the first to heed the call, and due to his Irish ethnicity, he jumped at the opportunity to join the "Fighting 69th." Although there were as many influences and impulses to serve as there were doughboys, Hogan identified and exemplified many of the important factors that drew men into the ranks during the war. Patriotism, faith in the cause, friendship, excitement and escape, ethnic pride, and the desire to "measure up" as men drove thousands of doughboys, like Hogan and his comrades, to more or less willingly face the dangers and exertions of war.[11]

As with their Civil War veteran fathers and grandfathers, a large number of men volunteered in the spring and summer of 1917 because they were caught up in the excitement and immediacy of the moment. Tensions between the United States and Germany had steadily mounted since 1915, and although the debate about the nation's role in the conflict and its lack of military preparedness had grown raucous, the nation's entry into the war was something of a psychological release. The nation's youth came of age during the presidency of Theodore Roosevelt, and visions of his service with the Rough Riders shaped their perceptions of war as an exciting, manly, and glorious endeavor. The bellicose ex-president himself maintained that "no triumph of peace is quite so great as the supreme triumph of war" and concluded that serving in the ranks would end the threat of class warfare, turn the nation's youth from the path of physical and moral decay, and reinvigorate democracy. To a very great extent, the volunteers of 1917, and even many of the draftees who came later, were adherents of the Rooseveltian idea of the "strenuous life" and of the vision of "muscular Christianity." War was to be the supreme test and an escape from button-down, boring, everyday life and was something that they damn sure were not going to miss.[12]

As early as March 1917, the Wilson administration had already concluded that in the case of a war with Germany, the nation would raise its wartime army mainly on conscription. Given popular sentiment and the long-standing American volunteer tradition, the administration was at first reluctant to close off all paths to voluntary enlistments.[13] Under the Selective Service Act of 1917, signed by Wilson on May 18, 1917, any man could continue to voluntarily enlist in existing Regular Army or National Guard units if they so chose. After Congress amended the act on December 15, 1917, only men who had not yet been called to register for the draft could volunteer for the army, but even those already registered could still opt to enlist in the navy or Marines. On August 8, 1918, this loophole was also closed and all voluntary enlistments ceased until the end of the war. The reason for the slow closing of voluntary enlistments was to allow the selective service system to work as intended: to keep the nation's military and industrial mobilization on a rational and efficient path.

Unsurprisingly, the surge of excitement that accompanied the beginning of the war generated the greatest number of voluntary enlistments. During the war, the army and National Guard accepted 877,458 men as volunteers.

Nearly half of the volunteers (437,136) entered the service between April and August 1917. Except for a spike in enlistments in December 1917, when 141,931 voluntarily joined the ranks, after August 1917 the number of volunteers pre- cipitously declined.

The jump in enlistments in December, the highest monthly total during the war, was due to the changes to enlistment policies in the Selective Ser- vice Act noted earlier. The men who enlisted in December saw it as their last chance to have some degree of control over the terms and conditions of their service. By enlisting rather than leaving everything up to the needs of the draft, the December volunteers could at least choose their arm or branch of service and sometimes their units.[14] The December volunteers' motivations would not have come as a surprise to Paul Landis and Edgar Hastings. During the war, Paul Landis rose from private to battalion sergeant major in the 3rd Division. He enlisted on June 6, 1917, because "the draft was imminent and I wanted to select my unit, which was the Cavalry as I loved horses and de- tested marching." Despite his early wishes, Landis landed in the field artillery. To Edgar Hastings, it plainly came down to the fact that "I would have been drafted in September and I wanted to select my field of service." As will be discussed, the draft still carried negative connotations for many Americans due to the Civil War, and many soldiers enlisted while they could to avoid the stigma of being a draftee. As one soldier admitted, he volunteered because he "did not want to be called a slacker."[15]

One of the men who were caught up in the excitement of the time was F. L. Miller. He recalled that in the spring of 1917, "There was a crusading spirit in the air." He was on spring vacation from college and was caught up in an atmosphere where "bands were playing martial music on the courthouse squares" as "proud fathers and tearful mothers" saw their boys off to war. Although his mother had forbidden him from joining the army, he rushed to Fort Sheridan in an attempt to enter the first Officers Training Camp (OTC). Upon being informed that the camp had its full quota of candidates, he took a train to Little Rock, Arkansas, to try for a slot in another OTC. He rational- ized his decision based on the fact that his college's president promised that all students who joined up would receive passing grades in all their classes. As Miller was then failing calculus, he figured he had nothing to lose. More im- portantly, he did not want to miss out on the biggest event of his generation.[16]

Some volunteers had grown up with a romantic vision of war and soldiering and saw the war as a way to finally live out their visions of martial glory. Donald Kyler admitted he joined due to "enthusiasm for soldiering and patriotic fervor, as influenced by my grandfather (a former soldier) and other members of my family." Kyler would get the adventure that he sought, fighting with the 1st Division's 16th Infantry throughout its long and bloody service in France. Another infantryman claimed that he enlisted because "I had been fired about reading of soldiers especially 'the Liberty Boys of '76' and had always wanted to be a soldier."[17]

To some, the war was to be the time to sow their "wild oats," see the world, and escape their staid and prosaic existence. This could be a powerful motivator for bored youngsters who chaffed against the sameness of their farmyard or shop floor. Glendon Armstrong confessed that he was "tired of monotony" in the civilian world and enlisted in the National Guard to flee his workaday life. The excitement of the moment and the enthusiasm of the local community also played a role in the motivations of some. For example, one doughboy sheepishly admitted that he volunteered "To show off—no other reason." When one cavalryman was asked why he served, he reflected the sentiments of many of his peers by simply replying, "I suppose it was a desire to travel some, learn something of a life that looked and sounded exciting to a teenager at the time." Although thrill-seeking seemed to be common among the early war volunteers, many draftees were also driven by wartime excitement to serve. While Harry House waited to be called by the draft he still went to war willingly, noting, "Like any kid of 22 I looked for excitement and got it."[18]

Some of the most ardent men wishing to join the ranks in 1917 were actually mere boys. As twenty-one was the age of maturity in most states and the legal federal voting age, the Selective Service Act initially restricted the draft to men between twenty-one and thirty. On August 31, 1918, Congress expanded the age range for draftees to eighteen to forty. The army's minimum age of enlistment in 1917 was eighteen, but it would accept boys as young as seventeen with their parent's permission. As with many of their older comrades, in 1917 underage youths believed that if they did not act to get into the service they would miss out on the single greatest event of their lives. Soon after the United States entered the war, Alonzo LaVanture pleaded with his father to allow him to join the local National Guard company. When his father refused to sign his enlistment papers, LaVanture traveled to Harrisburg, Pennsylvania, and convinced one of his friends to forge his father's signature. He believed that "there was a war on and I was afraid I would miss something." One underage boy who ended up in the 1st Division avoided a confrontation with his parents by merely forging his father's signature on his enlistment form. Even if a young man met the minimum age requirement, it was still up to the recruiter whether or not they would accept an eager youth into the service. Ralph Williams was impatient to serve but found that, when he tried to enter the military in April 1917, the recruiters were not swayed by his enthusiasm. He remembered, "I had difficulty in selling myself to the recruiter, since I was only five foot four and weighed 112 pounds . . . I tried the Marine Corps, and was laughed at, then the Regular Army Recruiter told me to go home and hang onto my mother's apron strings." He waited until he turned nineteen a month later and was relieved when he managed to squeak through his effort to enlist at a third recruiting station.[19]

It is not certain how many underage youths eventually worked their way into the military by hook, crook, or the sympathy or negligence of a recruiting sergeant. However, the enthusiasm and spirit of adventure that motivated those youths also seemed to have generally turned them into good soldiers. That same zeal and eagerness also came at a price. Albert Scott, of Brookline, Massachusetts, managed to bluff his way into the army at age fifteen in 1917 and found himself in France before the end of the year. Although many of his squad mates knew that he was underage, Scott was a good soldier and his comrades decided to look the other way. When he was killed by a sniper on the Marne front on July 18, 1918, he was still three months shy of his seventeenth birthday.[20]

Of all the services, the Marines seemed best positioned to draw those men most seeking adventure and who were eager to get to France. The Corps was able to capitalize on a marketing scheme that appealed most directly to this demographic: joining the Marines would be the fastest way to get to the front. A Texan claimed that he enlisted in the Marines in June 1917 because "Back home the glaring posters had read 'First to Fight!' 'First on Land and Sea,' 'France in 90 Days,' and the like . . . Every man in that group wanted to fight, or thought he did." At the same time, Anders Peterson was considering joining the Ohio National Guard when a Marine recruiter persuaded him to enlist in the Corps because the Marines "would be the first to go" overseas. Nor did the young Marines' enthusiasm for their choice of service seem to wane over time. As the end of his training at the Marine Barracks at Mare

Island, California, approached, Lloyd Short informed his father in late April 1918, "We are all getting anxious to go to France and take a wallop at some germans." Three weeks later he bragged to his aunt about his pride in serving in the Corps because, "When Uncle Sam is in trouble we are always the first to go."[21]

If the desire for adventure and to see the world drove some to enlist, others were driven by pure necessity. A case in point was Richard Atkinson. Throughout 1916 and 1917 he had drifted from one day labor job to another in North Dakota, Montana, and Canada. His vagabond existence left him perpetually short of cash. Finally in January 1918, he announced to his family that "Owing to the shortage of work [I] have decided to join Uncle Sam" and soon landed in the 324th Machine Gun Battalion of the 83rd Division then training at Camp Sherman, Ohio. Atkinson was not alone in joining up due to financial difficulties. A veteran of the 1st Division admitted that he ultimately entered the ranks because "no other jobs [were] available." Given the boom in wartime industrial and agricultural production and the removal of several million men from the workplace due to military service, it is somewhat surprising that these men had trouble finding work.[22]

Some young or underage men also felt compelled to enlist due to economic hardships or the hope for personal betterment. Lionel Harmison was fifteen when he lied about his age to enlist in 1917. His mother was the widow of a Civil War veteran who was having difficulty making ends meet on the pension she received for her husband's war service. He joined so he could supplement his mother's meager subsistence with a steady military paycheck. John Miholick had also a hard life in the years leading up to the Great War. When his mother died when he was thirteen, he dropped out of school at the sixth grade and went to live with his eldest sister in Chicago. With his life going nowhere fast and "anxious to be in action," he lied about his age when he enlisted two weeks after the United States entered the war. At 114 pounds, he was under the minimum weight to be accepted into the service. The understanding recruiting sergeant let him pass, noting, "good old army stew will fatten you soon." He ruefully admitted that after a few months of hard training, he "wished I stayed home" and was so homesick that he considered telling his superiors about his true age.[23]

The lure of comradeship, the obligations to friends and family, and peer pressure have always been some of the strongest motivations that have drawn men to military service. Before the grinding impersonal machine of the draft turned the army into an anonymous mass of similarity, the desire to serve with one's buddies and family members was one of the most powerful inducements to enlist. This wish to serve with those one knows also had an important military benefit. To a greater or lesser degree, the success of all military units is built on their ability to create mutual trust, confidence, and cohesiveness in their squads, platoons, and companies. It is vital for these small units to develop and preserve a close-knit primary group identity to satisfy the individual's physical and psychological need to create a built-in resistance to the innate stresses of combat. Basically the soldier must believe that his comrades "have his back" when the going gets rough. Those who went off to war in 1917 and 1918 with their friends were already well down this path before they even put on their uniforms.

One of the most effective recruiting posters used by the 69th Regiment, New York National Guard (soon to be the 165th Infantry), simply stated, "GO TO THE FRONT WITH YOUR FRIENDS. Don't be drafted into some regiment where you don't know anyone." The allure of this straightforward message was illustrated in the case of Horatio Rogers. He was a Harvard sophomore when the war began, had been an avid participant in the university's cadet corps, and had attended the Student's Military Training Camp at Plattsburg in 1916. Although Rogers was well positioned to receive a commission, he opted to enlist as a private in the 1st Artillery Regiment of the Massachusetts National Guard. Although he admitted that he was never exactly sure what had led him to enlist, the fact that several of his acquaintances had already joined the unit certainly influenced his decision. He confessed that he was somewhat sanguine about joining the artillery but rationalized that he would still much rather be "blown up among his friends" than run the risk of joining the infantry and "being bayoneted and left out in 'no-man's-land'" by feckless comrades he did not know. After opting to enlist with his friends he admitted that he was "relieved that there was nothing more to be decided."[24]

Of course peer pressure and the fear of being left out of an important event in the group's life certainly pushed impressionable young men into a precipitous leap into uniform that a moment of more sober and private reflection may have prevented. A soldier in the 89th Division admitted that he joined merely "because all my buddies did," while another member of the unit felt the pull "to heed the call to duty and join my friends to defend my country." Membership in sports teams, colleges, and other activities or institutions that brought men together seems to have rapidly accelerated this trend. The Commander of the Southern Department telegrammed Brigadier General Joseph Kuhn, the Chief of the War College Division, in mid-April 1917 that he had ninety graduating students from the Texas A&M class of 1917 who were all clamoring to enter the service and receive commissions and believed that "probably thousands from similar schools would respond if called upon." This sentiment was not limited to college men. A veteran of the 33rd Division maintained, "Many of my friends at the time were going into the service and we all thought it was the proper thing for young men to serve their country in time of war."[25]

The Selective Service Act's stipulation that voluntary enlistments would be limited to existing National Guard and Regular Army units left the guard particularly well placed to attract those wishing to serve with their friends and family members. National Guard units were local institutions whose officers and soldiers were often the acquaintances of potential recruits. While this made it easier for those wanting to serve together to find a "home" in a local guard unit, the clubbiness of these organizations came at a cost.

Colonel Frank Hume, commander of the 103rd Infantry, was known to break down and cry after reading his unit's casualty reports because he had to write letters home to his friends and neighbors informing them of the loss of their sons, fathers, and husbands.[26]

The greatest danger with having friends and family serve together was the effect that casualties among the group had on unit morale and on the local communities. On April 17, 1917, Duncan Kemerer, his brother Lloyd, and six of their buddies from Export, Pennsylvania, headed to nearby Oakland to enlist in the National Guard. Lloyd and one of the other men were turned away after failing the physical. Of the six accepted into the 111th Infantry, two were killed in action near the Vesle River in August 1918, and three others, including Duncan, were wounded during the war. Only one of the six men who enlisted at Oakland returned home unscathed. These losses fell hard on their small Southwestern Pennsylvania town.[27]

The peer pressure and desire to be part of something bigger than themselves that drove many men into the service were also tied to the larger American social definitions of honor and manliness. At the time of the Great War, Americans generally equated manliness with physical and moral courage and a sense of honor with personal reputation. These visions of machismo and expected behavior meshed seamlessly with Theodore Roosevelt's secular ideas of the "strenuous life" and with the burgeoning concept of "muscular Christianity." In both visions, the test of war would rescue, ennoble, and purify the nation's men from their precipitous slide into unsexed foppishness brought about by narcissism, materialism, and the extravagance of modern industrial society. These sentiments were prevalent in the army's prewar officer corps. One officer denounced the fact that "our millions are untaught, not only in the arts of war but [also] in the art of taking care of themselves. Fifty percent of them could not go fishing without endangering their lives through ignorance" and viewed military service as the only sure means for the country's males to truly achieve "the dignity of manhood." This officer was not alone in this belief. Soon after the United States entered the war, the *Dallas Baptist Standard* proclaimed that the conflict was "an antidote for the effeminacy and decay of luxury" that weakened the nation's youth.[28]

The alarmist views of both the officer and the editor of the *Dallas Baptist Standard* were unfounded. If, as Roosevelt maintained, war was the ultimate test of manliness, then being seen by one's peers as a "man among men" was also inextricably linked in the minds of many recruits to the era's code of honor and gender identity. This was the case with Mervyn Burke, who enlisted in the army with his parent's consent at age sixteen, a few months prior to the United States entering the war. He found life in the service "a strange new world" where "everyone in it was older than myself but I was treated as an equal and expected to carry my share" despite his tender years.

In this, the doughboys' beliefs on manliness and individual honor were closely related to the views of the World War II GI generation. Samuel Stouffer and his fellow researchers found that it was vital for a GI to be recognized as a "true man" by the other men of the group. Soldiers felt driven to exhibit the characteristics of courage, endurance, toughness, and a lack of squeamishness to prove their worth to the group and to maintain their self-respect.[29]

Being a man also meant living up to the man's role of warrior and protector of women. Just before sailing for France, the mother of one officer told her son, "Kill them . . . but don't let them get you." The man recalled, "She was a Spartan mother, reared in the midst of the War Between the States. For her, a man-child was born to fight, and a mother to weep alone."[30] These beliefs were also evident in the letters that Ernest McKeighan wrote home to his wife shortly after his National Guard unit was federalized in the summer of 1917. On August 31, 1917, he penned,

> The job *has to be done* and the sooner we get there and whip our foes the sooner we will get back to our recompense, our women's and children's arms, whom we know are safe from the terrible things visited on weak and helpless . . . women. Those that have to die do so happy in the knowledge that their helpless ones at least can fight *their* battle unharassed by brutes in human form.

He later expressed his dissatisfaction with members of his unit and their wives who were falling short of his expectations of proper behavior. "There are a few 2nd Lieut's of very tender age who have cold feet and would like out but the older officers are standing fast and are determined that this country and its women and children *shall be safe*." While denouncing those who were failing to play their gender roles, he was all praise for those who did, noting, "The women are a constant source of wonder to me, with their bravery and devotion. Have only heard of one who is trying to get her husband . . . out."[31]

The desire to live up to the expectations of manliness was a powerful inducement to serve. In fact, one wartime recruiting poster directly proclaimed, "The United States Army builds MEN" and showed a soldier contemplating the globe while the allegorical figures of "Crafts," "Character," and "Physique" looked on. In one of the war's more famous images, Howard Chandler Christy portrayed a girl wearing a sailor's uniform, stating, "Gee I wish I were A MAN, I'd join the Navy," the not-so-subtle message being if she would join, what excuse would the average male have not to enlist? The belief that military service was a good thing for the nation's males was not lost on the soldiers themselves. Upon hearing that two of his ne'er-do-well acquaintances were joining up, one doughboy commented, "I hope it makes men out of them for the army is a savior of a good many men and boys that have been wayward." Another wrote home that a neighboring mother could "Be proud that she has given two boys to the service . . . The last time that I saw them they looked more like real men than they ever did before. Their jaws were set and their eyes flashed as if they had a purpose in life and meant to carry it out."[32]

Of course the demand to live up to the nation's and their comrades' vision of proper manly behavior and honorable service brought with it great emotional and physical stress. A soldier in the 32nd Division replied to his mother's concern over the strain of his military service by retorting, "You think this artillery is too heavy for me. Well suppose it is. Should I give up? Not me, I will stick it out if I get knocked to kingdom come . . . It is do or die for me. No white feather here on my part." In April 1917, June B. Smith was torn by a host of conflicting emotions and obligations as he considered whether or not to enlist. As he explained in a letter home,

> Well mother the war looks quite bad . . . I don't know just what to do my-self about it for the last two weeks I have thought about it a good deal. It looks to me as if it is the duty of every young man to do his part but what his part or mine is I can't quite make up my mind. It is a very big ques-tion to answer. Tonight I feel like I should step out and do something but I think that it is caused by a letter I received from one of the fellows at school. Two of them have gone and some more are expecting to go.

Ultimately the call of manhood, honor, and comrades won out and Smith duly enlisted.[33]

The conception of manliness also carried with it the assumption that "real men" would also display courage when facing the foe. This, of course, placed much mental strain on those entering the service. The Yale psychologist William Hocking noted in 1918, "Many men suffer, during their training days, from a fear of fear. They hope they will not funk when the time comes; but they are not inwardly sure of it." While the notion of fear and courage will be discussed later in the work, it was still important to those who entered the ranks to be seen as manly and courageous by those around them. Brothers Frank and Al Fraas managed to meet in New York just before Frank sailed for France in May 1918. In a letter to their sister posted shortly after Frank's depar-ture, Al addressed her concerns about Frank's willingness to fight. He noted,

> Now you don't need to think that anyone with the name of Fraas, even though it does sound German, has got any yellow inside his shirt. He and all the rest of the fellows, are just like school kids, who have been practic-ing for a ball game or something they are anxious to get in. They say that they have been waiting and working like slaves for a long time, and now they want to show the Kaiser what they have learned. Frank says that he wouldn't miss the chance of going over for anything. He says we have all got a time to go West, and we won't go till the time comes. He said to me "Well Al it will all be over pretty soon, and won't you and I have some things to talk about when we are all home together again."

The desire of young men like Fraas to prove that they had no yellow streak down their backs sometimes came at a price. Frank Fraas was killed by shell-fire in the Argonne on September 29, 1918.[34]

In our more cynical age it is perhaps far too easy to dismiss the role that patriotism and the obligations of citizenship played in getting men to serve. These impulses not only encouraged the volunteers of 1917 to join up but also seemed to have made the war's draftees more amenable to their lot. The sense of patriotism and duty may have been reflexive, but it was earnest. "It was a sincere effort to come to the military assistance of My Country," an infantryman in the 35th Division later recalled, and to "preserve the ideals in which I believed." Another doughboy maintained, "I thought the war was justified and I am an American citizen whose ancestors fought in every war since the Revolution." Paul Rhodes opted to enlist in the 103rd Infantry in the summer of 1917 despite the fact that he was leaving behind an ailing wife and a newborn daughter. He justified his decision to his sister by explaining, "I have left home, wife and loved ones to come way over here to France to fight for all I have left behind . . . But the words came to me saying 'Your country needs You,' so I had to go."[35]

The patriotic impulses that drove men like Rhodes were so strong that some men went to great lengths to get into uniform. Frederick F. Seidel "felt it was my duty" to serve but had a hard time getting the army to take him. He made three attempts to enlist over a six-month period but was rejected each time by army recruiters due to his size and physical condition. Ultimately he had his family friend, who also happened to be the president of the local draft board, pull some strings to get him in the service. Similarly, after he had been turned down by the navy for having a heart murmur, Glenn L. Denton tried his luck with the army. Although he admitted that he was "frightened" at the prospect of going to war, he "wished to do [my] duty."[36]

Closely related to patriotism and a sense of duty was the soldiers' faith in the justness of the nation's cause and its political goals for the war. It is hard to state with any precision how many soldiers were politically conscious and understood the major issues of the day. To be sure, some soldiers later rejected any idea that the doughboy generation was motivated by any great and lofty goals or agendas. One veteran argued, "The American soldier was not the introspective Russian novelist that certain war fiction would have us believe. He appears . . . not to have been concerned at all about the status of his soul, nor

Photo 1: Emil Johnson (far left) and his buddies pose for a photograph before heading off to training camp in 1917. Like many young men, Johnson and his friends seemed proud to heed their nation's call. Source: author's collection.

the many muddled causes that have dragged him out of an Alabama back-lot to make the world safe from anything in particular." He believed that in the end the doughboys' "primary, and frequently his only, questions in regard to the murderous trade to which he found himself apprenticed were: (a) 'When do we eat?' (b) 'Where do we go from here?'" Although there was much truth in the soldier's observations, they were recorded eight years after the Armistice and perhaps reflected the disenchantment that had slowly crept into the nation's long-term evaluation of its wartime experience. Even so, William Langer later recalled, "I hardly remember a single instance of serious discussion of American policy or of larger war issues. We men, most of us young, were simply fascinated by the prospect of adventure and heroism." As late as 1918, some AEF officers were also convinced "that too many of our men do not really know for what they are fighting."[37]

The apparent lack of political consciousness in these two soldiers did not mean that a faith in the cause was minimal or nonexistent. In fact, the dearth of education and understanding of some of their comrades exasperated the more ideologically driven soldiers while also strengthening their convictions. As volunteer Fred Sasse complained, "The selective service act called to arms thousands of men who knew absolutely nothing about the principles for which we were fighting. Many thought they were fighting for Wilson; some said they were fighting for France, while others would not have been surprised to hear that they were fighting for Richard III or July 4th." He moralized, "The soldier who did not realize that he was doing patriotic, Christian duty was one to be pitied, as much as a slacker is to be despised."[38]

Despite Sasse's convictions, it must be noted that American opinions about the war had undergone a steady evolution since 1914. Although mass opinion polls had yet to appear by the First World War, the results of a *Literary Digest* poll in late 1914 of 367 American newspaper editors reveal something of the general American feelings of ambivalence about the conflict. When asked which of the European belligerents most held their personal sympathies, twenty of the newspapermen supported the Germans, 105 voiced sympathy with the Allies, and the remaining 242 responded that they held no particular preference or sympathy for either side. The results of the poll led its authors to conclude that "the sympathy on either side is that of a distant observer. No belligerency is evident anywhere." Most of the editors believed that their personal views corresponded with the general outlooks of their readers.

While it is perhaps overly simplistic to use the editors' responses as a specific gauge of popular American opinion in 1914, the poll did point to the divisions and uncertainties of American attitudes on the war and its combatants. As war engulfed Europe in August 1914, many Americans viewed the event as a distasteful and self-destructive blunder of the decadent Old World. Wrapped in the Progressive Era's faith in societal advancement and science, Americans watched with dismay and regret as the "finest flower of Western Civilization" consumed itself in an orgy of destruction and brutality.[39]

The ambivalence with which many Americans viewed the war in 1914 set the stage for a bitter debate throughout 1915 and 1916 about the nation's role in the conflict. On the one hand, some Populist, socialist, and Irish, German, and Eastern European immigrant groups wanted the United States to stay out of the conflict due to their distaste for militarism, sympathy for the Central Powers, or great antipathy for Britain and Czarist Russia. On the other hand, many old stock Anglo-Americans viewed German actions in France, Belgium, and on the high seas as both a threat to civilization and democracy and a direct danger to American national interests. These conflicting views played out in the often vicious battles over preparedness in 1915 and 1916. An unrelenting stream of Allied propaganda and the publicity surrounding the sinking of the *Lusitania*, and other real or imagined German acts of barbarity, certainly colored American opinion about the war and its combatants. Clarence Mahan, who would ultimately be in the first American contingent to reach France, remembered this steady change in perception in his small town:

> We were quite ignorant of the world outside of Indiana and Europe was far, far away . . . there was an Atlantic Ocean wide and deep between us and Europe which kept the safe. Our newspapers soon began to publish more war news, blaming Kaiser Wilhelm of Germany. He was pictured as the devil himself, the Beast in the Bible's Book of Revelation, who wanted to conquer the world.[40]

By the spring of 1917, German strategic blunders, culminating in its resumption of unrestricted submarine warfare, and the interception of the Zimmerman Telegram had turn the tide of American attitudes against Germany and toward war.

Aided by the work of the Committee on Public Information (CPI), the nation's wartime propaganda agency, many doughboys entered the service believing that they were fighting to protect democracy, defend small nations from German militarism, and save the world from German hegemony. Few would have doubted the commitment of Charles Clement to the nation's political goals when he rushed to enter the first Officer Training Camp at Fort McPherson, Georgia, in June 1917. As he was preparing to leave for France in April 1918, his faith in the cause remained undimmed. He proclaimed, "The Allies *must* win; and every true American is glad of the opportunity to pay whatever price may be exacted that Prussianism may be annihilated forever and that Democracy may live." One Marine proudly admitted that he enlisted "to save the world for democracy, to keep the Kaiser's crowd from overrunning the U.S.," and to prevent the "abusing of women & girls as reported from the Low Countries." Similarly, an 89th Division doughboy stated, "I wanted to save America from Germans bent on world domination."[41]

Moved by the importance of the day in American history, Milton Sweningsen wrote home from France on July 4, 1918, that he had been "thinking during the day of how our old forefathers ... fought for liberty way back in 1775–76." He then reflected on what he saw as the great differences between the United States and its German enemy. Sweningsen concluded that the present conflict centered on the fact that while the United States stood for the noble cause of individual liberty, Germany "has replaced that ideal by the less high one of territorial aggrandizement." Likewise, William Roper later admitted, "I was adventurous, idealistic and patriotic and wished to make the world safe for democracy as President Wilson proclaimed." He also confessed that he had "been deeply moved by a film [*Hearts of the World*], portraying Dorothy Gish ... being brutally treated by the 'Huns.'" Sweningsen and Roper were not alone in the belief that the United States stood as a bulwark against tyranny. A soldier from the 82nd Division maintained that he and his comrades were motivated by the "very high ideas for which they were willing to fight."[42]

Although the previous statements have indicated that many doughboys were ideologically committed to the nation's cause, it is impossible to determine with any accuracy how many soldiers shared their beliefs. How deeply the average American soldier understood the causes of the war, and their dedication to the cause, was a constant concern to the nation's military and political leaders throughout the conflict. The Military Intelligence Division (MID), Commission on Training Camp Activities, and the War College Morale Branch all worked to monitor the attitudes of the doughboys toward the war and their service and to develop in them a proper patriotic political consciousness. The representatives of these organizations often blamed unit officers for failing to train and encourage their soldiers to accept the "right" position on the war. Reverend A. B. Cohoe, a representative of the Morale Branch, denounced an officer for admitting "My chief fear has been that after we get over there and do a little fighting, it will all begin to seem like damn nonsense." Another officer reported of his soldiers, "They know that they're here to can the Kaiser, and that's all they need to know . . . After a man has been here two months, the worst punishment you can give him is to tell him he can't go to France right away. The soldier is a man of action; and the less thinking he does the better."[43]

To counter these trends Morale Branch representatives set up classes, brought in CPI speakers and publications, and showed anti-German films and theatrical performances to encourage "right" thinking by the soldiers. In September 1918, the Camp Gordon Chaplain-at-Large, Samuel Black, informed the Morale Branch of his intent to "carefully instruct the men in the causes which led America to enter this War . . . mentioning the atrocities of Germany and the gross injustice she is showing toward all nations of the world . . . and show the men that similar treatment may be expected by us if Germany gains control over us either by victory or by a German peace." To ensure that the doughboys were insulated from enemy propaganda and antiwar, socialist, or Bolshevik ideas, Military Investigation Division (MID) operatives in stateside posts and the AEF searched out the agents of disloyalty and their publications. In fact, in their weekly reports to the chief of the MID, post intelligence officers (who also often acted as the post morale officers) were required to comment on disloyal activities and the presence of "enemy or pacifist propaganda" at their locations. For example, on March 11, 1918, the intelligence officer at Camp Devens, Massachusetts, reported that he had found a tract from the International Bible Students Association in a YMCA hut that contained "many pacifist, socialistic and even anarchistic teachings." That same month, the acting intelligence officer of the 91st Division at Camp Lewis, Washington, informed his superiors that he had uncovered a plot by the Industrial Workers of the World "to organize soldiers with sympathy for the I.W.W. and spread dissention within the division" and claimed that he had thwarted their efforts to "distribute a large amount of seditious literature." The intelligence officers were often aided in their crusade against disloyalty by the representatives of the various soldier aid and welfare societies in the camps. One Library War Service librarian was commended by intelligence officers for being "on the lookout constantly for objectionable books, also for brochures or pamphlets which may be sneaked into the library and left there as propaganda."[44]

Was the War Department justified in its concerns over the political commitment of the doughboys? The existing evidence offers a mixed answer. In January 1919 the Morale Branch directed its officers to survey soldiers awaiting discharge as to their opinions of their military service and the war. In response to this directive the morale office at Camp Grant queried a select group of sixty men. When asked why the country was at war, forty-four responded that the nation was fighting "to make the world a better place to live in," with nearly half stating specifically that the goal was to preserve the "United States from overthrow" and thus "save ourselves from the fate of Belgium." The others in this group specifically noted that the United States was fighting to save the world from German domination, to protect small nations, to make "Germany into a free republic," to "conserve world morality," to give working men a better chance, to end the "divine right of kings," and to "promote the brotherhood of man." Thirteen other soldiers maintained that the United States entered the war for the "redress of wrongs committed against us," to end German "ruthless warfare and propaganda," to protect freedom of the seas and commercial rights, and to maintain national honor and to "hold the respect of the world." Despite these rather ideologically solid answers, the officer conducting the survey still noted of the average recruit "in a great many cases he neither knows very much nor feels very strongly about his duty and opportunity in making the world safe for 'democracy.'"[45]

Up to this point, this chapter has focused on what motivated the doughboy generation to serve. It must be made clear that, at the time, few of the men were actually asked their opinion of the subject. To a very great extent, the passage of the Selective Service Act in May 1917 made the question largely moot. As one officer noted,

> Some of the individuals, a very few, wanted adventure, even though it was accompanied by danger. Most of them had led placid lives of routine, and wished but to be permitted to continue the even tenor of their ways. Suddenly, their Government said, "I want you, and you, and you." Draft-Boards

did the selecting and personal preference was not taken into account. The Government needed them and took them for its use.

Of the 4,178,172 soldiers that the army mobilized for the war, 2,810,296, or over 67 percent, were draftees. From June 1917 to November 1918, the selective service system enrolled 24,234,021 men for possible military duty, which the army Provost Marshal General Enoch Crowder claimed represented 44 percent of the nation's total male population.[46]

The Wilson administration opted to raise the nation's wartime army using conscription based on the lessons that it had gained from Britain's efforts to build its military and from Progressive Era faith in efficiency, fairness, and corporateness. Realizing that the nation was embarking on a mass industrial war, the administration understood that the draft had to balance the need for military manpower with domestic industrial, agricultural, and societal needs. Keenly aware of the outcry that the draft had provoked in the Civil War, the administration made the wise and crafty decision to leave the administration of conscription, which would include the all-important decisions of induction and deferment, to local draft boards. In theory the local citizens on these 155 district boards, 4,648 local boards, 1,319 medical advisory boards, and 3,646 legal advisory boards knew the conditions and circumstances of the men who appeared before them and thus were the most fair and impartial judges of who should be sent into the military.[47]

The intent of the selective service was to be just that: selective. The War Department and the Selective Service Acts first established the minimum physical, mental, and moral requirements for those to be inducted. The Selective Service Act of May 1917 decreed that draftees were to be drawn from men age twenty-one to thirty-one. On September 12, 1918, the age requirements were expanded to include men age eighteen to forty-five. The original Selective Service Act also excluded "morally deficient" individuals from the draft, mostly because the army feared that these men would be a constant source of disciplinary problems. The law targeted those men convicted of felonies or other "infamous crimes." Some boards seemed to have been willing to listen to the cases of those men who sought military service despite their criminal pasts, but, in the end, 70 percent of "morally unfit" registrants received exemptions.[48]

In an effort to balance all of the nation's wartime manpower needs, the local boards categorized the enrollees into five classifications based upon the individual's importance to the overall war effort. In the end, all of the men inducted came from Class I, those whose "military duty would least disturb the domestic and economic life of the nation." On May 17, 1918, the government further amended the selective service by adding the so-called Work or Fight directive. This edict allowed boards to change the draft classification, revoke any deferments, or alter the call number for any registrant it deemed to "be an idler or to be engaged in a nonproductive occupation." Although this change to the rule brought in only a few more men, the army provost marshal claimed that it did force 137,255 men into jobs that more directly tied in to the war efforts than had their previous endeavors. At least one man used the Work or Fight directive to his own purpose. After his wife had previously refused to grant her consent to his enlistment, he simply quit his job, knowing that the local board would then use the new rules to draft him. The record is mute as to whether, following the young man's cunning plan came to fruition, the couple lived happily ever after.[49]

In the interest of fairness and kindness, the local boards were also empowered to grant deferments and exemptions to those unable or unwilling to do military service due to being the sole provider of their parents, wife, and children, or for other compassionate grounds. During the war, local boards granted over 76 percent of deferment requests that they received. The requests for exemptions could be heartbreaking or humorous. One man could have claimed exemption from the draft based upon the dependency of his wife and children, but his spouse would not have it. She dragged him before the local draft board and forcefully led him though the registration process. When the board chairman asked her why she was so adamant about sending her husband into the army, she replied, "My man sits around all day while I take in washing to support him and the kids. I'm getting tired of it, and so he's going to war, where he will support himself." The board agreed with the aggrieved wife and even consented to sending the man away to camp the next day. In another case, a man made the blunder of trying to get his mother-in-law to testify before the board to gain him a deferment due to dependency. When she appeared, she angrily informed the chairman that the man had abandoned her daughter and had not paid her a cent in two years. After her testimony, the board recorder noted, the shiftless man "looked at his mother-in-law, and then thought about the German bullets; and with beads of perspiration on his face said he would join the Army." Not all of the appeals of women to the draft boards were so humorous. One woman from New York City wrote to the local board that her jobless husband beat her so badly that a judge had ordered him out of their house. However, the ruling had not prevented further beatings as the man forced her to provide money for his upkeep and rum. Her simple and heartbreaking plea to the board was "I ask you in the name of God see that my husband is sent to the front to fight the Germans and not a defenseless woman."[50]

Although the draft of 1917 to 1918 was perhaps the most fair in American history, it was not without its failings. The broad discretion that the federal government gave to the local boards in determining exemptions and inductions did lead to abuse and the uneven interpretation of the selective service regulations. For example, while some boards were overgenerous in granting exemptions to married men, others demanded very strict and exacting evidence of dependency before changing a married man's status. Some men certainly took advantage of the apparent marriage dependency loophole in the draft law and hoped to sway their boards to grant exemptions by seeking wives. The prejudices and racial views of the board members also influenced the decisions of the boards. African Americans, immigrants, and other ethnic minorities were often unfairly treated when it came to inductions and exemptions. Arthur Barbeau and Florette Henri discovered that African Americans, particularly in the South, were much more likely to be selected for military service and much less likely to be granted exemptions from the draft than their white comrades. The local draft board for Fulton County, Georgia, for example, only granted six of 202 exemption pleas from African American draftees while simultaneously allowing 526 of the 815 requests from white selectees. José Ramíez notes similar patterns of discrimination in wartime Texas against Tejanos and Hispanic immigrants. Furthermore, the belief that "alien slackers" were avoiding their duty as residents (and perhaps as future citizens) of the United States and were occupying lucrative wartime jobs while more patriotic men were at the front often colored how draft boards dealt with immigrant selectees.[51]

There can be little doubt that for whatever reason they chose to enlist, those who volunteered in 1917 were dedicated to serve. But did the draftees share the volunteers' commitment? The Wilson administration claimed that the selective service would be a draft of the willing: "a selection from a nation that volunteers in mass." It was clear, however, that some Americans were not eager to don uniforms. Despite the Provost Marshal General's desire to quantify every aspect of the draft using facts, figures, and charts, the looseness of his definitions and the ever-changing status of the men involved make it impossible to determine with any accuracy how many Americans actively tried to avoid the draft. Depending on how one parsed the definition of "slacker," "deserter," or "delinquents," you can come to a great disparity of numbers and percentages of draft resisters. John Chambers estimated that while twenty-four million men registered for the draft, another 2.4 to 3.6 million men avoided service by simply failing to register at all. That would mean that around 10 to 15 percent of those liable for service evaded the draft. Provost Marshal Crowder classified an additional 363,022 men as deserters because they failed to report before the draft board, did not report for induction, or absented themselves from the military en route to camp. Adding together these deserters with those men who failed to register, then upward of 16 percent of those eligible tried to avoid military service in some way. This work focuses on those who did serve rather than those who did not, but these numbers demonstrate that there was an undercurrent of discontentment in the nation that had to have colored the attitudes of some of the men caught in the draft's net. Certainly, as will be seen, the actions and statements of some of the soldiers that follow and the AEF's straggler crisis in the fall of 1918 demonstrate that not all doughboys were as committed to the cause or happy about their service. Yet at the same time, few soldiers, it seems, doubted the justness of the nation's cause and most were at least reconciled to their lot in uniform.[52]

For perhaps the majority of reluctant doughboys, the desire to avoid military service was driven by personal family concerns. A man who ended up in the 3rd Division, for example, stated that he did not want to go because his wife was pregnant when he was inducted. Lunie J. McCarlry of Norman, Oklahoma, was another case in point. Having recently married, the twenty-eight-year-old Lunie wanted nothing more than to settle down with his fifteen-year-old bride, Lillian. When he was drafted in September 1917 and sent to Camp Travis, Texas, Lillian even followed him to camp and took up residence in nearby San Antonio. The pair seemed quite close, but the fleeting opportunities they had to meet while Lunie was in training and the imminent threat of his posting to France seemed to make Lillian miserable. As she explained to her sister-in-law, "I would be the happiest human on the earth if I could only bring my Darling home and live once more as we did before he had to leave."[53]

Lillian's unhappiness certainly drove Lunie to despair and encouraged him to seek a way to exit the service. On February 12, 1918, he wrote home to his sister, "what are they doing about getting me out . . . you don't know how Bad i want out and if there is a chance i want out." His desire to avoid service and the fact that Lillian was now pregnant drove him to a desperate act a month later. Just as he was to be sent in a levy for overseas service, Lunie went into San Antonio and got so roaring drunk that he missed his movement order and was locked in the guardhouse. As he explained to his sister,

> i wanted them to put me in [the guardhouse] for i sure was France Bound and i don't want to go to France for dear sister you know France means death don't you and dear sister i am not going to go until my sweet darling wife get well. i had just as well die here as to go to France and get killed over there . . . tell the Boys to send me to hundred dollars for I am going over the hill.

Notwithstanding Lunie's plots and plans, the army had other plans for him, and in May 1918 he sailed for France as a member of the 110th Infantry.[54]

Some men wanted to avoid service for more base reasons. Benson Oakley was making good money working for the Curtis Aircraft Company in the summer of 1917 when he received a bit of unwelcome news. Despite the company's government contracts, he informed his fiancée, Helen Chadwick, that he was "sorry to learn that the employees here are not exempt in the draft, so presume I shall have to return to Norwich next week, unless they reach their quota . . . SHERMAN WAS RIGHT! WAR IS HELL." Oakley married Helen in October 1917, but neither his war production job nor his new marital status prevented him from being inducted in March 1918. After failing to get a commission from the Camp Hancock Officer Training Camp, he departed for France in July 1918 as a corporal in an ordnance company. Similarly, one of the first men drafted from Harrison County, West Virginia, was far from happy to be conscripted because he "was accustomed to earning fabulous wages" as a handcraft glass worker and didn't "relish the idea of risking his life for thirty dollars a month." The lack of enthusiasm that C. P. Stowers had for the service was reflected in a letter that he sent to a friend July 24, 1917. He lamented,

> My number is 792 drawn in the eleventh hundred so you can easily see that we have not got much of a chance getting out of it. I do not know whether I can claim exemption on the grounds of sole support of my mother. I do not care so much of going to Europe but I do hate to think of lying around in a training camp for five or six months or perhaps a year . . . It seems pretty tough but I guess it cannot be helped . . . Well [I am] hoping that you will be fortunate enough to keep out of it.

Yet, despite all the dread and antipathy evident in the correspondence of men such as Oakley and Stowers, they, and thousands of other hesitant soldiers, still did their duty in the end.[55]

The army was aware of the reluctance of some men to serve and developed a creeping fear and uncertainty that its ranks harbored large numbers of disloyal, disaffected, or weak-willed soldiers. Morale and intelligence officers were required to monitor the soldiers at stateside training camps and in depot units in France and to report to the MIB the names and offenses of any men that they believed were unfaithful or untrustworthy. These officers were aided in this endeavor by a large contingent of informers and special agents who actively tried to ferret out culprits by listening in on their fellow soldiers' discussions and by attempting to engage suspects in conversations. Their reports reveal that numerous doughboys were falling short of being "100% American" or patriotic "Pershing's Crusaders."

Jessie Wyatt was both loath to serve and far too chatty for his own good. During his training at Camp Pike, Arkansas, he openly admitted to a special agent that "fighting was not to his taste" and that if he were taken prisoner he would tell the enemy anything they wanted to know "if the telling would save his life." His frankness brought him to the attention of army intelligence officers who continued to monitor his behavior after he arrived in France. The same month, the special agent reported that George Eagle bore further surveillance because the man admitted that he believed that he would be killed if he went to the front and did not want to run that risk because his wife was expected to soon give birth to their child.[56]

Some of the soldiers objected to being forced to serve due to political or ideological reasons. In March 1918, Harry Schrand was hauled before a court martial for making contemptuous and disrespectful remarks against the president. Schrand proclaimed that Wilson was a "bum" and a "capitalist" who had involved the nation in the war by "loaning all the money in the U.S. to the allies." He concluded that "President Wilson was a grafter and that this war is carried on by grafters."[57]

Those unhappy about the prospects of military service could sometimes take drastic steps to avoid fighting. The provost marshal general noted that men tried to avoid the draft by self-mutilation or by various ingenious means of simulating serious medical conditions. Some men added egg albumen or glucose to their urine, took medicines to artificially increase their heart rates, or used food coloring to make it seem that they were coughing up blood. The efforts to dodge service did not end for a few men even after they had been inducted and shipped off to camp. In December 1917, a soldier at Camp Gordon reported that one recent draftee from the "hill country" refused to don a uniform or perform military training. The reluctant recruit's officers responded by making him clean latrines and work on a wood detail for the company kitchen. While working in the kitchen, he cut off the trigger finger of his right hand. As the authorities could not determine if the act was premeditated or merely an accident, they chose to discharge the man from the service. Charles Parker was not so fortunate. After cutting off two fingers to avoid military service in September 1918, a court-martial at Camp Jackson sentenced him to twenty years confinement at the military prison at Fort Leavenworth. The same month, another Camp Jackson soldier was sentenced to ten years hard labor for "refusing to submit to an operation that would fit him for military service." After he relented and had the procedure, the authorities reduced his sentence to six months confinement at the post stockade and forfeiture of pay. These incidents paled in comparison to the drastic steps taken by one man at Camp Thomas, Kentucky. On August 6, 1917, Private James Miller wrote to his parents, "We had a little excitement here yesterday. A recruit came in and passed the exams and was accepted so he pulled out a gun and shot the top of his head off. Nice way to get out of trouble."[58]

Military authorities were most concerned about the loyalties and commitments of the nation's immigrants. Their demand for "100% Americanism" stemmed from the belief that anti-Allied, pro-German, pacifist, or socialist tendencies within the immigrant community had the potential to undercut the nation's war efforts or otherwise provide aid and comfort to the Republic's enemies. The MID instructed its operatives to keep a close watch for discontented or disloyal aliens. In March 1918, intelligence officers at Camp Grant interviewed 492 recruits who they deemed to be not "thoroughly Americanized," due to their foreign birth or foreign parents. Of these soldiers, 340 declared that they were unconditionally ready to serve, 137 stated that they were only willing to serve within the United States, and 150 proclaimed that they were "unwilling to fight for America under any consideration." The officers concluded that this "lack of loyalty is in direct proportion to lack of intelligence" and blamed this failing on the fact that most of the men had entered the army from the "foreign colonies" in Chicago "where American ideas and education have not permeated, and where socialism, pacifism and ignorance are rife." While one officer believed that the benefits of army life and interaction with the "more intelligent comrades" were slowly changing the immigrants' attitudes, he recommended that the Military Intelligence Section needed to employ "aggressive methods to complete this work." Some officers also feared that darker forces were at work among some immigrant groups. They maintained that the discontentment with military life shown by Russian immigrants was due to Bolshevik propaganda and the aliens' belief that the United States had basically declared war on Russia for having abandoned the Allies.[59]

Such investigations were not limited to the United States. On September 12, 1918, alone, one agent in France reported to the 83rd Division's intelligence officer that seventeen recently arrived replacements demonstrated reluctance to fight or serve. This group consisted of six Germans, four men from the Austro-Hungarian Empire, two Russians, four Italians, and a Turk. When questioned, most of the Germans and Austrians stated that they were reluctant to fight out of fear of killing their kin. It is interesting to note, however, that for many of these men their reluctance to serve was conditional. The Austrians, for example, felt no compunction about fighting the Germans. Interestingly, although the Turkish soldier in the September 12 report had a brother in the Ottoman army he claimed that he would rather fight the Turks than the Germans. The reports to the 83rd Division's intelligence officer in the summer and fall of 1918 also reveal that a number of Italians were reluctant to serve in the American army but were willing to transfer to Italy to fight in the Italian army.[60]

The army's tolerance and treatment of dissenting immigrant soldiers varied greatly from camp to camp. As the 82nd Division received most of its draftees from the Northeast, Camp Gordon received large numbers of non-English-speaking immigrants throughout the war. Many of these men arrived in camp sullen, disobedient, and unwilling to serve overseas. The camp's leadership took a rather enlightened view in handling these troops and established a development battalion under the command of Lieutenant Stanislaw Gutowski where the reluctant warriors were given English classes and drilled by officers and NCOs speaking their own languages. In July 1918, the situation improved to the degree that 85 percent of the men were now "enthusiastic and content" and willing to fight in France.[61]

Throughout the war, the army was most concerned about the loyalty of the Germans and German-Americans within its ranks and their willingness to fight against their European kinfolk. In 1917, Illinois Congressman Frederick Britten proposed legislation in House Resolution 5184 that would have allowed German-Americans to apply for an exemption for overseas military service. Britten, who had been one of the fifty representatives that voted against the war, aimed to spare the constituents in his heavily German Chicago district from the trauma of taking up arms against their people. Britten's cause was taken up by the pro-German journalist and publisher George Viereck, who used his newspaper, *Viereck's American Weekly*, to drum up support for the legislation and to canvas opinion-makers for their views on the subject. Those who favored Britten's efforts believed that forcing German-Americans to fight not only would be soul-crushing for the individual but also would create morale and discipline problems in the army. Joe Condremanny wrote, "You cannot expect the same enthusiasm of a soldier in his work when he is asked to shoot, maybe, his own brother—or any of his kin . . . Let them stay here, where there is plenty of work to do." Harvard University's W. P. Dudley simply stated that "anyone who believes himself to be engaged in slaying his relatives and is worried about it, would be a very inefficient fighter, hardly worth his arms and transportation."[62]

Some German-American soldiers certainly agreed with these arguments. In October 1918, one stated to a covert intelligence operative, "I have uncles and cousins in the German army and do not want to fight against my own people. I do not want to go to the front and if I am sent there I will refuse to fight or be of any service whatsoever. I will try to be taken prisoner by the Germans. I do not like the army and I do not like the United States." In another case, Captain Felix Campuzano, whose mother was German, was cashiered from the service after admitting to his battalion commander that "it was very hard for him mentally to . . . fight against a people whom he had been taught to love and revere." Campuzano was not the only officer whose statements or parentage drew the scrutiny of army officials. The AEF revoked the commissions of two other officers suspected of disloyalty, and the AEF Military Intelligence Section investigated at least sixty-five other officers for various allegations or suspicions of holding pro-German sympathies or other opinions that were un-American. Reflecting the tenor of the times, most of these investigations started with a letter or anonymous tip that expressed some doubts about the officer's heritage, attitudes, or actions. Most of the officers were accused of holding pro-German sympathies prior to the war or of having had family members known for their German sympathies. A lieutenant was investigated merely for the fact that his father was a naturalized citizen of German birth who did not want to see his son enter the service and had refused to buy Liberty Bonds.[63]

The argument that German-Americans should be in any way exempted from the service did not sit well with most Americans. Reflecting these sentiments, Theodore Bilbo, the governor of Mississippi, announced, "An American citizen, no matter where he is from or to whom he is related, if he is not willing to answer the call of the Nation and sacrifice his all, going wherever duty calls him, is not worthy of the blessings that he enjoys under the American flag." He went on to declare, "Strictly speaking, there are no German Americans, and if a man hesitates to fight for America in this crisis because of his relationships, he should either be interned or shot at sunrise." The Princeton professor H. C. Warren angrily argued, "It is my conviction that any American who is not willing to serve his country in the trenches should be placed in a concentration camp." The German-born former solicitor general of the United States, Frederick W. Lehmann, whose two sons had already volunteered to serve, maintained that exempting German-Americans from combat duty would ultimately damage the group's standing in the nation and that "lines of discent [sic] shall become perpetual lines of cleavage" that would only confirm the suspicions of the more rabid elements of the 100 percent Americanists.[64]

Although some immigrants were reluctant to fight, the fears that army and government officials held about the loyalty of aliens and "hyphenated-

Americans" were largely unfounded. An intelligence officer in France reported on October 31, 1918, that the German-American doughboys in two infantry regiments that had recently arrived "Were willing to fight the Germans" and that they had informed his operatives "that their parents want to see this war to a finish. They said that the defeat of the German government will be a blessing to the people of the country." Even Provost Marshall General Crowder had to admit of the immigrant draftees, "The great and inspiring revelation here has been that men of foreign and native origin alike responded to the call to arms with a patriotic devotion that confounded the cynical plans of our arch enemy and surpassed our own highest expectations."[65]

Crowder should not have been surprised at the willingness of immigrants to serve. In fact many of them viewed military service as a means of proving their loyalty to their adopted land and showing that they were just as "American" and deserving of the nation's blessings as the native born. The Dane Knud Olsen was a case in point. Although he was an unnaturalized alien from a neutral country, and thus exempt from service, he made no complaint when he was drafted. He even concealed his status when his captain asked all of the men in the company who were from neutral countries to step forward on the day prior to their departure for France. Olsen recalled, "I smelled a rat—so I stayed where I was. The next morning I was on the boat to Liverpool," while those who had stepped forward spent the war in the States. After arriving in France, Olsen's company commander discovered Olsen's neutral status and planned to send him back to the States for discharge. When Olsen threatened to desert and join the Canadian or Australian armies if the captain followed through with the plan, the officer relented. Afterward he proudly asserted, "I earned the right to my citizenship by being willing to die for my country."[66]

Other nondeclarant immigrants followed a similar path as Olsen. George Lokides had immigrated to the United States from Greece only three years prior to the war and spoke very little English. However, he stated that he willingly entered the service "for love of my new country." Immigrant Elmer Jacobson joined to defend "the best nation on earth against tyranny and to preserve Freedom-Justice-and Democracy for myself & coming generations." Lokides and Jacobson were also motivated to serve because the military offered a quicker route to citizenship. Congress passed a naturalization reform act on May 9, 1918 that eased the path to citizenship for aliens in uniform by shortening residency requirements and exempting the soldiers from some other statutory qualifications to streamline the process. These reforms quickly bore fruit. In August 1918, over one thousand alien soldiers were granted their citizenship during a patriotic parade at Camp Dodge, Iowa. The willingness of the immigrants to serve did seem to ameliorate some of the distrust of Anglo-Saxon America. One officer witnessed a ceremony where six hundred "enemy alien" soldiers were made U.S. citizens. He was impressed that "these men, drafted last fall, could all have received their discharge because of alienism, but have chosen to see the game thru, and were overjoyed at the chance to get their citizenship."[67]

Immigrants were not the only group seeking to use military service as a means to gain full citizenship and their rightful place within American society. African and Mexican Americans also viewed the war as a venue to show white society that they had every right to the equalities, protections, and opportunities promised by the Constitution and the Republic's avowed values. Charles Huston explained his decision to volunteer for the African American Officer Training Camp in Fort Des Moines, Iowa, by noting, "I was determined that if I lived I was going to have something to say about how this country should be run and that meant sharing every risk the country was exposed to." Another African American maintained that he joined "to protect my country," and added that he and his comrades were "proud of our part we played" in the war, for our country." Mexican American elementary school teacher José de la Luz Sáenz wrote in his diary on March 18, 1918, that his service brought with it "the hope for a better future for our people who have been unjustly treated and scorned for so long." In a letter to a friend in April 1918, he explained, "My country's calling pulled me away from teaching the children of my *raza* and placed me where I can insure their honor, their racial pride, and a happier future. I am a man in arms, I will kill, I will help in killing, and I will do everything to save the nation." Like many other ethnic soldiers, Sáenz later used his military service as a moral lever to make the point that "making the world safe for democracy" started at home.[68]

Despite all the internal and external motivations and pressures to serve, there were still large numbers of men who simply refused to bend to the nation and the army's will. The Selective Service Act provided only limited grounds for exemption from the draft due to conscientious objection. The original act only allowed men belonging to the thirteen denominations that the government recognized as having long-standing and clearly stated religious creeds that opposed war and killing to request exemptions. Ultimately, 56,830 of the 64,693 men who applied for exceptions on religious grounds or conscientious objection had their applications accepted by local and district boards (87.7 percent). The men whose claims the boards rejected had little recourse other than appealing their cases up the chain of command and eventually, if needed, to the president.[69]

As the Selective Service Act made no provisions for conscientious objectors for other than religious grounds, if the appeals of those men who sought exemption due to their individual objection to war were rejected by the local board, it was left to their commanders to decide these men's fates once they arrived in camp. The vagueness of the system led Wilson to issue further regulations to the army on March 20, 1918, that allowed commanders to assign those claiming conscientious objector status to noncombatant duties in the medical corps and to engineer and quartermaster units assigned to duties in the rear zone of operations. However, the regulation still allowed commanders to court-martial any man who refused to accept service as a noncombatant or refused to obey any lawful orders. During the war, commanders tried and convicted 371 contentious objectors for various offenses under the Articles of War related to their refusal to serve or to obey orders. The average sentence for these offenses ranged from ten to twenty years hard labor, with one soldier being sentenced to fifty years and another to be shot for desertion (later reduced to twenty-five years in prison).[70]

When the draft boards failed to settle the matter of a conscientious objection, it fell upon the gaining commander to adjudicate the case. In June 1918, officials at Camp Gordon held a board of inquiry to determine the fates of the 173 men who claimed conscientious objector status at that post. Although the attitudes of local commanders colored how they approached these cases, the results of the Camp Gordon board generally reflect the tack the army took in investigating and deposing of such matters. The board found that twenty-three of the men who refused to accept any military service had valid religious grounds for their objections and were thus furloughed. Seventy-two other men were judged to have held sincere enough beliefs to claim objector status but accepted the army's offer to perform noncombatant duties in the ranks. In fifty-four cases, the board did not believe that the men's claims to conscientious objector status were sincere or valid and directed that they be assigned to any duty the army saw fit. Twelve men withdrew their objections and returned to the ranks before the board met. Although eight men claimed to be citizens of enemy or neutral nations, the board decided that the soldiers had no grounds for exception and sent them back to their units. The board doubted the sincerity of the four remaining objectors but decided to send them to the military prison at Fort Leavenworth for further examination. The opening up of options other than bearing arms also worked in other locations. Most of the men reported as being conscientious objectors at Camp Devens were coaxed into willing service by transfers to noncombatant assignments in medical units. On August 19, 1918, thirteen other objectors were allowed to forgo military service if they agreed to serve as agricultural workers on local farms.[71]

As the attitude of the local commander determined the approach that a given camp took when dealing with conscientious objectors, the treatment of the individual objector ranged from genteel persuasion to out-and-out brutal physical coercion. The intelligence officer of the 85th Division reported on May 18, 1918, that the conscientious objectors at Camp Custer were "being handled with considerable tact and quite a number of them are beginning to see the light." To convince objectors to accept the justness of America's cause and to submit to military service, officials at Camp Gordon forced the men to watch D. W. Griffith's anti-German melodrama *Hearts of the World*. At the end of the show, a chaplain "made a stirring appeal to the men urging them to change their minds and express their willingness to help in the War for Humanity and signify their change by rising." When none stood up, they were greeted by "the jeers and hisses of the real soldiers" in the audience. After a later showing of the movie, the camp morale officer claimed that three soldiers had a "change of heart," with one stating, "I have now overcome those principles which I possessed and am now ready to give my all or make any sacrifice and at any hazard for my country." In the end, the army claimed that approximately 80 percent of objectors ultimately accepted military service once they arrived in their training camps.[72]

If the camp commander took a dim view of conscientious objectors he could make life rather grim for the resister. Former Army Chief of Staff Leonard Wood was particularly harsh on objectors at Camp Funston, Kansas. He stated flatly that he viewed the resisters as little more than "enemies of the Republic, fakers, and active agents of the enemy" and turned a blind eye when the officers and men under his command used beating, humiliation, and hard and unpleasant duties to persuade the reprobates to accept their martial lot. One of the camp's pacifist objectors, Otto Gottschalk, was stripped, beaten, and forced to drink stagnate water from a ditch by his supposed comrades for his beliefs. The American Civil Liberties Union later claimed that as many as seventeen objectors died during the war as a result of the treatment that they received while under army control.[73]

In May 1918 an officer at Camp Custer admitted that he had "come to the conclusion that the few 'dyed in the wool' objectors are simply 'yellow.'" It is interesting to note that the majority of the soldiers in the army seemed to have shared this belief and took a decidedly jaundiced view of the objectors within their ranks. One chaplain reported, "most of the men have no patience with the men so classified and do not favor leniency" in the handling of conscientious cases. Much of the brutality heaped on the resisters was dealt by the hands of their fellow enlisted men. Officers certainly ordered, encouraged, or at least turned a blind eye to such behavior, but the troops themselves were the acts' willing executors. Irving Crump noted that the life of conscientious objectors in his camp was "no merry one," for they were "mighty unpopular, as numerous black eyes attest." He observed that "Everyone takes the slightest opportunity to emphasize their displeasure at the stand these men have taken." Some soldiers serving at the Camp Lewis base hospital grew exasperated when a number of the conscientious objectors assigned to their unit refused to wear the uniform. In April 1918, a group of the irritated troops marched "two of the most bothersome objectors" to American Lake at night, stripped them, and "offered them the choice of walking home nude or putting on the uniform." Although the two donned the military clothing, elders of the Mennonite Church arrived a few days later to investigate the event and the army was goaded into disciplining those who had committed the harassment. The treatment of these objectors was mild in comparison to what befell Sheldon Smith. When Smith refused to don his uniform, troops from his unit took him to the bathhouse, stripped him, scrubbed him down with a broom, beat him with belts, doused him with ice-cold water, hung him by a rope around his neck until he could not breathe, and held him on his back with his mouth forced open while cold water poured in, and finally made him get on his knees and kiss a small American flag.[74]

How did Smith's "band of brothers" degenerate into the *Lord of the Flies*? Again it is fair to say that most doughboys believed in the nation's cause and viewed any reluctance to serve as at best misguided selfishness and at worse disloyal and treasonous. This view was reinforced by wartime hysteria and the hyperpatriotism pushed by the Committee on Public Information. The other reason is sadly more human in nature. After more or less willingly giving up their own peacetime pursuits to enter the service, the doughboy enforcers saw little justice in having any of their peers escape the fate that those in uniform had already accepted. Both of these attitudes were reflected in a letter written home by George O'Brien upon hearing that a former friend had sought to avoid service. "So Rudie is a big enough coward to ask for an exemption," O'Brien exclaimed. "The dirty yellow slacker. It is a wonder he cares to live in this country if he does not care to fight for it. I sure have lost respect for him . . . I wonder if he doesn't find a hole, crawl into it and pull it [in] after him." For whatever reasons that O'Brien and the other legion of doughboys had to serve or, like Smith, attempt to avoid service, their lives were going to change as they entered their training camps and prepared for war.[75]

3

"Oh! How I Hate to Get Up in the Morning"
Life in Training Camps

The recruit found the interviewer's question to be unsettling and it brought the young man to the sudden realization that becoming a soldier had serious consequences. It might have been the matter-of-fact tone of the query or its detached finality that was so disconcerting. "If you are shot and killed to whom do you wish six months' pay to be sent?"[1] With this, a physical, and the oath of service, Irving Crump, Conscript 2989, was in the army. As with many thousands of Crump's peers, the transition from being a civilian to a soldier started in the training and mobilization camps that sprang up across the United States in the summer and fall of 1917. These camps were intended to quickly receive, process, assign, train, and indoctrinate the nation's military manpower and from it build an expeditionary army for onward staging and combat in Europe. In much of this endeavor, the Republic was woefully unprepared.

The army intended that the local draft board would put the "selective" into the selective service by determining the regional balance of civil and military manpower needs, adjudicating humanitarian and societal conflicts with the individual's military service, and certifying that the drafted man met the army's basic physical requirements. The local board also coordinated the transportation of their draftees to the training camps. One of the more important roles that the local boards played was to preserve the idea that the draft was just another form of volunteering expressed in the individual's willingness to do their duty by enrolling and submitting to the will of their local community. To cement this bond between the draftee, the community, and the nation's overall war effort, the local boards and the communities that they represented often organized the giving of communal gifts and elaborate departure ceremonies to send their men off to war. In a scene repeated across the country, the draft board of Harrison County, West Virginia, bid Paul Maxwell and two other men of the county's quota a heartfelt farewell with a round of "hand shakes and well wishes" and an enthusiastic ceremony at the train depot attended by "every able bodied person in town." As had been the case with the Civil War volunteers of 1861, many of the gifts that the locals and family members showered on those leaving for the army were of limited utility. One draftee recalled, "the local Board did things up mighty well. I find myself possessed of a razor, razor strap, wrist watch, two pocket knives, unbreakable mirror, drinking cup and lots of other things that I never expected to own or need."[2] However, in these cases, it really was the thought that counted, and the gifts and the celebrations left lasting impressions on those departing and went far to reconcile the draftees to their fates.

So who were these men heading off to war in 1917 and 1918? In line with the ideas of the Progressive Era and the scientific age, during the war the army collected a massive amount of anthropological data on its soldiers. From this study, we know that by and large the new army comprised young, unmarried, and relatively footloose men. The average age of the doughboy was 24.89 years old. Men aged twenty to twenty-five made up the greatest demographic in the American Army, composing over 57 percent of all soldiers. Those aged twenty-six to twenty-nine were 25 percent of the force, while those over thirty or under twenty made up only 12 and 6 percent, respectively, of the remaining manpower. In its census the army also discovered that it had at least 16 fourteen-year-olds, 140 fifteen-year-olds, and 935 sixteen-year-olds in its ranks. It should be no surprise men aged twenty to twenty-five would have been the largest age group. In many ways, that is, the perfect military demographic for these men would have had enough maturity to take to the army's discipline and training while also having the physical stamina for the rigors of army life and combat. As importantly, they were not yet old enough to develop a sense of their own mortality or to have built the attachments and entanglements of civilian life to give them too much pause to think when the shells and bullets started flying.[3]

The selective service regulations stipulated that the minimum allowable height for draftees and volunteers was sixty-one inches and the maximum height was seventy-eight inches. The regulation further stipulated that "to be acceptable men below 64 inches in height must be of good physique, well developed, and muscular" and that boards should reject anyone over six foot, six inches unless they were "exceptionally well proportioned." The army imposed these standards because it believed men under sixty inches were "not capable of carrying the weight of the proscribed equipment" and very tall men were too prone to varicose veins and heart trouble. To meet its growing manpower demands, in January 1918, the army lowered its minimum height standard to sixty inches. The army also set its minimum acceptable weight for a recruit at 118 pounds (raised to 120 in 1918) and its maximum weight at 211 pounds. It maintained that men below 118 pounds would have difficulty carrying their packs, rifles, and other equipment, while those over 211 pounds would be "too unwieldy for rapid movement." The regulations, however, did allow doctors to accept men who did not fit these restrictions when the subject was "active, has firm muscles, and is evidently vigorous and healthy."[4]

The army also conducted a detailed study of an additional 100,000 troops to gain an appreciation for the overall health and physiological measurements of its soldiers. It determined that the average height of the doughboy at demobilization was 67.72 inches tall. The study further found that the "tall Texan" was no mere myth, as soldiers from that state were on average an inch taller than their fellow Americans. Southerners were generally taller than soldiers from other regions, "while the men of Connecticut, Pennsylvania, New York, Massachusetts, and New Jersey have an average short stature." The statisticians in part attributed these discrepancies to the influx of poor and often malnourished immigrants into the urban northeast in the decades leading up to the war. The weight of the average doughboy upon induction was 141.54 pounds and he tended to add three pounds prior to demobilization. Lastly, the average chest circumference for the men was between 34.63 and 34.96 inches.[5]

So what of these men's backgrounds? The initial burst of volunteering and the subsequent draft brought into the ranks a wide swath of American men from across the socioeconomic spectrum. In 1917 one in three Americans was a first-generation immigrant, and one in five draftees was foreign born. A survey in 1919 of the prewar occupations of 592,854 veterans also found that the largest number (112,523) stated that they were farmers when they entered the service. This should not have been a surprise, as it was not until the Census of 1920 that for the first time in American history more Americans lived in urban than in rural areas. The next most prevalent occupations were "horsemen" (forty thousand), clerical workers (forty thousand), laborers (thirty-eight thousand), mechanics and machinists (twenty-six thousand), chauffeurs/automobile operators (twenty-six thousand), and factory workers (sixteen thousand). The draft also brought in an interesting mix of skills and capabilities. At Camp Lee, Virginia, one officer reported that in one 150-man company, 105 soldiers knew how to drive a Ford when they entered the service, but a similar company recruited from the Virginia upcountry had thirty men who could not read or write.[6]

A census from March 1918 of the prewar occupations of the enlisted men of the 164th Infantry allows us to refine this broad accounting of the soldiers' backgrounds and to illustrate the variety of jobs and the relative social position held by a random sample of doughboys. The 164th Infantry originally comprised men drawn from regiments of the North Dakota National Guard. It was originally part of the 41st Division, which in turn was composed of guardsmen from Colorado, Idaho, Montana, North Dakota, South Dakota, New Mexico, Oregon, Washington, and Idaho. When the division arrived in France, the AEF GHQ turned it into the 1st Depot Division and used its units as replacement detachments or to serve as the elements that formed the AEF's general administrative support backbone. The 164th Infantry became the support unit for the AEF schools around Valbonne. It is not unexpected that the occupations given for the soldiers indicate the rural nature of North Dakota and the other western states from which the 41st Division drew its troops. For example, 28 percent of the men were farmers. Although units drawn from the northeast and the nation's cities would have certainly reflected a greater occupational diversity than that of the 164th Infantry, the unit still displayed a surprising variety of backgrounds within its ranks. The occupations that its doughboys gave are still an indication that American society was undergoing a rapid pace of modernization during the period. The occupations given for the 330 men are listed in table 3.1.[7]

Given the general youth and background of the recruits, it is not surprising that their travel to camp often resembled rolling fraternity parties. Soon after pulling out of their hometown train station, one man recalled that he and his fellows "acted more or less like a football squad going to battle with a neighboring high school or college team" and that they passed the time

Table 3.1. Prewar Occupations of the Enlisted Men of the 164th Infantry Regt.

95 x Farmers	4 x Electricians	2 x Telegraph Operators	Jeweler	Salesman
52 x Laborers	3 x Bakers	2 x Telephone linesmen	Lathe operator	Saloonkeeper
16 x Students	3 x Postmen	Assistant Baggage Master	Locomotive fireman	Shoemaker
12 x Store Clerks	3 x Railroad Brakeman	Bank Cashier	Lumber yard foreman	Steam engine fireman
9 x Automobile Drivers	3 x Ranch hands	Bartender	Lumber yard manager	Steam fitter
8 x Railroad Workers	3 x Teamsters	Blacksmith	Machine operator	Steeplejack riveter
7 x No occupation given	2 x Accountants	Boilermaker	Milkman	Stone mason
7 x Painters	2 x Billposters	Cabinet maker	Miner	Storage battery man
6 x Automobile mechanics	2 x Building contractors	Cattle buyer	Musician	Streetcar motorman
6 x Butchers	2 x Foremen	Fireman	Newspaper editor	Tailor
5 x Horsemen	2 x Industrial Mechanics	Gas & steam repairman	Oil field worker	Tractor operator
5 x Teachers	2 x Lino-type operators	Grain & coal dealer	Photo developer	Waiter
4 x Barbers	2 x Medical students	Harness maker	Pipefitter	Wholesale grocery dept. manager
4 x Bookkeepers	2 x Pharmacists	Horse & cattleman	Plumber	
4 x Carpenters	2 x Plasterers	Hotel clerk	Postal clerk	
4 x Cooks	2 x Printers	Janitor	Restaurant manager	

Source: NARA, RG 120, Records of the AEF, G5 Schools-Army Candidate Schools, Box 1634, File 319.1, "Vocational Qualifications of Men."

singing songs and generally having a rowdy good time. On the train he had time to assess his new comrades, noting, "It was some 'Coxy' army all right. Some were dressed in their best, while others wore their working clothes and overalls. Some wore stand-up collars, as if they were going to a 'pink tea' party . . . Straw hats, derbys, caps, etc., were all in evidence." The festive atmosphere on many of the trains was enlivened by the free flow of alcohol brought on board by the recruits, handed out by well-wishers along the route or obtained at the short stops along the way. Paul Maxwell noted that his train from "dry" West Virginia was relatively sedate, but "once we reached Cumberland, Maryland all hell broke loose. Maryland is a wet state and the several saloons across the street from the Cumberland depot had not yet closed for the night." One of Maxwell's companions "made a bee line for the nearest one and within a few minutes returned with an ample supply of hard liquor to fortify him for any ordeal he was likely to encounter."[8]

Railroad owners complained that rowdy and intoxicated draftees often damaged railroad property during their trips to the mobilization camps. As the draftees wore civilian clothes during the journey, the railroads found it difficult to identify the culprits from the mass of other similarly clad passengers. This problem grew to such an extent that on July 31, 1918, the army ordered that every recruit would be given a brassard to stitch on their sleeves during the journey to indicate that they were in the service. As the Selective Service Act prohibited the sale of alcohol to men "in uniform," the brassards were also intended to prevent the draftees from obtaining the evil elixirs that were the root cause of so much of the rail-borne hooliganism.[9]

The high spirits that often accompanied the recruits' travel to camp were also encouraged by the reception that they received from local communities en route. The volunteers and conscripts traveling throughout the United States in 1917 often noted that they were greeted at train stops by enthusiastic crowds who showered them with food, small gifts, and well-wishes. Although public outpourings seemed to have waned somewhat during 1918, public support for the troops never disappeared. Floyd Sosey wrote to his mother on June 20, 1918,

> The old farmers would drive in to town from miles around just to see us go by, and if we stopped they would crowd around and shake our hands and

Photo 2: This group of draftees from Tracy, Minnesota, prepares to report for service on February 25, 1918. They have all been issued campaign hats to signify that they have been inducted into the service and were under military law and discipline. The signs in the back of the crowd assure the men of their community's support, with one boasting, "Good Luck Boys. We are buying government bonds to Back You Up." Source: author's collection.

give us fruit cakes etc. We had to put guards around the train after we got in the eastern states to keep the crowds away. At every station there would be automobiles full of girls giving away Candy, Cakes, Ice Cream, Nuts, Post Cards, Stamps, Cigars etc, and also their addresses which the fellows would fight over.

Private Walter Shaw had a similar experience and, like Sosey, was most over-joyed by the attention that he and his comrades received from the fairer sex. On June 9, 1917, he gushed, "The girls are just crazy about soldiers. When ever we got off the train they just simply grabbed us around the neck."[10] Interestingly, westerners Shaw and Sosey noted regional differences in the local welcomes they encountered. Both believed that people in the eastern half of the nation were more hospitable than those of their own region, with Sosey declaring, "The people here in the east are the most patriotic that I ever saw. There is just about twice the feeling here that there is in the west." Despite these variations, however, the encounters between the recruits and the locals on the way to camp reinforced the belief of the soldiers that their cause was noble and that their service was appreciated by the Republic.

The frivolity that the recruits often experienced en route to camp quickly disappeared upon their arrival. While men in National Guard units generally had built-in support structures of friends and family members to ease their paths to military service upon mobilization, the conscripts of 1917 and 1918 were generally cast adrift in a sea of strangers in a completely alien environment. Irving Crump's first disappointment came when he was separated from the other boys that had been drafted from his home district and placed in a group comprising mostly immigrants. He lamented, "Never in my wildest flights of fancy can I picture some of these men as soldiers. Slavs, Poles, Italians, Greeks, a sprinkling of Chinese and Japs- Jews with expressionless faces, and what not, are all about me. I'm in a barracks with 270 of them, and so far I've found a half dozen men who speak English without an accent."[11]

Upon being thrust into an unfamiliar environment with no friend at hand, the rookie's first days in camp were often disorienting and depressing. As one recalled, "Besides being all tired out from your long journey, you are hungry and everything about it is strange, bewildering, incomprehensible. As you stand in line waiting your turn, you are joshed by the soldiers loafing about. You know nothing about anything. You feel as green as the proverbial bitterbash. You don't know who's who, or which is when . . . everything is very strange." The greeting that new arrivals received from the men in the camp did nothing to lighten the mood. Crump and his party were met by gangs of soldiers who happily dispensed the warning, "Oh, you rookey. Wait, just wait; you'll get yours! Oh, the needle." He later admitted, "I had a vague idea what the 'needle' might be, but it wasn't pleasant to hear about it from everyone I met." The sergeant in charge of his group only made things worse by answering the rookies' queries with more dire explanations of what awaited them. This welcome and the newbies' homesickness made their first night in camp miserable. In fact one recalled that a number of men in his barracks actually broke down in tears at the thought of what awaited them.[12]

Crump's experience seems to have been typical. Men who had been in camp only a few days or weeks tended to delight in tormenting the new arrivals. The "veterans" generally expressed all the horrors that awaited the "fresh fish" and particularly dwelled on the pending tortures of the physical examination. Reflecting perhaps the great failing of the human condition, the hazed novices that arrived on day one quickly became the "veteran" hazers of those arriving on day two. Although he himself had only been in training for two months, one soldier reported to his brother in November 1917, "There are all kinds of new rookies coming into camp at the present time, and it must seem funny for them to see all us guys in uniform because you can tell how they size us up when they see us." He amused himself by harassing the new men while they were going through their first exercises and enduring their inoculations.[13]

There was certainly a degree of psychological dislocation that accompanied every man's transition from civilian to soldier. In the fall of 1917, a Regular Army officer observed, "Habit is the strongest element in the lives of most men, and in wrenching from him his daily habits of eating, sleeping, working, playing, meeting his friends, expressing his opinions, we play havoc with the recruit's world." He was not alone in this belief. After visiting army camps in the United States and France, the Yale psychologist William E. Hocking noted, "The loss of personal freedom is something that the soldier never entirely ceases to feel, and its mental effects are far reaching. In many ways he has to unlearn the imitative of civil life, and to disuse the constant preoccupation of the independent man—the *making of plans* for the morrow, and for the weeks and months ahead." Although Hocking focused mainly on the experiences of enlisted men, this disruption of everyday life and patterns also applied to new officers. John Castles was a law school student and recent Yale graduate when he decided to accept a commission in the African American 369th Infantry. Although he had joined with great enthusiasm, in June 1917 he admitted, "It's a funny feeling, this going to war, feeling that you can't make plans or anything, and that all the life that you've loved for twenty-four years is suspended for an indefinite time and may never be resumed."[14]

The fact that they were mere cogs in the collective army machine was generally brought home to the recruits in their first days in camp. The sometimes-arbitrary nature of military authority and their relatively powerless status in the system were made evident to them in how they were assigned and treated. The hustled pace of army life was made clear to one soldier the moment he arrived on the train. "Before anyone could move," he recalled, "a Second Lieutenant, fresh out of training school, entered each end of the coach barking orders a la Black Jack Pershing." His party of recruits was immediately set to work in the pouring rain, without any raincoats or ponchos, moving piles of lumber from one spot to another only a mere hundred yards away. The fact that "rank hath its privileges" was not lost on the new soldier. While he was soaking wet, the officer supervising the detail was decked out in a rubber hat, coat, and boots. During his first week in camp, Lyman Varney received a similar object lesson. "At morning roll call the sergeant asked all men who could type to step out. I and several others did and we ended up cleaning mule barns." Cornelius Freely found the way that the army managed people to be rather perfunctory and impersonal. In a letter home dated June 15, 1918, he observed, "You get very little chance to talk as they . . . put you where they please." When it came to his assignment in the regiment, the personnel sergeant glanced at him and said, "you are a bookkeeper and you can run a typewriter," and assigned him to be a headquarters company clerk without any further thought or questions. Varney, Freely, and the millions of other men who filled the ranks had to come to grips with the fact that while they were in uniform their lives would be dictated by the needs and whims of the service. The overarching goal of the training camp was to transform them from relatively free-acting, self-regulating individuals into parts of a larger collective body whose actions were intended to be mere extensions of the will of its commanders.[15]

After their discordant welcome to camp and their first brush with military discipline, the recruit's first great hurdle was the physical examination. The army was very concerned about the physical and mental capabilities of its growing legions. In theory, the physicals the recruits were given in camp should have been a rather perfunctory process, as they had been given physical examinations by the draft boards. In fact the selective service's "Standards of Physical Examination" made clear to the local doctors, "To make a good soldier, the registrant must be able to see well; have comparatively good hearing; his heart must be able to stand the stress of physical exertion; he must be intelligent enough to understand and execute military maneuvers, obey commands and protect himself; and must be able to transport himself by walking as the exigencies of military life demand." However, the army found that great variations in the physical examinations conducted by the local boards and the desire of some attending physicians to turn blind eyes to the defects in enthusiastic registrants made it prudent to send its recruits through another, more rigorous round of physical examinations upon their arrival in camp. Doctors at Camp Devens, Massachusetts, for example, claimed that Boston draft boards had sent them one man with only one hand, another with only one eye, and one more who was nearly dead from heart disease. Medical examinations of 14,244 draftees from Ohio and Illinois conducted at Camp Gordon in July 1918 found that nearly 12 percent of the men had to be rejected for physical defects or injuries that should have been caught by any competent draft board physician. The examinations in camp basically started from scratch and checked the recruit's balance, reflexes, hearing, feet, and eyesight as well as the man's overall dental, genito-urinary, and skeletal-muscular health. The examiners also quizzed the recruits on their mental state and nerves. At the end of the examination, the doctors then classified the recruits as Class A, physically fit for all service; Class B, fit for all service after some minor physical defect was corrected; Class C, fit only for stateside service; or Class D, unfit for any service and must be discharged. During the war, draft boards classified 70.41 percent of their enrollees as Class A, 2.76 percent as Class B, 10.58 percent as Class C, and 16.25 percent as Class D.[16]

The army sought to make the system as efficient as possible and established an assembly line process whereby the men moved in groups through a battery of doctors and attendants at various stations and checks. Fred Sasse noted that his group of 250 men was completely examined within a space of about two hours. For many soldiers the most disconcerting aspect of the inspection was that most of the process was done while the men filed through stark naked. Still, some found the process as humorous as it was intimidating. One wrote home from Jefferson Barracks, Missouri, on April 17, 1917, "We were taken to a room and stripped and lined up 50 of us at once [and] inspected from head to foot for defects. I think I passed 100%. We had to hop on one leg around the room then on the other it was real funny."[17]

Although some men certainly hoped that the physical examination would lead to their quick discharge, large numbers feared that the exams would cut short their dreams of military glory. As one nervously wrote home, "Tomorrow we are to be examined by the Federal Dr. I'll know to-morrow night whether I'll be taken or not if not you may see me soon." The fear of failing drove some soldiers to resort to cheating and other ruses to increase their chance of being accepted. When Lyman Varney tried to enlist in June 1918 he was rejected due to poor eyesight in one eye. This, however, did not stop the army from drafting him the following month. To avoid rejection during his physical in camp, when the doctor asked him to cover one eye and read the eye chart, he started with his good eye. When directed to change eyes, he simply made a motion of changing hands and continued using the sound eye. Although the army intended for the physicals in camp to be objective, some doctors still bent the rules to allow a physically unqualified but eager youngster into the ranks. One soldier had tried to enlist when the war broke out, but his five-foot-one height and 110-pound weight disqualified him. He still managed to be drafted in September 1917 and to skate past the draft board examination. Upon reaching Camp Lee, Virginia, he admitted to the examining doctor his true weight and his fervent desire to serve. He was quite happy when the physician instructed his clerk to record 130 pounds, the minimum acceptable weight for a recruit, in his file. Not all of these seemingly sympathetic actions by the physicians turned out so well. One such local doctor turned National Guard surgeon passed Joe Zwinge fit for duty, even though the recruit was stone deaf. Zwinge was a hard worker and a fine companion and the doctor wanted to be a "good fellow." Unfortunately, Zwinge's deafness later prevented him from hearing a shell and thus taking proper cover in the Chemin des Dames sector in April 1918. He was killed when the unheard shell sent a splinter between his eyes.[18]

True to the shouted warnings of the wags that greeted the new men upon their entry into camp, the battery of inoculations proved to be the most harrowing ordeal of the examinations.

Until the medical revolution of the late nineteenth and early twentieth centuries, disease had been the great scourge of armies. Following the latest medical research, the army intended to keep disease to a manageable problem by ensuring that its recruits were vaccinated to prevent typhoid, paratyphoid, and small pox. During the influenza epidemic of 1918, the army also gave out over 1.5 million pneumococcus lipo vaccines and a limited number of experimental staphylococcus and streptococcus vaccines. The antityphus vaccines were the most feared by the soldiers. It was administered in three shots given over two days. As James Miller informed his mother, "I get my second shot tomorrow. Its supposed to be the worst of the three. Makes some of the boys pretty sick." Miller's fears were justified and he became violently ill after the inoculation. Another recruit recalled that after getting the shots his arms grew red and swollen around the injection site and that he suffered from a very painful backache and a high fever. The side effects of the vaccinations were so bad that it was the army's general policy to give the new recruits no duty for twenty-four hours after the immunizations.[19]

In addition to certifying that the recruits were physically fit for service, the army also embarked upon an unprecedented effort to ascertain the mental capabilities of its soldiers. On April 6, 1917, a group led by Robert Yerkes and Harvard University ROTC instructor Captain S. B. Bowen met at Cambridge, Massachusetts, to study the possibility of using the new science of psychology to aid in classifying military manpower. The group's efforts led the American Psychological Association to petition the army surgeon general to adopt the mental testing of men mobilized for the war. In late August 1917, Secretary of War Newton Baker approved the use of mental tests in an experimental evaluation of officers and enlisted men at Camps Devens, Dix, Lee, and Taylor and authorized the army to hire or commission a handful of psychologists. Yerkes himself was given a direct commission to major and allowed to carry out four weeks of testing to demonstrate the viability of his plan.[20]

Over the course of the war army psychologists gave standardized mental tests to 1,726,966 officers and soldiers, or nearly half of the men in the army. At the time this was the largest effort to test the mental abilities of humans in history. In many ways, the testing represented the acme of Progressive Era thought: the use of science and organization to gain efficiency and to solve social problems. The testing reflected the era's belief in Social Darwinism and the "scientific management" of workers propounded by Frederick Winslow Taylor. The tests promised the army the ability to dispassionately and quickly "pigeon hole" its recruits into their proper jobs and places within the ranks. Yerkes and his fellow psychologists were certain that their tests had unlocked the key to objectively determining the degree of an individual's intelligence and were unafraid to make sweeping claims about what the test showed about the state of American mental acuity. Yerkes himself proudly proclaimed, "These group examinations were originally intended, and are now definitively known, to measure native intellectual ability."[21]

The data that the psychologists collected led them to some interesting conclusions. Some 30 percent of draftees were classified as illiterate due to their inability to "read and understand newspapers and write letters home." The tests also showed great regional variations in literacy, with northeastern native white soldiers generally scoring the highest in overall intelligence and English-language skills. For both officers and enlisted men, southern and midwestern native white soldiers tended to score lower than native white soldiers from the northeast and the Great Lakes states. Examinations conducted at Camp Devens, a post that received most of its soldiers from New England, revealed that 16 percent of native white soldiers were illiterate. Tests at Camp Jackson, South Carolina, a post that received most of its soldiers from the South, showed that 7.9 percent of northern native whites and 36.5 percent of southern whites were illiterate. The tests also revealed issues with the literacy and English-language skills of immigrant soldiers, and over half of these men had to take the test that Yerkes and his fellows had developed for illiterates. Immigrants from Northern Europe scored the highest on the tests among alien groups, with men from England and Holland ranking at the top in intelligence. Soldiers from Russia, Italy, and Poland had the greatest number of men in the "inferior" or "very inferior range."[22]

The psychologists' findings on the intelligence of African American soldiers were a typical reflection of the attitudes and assumptions of the era. The testing generally showed that black draftees scored lower than native and most immigrant whites and had higher rates of illiteracy. For example, 79 percent of African Americans tested at Camp Devens and 83 percent at Camp Lee were categorized as illiterate. The data also suggested that northern blacks were more intelligent than those from the South. In a very limited pseudoscientific study, the psychologists also determined that lighter-skin-toned African Americans tended to be more intelligent than their darker hued comrades. A detailed examination of 100,000 soldiers further determined that the "mental age" and "average intelligence" of the white soldiers tested was equivalent to a thirteen-year-old, while that of African Americans was just under a ten-year-old. Although Yerkes never came out and stated it, all of the data that his colleagues collected tended to reinforce the popular belief that whites were inherently more intelligent than blacks. Yerkes and his fellows, however, passed quickly over some data that suggested that some northern blacks scored above some Southern whites in the test.[23]

The army used the mental tests to try to put the "right peg into the right hole," and the exams became one of the tools for selecting noncommissioned officers (NCOs) and officer candidates. It is interesting to note that the examinations tended to bear out the army's social assumptions about the linkage between intelligence and a man's suitability for increased rank and responsibility. The examinations followed a pattern where test scores all fell out according to rank. In other words, majors scored higher than captains, who in turn scored higher than lieutenants, and so on. Privates generally scored lower than every rank above them. Yerkes claimed that this phenomenon had nothing to do with education. He repeatedly stressed that the exams were "to some extent influenced by educational acquirement," but "in the main the soldier's inborn native intelligence and not accidents of environment determine his mental rating or grade in the army." To prove his point he compared officers with the equivalent of an eighth-grade education to "native born white recruits of high school and college education." The end result was that the undereducated officers still did slightly better on their intelligence tests than did their more highly educated enlisted soldiers. Even officers in the rank of major who lacked a solid educational background scored higher than captains and lieutenants with a greater degree of formal education. Yerkes made no real effort to explain this phenomenon other than to assert that "It is evident that the examination is measuring other qualities, in which officers stand above recruits, to a greater extent than is measuring education."[24]

The greatest problems with Yerkes's psychological tests were that they were culturally biased and, contrary to his assertions, greatly dependent on a degree of general education to correctly answer the questions. This was particularly true of the "Alpha" test that was given to literate soldiers. The testing consisted of a fifty-minute-long battery of eight different exams, each focusing on a different intellectual skill. Test Two, for example, asked the student to answer mathematic word problems such as "A certain division contains 3,000 artillery, 15,000 infantry, and 1,000 cavalry. If each branch is expanded proportionally until there are in all 20,900 men, how many will be added to the artillery?" This problem would have required both an understanding of mathematics and of the concepts of ratios and proportionality. Test Three was a multiple choice test designed to determine the soldier's level of "common sense" by asking, "Why is it colder nearer the poles than near the equator? Because, A. the poles are always further from the sun. B. the sunshine fall obliquely at the poles. C. there is more ice at the poles." Test Four asked the examinee to establish whether two words were synonyms or antonyms.

Examples included "vesper—matin," "aphorism—maxim," and "encomium—eulogy." Again, the student had to have a well-developed vocabulary to score well on these questions. The most culturally skewed of the tests was Test Eight. This test assessed the examinee's ability to recall facts. Questions drawn from one version of these tests included

> The Wyandotte is a kind of A. horse B. fowl C. cattle D. granite
> "Hasn't scratched yet" is used in advertising a A. duster B. flour C. brush
>   D. cleanser
> Rosa Bonheur is famous as a A. poet B. painter C. composer D. sculptor
> The bassoon is used in A. music B. stenography C. book-binding
>   D. lithography
> The number of a Zulu's legs is A. two B. four C. six D. eight
> The scimitar is a kind of A. musket B. cannon C. pistol D. sword
> The Knight engine is used in the A. Packard B. Lozier C. Sterns
>   D. Pierce Arrow
> The author of "The Raven" is A. Stevenson B. Kipling C. Hawthorne
>   D. Poe
> Isaac Pitman was most famous in A. physics B. shorthand C. railroading
>   D. electricity
> The ampere is used in measuring A. wind power B. electricity
>   C. water power D. rainfall

Although Yerkes downplayed the role of education in intelligence, it is clear from the various questions that the exam results would reward white, educated, middle- and upper-class men. A survey of 69,748 recruits determined that the median length of schooling was 7.7 years for whites and 4.6 years for blacks. Given the quality of schools in the era's South and parts of the West, and the suppression of African American education in many regions of the nation, it is little wonder that some soldiers of all races had trouble answering these questions.[25]

The "Beta" tests for illiterates or those soldiers lacking basic fluency in English were a bit less biased. It consisted of ten tests and, like the "Alpha" test, was to be conducted in fifty minutes. In one test the examinee was presented with ten jumbled frames of a steamship and he was required to properly reassemble the frames into a correct picture of the ship. Other tests required the soldier to make a cube or the parts of a human face from separate features or to properly navigate a maze. In the last two tests the soldier had to arrange a series of pictures in a logical order so that they told a complete story.

The attitudes of the soldiers about the exams varied. Fred Sasse believed that the tests were a wonderful breakthrough in placing the right man scientifically into the right job. Many soldiers, however, viewed the test with a more jaundiced eye. One wrote, "For most of us the army psychological examination was the first and only such amusement we have ever had. We distinctly remember, at the officers' signal how we glanced at the long sheets of questions with foolish interrogations, and how we romped through the examination with a sneaking feeling that we were playing in the kindergarten." One officer candidate called the tests "the nut exams" and lampooned them for supposing to show a "high order of intelligence by answering such questions as, 'How many legs has a Papuan?'"[26]

Freshly inoculated and certified healthy and, after accurately determining the number of legs possessed by the average Zulu or Papuan, judged mentally fit for military service, the recruits now embarked on the true purpose of the camps: to discipline and train them for combat. But before that could occur, the camps themselves had to be built. With the federalization of the National Guard and the looming call up of the selective service men, in the late spring and early summer of 1917 the army had to scramble to build the infrastructures of sixteen National Army and sixteen National Guard cantonment camps.[27] While Camps Funston and Doniphan would be constructed on the Fort Riley and Fort Sill reservations, most of the camps were built on underdeveloped National Guard training areas or land that had never seen previous military use. As the army desired to construct camps in locations that offered cheap land and a climate most conducive to year-round training, it is not surprising that over half of the cantonments were in the South or Texas. Reflecting the old real estate adage that location is everything, the army camp planners did a good job in selecting the sites for their posts. Of the thirty-two original camps, nine are still in use by the Regular Army and eight more are being utilized by the Army Reserve or National Guard.

The building of the camps was a monumental undertaking. The army basically had to build from scratch thirty-two completely new towns, each with their own housing, water, power, sanitation, health, food, transportation, supply and administration systems, and, of course, the ranges, drill fields, and other training areas needed to prepare units for combat. Given the still recent memories of the wild western mining boomtowns, Major Granville Fortesque sought to convince the American people in the November 1917 *National Geographic* magazine that the army sought to avoid "the garish, irregular outline of the bonanza camp, that symbolized its equally loose and careless organization" in constructing its training encampments. Everything in the camps' creation was to be based on the "fundamental element of military life—order through efficiency."[28]

The scale of the army's efforts to build the camps is reflected in sheer numbers. In August 1917 the nation spent more on erecting the training camps in one month that it did to fund one year of work on the Panama Canal at the peak of its construction. Camp Lewis, Washington, would ultimately grow to be the army's largest cantonment. At its peak occupation it housed 47,650 men and stabled fifteen thousand horses. Within a short time of its construction, Camp Meade became the second largest "city" in Maryland, surpassed only by Baltimore. Camp Funston's population of over forty-one thousand soldiers rivaled that of the state's capital in Topeka. In one day at Camp Dodge, Iowa, builders unloaded nearly 1.9 million board feet of lumber for building construction. To build Camp Funston the army brought in over forty-eight hundred carpenters, electricians, and plumbers. These men worked seven days and sixty-five hours per week to prepare the site for occupation. At Camp Shelby, Mississippi, the builders had to remove over 180,000 stumps to make way for the camp's new building and drill fields. Despite being one of the smallest camps, the facilities at Camp Devens, Massachusetts, still produced twenty tons of ice and eighty thousand pounds of bread daily and had refrigerated storage for 120 sides of beef.[29]

To speed and simplify the process of building the camps, the army crafted a standard set of blueprints for every conceivable structure, be it barracks, stables, headquarters, or hospitals, that a cantonment would need. The standardized 120 foot by forty foot wood-framed barracks building was intended to house a complete company of 150 men. Unfortunately, after the construction was complete, the army increased the size of the infantry company to over 250 soldiers. The barracks were two-story buildings with integral space for the kitchen, mess hall, supply room, and company administrative offices. The soldiers lived in open squad bays that were lit by electric lights and heated by wood- or coal-burning stoves. The soldiers slept on individual iron cots or wooden two-story bunk beds lining both walls of the bays. The mattresses were filled once or twice a month with straw and the soldiers were issued two blankets for warmth. On very cold nights, they could add additional warmth by covering their bunks with the issue overcoat. Only the highest-ranking sergeants had their own rooms; the other NCOs bunked with the men. The soldiers did their laundry, morning absolutions, and bathing in detached bath houses. Officers lived apart from their soldiers in standardized 150 foot by twenty-five foot single-story buildings. In concession to their ranks, each officer had his own room.[30]

Although the army did yeoman's work in attempting to have the camps ready in time for the arrival of their first soldiers, shortages of supplies and the confusion and muddle that accompanied the opening months of the war still caused delays and problems. As they tended to arrive in camp prior to the draftees, in the spring and early summer of 1917 National Guard units usually bore the brunt of these difficulties. Since their barracks had yet to be constructed, the guardsmen generally spent this period living in tents. One Pennsylvania soldier reported home in September 1917 that he and eight other men were living in an eighteen-square-foot tent and were hurriedly putting in wood flooring and electric lights in anticipation of the coming fall and winter. Another guardsman discovered that his mobilization station near New Orleans was in reality "a cypress swamp" that the soldiers had to drain and clear as they occupied the area. Despite their efforts to improve drainage, after heavy rains the floor of his tent was six inches deep in water. One of his soldiers on guard duty even "killed an alligator during the night thinking that it was a German creeping up on him."[31]

Soldiers often complained that their early days and weeks in the camp were spent in hard labor preparing their camps for military use. Soon after arriving in camp, Irving Crump was put to work pulling stumps around his unit's area. As he and his comrades were still in the civilian attire that they had arrived in, the work quickly made a hash of the only clothing that most of the men possessed. Upon arriving at Camp Dodge in September 1917, another recruit discovered that since "the camp was not ready for us" he and his comrades mostly worked to turn a cornfield into a parade ground. As with Crump, the uniform shortages at Camp Dodge meant that for several weeks,

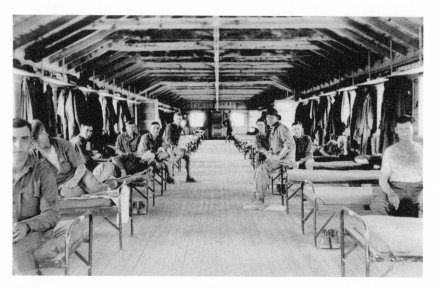

Photo 3: The spartan interior of a newly constructed army barracks. All of a soldier's meager possessions were placed on a small shelf or hung from his bunk or hooks on the wall. Source: author's collection.

the young recruits had to perform their duties in whatever shoes and clothing that they had brought with them from home.[32]

The locations of the camps themselves added further misery to the soldier's life. Few of the camps would have been considered garden spots. Complaints about the weather, terrain, and other conditions in the posts frequently pepper the letters that the men sent home. A soldier arriving at Camp Jackson, South Carolina, noted that the weather was so hot that "a man from here would freeze to death in hell. Believe me no kidding it is hot down here. No grass all sand the tree grows so dam high and far apart there is no shade." The heat led his commander to create a work schedule that mandated a half hour of rest for every half hour of labor. Another doughboy found the area around Fort Riley and Camp Funston to be "desolate looking . . . [where] all you can see are hard hills every way you look." He informed his mother, "I don't like the country around here very well one day is nice and warm and the next it is cold and windy. I hope they ship us out of here soon as a fellow couldn't get in a place much worse than this." After a stint at Camp MacArthur, another doughboy only half-joking wrote his sister, "If I had a home in hell and a farm in Texas, I'd go home that is how much I like the state. Its no good for raising crops so they made a camp down here. They feed the chickens cracked ice so they don't lay hard boiled eggs." In early November 1917, Floyd Sosey wrote that at Camp Kearny, California, "There is just as much dust as ever and you have to take a bath every day unless you want to look like a nigger." He grumbled that even though it was getting very cold, it was not until December that the engineers finally installed warm water in his unit's bathhouse.[33]

The situation was even worse at Camp Doniphan, Missouri, where the soldiers of the 35th Division had to cope with a shortage of water. In early September 1917, one soldier claimed that some of his comrades had gotten so sick from the camp's water that the soldiers now had to boil it before drinking. A month later Private Franck Fraas wrote home that the scarcity of water was so great that the rumor was that if it did not rain in ten days, "we are going to leave here." While the rumor proved false the post still faced a crisis. On October 26 Fraas groused to his mother, "Had devil of at time yesterday—couldn't get water even to wash in of course the wind was blowing we came in from drill dusty and dirty couldn't wash . . . cooks couldn't get water even to make coffee with."[34]

The winter of 1917–1918 was particularly cold and inclement. Deep snows blanketed the nation and brought freezing temperatures and accumulations of frozen precipitation to camps as far south as Georgia, Florida, and Texas. These unanticipated cold snaps made life in the camps even more miserable for the novice soldiers. In "sunny" Camp Kearney, California, in early November 1917, Floyd Sosey informed his mother, "I was on guard a couple of nights ago and had a post about fifteen miles out in the wilderness. I sure was colder than the devil out there. There was no danger of going to sleep on guard because you had to walk like thunder all the time to keep from freezing to death." A month later he further lamented that it had grown so cold that the army had issued each man extra blankets so that they wouldn't freeze at night.[35] At Camp MacArthur, just outside of San Antonio, Texas, the horrible weather made one doughboy particularly thankful for the woolen goods that he had received from friends and family back home. On January 13, 1918, he reported,

I got a package from . . . the Red Cross which contained a sweater knit by Mr. J. H. Dixon . . . socks by Mrs Virginia and wristlets from Mrs M. V.

Sheppard . . . It sure was a nice present and came in just right for last Thur
it started to rain and turn cold. We live in tents & had to stay up all night
to fire our stove. It was snowing and blowing so hard we had to have all
our clothes packed expecting the tent to go away. It snowed a foot & the
thermometer stood [at] zero . . . I sure put on the warm clothes as soon as
I got them.

The boredom of being kept indoors for days or weeks at a time by the weather
turned into a different form of misery when the melting snows turned the
drill fields of the raw camps into seas of mud. From "Marius's Mules" of
ancient Rome to the Grognards of Napoleonic France, it has always been the
special purview of soldiers to bitch and grumble. Despite all of the privations
the army was not a garden party and, by the fall and winter of 1917, the camps
were basically complete, and it was time to get on with training.[36]

It can be said that the new soldier and Marine's adjustments to military life
were marked by some continuities from their civilian lives as well as some jar-
ring discontinuities as they were immersed into what was still essentially an
alien society. Turn-of-the-century American civil and military societies were
essentially hierarchical in organization, deference, and rewards and privilege.
Given the age of the recruits and the increasingly urban and industrial bent
of American society as a whole, few entered the service without having experienced a curtailment of their individual freedom and the reality of "working
for the man." In fact, army officers often selected their NCOs from those
men who had previously held minor leadership positions in civil life. Major Charles Tips maintained that "men who have successfully handled six to
eight men in civil life as a boss of a group of farm hands, or as the foreman
of a small department in some factory, will almost invariably make good corporals, and men with relatively more experience will, in most cases, qualify to
fill relatively higher positions."[37]

Despite the transference of similar worker-boss patterns from the civilian
to the military world, they were still fundamentally different in their function, outlooks, and rules. No disgruntled soldier could quit his army job. A
labor dispute in the army was called a mutiny, and the strike organizer was
subject to the death penalty. In theory, the military still operated under premodern ideas of paternalism and noblesse oblige. The bastions of tradition in
the old army maintained that a good and effective company was one modeled

on a happy family where the commander and first sergeant were stern but benevolent parents. In one of the most widely read advice manuals for new officers, Colonel James Moss informed the nascent leaders, "With regard to his company the Captain stands in the same light as a father of a large family of children. It is his duty to provide for their comfort, sustenance, and pleasure; enforce strict rules of obedience, punish the refractory and reward the deserving . . . He should by word and act make every man in the company feel that the Captain is his protector."[38] Thus, army life was essentially paternalistic socialism, not a democracy.

Although the military culture was paternalistic, the recruit was still at the mercy of those placed above him, and these leaders' definitions of paternalism governed the soldiers' lives. Soldiers and Marines often commented on what they termed "hard-boiled" leaders and instructors. The "hard-boiled" were generally long-service officers or NCOs (which over the course of the war could also mean someone who had been in the service slightly longer than the recruit) who sought to train and discipline their young charges with the judicious or injudicious use of salty language, punishments, pushes, and blows. Upon reporting to Parris Island for his basic training, Warren Jackson was quickly impressed by the rough discipline meted out by the Marine Corps's NCO:

> Upon the slightest mistake made by one of the men, Sergeant Bunch cursed furiously . . . The use of physical violence by sergeants was not uncommon in some of the companies . . . After swearing at the man for a while, it was not uncommon for the sergeant to call the man out of the ranks and force him to run until his tongue hung out, while the other men looked on, wondering whose turn it would be next. Returning the man to his position, he would probably swear at him some more, and if the sergeant got tired he would probably then turn the man over to one of the corporals, who in turn swore at him a while "to put a little discipline in him." Once or twice, Sergeant Bunch told me to "wipe a smile off my face," but that was as far as the correction went. Also the smile.[39]

These NCOs believed that the best way to care for their military wards was to instill the proper obedience and toughness in the recruits that would prepare them for the challenges that lay ahead.

Every soldier and Marine adjusted to military life and the experiences of training camp differently. Some took well to the new environment; some were shocked or rebelled at the government's impositions into their lives; and some merely saw the service as a change of circumstances, something to be endured. Most realized that the military operated under different rules, standards, and expectations from the civilian world and that their service was going to change their own perceptions and ways of living. One novice Marine marveled that at basic training "we were indeed in a new world with new values. A man was not known by what he possessed or had done in civilian life. The question was what could he do and what did he do *then*." In November 1917, a soldier in the 35th Division informed his mother, "When I get out of this Army I sure will be a different fellow. I can see for myself that I have changed from a boys viewpoint to a mans and I am just as serious as an old judge. This Army life sure has brought me out of the kinks and made me look at things in a different light altogether."[40]

From the moment they arrived in camp the soldiers learned that the military ran by its own set of regulations and that it placed value on things that sometimes seemed trivial to the recruits. To keep everyone apprised of the laws and policies that governed their everyday lives, one soldier informed the folks at home that "they gather you ever so often and read the rules to you about war and about different things." Ignorance was not accepted as an excuse for violating the myriad of orders and regulations that ran the army. The soldiers often commented on the army's fetish for neat and orderly appearance and cleanliness. One man complained to his brother, "in the morning we all have to do what they call police duty, go all around the barrack and pick up all paper and chew of tobacco and stumps" of cigarettes, a task that he believed was rather demeaning and pointless. Mike Scheck warned, "If you don't keep clean in the army they get a detail of men with scrub brushes and give you the most rubbing in the world." Men who failed to live up to the new norms of cleanliness and behavior alienated their peers both by their personal slovenliness and through the collective punishments that often befell the group when any part of their barracks failed to pass inspection. In such cases, as Scheck alluded to, the offending party was summarily and brutally brought back into line by a direct form of peer pressure.[41]

As many of the nascent doughboys had never been away from the loving care of their female folk before, they quickly had to learn the rudiments of "woman's work": washing clothes, sewing, and general housekeeping. Some of these lessons came hard. After washing his flannel shirt in hot water, one soldier discovered that when it had dried it had shrank so much that it was now far too short for him. A female friend of Andy Magnus teased him for the skills he was picking up in the army. She noted, "What a help you will be to your mother when you come home! Learning to *wash* and now learning to *iron*. Some housekeeper!" Despite the disconcerting change in gender roles, most soldiers accepted their newfound skills with equanimity. In fact one soldier joked to his sister, "They sure learn us how to keep clean in the army. When I get home I will show Ma how to do some real washing."[42]

As the training camps began to fill up in the summer of 1917, Regular Army officers James Moss and William Waldron published a small book titled *What Sammy's Doing*. Their audience was the mothers and fathers of America and the book was to serve as both a primer to the parents of their sons' life in camp and an assurance that the doughboy's military experience would be wholesome and a positive transformative experience. Moss and Waldron guaranteed that military training would instill in their sons "self confidence and self respect, self control and orderliness" and build a person who "heads law and order." Furthermore the soldier will return with "sturdiness, loyalty, sound body, good digestion, handiness, steadiness, strength, hardiness," and "endurance." In other words, the sons that they had entrusted to the army would come back to them as better citizens and men.[43]

Many men in the training camps agreed with Moss and Waldron's rosy assessment of army life and viewed their experience in a positive light. On October 13, 1917, machine gunner Ira Wilkenson wrote his sister, "If I didn't like the Army I guess I would be crazy. But I like it, and am not ashamed to own it a bit." Another informed the folks back home, "I suppose Ma thinks the army is a bum life, tell her it aint and all the soldiers here are happy always raising hell and they cant wait until their time comes that they can go overseas." While waiting to sail for France, Paul Andrews, a Jewish kid from Brookline, Massachusetts, informed his aunt, "I have gotten into the swing of things and am beginning to like it. It was pretty hard at first but we are getting hardened to the work and it seems easier than it was at first . . . On the whole it is a good life plenty of fresh air, and up at a quarter of six and into bed at nine, and I feel great. The best that I have felt in a long time."[44]

Like Andrews, many of the rookies admitted that adjustment to army life was hard at first but that they had grown accustomed to it over time. The soldier's correspondence often tried to make clear to the home front that no matter how much the troops might be enjoying camp life, the army was no Sunday cotillion. A soldier in the 310th Infantry informed his brother-in-law,

> Camp life is great. I like it best as far as training is concerned but believe me we have been doing some hard drilling in the last two weeks only 8 hours a day. A person at home cannot understand what it is to stand out on that field all day and drill with only 2 rests, working in a shop is nothing compared with training. The sun is so hot that some of the fellows keil over.

Another assured his friend, "Army life is kind of tough but we get plenty to eat and enough sleep . . . We drill almost every day and lots of men can't stand it and they fall out of ranks but I can stick it out easy." In a similar vein, Dewitt McIntyre wrote home from Camp Hancock, Georgia, in September 1917,

> Our camp is getting better every day and our work is getting easier. It was not too pleasant for a while. It took us a while to get acclimated and instead of drilling we had to clear a woods and were covered with poison ivy, and there was trouble in the kitchen—we of course were the ones who suffered, but we have our land cleared now and our tents are up in good shape.

The soldiers' boasting of their newfound ruggedness sometimes backfired. One female friend chided a prideful doughboy for getting a "swelled head" now that he was in uniform, and teased him by noting, "it must be pretty tough work and especially for you fellows that never had any hard work to do."[45]

The soldiers that seemed most content with being in the army were those who believed that the training that they were receiving was setting them up for better opportunities in civilian life. Soon after arriving at Camp Sherman, Ohio, in July 1918, one man assigned to the base hospital was trained to work in the field of bacteriology. He was excited at the posting and informed a friend, "this is a wonderful place for experience and believe me I am going to take advantage of all opportunities which present themselves." Likewise, Mike Scheck learned to be an automechanic while stationed at Camp Johnston, Florida, and happily told his sister, "I'm getting to like this camp very much, a fellow [has] got a good chance to learn something around here they have got all kinds of trade schools here and I expect to be a supply sergeant soon."[46]

Despite these fortuitous circumstances, army life was also about learning to live with disappointment. Many soldiers quickly learned that the "needs of the service" trumped individual desires in most cases. As he had experience in clerical work, Cornelius Freely was temporarily assigned to in-process other recruits upon his arrival at Camp Seviers, South Carolina. Given his skills, he ultimately hoped to be given a desk job in the quartermaster corps. Instead, he wound up serving as an infantryman. Despite this setback, he remained hopeful and informed his girlfriend, "Don't you go and worry about me being in the infantry as they can make better use of me than just shouldering a gun." Upon being assigned to work with signal pigeons, another soldier sent his mother a melodramatic and inaccurate missive stating that he was glad that he had taken out War Risk Insurance because in his new line of work, "I am classed as a spy by all warring powers and receive only time to say my prayers if they get me."[47]

As could be expected, not every new soldier was happy with his lot. Being torn away from family and good jobs to face the hardship of military service and the possibility of violent death did not sit well with everyone. Some soldiers were also dissatisfied with camp life for the same reasons that such a living had discontented their Civil War predecessors. They had joined to fight and have adventure, not to march around and pick up cigarette butts on monotonous stateside camps. An engineer soldier at Fort Thomas, Kentucky, complained on July 29, 1917, "I've wound up my second week around here and am almost ready to move. I get my third and last shot in the morning and am expecting marching orders this week. I hope they do come along for I'm getting a bit tired of this place. Too much loafing and too little soldiering. Too many smart recruits." In October of the same year June B. Smith groused, "We thought that we would leave here within a month but the way things have turned out it will be several months before we go and really I don't think that we will ever see France unless we buy a ticket and take a trip over to see the sights some later years." Smith did not realize how good he had it. Within a year he and his 35th Division comrades not only had his longed-for all-expense-paid trip to France but were also enduring a pounding from the Germans in the Meuse Argonne.[48]

Not all of the soldier's time in camp was dedicated to training. At the end of the duty day, once the soldier completed any required cleaning or other duties, he was generally free to partake of the educational, spiritual, or entertainment possibilities offered in the camp. Fred Sasse and his comrades, for example, were allowed to be away from their company area two evenings a week until midnight if duty and the training schedule allowed. Additionally, they could apply for a pass on Sundays that allowed them to leave post from reveille to midnight. However, his commanders only issued a small number of these passes each week, and any infraction of the rules removed a man from consideration. Under certain circumstances, commanders allowed soldiers to take leave for up to ten days or could grant them furloughs for anything in excess of ten days. Generally officers would only grant furloughs for some dire circumstances such as a serious sickness in the soldier's family.[49]

A later chapter will discuss the military's efforts to build and maintain morale, but, as these endeavors played a major role in the soldier's life in camp, a few words on the subject are in order. Unit commanders and various welfare organizations, such as the Salvation Army, Knights of Columbus, and the Young Men's Christian Association, subscribed to the belief that idle hands were the devil's workshop and sought as many wholesome activities and diversions as possible. Most units fielded an array of sports teams and even put on expeditions in the local community. For example, in November 1917, the 35th Division football team played against the nearby University of Oklahoma. The welfare organizations also took the lead in establishing links to the local community and organizing mixers and dances. After one such event, a Marine training at Mare Island, California, enthusiastically related to his father, "We had a big dance down at the navy yard here last night about a thousand girls from Frisco were over and we all had a fine time."[50]

Not all such endeavors to cater to the recruit's needs were so successful. Soon after the establishment of Camp Funston, two entrepreneurs from Sioux City, Iowa, approached the army with a plan to establish an entertainment and shopping arcade to serve the troops. These two were to pay for building the "Zone," as the arcade was known, with 10 percent of any profits from the business going to the Camp Post Exchange Fund. Although the intent of the enterprise was to cater to the soldiers' needs and contribute to morale, T. P.

Smith, a social welfare volunteer in the camp, claimed that army officers were in collusion with the entrepreneurs to make money at the soldiers' expense. Smith noted that the Zone's owners had worked to undercut the efforts of the YMCA and the camp Liberty Theater to hold free boxing events and to bring in inexpensive movies and theatrical shows. He reported that "The Zone owners are getting away with high prices, poor service and cheap merchandise, because they have protection enough from some military source" and that "50,000 boys are being exploited for the profit of two rather questionable business men." When Smith complained of the poor quality of the shows in the Zone, one manager retorted that he could always fill the house by giving the boys "a few cheap untrained chorus girls" who provided "a few indecent lines and gestures."[51]

Some soldiers and Marines chose to seek their entertainment in the civilian communities outside of camp. The availability and quality of these diversions varied greatly depending on the size of the local community, their long-term relationship with the military, and the overall attitudes of the civilians toward the doughboy newcomers. In communities with long-standing military posts the locals sometimes viewed the arrivals as merely the latest in a long line of soldiers or Marines who had the potential of being nuisances or business opportunities. A Marine was disappointed at the reception he received in Galveston, Texas. "I don't like the people here at all," he complained. "They aren't one bit cordial or inviting. It seems as if this is an old army post and the boys before have raised such havoc that the people have shunned the soldier ever since." Other soldiers were equally irritated when the locals were not used to having soldiers in the neighborhoods and viewed the troops as their own form of entertainment. This prompted a soldier in a post in Kentucky to carp to his mother, "People just crowd out here Sundays to see the animals. Especially at mess call in the evenings, they line up around the mess hall to watch us feed."[52]

Over fifty years after the Civil War, the heirs of Johnny Reb and Billy Yank still found the regions of their former foes to be somewhat alien. A northerner wrote from Camp Hancock, Georgia, in April 1918, "This is quite a nice place but you know [I] would just as well be up North somewhere where the people are civilized." Southerners, on the other hand, often found the industrial cities of the North to be noisy, crowded, and equally uncivilized.

In some cases familiarity brought an end to age-old animosities. On September 11, 1917, Private Dewitt McIntyre noted that in Augusta, Georgia, "at first the boys here were not well satisfied with the cool treatment of the Southern people and the citizens here, [they] thought us just as cool. But they are making an effort to get acquainted with us." Two months later he informed his mother, "Yesterday I was invited down to Augusta for both dinner and supper. The people treated me fine. They have a Victrola and a great many of our records. We had hot turkey for dinner and cold turkey for supper." With dinner over, the family took him on a pleasant three-hour automotive tour of the area.[53]

Despite all the allure of shopping and entertainment that the local community might offer, for many soldiers like McIntyre the best off-post experience was being taken in by a local family for a home-cooked dinner and other prosaic activities. In these settings the soldier could momentarily forget the tribulations of army life and enjoy something that felt like the civilian lives that they had left behind. In fact many soldiers simply wanted to leave camp just to leave camp, to get away from the military altogether for just a short while. Unfortunately, given the large military populations that sprang up across the nation, those seeking this escape were often disappointed. A soldier at Camp Kearny, California, observed, "San Diego is seventeen miles from here and it only costs fifty cents [for] the round trip. Only about one person out of six on the streets are not in uniform so you can see for yourself what a big bunch of men there are here. There are twenty-five or thirty [train] car loads of men coming in every day from all over the United States." A temporary escape from camp did not remove the soldier from Uncle Sam's watchful eyes. At all times, the soldier on pass, leave, or furlough had to carry the proper documentation to prove that his absence from camps was valid. Soldiers were also generally prohibited from wearing civilian clothes on or off posts. This made the soldier readily identifiable to the MPs, who seemed to relish in constantly stopping and asking doughboys on the street to see their papers, especially, some complained, if the soldier was escorting a female companion.[54]

Whether seeking amusements or buying the various necessities and small luxuries associated with army life, one of the constant concerns of the doughboys was with their pay. Under the pay table authorized on March 1, 1918, a lieutenant general received $916.67 a month in pay, while a major general made $666.67, a brigadier general $500, a colonel $333.33, a lieutenant colonel $291.67, a major $250, a captain $200, a first lieutenant $166.67, and a second lieutenant $141.67. For enlisted men on their first enlistment (which included the vast majority of the war's soldiers) a private was paid $30 per month; a private first class $33; a mechanic or corporal $36; a horseshoer, cook, or line sergeant $38; a band or color sergeant $44; and sergeant majors and first sergeants made $51. Some enlisted men with very technical skills received considerably higher pay. For example, master signal electricians and master aviation mechanics in the Air Service pocketed $121.50 per month.[55]

The relatively low pay of the lowly private led many to call themselves "dollar a day professionals." In fact one ditty that made the rounds in the AEF lamented,

Hip, hip, I had a good job and I quit.
A dollar a day
Is damn good pay
For a guy that shovels shit!

There were grounds for the doughboys' complaints. While the private was earning a dollar a day for twenty-four hours of service, due to the wartime production boom, in 1918 the average factory worker was earning 53 cents an hour ($4.24–$6.36 per day); a miner was earning 67 cents an hour ($5.36–$8.04); and a construction worker was bringing home 57 cents an hour ($4.56–$6.84 per day). Although wartime inflation cut into the civilian worker's buying power and the military provided free food, clothing, shelter, and medical care for its enlisted men, there still remained a great disparity between those keeping the home fires burning and those fighting to make the world safe for democracy.[56]

It is devilishly difficult for a mathematically challenged historian to offer an accurate estimation of what the doughboy would earn if converted to today's currency. However, it is possible to provide an idea of the soldier's buying power based upon the price of common items in 1917 and 1918. In 1918 a five pound bag of flour cost thirty-four cents; round steak was thirty-seven cents a pound; bacon fifty-three cents a pound; a dozen eggs cost fifty-seven cents; and the national average for a half gallon of milk was twenty-eight cents. Additionally, a box of Kellogg's Corn Flakes cost eight cents a box; Campbell's tomato soup was ten cents a can; Coca Cola cost five cents a bottle; and a doughboy could enjoy a sixteen-ounce Hershey Bar for three cents.[57]

Although American soldiers seldom thought that their wages were princely, they were well paid compared to their European counterparts. The gross pay of the American private was $360 per year while his British and French comrades made the equivalent of $89 and $20 per year, respectively. The long-suffering Poilu earned only a franc per day, which was roughly equivalent to twenty American cents in 1918. To put the French soldier's pay into perspective a pack of cigarettes cost him approximately forty centimes (one hundred centimes to the franc) and the minimum fare for all taxis in Paris in 1918 was seventy-five centimes.[58]

If the doughboy was wealthy in comparison to the war's other combatants, it seldom seemed so to him. The process of being paid itself was straightforward. On payday the soldiers were called into a room in small groups where they were met by two or three officers and an armed guard. One officer read off the soldier's full name and checked him off the payroll. The next officer counted out the soldier's pay taking into account any stoppages or forfeitures due to allotments or legal actions. The last officer recounted the money to ensure correctness and issued it to the soldier.[59] It was work of the second officer in adjusting stoppages and forfeitures that cut into the paychecks remorselessly. Although the government sought to follow Lincoln's admonition to "care for him who shall have borne the battle and for his widow and his orphan," it still expected the soldiers to help with the lifting. The government and military sought to blend the altruism of the Progressive Era with the traditional American faith in sturdy self-help. Since the nation was conscripting men to serve, it owed them and their families a safety net in case of death or serious injury. This was evident in the War Risk Insurance Program. The insurance offered a soldier or his survivors up to $10,000 in the event of his death or permanent disability connected to his military service. While officers often browbeat and strong armed their soldier to sign up for this "voluntary" coverage, the generous premium in relation to the solder's outlay, coupled with the uncertainly of the future, led most soldiers to opt for the coverage. The adjutant general reported that by February 1918 over 95 percent of soldiers had signed up for the insurance. Marine Raymond Stanbeck reflected most doughboy attitudes when he chose to take the maximum coverage of $10,000 with its monthly cost of $6.60 being deducted from his pay. He reasoned, unsentimentally, "the government bets $10,000.00 to your 6.60 in the gamble of death. We have awful dangerous work ahead and I feel as if it is best to be prepared."[60]

The government was also determined to ensure that its soldiers would live up to their responsibilities at home while in the service. As with the insurance, the government would subsidize payments to a soldier's family, but the military required the man himself to allot at least half of his monthly pay to maintain his dependents. If a soldier had a wife (or divorced wife receiving alimony) with no children, the government would match the soldier's mandatory allotment with an additional $15 per month. If a soldier had a wife and one child, the government paid the family $25 per month. A wife with two children received $32.50 per month. Families with more than two children received $32.50 plus $5 per month for each additional child. Thus a wife with four children would be given $42.50 per month in addition to her husband's allotment. The government also made allowances for soldiers who were the sole or major financial supporter of their parents or siblings. The government paid $10 for one dependent parent, $20 if the soldier supported both parents, and $5 dollars for each additional dependent sibling, after the soldier started his own allotment for the family's maintenance.[61]

Last, the doughboy's pay was further eroded by allotments for Liberty Bonds, payment for laundry services, and fines due to disciplinary proceedings. As with the War Risk Insurance, officers and other officials pressured soldiers to subscribe to Liberty Bonds and those who refused to buy were deemed unpatriotic by their leaders and many of their peers. All of these deductions added up and left the soldier with little coin in his pocket on payday. For example, Henry Schulz was left with only $18.30 from his monthly pay after the deductions for his insurance and Liberty Bonds. He sent most of this remaining pay to his brother for safekeeping and home expenses. Schultz was still better off than Paul Rhodes of the 103rd Infantry. In a letter to his sister in June 1918, he complained, "It's payday today but a whole lot of good that does me," due to the fact that after sending $35 home to his wife in mandatory and voluntary allotments he was left with only four dollars and some change. Not all doughboys were unhappy with the stoppages. The Marine Corps instituted a policy where it would withhold half of the pay of Marines deploying to France and establish a savings account for them earning 4 percent interest that would be paid upon their discharge from the service. Raymond Stanbeck believed that this was a fair system, claiming that although he could take care of his own finances, for many of his more improvident comrades, "It is good that the government keeps half their pay."[62]

Some of the soldiers' complaints about their pay were due to other issues. At times doughboys believed that local civilians and even some of the official outlets in camp sought only to separate the men from their meager wages and inflated prices to meet growing demand. One doughboy, for example, questioned the patriotism of the people in Waco, Texas, because "everything you want to purchase costs like fury. I think the merchants here load it on as much as possible." Sometimes the problem was simply not getting paid at all. The military's massive expansion and the systemic problems with mobilization meant that getting the soldiers paid was a lower priority than getting them feed, clothed, and housed. One despondent doughboy begged his father from Camp MacArthur, Texas, in March 1918 to send him "a lot of Durham smoking tobacco" because "my company has not been paid in nearly two months, everybody is sore and broke." These lapses in pay were also due to the frequent reassignment and moving of soldiers within the United States. After not receiving any pay for two months, another soldier hoped that he would still be in Camp Merritt, New Jersey, between the first and fifth of July 1918 as that was the only time when the paymasters held the camp's paydays.[63]

Before closing on the issue of pay, it should also be noted that the soldiers themselves were frequently the source of their own financial woes. Paydays often resulted in spending sprees in post canteens and exchanges or in off-post establishments. After one such splurge and an effort to help out a comrade, a doughboy confessed to his mother, "We got paid yesterday, I drew 13.60 and have got 2 left of it. I loaned out 6.50 but don't suppose I'll ever see it again." As with armies throughout history, other camp diversions were specifically designed to strip the unwary or unlucky of their cash. "Pay-day to-day and I can hear dice rolling from all quarters," George Browne explained in a letter to his folks. "Also the sound of money changing hands. It really is funny to see what fools some people can make of themselves." Another recruit simply told his mother, "Most of the fellows here are nice fellows. Some of them are crooks and gamblers. The tent next to mine is the official gambling hall of the company. The rule is gamble all that you want to but don't quarrel."[64]

In the end nearly four million men passed through the nation's training camps during World War I. Each individual's experience in camp was unique, but all of the camps were designed to mold the individual into the military collective. Some men hated and resisted the process, others relished their new lives, and most perhaps fell somewhere in between these poles. All, to some extent, were changed by the process and experience as they merged into a culture that was very alien to their previous lives.

4

Learning "The Savage Game"
Training in the United States

In September 1918 Private Ed Guiss admitted to his sister that he had relished a quiet walk in the woods of Camp Dix, New Jersey, because he was away from the sound of his comrades involved in the "savage game" of taking bayonet practice. "If you are a short distance and hear them in their savage grunts and yelling and growling," he related, "you would think you had gone back five thousand years and were somewhere in the wilds of America or Europe." Still, he laconically confessed, "I have gotten far enough in the training to learn how to pull a bayonet out of a man without losing my balance." John Nell had similar reservations. "None of us young recruits had ever thought for one moment in our life to shoulder a rifle and go hunt human beings. We had never contemplated shooting down a man, or killing him in any way we could, and then leaving him where he fell." He mused, "It was just too horrible to think in this manner, yet this is exactly what we were training and preparing to do." Guiss and Nell had entered a strange new world of different values and expectations, one that often turned the ethics and strictures of the peaceful civilian world on its head.[1]

The previous chapter focused on the soldier's life in camp; this one centers on the true purpose of the training: teaching the soldier how to kill, or aid in killing, and gaining the discipline to do both while accepting the possibility of one's own death. Military training seeks to strike a balance between inciting the primal violent urges to "hunt human beings" that Guiss and Nell discussed and the practical need to harness those urges in a disciplined manner to achieve the goals of the military operations and state policy. The training camps sought to teach the recruit how to use his weapons and tactics to most effectively and efficiently kill, capture, or dishearten the enemy; how to follow orders and work as a team; and how to overcome the instinctual fear of death and injury and to physically, mentally, and morally prepare the individual to endure the strains and privations of combat.

Prior to the war it was an article of faith among Regular Army officers that they could turn the average American into a soldier in 120 to 180 days. In fact, in testimony before Congress in January 1916, Major General Leonard Wood proclaimed that recruits "could be trained very well in six months if assembled in large training camps alongside of full-strength organizations of regular troops and under the instructions of carefully selected officers of the Regular Army."[2] Unfortunately, as the first recruits arrived in camp the army was woefully short of regular organizations and officers to turn Wood's boast into a reality. The War Department realized that it was facing a monumental task and believed that the best way forward was to institute a standardized and mandatory training plan for all divisions. On August 27, 1917, the Army General Staff issued *Infantry Training*, its initial plan for training the growing legion of men gathering at the training camps. *Infantry Training* delineated the responsibilities of commanders at all echelons for the training of their soldiers, mandated the establishment of thirteen divisional schools for specialists, and provided a weekly training plan for the instruction of infantry and machine gun companies. The total course of instruction was to take sixteen weeks, and its stated goal was to create units able "to take their places on the line," with a "minimum of training in France." On December 20, 1917, the War Department extended the standard training plan from sixteen to eighteen weeks mostly to address Pershing's concern that the original regimen placed too much emphasis on trench warfare and not enough on "open warfare."[3]

The original sixteen-week training plan was to consist of 640 total hours of instruction. Of this time, the soldiers were to spend forty-one hours in bayonet training, fifty-six hours in close order drill, fifty-seven hours in extended order and trench warfare drills, and twenty-seven hours in trench construction. All soldiers were to spend thirty-one hours in hand grenade training and six hours of familiarization training on machine guns, automatic rifles, and the other weapons of trench warfare. Weapons specialists (automatic riflemen and machine gunners) were scheduled an additional eighty hours in range firing, while other members of the company spent that time in additional trench warfare training. Gas warfare and defense accounted for only fourteen hours of the training plan. The training of the division was to be progressive, with the instruction of each level building upon the work done at the lower echelon. Training started with the individual and moved step-by-step to the company. Once the companies were trained, the last two months were intended to focus on regimental, brigade, and division operations.[4]

Based upon the War Department's standardized plan, the training in the camps was to follow a strict daily and weekly schedule that was intended to govern every moment of the soldier's life in camp and make the most effective use of valuable time. The man's existence was to be an orderly process, from the moment that he awoke to the moment that he went to sleep, designed to systematically care for his bodily needs and preparation for battle. As one soldier described his average day to his girlfriend,

> We are out of bed at five A.M. We have three or four bands here and they start playing the bands and march up and down the Co[mpany] streets. We then stand the roll call eat breakfast at about six forty five, then are called out for setting up exercises. That means physical culture. We get about an hour of that and then practice with our guns and so on until dinner. Then we drill until four, wash up, stand retreat at five thirty and eat our supper at about five forty five. This is a gay old life. But I can assure you that we would all prefer home life and a dear sweet girl to go and see when you want to.

As the soldier mentioned, the office and factory time clocks of civilian life were exchanged for the bugle calls that signaled the beginning and end of the day, meal times, and all-important events in between. Due to the regimentation that accompanied these brassy siren songs, many doughboys found kinship in the lyrics of Irving Berlin's "Oh! How I Hate to Get Up in the Morning" from 1918. Berlin, who was himself a soldier in the 152nd Depot Brigade at Camp Upton when he wrote the song, threatened,

> Someday I'm going to murder the bugler,
> Someday they're going to find him dead;
> I'll amputate his reveille
> and step upon it heavily,
> and spend the rest of my life in bed.[5]

As with all organized armies since the seventeenth century, the dough-boy's military training started with close order drill. Marching and drill served two major purposes: it taught soldiers how to move as a mass in the most rapid and efficient means possible while performing the vital role of welding individuals into a collective whole. Drill was the building block of training, for it taught soldiers how to immediately respond to a command without thinking or questioning. It built a reflexive Pavlovian "muscle memory" that was intended to condition soldiers and their units to cope with fear and un-certainty by ingraining a near-instinctive response to the various stimuli of combat. For an army wrestling with undertrained leaders and shortages of weapons and other equipment, close order drill had the key benefit of being cheap, easy, and unconstrained by resources.

But as with all good things too much drill was a bad thing. Due to the sys-temic problems of mass mobilization to be examined later, drill often became the substitute for training rather than being simply a means to the ends of discipline. Shorty after the Armistice, the Morale Branch conducted a survey of the attitudes of returning officers about their military service. A number of these officers complained that the army's emphasis on drill actually under-mined its efforts to create a combat-ready force. An infantry captain reported that the training of his unit was "forced" and "mechanical" and offered "little or no appeal to the initiative and imagination of enlisted men and junior officers." Another lamented, "Regular Army training has killed ambition and progressiveness in all except the exceptional man." One engineer lieutenant's critique of training was even more direct and devastating: "Too much stress [was] put on form, ceremonies, close order drill and other West Point relics of the Roman phalanx age" and "too much valuable time [was] spent teaching *squads right* and not enough making a man able to use any type of machine gun."[6]

In addition to open and close order drill, the army and Marine Corps also devoted an average of an hour or more per training day to physical fitness. The goal of this training was to build up the soldier's stamina, endurance, and ability to bodily perform the marching, crawling, running, jumping, and equipment carrying required in battle. The army had embarked upon a fit-ness craze in the 1890s and had strived to codify the exercises designed to best prepare its soldiers to remain healthy and fit for war. By World War I the result was encapsulated in its *Manual of Physical Training*, which not only described and illustrated the various exercises but also provided a schedule for progressively building the soldiers' strength and stamina. During the war, physical training was usually done in the morning before breakfast in mass formation. The soldiers seldom had any special exercise apparel and performed the training in their issue boots and uniforms. The training started with "setting up drills," a selection of the seventy-seven different exercises, stretches, and movements outlined in the *Manual of Physical Training*. The exercise leaders would then supplement the "setting up drills" with jumping and leaping exercises, running, and the use of barbells, Indian clubs, rings, and bars when that equipment was available.[7] The army also put much stock in individual and team athletics as tools for building spirit, aggressiveness, teamwork, and group cohesion. On July 15, 1917, a Rainbow Division soldier reported from Camp Mills, "There is always a ball-game going on here and usually two or three. Sat[urday] afternoon is always a big time. Foot-racing and all sorts of athletic events. Last night there were three boxing matches." Football and baseball were the perennial favorites of doughboy team sports. George Browne recalled, "Baseball is, of course, **the** game. It doesn't take long to get one started when the men are off duty. Back of the barracks there is a game going on most of the time." Browne was not exaggerating. The morale and intelligence officer for Camp Jackson reported that during the week ending October 21, 1918, 35,237 soldiers in the camp had played 1,650 games of baseball. Basketball and football came in at a distant second and third with only 667 and 662 games each. He further estimated that over 169,550 soldiers had participated in some form of athletics during the week. One does wonder, however, how the troops found the time and energy to train given all these activities.[8]

Athletics also served other functions in camp. A recruit noted that his officers marched his company en masse to athletic events "to get the men interested in sports and to take their minds off the routine of camp life." These events also inadvertently broke down the social distinction of the recruits. Browne was surprised that "one sometimes finds a man who has never gone to college, but who might have become a world champion with proper training." Many officers put much faith in boxing matches as a way to toughen their soldiers and to serve as a safety valve for solving personal animosities between men living in too close of quarters. Sometimes, leaders allowed the privates to challenge their NCOs to friendly, or not-so-friendly, rounds in the ring. A doughboy recalled that he and his comrades were cheered when one of their number beat up the company mess sergeant during one of the unit's boxing smokers.[9]

One of the other stock training events in the camps was route marches. As much of the army traveled on its feet as it moved from place to place, these events progressively increased the length of the route to be traveled, the type of terrain the unit moved across, and the amount of gear that the soldier carried on the march to prepare the individual and unit for the actual conditions they would face during military operations. The route marches were intended to harden and acclimatize the men physically and mentally to long, hard slogs with heavy packs and little food and water. The army expected that for a regular march with full packs the infantryman could travel two and a half miles an hour, covering approximately twelve to fifteen miles a day. A "forced march" increased both the rate and the distance of the movement, speeding the doughboy along at three miles per hour and covering up to twenty-five or thirty miles a day. The army intended that during the first hour of the march there would be a fifteen-minute rest period so the soldiers could answer the call of nature and make any needed adjustment to the pack or boots that the marching had revealed. Thereafter, the soldiers were given a ten-minute rest at the end of every hour. To limit the lengthy process of refilling canteens on the march, to keep the men from drinking from impure water sources, to inure men to scarcity, and to prevent them from falling out of the line to urinate, the soldiers were trained to take only small sips from their canteens to rinse their mouths while marching or resting. In fact the *Manual for Noncommissioned Officers and Privates of Infantry* stated that the soldier's one-quart canteen of water should be sufficient for one day of marching. As can be imagined, route marches with all their exertions, blisters, and lack of water were far from pleasurable events in the life of the average doughboy.[10]

Since the 1870s, the Regular Army had developed a particular mania for marksmanship training. Pershing's faith in "open warfare" stemmed in no small part from the regulars' faith that shooting was a particular American forte. He made this clear in the directive that he issued in October 1917 for the training of all arriving divisions: "The rifle and the bayonet are the principle weapons of the infantry soldier. He will be trained in a high degree of skill as a marksman both on the target range and in field firing." Reflecting this predilection, during their stateside training soldiers were to receive forty hours of musketry and the fundamentals of the rifle followed by eighty hours of individual, squad, and platoon firing.[11]

The army instructed the recruits in how to fire from the prone, kneeling, sitting, and standing positions and evaluated them on slow and rapid firing. While the regular marksmanship course fired at ranges up to six hundred yards, many wartime recruits had to make do with the "special" course of firing, whose maximum range was three hundred yards. In the "special" course, the soldier went through four iterations or tables of firing, each with differing size targets and conditions. For example, on table 1, the men fired at large four-by-six-foot targets, firing fifteen rounds from two hundred yards (five rounds each from the prone, kneeling, and standing positions) and ten rounds from three hundred yards (five rounds each from the prone and sitting positions). Table 1 was classified as "slow fire," so the firer had as much time as he needed to complete the course. Table 3, on the other hand, was a "rapid fire" course, and the shooter had to fire all of his rounds within a prescribed amount of time. In table 3, the soldier had one minute to fire ten rounds at two hundred yards into a target that replicated the head and shoulders of an enemy soldier, and then a minute and ten seconds to fire ten more rounds into a similar target at three hundred yards. The target and time constraints of the rapid fire tables were to replicate shooting in combat.[12]

All of this looked fine on paper; it was a far different reality on the ground in the training camps. Throughout the summer and fall of 1917 the army faced an acute shortage of rifles and other weapons. To make do after the Ordnance Department was unable to fill the demand for the standard M1903 Springfield rifles, the army quickly contracted for a substitute weapon, the M1917 rifle (more on this in chapter 10), and issued its obsolete Krag rifles for training. As a stopgap measure, the army further purchased twenty thousand Canadian Ross rifles, a weapon that Canada had removed from frontline service due to failure under combat conditions, and 280,049 Russian Mosin Nagant rifles that the U.S. government had obtained from the American contractors who produced them after the Russian Revolution interrupted their delivery, just to give the American soldiers some weapon with which to drill. Even these emergency actions fell short, and in some camps men were forced to drill with broomsticks and boards to simulate rifles. The officers at Camp Gordon, for example, turned to local sawmills to create the wooden weapon that the soldiers in the 82nd Division mockingly called the "Camp

Photo 4: Rifle marksmanship training circa 1917. Although the army placed great stock in marksmanship, the shortage of rifles, quality ranges, and instructors often hindered its efforts to properly prepare its doughboys for combat shooting. Source: author's collection.

Gordon 1917 Model Rifle." The weapons shortage was so extreme that some of the 82nd Division's soldiers did not receive actual rifles until early February 1918, six months after the unit's formation. The 82nd was not alone in this dilemma. Rifles were in such short supply in the 36th Division that they had to be rotated around its infantry regiments just to complete the required marksmanship training. The situation was even more dire in the 4th Division. In order to fully equip the 3rd Division and other units preparing to sail for France, the army stripped the 4th Division of all its weapons even though the latter had just begun its systematic unit training. The replacement rifles for the 4th Division arrived so late that the 39th Infantry Regiment and a battalion from the 58th Infantry were unable to complete even the basic firing course before the division sailed for France.[13]

Although many doughboys welcomed the arrival of rifles as a clear rite of passage to becoming real soldiers, the weapons also imposed new burdens upon them. Soon upon arriving at Fort Bliss, Texas, a sergeant brought Leslie Martin a rifle so "dirty and rusty" that he "thought that it must have been stored away since the Civil War." After spending four days cleaning the weapon, he was ordered to turn it in for a new one. He later recalled philosophically, "I don't know what they did with those old guns, probably threw them in a barrel of water so they would be good and rusty for the next bunch of recruits." Unlike Martin's piece, most soldiers found that their rifles arrived coated in cosmoline, a nasty and viscous metal preserver that required hours of scrubbing to remove it from the weapons. The process generally resulted in the thick goo simply being repositioned from the rifle to the cleaner. Once cleaned, the rifle continued to draw liberally upon the trooper's time. One trainee reported to his brother from Camp Lee, Virginia, in May 1918, "We got our guns on Monday it sure is some job to drill with them it is so hot down here and the dust is bad you got a hard time to keep them clean but you have to shine them up or on the wood pile you go or in the kitchen for a day" of extra duty.[14]

The first drill with the rifles also brought many unwelcome realizations. As one man recalled, "We drilled until our arms ached, and rifles that weighed about eight pounds at the beginning of the drill seemed to have increased to fifty pounds and felt as long as telephone poles." To add injury to this insult, during his first rifle drill with weapons, a careless man in the rank in front of Irving Crump turned suddenly with the rifle on his shoulder bent at too low of an angle, hitting the unfortunate Crump hard on the mouth with the rifle's muzzle. Crump reported that he now had "a split and considerably puffed lip and a lose tooth to my credit in this horrible war." This event, however, was Crump's coming of wisdom and the next time that his unit drilled with rifles and mounted bayonets he stayed well clear of his careless comrade. The advent of rifles into training also allowed officers to conduct "Swedish drills" during physical exercises. These were calisthenics performed using the rifle as an ad hoc set of barbells and Indian clubs that were guaranteed to tire man and muscle.[15]

On the rifle range the powerful 30.06 cartridges that the rifles fired proved an unwelcome surprise to many of the novice firers. "We just got back from the rifle range which is six miles from camp," a soldier reported to his family in November 1917. "We hiked out there and stayed four days, shot about one hundred shots a piece . . . My old shoulder is Black & Blue." A Marine complained to his parents, "the heavy shooting rather gets my goat for I am too used to one of those twenty-two [rifles] and the shot gun." He observed, "There is a whole lot of learning to shoot with one of our rifles . . . You ought to see the bunch, black eyes, skinned cheeks and noses, sore lips and all that for [the rifles] will get unruly if they aren't held properly."[16]

The seriousness with which the army and Marines took marksmanship led to dire predictions of what befell those who fell short on the rifle range. A Marine recruit noted that "There were dark rumors that if a man's score fell below 202 [the minimum rifle qualification] he would be forced to remain in the kitchen, or do other work foreign to fighting." One soldier wrote to a friend that he was told that any man who failed to qualify with his rifle would remain in the United States in a depot brigade and fretted that it would "be awful if I couldn't go across." Some officers sought to raise their unit's scores by offering incentives. In one company the commander ordered that those who qualified would not "have to do guard duty or other kind of extra work for 1 month." Both branches offered extra pay for those soldiers or Marines who scored high on the range. While training at Mare Island, California, Lloyd Short had high hopes of shooting well enough to become an expert rifleman so he could collect the extra five dollars a month that accompanied the feat. He noted that if he fell short on the rifle range, he might still earn three dollars extra as a sharpshooter or two dollars more as a marksman. Other men had less mercenary reasons for wanting to qualify. Although another Marine was happy with the bump in pay he received for qualifying as an expert rifleman, he was most excited that the feat "helps my standing and what is more it gives me a medal to wear."[17]

As rifle marksmanship proceeded with varying degrees of fits and starts, the army faced even graver shortages of artillery, machine guns, and other specialist weapons. At the outbreak of the war, the machine guns and artillery pieces in the army's arsenal were few in number and mostly obsolete. While the war in Europe had already demonstrated that artillery was the biggest killer on the battlefield, in April 1917 the U.S. Army fielded only 604 field guns and 180 heavy howitzers. Few stateside artillerymen had ever seen, much less fired, the French 75mm and 155mm guns they would later crew in France. In fact, during the French Military Mission's inspection of training camps in the United States in February 1918, they were shocked to discover that the only cannons at Camp Beauregard, Louisiana, were seven muzzle-loading guns from the Civil War. When not fortunate enough to have even obsolete cannons to train on, the gunners had to be contented with practicing crew drills on logs mounted on old wagon wheels.[18]

These shortages hindered the training of artillerymen to even a greater extent than it did the infantry. The development of massed indirect artillery fire between 1914 and 1918 was truly revolutionary, and the U.S. Army was well behind the times in the development of artillery doctrine. The war had caught the American artillery flat-footed and it had to scramble to catch up. For the most part, shortages of guns and the artillery's steep learning curve meant that most American artillerymen departed for France woefully unprepared and undertrained for the realities of the Western Front. In the 90th Division, for example, artillerymen only received, and had a brief chance to fire, their guns in March 1918, mere weeks before the unit departed for France. One 77th Division soldier later lamented, "No explosives were ever handled at Upton, and the only real benefit the cannoneers received from their training there, was a slight inkling of how a gun crew was formed, how it functioned on a drill field, and the manner in which indirect fire was conducted."[19]

Trench warfare had also elevated the importance of the machine gun and had led to the hasty development of new weapons such as trench mortars, automatic rifles, modern hand and rifle grenades, and a host of other implements of destruction. However, the American army of 1917 was still saddled with the tools and mired in the conceptions of warfare that had characterized combat in August 1914. The war's other major combatants had been forced to pay a steep tuition during one of the most revolutionary periods in military history to learn the realities of modern high-tech mass warfare. The American Army had a lot of catching up to do and it was ill positioned to do so. The 82nd Division's chief of staff, Colonel G. Edward Buxton, recalled,

> The training of specialists in the United States was necessarily of a theoretical character. The Divisional Automatic Rifle School possessed about a dozen Chauchat rifles; the regiments had none. Colt machine guns were issued to machine gun companies, although this weapon was never to be used in battle. The Stokes Mortar platoon never saw a 3-inch Stokes Mortar while in the United States, and the 37-mm gun platoons possessed collectively one of these weapons during the last two or three weeks of their stay at Camp Gordon. A limited number of offensive and defensive hand grenades were obtained and thrown by selected officers and

non-commissioned officers at the Division Grenade School. The men of one regiment witnessed a demonstration where four rifle grenades were fired.

The 82nd Division was far from alone in these tribulations. Through much of its training in the United States, the machine gun battalions of the 36th Division had to make do with training on a handful of obsolete Colt and Benet-Mercier machine guns: weapons totally unlike any of those in operation, maintenance, and employment that they would eventually use in France. In 1915 the French fielded the Chauchat automatic rifle to give their attacking infantry more firepower to suppress German defenders. By 1917 similar weapons had also become a vital standard in the British and German armies. After slowly recognizing the importance of these weapons, the War Department ordered a number of Chauchats from France and decreed that each division would have 768 automatic rifles. Unfortunately, numbers on a chart seldom parlayed into weapons in a soldier's hand. When the French Military Mission inspected eighteen American divisions undergoing training in the United States in February 1918, they found that seventeen of the units had thirty-two or less of the rifles on hand. The French further reported similar shortages of trench mortars and the other modern tools of war. All of these scarcities hamstrung the realistic training of the doughboys and exacerbated the army's already difficult task of preparing for war.[20]

The next challenge for the army was finding qualified instructors to teach the gathering legions the fine details of killing their fellow man. The miniscule Regular Army was unprepared to aid much in this endeavor. On May 22, 1917, George Marshall wrote an acquaintance, "We are suffering from a serious lack of sufficient officers and non-commissioned officers of the regular army, particularly at the larger headquarters and training camps." The Regulars attempted to provide some relief to the expanding National Guard and forming National Army units by providing them a sprinkling of regular soldiers to assist in training. The results were rather mixed. One officer reported that the thirty-four Regular NCOs assigned to the 353rd Infantry were vital to the early organizing and training of the unit. Another soldier informed his parents, "I believe the top Sergeant is the best authority and has more of the military deportment than any of our officers. He is firm but just and knows the drill very well. He has been in the regular Army for 8 years . . . is a nice clean fellow and never forgets himself or his responsibilities. I think most of the men would fight for him now." Other units were not so pleased with the new arrivals. Many of the Regular NCOs were in fact recently promoted privates with little more military knowledge than those they were sent to train. Others had poor opinions of the guardsmen and draftees under their charge, were unhappy with their new assignments, or had been reassigned from their previous commands to rid their units of troublemakers. A sergeant assigned to the 306th Field Artillery went so far as to go AWOL in order to be demoted and returned to his original unit, where he could serve with his buddies.[21]

With only limited assistance from the Regulars, the training of the new or expanding formations generally fell to newly commissioned officers. These men were usually products of three-month Officer Training Camps (more on this in chapter 12) with only an incomplete and inexpert grasp of the military essentials that they were imparting to those under their command. These officers admitted that they frequently stayed up late to teach themselves the tasks that they would have to impart to their soldiers the very next day. The results were predictable. The acting 83rd Division intelligence officer reported on April 1, 1918, that the quality of training in the unit had grown so poor that it was beginning to harm morale in the unit. He blamed much of this on the fact that "many of the officers have reached the limits of the powers of their imagination, their instruction is going monotonous and has assumed too much the character of repetition without the introduction of new material so essential to keeping the interest [of the men] alive." It wasn't that the officers were not dedicated or trying their best; it was simply that systemic problems with mobilization and the army's unreadiness to wage modern war had left the leaders woefully unprepared to know how and what to train. As one officer admitted, too often his unit's training "was a case of the blind leading the blind." Although both the French and British sent combat veteran officers and soldiers to assist the Americans in their training, they were few in number and their potential was undercut by senior American officers who chaffed at any suggestion that the foreigners might have a better grasp of warfare than the long-service defenders of the Republic.[22]

Realizing that it had fallen far behind in the realm of military science, the War Department scrambled to catch up. At first the problem was a lack of technical, doctrinal, and tactical publications to aid in the training of the new units. To address this shortfall, the War Department, the Army War College, and the AEF embarked upon a riot of uncoordinated field manual publishing. Mostly these entities merely translated and republished British and French manuals and made little to no effort to reconcile the nuances and inconsistencies among these works. Left to their own devices, unit leaders often picked through the smorgasbord of varying tactics to instruct their troops based upon local situations or the whims, prejudices, and predilections of the commander. This, along with the constant debate over the proper mix of "trench warfare" versus "open warfare" training that the soldiers should receive in camp, made the tactical training of the divisions an idiosyncratic endeavor.[23]

Although the details of the tactical training varied widely from unit to unit, all divisions still tried to make their training as meaningful and realistic as possible for the soldiers. Despite Pershing's constant carping that divisions needed to be prepared to wage open warfare, the War Department still insisted that the units devote a large portion of their training to trench warfare. This was based on the assumption that the war in the trenches would continue to typify combat in France for the foreseeable future. Aided by Allied officers, sent to aid the instruction of the Americans, division commanders constructed elaborate trench systems in all of the major training camps and rotated their units through training focused on how to defend and assault earthworks. Given time and resources, trench warfare training in some units provided their novices with realistic preparation for combat. For example, the commander of the 27th Division, Major General John F. O'Ryan, required that his units practice attacking enemy trenches while the division's artillery units fired live shells for preparatory fires and a rolling barrage forward of the assaulting infantry. Trench warfare instruction in other units was not always as well planned or effective. During a night bayonet training exercise that simulated a trench raid, some soldiers accidentally stabbed men in the proceeding wave in the rump. After that debacle one soldier laconically noted, "night raids were dropped thereafter." Another soldier reported in July 1917, "For the past week we have been studying barbed wire entanglements and trench warfare as it is now fought in Europe; and believe me it is some study. We charge from one trench to the next, stabbing the dummies as we go in with our bayonets, occupying and investing the trench and then go on to the next." The 28th Division's Chester Baker likewise described his training as "leaping from trenches, racing across open areas, and thrusting our bayonets at targets we'd constructed." Unfortunately, far too many French, British, and

Germans soldiers had already found to their dismay that taking trenches was far more difficult than charging "from one trench to the next."[24]

Based on soldier accounts and photos taken during stateside training, practice in open warfare seems to have suffered from even a greater lack of realism. A 77th Division soldier noted that his open warfare training was "nothing more than wild games of hare and hound, pursued without the slightest regard for military regulations." Private George Browne sent this description of his field training to the folks at home,

> We had a practice march and engagement . . . I was on second line of advance guards on the left flank. We had to keep abreast of our company and watch for the enemy . . . The great trouble was we were in heavy marching order and the heat was not to my liking. About three miles out we spotted the enemy and then the fun started. We have signals to advance and halt— no commands. We'd run a ways then fall down then up and run again. Imagine those heavy packs and rifles.

It was all great "fun," but not perhaps the best way of preparing soldiers to face a skilled and deadly enemy. After seeing battle, a 1st Division soldier stated that his training in the United States was "not realistic" and that it "did nothing to equip us to take care of ourselves as a combat soldier."[25]

As the use of poison gas had become a feature of warfare on the Western Front, the army also had to rush to train its soldiers how to fight and survive on a gas-contaminated battlefield. As with so much else in 1917 and 1918, gas training was constrained by shortages of equipment and qualified trainers. Although the army quickly adopted an improved version of the British Small Box Respirator, difficulties in production meant that the American masks did not start leaving the factories in sufficient numbers until April 1918. These shortages meant that the first six divisions that departed for France received little to no gas training before arriving in the AEF, and the training of units leaving in the spring of 1918 was sketchy at best. Archibald Hart recounted that his unit's total gas training consisted of a few lectures and a few days of marching to and from the drill field wearing gas masks. One of the subjects taught to a 28th Division soldier when he attended a ten-day gas warfare school was how to identify the various poison gases. The training was rather basic. He remembered, "I learned to tell most of the gasses by smell, for instance, some smell like different fruits, and of course mustard like mustard which it was named after, and also what were the effects of each and their preventatives and treatments."[26]

As expertise and the number of masks on hand increased, gas training slowly improved. Ultimately, most large posts constructed "gas houses" where the soldiers would gain confidence in their masks and training by being exposed to tear and diluted chlorine gases. This usually entailed having the soldiers wearing masks enter a gas house filled with tear gas and then requiring them to remove their masks to "prove" that the respirators actually worked. Some units further endeavored to make their instruction in trench and open warfare as realistic as possible by incorporating chemical agents into their field training. Troops training at Camp Gordon were subjected to simulated gas shell and cloud attacks while practicing occupying trenches. Camp Devens took chemical training even further when its Gas Defense School exposed soldiers training in the post's mock trenches to simulated gas attacks using chlorine gas in the open air. Although training with deadly gases was certainly risky, the realism of the event forced the soldiers undergoing the instruction to take gas defense seriously.[27]

Other factors also conspired to hinder the stateside training of American divisions. The fear of the spread of contagious diseases and the outbreak of Spanish influenza brought instruction to a standstill in many units as soldiers spent weeks in quarantine. As disease had long been the great destroyer of armies, the War Department was certainly justified in this cautious approach, but it still cut into a unit's valuable training time. Generally, the members of a barracks, tent, or small unit underwent a two-week or twenty-one-day quarantine as soon as one of its residents came down with measles, influenza, or other communicable diseases. However, the quarantine clock reset as soon as anyone else also contracted the sickness. A soldier reported that one of his comrades at Camp Hancock thus lost over five weeks of training when he and his tent mates were quarantined. The army estimated that the influenza epidemic alone resulted in the loss of 8,743,102 total man-days of training.[28]

The extremely inclement weather of the winter of 1917–1918 also disrupted training as major snowfalls and frigid temperatures covered much of the nation for weeks at a time. An officer in the 4th Division training at Camp Greene, North Carolina, estimated that only sixteen days between December 10, 1917, and March 4, 1918, were suited for outdoor training. By February 1918 constant poor weather at Camp Sherman, Ohio, meant that the 83rd Division was nearly five weeks behind in its training plan. Combat training is a vigorous, hands-on affair, and officers found it devilishly difficult to train and practice marksmanship, unit tactics, and trench warfare in the comfortable confines of a company barracks.[29]

The War Department's training plans initially envisioned that the majority of doughboys would be trained in their units by their organic platoon and company leadership. Thus, the divisions in each of the training camps were largely responsible for planning and conducting their training and for providing the personnel and equipment overhead for all needed specialist schools. However, when the divisions deployed to France, they dismantled this infrastructure and thus forced the army to stand up a number of depot brigades to receive, process, and train replacements. Under the best circumstances the often undermanned and ill-equipped depot brigades barely accomplished the tasks given to them. Unfortunately, under the crush of unexpectedly high casualties in the summer and fall of 1918 the training of replacements all but broke down. On July 23, 1918, the Camp Devens intelligence officer warned, "The enormous size of the companies of the Depot Brigade, varying from 300 to 450-odd in the past week, with a prospect of an increase to over six or seven hundred next week, upon receipt of the new draft, makes the conditions very difficult . . . taxing the strength of the depleted corps of officers and noncommissioned officers to a great degree." He went on to note, "The strain on the officers and noncommissioned officers is reflected in the men," but added hopefully that the "situation will doubtlessly adjust itself within a fortnight." He was right to be concerned about the depot's leaders. All too often, the officers and NCOs that the divisions left behind to man the depot brigades were those who were unfit for combat or considered to be dispensable (or otherwise lacking) by their units when the divisions deployed overseas. These instructors often proved ill suited and ill prepared to train the recruits in their care.[30]

As the Depot Brigades struggled to keep ahead of the flood tide of draftees and were beset by a constant demand to ship large levies of replacements overseas, the training of the recruits naturally suffered. Fred Takes was one of the soldiers who experienced this breakdown. He was inducted on February 21, 1918, and sailed for France on April 22. During that brief time he was shifted from Camp Dodge to Camp Gordon before moving to Camp Upton to catch a ship for France. He was at Camp Dodge for two weeks before he was even issued a uniform and rifle. Most of his stateside training was limited to close order drill. Takes's experience was far from unique. Edmund Grossman recalled that pressing needs for overseas manpower meant that he "received only three weeks of training from induction until [going] overseas." Takes and Grossman still had it better than a soldier in the 1st Division who reported that he was "shipped over [to France] twelve days after enlisting." What transpired in the training of replacements in the summer and fall of 1918 was a near-criminal failure to prepare soldiers for war.[31]

The United States pulled off a minor miracle during World War I by inducting over four million men into the service and eventually shipping half of them to France. This was accomplished in the face of monumental challenges, the nation's systemic problems with mass mobilization, and even the baleful influences of Mother Nature. But this minor miracle came at a cost. Despite the War Department's best hopes, the planned standardization of unit training broke down under the weight of local training camp realities and circumstances. This meant that American divisions arrived in France with great variances in their tactical skills and capabilities. The good or the lucky managed to bridge the shortcomings in their stateside training upon arriving in France; the hapless or dim ultimately received their missed training the hard way. As always, it was the soldier who paid the price when the Republic, its army, and his leaders failed to provide the tough and realistic training that he needed to survive and thrive in battle.

5

Of "Canned Willie," "Slum," and Hard Bread

The Doughboy's Food

Army life, especially in combat, generally reduces a soldier's most important concerns to fulfilling the lower end of Abraham Maslow's hierarchy of needs. In this stripped-to-the-bare-essentials world, food, water, clothing, shelter, warmth, and sleep become the all-encompassing obsession. Given the vital importance of these very basic realities and concerns to the average doughboy, it is worth spending time to understand what the soldiers ate, what they wore, and how they were housed.

Of the items that fell under what Maslow termed "basic psychological needs," food and water took pride of place for the doughboys. On paper, and generally in reality, the American soldier was well fed both in the States and in France. The great output of American agriculture allowed the United States to feed its own legions and supplement the larders of the Allies. Under the leadership of Herbert Hoover, the nation's Food Administration mobilized the public to more or less voluntarily curb civilian consumption. Voluntary "meatless" and "wheatless" days and the high wartime profits that encouraged agricultural production helped to provide the boys in the ranks ample amounts of good-quality food. As we will see, however, it was in combat, the time when soldiers needed the restorative power of rations the most, that the rations system broke down.[1]

The scandal of "embalmed beef" during the Spanish American War, the development of the science of nutrition, the revelations of the unsanitary conditions in the American food industry in Upton Sinclair's *The Jungle*, and the Pure Food and Drug Act that followed all led to major reforms in how the army fed its soldiers between 1900 and 1917. The army's two major prewar reforms that changed the way that American soldiers were fed were the establishment of the Cook and Bakers School at Fort Riley in 1905 and the publication of the *Manual for Army Cooks* and the *Manual for Army Bakers* in 1910 and 1916. The Cook and Bakers School taught the basics of managing rations, running mess halls, and the preparation of nutritious and sanitary meals. The manuals provided guides for mess sergeants for planning daily and weekly meals and provided detailed recipes and instructions on how to prepare food. The immediate problem of food preparation in 1917 was not recipes, however, but a severe shortage of trained cooks. To meet this emergency, the army accepted an offer from the Hotel Keepers Association of America for a loan of thirty-six hundred cooks to fill in until each division could stand up cook and bakers schools to train their own chefs.[2]

Throughout the war, the doughboys were fed a variety of types of rations determined by the nature of the operation or environment in which they found themselves. When in barracks or training behind the lines, most soldiers were fed the garrison ration. As these rations were cooked in mess halls with regularly established meal times, on the whole the food was of good variety, quality, and quantity. It contained some degree of fresh meat, bread, and vegetables. The company mess sergeants planned out the daily and weekly meals for that unit and were given a strict budget to "purchase" food from the central post commissary depot for feeding the troops. The cooks could serve whatever they wanted, within the confines of the cook's and baker's manuals, as long as they stayed within their budget. In garrison, the army expected company mess sergeants to feed their soldiers on approximately twenty-six to thirty-two cents a day.[3]

As with so many things in the American army, what the soldiers actually ate in garrison differed greatly depending on the prevailing supply situation and the skills and creativity of the company cooks. Many of the complaints about stateside food stemmed from the mess sergeants' fears of busting their budgets. To be on the safe side of the bottom line, some mess sergeants opted to serve lower-cost items such as corn flakes, potatoes, canned items, and watery stew rather than spend their budget on fresh meat and vegetables. The troops were quick to size up their cooks and to express their discontentment when they felt that their food was poor. One complained,

Each company had its own kitchen. Although some companies had excellent cooks with imagination, our cooks certainly did not. They fed us on stew for breakfast, lunch and dinner. We called that stew "Slum." It was not good but we either ate it or went hungry. It really griped us when we found that cooks and other companies tried to have different delicious foods even cakes for their men.

Despite these complaints, army life agreed with many men. Whatever shortcoming in quality or variety, the doughboys in garrison were still receiving three regular meals a day: a novelty for some men. Letters home frequently announced how much weight the soldier was putting on in the service. For example, one doughboy that arrived at camp weighing 134 pounds bulked up to 162 pounds in eight months, most of it, so he claimed, in muscle.[4]

In garrison the army intended that the soldiers receive a balanced diet to give them the needed nutrition for the physical demand of training. The fare was simple and rather bland and was to provide each man approximately 4,199 calories a day. The following descriptions give some sense of the types of meals the doughboys received in camp. A sample illustration of a daily menu given in the *Manual for Army Cooks* consisted of corn flakes, baked sweet potatoes, cantaloupe, bread, egg omelets, coffee, and milk for breakfast, Spanish-style fish, mashed potatoes, cream peas, sliced tomatoes and onions, bread and butter, and tapioca pudding for dinner, and El Rancho stew, steamed rice, assorted rolls, stewed tomatoes, apple pie, and ice tea for supper. Major Ganville Fortesque told the readers of *National Geographic* that the recruit's breakfast comprised steak, potatoes, rice, bread and butter, and coffee; "Dinner will be stew, with mashed potatoes, boiled onions, peas, bread and butter, pudding or pie for desert, and tea, coffee or lemonade to drink," while "Supper will consist of fried bacon, cold canned salmon, potato salad, a vegetable, bread and butter, and peaches or some other preserved fruit." Colonel James A. Moss informed the doughboy's loved ones that an average day's meals consisted of apples, Irish stew, hot cakes and syrup, butter, bread, and coffee for breakfast, vegetable soup, pork and beans, coleslaw, sliced onions, pickles, bread, and coffee for dinner/lunch, and meatloaf, hash brown potatoes, stewed tomatoes, bread pudding, bread, and ice tea for supper.

Of course not all soldiers enjoyed such tasty repasts. Paul Maxwell's first meal at Camp Lee, Virginia was made up of "fat salt pork cut into half inch cubes and fried over a wood fired stove until their temperature reached approximately that of the body, potatoes cut exactly like the pork and half fried (you couldn't tell the pork from potatoes by sight and they both tasted like hell in a different way), very good bread and what passed for coffee, army style." When given his first meal upon arriving at the receiving barracks, the Cornell student turned soldier Frank Faulkner found "the dishes did not look very appetizing and since the food was slum and pretty sloppy and everything even to the dessert was put in the same tin, my first taste of army life was quite discouraging and I thought that I would have to be very patriotic indeed if I could endure that." However, Faulkner still admitted, "but, later on the front I would have considered myself lucky if I could have had something half as good."[5]

Despite the complaints of soldiers such as Maxwell and Faulkner, the army still made a monumental effort to properly feed its troops. Many posts established garden plots to provide their soldiers fresh vegetables. For example, the commander of Camp Gordon placed sixty acres of camp land under cultivation and rented out an additional 240 acres in nearby Norcross, Georgia. While the farm plots were initially worked by American soldiers, the farming was ultimately turned over to one hundred interned German prisoners.[6]

The quickness and efficiency with which the army fed large numbers of men simultaneously impressed many of the new soldiers. An artilleryman informed his mother, "It is some sight to see 2500 men fed in one building [in] about 20–25 minutes. It is hustle, hustle, hustle." Another at Fort Riley marveled that his mess hall fed between four and five thousand men a day and that to supply the ingredients for such massive meals he had helped to peel nine sacks of potatoes and cut up "a lot of beef" while assigned to kitchen duty.[7]

Eating in the army required the recruits to make adjustments to their dining rituals. The soldiers generally had no silverware or plates other than their issue mess gear. The two-part mess tin did duty as the soldier's dish, soup bowl, and trencher while the canteen cup held all beverages. Keeping all three of these unhandy aluminum items balanced while moving through the chow line and then on to the tables required a great degree of dexterity. Army meals also came with their own regulations. A soldier recalled that "the cardinal rule" in his mess hall was "to take what you can eat, but eat what you take. No wasted food allowed. The medical officer inspected the kitchen cans every day to see if food was being discarded." The other great rule was sanitation and hygiene. As the soldiers exited the mess hall they had to separate any refuse from the meal into containers so it could be reused for other purposes (feeding pigs and the like) and then they were required to scrub out their mess equipment in a can of hot soapy water and then rinse the gear in a can of clean hot water.[8]

If the garrison ration was generally filling but bland, the army did make a major effort in both the United States and overseas to provide the troops a feast for the Thanksgiving and Christmas holidays. The military's efforts to replicate the festivities of civilian home life with rich food, entertainment, and small gifts were appreciated by the doughboys. Frank Fraas wrote his mother an enthusiastic account of his unit's holiday at Camp Doniphan:

> We sure had some Thanksgiving, never had so much to eat in all my life, we had a regular banquet—one that the Baltimore [Hotel] would have had to fight hard to beat. The mess hall was all decorated in red white and blue had autumn leaves palm branches and cedar strung around the walls. Accrost one end they built a stage—had red curtain which is the artillery color. In the center was the letters Batt C 129 done with leaves and branches, it sure was keen . . . we had brand new white peoples dishes to eat out of. Cooks were all dolled up in white, everything set out on the table all you had to do was eat and that we did.

His recollections of Thanksgiving were particularly poignant for it was the last that he would enjoy; the young Missourian was killed in action in the Meuse Argonne on September 29, 1918.

Another doughboy remembered that his mess sergeant, cooks, and officers made a great effort to make his unit's Christmas dinner in 1917 a memorable and enjoyable event for the troops. The cooks decorated the mess hall and the officers arranged for a band to play during the dinner. The menu consisted of pickles, green olives, and celery as relishes, a cream of tomato soup with Oysterettes crackers, roast Vermont turkey with cranberry sauce, roast pork with apple sauce, a vegetable selection consisting of creamed corn, candied yams, French peas, asparagus tips, and mashed potatoes, two types of salad, bread and butter, and assorted fruits and nuts. For dessert the soldiers could choose from mince or pumpkin pies, English plum pudding in brandy sauce, ice cream, and a coconut layer cake. The meal ended with hot chocolate, coffee, cigars, and cigarettes.[9]

The army seemed to have made even greater efforts to provide holiday cheer for the doughboys in Europe. Sergeant Elmer Straub was one of those rare soldiers who spent two Christmases in Europe. On both occasions, he, his comrades, and their officers tried to enjoy the holidays as best as they could. For the Christmas of 1917, they decorated their mess hall and billets with pine, fur, holly, and mistletoe and on Christmas Day had a dinner consisting of "Turkey, mashed potatoes, gravy, dressing, biscuits, butter, jam, sugar, coffee, cream, pie, dates, cake, fruit salad, nuts and cigars, just about all we could eat." That evening they made the rounds of the camps singing Christmas carols and then returned to their billets to eat some more. With the coming of peace a year later, Straub found the Christmas of 1918 to be even more festive. The soldiers had decorated their mess hall with a Christmas tree, evergreen boughs, and colored crêpe paper. Christmas dinner consisted of chicken, duck, potatoes, gravy, slaw, dressing, butter, bread, coffee, sugar, milk, applesauce, puddings, pies, and fruits. The festivities were further enlivened by a bar stocked with two thousand liters of beer and a selection of wines and champagne. Straub admitted, "I set down to drink as I never had before" and claimed that he and his fellow sergeants downed twenty-seven quarts of wine and Rhineland champagne on Christmas night. Likewise, a Marine reported,

> Xmas day was spent much differently than usual. I was on guard the night before and did not get up until nearly noon. The rest of the day was spent sitting around doing nothing. For a wonder it did not rain that day and it was quite warm. It was warm enough for baseball. They gave us a good dinner, it consisted of chicken, mashed potatoes, salad, celery, gravy, coco, bread and butter, cake, apple, nuts, a can of candy, and tobacco . . . The Y.M.C.A. gave each of us a box. It contained two bars of French chocolate, two packs of chewing gum and two packs of cigarettes.

"Christmas here was wonderful," Private Howard Andrews noted while recovering from wounds at Base Hospital 11. The patients had decorated the wards and enjoyed a chicken dinner. The celebration ended with the Red Cross giving the troops "A pair of sox filled with nuts, cookies, figs, cigarettes, matches and two handkerchiefs."[10]

Of course not every day was Christmas nor every soldier's meal as bountiful as those in garrison. When traveling and in action the doughboys' fare was much less rich and enjoyable. The soldiers spent much of their time in France moving from place to place. Feeding troops in transit presented unique challenges. Like most of the armies of the time, the Americans had developed mobile field kitchens that allowed company-sized units to provide cooked meals while on the march. The standard Liberty Rolling Field Kitchen was a single-horse-drawn wagon with a wood-fired stove and boiler and bake oven. It was designed so the company cooks could prepare the meal prior to the march and have it actually cook while the wagon moved with the marching column. At the end of the march, the soldiers would then be issued a hot meal generally consisting of some form of stew and coffee. In fact, this easily prepared stew, universally termed "slum" by the troops, was so ubiquitous that it could easily be termed *the* meal of the AEF. As one doughboy wrote in *Stars and Stripes*, "Everyone knows that there are at least three kinds of slum— the watered kind, the more solid variety and the occasional special kind that wears a pie crust. The Marines describe these three types in sea-lingo 'slum with the tide in,' 'slum with the tide out,' and 'slum in an overcoat.'" Whatever its variations, the troops quickly grew tired of it. One complained, "The beef issued in the American Army was very good, but when our kitchen received a side of beef, instead of cutting it into small steaks and using other parts to prepare pot roasts and such, they just made stew of the whole side of beef. We were stewed to death."[11]

Feeding the troops while traveling by rail across France also proved to be a challenge. Under wartime conditions, rail travel in France was slow and often accompanied by frequent and lengthy stops in sidings as trains with higher priority moved ahead of troop trains. Some enterprising mess sergeants tried to provide their units with hot meals by operating their field kitchens from the train's flatcars. The cooks then scrambled at the stops to issue food to the soldiers stuck in the boxcars. Other mess sergeants did not bother with this trouble and simply issued cold travel rations to the soldiers or relied upon army contracts with French railroads to provide some limited foodstuffs at selected stations. Soldiers often resented this arrangement. A writer to *Stars and Stripes* complained that food that his sergeant provided was "of the keepable variety—bacon, hardtack, one can of beans for every three men, one can of jam for every seven, one pickle for every two, possibly a hunk of cheese all around. In addition the mess sergeant spreads something about hot coffee being contracted for at several stations along the route. This is usually plain bunk." Newly arrived troops quickly learned that it was best to look out for their own needs when traveling by rail. A lieutenant recalled,

> We . . . were locked in compartments . . . with no access to water, food or latrines from about 4 A.M. until about 10 A.M. when we stopped in a railway yard at Rouen for fuel and water *for the engine.* One or two had canteens with them, so foraging parties went out and came back with water, loaves of bread, some cheese and much wine. We did not reach our destination until after dark. We found one shop open and managed to buy some tangerines. Never again did I travel by troop train without a canteen full of some liquid, and at least a few chocolate bars.

As he noted, troops with time and money supplemented their poor travel rations by buying items from the locals, but these foraging forays were limited by the fact that the stations tended to be "over grazed" by previous troop trains and the fear of being left behind if the train pulled out without warning.[12]

If the American soldier was often critical of his own rations, he was even more unsparing of those of his allies. This was particularly true of the Americans who received British rations while training or serving with the British Army. Fred Takes, an automatic rifleman in the 325th Infantry, is a case in point. His wartime diary is filled with a meticulous accounting of the quality, quantity, and types of rations that he consumed in France. He was scathing in his denunciations of the British rations he was issued while his unit trained with their army in May and June of 1918. On his first day of training with the British, he was surprised that his entire food for the day consisted merely of "one thick cracker, piece of cheese and a hand full of raisins." The British rations did not improve much thereafter. On May 27, 1918, for dinner he was issued "one thick cracker" and a can of corned beef and a bit of coffee and jam. Four days later, his dinner was merely, "3 teaspoons of stew, a little piece of cheese, one slice of bread, jam and coffee." After receiving the food, Takes noted ruefully, "wish I could have had just again that much." During the thirty-six-hour train ride back to the American zone after completing his unit's training with the British, he subsisted on only a breakfast of "a slice of bread, butter, & two tablespoons of rice," and "two bites of bread and a few little crackers" and a half can of corn beef for the remainder of the journey. He wasn't truly happy until June 21, 1918, when his regiment started drawing

American rations. Takes noted gleefully, "We get a bigger slice of bread and syrup once in a while, and get more eats all around." The other thing that irritated the American soldiers serving with the British was that they were issued tea rather than coffee. On the positive side, some doughboys did get to partake in the British Army's issue of rum to soldiers going into or out of combat or otherwise involved in arduous duties. In fact an American officer in the 27th Division, a unit that fought with the British throughout the war, claimed, "The issue rum, in addition to its medicinal qualities was a strong factor in maintaining their morale."[13]

Whether moving by rail or training with the Allies, the ultimate goal of the American Army was to get into battle. It was here that the feeding of the doughboys became complicated. In theory, the soldiers' rations in combat were to be as close to that of the garrison rations as possible. General Orders 18, issued on July 28, 1917, stipulated that the field ration for the AEF would consist of twelve ounces of bacon or sixteen ounces of canned meat, sixteen ounces of hard bread, four ounces of beans, eight ounces of potatoes, 1.28 ounces of dried fruit or jam, 1.12 ounces of coffee, 3.2 ounces of sugar, a half ounce of milk, and a small amount of salt and pepper. The order further directed, "Fresh beef will be issued to the exclusion of canned meat whenever it is available," and allowed the issue of fresh vegetables if they could be procured locally. Later directives allowed for a vast array of substitutes, such as canned salmon and tomatoes, for the stated meat and vegetable rations. During the winter months (November–March) or when the troops were engaged in "hard manual labor of eight hours or more per day," the AEF allowed for a 50 percent increase in coffee, 25 percent increase in meat, and 33 percent increase in sugar per man.[14]

Whenever possible, the field rations were to be consolidated so the company field kitchens could provide soldiers in combat with hot meals. The kitchens were to be set up immediately behind the reserve trenches or the most secure and concealed position behind the forward fighting lines in open warfare. Supplying hot food to the fighting doughboys, however, presented three main difficulties: distributing food from the supply dumps to the field kitchens, keeping the kitchens in contact with the troops during mobile operations, and physically bringing the rations forward from the kitchens to the firing line. The problems of supplying rations to the kitchens and with the field kitchen keeping up with attacking troops were evident in the AEF's first major operations in the summer of 1918 and grew to crisis proportions during the Meuse Argonne. The wood-burning cookers in the field kitchen created clouds of artillery-attracting smoke that required them to remain a safe distance from the front. As their officers moved forward with the fighting troops, the cooks were left with little leadership and only a tenuous grasp of their company's movements and locations. Resourceful and dedicated cooks charted the uncertain flow of the battle from scanty reports from their officers and from men carrying wounded to the rear and then did their best to send rations forward. The other alternative was for the officers at the front to send carrying parties to the rear to bring the food back to the fighting line. Both systems were prone to fail under the realities of the fog of war. A machine gunner with the 1st Division informed his sweetheart, "Nobody knew where anyone else was—it was impossible. Why we didn't even see our own kitchen for over a week and chow had become an unknown factor— something found by the process of elimination—elimination & kilometers via hob nails."[15]

If the mess sergeant was not resourceful or required more supervision than was possible under combat conditions, the rations system for their units broke down completely. Soldiers were quick to denounce mess sergeants who failed in their duties and cooks who did not know how to cook. The mess sergeant in Albert Ettinger's company had been appointed to his position because he had been a New York City market inspector prior to the war. The sergeant supervised three cooks, one who had been a veterinarian before donning Uncle Sam's uniform, another a Wall Street runner, and another a hobo. Their collective failure to master the basics of the culinary arts made the lives of the soldiers in their company miserable. Ettinger admitted that he longed for one of "those few enterprising mess sergeants who had been cooks or chefs in civilian life and who knew how to forage for fresh fruits and vegetables."[16]

Sadly, Ettinger's lament over poor cooks was far from unique. "We subsist on stuff called 'camouflage' by the men because it looks like and tastes worst than our camouflage nets would have tasted had we put them in a pot of water and boiled them," one soldier groused of his rations in the Argonne. "It keeps one's bowels in a constant state of uproar." One hapless mess sergeant earned the ire of his doughboys when he mistakenly used a bulk issue of foot powder instead of flour in his cooking. Other mess sergeants irritated the soldiers by their fraud and selfishness. The shortages and privations of war-torn France offered an unscrupulous mess sergeant an ideal situation for padding his own wallet or increasing his comforts. Soldiers frequently claimed that their mess sergeants and cooks kept the best food for themselves or sold or traded their unit's rations for wine or other luxuries for their own use. One culinary lothario used his access to rations as an aid in seducing the women in the villages where his unit was billeted. Soldiers in the 16th Infantry were overjoyed when their company commander caught the mess sergeant selling the unit's food and candles. The sergeant got his comeuppance after the captain busted him down to private and set him to work as the "kitchen police" doing all the scullery work of the mess.[17]

Not all of the problems with provisioning the troops rested with the cooks and mess sergeants. Without much training in basic unit administration and with their minds occupied by the more-pressing matters of combat, officers sometimes failed to even think about their ration arrangements. After two days without receiving hot rations, Captain Thomas Barber belatedly remembered that he had instructed his kitchen to remain in place until he ordered it forward.

Major Merritt Olmstead noted that the 5th Division's lackluster performance in combat in the Argonne was due in part to the failure of small-unit leaders to devote "personal attention to the supply of food" to their men.[18]

Even when officers were more conscientious than Barber or those of the 5th Division, simply getting food to the frontline troops was a chore. Whether in the trenches or in open warfare, transporting rations forward required a tremendous amount of manual labor. The ration-carrying parties carried the food forward by hand through the warren of communications trenches or the shell-torn and tangled ground of the front lines. To make matters worse, to avoid the all-seeing eye of enemy observers and the shellfire that invariably resulted from being discovered, the parties generally brought rations forward under the cover of night. The Americans adopted the French practice of sending hot food from the field kitchens forward to the front in "marmite cans," heavy tin containers that could be sealed and insulated by packing them in baskets lined with straw. A full marmite weighed approximately twelve to fifteen pounds each and provisioning a company in the line required eight to twelve cans. A single member of the carrying party could carry two cans with much difficulty and frequent stops. Two men could carry three to five cans if they ran a pole through the marmite's wire bail handles and lifted the weight on their shoulders. Despite all of this exertion and good intentions, all too often the rations still reached the soldiers cold and congealed. Delivering cans of food and dry rations to the soldiers in the line also presented problems. As with the marmites, canned meats, vegetables, and hard bread were heavy and bulky. These rations were generally brought forward by the carrying party in sandbags.[19]

At times, soldiers at the front received fresh bread from bakeries set up in the Advanced Section of the Services of Supply (SOS), the AEF's forward logistics organization. By the time of the Armistice, there were sixty-nine bakery companies operating in the AEF and by November 30, 1918, they were able to produce over 1.8 million pounds of bread per day. As with everything else involved in feeding the troops, the greatest challenge with the fresh bread ration was getting it to the front. Most of the bakeries were located in depots far removed from the front and their products were shipped to the divisions in boxcars and trucks with little thought of cleanliness or protection from the elements. Upon arrival at the forward supply depots, the bread was often unceremoniously dumped on the ground while awaiting further distribution to combat units. During the Meuse Argonne offensive, divisional sanitary officers complained about the "lack of care and handling of bread at the dumps" and said that the bread was "hauled in dirty trucks and carelessly handled" and that it was being moved "without being sacked or protected." On October 10, 1918, an inspector general officer with the First Army discovered that between three hundred and five hundred loaves of bread for the 91st Division had been left in a pile beside the road without any shelter from the weather. He reported that "the bread is now soggy and can probably not be used for food." After retrieving bread dumped in a similar manner, one doughboy noted philosophically, "We learned not to be very particular about our food."[20]

After retrieving the bread from the rations dump and field kitchens, the loaves still had to make the arduous trip to the front line. It was either bundled forward in sandbags, or strung through a string and worn like a bandolier, or skewered on a long pole carried on the shoulders of two men. A sergeant in the Meuse Argonne reported that he carried thirty loaves of bread, weighing two pounds each, to his troops in the line in two large burlap bags that he had tied together and slung over his shoulders. There were a few major problems

Photo 5: Forward ration dump near Samogneux, France, for the 102nd Infantry, 26th Division, October 27, 1918. The pile of bread in the lower left corner is being loaded into a supply wagon using the "fire bucket method." This was far from hygienic, but given the problem of supplying the troops at the front, dirty bread was better than no bread at all. Source: Frank Mackey and Marcus Jernegan, *Forward March* (Chicago: Disabled American Veterans of the World War, 1934), 371.

with these methods of transportation. The bread was exposed to the elements throughout its progress forward and any missteps that the carrying party made inevitably added a coating of muck, dirt, or wetness to the food. The bread was also subject to contamination if at any time it came into contact with gas. Men in one Marine company were sick for several days after being served bread contaminated by mustard gas.[21]

The AEF's senior leaders fully understood that combat conditions and difficulty in moving provisions would sometimes make supplying troops with hot and fresh rations unfeasible and thus devised trench, reserve, and emergency rations to meet those situations. The trench ration was issued to men garrisoning trenches and was only to be eaten if the kitchens were unable to bring up normal field rations. The trench rations were packed in large, galvanized tin cans designed to feed twenty-five men for one day and to keep the contents safe from spoilage and gas contamination. The ration consisted mainly of canned meat (corned beef, sardines, or salmon) and hard bread and an allocation of soluble coffee, sugar, salt, solidified alcohol to warm the rations (akin to modern Sterno), and cigarettes. It is interesting to note that the soluble coffee used in the trench rations saw its first major use in World War I. In 1910 George Constant Washington founded a company to make instant coffee. Although he was not the first to produce soluble coffee, Washington was the first to mass-produce and market the product. The army saw advantages in using instant coffee over the more traditional variety because it was much easier to transport than bulky coffee beans and was immediately ready to be used by the soldiers without the need for any lengthy brewing. Once the war broke out, the War Department cornered the market on Washington's soluble coffee and thereafter monopolized most of his production. Although soldiers seemed to have preferred fresh coffee, they quickly learned that in Uncle Sam's service, beggars can't be choosers.[22]

In combat the doughboys were also issued reserve and emergency rations. As the name implied, the reserve ration was to have been the soldier's edible insurance policy if the normal flow of food from the field kitchens was interrupted. Providing roughly thirty-three hundred calories, a single reserve ration was to provide the doughboy with enough food for a single day of fighting. The ration was heavy and bulky, as it consisted of a one-pound can of meat, two eight-ounce tins of hard bread, 1.12 ounces of ground or soluble coffee, 2.4 ounces of sugar, and a small issue of salt.

In advance of an operation, the soldiers could be issued three to four days of reserve rations, but the configuration of the soldier's pack made storing and carrying these extra foodstuffs difficult. Given the reoccurring difficulties in getting hot food to the fighting troops, it is not much of a stretch to state that the reserve ration was the combat meal of the AEF and the true forerunner of the C Rations of World War II, Korea, and Vietnam as well as the Meals Ready to Eat of more recent times.[23]

Given the reserve ration's importance in the daily life of the combat soldier, it is prudent to give some description of its major components. The meat in the reserve ration was usually canned corned beef or canned salmon. The corned beef, nicknamed "bully beef" or "Corned Willy" in dubious honor of the Kaiser's son Wilhelm, was exceptionally salty and when opened cold contained a thick pad of congealed fat at the top of the can. Americans also quickly picked up the French Poilu's habit of calling his meat ration "monkey meat" due to its uncertain origin and somewhat odd taste. After noting that some of the meat was in fact beef from Argentina, one soldier still contended that it was "either boiled llama or some other South American animal which the natives coax from its lair and drive into the can." Dough-boys invariably nicknamed their canned salmon "gold fish." Whatever the meat ration was called, it grew quite monotonous over time. As a soldier from the 310th Infantry wrote his sister shortly after the Armistice, "I can eat most anything now. But keep away that corn willy and salmon as we have had our share of it."[24]

Whenever possible, canned vegetables were also to be included in the re-serve ration. The vegetables consisted mostly of pork and beans, peas, corn, string beans, and stewed tomatoes. Canned stewed tomatoes, however, were the most common vegetable issued. In fact the army bought 45 percent of the nation's tomato crop in 1918 and issued more cans of tomatoes than all other vegetables combined. The doughboys were rather ambivalent about the vegetable but did state that the juice in the tomato cans did help to slake their thirst when their water supplies ran short.[25]

The hard bread in the reserve ration was the descendant of the hardtack of the Civil War. Hard bread was a simple two-inch-by-two-inch cracker made from flour, salt, and water. The crackers were slowly baked at low tempera-ture to leach out as much moisture as possible to aid in preservation. This process also led to the cracker's legendary hardness. Hard bread came packed in a sealed eight-ounce tin that protected the crackers from moisture and gas contamination. A Marine maintained that his hard bread "had the physical characteristics of a brick" and joked that a fort made out from the material "would be impregnable." Private James Miller went so far as to claim that he had to have four teeth filled after eating too much of the English variety of the rations. As with their Civil War predecessors, soldiers tried to make the hard bread more soft and edible by dipping it in coffee or crumbling it in the grease left over from their meat rations before eating it. Given all of the head-aches associated with obtaining clean and edible fresh bread, some soldiers actually preferred to be issued the canned variety.[26]

When all other forms of substance were exhausted, the soldier's last re-course was his emergency ration. The emergency ration came in a sealed tin can measuring just under six inches long, three inches wide, and nearly two inches deep and was, as the label on the can claimed, "Calculated to sub-sist one man one day, maintaining his full strength and vigor." The ration's compact size was designed to fit inside the soldier's lower tunic pockets. It contained three three-ounce cakes of a mix of compressed beef powder and cooked wheat that could be eaten dry, turned into soup when mixed with three ounces of water, or fried like bacon. The can also held three one-ounce bars of chocolate. The doughboys often called the emergency rations "Armour" rations after its major manufacturer, or followed the British example of naming them "iron rations." Given the nature and intent of the item, the emergency rations were only to be eaten "by order of an officer or in extremity."[27]

One of the most important parts of the soldier's combat rations was fresh water. Water, that most basic of life-sustaining substances, presented its own immense challenges of resupply during the Great War. Even before the war, industrialization and centuries of intensive farming and human waste disposal had already made much of the water in France unsafe to drink. In fact the poor quality of water in large towns such as Toul, Tours, and Cherbourg forced the army to use specially designed gravity filters or chlorination or to boil the water supply before it could be used by the American soldiers stationed in those locations. The problem of obtaining clean water at the front was further exacerbated by the inherent nastiness of war, as a group of officers living in a dugout near Mountfaucon discovered in October 1918. As they had occupied the position at night, it was not until the morning that they found a decapitated head of a German soldier in the well from which they had drawn their drinking water the evening before. During the 28th Division's attack on Fismette, commanders informed their troops not to drink from any of the water sources in the sector of their advance because the Germans had poisoned the wells and gas had contaminated the streams.[28]

Due to all of these factors, potable water at the front was usually in short supply. Recognizing this problem, the AEF had one unit, the 26th Engineers, whose sole responsibility was to build the infrastructure and operate the various systems for providing the AEF its water. The unit accomplished great feats of engineering, including building two purification plants, each capable of producing fifty gallons of pure water per minute to supply the 2nd Army. This, however, was not enough and division and corps commanders instructed their medical and sanitation officers to certify the safety of all water sources in their areas and insisted that all water for human consumption had to be boiled or chlorinated before it could be used by the troops. Although these measures worked well in settled base locations, they proved to be impractical in mobile warfare. The greatest problem was getting the water to the soldiers in the line for the simple reason that water is bulky and heavy. The soldiers were issued a single one-quart canteen to carry their day's supply of water. Seasoned doughboys quickly discovered that this small allocation was not enough for troops engaged in active fighting and thus tried to add an extra American or French canteen to their combat load. While this expedience offered a short-term solution, once the canteens ran dry, the soldiers still had to find some source of potable water to refill their stocks. In theory, fresh water was obtained from the large water carts that accompanied each company's field kitchen. Water was to be brought to the front by carrying parties in large tin cans or buckets or by returning filled canteens with the daily food rations. As each full canteen weighed 2 pounds, 9.5 ounces, bringing forward a brace of ten to twenty canteens strung like a necklace or bandolier from the chains that connected the canteen cap to its body was a chore. When coupled with combat losses, the manpower required to deliver water to the firing line could become prohibitive. An officer in the 35th Division admitted that during the fighting in the Meuse Argonne, he could not afford to send a detail one mile back to the nearest water point because it would require too many men and "the line was too thinly held."[29]

Shortages of water added to the doughboys' miseries throughout the AEF's operations. The composition of the food rations themselves added to this litany of woe. During the fighting in Belleau Woods one Marine recalled that his unit subsisted on canned hard bread and corned beef. "Had water not been so scarce," he lamented, "this meat would have done very well as a substitute for something to eat, but it was salty as brine. When a fellow ate this monkey meat he was ravenously thirsty." As water is a necessity of life, when the army failed to provide it, the soldiers resorted to whatever sources were at hand to fill their needs. This had predictable results. During the fall of 1918 division inspectors and medical officers constantly reported that the soldiers in their units were falling sick from drinking contaminated water, and dysentery became the signature malady of the Meuse Argonne campaign. An officer in the 137th Infantry admitted that after only a day of fighting in the Argonne, "Canteens were soon emptied, and they drank water wherever they could find it—in shell holes, crevices, and in fact any place that water was obtainable. The eating of cold rations out of unwashed mess kits, this drinking of foul water, and the exposure and strain, caused every man to suffer from dysentery." This observation was not unique. A private later wrote, "most all of us had dysentery from eating spoiled food and drinking unsafe water running down ditches." The situation grew so dire in the 91st Division that its chief surgeon reported on October 19, 1918, that "none of the men" in the unit "were fit for duty owing to dysentery, fatigue and stomach trouble" caused mostly from drinking bad water.[30]

Getting fresh water to the troops was just part of the larger problem of supplying sustenance to the fighting troops. We have already alluded to the general difficulties in bringing heavy and bulky rations forward to the fighting lines. But what effects did these difficulties have on the AEF's operations? Food was of course essential to maintaining the doughboy's endurance, performance, and morale in battle. Doughboys in combat frequently complained that they went for long stretches without hot food and, at times, without any food at all. These shortages slowly sapped the troops' vitality and led to a decline in their health. An officer in the 79th Division stated that it was impossible to bring up any supplies during his unit's initial fighting in the Meuse Argonne. The soldiers had quickly consumed the reserve rations that they carried in their packs and subsequently after four days in the line, "the troops were in a pretty exhausted state." In another instance, despite the best efforts of their mess sergeant to move rations forward between October 12 and 14, 1918, the doughboys of Company H, 126th Infantry, subsisted exclusively on the small quantities of hard bread and canned corn beef that stretcher bearers could bring up when they returned to the front. On October 15 the only supplies that made it to the company were hard bread and bandoleers of ammunition. When the company commander tried to resolve this dire situation by sending back a large ration party on October 16, the cumulative effect of food shortages and fatigue at the front thwarted his plans. He discovered that the men were "too tired, wary, and weak to carry the marmite cans of hot food thru the back area brush and shell holes" and the only food that the frontline troops received was again hard bread. Another infantryman from the same division simply reported that by October 19, 1918, the "lack of food caused me to be very weak."[31]

The composition of the reserve ration itself often exacerbated the decline in the doughboys' stamina and health. Shortly after the war, an infantry officer informed the Morale Branch that the army needed a "reserve ration more suited to the stomach than canned beef," and opined, "we could never keep our strength up on it alone." Soldiers' letters, diaries, and memoirs frequently comment on the number of days where their units lived entirely on corned beef and hard bread. This diet was long on calories but short on balanced nutrition. In fact after days of short rations one soldier wrote to his mother, "I wish I had some of that food now that I used to refuse to eat when I was a kid," and added apologetically, "I'll eat all the carrots you'll ever give me in the future." It has been said that the infantryman's three greatest concerns in combat, besides, of course, being killed, are "sleeping, slopping and shitting." Prolonged eating of the reserve ration negatively influenced all three. In late September 1918 the chief surgeon and sanitary officer of the 26th Division informed his commander that during the unit's recent combat operations, "the food supply was scanty at times" and "was not gotten to the men at the front positions in as good quantity or condition as could be desired." He blamed this "ill-balanced diet" on an outbreak of urticaria (hives) in the division. Another division surgeon reported in October 1918 that too much meat ration, combined with "insufficient fresh vegetables and dried fruit," had caused endemic "constipation throughout the command." Between the dysentery caused by bad water and constipation caused by poor diet, the poor, bloody infantryman, specifically his stomachs and bowels, could not catch a break.[32]

It should be noted that many of the failings of the ration system were beyond the ability of a unit's cooks to fix. Although many (if not most) dough-boys complained about their mess cooks, scores of soldiers also praised their mess details for the efforts that they did make to get them food under the difficult conditions at the front. One 1st Division soldier claimed that bringing rations forward was even more dangerous than patrolling in No Man's Land. He believed that his unit's cooks were "real men" who could always be counted on to be on time to meet the rations-carrying party and "tried to make it as good as they could for us," by doing extra things such as wrapping candles in straw to prevent breakage and wrapping the company's bread rations in French newspapers to keep the fibers of the sandbags in which the bread traveled from sticking to the food. Many mess sergeants tried to make the best of a bad situation. After becoming separated from his unit during the transportation muddle of the St. Mihiel offensive, a mess sergeant from the 76th Field Artillery opted to set up on the side of the road and dole out his food to any passing hungry doughboy rather than let his rations go to waste. A Tank Corps officer joked that the cook was "his friend for life" after enjoying the sergeant's largesse following days without eating.[33]

Unfortunately, ad hoc methods like those employed by the 76th Artillery's mess sergeant could not overcome the systemic problems of feeding an army in battle. When faced with short rations, the troops improvised as best as they could. After having eaten all of their emergency rations, some Marines at Belleau Woods were forced to rummage through the packs of the dead for food. One admitted, "I would not greatly relish food that had been in close proximity with a corpse for several days but when a fellow is really hungry, such a consideration is of no consequence." Sometimes the enemy provided what the American military could not. The wholesale capture of German kitchens, rations, and livestock during the St. Mihiel offense provided a welcome respite to the soldiers' short or otherwise drab fare. One 26th Division soldier noted, "We found several cages of live rabbits, some hens, some big tubs of honey, and a wagon of good German fodder for the horses . . . We found some salt fish which we loaded in, and a lot of condensed soup in long cloth bags . . . We saw German hardtack here for the first time. It was like sweetened oyster crackers, very hard, but easy to eat." The company cook Harry Ricket likewise made the best possible use of the German slaughterhouse, storehouse, and garden that his unit had overrun. He discovered that while the German flour was of too poor a quality for making pies and pastries, it worked fine for pancakes and biscuits. He noted that with the abundance of rabbits, chickens, and vegetables that the enemy had left behind, his troops were "living like lords."[34]

If the dead or the Germans could not fill the larder, American soldiers were not hesitant to forage food from French civilians. A veteran of the 1st Division confessed, "Close to an active fighting front there were always villages and buildings which had been abandoned by the people. If there was anything of value therein, particularly if it was easily carried or eatable, it was usually taken by certain of our members. We found fruit on trees in orchards, dug potatoes in gardens, and caught a few chickens. And wine was not overlooked either." While this method of provisioning was understandable given the circumstances, it often came at the price of cordial relations with the locals as well as good military order and discipline. During the Aisne-Marne operation, the 2nd Division's provost marshal stated, "The difficulty of getting the food to the troops soon resulted in looting for the men were searching the whole country for deserted chickens, rabbits and scant food supplies left by the villagers. Looting and straggling went hand in hand for it was noticed that in nearly all cases where arrests were made the looter was found also to be absent without leave from his organization." Such foraging also strained the Americans' relationship with the frugal French peasants in their paths.[35]

When the army failed to live up to its end of the social contract, the dough-boys often felt justified in taking matters into their own hands to fill their bellies. As the 2nd Division military policeman pointed out, American soldiers felt little compunction about leaving the ranks to obtain food when the AEF's supply system broke down. Horace Baker readily admitted that "pangs of hunger" drove him to go on "an exploring trip" out of the front lines to obtain something to eat. After stealing a large can of corn beef from another unit's field kitchen, Baker commuted back to the front with his booty. The supply situation grew so dire in the Meuse Argonne that sometimes even officers were complicit in straggling. After days without receiving rations, one company commander led a party of eight of his men on a foraging expedition for food.[36]

Despite reports of straggling, it is far from certain that the AEF's senior commanders were actually aware that there were problems with getting rations to the troops at the time. Although division medical officers often commented on issues with rations, the reports by division inspectors general during the Meuse Argonne fighting seldom mentioned troubles with feeding the troops. For example, between October 6 and 18, the 82nd Division's inspector general, Major Edward Buxton, was upbeat about the division's supply situation and even reported on October 11, "Men in the front line get one hot meal at night; men in the support battalions get two hot meals per day. Fresh beef has been supplied three times a week." The same day that Buxton submitted this report, Fred Takes, a doughboy in the division's 325th Infantry, recorded in his diary that after days without any rations he had to resort to looting the dead in search of food. "On a dead German I found a loaf of bread in his pack," he wrote, "It was very black and heavy. I cut the outside of the loaf off and I and a few others ate it." After two more days without eating, he left the fight to scrounge for food. This discrepancy between what was reported at the AEF's upper echelons and what was being lived by the soldiers was due to the inherent limitations of field communications at the time and the failure or inability of senior officers to make it far enough forward to the fighting to see for themselves what the troops were actually enduring.[37]

Although the AEF tried to untangle its supply situation and improve the provisioning of its soldiers, getting rations to the combat troops remained a challenge to the end of the war. Private Gilbert Max of the 77th Division's 307th Infantry recorded in his diary on November 8 that he had "Nothing to eat for 3 days except bully beef and hard tack." Even the veteran 1st Division had problems feeding its doughboys. In November 1918, the division's chief surgeon reported, "because of the movement of troops and transportation conditions the quality and quantity of the rations have been generally unsatisfactory." Interestingly, it was not until after the fighting ended and the AEF was able to take stock of its operations that the truth about the soldiers' combat rations came to light. Shortly after the Armistice the AEF inspector general admitted, "There were cases during the last offensive when soldiers in the front lines did not receive hot meals for periods of four to five days." He blamed these shortfalls on shortages of carrying utensils for bringing the food forward and on the failure of junior officers and mess sergeants to make providing hot food a priority. This passing of the buck by the top ranks of the AEF was both unfair to the junior leaders and a cold comfort to the soldiers themselves.[38]

Of course not all of the AEF's soldiers suffered from shortages of food like those listed earlier. From the creation of the first armies to the present day, the common complaint of combat soldiers has been the disparity between their daily existence and the "easy life" of those serving "in the rear." This accusation is an ancient refrain mostly because it contains more than just a small element of truth. In a survey of officers awaiting demobilization, one infantryman bitterly noted, "Rations for line companies are in my opinion tampered with," and claimed "that the S. O. S. Troops in different supply bases had the choice of rations" and got the pick of "cigarettes, hindquarters of beef, [and] candy." The monthly sanitary reports that the AEF required all of its units, bases, and depots to submit detailing the conditions of the food, clothing, shelter, and general health of the soldiers in their organization generally highlight the inequality between the rations available in the AEF's front and rear. For example, while combat units in the line in November 1918 frequently reported on the poor quality and quantity of rations the combat troops were eating, the chief medical officer for the massive AEF army schools area in Langres reported that his soldiers were living in warm, clean barracks and were receiving "quality good, ample quantity" food including "plentiful" "fresh meat, bread and vegetables." The AEF's efforts to address its acknowledged problem of getting fresh vegetables to combat troops also fell short of its goal. The AEF Quartermaster Corps operated a Garden Service that ran fifty-eight vegetable farms, which included one on the grounds of the palace of Versailles. By the time of the Armistice, these farms had produced approximately seventy-five million pound of vegetables. While some of this food fed those convalescing in the AEF's hospitals, much of it went to feeding soldiers in places like Langres and other locations in the vast expanse of the SOS; little of it made its tortuous way to the fighting men.[39]

Before leaving the topic of food, it is important to discuss one other source of substance for the doughboys: the local French community. The American soldiers were among the best paid of the war's combatants and French civilians were quick to profit from doughboys with deep pockets who sought an escape from monotonous and ill-prepared army rations. On June 25, 1918, Fred Takes recorded in his diary that he and four of his fellow chowhounds had a feast consisting of a bit of beef, two-dozen eggs, bacon, butter, and potatoes at a French house. They received this feast for the paltry sum of five francs a head. When all parties were on cordial terms, the eating arrangements between the Americans and French could become quite symbiotic. Some soldiers were put off by being served horsemeat by their French host, but one soldier admitted that given the culinary skills of the Gallic people, most Americans could not tell it apart from real beef. When billeted in the barn of a woman in Naives in December 1917, members of a platoon from the 165th Infantry were treated with apples, cheese, and fresh milk from the farm's larder. In return the soldiers did odd jobs around the farm and offered the woman and her three children candy and canned corn beef and salmon from their rations. Other troops were not as fortunate. A lack of money or language skills to barter with the locals often proved a hindrance to the Americans' quest for local food. In a letter to his mother a lieutenant protested, "I have a great deal of trouble in France because I can't speak French. Anything you order to eat turns out to be either snail or eggs."[40]

In the final analysis the centrality of food to the doughboy's life and his attitude toward army rations are best summed up in a letter sent from Private

Wallace Mansfield to his mother while he was recovering from gas poisoning in France in 1919. He recounted that he whiled away one hour giving his fellow convalescents an "account of what we have to eat back on the farm in Ga." He confessed,

> I got everyone homesick and they threatened to gag me if i did not shut up talking about the good things to eat over there. I've eaten canned salmon, corn willie, and rice until my mind goes wandering off to home every single meal i eat. I want some fried ham and eggs, and chicken, and milk and butter and cake, and boiled beans and potatoes, and lettuce, and pie and most of all some cornbread. Say i uster think we didn't have good things to eat. I see I was a liar and a fool now, "I'll" kick no more as long as I live.[41]

6

Of "Tin Hats," "Little Tanks," and Entrenching Tools
The Doughboy's Clothing and Equipment

Following just behind food in the doughboy's' hierarchy of needs was his uniform and equipment. Along with food, these things constituted the basic tactile realities of the soldier's everyday life. As with nearly everything else in the American Army of the time, the type, quality, and quantity of the soldier's clothing varied widely depending on time and location.

If, as it has been argued, clothes make the man, then it must follow that to some extent the uniform makes the soldier. As the army suspended the production and issue of dress uniforms during the war, we will focus on its service (work and combat) uniforms. To be effective, a combat uniform must be durable, suited to the climate and geography of the area of operations, and comfortable, and, in a battlefield dominated by very lethal weapons, it must offer a degree of concealment and protection. The American Army uniforms of the Great War accomplished some of these tasks admirably but fell far short in others. The army entered the war with two major models of service uniforms: the M1910 cotton uniform and the M1912 wool uniform. The M1910 uniform was made from heavy-duty tan khaki cotton that had the weight and durability of canvas. The uniform was to be worn during the summer and in locations such as the American Southwest, the Panama Canal Zone, and the Philippines, where the climate dictated lightweight and cool dress.

Although the M1910 cotton uniform saw extensive use in the United States during the war, it was a rarity in the AEF. Given the pressing need to efficiently use every inch of shipping space, the AEF

GHQ maintained that having two different types of uniforms was a luxury that the AEF could not afford. There were also practical reasons for mandating wool uniforms in the AEF. As wool was much more durable than cotton, wool uniforms would further help to ease the perennial problems with shipping by reducing the wearing out of clothing and thus the amount of uniforms needed in France. While temperatures could rise to uncomfortable levels during French summers, on the whole its climate in the areas of the Western Front is cooler and wetter than that in much of the United States. This was important because wool retains its warming properties when wet. On the down side, wool does not readily shed water or dry rapidly. As such, an already heavy wool uniform will double its weight when wet and make life just that much harder on the soldier. Furthermore, wool tends to develop a God-awful stink when not frequently or properly laundered.[1]

The M1910 and the M1912 (and the M1917 that replaced it) shared the same cut and design. The tunic had two external breast and two external hip pockets and a choker collar. The breeches were wide at the hip and tapered at the ankles, much like riding pants or jodhpurs. The breeches were to be worn with canvas leggings or spiral puttees and were to fit tight around the ankles. To achieve this snug fit, the bottom of the breeches was closed with eyes and laces like those on lace-up shoes. The tunic was to be worn over a flannel shirt with a stand and fall collar that buttoned only to the midchest. In very hot weather, commanders could authorize their soldiers to wear the flannel shirt and breeches with no tunic. This combination was worn in combat by some units of the AEF in July and August 1918.

In an effort to ease production and conserve materials, in 1918 the army adopted the M1917 wool uniform. This uniform retained the cut of the M1912 but simplified production by eliminating some of the stylistic elements of the earlier tunic and by using a rougher quality of wool in its construction. Like its predecessor, the tunic had a five-button front and a full lining made of khaki-colored cotton. Due to the vast array of wartime producers of wool and dye, the color of the uniforms varied considerably, ranging anywhere from a dark olive drab to a yellowish brown. As units might receive differing lots of tunics and breeches, their soldiers sometimes presented a two-toned appearance guaranteed to drive a prewar Regular NCO to the edge of despair.

The combination of the choker collar and the breeches in the M1917 uniform made it the most uncomfortable combat dress of the American Army in the twentieth century. The tight fit at the calf of the breeches hindered the circulation of blood to the lower leg and contributed to foot chills and trench foot. The unlined choker collar was an apt description, as it was stiff and close fitting and often brought its coarse wool directly into contact with the soldier's skin. Many soldiers in the AEF echoed Private Walter Wolf's criticism that the "tight collars always hurt" and made the movement of the neck uncomfortable. The complaints of the soldiers grew so great that the AEF issued General Orders 122, which allowed the troops to wear the stand and fall collars of their flannel shirts over the choker collars of their tunics. Unfortunately, some officers objected to the unsightly appearance of this practice and banned it in their units.[2]

Based on complaints from the field and the desire to save money and materials, the army attempted to make some changes to its uniforms in the spring of 1918. To address issues with the tapered ankles of the breaches, the army introduced the M1918 straight-leg trousers. The new blouse changed from sixteen-ounce wool to eighteen-ounce wool to make them more durable and increase their warmth. Also, the new M1918 tunic dispensed with the four external patch pockets in favor of four internal pockets to decrease the overall amount of wool used in the production of the garments. In a further effort to conserve wool, the AEF decreed that NCO rank chevrons would only be worn on the right sleeve, rather than both sleeves. Problems with production delayed the issue of the new M1918 uniform and the M1917 remained the standard service dress of the AEF throughout the conflict.[3]

Both the M1917 and M1918 uniforms came in for their share of criticism from the soldiers. In a common refrain, a 1st Division veteran complained, "Our uniforms could not measure up to the French and British in texture and quality." When queried on his opinions of the service, one returning officer grumbled to army researchers, "Not enough attention is paid to the quality of uniforms, etc. worn by the enlisted men. We have the poorest and shabbiest uniform of any nation and yet we pay more for it," while another stated, "The present uniform is really uncomfortable," and urged the military to adopt a service dress similar to that of the British Army. A prewar Regular carped that his uniforms were of "inferior quality, poor fitting with little thought to comfort and looks."[4]

All of these objections had merit. In the rush to fill pressing army contracts and maximize profits, wartime contractors sometimes skimped on the quality of the materials that they used in the production of uniforms. Even with the most dedicated contractor, the wool was generally quite coarse and itchy. In fact one Marine went so far as to describe his uniform as "rough as a coyote's coat." The open weave of the material was also perfect breeding ground for lice, fleas, and other body vermin.[5]

Two of the banes of the soldier's existence when it came to uniforms were leggings and spiral puttees. These items were worn over the bottom of the breeches and the tops of the boots and were intended to add warmth and support to the ankles, to protect the cuff of the trousers from wear, and, most importantly, to keep sticks, stones, mud, and other debris from entering the top of the boots. The leggings were a one-piece canvas shaft that wrapped around the lower leg and were laced together by a complex arrangement of hooks and eyes. It was "some job to get them on in the morning," a doughboy admitted, which caused much consternation in the ranks when the troops had only ten minutes to get dressed and in the ranks for roll call. The use of leggings was much more common in the United States than in France. In the AEF, most doughboys followed the French and British practice of wearing spiral puttees. The spiral puttees were two rolls of wool wraps, constructed much like an Ace bandage, that were approximately three inches wide by eight or nine feet long. The soldier wound the puttees around his leg by starting at the top of the boot and winding the wrap from the ankle to the knee with each rotation progressively overlapping the previous wrap. The puttees were secured at the knee by a cotton tape sewed to the end of the wool. Properly applying the puttees required time, patience, and a bit of skill. If they were wrapped too tight, they would interrupt the flow of circulation to the feet; if too loose, the puttees would come unwound and the soldier would be trailing several feet of wool behind him. It is best to leave it to Private Elmer Stovall for the final comment on the puttees. He called them "an abomination" and grumbled, "whoever wished those things on the service should have been made to wear them every day for five years."[6]

The army also issued additional clothing items for cold weather. The doughboys' most common defense against the cold was the greatcoat: a double-breasted, heavy-weight wool overcoat that reached mid-ankle. It had a stand and fall collar that could be turned up and buttoned to protect the wearer's neck and parts of the face from chills. It was exceptionally warm but was also heavy and tended to restrict the solder's movements. In combat, the long tails of the coat tended to become caked in mud, further adding to the already ponderous weight of the garment. Some soldiers attempted to remedy this problem by cutting down the skirts of the coats. This practice, however, ran one Marine afoul of his officers, who promptly fined him three days' pay for damaging government property. Doughboys who were engaged in work that required much mobility or prevented the wearing of the bulky overcoats, such as truck drivers and tankers, were issued short mackintosh-style coats or leather jerkins. The leather jerkin was a sleeveless, single-breasted, thigh-length leather jacket that was lined with blanket wool for warmth.[7]

Perhaps the soldier's most important uniform item was his boots. Despite advances in railroad and motor transport, combat soldiers still traversed the battlefield and its environs on their feet. Obtaining the proper fit for boots was so important that the army had embarked upon a scientific study of feet prior to the war and had issued specialty equipment and thick instructions on accurately measuring and fitting the issue boots. At some posts, when the men were being fitted for shoes and boots the supply sergeant made each carry a fifty pound bag of sand to make their feet spread to their widest extent. Then the sergeant would take a series of measurements from the men's feet and consult a standard chart to determine the correct size of boot for each man. The chart generally recommended boots that ran two or more sizes larger than what the men had worn in civilian life. This allowed for the wearing of the heavy army wool socks and for the men's feet to expand after weeks of marching. Although one recruit was at first alarmed at the supply sergeant's seemingly ill-fitting handiwork, he later admitted that his boots ultimately felt "more comfortable than any shoes I have ever owned." Not all supply sergeants were this careful in properly sizing the new men's boots. Upon arriving in camp, Lyman Varney recalled, "They ran us through a very large warehouse where there was a pile of shoes tied together in pairs, you were told to keep moving but grab a pair. You had no time to look at the size. Your only hope was to trade until you got a near fit."[8]

The standard combat boots in the AEF were the M1917 trench boot and the M1918 "Pershing" boot. Both were based on French designs and were ankle-length "rough side out" boots with hobnails on the soles and small horse shoes on the heels. The hobnails were primarily used to help extend the life of the shoes and to offer some grip on slick terrain but made marching on

French cobblestone roads something of a trick. The boots were waterproofed by applying liberal coats of drubbing, or in a pinch, the leftover grease from the soldier's meat ration. The army fielded the M1918 "Pershing" boot to correct some of the shortcomings of the M1917 field boot. The new boots were of heavier construction, were intended to be 50 percent more durable than the old boot, and were made wider to accommodate the wearing of more socks in cold weather. They were also so heavy, stiff, and clunky that the boots were nicknamed "little tanks" by their foot-weary wearers. When stocks of American-made boots were short, the AEF sometimes issued French and British boots. The British boots met with nearly universal condemnation from those who were forced to wear them. After some soldiers in his unit were issued British boots, the 90th Division's sanitary officer complained that the boots were so ill fitting and poorly designed that "many men have fallen out on the march on account of blisters, excoriations and pains in the ball of the foot." In France, the army made no effort to provide any light-duty or casual footwear. However, when resting out of the line, some men took matters into their own hands and followed the customs of the locals. Walter Shaw, for example, informed his mother in January 1918, "I have a pair of wooden shoes I wear when inside during the evening," and noted, "They rest your feet."[9]

Officer uniforms were of the same style as those of the enlisted troops. But as officers had to purchase their own clothing and equipment from clothiers such as Brooks Brothers, their uniforms were made of broadcloth, gabardine, or serge and were lighter and of higher quality than those worn by their men. To distinguish officers from the men, the officers' uniform had a narrow braid sewn round both cuffs and the officers' rank insignia was pinned on each shoulder strap. Enlisted mens' uniforms also had two round brass disks on each side of the collar (one with the letters US and NG or NA for National Guard or National Army, and the other with the man's branch or arm of service), while the officers' uniform had the letters "US" and the insignia of the officers' branch or arm on each side of the collar. Officer footwear often consisted of calf-length riding boots or high lace-up trench boots. Officers wore greatcoats of similar design to those worn by the troops, but, following the path of their Allied counterparts, often chose to purchase trench coats. The trench coats were popular because they were warm, lightweight, and waterproof. As the war progressed, pilots and other members of the AEF Air Service also took to aping the relaxed dress and styles of their British and

French flying comrades. This practice grew so common among the flyers that in September 1918 the AEF GHQ reiterated its ban on the wearing of garments with "split coats, bellows pockets and roll collars" and other violations of uniform regulations.[10]

The officer uniforms had some major drawbacks. First they were expensive and not readily replaceable if worn out or damaged in France. The officer uniforms and trench coats were generally a lighter shade than those worn by the troops. This, combined with distinctions such as high trench boots, braid, and insignia, tended to make the officers more conspicuous in battle. The AEF quartermaster department tried to remedy these problems by employing French tailors to make readymade officers' uniforms to replace those worn out in service. Furthermore in January 1918, the AEF GHQ allowed officers serving in the Zone of Advance to be issued "all articles of the enlisted man's uniform and equipment that they may require" to make the wearers better able to blend in with their troops. At the end of the combat mission, the officers were to turn in the borrowed items and return to their regulation officer apparel. Although the order stipulated that the enlisted uniforms had to still have the cuff braid and insignia that identified the wearer as an officer, some leaders chose to ignore that directive in combat to enhance their survival.[11]

Another important item of officer apparel was the Sam Browne belt: a leather waist belt with a single chest strap that ran across the wearer's left shoulder to his right hip. Soon after arriving in France, Pershing mandated that all AEF officers wear the Sam Browne belt to spruce up his officers' appearance and make their status readily identifiable to both American and Allied soldiers. Officers were to wear the Sam Browne belt at all times except when actually going into combat. The belt became so ubiquitous that "Sam Browne" became the soldiers' nickname for all officers. Although many American officers liked the way the belts looked, they were irritated that the cost of the expensive new accouterment came out of their own pockets. Even the well-heeled George Patton complained to his wife about the expenditure. The greater irritation for officers was the fact that the Sam Browne belt was strictly prohibited from wear in the United States, and those returning from the AEF during and after the war had to shelve the costly item.[12]

The final uniform item in need of discussion is the soldiers' headgear. The primary combat headwear in the American Army at the start of the war was the broad-brimmed, Montana-peaked M1911 campaign hat. The campaign hat was designed to protect the wearer's head and face from sun and rain and had proven to be well suited for an army focused on policing the nation's overseas empire and protecting the southern border. With the advent of the steel helmet, the campaign hat's days were numbered in the AEF simply because once the soldier donned his helmet there was no easy way for him to store the rigid hat. As the doughboys still needed some form of noncombat headwear, the AEF adopted the ungainly and rather ugly overseas cap. The overseas cap was a visorless envelope of wool cloth whose only redeeming quality was the ease with which it could be stuffed in a pocket or pouch when the soldier was wearing his helmet. The caps were not well received. The arrival of the overseas caps prompted one soldier to write home, "They gave us new caps to wear the kind you see on a monkey with the grind organ man." A doughboy in the 32nd Division informed his mother in May 1918 that he was now "as brown as an Indian" because his overseas cap offered no protection from the sun. He further complained, "Those caps look like a sauce pot up side down." The army tried to improve the appearance of the caps by ordering the sides of the crown to be sewn together to give them a tent-like rather than a bowl-like appearance, but this did little to endear the hat to the troops. The only redeeming quality of the overseas cap for the soldier was that upon his return to the States it advertised that he had served in France. As for the campaign hat, they remained a common item in the United States but grew increasingly rare in France after 1917. Most of the hats that reached France were ultimately turned into the SOS for salvage, where they were cut up and used to make felt hospital slippers.[13]

The doughboys' headgear in battle was the M1917 steel helmet. The helmet was a copy of the British Brodie helmet and consisted of a steel dishpan-shaped shell, with an adjustable oilcloth liner and leather chin strap. The helmet was designed to stop low-velocity shell fragments and could only stop rifle bullets if their power was mostly spent. This fact was not universally understood by the troops. Ernest Sherwin claimed that his unit's first casualty came when two drunken soldiers argued over whether or not their newly issued helmets would stop a bullet. "One of the soldiers put the helmet on and the other stood a short distance away & shot. The bullet hit just above the rim in front and came through the back." The helmet perched precariously on the soldier's head and tended to ride back on the skull or ride forward over the eyes when running and during sharp stops. Whether soldiers in the AEF nicknamed their helmets "tin hats," "tin derbys," "battle bowlers," "tin lizzies," or even "steel Stetsons," they appreciated the headgear for the limited protection it provided and because wearing a helmet symbolized the soldier's status as a creature of the front. As one soldier boasted to his sweetheart back home upon being issued his "new tin hat," "they make a fellow look like a rough customer."[14]

The Marine Corps had their own distinctive uniform during the war. Although it had a similar cut to the army's M1917 uniform, the Marine uniform was distinguished by its pleated breast and billow hip pockets and its deep-forest-green color. Although the Marines arrived in France wearing this unique apparel, the AEF GHQ dictated that to save shipping space once the Marines' clothing wore out it would be replaced with army uniforms. As the Marines took great pride in maintaining their distinctiveness, they lovingly attempted to patch together their forest-green uniforms as long as they could. When the fear of nakedness finally induced the Marines to say farewell to their tattered forest greens, they sewed on their USMC buttons and stripes to the new, hated army khaki uniforms to broadcast the fact that they were not the average army doughboys.

Although the military had problems with the design and quality of its uniforms, its greatest challenge in 1917 was simply having enough clothing to issue to the expanding legions. As with most articles, the army had only limited stocks of uniforms on hand when the first draftees, guardsmen, and volunteers began arriving in camp in the summer and fall of 1917. A recruit noted that most men in his camp did not receive uniforms until one to three weeks after they arrived. In the meantime they all drilled in the civilian clothes in which they had arrived. It took the army nearly two weeks to issue Henry Schulz and his comrades at Camp Dix, New Jersey, their first sets of uniforms. But even then, there were still shortages of clothing. When he sent his civilian clothes home, he informed his father that he would have to keep his civilian underwear, for the army had no replacements to issue him. Some commanders, such as the 89th Division's Leonard Wood, did the best they could under trying circumstances. Wood ordered his quartermaster officers to buy blue denim overalls to give the new soldiers some form of uniform to wear while training. The records of the 91st Division give some indication of the magnitude of the clothing shortages. As late as March 11, 1918, the division

Photo 6: Common uniforms of the AEF. The two army soldiers in the photo on the left wear the M1917 wool uniform. The man on the left wears the overseas cap and spiral puttees. The small chevron on his right sleeve indicates that he was also wounded in combat. The soldier on the right wears the campaign hat and canvas leggings more commonly worn by soldiers stationed in the United States. The Marine in the photo on the right wears the standard USMC forest green uniform and his campaign hat carries the "Eagle, globe and anchor" insignia of the Corps. Source: author's collection.

morale and intelligence officer reported to the War Department that his unit still had only 60 percent of the breeches, 47 percent of the tunics, and 72 percent of the field boots needed to clothe the division. Throughout the period, this division quartermaster complained that the War Department was consistently sending batches of uniforms and boots that were too small to be issued or were the cotton uniform instead of the requested wool uniforms. He also sheepishly admitted that part of the shortage of trench boots resulted from many soldiers in the notoriously wet Camp Lewis environment accidentally destroying their boots by placing them too close to open fires in an effort to dry them.[15]

Prior to the war the army had tried to increase its efficiency by working out a scientific method for determining the size and number of uniforms that it would require to properly clothe an average population of recruits. Based on these studies, the War Department issued twenty-two sizes of blouses and twenty-four sizes of breaches and planned to build larger stocks of what statistically should be the most common sizes. Given wartime shortages and the press of time, the rationale behind this mathematical exactitude was lost on the supply sergeants who issued the uniforms. Most doughboys recalled that this was a hurried process where the harried supply sergeant visually sized up the recruit who appeared before him and threw the man pants, tunics, and other items based on the sergeant's best guess of the rookie's size, or simply gave the man whatever he had available on the shelf. For Private Fred Neff, the process was not without its humor:

> We all get in a row and get a Barracks Bag, and they look at you and pick up a pair of pants and throw them in a bag if they fit alright O.K. if they don't you are shit [out] of luck . . . My bunk mate is a small fellow, he got a pair of pants that he can wrap around twice and button in the back . . . I had to laugh this morning to see the sizes some of the fellows got. One size for all big and small.

Likewise, a soldier in the 82nd Division bitterly joked, "We were issued those 'tailor made' uniforms guaranteed not to fit . . . The clothing was shoddy wool and the tailoring equally poor." After completing the haphazard issuing of uniforms, the recruits were then left on their own to swap uniform items around with their squad mates to find the best fit. This system of swapping seemed to work in most cases, but two soldiers in Irving Crump's company, appropriately nicknamed "fat" and "shrimp," could not be fitted with standard-sized uniforms, so the unit quartermaster had to order tailor-made clothing for them.[16]

The shortages of uniforms meant that many recruits were clothed in a mixture of summer cotton and winter woolen uniform components. This caused some angst among the recruits because they would not be able to receive a pass to leave post without first passing a rigorous inspection that required the soldier to be in a complete and proper uniform. "I have about all the clothing now that I can use except the Army regulation [ones]," a Camp Funston doughboy complained, "I haven't been issued but one pr. of trousers and no O[live] D[rab] coat. So before I come home I must have more than that but they are short and not have enough to give everyone a suit." Another recalled that this situation led to a riot of bartering and exchanging as the men in his barracks tried to make up their shortages before inspection. An underdressed pass recipient could make up his sartorial deficiencies by "renting" an overcoat from one of his fellows for a dollar or a coat or trousers for fifty cents apiece.[17]

Despite the shortages and the motley appearance of the troops most doughboys seemed to take great pride in being in uniform. Reflecting this attitude was a letter that one cheeky doughboy sent to a Norwich, New York, clothier upon receiving an advertisement for their civilian wares.

> While I appreciate your thinking of me. I am glad to say that I have changed my tailor and will not require your services until peace is declared. U.S. & Co. are now supplying me with some very nifty suitings of khaki which I find best adapted to my present line of business. They don't get shiny in the seat of the trousers for the simple reason that I never have time to set down. They are also supplying me with headgear, their latest in the line being a derby like affair with a stiff steel crown which affords me better protection against the elements and shrapnel than anything any civilian hatter has furnished me.

One of the first things that many new recruits did at their first opportunity was to have photographs taken of themselves in their new uniforms to send home to their families and sweethearts. Some were not content with the fit or quality of their issued duds and bought tailor-made uniforms or paid to have their government uniforms specially tailored. One such soldier from Fairbury, Illinois, spent $18.40 for a tailored uniform because "the one that Uncle Sam issued me wasnt exactly a good fit or very fine material." Reflecting the pride he felt in his new status as well as in his new duds, he admitted to his family, "Just between you and me, I wouldnt mind sporting it in Fairbury."[18]

As the soldiers completed their training and moved on to France, they came under the jurisdiction of John J. Pershing, a notorious stickler for the proper military appearance of his soldiers. One of the AEF's initial general orders issued soon after the arrival of the first American troops in France admonished,

> The conditions under which our troops are serving in Europe are such as to require the most scrupulous observance of the Uniform Regulations. Not only is the disciplinary effect of mixed and careless dress bad, but the

conspicuous position in a foreign land which our officers and men occupy makes every slouchy officer and man a reflection on the whole American Army . . . The clothing allowance having been suspended during the war, clothing issued to men remains the property of the Government and while the Government's interests must be safeguarded the determination by company commanders of unserviceability of clothing will be made liberal, under the necessity of neatness and smartness of appearance for disciplinary effect.

Despite Pershing's prickliness on the matter, conditions in France and the ongoing shortages of clothing made Black Jack's edicts difficult to enforce. Uniformity was not always a priority in some units or even possible given wartime realities. One engineer unit wore such a mélange of uniforms that one observer nicknamed it "Villa's Bandits" after the motley appearance of the Mexican guerrilla leader's band. He noted that the unit wore "American sombreros, or steel helmets, and others wore French or English headgear of various types. There were men with leather puttees, men with spirals, men with canvas leggings and men with no leggings. One corporal sported a pair of rubber boots. They were just as variegated as the breeches and blouses." Had he seen the unit, Pershing surely would have been most displeased.[19]

Problems with clothing only grew worse when the AEF entered active combat. The battlefield was rough on uniforms and getting replacements for worn-out or damaged clothing to the troops during active operations was even more difficult than bringing up rations. An artillery officer on his first day of action in the Argonne experienced this reality after having the misfortune to tear his pants from the crotch to the knee on barbwire and shortly thereafter losing the heel on his trench boots. Days later he felt it fortunate that he was able to at least replace his damaged boots with those of a dead German, even though he knew the old legend that "one who wears a dead man's boots takes over all his troubles." Likewise, after tramping through the battles of St. Mihiel and the Argonne, Thurmond Baccus's shoes were so worn that he also scavenged a pair from the German dead. These soldiers were not alone. In November 1918, the 1st Division's sanitation officer reported that shortages of boots and a lack of proper sizes had led to a rash of foot problems and that some men had been reduced to march in "rubber boots or galoshes, or with no soles on their shoes." This problem was also reported by the 36th Division.[20]

Generally, it was not until a unit rotated from the front to a rest area that the troops were issued fresh uniforms. Although the doughboys were happy to receive clean new clothing, this system was not without its problems. On October 26, 1918, the inspector general of the 32nd Division reported that upon coming out of the line, "only four sizes of breeches and three sizes of coats can be obtained. This is of course better than nothing, by far but it is difficult to get good fits for men with such a limited number of sizes available." In November 1918 sanitary inspections of the 81st Division revealed "practically all of the infantry regiments are without a change of underclothes and the condition of the outer clothing of the men is more or less ragged and worn out." When the division commander pressed his quartermaster for a solution to this problem, the supply manager claimed, "There has been made by this office every possible effort possible to obtain clothing since arriving in France, but without success." Although the quartermaster had sent repeated requests to the SOS clothing depot in Is-sur-Tille for the items, the division's frequent moves between August and November 1918 had led to the belated arrival of needed clothing at locations long departed by the unit.[21]

As with rations, some combat troops complained that their clothing woes stemmed from rear echelon troops who received the first pick and the best quality of uniform items. One officer denounced the fact that "Goods, such as trench coats, trench boots and the like, did not reach commissaries at the front until after every Quartermaster was fully equipped, despite the fact they were badly needed." He was not alone in his bitterness. While temporarily halted in the Argonne region in early November 1918, a company of Marines received a long-awaited resupply of clothing to replace their battle-scared garments. Unfortunately they found, "as was frequently the case, the clothes had been picked over long before they got to the men at the front, and the bulk of what was left consisted of over and under sizes." Likewise, when Burt Richardson's unit was issued new uniforms after coming out of the line, he was dismayed to be issued clothing that was too large for him. When he complained, his supply sergeant retorted, "Well, damnit, this isn't any department store! Trade around until you get some to fit." The complaints of these soldiers had merit. While the combat divisions reported shortages of boots and clothing, in November 1918 the airmen and ground crew of the 1st Pursuit Group were being supplied with "gum boots, or Arctic over shoes, rain coats, and an ample amt. of good clothing." All of this is not intended to besmirch the reputation of the AEF quartermaster service (no matter how much it may have deserved it) or to fault the tremendous efforts made by the War Department to clothe its soldiers under very difficult conditions, as much as it is to remind the reader that it is the special purview of all soldiers, and combat soldiers in particular, to bitch about the realities, inanities, and privations of their daily lives.[22]

A discussion of the soldier's uniform is not complete unless it is also accompanied by a description of his individual equipment. Throughout the war the doughboys used the M1910 equipment set. The army intended the M1910 to be a self-contained accouterment system that would allow the soldier to comfortably carry everything he needed to live and fight. The set was made of a strong, durable, and relatively waterproof woven cotton material. The basic M1910 system consisted of a ten-pocket rifle belt that carried one hundred rounds of ammunition in five-round stripper clips, a haversack with shoulder straps that snapped into the rifle belt, and a pack carrier. The rifle belt contained rows of grommets to allow the canteen, first aid packet, and various other implements to be added as the situation dictated. The haversack contained the soldier's combat rations, toilet items, a spare shirt, change of underclothing, messkit with knife, fork, and spoon, and the soldier's small personal items. The soldier's bayonet and entrenching tool were hooked to the outside of the haversack. The pack carrier was attached to the bottom of the haversack and, if the soldier's officers believed that the battle would be relatively short, it could be removed prior to going into combat to lighten the soldier's fighting load. The pack carrier contained the soldier's blanket, any remaining extra clothing, tent pegs, and a folding tent pole, all rolled inside the soldier's shelter half to make the bundle waterproof. When not worn, the soldier's overcoat was strapped to the pack. In addition to the rifle and complete uniform, a fully equipped infantryman carried the following (the numbers correspond to the items in photo 7):

1. Ammunition belt
2. Bayonet and scabbard
3. First aid pouch and packet
4. Entrenching tool, pick, or wire cutters
5. Haversack with mess kit pouch
6. Pack carrier
7. One or two blankets
8. Wool overcoat
9. Raincoat or poncho
10. Shelter half, five tent pages, and folding pole

11. Aluminum one-quart canteen in
    web carrier
12. Aluminum canteen cup
13. Condiment can for coffee, sugar,
    and salt
14. Messkit/meat can
15. Bacon can (often discarded)
16. Knife, fork, and spoon

17. Reserve rations and sealed
    emergency ration tin
18. One extra set of underclothing
19. Two extra pairs of socks
20. Toilet set (comb, toothbrush,
    soap, razor set, extra
    shoelaces)
21. "Housewife" sewing set

Going into combat, infantrymen were also issued one or more disposable cotton bandoliers containing sixty additional rounds of ammunition in five round stripper clips. In theory the M1910 equipment set balanced the soldier's load and distributed the weight evenly between the waist and shoulders. In reality most of the weight still hung uncomfortably from the shoulders and the pack, especially when using the long pack carrier, sat awkwardly on a narrow part of the back, and banged into the buttocks when marching. Each eight-man squad also had a squad bag that was to be transported in the company wagons. In this bag, each member of the squad was to have a pair of pants, two pairs of socks, a complete set of underclothes, a shirt, and an extra pair of boots and laces.[23]

Upon arriving in France the doughboys received even more items, such as gasmasks, wire cutters, and trench knives to prepare them for combat. All of this added up to a prodigious weight for the infantryman to carry. As Charles Minder noted, "the pack we have to carry now with all the extras is something brutal. It weighs almost ninety pounds." The always sensitive Minder worried about the ability of some of the unit's 110-pound soldiers to carry the burden and argued that, had the teamsters in New York City so overloaded their horses, the Society for the Prevention of Cruelty to Animals would have had them arrested. In reality, the soldier's full marching pack weighed in between sixty-five and seventy-five pounds, but, as the average weight of the doughboys was a little over 141 pounds, this was still quite a burden. As a soldier in the 35th Division joked, "If I ever get back I will be a regular pack mule," and then compared his existence to a Bible passage from John 5:9 where Jesus commanded a lame man to pick up his pallet and walk.[24]

The AEF GHQ understood that the soldier's need for greater mobility in battle required a lightening of their load. In May 1918 it published a list of

Photo 7: The soldier's burden: the M1910 pack and its contents. Source: author's collection.

"Over the Top Equipment" to give commanders guidance on "those articles which are likely to be carried by the different armed groups of infantry men in offensive operations from the trenches." In addition to his uniform, his rifle, his helmet, a French M2 gasmask and Small Box Respirator gasmask, the rifleman was to carry the pack without the pack carrier, complete mess gear (meat, bacon, and condiment cans, knife, fork, and spoon), two canteens, first aid pack, entrenching tool, rifle belt with one hundred rounds of ammunition, a disposable bandoleer with an additional sixty rounds of ammunition, a can of solidified alcohol for heating rations, a can of foot powder, two reserve rations, and two sandbags. If followed, these instructions should have reduced the doughboy's combat load to a more manageable forty to forty-five pounds.[25]

However, there were great variances between what the AEF GHQ dictated and what the doughboys actually did. An article from July 26, 1918, in *Stars and Stripes* posed the question, "How much does a Yank take into the line?" The author quipped, "It all depends on the Yank. In one squad you will see a

How It Feels, During a "Hike," in Full Marching
Order, and Wearing Our "Cinderella" Army Shoes

Photo 8: As the photo on the right indicates, the humor in the postcard on the
left was not far off the mark. The soldier in the photo wears the full M1910 pack,
complete with a spare pair of boots. Even as shown here without the helmet,
gasmask, and rolled greatcoat, the soldier's pack was a ponderous load. Source:
author's collection.

man carrying a full pack, including extra shoes and overcoat, and wearing a
whole string of corned Willie cans much as a Fiji Islander wears a loin cloth.
Another man in the same squad will go up minus his blouse and carrying
only a blanket, gasmask and helmet." As with their Civil War predecessors,
the doughboys soon followed Stonewall Jackson's maxim that "the road to
glory is not accompanied by much baggage." For infantrymen in particular,
life was punctuated by a steady process of acquiring and shedding the gear
and other impedimenta that encumbered their weary foot-borne existence.
The infantryman evaluated every article based on its weight and perceived
utility to the user. Those items that carried too much of the former or too

little of the latter quickly littered the countryside of France. Before going into action, the soldiers of the 306th Machine Gun Battalion reduced their load by carrying their haversacks and taking only their overcoats, raincoats, reserve rations, and toilet articles. Everything else they left behind rolled in their discarded shelter halves. An MP observing the infantry marching to the front in September 1918 noted that despite the cold and wet, "mostly the boys have discarded their overcoats [and are] just wearing their blouse and slicker."[26]

Sometimes, however, this reckless lightening of the load brought later regrets. A few weeks prior to going into action at Belleau Woods, Warren Jackson's unit was issued army entrenching shovels and picks for the first time. Although these implements were relatively light and portable, Jackson and his fellow Marines deemed them "to cumbersome to carry and always in the way." Despite the admonitions of their officers, the Marines "accidently" lost the tool along the route. When later faced with German rifle, machinegun, and artillery fire at Belleau Woods, Jackson ruefully confessed, "At that hour if a million dollars been placed on my right hand and one of those once-despised army shovels put on my left, and I given my choice, I would have rejected the million in the twinkling of an eye." As will be seen, other soldiers also came to lament their cavalier discarding of greatcoats and rain jackets in the warmth of September 1918 when the weather turned wet and cold in the Meuse Argonne.[27]

The officers and first sergeants in an infantry company carried a much lighter load than their riflemen. Going into battle, the leaders were to carry a helmet, a French M2 gasmask and Small Box Respirator gasmask, complete mess gear, first aid pack, field message book and pencil, flare pistol with six cartridges, a M1911 pistol (with pistol belt, holster, ammunition pouch, four pistol magazines, and thirty-five rounds of ammunition), luminous compass, field glasses, trench knife, two reserve rations, luminous dial watch, and a whistle with chain.[28]

Officers tended to complain less about the weight of their equipment but much more about its cost and its true need. As with their uniforms, officers had to purchase most of their own field equipment. This could become a very costly endeavor. At a time when a lieutenant was being paid between $166.67 to $141.67 a month, Lieutenant James Dalgren informed his girlfriend that he spent $150 on additional equipment and gear that were required for overseas service. Manufacturers and outfitters offered all kinds of sleeping bags, map cases, flashlights, camp stoves, and other "useful items" to the unwary officer and their concerned family members. The War Department was not much help in directing the novice leader in making prudent purchases. One officer made his displeasure of this fact clear in an army survey, noting, "many officers have been misinformed as to [the] proper equipment for line work and many have gone beyond their means to obtain such and never needed it or could not take it with them."[29]

Given the amount of equipment that officers garnered, it is no surprise that they also underwent a process of lightening their baggage before campaigns. As army regulations allowed officers more baggage and space on wagons for transporting it than enlisted soldiers, some officers acquired quite a bit of extraneous gear and other articles along the way. The inventory of items that Lieutenant C. L. Crane left behind with a French family in Aubiére when his artillery unit moved to the front on July 30, 1918, gives an indication of the variety of objects that an officer might amass and discard on active service:

Fist aid packet with 3 scissors,	16 misc. books
a nail clipper and tweezers	Map of France
2 pair light kid gloves	Pair of goggles
2 pair heavy kid gloves	12 Books of notes
Whisk broom	Foot ruler
2 hairbrushes	Signature blotter
Chamois cloth	Complete toilet set
4 belts	Box of Cuticura soap
2 Hunting knives	7 pairs light socks
Small vase	9 pairs heavy wool socks
Package of eyelets	Carton of matches
Microscope	Carton of Fatimas (cigarettes)
Screwdriver	2 heavy wool and 3 lightweight union suits
Razor	4 sheets and a pillowcase
Field knife and fork	Cigarette holder
Set of drawing instruments	Pair of pajamas
2 tubes of toothpaste	Knife

Corncutter	2 suits of summer underwear
Paperclip	3 face towels and 4 bath towels
Extra cap chinstrap	Muffler
Pair of rawhide shoestrings	Sweater
Box of pencils (etc.)	2 pairs of cloth
English dictionary	Khaki suit
Old pocketbook	Khaki pants
Big red envelope of souvenirs	Face cloth
Pair of canvas leggings	2 wool shirts
Barracks cap	Barracks bag
Map of Paris	Suitcase
Souvenir book of Paris	Boy Scout knife
24 army issue/semi-official	Campaign hat
books/publications	Photos of troops and guns
Bathing suit	Case of envelopes

Why Lieutenant Crane believed that he needed a microscope in France is an interesting question whose answer has unfortunately been lost to time. What we do know is that he was far from being alone in his efforts to shed the unnecessary encumbrances of his military life. "As an officer going overseas, I had to buy 2 trunk lockers of clothes, etc., most of which I never saw again after my first trip to the front," an officer in the 1st Division recalled. Having learned this hard lesson, from then on his baggage was reduced to a "bed roll, sleeping bag, folding cot, rubber and leather boots."[30]

After living through a few days of combat one doughboy boasted, "It is surprising how little one needs for existence when he must carry everything he owns in the world, even his next few days' meals, and the water he will drink." After this pairing down, this newly minted veteran still concluded,

> It is only in novels that a soldier steps with a springy and heroic tread. A regiment at the front marches as a great serpent uncoils, slowly and weightily. A heavy pack crushes the carrier's shoulders, its straps cut into his flesh, his steel-shod shoes crash with jarring impact upon the stony roads. The marching gait is the stride of a truck horse, stiff, jolting, and mechanical, though processing a labored rhythm. The men's faces grow grey and dust-covered, the sweat cakes upon their skin; the heavy sagging cartridge belts make sores on their thigh bones.[31]

As they marched off to battle in their itchy, uncomfortable wool uniforms with their bouncing dishpan helmets and equipment weighing upon them, the doughboys certainly had much reason to complain. Yet despite the problems with the supply system and with the design of their clothing and accouterments, the army had still ensured that these latter-day American "Marius's Mules" were marching off tolerably clad and outfitted for battle.

7

Be It Ever So Humble
The Doughboys' Shelter

Having discussed food and clothing, it is time to turn to the last of the doughboy's great Maslovian concerns: shelter. Although the requirement to find a place of warmth, rest, safety, and protection from the elements and from enemy fire was third on the soldiers' list of needs, it was still an important part of their everyday life. As the soldiers' housing while stationed in the United States was covered in chapter 2, this chapter will focus on the kinds of shelter the troops used while living and fighting in France. From tents to ancient barracks, foxholes, barns, dugouts, and even the occasional château, the doughboys found themselves living in a vast array of lodgings during their tour in Europe. The types of shelters the soldiers occupied depended greatly upon their location and duties and whether they were in the midst of training, travel, or fighting.

Despite the presence of established French barracks, camps with semipermanent huts, and the possibility of billeting troops on the local civilian population, a surprising number of Americans spent at least part of their time in France living under canvas. Large tent cities on the outskirts of the AEF's receiving ports or in Allied training areas, such as the vast British camp at Etaples, temporarily housed doughboys assembling from the docks or learning the trade of modern war. Under the press of events in 1918, some of these tented camps in the ports and in the burgeoning sprawl of the SOS became the permanent billets for doughboys living in those locations. In most cases the army tried to make the tents more comfortable and sanitary after it became clear that their occupants would be in them for the long haul. One engineer happily informed his mother in February 1918, "I've moved into my new tent which has board walls and a floor and double decker bunks, making it roomier, cleaner and much more livable." However, these improvements did not always reach all members of the AEF equally. Although they were stationed for months in Donzy, the AEF made only tentative efforts to properly house the African American soldiers of the 321st Labor Battalion. Upon their arrival in France, these doughboys lived in two-man shelter tents, and it was not until November 1918 that they were housed in pyramid tents and had, for the first time, access to a purpose-built bathhouse. Five soldiers lived in each tent and slept in wooden bunk beds. In October, a sanitary inspector likewise found that the 324th Labor Battalion's soldiers were living in eight-men tents while their white officers were housed in a large stone house.[1]

In some cases the duties of a given unit required its soldiers to live in tents. Field hospitals, mobile repair shops, and units serving in forward supply dumps all required an ability to pick up and move as the flow of battle dictated. This generally left these units with little other recourse than to shelter their soldiers in easily transportable and quick-erected tents. For example, while supporting the Argonne offensive in October 1918, the troops assigned to Mobile Hospital 1 were living in pup tents while their NCOs and officers were lodged in more spacious marquee tents. However, even these semi-itinerant units were quick to occupy better quarters if the opportunity presented itself. In October 1918 the soldiers in Mobile Hospital 2 were being billeted in a "medium size château and four large frame huts" with access to showers and a laundry.[2]

If life in tents was better than sleeping out in the open, it was not without its dangers and discomforts. Even the best of tents were drafty, cold, and of doubtful waterproofing if not constantly maintained. To keep the occupants warm, the army installed wood- or coal-burning stoves in the large wall and pyramid tents. If not properly operated and watched, these stoves presented fire and other health hazards. When one of his comrades started a heating stove in their tent in the middle of the night without checking to ensure that the flue was open, Raymond Stanbeck and his tent mates nearly suffocated to death. He informed his family, "I managed to wake up the other two and put the stove out, then lit for the air and stood and coughed about a half hour. After we got the smoke out we went to bed again, but in the morning—our faces were just like niggers and everything in the tent was black."[3]

The most common tent used in the AEF was the shelter tent, also referred to as the "pup" or "dog" tent. Each combat soldier was issued with a shelter tent half, a folding tent pole, and five pegs. The soldier and his comrade would button their shelter halves together to make a small two-man tent that measured roughly 6.5 feet long, 3.5 feet tall, and 5.5 to six feet wide. As the shelter tent was open on one end and had no floor, the doughboys had to use their raincoats, rubberized ponchos, or greatcoats to seal the opening or cover the muddy ground. The army issued no sleeping bags and the troops had only their blankets and greatcoats to keep out the cold. Although the shelter tents were made to house only two soldiers, some doughboys discovered that by pooling their resources they could accommodate three. This was a very tight fit, but the third man's shelter half could then serve as a door or a floor to the tent and the men could huddle under all three of their blankets for warmth. The shelter tents were generally the only cover readily available to the average soldier while on active campaigning. Despite this fact, soldiers going into battle frequently left their shelter halves and pack carriers behind in the unit supply train or simply discarded them to lighten their combat load.[4]

Large numbers of American troops spent at least some time living in established French caserns or in permanent camps with purpose-built barracks. Doughboys often found the barracks buildings in the old French caserns gloomy and shabby and failed to appreciate how wartime stresses had contributed to things "going to seed" in France. The solidly built barracks were certainly without many frills and comforts. This was the case in the French artillery school at Coëtquidan, a camp that had served the French army since the time of Napoleon. Like many French barracks, the buildings in the school were long, single-story stone structures whose whitewashed interiors contained only rows of bunks along each wall and a centrally located coal stove. Each building had running water provided by a hydrant located on the outside of the building. The doughboys were most amused by the camp's sanitation system. An artilleryman recalled that the camp's latrines were

a curious structure of iron and concrete with an impressive flight of broad steps leading up to it. It suggested a public monument of some sort. At the top of the steps were several iron half-doors, each giving access to a small cubicle. The floor of each cubicle was of cement, with a hole in the center. Walking around the monument I found a large row of galvanized barrels under the cubicles . . . We christened it "Grant's Tomb." Every day the cans were emptied into a great vat on two wheels drawn by a Percheron horse, and this equipage was known to us as the "Honey Cart."

Of his French barracks, another solder quipped, "You should see our bachelor apartments: quite modern in every respect—erected about the time that the 'she wolf' found Romulus & Rhemus . . . We have labeled the oldest & most exclusive 'Hotel de Cobweb.'"[5]

Despite the Americans' criticism of the French camps, the shelter that they provided was still better than the living arrangements enjoyed by most doughboys throughout the war. In many cases the French barracks were also far superior to the barracks erected by the Americans themselves. This is borne out by the reports submitted each month by American unit medical and sanitation officers to the AEF chief surgeon's office. These reports offer a fairly complete picture of the housing, mess, and bathing facilities and the general sanitary conditions that doughboys encountered across the AEF. The soldiers of Base Section 5 in Cherbourg, for example, lived in "old French stone barracks" that their medical officer deemed "primitive but fairly well adapted" for use by the Americans. Service of Supply troops stationed at Camp Victor Hugo near Gare St. Charles lived in a large, forty-room stone and masonry building and two ample-sized wooden barracks. The barracks had hot water for showers and laundry. The only downside for these men was that the local French water supply was of poor quality and thus had to be sterilized to make it potable. At the American-run Camp Pontanezen, the receiving camp for men and units arriving at the port in Brest, the conditions were much worse. The camp was notoriously dirty, muddy, and inhospitable. As late as November 1918 the camp was still billeting troops in unfloored and unheated wooden barracks and tents on locations where the "ground is saturated with water and natural drainage is nil." The camp's kitchens and mess halls were likewise without flooring and the accumulation of rotting food dropped and then ground into the muck of the ground left them with a "most disagreeable odor." There were no showers in the camp and its only toilets consisted of "pit latrines, latrine cans or saddle trenches."[6]

As noted earlier, the doughboys sometimes found themselves living in wooden barracks that the American Army had built to house troops in its permanent bases, camps, and depots. These barracks generally followed the standardized floor plans of those built in the camps in the United States. Barracks built for transient troops, like those described earlier for Camp Pontanezen, often suffered from a lack of upkeep and comfort simply due to the population that they served. This was not the case for camps occupied by more sedentary units. When soldiers and their officers realized that their units would be in a given location for a long duration, they set about to make their living areas as nice, clean, and comfortable as possible. The air service troops of the 1st Pursuit Group at the airfield near Rembercourt were a case in point. They lived in barracks with wooden floors and two-tiered bunk beds with ample floor space and four stoves per building. The flyers and their mechanics enjoyed the use of a mobile shower system that allowed them to have at least one hot bath a week. A cynical ground-pounder might note that the American Air Forces' quest for creature comforts seems to have had very early roots.[7]

When training or serving with the Allies, American soldiers sometimes found themselves living in more novel surroundings. In early May 1918, the soldiers of the 306th Machine Gun Battalion were billeted in British army Nissen huts. These huts were designed by British Major Peter Norman Nissen in 1916 as a cheap and fast way to mass-produce needed troop billets. They were constructed of semicircular corrugated sheet metal sections that were engineered to be erected in four hours by a party of only six men. When buried or covered with dirt, they also served as bomb shelters closer to the front. They were the predecessors of the famous Quonset huts of World War II and were similar to the Adrian shelters used by the French army during the Great War. An American machine gunner described them as being "like great big sewer pipes cut in half with openings at both ends" that were "about fourteen-feet wide at the bottom, and about seven feet high in the center." His hut had wooden floors and space for twenty-six soldiers. He claimed that "the men all prefer these corrugated huts to French barns."[8]

The machine gunner's comments about French barns points to another source of billets for the American soldiers: the civilian populations in areas where the AEF operated. The État de Siége acts of 1849 and legislation passed in 1877 had long given the French Army sweeping wartime powers over local governments and civilians. These acts, which were further expanded and codified during World War I, provided the legal basis for Allied armies to requisition needed supplies and quarter troops on the civilian population. The AEF's process for requisitioning or using civilian-owned buildings, and for compensating their owners, was established in great and painful detail in General Orders 18, issued on January 31, 1918. In areas under constant American occupation, the AEF assigned permanent town majors to supervise and coordinate billeting and requisitioning with the mayors and French Army liaison officers of the local village or commune. In other cases, units appointed their own acting town majors to perform the same function. The town majors were to coordinate with arriving units to determine their housing, stabling, water, and sanitary needs, assign French assets against those needs, and oversee the compensation that the French civilians received for the use of their property and any damage caused by the American occupation. The Americans were also entitled to the locals' forage for the army's animals, straw for bedding, wood or coal for heating and cooking, and access to the community's mills, ovens, wells, and laundry facilities.[9]

Although French law allowed the quartering of troops in private residents, in practice only the AEF's officers and senior NCOs were billeted in French homes. Lucky indeed was Sergeant Benjamin Heath who found shelter in a French house with "a soft downy feather bed to rest our weary bones in at night" during the Argonne fighting. Unlike Heath, soldiers generally had to make do sleeping in barns, outbuildings, warehouses, and the occasional town school or church. Under French and AEF regulations, a householder was to be paid a franc a night if he or she provided an officer a room with at least twelve cubic meters of airspace containing a bed with a mattress, box springs, sheets, and at least one blanket. If the owner provided an NCO or soldier a room and bed, they were to be given twenty centimes a night. The civilians would be compensated five centimes per soldier per night if they only provided shelter for the troops in their barns or other nonresidential structures.[10]

In villages close to the front that had experienced a steady stream of soldiers since 1914, it was not unusual to find some barns and outbuildings that had been converted into makeshift barracks through the installation of bunks. These were simple multitiered arrangements stacked three to five bunks high with wooden slats or chicken wire nailed to posts to comprise the mattress of the bed. In most cases, however, the barns where the soldiers stayed lacked these rough amenities and the men merely bedded down in the straw and hay in the barn's loft. Although some doughboys found barn living homey and comfortable, many maintained that poor upkeep made the barns cold, drafty, and filled with lice and other unpleasant vermin.

Chapter 9 will discuss the American soldiers' relations with the French people, but when it came to billets, it is important to note that the reception that the Americans received, and the comforts they enjoyed, depended on the attitudes of the locals. In a war-weary population that had seen hordes of soldiers tramp though their communities, the behavior of the doughboys, and those who had preceded them, colored French perceptions and interactions with the Americans.

Where the Americans were respectful of French property and local sensibilities and worked to build a symbiotic relationship with the locals by helping the people with chores, the doughboys could be welcomed as members of the family and their stays made as pleasant as possible. However, if the troops failed in these areas, the results were predictable.

Footloose young men facing the possibility of sudden violent death tended to play fast and loose with army regulations and local morays. The doughboys all too often placed their own temporary needs and comforts above the desires of the civilians when living in small towns. The number of barns and other buildings destroyed by fires caused by American soldiers grew so large that in March 1918 the AEF GHQ had to issue a decree stating, "The striking of matches, smoking and the use of uncovered lights in rooms in which straw, hay or other easily inflammable substances are stored are forbidden." As the Jewish chaplain Lee Levinger observed, "The French country people did not like our soldiers over much. The soldier of any nation was rather noisy, rather rough, and had no idea whatever of property values. He took anything he needed, simply 'finding' it, the worst possible trait to thrifty French country people." The French often saw the American soldier as "ignorant of ordinary politeness, a wild Indian, the brother of the savages still supposed to be thronging our plains."[11]

By regulation the American town major was to investigate and document all damage claims made by French civilians against American soldiers living within their areas. These claims were to be submitted prior to the unit in question leaving the town so the guilty parties could be held responsible (and financially liable) for their misdeeds. In practice this was not always easy to do. Language barriers and the lack of sympathy of the town majors and unit officers for what they saw as rapacious and unjustified French demands often hindered the compensation process. Clever soldiers could also derail the process. As his unit was departing the village of Champlitte, an American NCO was approached by an irritated French woman with a complaint that three American soldiers had not paid for their lodgings. When the American asked the French woman if she could identify the soldiers, she produced the required billeting chit inscribed with the miscreants' names: John D. Rockefeller, J. P. Morgan, and Henry Ford.

As these titans of industry could not be ferreted out of the ranks, the woman received nothing.[12]

The AEF continued to billet its soldiers on the civilian population when it occupied its sector of the Rhineland after the Armistice. Troops occupying German territory often found a marked increase in the comfort of the lodgings. Sergeant Hank Gowdy, of the 42nd Division's 166th Infantry, was even lucky enough to find himself billeted in a castle in Roaldseck, where he enjoyed sleeping in a room with silken coverlets, a plush chaise lounge, and jeweled bedside lamps. Although Gowdy's experience was the exception, the majority of soldiers still benefited from access to warm, dry, and comfortable shelter that surpassed their previous experiences in France.

A great deal of this change in condition was due to the fact that it was much more common for the doughboys to be quartered in German homes than had been the case in France. It is interesting to note that the AEF policies worked somewhat at cross-purposes when it came to billeting. General Orders 218, issued on November 28, 1918, as the first American units were entering Germany reminded the troops that the United States was still at war and forbid any fraternization with the locals, but also directed them "to so conduct yourself in your relations with the inhabitants of Germany as will cause them to respect you and the country you have the honor to represent." At the same time other policy memorandums stated, "The commanding general also directed that every male German between the ages of fifteen and sixty, who was not in ill health, should give up his bed if American soldiers billeted in his house lacked them." How far this policy was carried out depended on local commanders and the doughboys themselves. A corporal recalled that while he and two of his comrades shared a room in a German home from January to July 1919, the son of the owner, himself a recently returned veteran, slept on the floor while the Americans occupied the two beds. Other doughboys were more considerate than these troops and sought to impose themselves as little as possible on the conquered people. While marching into Germany in December 1918, José Sáenz and his comrades politely rebuffed repeated offers for beds made by the owners of the homes in which they stayed. But when his unit was settled in Lösnich and it became clear that he would be wintering in Germany, even Sáenz swallowed his scruples and accepted a room and bed in a German residence. All in all the billeting of American soldiers in German homes went smoothly. The unfortunate side effect, from the AEF GHQ's perspective at least, was that the close contact between the two groups made the army's antifraternization decrees moot.[13]

Barracks, barns, and private homes aside, the last aspect of lodgings that must be covered is how the doughboys sought shelter in combat. The forms of shelter available to the soldiers in battle depended largely on the types of operations that their units were waging. Troops occupying trenches, especially those in long-established parts of the Allied lines, had access to more extensive and elaborate forms of shelter than those constantly moving forward in attacks.

All of the AEF's combat divisions spent some time defending portions of the French or British trench lines. As some of these works had been continually occupied since 1914, the Americans benefited from the years of labor that the Allied troops who preceded them had devoted to adding some degree of comfort to their troglodyte existence. The Allied frontline, support, and reserve trench systems were honeycombed with bunkers and dugouts designed to protect the soldiers from shellfire and the elements. The construction and sophistication of these shelters differed greatly depending on the soil, the access to building materials, and the degree of activity on the front where they were located. On the low end of the comfort and protection scale were the "funk holes," mere alcoves cut directly into the side of a trench to provide an individual sitting in it a minimal degree of cover. They were mainly intended for soldiers on guard duty in the trench. A soldier's only protection from the elements while occupying a "funk hole" was to huddle into the cut as far as possible and then drape himself with a blanket, greatcoat, or poncho. As the "funk holes" seldom contained any support to hold back the earth, rain or shellfire sometimes led to their collapse. In May 1918, a soldier in the 2nd Brigade, 1st Division was suffocated to death when his "funk hole" caved in during a bombardment. To prevent this kind of tragedy, the "funk holes" were sometimes further protected from shellfire by being roofed by a semicircular corrugated steel covering known as an "elephant shelter."[14]

Bunkers, shelters, and dugouts were more substantial structures made by digging a shaft and a gallery into the ground where the soil permitted (termed a "cave shelter" in AEF publications) or by excavating a dugout, a relatively shallow gallery over which was constructed a bombproof roof. Cave shelters needed to be dug approximately fifteen to twenty feet below ground. To protect its inhabitants from a 105mm shell, dugouts had to have a roof of steel rails, covered by a yard of earth and a further "bursting layer" to absorb the shell's energy consisting of a layer of logs, sheet iron, gravel, or stones. All bunkers and dugouts were to have at least two exits and were to be constructed in a manner that allowed its occupants to race outside to respond to an enemy attack.[15]

The dugouts and shelters were built primarily with protection from enemy shellfire in mind. The soldiers' coziness was a secondary concern. A shelter's degree of comfort depended on the area's climate and geology as well as the ingenuity of its occupants. In wet weather or in regions with a high water table, they would be soggy and disagreeable. "We are in a place like a swamp and living in dugouts under the ground," a 26th Division soldier wrote his sister. "We have to pump the water out of them two times a day." An artilleryman only half-jokingly noted, "The 'dug-outs' look like frail piano boxes on end, roofed with tin to make them bombproof. Each time we fired a gun fifty-seven rafters caved in. Each dugout was equipped with running water. Sometimes it ran down the walls more often through the door." Other elements of construction also added to the discomfort of the bombproofs. Leslie Martin quickly made the discovery during his first stint in the trenches that the "ceilings weren't too high" in the shelters, "and if one didn't keep his helmet on, and raised up real quick, [it] just nearly knocked your brains out." To add to the misery, the shelters frequently were home to legions of rats and lice.[16]

Given time and resources, the shelters could become quite livable. A Marine was amazed at the work that the French soldiers had put into the bunker his unit occupied:

> A steep flight of stairs led to what appeared to be a room below! And forty feet down was an oblong room, running parallel to the trench above. The place was roughly boxcar shaped. With a low ceiling the room was about

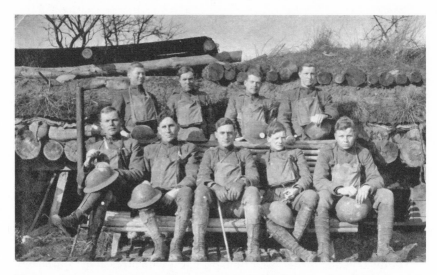

Photo 9: A group of engineer officers posing in front of a log and earth bombproof shelter in the reserve trenches. Such shelters were common at the front and were made as comfortable as time and resources allowed. The stovepipe on the left indicates that this bunker was at least heated. Source: author's collection.

four foot wide by fifty or sixty feet long. Running the length of the room, and on the side opposite where we entered, was a double-tiered row of bunks nailed to the floor and wall. These consisted of a board frame with some improvised wire nailed to them as springs . . . It had been a glorious surprise to find this room below, protected from the weather and shells.

The structure was also warmed by a wood-burning stove. Some shelters even had electric lights and lavish furnishings, such as tables, chairs, gramophones, and crockery, which successive waves of occupants had looted from nearby abandoned houses.[17]

Some men actually seemed to like the rough living that the dugouts provided. The simplicity of his new living arrangements made Lieutenant James Dalgren reconsider his wild and spendthrift peacetime ways. He confessed to his sweetheart, "Now I regret it all. Here I am in a shelter 16 ft. square with the ground as my floor, a cot with a few blankets, a piece of a stove picked up on the road as my fireplace, a candle for my light and yet without finery and extravagances . . . I am more content and healthier." It is doubtful, however, that many doughboys shared the outlook of this Thoreau of the Trenches.[18]

The drawbacks and discomforts that the doughboys encountered living in dugouts paled in comparison to those that they faced when engaged in open warfare. When engaged in combat outside of the trenches, the doughboys were left to their own devices to wage a battle against the elements that was as desperate as the one against the enemy. Generally, the soldiers' shelter in open warfare consisted of what they could construct using their entrenching tools and whatever else they carried on their persons. It is again the unit medical and sanitation officers who offered the most accurate, if somewhat terse, assessments of their soldiers' living conditions in battle. For example, at the end of October 1918, the 3rd Division's sanitary officer reported, "Troops were at the front during the entire month. There were no billets. Men lived in dug outs, ruins, and shelter tents, pitched over pits." This was a common experience for the divisions operating at the same time in the Meuse Argonne. For infantrymen, machine gunners, and other soldiers closest to the fighting, shell holes or one- to three-man foxholes tended to be their only shelter from the weather and enemy fire. In such cases, overhead cover was provided by raincoats, ponchos, branches, or whatever else the troops could improvise.[19]

In his great wartime novel *Under Fire*, the veteran French infantryman Henri Barbusse wrote, "Damp rusts men as it does rifles; more slowly, but deeper." This observation was borne out during the American campaigns of 1918. Captain Clarence Minick, a company commander in the 91st Division's 361st Infantry, recorded in his diary for September 28, 1918, "Rained hard. No shelters—only 'foxholes.' I slept in a hole with 3 inches of water in it . . . No one in Co. G will ever spend such a more miserable night if he lives for three centuries." Sometimes the soldiers' own "live for today" outlooks and action hurt their ability to create shelters for themselves. To lighten their load, an infantryman observed, some of the members of his unit "threw away their raincoats and overcoats when they went over the top, so that later they had nothing at all to protect them from the cold and the wet. They went for days and days, sleeping in shell holes filled with ice-water." In such situations the only thing that the soldiers could do was to endure as best they could. An Iowa doughboy tried to make his wet foxhole more livable by lining it with the uniforms taken from dead Germans. After a similar experience of living in the rough, another soldier simply told his mother, "[I] have been sleeping on the ground lately. I don't think I will ever know how to sleep when I get back to a good bed."[20]

Those who could found other ways of obtaining shelter in combat. The infantryman turned truck driver Clarence Mahan found his new life in his unit's supply company to be a mixed blessing. He later noted, "Although our trucks were always targets for the Germans we had advantages the infantry did not have, a place to sleep whenever we could stop working. Our truck had wooden sides and a canvas top and we always tried to keep a good supply of blankets. This was better than sleeping on the ground as I had to do in the infantry." During both the St. Mihiel and Meuse Argonne offensives, captured German facilities also provided for the doughboys' housing needs and offered the Americans welcome respites from sleeping in foxholes. The enemy's efforts to quarter their troops often impressed the doughboys. "You should have seen some of the dugouts the Germans had," June Smith explained to his mother. "They had been up on the line for about three and a half years and had things fixed up to stay a long time. Some of them were concrete, had hot and cold shower baths, and everything else you could think of." The machine gunner Franklin Schall also wrote home in October 1918, "At the present we are located in a place which the Germans held since 1914 but were driven back. The wooden shack in which we are staying and the bed in which I sleep and I am now writing this letter was built by Fritzie. Fritze also had the place all wired up. A high transmission line runs into it and most of the shacks were electrically lighted." But such pleasant interludes were fleeting and both Smith and Schall soon found themselves living out in the elements like most other combat doughboys for the remainder of the war.[21]

8

"Good-Bye Broadway, Hello France"
Life on Board a Ship for France

The World War II generation called it "hurry up and wait": the special purview of militaries to go through bouts of frenetic activity followed by long periods of lull as the organization's nervous system catches up to it muscle movements. "Hurry up and wait" governs all aspects of an army's endeavors, but it seems to be at its most nerve-wracking and irritating to soldiers when getting ready for a major deployment and on the eve of combat. As moving over two million American soldiers to France was a major undertaking conducted in the face of shipping shortages, bureaucratic inertia, and the inherent friction that such mighty migrations produce, "hurry up and wait" was a phrase as applicable to 1917–1918 as it was to the GI generation.

The wartime fear of spies and U-Boats meant that deployment and shipping information was generally withheld from the troops until the last possible moment. This all but ensured that the training camps became a hotbed of rumor and gossip as the soldiers tried to predict their futures from the cryptic pronouncements of their officers and daily orders. From these divinations the soldiers tried to give their friends and family some idea of when they would depart. Reflecting this, Harry Callison wrote his mother in April 1918,

> The rumor here is that they need men so bad in France that the whole bunch of us will go as soon as the plans are finished. About a month ago each Capt made out an "indispensable list" of men needed to train the next draft. The Division adj[utant] says now that America's only indispensable list is in the trenches. So, I again advise you that we are bound for France how soon I don't know.

Based on what he had heard, another solder confidently informed his sister, "From all indications we will be on our way about Thursday. We don't know where, but do not think to France. The dope is to Siberia by way of Hwaiian [*sic*] and Philippine Island." Like many camp rumors, his information proved to be wrong and he was soon bound for France. The coming of army wisdom or hard experience led some soldiers to become inured to all of the tales of an imminent departure. "Rumor has it that we leave here shortly for France. Rumor tells a lot of lies tho,'" James Miller penned to his mother. "We may be here for two months. I wont be able to tell you when we leave when I do know, tho.' Mr Censor will tend to that." Even Miller succumbed to the lure of rumors and informed her three weeks later, "We are still in the U.S.A. tho' everyone expected us to be gone by now. I'm pretty sure tho' that we leave here on Sunday. The boys have it all doped out that way, anyway."[1]

The constant preparation and waiting created a nervous tension in the ranks while they awaited orders to pack up and leave camp. The army's tendency to strip certain units of men to fill the ranks of other units getting ready to sail and a lack of information from commanders to their soldiers exacerbated these anxieties. After fifteen men in his hospital unit had their departure for the port unexpectedly halted, George Hetrich observed sarcastically, "They should be on their way now, but why the delay, no-one knows. You never know the reason 'Why' in the army." The delays were even more maddening for a soldier in Kansas. He informed his brother, "I am still in Ft. Riley we were all loaded on the train and ready to go day before yesterday but for some reason they took us off again. I don't know when we will leave now." A 7th Division soldier viewed the inevitable waiting with a greater equanimity and seemed to enjoy the fact that he and his comrades were "doing nothing but Eating, Sleeping & Hiding around to Keep out of Details" as they awaited orders.[2]

The receipt of final orders to sail for France unleashed a torrent of activity by the units in the training camps. Equipment slated for overseas service had to be packed and crated for shipment while excess items had to be disposed of or inventoried and signed over to those staying behind. This would prove more difficult for National Guard units whose initial mobilization camps were often in close proximity to gift-bearing family members and well-wishers. An artilleryman in the 26th Division recalled,

The day was spent in striking tents and packing them, and cleaning and packing equipment . . . The work went on half the night—a bitterly cold night as September nights can be—and all packed up we tried to sleep as close to big bonfires made mostly of the pajamas, bellybands, excess socks, books, and the mountains of non-portable trunks which everyone had accumulated. It would have taken a dozen barracks bags to transport the junk that each of us thought he needed, and it was bitter moments when we had to choose what valued articles to leave behind.

Commanders also combed out their personnel, winnowing out those soldiers who were unfit for deployment or were otherwise needed to maintain the war effort at home. As units neared departure, the War Department hurriedly filled vacancies in the ranks with fresh levies of men. These new arrivals were hastily added to the company rolls and integrated into units as completely and smoothly as the press of time allowed. All of this frenetic activity was accompanied by a great degree of labor, excitement, and confusion. In a hurried letter, one doughboy informed his sister, "Tonight the 135th Inf has one foot at Camp Cody and the other reaching out we know not where. The only thing we know is that there is a train on the track about a half mile long and we are going tomorrow . . . We have been working our fool heads off, getting up as early as four o'clock or 3:30 and going until bed time."[3]

Depending on the predilections of a unit's officers, the planning that had gone into the comfort of the men on the journey, and the individual doughboy's own attitude about going to France, the train trip from the training camps to the ports could be a sorrowful or exciting time. As his officers had made little coordination for hot meals along their route from Fort Riley to Camp Merritt, Bernard Bockemuehl informed his mother that he had been spending much of his money on food at the railroad stops, "as the feed was pretty poor all we got on the train was canned stuff served cold." This was not Mike Scheck's experience as his unit spent fifty hours moving from Camp Johnston, Florida, to Camp Merritt. Scheck wrote his sister, "I saw some great sights on the trip and the red cross treated us to cigarettes, candies and all kinds of nice things . . . We raised cain on the whole trip and the people cheered us great all along the coast."

When their officers weren't looking, some soldiers took further steps to ensure an enjoyable trip. On the journey to Camp Upton, New York, the train's porter sold a doughboy and his comrades "red eye" whiskey for $10 a quart or $5 a pint. Although the soldier resented the price gouging, he admitted, "I looked at the 5 [dollars] and then at the pint but I had to have it and drank the damn thing [all by] my self."[4]

Although doughboys sailed for France from Norfolk, Newport News, Baltimore, Philadelphia, and other ports along the Atlantic coast, the majority of them departed from docks in and around New York City. In fact, the commander of the nation's troop transport effort, Major General David Shanks, claimed that over 1.7 million of the doughboys who went to Europe left from these facilities alone. To ship these numbers required a monumental effort, and at the peak of their operations, some twenty-five hundred officers, seventeen thousand soldiers, and fourteen thousand civilians worked at the ports and embarkation camps around New York City to ship the doughboys overseas.[5]

The docks of New York were fed by a steady stream of doughboys arriving from the Camp Upton, Camp Merritt, and Camp Mills embarkation camps. As the army intended these camps to be only temporary stops for units undergoing their last preparations for overseas service, until the late spring of 1918 they had few amenities. As problems with shipping and eleventh-hour arrival of needed replacements required some units to remain in the camps from one to four weeks, the initial shortages of amenities added to the soldiers' woes. One complained that Long Island's Camp Mills was built in "an area that had wisely been considered as unsuitable for human habitation by local construction engineers" prior to the war. In the wet and cold winter of 1918 it was muddy and miserable for those living in tents while waiting to ship overseas. It was not until the summer of 1918 that the camp's tents received wooden floors.[6]

In the embarkation camps, units underwent their final shakedown inspections, equipment issue, and assignment to ship manifests. To the soldiers these ceaseless rounds of administrative activities quickly grew tiresome. "This camp is just one big inspection after another," a soldier complained to his mother in June 1918. "First it is Physical then it is clothes etc from the time we get up in the morning until we go to bed at night." To correct the clothing and equipment shortages that had plagued the training camps in 1917 and early 1918, some of the inspections were intended to identify any remaining shortfalls and to issue the departing troops complete and serviceable sets of kit. The army mandated that "troops designated for overseas service will be provided with at least two suits of O[live] D[rab] woolen clothing, light wool socks, overcoats, field shoes, winter gloves, woolen underwear and three blankets each." Given the preciousness of shipping space, the inspections also sought to remove unnecessary items from the individual's and the unit's baggage. For service overseas, corporals and privates were allowed to take seventy-five pounds of baggage in addition to their combat equipment. Sergeants were permitted one hundred pounds, and company grade officers 250 pounds of baggage, which included their basic combat equipment and all "professional books and all necessary clothing and bedding for extended field service." Officers in the rank of major to brigadier generals were allowed four hundred pounds of baggage.[7]

While going through the assorted details associated with sailing, some troops had the opportunity to visit New York City. The commander of Camp Mills initiated a pass system that allowed up to 20 percent of the soldiers in the camp to enjoy a full twenty-four-hour pass in New York if the commanders of the units awaiting embarkation were amenable to granting leaves. As over half of the nation's citizens still resided in rural areas when the United States entered the war, the city was a bewildering source of wonderment to the country lads who visited. From Camp Mills an excited Harry Callison wrote home, "I have seen the tallest part of New York from a distance when we ferried over. Also saw the Statue of Liberty, this is certainly some sight for an inlander like myself." He added, "I went over to Brooklyn with one of our sergeants and we went to Coney Island. They certainly have some swell turnouts here." Given their deeper pockets and perhaps more cosmopolitan views, officers had the chance to drink more deeply of New York's amusements. A lieutenant with the 82nd Division admitted to having a ball while waiting at Camp Upton. He and a few of his fellow officers lived it up in New York and stayed at the Biltmore, ate at fine restaurants, took in Ziegfeld's Follies, escorted some "Ziegfeld girls" out on the town, and "danced and celebrated generally." His reaction to the great metropolis was mixed. "I saw the Statue of Liberty for the first time. How impressive that emblem of freedom! What a welcome to every people into the greatest country on earth. I was deeply impressed by the view of our great New York." However, like many other soldiers from the heartland, his overall impression of the city was more restrained:

Saw the bright lights of Broadway for the first time. Some lights. Some heterogeneous mass of humanity. Derelicts. Degenerates. High flyers. Red nosed old rogues. Bankers and chorus girls. Distinguished actors. Society women. Newsboys and chauffeurs. All basking in the calcium glare—for what, I don't know. The skyline of this great metropolis is more impressive than its sidewalks.

Whether they loved, hated, or were left with a mixed opinion of the great metropolis, New York certainly left a lasting impression on those doughboys who encountered it for the first time.[8]

Some soldiers liked New York so much that they went AWOL or overstayed their passes to see the sights. Many units reported that the number of their soldiers AWOL spiked when they reached the major embarkation ports. For some the desire to see friends and family one last time before sailing was more compelling than mere army discipline and regulations. This was particularly true for soldiers whose families and friends lived in the New York City area. After being turned down for a forty-eight-hour pass, the New Yorker Albert Ettinger took matters into his own hands by going AWOL from Camp Mills to see his parents. He was not alone in his mischief. Upon being sent to the guardhouse upon his return from his illegal trip home, he found it occupied by six other soldiers from his company who were guilty of the same crime. The number of soldiers AWOL from the embarkation camps grew so great that the commander of the area posted notices in the New York papers and throughout the city imploring family members and friends to ensure that the soldiers did not overstay their passes and to shame them into returning to camp. The commander also established a stockade within each camp to hold those men who had gone AWOL and missed the sailing of their units until such time as they could be placed on another transport.[9]

The fear of losing soldiers to AWOLs and desertion led some unit commanders to prohibit their soldiers from leaving the dreary embarkation camps. Given this fact, the army belatedly worked with the Red Cross, YMCA, Knights of Columbus, Jewish Welfare Board, and other relief organizations to establish canteens, gyms, and recreation centers to give the troops something to do while waiting to sail. With their closeness to the reigning entertainment capital of the nation, the camps around New York were also able to bring in a great variety of entertainers and vaudeville acts to amuse the restless khaki masses. Some of these shows were better received than others. This became clear to an officer who was tasked to fill a three-thousand-seat auditorium at Camp Upton with troops from the 82nd Division in order to listen to Madame Francis Alda, the star of the Metropolitan Opera. He quickly found that "Her 'million dollar voice' did not appeal to the uneducated tastes of our boys, and I had to lock the doors after about three songs to keep the audience inside." One of the most important services that the welfare agencies provided in the embarkation ports for the morale of the soldiers and their families was the "Hostess Houses" they built to lodge relatives who wished to see their boys one last time before they departed for war. These became poignant backdrops for farewells, family reconciliations, and even the occasional last-minute wedding. In one case a young lady arriving at Camp Merritt with her wedding dress in her valise was inconsolable because she had arrived a bit too late for her anticipated nuptials. Her fiancé had boarded ship the night before and was scheduled to sail in a few hours. The woman's distress so moved the camp inspector that he drove her to the dock and had the soldier momentarily removed from the ship so the wedding ceremony could be held immediately on the dock.[10]

When at last the day arrived to board ship, "hurry up and wait" gave way to bewilderment as many doughboys encountered the completely alien environment of a ship. The Missouri-born landlubber William Triplet found his hurried introduction to the nautical world to be disorienting. Like that of most doughboys, his embarkation started with his unit mustering in a large warehouse opposite the docks for the last-minute inspections and roll calls. From there he was hustled up the gangway to the ship. Upon entering the vessel, he and his party were escorted by a member of the ship's company through the labyrinthine maze of decks and ladders until they reached their berths deep in the bowels of the vessel. There they found rows of improvised three-tiered bunks that would serve as their homes for the voyage.[11]

To help counter the landsmen's natural bafflement and allow the soldiers to slowly gain their bearings, as they boarded the ship the troops were presented a card that listed the compartment, deck, and bunk assignment for the trip as well as the location of, and directions to, their abandon-ship station. On the back of the card was a lengthy list of the rules that were to govern their life afloat. These rules were intended to make the journey safe for all and lessen the possibility of U-Boat attacks by limiting when and where soldiers could smoke, the places that they could go on the ship, and how they were to dispose of garbage so a submarine could not track the ship by any trail of debris left in its wake. One such card concluded with the positive note: "IN CASE OF ABANDON SHIP, REMEMBER THERE IS LOTS OF TIME." Upon boarding, the soldiers were also given a postcard that contained the simple message "The vessel on which I sailed has arrived safely overseas." The doughboy was to address the card to his family and then deposit it in a designated mailbag. These bags were left in the port upon the ship's departure. When the ship reached its destination, army officials wired the news back to the States and the stateside port authorities released the mailbags for delivery.[12]

The soldier's life aboard ship and the time it took him to make the passage to France differed greatly depending on the type of ship on which he sailed. William Clark and the men of the 104th Machine Gun Battalion went to France in the SS *Calamares*, a true "banana boat" whose prewar existence was devoted to running fruit from Central America to the United States for the United Fruit Company. The small ship still stank of bananas when the twelve hundred men of the battalion came on board. The berths consisted of three-tiered bunks that had been improvised in the ship's hold using wooden two-by-fours and chicken wire. Over the course of the war, nearly 49 percent of American soldiers went to Europe in British ships. These ranged from the majestic passenger liners *Olympic, Aquitania,* and *Mauretania* to the tramp steamers that had plied the oceans carrying the assorted goods of the British Empire. More troops traveled on the later than the former and generally found the voyage to be decidedly unpleasant. Another 45 percent of doughboys made the trip on American-flagged ships, including twenty large German passenger liners and steamers that were seized by the U.S. government in American ports in April 1917. One of these German ships, the SS *Leviathan* (formerly the Hamburg-America Line's *Vaterland*) became the queen of the transport fleet by moving 96,804 soldiers to Europe in ten sailings. Until the shipping crisis of the spring of 1918, life aboard the larger British, American, and former German liners was relatively pleasant for the soldiers on board. If nothing else, these fast ships were capable of making the passage to Europe in around seven days, while the average time for other steamers was twelve to seventeen days. It took thirteen days, for example, for elements of the 82nd Division to make the trip from New York to Liverpool aboard the British steamer *Karmala* in April and May 1918.[13]

The panic that accompanied the German spring offensive of 1918 caused a major and hurried spike in the shipping of American combat units overseas. Every possible ship was pressed into service to meet this demand. The British even consented to transporting soldiers in their naval ships used to escort the Atlantic convoys. This push contributed to the discomfort of the soldiers involved. Major General David Shanks admitted that "there was considerable over assignments" of troops to berthing space, "amounting in some cases to as much as thirty percent" over the specified capacity of some vessels. Vice Admiral Albert Cleaves, who oversaw the ships of the American Transport Service, claimed that during the shipping crisis he was able to actually increase the number of troops carried on the largest ships by 40 to 50 percent using the simple expedient of "turn-in-turn-out" or "hot bunking" berthing. A given bunk was thus never empty as two men took shifts sleeping in the same berth. By this trick, the liner *Leviathan* increased the number of troops it could carry from seven thousand to ten thousand, and actually surged to over fourteen thousand men on one trip. Cleaves rationalized this move by maintaining that these ship's great speed and faster passage ultimately lessened the overall discomfort of the doughboys that they carried. The sardine-packed doughboys did not agree. One soldier reported that troops were crammed so tightly on the *President Grant* that "you couldn't talk without biting off somebody's ear." However, the crowding paid off and the peak months for transporting troops to France occurred from May to August 1918. In July 1918, the high point of American troop movements, 311,359 soldiers sailed for France.[14]

Once at sea the doughboys' lives tended to become a steady refrain of seasickness, homesickness, and boredom. The realization that the ship was taking them to a dangerous and unknown future weighed on the minds of many. As his ship passed the Statue of Liberty, a soldier in the 137th Infantry "wondered if ours would be the luck to see this wonderful piece of art again." While they came to grips with their fate, the doughboys also had to reconcile themselves to the tedium and discomfort of life afloat. For safety and security, the troops were allowed to smoke only on deck and could only be on deck during daylight hours. At night the portholes were closed, the lights were out, and smoking was prohibited from dusk until dawn. As soon as the troopships entered the submarine zone, most required that their occupants wear life belts at all times. These contraptions usually resembled fat "doughnuts" worn around the soldier's waist and secured by crossbelts running across his shoulders. They made the ship's already tight accommodations even more difficult

Photo 10: Berthing quarters on a troopship. Unlike those on the right, the men standing against the bunks have disobeyed orders by removing their lifejackets, perhaps to have more room and comfort in the close confines of their billets. Source: author's collection.

for the soldiers to navigate. This was particularly true when it came time to eat, as the cumbersome devices often upset tables as the soldier maneuvered or sat down in the mess, sending his, and his comrade's, food flying.[15]

Like many soldiers, Clyde Eddy found his passage to France in August 1918 to be particularly uncomfortable. He and five hundred other soldiers were packed in a small hold several decks below the steamer's promenade deck. They had been ordered to wear their complete uniform at all times, including their rifle belts with canteen and first aid pouches. In the sweltering heat the doughboys also had to always wear heavy padded life jackets. The ship's crew enforced strict fresh-water rationing and the soldiers had to resort to using coffee for shaving water. Eddy had one cold salt-water bath during the trip. He memorialized his voyage in a short poem,

> What Sherman meant was clearer now than ever,
> Since I have slept in canteen, shoes and pants,
> He was righter than he knew because he never,
> Took passage on a troopship bound for France.

Eddy's comments about water and washing are notable. As many of the ships used for transport were not originally built to carry large numbers of passengers, they often lacked large stores of water and were woefully short of latrine/head and bathing facilities. Although this situation was better on the large liners, even on them most soldiers were lucky if they received two saltwater baths during their passage. As the troopship *Agamemnon* had only seventeen shower heads available to serve its thirty-five hundred passengers and crew, it was customary, when the weather permitted, to do a mass bathing of men on its deck using cold salt water sprayed from hoses.[16]

As with most things in the American Army, at sea rank continued to have its privileges. When it came to berthing, food, and the freedom of the ship, officers tended to enjoy a much better life than that of their men. Soon after arriving in France, Lieutenant Dewitt McIntyre fairly gushed to his folks, "Our trip across the Atlantic was the finest thing I have ever had. We traveled on one of the largest ships afloat. And I travelled 1st class and the government paid all my expenses." While his soldiers lived in the ship's cramped hold, another lieutenant spent his voyage in a four-berth stateroom with one other officer and lunched in a well-stocked officers' mess. On reaching the harbor, he reported, "The trip over was wonderful . . . No trip could be more enjoyable." He bragged, "The scotch was plentiful and the food excellent," and then pronounced that it was "the damnedest pleasure trip I ever took!" Some officers regretted the disparity between their living conditions and those of their men and made efforts to ameliorate the more glaring discomforts of the troops. In the end, long-standing military traditions designed to keep up social barriers between the leaders and the led, and the realities of wartime shipping, limited what even the best-intentioned officers could do.[17]

Not all of the troops' time was spent idling away in their cramped quarters. Some of their time was spent in physical drills, in mandatory (sometimes daily) abandon-ship drills, and in various housekeeping, maintenance, and security details that were required to keep the vessel in good order. Due to these kinds of work parties, Private Tom Carroll experienced a particularly unpleasant trip across the Atlantic in June 1917. Since he did not suffer from seasickness, his sergeant assigned him to "puke detail," where, "equipped with a small bucket and a piece of tin," he roamed the decks "scooping up retchings." He then carried this nasty mix to the boiler room to be burned, as nothing was allowed to be thrown overboard for fear of giving U-Boats a trail to follow to the convoy. This was just the start of Carroll's woes. After being charged as a thief for buying two purloined oranges from one of the ship's crew members, his punishment was to assist the crew in hauling coal from the ship's coal bunkers to the engine room. During this muscle-draining exercise the soldiers on the detail wore only their underwear to keep their uniforms from being ruined by the ubiquitous coal dust. Afterward the miscreant coal-haulers were given a cold saltwater shower "with a supposed salt water soap that was like a piece of marble and had the same cleansing effect on our dirt." A similar detail of soldiers on board the *Antilles* shifted eighty-nine tons of coal on a single day.[18]

The most common duty on the ships, however, was the submarine watch. This required a continual party of men to be on station at various points around the ship to scan the seas for periscopes and give advance warning of the telltale wakes of torpedoes. The soldiers generally stood a five-hour watch. To keep them as alert as possible, the soldiers spent one hour at rest for every hour spent actually observing their sector of the ocean. To keep this watch, the *Antilles* required a daily detail of 150 enlisted men and fifteen officers. Although the submarine watch was usually a monotonous assignment, at times it could be quite frightening. One soldier was ordered by his captain to conduct his two-hour watch in the ship's crow's nest. Unfortunately, he was afraid of heights; the crow's nest was seventy-five feet above the water, and the ship was violently pitching. Although he made it to the base of the nest, he was unsure of how to climb from the unstable rope ladder to the perch. Eventually the ship's captain had to send a sailor aloft to help the frantic doughboy scale the last few feet.[19]

As was the case on land, one of the soldier's main concerns at sea remained food. The food on American ships, especially on the large liners, tended to be rather good and plentiful. However, the doughboys consistently complained about the quality and quantity of food that they were served on British troopships. One wrote that the English cooks "simply starved us to death" by the stinginess of their rations. Another stated that throughout his voyage his breakfast consisted of a monotonous menu of bread, bacon, orange marmalade, and tea, all eaten while standing at a chest-high trestle table. The rest of the meals consisted of Australian jackrabbit stew, which the soldiers claimed was actually kangaroo meat, and "a morsel of boiled potatoes or carrots, a slice of dense gray bread, a sliver of cheese, the ubiquitous orange marmalade with a high portion of peel, and tea." Charles Minder was equally disgusted at the quality of food that his unit received on the British tramp steamer *Koroa* in April 1918. He noted, "We have a couple of cockney Englishmen cooking for us, and it's a shame that they get away with it, because they cannot cook decently at all. The coffee is served in a big garbage can. There probably never was any garbage in it but when you see them dip the coffee out of it, your stomach turns just the same." What irked Minder the most was that while he believed that "animals on cattle boats had better quarters" than the enlisted men, the officers were enjoying life with nice dining and staterooms. He observed that when the officers were being fed roast chicken, pies, steaks, and pudding, the troops were eating beef stew consisting largely of water and flour. Only after a fellow soldier staged a minimutiny by refusing to eat the swill that he was being fed and threw his messkit to the deck did the food for the enlisted men nominally improve. It should be noted that some officers took an active role in combating the poor food the soldiers received. On June 19, 1917, Colonel Beaumont Buck recorded in his diary, "I have a sample meal of the soldiers' mess sent to my room daily. This meal started off poor and scant, but I have gradually made the transport Q[uarter] M[aster] come across with good meals for the men."[20]

What angered officers and soldiers the most about food was when the ship's crew tried to profit from the troop's discomfort. It was not unusual for members of the ship's company to carry on a black market trade in alcohol and foodstuffs with their needy passengers. After discovering that members of the vessel's engineer mess were selling sandwiches to his soldiers, Colonel Buck raised hell with the ship's captain to put a stop to the practice. On another British troopship a steward made a healthy profit by selling the hungry doughboys roasted chicken stolen from the officer's mess for $5 a bird. One soldier got the last laugh on the greedy gob by posing as an MP and confiscating both the cash and the bird when the steward appeared to complete the transaction.[21]

For far too many doughboys, food was the last thing on their minds. Soldier accounts frequently noted the presence and persistence of seasickness in the ranks. One Marine was so seasick that he tried to refrain from eating during the entire voyage. This did not help, for he found that "the very odor of food halfway across the ship was very sickening." One France-bound artilleryman was so seasick that he swore, "If I'm ever on land again, by Christ,

I'll come home by way of Siberia, if I have to crawl on my hands and knees."
Walter Shaw admitted to his mother that he was seasick for most of his voyage, and the absence of appetite and constant purging caused him to lose twenty pounds on the voyage.[22]

The other great shipboard plague was boredom. Although the army had worked with the various welfare agencies to provide recreation in the ports, it was slow to realize that the troops were in just as much need of diversions aboard ships. It was not until late March 1918 that the YMCA began placing at least two of their secretaries on each troopship to look after the welfare of those afloat. In the larger liners the troops benefited from libraries, sporting matches, and games and even had access to movies and music from bands. They also contained well-stocked canteens to provide candy, cigarettes, and other comfort items at near-cost prices. During a single passage, the troops and crew of the *George Washington* spent between $45,000 and $50,000 in the liner's canteens. Additionally, the military sought to give the troops spiritual comfort during their voyage. Over the course of the war, the commander of the port of embarkation created a pool of chaplains to accompany any ship not already served by an ordained navy or army officer.[23]

Of course many, if not most, doughboys did not enjoy this level of wholesome activity and access to entertainment. Letters sent by Private James Miller to his family neatly capture the monotony and lassitude that many, if not most, soldiers coped with during their passage.

> There are about 2500 of us on board and we are having some slow time. There is nothing to do and no place to go. We had some boxing matches on deck yesterday and, I suppose, some more today. We eat and sleep and look around and wonder where we are going. It's mighty cold out here. I wear my mackinaw morning and evenings and nearly freeze. My hands are so cold now I can hardly write. I bought a Kodak in Washington but we are not allowed to use them on the boat . . . There are lots of things I'd like to tell you about but I know it wouldn't get by the censor. I doubt if all this gets by. Since this is a British ship we are not getting as good treatment as Uncle Sam would give us.

The ennui these conditions inspired and their effects on the troops were evident in a letter he posted from Halifax, Nova Scotia, as his ship waited to join a convoy. "We left New York harbor Sunday night a week ago and arrived in Halifax harbor early Thursday morning. We have been here in Halifax ever since. Talk about being tired! We are not allowed off the boat and can see the town about half a mile across the water. We amuse ourselves as best we can but the boys are getting grouchier and grouchier." Miller's experience was far from unique. A 1st Division soldier recalled that "time hung rather heavy on our hands, and I don't remember any reading material being available. There was no daily news bulletin from the wireless room." With nothing else to do, some troops on the steamer *Koroa* passed the time in endless card games. In under a week one cardsharp had managed to win $410 from his comrades. The wagering grew so bad that one soldier compared the ship to a "Yukon gambling dive."[24]

Beneath the boredom was the possibility of the voyage ending badly with a U-Boat attack or some accident at sea. This prospect was brought home to the doughboys with every abandon-ship drill, submarine watch, and day spent wearing uncomfortable life preservers. The ship's crewmen sometimes worsened the tensions on the vessel by having fun at the landsmen's expense. An officer in the 35th Division noted that his Midwest soldiers' unease at being at sea was compounded by "horrible tales of submarine sinkings, of floating mines, of terrible storms, of battles at sea kept secret by cruel censors" told them by the ship's crew. At other times the soldiers themselves contributed to the group's apprehensions. On their third day at sea, one of Charles Minder's fellow soldiers earned the ire of his comrades by reminding them that the *Titanic* had sunk exactly six years ago to the day. As it "wasn't a very pleasant subject to bring up when everyone on board is worried about being sunk by a torpedo," he recalled, there were calls to throw the miscreant overboard. In the face of the German threat some doughboys clung to wishful thinking. When assigned to sail on a seized German ship, one doughboy wrote his sister the hopeful note, "The Germans will not sink her if they do they sink their own boat."[25]

The fear that the U-Boats inspired at times provided moments of humor that helped to break the tension. During one submarine alarm a particularly snobbish and odious company commander rushed on deck full of terror wearing a brightly colored inflatable lifesaving suit. These suits were private purchase items not readily available to the soldiers. That, combined with the man's outlandish appearance while wearing it and his panicked demeanor, instantly made the officer a figure of ridicule. One soldier reported that as soon as the officer appeared he was met with "a great woop and holler of scorn and derision" and from that day onward he was merely "a captain in name only."[26]

It is interesting to note that the letters, diaries, and memoirs of the doughboys abound with harrowing tales of U-Boat attacks, narrow escapes from torpedoes, and great duels between escort ships and submarines. Colonel Beaumont Buck recorded one such incident in his diary on June 26, 1917:

> Submarine sighted at 1:40 P.M. Our port bow guard destroyer was very near it & gave the signal and swerved sharply to the left. The submarine passed, below surface, between our ship and the *Lenape* (on our port side) then swung off to its right (our left). A broad streak of bubbles was all that was seen. The signal "submarine" was repeated by our ship . . . The men behaved splendidly. Not the slightest sign of excitement anywhere. About 2:15 P.M., I was on the bridge with Capt. Boyd and Lieut. Commander Ghent [and] discovered a puff of white smoke on the surface of the water, port bow, 500 yards from our ship—a slight streak on the water passing from this point towards our stern was discernible. Comdr. Ghent thought it a torpedo.

Buck claimed that an American destroyer escorting the convoy immediately responded to the attack and sank the U-Boat. In many American accounts the results were the same: close calls followed by the ultimate demise of one of the "Kaiser's Pirates." Had, in fact, the Germans lost as many U-Boats as the Americans reported, the Kaiser's navy would have completely run out of submarines by the first quarter of 1918. Some of the Americans were a bit more unconvinced about the purported attacks. When ships in the convoy began firing at a suspected U-Boat, what resulted, in the words of one 35th Division soldier, was "a veritable Chinese fire drill," where "no one was lining up at the boat stations as prescribed, just crowding the rails to see the show." In the end, "the gunnery was very rapid, horribly inaccurate, and totally without regard for friendly ships in the line of fire beyond the target." At the conclusion of the excitement it was discovered that the "periscope" was merely a piece of floating debris. To be fair, it does seem that these more cynical views of submarine attacks were written by soldiers in the safe hindsight of the post-Armistice world.[27]

While it is easy to downplay the hysteria that the U-Boat threat created in the minds of the doughboys making the Atlantic crossing and their tendency at times to exaggerate their close calls, the threat was real and at times turned quite deadly. This was brought home to one American when his ship encountered a lifeboat containing two bodies from a British vessel sunk a few days before. Although rare, U-Boat attacks on American troopships did occur. The first American troopship sunk by enemy action was the *Antilles*, which sank in less than five minutes after being torpedoed on October 17, 1917, taking with it sixty-seven men, including sixteen soldiers returning to the States. Fortunately, like the *Antilles*, most of the troopships lost to U-Boats occurred on their return voyage from France. Such was the case with the *President Lincoln*, which was torpedoed on May 31, 1918, with a loss of twenty-six men out of a complement of 785. Likewise, the *Mount Vernon* managed to limp back to Brest after being torpedoed on September 5, 1918. Thirty-six men were killed and another thirteen were injured by the torpedo's explosion.[28]

Some ships, however, were attacked while they were still laden with troops. The *Moldavia* was hit off the Isle of Wight on May 23, 1918, while bound for St. Nazaire with a load of 480 soldiers from the 4th Division. The torpedo struck a compartment occupied by B Company, 58th Infantry, killing fifty-four men in the confined space. Sadly, all but one of the fifty-six men killed in the attack came from the unfortunate company. The attacks on the France-bound liners SS *Tuscania* and USS *Ticonderoga* were even deadlier. The USS *Ticonderoga* was carrying a shipment of horses and a crew of 124 U.S. Navy and 116 U.S. Army personnel when it was attacked by a U-Boat on September 30, 1918. The submarine attacked on the surface using its deck guns. This fire caused a large number of casualties and damaged most of the ship's lifeboats. After finishing off the ship with torpedoes, the submarine seized two of the *Ticonderoga*'s naval officers and left the ship's few remaining survivors in a single lifeboat and a life raft. In the ocean swells, the two boats became separated and the men on the life raft were never seen again. After four days adrift, the eleven sailors and fourteen soldiers in the lifeboat were rescued by the British steamer *Moorish Prince*. Only twenty-seven of the 240 who sailed on the *Ticonderoga* survived its sinking.[29]

The SS *Tuscania* was torpedoed by *UB-77* on February 5, 1918, off the west coast of Scotland while carrying 2,013 soldiers from the 32nd Division, 20th Engineers, and members of three aero squadrons to France. The attack occurred just after dusk. The darkness, the poor condition of some of the ship's lifesaving equipment, and the ship's proximity to a dangerous shore all combined to make the ship's sinking a tragedy. A member of the 20th Engineers recalled shortly after the Armistice:

> The earliest knowledge we had of the proximity of a German submarine was a decided shock which rocked the big ship from end to end. Simultaneously all lights went out and a deafening crash echoed and re-echoed through the ship. There was no question we had been hit, and so, life belts on, we rushed for our stations. Our boat drills had been perfunctory ones at the best . . . With all indications of a speedy sinking staring us in the face, we worked feverishly to lower the lifeboats and cut away the rafts . . . We discovered the boat tackle in many cases to be fouled or rotted and unfit for use. Some of the first boats we attempted to lower were capsized in midair, spilling their occupants into the icy water. The high seas running and the darkness made the rescue of these men almost impossible. Occasionally we got a boat away in good shape with nothing more serious than sprung planks or missing drain plugs . . . In all some thirty lifeboats were launched, and perhaps twelve of these were successful.

The ship's list prevented the launching of some lifeboats and the torpedo had damaged a number of others. After the few remaining boats had been launched, some six hundred soldiers still remained on board clinging to the rails of the ship. One of these unfortunates reported:

> The remarkable part of it all was that they took everything in a matter-of-fact sort of "well, what's next?" attitude. Occasionally a few would sing some little song, indicative of their feelings, such as "Where Do We Go From Here, Boys!" or "To Hell With the Kaiser." The absence of any panic, or effort and time in prayer was notable. A casual observer might, had he acquired a few snatches of the conversation, have thought the latter practice was being indulged in. A closer observer would have revealed a collection of wonderful expressions from vocabularies replete with all the known cuss-words in existence. The objects of the remarks were chiefly the U-boats, the Kaiser, the Germans and the authorities criminally neglectful of the safety of the troops.

Ironically, those left behind actually increased their chances of survival. A pair of British destroyers pulled alongside the *Tuscania* and carried those stranded to safety.[30]

The men in the *Tuscania*'s lifeboats, or those attempting to swim to safety, were at the mercy of the sea, the rocky shore, and fate. In addition to the elements, these men were even victims of the efforts to attack the offending submarine. As a survivor recalled,

> Lifeboats and rafts were drifting helplessly about. It was impossible to make any headway with the oars, as most of the boats were full of water, and there was such a heavy sea that any such effort was useless. In and out among these boats the destroyers raced, looking for traces of the submarine and dropping depth bombs where there were any suspicious indications. Each time one of the "ash cans" exploded the boats would shiver and shake with the concussion. Those men who were in the water were knocked breathless with each explosion, and in a few cases were rendered unconscious.

Driven by the winds and waves, many of the lifeboats that made it to the shore were dashed upon the rocks and cliffs of the Scottish Isle of Islay. In one case only eight men in a boat containing some sixty souls survived their abrupt landfall. In another instance, a boat with thirty-three men, including Everett Harpham and his best friend, was thrown upon the shore and it broke up on the rocks. Harpham was pulled under the water and smashed against the breakers before a large wave carried him to shore. Unfortunately, twenty-six of the men, including his friend, were not so fortunate. Two hundred and ten men of the *Tuscania* died in the incident, with most of the casualties coming from those in the lifeboats. The majority of the dead were soldiers with the 6th Battalion, 20th Engineers, which alone suffered the loss of ninety-five men.[31]

Some soldiers also lost their lives at sea due to accidents. To throw off the aim of U-Boat commanders and the probability of torpedo hits, ships in the Atlantic convoys moved on a zigzag course. These erratic movements, especially at night, increased the danger that ships in the convoys would collide. Seven soldiers were killed when the steamer *Brinkburn* tore a twenty-five-foot gash in the side of the troopship *Great Northern* on October 3, 1918. A much greater disaster befell the SS *Otranto* three days later. The *Otranto* was carrying 1,027 soldiers and crewmen when it was rammed by the SS *Kashmir* during a massive storm not far from where the *Tuscania* had sunk eight months before. As high seas and winds prevented abandoning the *Otranto*, its captain opted to await rescue from other ships. Through the heroic efforts of its captain and crew, the British destroyer HMS *Mounsey* managed to rescue over 560 men from the ship. Regrettably, approximately four hundred remained on the stricken steamer when the storm smashed it on a reef on the

Isle of Islay. Of those remaining on the ship, only twelve made it safely to the shore. The survivor Dave Roberts recalled,

> The waves carried me away from the ship, then one about as high as a house came over me and whirled me around like paper in a whirlwind. I went under. A Scotch lad got hold of a sailor and me and took us to a cottage. All I had left on was my underwear, pants and shirt-one sock. When we got to the shore, they put us to bed . . . The people there could not have treated us any better.

The wreck of the *Otranto* was the greatest maritime loss of American soldiers during the war. Of the 470 men who perished in the disaster, 350 were army personnel.[32]

Despite the toll taken by U-Boats and accidents, the deadliest threat to soldiers sailing for France was actually disease. The historian Byron Farwell estimated that only around seven hundred soldiers died as a result of enemy action at sea. This number pales in comparison to those who died of influenza and pneumonia during their voyage. Many soldiers arrived at the embarkation ports sick with influenza, and in the close confines of the overcrowded ships, it spread like wildfire. The fate of those aboard the *George Washington* in September 1918 was a case in point. The flu had already struck the embarkation camps in New York and medical officers had to remove 450 suspected flu cases from the ship before it even left port. Unfortunately, the contagion was already on board, and by the second day at sea the vessel's sick bays were crammed with over 550 new cases. Ultimately, seventy-seven soldiers on the liner died on the passage to Brest.[33]

In September and October 1918, the sickness was so great that it was as if a fleet of plague ships was descending upon France. The degree with which sickness hit the troopships can be tracked in the steady stream of reports sent from intelligence operatives to the 83rd Division's intelligence officer during that period. As the division served as one of the depot divisions that received the AEF's replacements when they landed in France, its officers were in a good position to gauge the health of the new arrivals. On October 8 an operative reported that the *France-Harve* arrived in Brest with seventy dead and 450 sick soldiers. A week later, soldiers estimated that the *Martha Washington* held five hundred sick and thirty dead, the *America* had arrived with eight hundred sick and thirty dead, and the *Pocahontas* made port with an additional seven hundred sick and forty dead. During its fifteen-day passage the British tramp steamer *Corona* was reported to have suffered seventy deaths. Although these soldier reports were sometimes inflated, they do show the magnitude of the problem. One of the more tragic cases of sickness at sea occurred on the voyage of the *Leviathan*. When it departed New York for Brest on September 29, 1918, the liner was carrying 9,133 troops. Within a day of leaving port, over seven hundred soldiers were laid low by influenza. This immediately overwhelmed the ship's 160-bed sick bays. By the time it reached France on October 8, ninety-one doughboys had died of influenza or pneumonia and a further two thousand were ill from the disease. Several of the sick later died in hospitals ashore. Ultimately Admiral Cleaves claimed that only 8.8 percent of the troops that sailed at the height of the influenza fell ill, and, of those infected, 5.9 percent died of the disease.[34]

Although Admiral Cleaves may have downplayed the lethality of the epidemic, he, and those who participated in the transportation of the AEF to France, had succeeded in accomplishing the greatest movement of American military manpower to date. Their monumental efforts would be surpassed only by those made in the Second World War. After crossing the Atlantic in 1917 and 1918, the flood of doughboys now faced the challenges of coming to grips with a determined foe and the somewhat alien cultures of the Old World.

9

"The French They Have Their Customs Rare, Parlez-Vous"
The Doughboys and the French and British People

The Great War marked the first time in American history that large numbers of the nation's citizens interacted with foreign cultures in their native lands. Prior to World War I, excursions outside the United States were limited largely to upper-class American travelers and businessmen and a handful of middle-class tourists, students, and missionaries. When the doughboys came into contact with French and British societies, they were, to use Samuel Clemens's apt phrase, "innocents abroad." Some had read about the places they would see, but few were truly prepared to be surrounded by people who often did not speak the same language and whose cultures, attitudes, and ways of doing things were quite different from those of America. Echoing the feelings of many soldiers, Cornelius Chandler wrote, "I had never been outside my general area of Georgia until I went abroad and I really didn't know what to expect."[1] By observing and interacting with the Europeans, the doughboys came to better understand and appreciate their own country. The Americans who entered Europe as "innocents abroad" returned home with new perceptions of themselves and their country's place and role in the world and generally a strong faith in the inherent superiority of their nation's way of life.

The doughboys brought to Europe differing, and at times conflicting, perceptions of the French and British peoples. The United States, Great Britain, and France had shared an uneasy embrace and a complicated history since the founding of the American Republic. Americans were by turns in awe of European cultural achievements

while simultaneously being repelled by what they saw as the social and political corruption and decadence of the Old World. Likewise a bumptious
faith in American exceptionalism and the inherent superiority of the nation's
institutions competed with the fear that the United States was a culturally
backward country bumpkin when compared to the glittering salons, museums, and artistic institutions of Europe.

American prewar attitudes toward France were generally ones of uncon-
cerned ambivalence. Historically, American relations with France lacked
the adversarial consistency of the United States' interactions with England.
American popular opinion of the French followed the ebb and flow of relations between the two nations. One of the key factors behind the continued American ambivalence and misunderstanding of France was the lack of
meaningful contact between the two peoples. Few French immigrants had
settled in the United States (in 1910 "French stock" made up less than 1 percent of the population) and relatively small numbers of French tourists had
visited America. The lack of direct cultural ties between the Americans and
the French hindered close relations and tended to create stereotyped perceptions of French society among the Americans.

Samuel Clemens remarked that France was the "highest modern civilization" and represented to him the pinnacle of "progress, and refinement." The
admiration that American artists, students, and intellectuals held for France
does not seem to have been shared by the average American. When the average American thought of France, which does not seem to have been very
often prior to 1914, his attitude was decidedly mixed. There was a popular
adulation of the Revolutionary War hero Gilbert du Motier, the Marquis de
Lafayette, and an appreciation for the role that France played in the American Revolution. These positive associations also contended with the popular
belief that the French were a worn-out and decadent race whose glory and
importance had passed. While the average American perhaps maintained a
vague awareness of French cultural superiority in learning and the arts, the
more prevalent perception was one of a France teaming with immorality,
corruption, and frivolity. The frequent changes in French governments and
episodes of popular unrest bewildered Americans and created the perception that France always teetered on the brink of a Paris Commune style of
anarchy. Moralists decried the French predilection for wine and other sensual
pleasures. Finley Peter Dunne's Mr. Dooley summed up this belief when he

pointed out, "Th' Fr-rinch ar-re not steady ayether in their politics or their morals." Even Clemens, who was no moralistic shut-in, had to admit after watching a Can-Can dance in Paris, "I suppose French morality is not of that straight-laced description which is shocked at trifles." These conflicting images of Lafayette and the Can-Can influenced the perceptions that the doughboys took with them to France.[2]

The doughboys' visions of France and Britain were also shaped by the events of 1914–1916. During that period, the growth of anti-German sentiment, Allied propaganda efforts, and sympathetic accounts of Allied valor and suffering by American reporters and observers slowly created the popular perception that the Allies' cause was a noble endeavor. American writers such as Wythe Williams went to great pains to present the French and British as noble fighters who were sacrificing their blood and treasure to protect the world from a new dark age. Angered at the prevalence of old stereotypes that continued to shape American attitudes, Williams derided his countrymen for viewing the French as "a frivolous people" after he witnessed the courage and moral certainty of a French attack on the ignoble Huns. Another narrator reported that in the crucible of war the French had been purified into a righteous role model: "The stirring thing is that France the frivolous, France the debonair, France the carefree and laughter-loving, has met the supreme ordeal of her existence in a manner to teach the whole world lessons of steadiness, of sobriety, of dogged courage, of concentrated efficiency, and of uncomplaining sacrifice." These visions of the Allies, and the concurrent outrage at the Germans for the *Lusitania*, use of poison gas, and other reputed underhanded tricks, certainly created a sympathetic and sentimental view of their cobelligerents in the minds of many American soldiers before they arrived in Europe.[3]

Given the insular nature of early-twentieth-century America, few doughboys entered the war zone with any realistic comprehension of Europe and the Europeans. Armed only with a schoolboy's perception of the world, one soldier remembered that he "expected France to be glamorous and romantic having read about Paris and Napoleon and his wars." Likewise, Levi Hemrick recalled, "In my younger days, it was true that given the chance of an expense paid visit to any city of his choice, any young man would have unhesitatingly chosen Paris, France. So, going to war also meant going to France, going to Paris, the city of my dreams." Reflecting their prewar preconceptions of European culture and morality, some doughboys expected to encounter a rich and advanced society, while others hoped to find France overflowing with "wild women." This last belief was so prevalent that the editors of *Stars and Stripes* scolded, "'Oo-la-la! This is France.' That is the impression which altogether too many men have on their mind upon their first arrival here. They have come over expecting to find a sort of international Coney Island, a pleasure resort."[4]

Once the soldiers landed overseas, however, they had to reconcile their preconceptions of Europe with the realities that they encountered on the ground. Upon reaching France in May 1918, Lieutenant W. A. Sirmon proclaimed,

> I was anxious to get my feet on the soil of France, for deep down somewhere within me there was a great love for this proud nation. France is to me the heroine in the romance of all the nations of all time. This feeling was born in me years ago when I read how her noble sons had defended America in its cradle. Today I am proud that I am one of the millions who will come to save our heroine from the clutches of the villain from across the Rhine.

Unfortunately, such idealized and romantic visions of France could seldom survive the harsh light of day. Soon after writing of his raptures about France, Sirmon's attitudes changed, and the young lieutenant became one of the more cynical observers of French society and culture. Levi Hemrick, who had waxed so eloquently about the France of his dreams, faced a similar letdown. He remarked,

> The quaint old cobble stones that surface the streets ... were soiled with human and animal droppings. It ... vanished any lingering dream of a land of ancient romance ... I didn't have the heart to let my mind pry or speculate about these people. Apparently ... these people had lost their pride and self respect ... It was pitiful beggars we had come to save.

It is perhaps not surprising that those who arrived in France with the most rose-colored expectations were often the ones who were most disillusioned with what they found.[5]

The degree of acceptance or disillusionment with France varied considerably among the American soldiers. It is difficult to chart with any precision exactly what the doughboys thought about the European civilians that they encountered. When studying soldier accounts, those who had particularly

positive or negative experiences with the foreign people that they encountered seemed to have commented on the matter. Large numbers of Americans
wrote nothing about British and French civilians at all. In the late summer
of 1918, the AEF Censor Bureau began opening the mail of American soldiers
to gauge doughboys' morale and attitudes toward the army, the war, and the
Allies. In January 1919, the AEF chief of intelligence specifically requested that
the Censor Bureau check the mail of soldiers in the 1st Army for a report on
these issues. The Censor Bureau focused on the mail of the 6th, 26th, 29th,
76th, and 82nd Divisions and came to the less-than-startling conclusion that
some soldiers did not like the French, others did, and many had no opinion
one way or the other. In fact, in the 6th Division only 1 percent of the soldiers mentioned the French people at all in their letters home. The report did
state, however, that while most doughboys seemed to get along well with the
locals, there were frequent negative comments related to the French about
"overcharging, immorality, unsanitary conditions in which they live and
forcing the same unsanitary conditions on the American soldier." It should
also be kept in mind that comments made by soldiers about the Europeans
in postwar memoirs and surveys may well have been colored by disillusionment with the flawed peace and by the nation's interactions with Britain and
France from the 1920s through the 1970s. With these caveats in mind, what
follows is an effort to generalize as many of the soldiers' attitudes toward the
French and British civilians as possible and to draw some tentative conclusions of the doughboys' perceptions of European peoples and societies.[6]

The doughboys' first impressions of France were as varied as their preconceived expectations. For better or worse, the doughboys' initial reception
from the local population and the physical environment they encountered in
their first weeks ashore often colored their later attitudes toward the French
and their society. Although the doughboys generally enjoyed a warm and
cordial welcome from the locals, their reception differed throughout the war
based on the number of Americans in the war zone and the military situation. When the first contingents of American soldiers arrived in France in the
summer and fall of 1917, they were greeted as heroes and showered with an
effusion of praise and affection by the French. Soldiers who arrived during
the spring and summer of 1918 still encountered an amiable population, but
the shock of the Ludendorff offensives had convinced many of the French
that the Americans had arrived too late with too few men to prevent a Ger-

man victory in the war. The doughboys who disembarked at this time often branded the French and British they encountered as defeatists. Soldiers passing through British and French ports in the fall of 1918 reported receiving even cooler receptions. By this time the AEF's ranks had swelled to over two million men, and Americans were no longer the novelty they were in late 1917 and early 1918. The doughboys perceived that since the tide of the war had turned decisively against the Germans, the Allied populations no longer needed or wanted the Americans in Europe.[7]

Despite this evolution in Allied attitudes toward the Americans, a number of doughboys remained excited by their contact with a different culture and embraced the French people. Donald Mitchell, for example, found the French warm and friendly and sympathized with their wartime suffering. His wartime journal often reflected his great affection for the country's "easy going people." One American was particularly overjoyed by one of his early encounters with the French people: "When we came into this town [the French] gave us good things to eat and even Brought out pails of water for us boys to drink. Gee you could tell by their actions that they are crazy over the American Soldiers. They seem to do and try to make us Boys happy. They gave us milk and cheese and apples and would not take a cent from us." Likewise, a private in the 28th Division wrote to his parents in 1918, "I like the French people. The men are very obliging and polite, and the women are beautiful. The American soldier is very popular with them."[8]

The doughboys' opinions toward the French also depended on their length of time in Europe, their proximity to the front, and their post-Armistice duties. Soldiers who arrived with the 1st Division in June 1917 and later served with that unit in the Army of Occupation had many more chances of interacting with European civilians than soldiers from the 38th Division who went directly to the front after arriving in France in October 1918. In some cases the longer time of interface with the locals brought a greater degree of understanding. The examination of the mail of soldiers from the 26th Division in January 1918 revealed "no animosity against the French people in general." Being stationed in ports, major transportation hubs, and production centers, soldiers in the Service of Supply also enjoyed more numerous and varied relations with the local populations than the more transitory combat soldiers.[9]

Units arriving after April 1918 went directly from the ports into quiet sectors of the front for training and then into combat in the summer and fall.

Soldiers in these units often had only a limited opportunity to interact with civilians because the front areas had been denuded of local inhabitants by the fighting and forced removals. The opinions of the late-arriving doughboys were influenced more by their post-Armistice contact with the local civilians than by the fleeting contacts made during the war. In fact, there was a general cooling of relations between the doughboys and the French following the Armistice. Doughboys' often complained that the French were ingrates who merely wanted to fleece the Americans out of as much money as possible once the dirty work was done. An officer reported that the French woman who owned his billets asked shortly after the Armistice, "Why didn't you go back to America? You and all the Americans? The war is over and we don't need you any more." This frustration was evident in a letter that D. S. Martin sent to his girlfriend in August 1919:

> Dear, you seem to think that I like those dam old frogs. No I do not, I hate them worse than ever you ever had time to. Well I will tell you that I have a [fight] with some of them every time I go down in Issustille that is the men, and the girls I would not let one of my dogs go with them . . . so please don't ever think I like a darn frog. The hell with France & the Frogs, I mean that . . . So Lucy when you think I am having a good time in France, you are badly wrong for I am not it is all bad times.

Although the main point of Martin's letter was to assure the girl back home that he was avoiding temptations, his bitterness toward the French still shines through. Relations between the French and Americans grew so frosty after the Armistice that in February 1919 the American liaison officer to the French Army in Germany reported that "American resentment against the French, which may have existed in embryo before, was brought to a critical point in the middle of December 1918." The Franco-American relationship was so strained that even German POWs noticed. One wrote home to Germany, "The Americans who are here also hate the French, no matter whether officer or men, and will never return [to France]. They curse from morning to night about the French people, and hate them like they do the night."[10]

General Hunter Liggett was a perceptive observer of the doughboys' attitudes toward the French and later termed the interaction between the two groups as a "broken romance." He noted,

France itself was a sorry disillusionment to the American soldier. That the fault was more the American soldier's than France's does not alter the fact. He sailed from Hoboken with a romantic picture compounded of the label, "Sunny France," and a musical-comedy conception of Paris. He found there an abominable winter climate unrelieved by American comforts, and a population farther removed from the pages of *La Vie Parisian* than the people of Berks County, Pennsylvania. Most of all, I think, he never got over the manure pile that is the brightest jewel of the French peasant's front yard.

Echoing the general's observation, a soldier in the 91st Division was so "disappointed in the level of culture of the people and their level of living" that he came to believe "the country itself hardly seemed worth fighting over." Like that of many other doughboys, these soldiers' inability to reconcile the actual with the ideal sometimes created a deep disillusionment with their allies, which only increased with time and exposure.[11]

One of the most common impressions that the doughboys had of their first encounters with France and Britain was the devastation that the war had wrought on their societies. The Americans' letters, diaries, and memoirs frequently mentioned the sobering and universal presence of women in mourning, the absence of local men in their twenties and thirties, and the changes in gender roles. As a private in the 42nd Division recalled, "By the time we got to France, the only males we would see in the villages were old men, young boys, and disabled French soldiers. The whole rural area was run by women. Women ran the farms, operated the stores and cafes." On the one hand, the Americans were shocked to see women doing men's work; on the other hand, it gave many doughboys food for thought on the unforeseen capabilities of women and a means for comparing the United States and France. The Kansan Walter Shaw brought these subjects up several times in his letters home. In October 1917 he informed his mother, "The women over here are expert bicycle riders, they sure have to work lots. I don't know what some American girls would do if they had to snap out this way." He followed this up a month later by observing, "The Peasant Girls aren't very pretty or small either but they can surely work. They quit school when 13 years of age. As a whole I don't think they are as progressive as U.S. girls. I think the French girls are the best workers."[12]

While some Americans took the lack of young and fit men in French towns and farms as an indication of the suffering and sacrifice that the war had imposed on France and became more sympathetic to their allies, others saw this as a sign that the Allies were "on the ropes." Earl Seaton, one of the first doughboys to arrive in France, believed that "the French were ready to quit" and felt an "urgent need to pep up the French morale." A military police-man came to think that "France was in terrible shape" after being mobbed by "poorly clad and frozen youngsters" begging for food when his transport ship docked at St. Nazaire in November 1917. These concerns even reached to the highest levels of the AEF. In his diary General James Harbord worried, "There is no doubt that the French morale is waning, as are their numbers. A people of about forty million have lost two million men, and mourning is everywhere." The perception that the Allies were played out later contributed to the doughboy's unshakable faith that it was the arrival of the Americans that ultimately won the war.[13]

For the handful of doughboys who had visited France prior to the war, the changes brought to the nation and its capital were particularly sad and distressing. One officer recorded in his diary in July 1918,

> I spent four days in Paris, staying at Meurice's, and a very different Paris I found it from the Paris of 1914, very few people in the streets; practically no taxis or fiacres; the boulevards quiet and few people upon them; women driving cabs and cars; the monuments and Arc de Triomphe, etc. all sand-bagged against the long range Bertha; prices horrible.

He was particularly incensed by the fact that he was now forced to pay eighteen francs for a champagne cocktail. Another American recalled,

> Poor France! The war smote hard upon her . . . In Paris the streets were deserted. By day one might see an omnibus, or might not. Occasionally an ancient taxi carriage drawn by an ancient horse, too decrepit for service of any sort at the front, might be encountered. By night the scene was dismal indeed. Few streetlights were burning–there was a great scarcity of coal.[14]

As most doughboys had no previous experience with Europe and the Europeans, it is not surprising that they measured the Allied societies they encountered against the social and economic conditions in America. How-ever sympathetic a doughboy might have been toward France and Britain, with the notable exception of the African Americans, the soldiers generally believed that their society was markedly superior to anything they encountered in Europe. This impression seems to have cut across sectional lines; even farmers from the rural South and West commented on the miserable condition of the peasants, the archaic nature of French agriculture, and the general backwardness of France and Britain when compared to the United States. The Americans pointed to the lack of indoor plumbing, stoves, and other modern conveniences along with the prevalence of outdated customs and practices, such as the way the French plowed their fields and cooked their meals on open fires, as evidence of their alleged backwardness. After his first taste of France, a doughboy wrote his mother in April 1918, "This is certainly an old-fashioned country, they do things here the way they have been doing for the last thousand years. All the poor people wear huge wooden shoes and I can't understand how they keep them on."[15]

These attitudes were also evident in a series of letters that Sergeant Elmer Lewis, of the 91st Division's 361st Infantry, wrote to his girlfriend, Goldie Little, in 1918 and 1919. Soon after arriving in France he noted,

> Things are so much different than they are at home, the rail road cars here looks like kid's toys the box cars are about as big as a ford automobile. Here in France the people . . . live in one room keep the pigs in one the cows in another and they keep the sheep, horses, and chickens in another. They are all under the same roof, so you can just figure out for your self what nice places they have.

A few months later, he reported, "Well Goldie France isn't very much like I pictured it would be. It is very beautiful but so quaint and old fashioned along side our own progressive Country." Shortly before sailing for home he ultimately concluded, "I don't think that you would like France, it is too old fashioned for Americans . . . only a few of the largest cities are up to date." Like many of his peers, when Lewis contrasted the United States and France, the later was found wanting.[16]

Rabbi Levi Levinger was an educated Francophile and insightful observer of the American relations with the French civilians. He maintained that much of the doughboy's negative views of France stemmed from their narrow exposure to the life of the French nation and their own parochial views. "No soldier admired the France of the war zone, with its ruined villages, its waste stretches, and its shell holes," he perceptively noted. "Neither did he care for the France of the rest areas, where he knew only the smallest villages, with the least attractive people to a young progressive from the western world." The France that most doughboys experienced was often limited to the small towns and villages that Levinger described. Supporting the rabbi's assertion, a doughboy in the 101st Infantry reported in January 1919, "All my time in France has been spent with the peasants—the bum class of French people and a feller loses his sense of respect. They don't live the way you or I do . . . They're the dirtiest lot that I ever put up with."[17]

Like this soldier, to many Americans, these peasant ways were the source of what they viewed as France's backwardness and ossified parochialism. "I can see the reasons for the Frenchman's antique ideas about things," one wrote in June 1918. "The country is full of little towns they are all behind the times and don't seem to have any system toward municipal improvements." Another found his days in a small French town to be stultifying. The town's only excitement was when a "cow gets rather frisky and runs kicking down the street followed by a French woman yelling frantically trying to head it off and get back into the barn." His most cutting conclusion was that "it certainly would be torture for one of us to have to live in a village like this for the rest of our lives." He was not alone in his dissatisfaction with French ways. In April 1918, a 42nd Division infantryman wrote his sister of France, "It is surely God's country—Because he is about the only one [who] would have it I think except the Frenchmen over here." A more sympathetic Marine simply told his mother, "As of yet I have not seen a great deal of France and have no right to criticize in any way but their customs are quite different from ours and some things seem rather queer to one who has never seen anything of the kind before."[18]

Coming from a nation that believed electricity and indoor plumbing to be the pinnacle of civilization, many if not most doughboys' perceptions of France were colored by their disapproval of the level of sanitation that they encountered in French towns and villages. With much condescension, one officer wrote home, "Naturally, such places are not long on sanitation, but there isn't much of that here except what we brought along with us." The French habit of placing manure piles close to the farmhouse was near universally noted in American accounts and often drew their substantial scorn. Some doughboys joked that local fathers would not assent to proposals of marriage for their daughters until the size of the grooms' manure piles were checked and given paternal approval. The soldiers also criticized the French for stabling livestock in rooms attached to their houses. Lieutenant Sirmon wrote that his billet in Landremont, France, contained "four hogs at the base of the stairs, two cows and as many calves under our bedroom, and fifty Belgian hares adjoining the parlor, creat[ing] an odor that challenges the most sickening fumes that chlorine or any other gas may produce." In fact one of the greatest of praises that a doughboy could give a French town was to compare it favorably to one in America. After visiting Aix Les Bains in June 1918, one wrote his parents that the thing that impressed him the most about the resort city was that it "really cues up to American towns in cleanliness."[19]

What made French sanitary habits especially onerous to the doughboys was the fact that the army's field hygiene regulations required them to bring their billeting areas up to an acceptable (that is, American) level of cleanliness. This required the soldiers not only to scrub down the barns and structures that they occupied but also to remove the garbage and clean the streets of the village. Of this distasteful duty, a soldier in the 28th Division remembered, "For the first few days all units were engaged in cleaning up their billets and putting American house-cleaning methods into practice; the change was certainly noticeable in many instances." Soldiers in an Alabama regiment responded to orders to clean up their town by sarcastically singing, "Good Bye, Broadway, Hello France! We've come to clean your streets for you." The soldiers naturally believed that they were being punished because the French were too degraded and lazy to keep their own houses in order. The French in turn resented the Americans' patronizing approach to their folkways and the army's removal of the locals valuable stash of fertilizer. The French complaints, however, were met with unsympathetic and hostile responses from the doughboys and their officers that often strained the relations between the Americans and the villagers.[20]

The still very Victorian Americans were also shocked by what they believed was the immodesty exhibited in French toilet habits. A young Marine was stunned to see an "old lady squatting in the streets" to answer the call of nature. Other doughboys were amused or scandalized by the French practice of building open-air urinals in their towns and cities. The Americans' criticism of these French ways of doing things eventually found its way into this verse of the popular song "The Mademoiselle from Armentières":

The French they had a custom rare, *parlez-vous?*
They shit and piss in the local square,
Hinky Dinky, *parlez-vous*[21]

The accumulation of these perceptions and observations left many dough-boys with the belief that France was socially and technologically behind the United States in most areas. The more charitable Americans described France and the French as "quaint" and "picturesque." Frank Holden, for example, enjoyed watching a French woman washing his clothes, noting, "What amused me most was the way she would beat the water out of the clothes with a paddle." Other viewed these practices, and French life in general, as completely lacking in modernity and any sense of progress. Some doughboys stated that France was over a hundred years behind the United States and agreed with a Massachusetts doughboy's observation that France was "old and decayed, not modern and up to date as [in] our country." Even the ever sympathetic Levinger lambasted the French for lacking "the luxuries which are so commonplace in America—electric lights, a bath tub, and the other conveniences of civilization."[22]

Nowhere were the American's attitudes and sense of their own superiority more clear than when they were discussing the state of technological development in Europe. Coming from members of an army that was so dependent on French and British weaponry, these attitudes were somewhat hypocritical; this did not prevent them from criticizing the decrepit and anachronistic state of Allied factories and infrastructure. The doughboys reserved their most disparaging and patronizing comments for the British and French railroads. They frequently disparaged the Allied trains and engines as being toylike or "dinky." A soldier noted that in France "everything seemed antiquated" and described a French train as a "little old locomotive that, with the date 1840 or 1850, we remembered having seen in school books." Another American wrote that British locomotives and rail cars were "small in comparison with those on our great railway systems" and recalled that "the small engine and coaches reminded me of little toy trains."

After the AEF imported American trains and rail cars to France, the negative comparisons grew. Doughboys expressed a smug certainty that the Europeans were awed by the power and majesty displayed by the American trains. Commenting on the American-built railway system and other construction projects, the YMCA worker Marian Baldwin wrote, "Our engineers are remaking France. The French people stand about watching with their mouths open." The sight of big American trains speeding across France left the doughboys with few doubts about the superiority of the society that produced such a modern and powerful machine.[23]

The arrival of the Americans in France unleashed a flood of money on the French economy. The greatest economic power on the planet spent huge sums of money in France and England to arm, equip, clothe, and sustain the AEF. The army employed over eighteen thousand civilians in France alone and embarked on construction and improvement projects in Europe that cost nearly twice as much as the building of the Panama Canal. The extravagance of the American military was also matched by that of its soldiers. As the best-paid soldiers at the time, the Americans became notorious for their profligate spending and their insatiable demands for local goods and services. Naturally, the locals sometimes viewed the Americans as cash cows to be milked to benefit the local economy. As one 81st Division soldier complained in January 1919, "Oh! these people are the limit, think all Americans are millionaires and soak them accordingly." The economic onslaught of the doughboys, however, could quickly overtax an area's resources. After the doughboys entered the small French town of Bellefontaine, James Murrin noted, "The soldiers literally took the town by storm, drank all the milk in sight, exhausted the limited wine supply and bought out the stock of goods which the little 'epicerie,' or general store, carried." The shopkeepers wanted to make a healthy profit while also protecting their local customers so they often kept some of their goods aside for civilian needs and created price scales that disadvantaged the Americans. A soldier in the 30th Division was irritated by the fact that one shop sold wine to the locals for only twenty cents while charging the doughboys $1.20 for the same item. The soldiers joked that items in French stores always carried three prices: one for the French, a slightly higher one for the British, and a very high price for the Americans.[24]

Perhaps unaware of their own complacency in the problem, the doughboys considered themselves economically ill used by what they saw as price gouging by the French. In the minds of the Americans, overcharging and other sharp business practices came to symbolize French dishonesty, duplicity, and ingratitude. Market interactions led many soldiers to the cynical conclusion that good relations with the French locals lasted only as long as the doughboys had money in their pockets and that their main goal was to make a fast buck at Uncle Sam's expense. A combat engineer wrote home shortly after the Armistice,

> As I have told you before that the French people who have a son in the army treat us fine but the others must think that we are made of money and rob us right and left. The gink that owns our billet wants his shack made into a mansion and demanded money for all kinds of old junk broken long before the war began. Say, I could have knocked him into the middle of next summer but his age saved him.

Another reported, "They simply soak and overcharge us whenever they can. An old lady Frog claims that the American stole 700 francs from her and her neighbor swears that she never had that much in her life . . . You can see what kind of people they are and there are few exceptions." After being cheated in a local town, an infantryman in the 77th Division remembered,

> I finally asked one French peasant woman how they could do this to brave men who'd come all the way across the ocean to help them. She smiled at me. *"Les Americans,"* she sighed, *"beaucoup d'argent."* . . . I think they really hurt the feelings of many of our men. After all, we were New Yorkers—we knew that all these jerk water towns would up their prices when we'd pass through. There's nothing a New Yorker hates any more than having a rube take him for a ride.

Efforts by American and French officials to rein in the overcharging of the doughboys fell far short of their goals, and the "hurt feelings" experienced by soldiers such as these New Yorkers led to deep disillusionment and bitterness toward France in some doughboys. One such soldier from the 26th Division railed against French ingratitude in a letter home written in January 1919: "I want to get away from these people. They rob you right and left and certainly rub it in any way they can even after all we've done for them."[25]

The soldiers' faith that the French were driven by a desire to fleece the Americans became so entrenched that a number of doughboys even believed the rumor that the French government charged the Americans rent for the use of their frontline trenches or were keeping them in France to rebuild the country after the war. In a letter opened by the AEF Censor Bureau shortly after the Armistice, an 80th Division soldier grumbled, "We finished what we came over for and those damn frogs have no use for us now except to repair their roads for them." These complaints grew so strident that *Stars and Stripes* and the French High Commissioner for Franco-American Affairs issued statements categorically denying the existence of "trench rent" or the deliberate use of the Americans as cheap labor. These efforts to shape the doughboys' attitudes did not seem to have much effect. "There seems to be a loathing among the Americans around here for the French," an infantry officer noted at the time of the *Stars and Stripes* article. "I know there is hardly a man who cares anything for them."[26]

One result of the doughboy's anger over being cheated by the French was their increased acceptance of petty thefts and other misdemeanors against French civilians. In fact French, and later German, officials accused the Americans of bringing a crime wave wherever they went. Not long after the Armistice, the French justice of the peace at Pont-a-Mousson complained to the French War Ministry,

> The Americans billeted in our houses, steal, pillage, burn and break our furniture, cave in our treasure boxes, and destroy our houses. The Boches burned cities and towns, the Americans are doing the same at Pont-a-Mousson . . . The manic [of the Americans] to steal, pillage and burn is so great that one cannot leave his home without being exposed to being robbed.

Although the justice's claims were somewhat exaggerated, it was clear that the doughboys were certainly not acting on their best behavior.[27]

As will be discussed in chapter 22, although the AEF's crime rate was never very high, some doughboys did seem to have believed that unfair business practices made the Europeans "fair game" for American retaliation. Sergeant Elmer Straub, for example, stole a watch from a French store and later walked out of a French restaurant without paying to "make things even with the French for their high prices." Soldiers of the 35th Division stole copious amounts of wood and honey from French beehives, knowing full well that "the French peasants regarded it as a high crime." American censors intercepted a letter in January 1919 where an artilleryman in the 77th Division confessed, "Most every good thing in our comfort we have to steal as there is no one interested in us or our comfort—[we] get away with a lot of stuff." Four months later a captain wrote *Stars and Stripes* and unashamedly admitted that his soldiers "stole honey and rabbits, smashed windows, tore down doors for firewood, shot wild boars with service rifles, with wonderful disregard to the safety of the French civique." He claimed that the Americans' antics grew so bad that some French soldiers told him "they thought it was safer at the front." Whatever the Americans' justification for this petty criminality, it can be assumed that their actions certainly undermined Franco-American harmony.[28]

Whether dealing with issues of money or folk life, much of the doughboys' lack of cultural understanding stemmed from their deficiency in French-language skills. "France wouldn't be so bad if you could understand this language," one soldier informed his sister. "I think I learn a word about every week. So I guess if we should have to stay in France about four or five years I might like it." Although some commanders had held French classes for their units while training in the United States, these seemed to have been ineffective in passing on anything more to the average doughboys than some very basic phrases. The war brought on a bonanza for the publishing of French primers, dictionaries, and language guides. One of the most popular of these was the *Parley Voo Booklet* published and distributed free to soldiers by the Kolynos toothpaste company of New Haven, Connecticut. Other guides were indexed so as to allow the soldier to select the phrase that he wanted to impart and then point out the translation to the French person with whom they were attempting to communicate. Private Edward Dolan used one such guide to get through his confession to a French priest. The session took over two hours due more to the process than to the number and severity of Dolan's sins.[29]

Although some Americans diligently worked to hone their French-language skills, most seem to have limited their explorations of European linguistics to the basics required for market bartering. As one officer recalled, "Soldier French was a wonderful thing, consisting of the names of all ordinary things to eat and drink, together with a few common expressions, such as 'toute de suite,' . . . and 'combien.' This prevented easy communication." The provincial nature of the American soldiers could turn even the most ordinary market transaction into a titanic clash of cultures, and the doughboys were linguistically unarmed for the meeting of parochial America with parochial France. A soldier in the 77th Division wrote his aunt in May 1918,

> Have had quite a few rather funny experiences with some of the places and farm houses trying to buy things and make them understand what we wanted. Usually two or three of us will be together each with a french book in our hands and will manage to get a sentence or two out. Take it from me it is a good thing for us that most of them know a little english or we would never get by.

Even Americans with some knowledge of European dialects often chose to work through interpreters rather than trust their language abilities. George Marshall, an AEF staff officer and future Chairman of the Joint Chiefs of Staff, declined to speak French when dealing with his Allied counterparts after he made an embarrassing language mistake during his first days in France. While attempting to make small talk about the weather to a French officer, Marshall remarked, "*Je suis tres beau aujourd'hui*," (I am very handsome today) instead of "*Il fait tres beau aujourd'hui*" (It is very beautiful today). The doughboys' lack of foreign-language skills prevented the Americans from grasping the subtle complexities of European societies and all too often led them to make uninformed and caustic pronouncements on France and the French. As one chaplain noted, "We were meeting in a strange land which some of us liked and some disliked, but which none of us could quite understand."[30]

Although much of the proceeding passages have cast a rather negative view of Franco-American relations, it is important to note that the doughboys often developed warm relations with the local civilians. The army's billeting arrangements and other exchanges brought the Americans into close contact with the French people. This frequently led to symbiotic relationships where the soldiers' assistance around the villages and in bringing in the harvest was reciprocated by invitations into French houses for home-cooked meals and other pleasant distractions from army life. Two railroad soldiers, for example, spent their free time repairing an organ that had been broken for fifteen years in a church in the town where they were stationed. American units also organized Christmas parties for local children and festivities on Independence Day and other holidays that encouraged comity and communion between the nationalities.

The arrival of young, green Americans in small towns elicited much sympathy from French mothers and fathers who had lost relatives or whose sons were at the front. In such cases, the novices became the surrogate sons of the household. "I am billeted with some French people," a 77th Division doughboy wrote home. "The madam or lady of the house is just like a mother to us boys and makes everything nice for us." Another told his family that he was a frequent guest in the home of an elderly French woman. He reported, "She certainly does treat me fine; lets me play on her piano and makes the finest coffee for me every time I go and visit her." The plight of French civilians that the AEF liberated during the St. Mihiel and Meuse Argonne offensives

Photo 11: Sergeant George Lawrence (with the child) and his comrades with French civilians, July 28, 1918. Although relations between the doughboys and the French could be rocky at times, the Americans often exhibited a soft spot for the French children they encountered. Source: author's collection.

also elicited great sympathy in the doughboys and tended to override their misgiving over French society. Private Luther Grover informed his sister on September 22, 1918,

> When our boys went over the top they took quite a few houses with french women and a few old men in them who had been prisoners of the germans for four years and a lot of young kids between 3 and four years old running around. So me and this other fellow that can talk french was down there the other day and we was talking with a young woman about 22 years old and she told us everything that they had to do and how they were used so I would not want to put it in a letter.

In such cases, complaints about price gouging and manure piles were forgotten.[31]

The doughboys were particularly friendly toward European youngsters and often played an active role in easing the suffering that the war inflicted on the children. In March 1918 *Stars and Stripes* inaugurated a program that allowed American units and individuals to "adopt" French war orphans. The newspaper noted that French children were the doughboys' "best friends on this side of the world," and under the program, a unit would subscribe five hundred francs to "feed, clothe and start toward an education and a useful life" a needy French orphan. When the program ended in June 1919, Americans had "adopted" 3,567 children and raised over two million francs for their benefit. Unofficially, the doughboys also gathered young human "mascots" wherever they went. One such mascot, a Belgian boy nicknamed William Jockey by the American railroad engineer troops who found him, wore a specially tailored U.S. uniform and took all of his meals in the company mess hall. The soldiers of the unit contributed two francs a month from their pay to cover the boy's food, clothing, and education. The soldiers' relations with European children offered great benefits to both parties. The children received needed help and care while the Americans obtained language lessons and an insider's leverage in the local communities. As one soldier admitted in *Stars and Stripes*, "money given to a small French boy has twice the buying power of the same amount tendered by a uniformed stranger." However, French authorities grew so concerned over the number of French boys running away from home or orphanages to follow the Americans that on October 28, 1918, the AEF GHQ issued orders to end the practice and directed units to turn the children over to local authorities.[32]

Although most of these soldier–mascot relationships were wholesome and beneficial for both parties, some doughboys seemed to delight in teaching the youngsters salty English words and phrases and other bad habits. The soldiers of Veterinary Hospital No. 1 in Neuilly-l'Evigue "adopted" the fourteen-year-old Emil Le Gros and provided him with a cut-down American uniform complete with the insignia of a second lieutenant. Unfortunately, on August 25, 1918, Emil's American buddies took him out drinking at a local café. When a major found him and an American soldier lying drunk on the main street of the town, he reported the incident to the local American commander and thundered, "If the adoption of French children as 'mascots' is to be permitted, it would seem that their training and character building ought not to be turned over to men who have no sense of moral responsibility." Another officer wrote to General H. A. Smith, the commandant of the Army Schools at Langres, that the woman who owned the house in which he was billeted was "very much upset" that her young son was being encouraged by local soldiers to "remain away from home during the night and most all day" and was being "taught very bad habits" by the Americans. Some soldiers even tried to Americanize their mascots and endow them with a sense of American superiority. One nine-year-old boy was "transformed into an American" to such a degree that he refused to acknowledge people speaking to him in French and demanded that his countrymen address him only in English.[33]

To some extent, the doughboys were tourists in France, and like any tourist, they could be obnoxious and contemptuous of local ways, but many doughboy tourists also gained a greater appreciation for the people that they encountered by marveling at the monuments and history of their civilization. Rabbi Levinger maintained that the doughboys developed a negative perception of France because "the average soldier did not meet the better class of French people" and because "he had little taste for the wonderful architectural and historical treasures of the country; he could not speak the language beyond his elementary needs." While there is some truth in this, the frequency with which the Americans wrote home about the very wonders that he lists undercuts his view. The doughboys' letters, diaries, and postwar accounts are liberally sprinkled with descriptions of castles, cathedrals, and historic events. "This is a very historic place," Dewitt McIntyre gushed to his mother in July 1918. "Caesar spent a summer battling with the Celts in this district. Some buildings of Gothic architecture have dates of 800 A.D. etc on them and they don't look to be 100 years old. And some of the peasants here still dress like the pictures I sent you." Numerous doughboys positively recounted the sites they visited, with locations like Joan of Arc's birthplace in Domrémy being particularly popular.[34]

The focus of many American doughboys' hopes and dreams of France was Paris. In 1917 and 1918 the City of Light was still the cultural and entertainment center of the world: a source of any soldier's possible desires. In Paris, the doughboys could see the sights, immerse themselves in museums, art, and history, or drown themselves in wine, women, and song. Lieutenant C. L. Crane of the 55th Coast Artillery had a wonderful time in Paris in early April 1918 touring the city and making the rounds of its cafés and restaurants. After spending a day walking the Champs-Élysées, visiting the Arc de Triomphe and the Eiffel Tower, and riding the Ferris wheel built for the 1898 Exposition, he recorded in his diary that the day was "the greatest spectacle of my life." A 1st Division infantryman recorded,

> Many of us were from the country or small towns and had always heard of Paris as such an unusual city with museums, beautiful woman, excellent wine and the Eiffel Tower. When the 16th Infantry blew in we found Paris all we had heard about it and more so. The women were nice-looking but no more so than the girls back home, but those girls were there and the girls in Paris were here. The girls out in the French countryside acted afraid of the American soldiers but not the girls in Paris. The 16th Infantry was not looking for museums. We did see the Eiffel Tower but we were more interested in the girls and French wine. We also had heard of the wonderful French food . . . We did not change Paris but the 16th Infantry was probably never the same. If for no other reason the memories of our visit to Paris were things to hold on to.

After the Armistice, George Tucker was so eager to reach Paris that he was even willing to delay his return to the States if he could see the city. "Some of the men in the company have already been to Paris, and from all accounts it sure is some town . . . After I have seen what I can of Paris in three days time they can send me home just as soon as they like." To these soldiers, the French could not be all that bad if they had created such a wonderful and vibrant city.[35]

As most Americans spent their time in Europe in France, this chapter has logically focused mostly on the doughboys' relationship with the French people. However, several thousand Americans served in Britain and nearly half of the AEF's soldiers passed through that nation on their way to France. Prior to the war people of the United States were far from united in their opinions of Britain. The South and New England were bastions of Anglophilia, and the nation's economic, intellectual, and political elite had voiced an admiration for Britain and her social institutions for decades. The pro-British attitudes of American financiers like J. P. Morgan and Andrew Mellon reflected the practical need to work within a British-dominated global economy and the predominance of English creditors in American markets. To politicians such as Theodore Roosevelt, Woodrow Wilson, and Edward House, and intellectuals such as Henry James and Albert Bushnell Hart, England represented social stability, economic security, and international might. Other Americans were much less impressed by the British. Their attitudes were shaped by nearly

150 years of viewing England as the nation's primary military and economic rival. To the Anglophobes, two wars, numerous territorial disputes, England's support for the Confederacy during the Civil War, and the competition for overseas markets made Britain "our natural enemy." To the ranks of the native Anglophobes were added Irish, German, and Russian immigrants with their own reasons for detesting Britannia. As late as 1914, the English expatriate Frederick DeSumichrast reported that the average American "saw her [England's] hand in nearly every disaster, domestic and foreign; he suspected her interference in every election that ran counter to his wishes ... and he rejoiced over her misfortunes, crowed over her mistakes." These prewar attitudes shaped the doughboys' perceptions of the British much as their preconceived notions colored their ideas of the French.[36]

Most doughboys remained in the British Isles for only a few days or weeks, and their first impressions of England were thus their last. As his unit passed through England en route to France, a machine gunner found Folkstone to be a "wonderful quaint town." He was delighted that "the English people were all very polite and kind," and noted, "They sure are glad to see the 'Sammies,' as they call us." While Britain garnered its share of negative comments, the doughboys' opinions of their Albion allies were more mixed and somewhat less derogatory than their views of the French. Part of this may have stemmed from the commonality of language. It must be noted that following George Bernard Shaw's observation that the United States and Britain were a people divided by a common language, American soldiers sometimes derided their British comrades' seeming inability to use the "mother tongue." Officers, perhaps reflecting the more Anglophilic attitudes of the American upper classes, commented more favorably on England than did their soldiers.[37]

This is not to say that the doughboys' judgments of the British were always positive. Many doughboys maintained that their reception from the British was less cordial than that of the French. The Americans especially resented the English condescension and their studied social distance. Some doughboys reported that they experienced hostility from the populations of Liverpool and Winchester in the summer and fall of 1918 because the locals thought that the Americans had merely swooped in at the last minute to "steal" the glory for winning the war.

A soldier in the 82nd Division said that his passionate dislike of the English arose because "they felt superior to us." An officer in the same division was struck by Britain's strict social stratification, noting,

> The class distinction maintained in England apparently has prevented the development of the middle class that we have in America. The gentle folk, I understand, are mostly athletic, and neatly built, and dress gracefully. The laboring class look stiff and hard, and seem to feel that anything that covers their bodies is good enough for commonplace ruffians like themselves. These two classes never overlap. A man is born into one class and cannot marry out of it, so there is no average between the two.

While personal relations between the British civilians and Americans seemed more strained and cool than those with the French, the Americans gave the British and their society a higher degree of respect than they afforded their Gallic allies. In narratives, usually written after their contacts with the French, the Americans hailed Britain's ability to maintain "its business-like aspect in spite of the war."[38]

The most important aspect of the doughboys' interactions with the Europeans was that many, if not most, of them returned home with a faith in American exceptionalism and the superiority of the United States and its institutions. After the United States entered the war, an unprecedented number of Americans had the opportunity to compare and gauge the relative social and cultural progress of the United States against other societies. This assessment led the victorious yanks to proclaim that the United States had won the war and under the assault of American "know-how" and youthful vigor, Europe's time had passed. Reflecting the fresh American attitude, General Liggett crowed,

> What really had happened was that the star of destiny, having been westward bound for many generations, finally had passed over the horizon of the meridian of Greenwich. Largely unperceived, we had come to equality with the world's greatest by 1914. We had finished conquering a new world and had consolidated our positions, and now we had, with our youth, our inventiveness, our economic isolation and our tremendous natural resources, perfected a new theory and practice . . . We should have passed Europe anyway, but the war had expedited the process.

This bumptious sense of nationalism was not limited to Liggett. While waiting to leave France in 1919, the future Vanderbilt poet and professor Donald Davidson's distaste for Europe reached a boiling point. The young doughboy concluded that "Europe is a hundred years behind the United States" and had little to offer or teach the Americans. Like many doughboys, Davidson in his time overseas had destroyed any lingering thoughts of the superiority of European cultures and societies over the United States. By 1937, his time overseas had prompted Davidson to declare to his students, "I insist on the uniqueness of the American establishment and on its separateness from Europe." In a very telling statement, the cultured and educated officer Quincy Sharpe Mills wrote his mother after serving several months in France that his greatest desire was to "get back to civilization." Like Liggett and Davidson, Mills had come to believe that civilization rested not in the ancient and decayed monuments of the Old World but rather in the skyscrapers, viewpoints, and institutions of the New World.[39]

By their social intercourse with the Europeans the doughboys had come to better understand themselves. The process was not always pretty, nor did it necessarily expand the Americans' cultural horizons. As Rabbi Levinger commented,

> We felt the travel, with its intended contact with other customs, language and people, would broaden our soldiers mentally and tend to break down the provincialism which has been often noticed in America . . . Altogether, knowledge of France, England and Germany made, on the whole, not for a greater appreciation of foreign lands, but instead for a greater appreciation of America.

Soon after the Armistice, the War Department Morale Branch directed its officers in camps in the United States to survey soldiers awaiting discharge on their attitudes toward their military service, their future plans, their allies, and their opinion of the United States. One morale officer at Camp Funston reported that soldiers returning from Europe maintained that "the United States is by far superior to any other country." Another noted that "practically all consider the United States the leading Nation" and that the countries that they had visited overseas were "several years behind our times." These perceptions often stayed with the doughboys for the rest of their lives. An old doughboy from the 26th Division later wrote in the U.S. Army Military History Institute's World War I Veteran Survey that while he was in France he learned "that America was far ahead of anything I saw or experienced overseas," while a Kansan recalled that he "saw nothing in Europe that I thought equal to what we had." The veteran Felix Stastny admitted, "I learned to love my country—I saw how the French lived and how we lived. There was no comparison. Ours is the greatest, the best the most wonderful and on God's earth." Comments like these were far from rare in the responses of other veterans.[40]

It is important to note that not all Americans evolved such a jaded view of Europe. African American doughboys developed perceptions and opinions of the French that diverged greatly from those of their white comrades. Unlike white soldiers, the African American soldiers did not indulge in deprecating European societies or expounding American superiority. To the black dough-boy, France was not a backward and decadent society but rather a bastion of racial equality. For the first time in most of their lives, the African American soldiers interacted with a white population that did not automatically shun, segregate, and marginalize them. Like white soldiers, the African Americans used the United States as a "yardstick" to measure French society. But, un-like their white comrades, black doughboys found the United States lacking in the comparison. Though racial attitudes in France were perhaps not as liberal as the doughboys believed, their treatment by the French was a vast improvement over their previous experiences in the United States. Against the backdrop of French equality, the black soldiers evolved a sympathetic view of France that was at odds with the attitudes of many of their white countrymen.

In many other ways, the African Americans' impressions of Europe mir-rored those of other doughboys. The African American officers Monroe Ma-son and Arthur Furr noted the poverty and dirtiness of St. Nazaire and even wrote that the French railroads were "joking reminders of pictures we knew as children in our histories and geographies of how people traveled in the early days of America." Looking deeper however, the African Americans in their critical comments did not carry the inferences of American cultural superiority inherent in many of the whites' observations. Negative opinions like those of Furr and Mason were relatively rare in African American narra-tives and constituted a noticeable departure from the trends evident in other black writings. When negative comments appeared, they were usually quali-fied by references to the war's harsh impact on France. As a soldier in the 92nd Division remembered, "My impression was not too good—France was in a very bad way and needed all the help they could get." Chained to a system that sought to keep them as a permanent underclass, the African American soldiers did not display the same faith in Progressive ideology as white Americans. The elite African American view of an evolving American society had less to do with the Progressive tenants of modernity, cleanliness, and moral regeneration (elements common in the white doughboys' critiques of Europe) than with the idea of social improvement through racial equality. Fortified by the belief that France represented a racial equality sorely lacking in the United States, the black doughboys were willing to overlook France's perceived faults. This dynamic was illustrated by the comments of a soldier in the 371st Infantry. His lasting impression of one French town was not that the dwellings failed to "present a very favorable appearance to the casual observer" but rather that "the inhabitants were all of the true democratic spirit, catering alike to all."[41]

The African American doughboys enjoyed warm relations with the French civilians and participated in the same social interactions with them as white soldiers. For instance, under the *Stars and Stripes* fund drive, black soldiers raised over three hundred thousand francs for "adopting" French war orphans. Doughboys in the 92nd and 93rd Divisions and the African American pioneer infantry regiments were quartered on French families much the same as other doughboys. The billeting arrangements encouraged interpersonal relationships and helped to dispel any negative perceptions of the African Americans implanted in the French by white soldiers. Unfortunately, African Americans serving in ports, depots, and other installations in the SOS rear area did not enjoy the same quality and quantity of interpersonal contact with French civilians as black combat troops. This was a very different norm from the personal interactions generally experienced by white soldiers in the SOS. The army went to great lengths to keep the black rear-area soldiers segregated from the civilian population. To prevent African Americans from experiencing the free and open contact with the locals so common among the SOS's white troops, the blacks met with "long hours, excessive tasks, little opportunity for leave and recreation, holding of black soldiers to barracks when in the same community white soldiers had the privilege of the town." However, the army's restrictive and oppressive procedures rarely succeeded in totally preventing social interactions between African Americans and the

French. Like their companions in African American combat units, the SOS's soldier-laborers mingled with the local population whenever they could and discovered new freedoms and racial attitudes.[42]

Along with its attempts to "keep the Negroes in their place" through segregation, the army worked to instill "Jim Crow" ideology in the French people. As W. E. B. DuBois ruefully noted, "The [white] Americans were thoroughly scared. Negroes and Negro officers were about to be introduced to French democracy without the watchful eye of American color hatred to guard them." Cognizant of the fact that the segregation of the African Americans was only a partial measure, the army worked to "educate" the French on the dangers of fraternizing with the black Americans and to build a "color line" in France. The message of white supremacy and black inferiority spread through official AEF command channels and, more insidiously, by word of mouth from white American soldiers. The most taboo subject was any relations between black troops and French women. Attempts to maintain a strict level of racial and sexual segregation were frequently taken to ludicrous extremes. After a group of black officers from the 167th Artillery Brigade danced with French women during a joint Franco-American charity ball, the commander of the AEF Artillery School in Vannes barred them from attending further goodwill events. Similarly, the white commander of the 804th Pioneer Infantry decreed, "Enlisted men of this organization will not talk to or be in company with any white women, regardless of whether the women solicit their company or not."[43]

At the request of the AEF General Headquarters, the chief French liaison officer to the American army issued a secret memo to French officers and public officials in contact with African American soldiers apprising them of American racial attitudes and suggesting rules of racial contact that would "avoid profoundly estranging American opinion." The memo remarked that white Americans were "afraid that contact with the French will inspire in black Americans aspirations which to them appear intolerable," and requested that French officers "make a point of keeping the native cantonment population from 'spoiling' the Negroes." The memo even went so far as to ask the French to refrain from shaking hands, eating, or talking with African Americans.[44]

While the AEF General Headquarters worked behind the scenes to manipulate French opinion, white doughboys officially and unofficially spread the gospel of racial hatred and inequality. White troops told French civilians that the African Americans were "servants of the white soldiers" and "so brutal and vicious as to be absolutely dangerous." After decrying the blacks' predisposition toward criminality, dishonesty, and immorality, one white soldier reportedly informed an astonished French woman, "They are not Americans; they are just niggers." Addie Hunton and Kathryn Johnson, two female African American canteen workers in the AEF, experienced this official and unofficial "smear" campaign against the black soldiers firsthand:

> The first post of duty assigned us was Brest. Upon arriving there we received our first experience with American prejudices, which had not only been carried across the seas, but had become a part of such an intricate propaganda, that the relationship between the colored soldier and the French people is more or less a story colored by a continued and subtle effort to inject this same prejudice into the heart of the hitherto unprejudiced Frenchman.

For the most part, the white Americans' endeavors to foster "Jim Crow" racial attitudes in the French people failed. One African American activist maintained, "The Negroes resented being publicly stigmatized by their own countrymen as unfit for association with decent people, but the French men and women much preferred the courtesy and bonhomie of the Negroes to the impudence and swagger of many of the whites."[45]

For their part, the French could not comprehend the depth of the Americans' racial animosity or the United States' segregationist ideology. A French liaison officer attached to the 371st Infantry stated that he did not "understand why Americans should treat one another so harshly and cruelly when it was momentarily expected that the division would be plunged into battle." The French displayed their support and sympathy for the African American troops by inviting them into their homes and by small acts such as French officers seating black doughboys at their tables over the protestations of nearby white Americans. Bertram Lawrence, an artilleryman in the 92nd Division, later recalled that unlike in the States, "In France Black Soldiers were accepted by the civilians with cordial and friendly gestures." Others observed, "A new equality was tasted at this time by these American colored men; they were treated upon an absolutely equal basis with other men," and were heartened by the fact that the French received black officers "with all social and military courtesy due their rank." Captain William Braddan likewise explained the

African American doughboys' affection for France by noting, "For the first time in their life they had been treated like men and the gentlemen that they were. They enjoyed liberty and were judged not by the color of their skin or texture of their hair, but by their real worth."[46]

Given their warm reception and treatment as equals by the French, the African American soldiers developed a much more positive view of France and a different take on American society than their white comrades. In some cases the black doughboys clearly preferred the company of the French to their own countrymen. Robert Stevens, a Louisiana farmer in the 803rd Pioneer Infantry, expressed bitterness at the attitudes of his fellow Americans and remembered that the French "treated us with respect, not like the white American soldiers." A 92nd Division machine gunner stated that he admired the French because he was treated by them "better than with our soldiers." William Colson, a black officer in the 367th Infantry, later wrote that the black doughboys "felt better within themselves because they were fighting for France and for their race rather than for a flag which had no meaning."[47]

As with white soldiers, the African Americans left France with a new impression of the United States and the world, but the two groups generally came to two different conclusions. To the black soldiers, their white comrades' declarations of American cultural superiority had a very hollow ring. One African American soldier wrote, "France will always be looked upon by American Negroes as the one shining example of democracy in this narrow world." In April 1918, William Braddan wrote home, "I am hoping that when the War ends, the same spirit of manhood that prevails here will [be] obtain[ed] over there." Another officer proclaimed, "These same black soldiers, held in abject ignorance so long in the United States, returned from France with something they had not possessed before. They learned first of all that uncompromising equality is the key to a long closed door." He believed that it was the duty of the returning African American soldiers "to act as an imperishable leaven on the mass of those who are still in mental bondage." To these African Americans, their contact with the French had brought the inequities of the United States into sharp focus. The black doughboys, who so admired the French for their notions of racial equality, were to be the vanguard of the long and painful battle for civil rights in America.[48]

For all races of doughboys, their interactions with Europe and the Europeans forever changed their perceptions and worldviews. Europe became a yardstick for the soldier to measure their own society. Many developed a deeper appreciation for the United States, while others, like the African Americans earlier, returned home with a deeper sense of the inequities within the Republic. The French, so the song stated, "They have their customs rare," but as many doughboys discovered in their travels overseas, so too did the Americans.

10

Of Trench Guns, Sho-Shos, and Trench Knives
The Doughboy's Weapons

War has a perverse way of unleashing the most creative juices of mankind. The greater the stakes are in a given war, the greater the levels are of ingenuity and innovation designed to kill one's fellow man. The fifty years between the end of the American Civil War and the start of the First World War witnessed one of the most profound periods of military technological change in human history. The advent of modern artillery, chemical explosives, smokeless powder ammunition, bolt-action magazine rifles, and the machine gun, just to name a few, meant that nasty lethal projectiles were now blanketing the battlefield at a markedly greater rate, volume, and range than ever before. For sake of comparison, while the Civil War infantryman was lucky to fire three rounds a minute to a maximum effective range of two hundred to three hundred meters with a rifled musket, his counterpart in World War I was capable of firing fifteen to twenty shots a minute to a maximum effective range of seven hundred to eight hundred meters.

Although the Boer, Spanish-American, Russo-Japanese, and Balkan wars all previewed the coming lethality of the battlefield, it was not until 1914 that the changes in military technology, when wielded by immense conscript armies, reached its critical mass. On August 22, 1914, alone, some twenty-seven thousand French soldiers fell dead before the scythe of German rifle, machine gun, and artillery fire. Other combatants faced similar losses. Nearly 28 percent of all the German casualties for the entire war occurred in August and September of 1914. Faced with these losses, short on replacements and stocks of ammunition, and needing to shelter the survivors from the enemy's firepower, the contending armies in France and Belgium began constructing a nearly unbroken line of trench works stretching over four hundred miles from the North Sea to the Swiss border. As these trenches solidified into a formidable defense in depth protected by thick bands of barbwire, the advantage on the battlefield shifted decisively to the defenders. The tactical dilemma that the trenches now presented let loose another burst of creative energy as the attacker wrangled with the problem of how to cross No Man's Land, break into the enemy's first belt of trenches, break through the subsequent belts of trenches, and then break out into the open terrain. The attempted solutions to this dilemma would birth some of the greatest horrors of the past century—poison gas, flamethrowers, tanks, and light automatic weapons—and create concepts of doctrine that still govern ground combat today.

These monumental technological and doctrinal changes were important to the doughboy because they governed the world in which they lived. Weapons were the tools of the soldier's trade, so to comprehend more fully the doughboys' daily life, one must also understand the tools that they carried. How much the weapons weighed, their capabilities and limitations, and how they were used are vital to understanding the doughboys' story for the simple reason that they were the implements that determined the soldiers' key realities: killing and dying. In the interest of brevity, this chapter will only cover the weapons used in an infantry regiment during the war.

The primary weapons of the American infantryman in World War I were the rifle and bayonet. In April 1917 the standard army rifle was the M1903 Springfield. It was one of the most elegant, handy, and accurate rifles that the U.S. military had ever fielded. Its 8.6-pound weight and 43.2-inch length made it lighter and less cumbersome than the rifles used by France, Germany, and most of the other European combatants. The weapon's powerful 30.06 cartridge could reach a maximum range of approximately thirty-four hundred yards and penetrate fifty-six one-inch-thick pine boards when fired at a distance of fifty meters. The cartridge, however, produced a vicious recoil, as one officer noted, equivalent to placing the hind hoof of "a healthy young colt . . . gently but firmly against your right shoulder, and allow it to kick you a hundred times each morning." The M1903 was a bolt-action rifle with a five-round internal box magazine. To load the weapon, the soldier opened the bolt, took a stripper clip holding five rounds of ammunition from his rifle belt, lined the stripper clip in the weapon's charger guide, pushed the rounds from the clip into the spring-loaded magazine using his right thumb, and then discarded the now empty clip. The combination of the smooth bolt action and the ability to rapidly reload the weapon meant that a trained rifleman could fire around fifteen aimed shots a minute. Although the weapon was sighted for up to 2,850 yards, it was rare for soldiers to hit, or even see, an enemy beyond three hundred to five hundred yards.[1]

The biggest drawbacks to the M1903 Springfield were that there were not enough of them on hand and that it was too well made. In April 1917 the army had less than six hundred thousand of the rifles in its inventory and the single plant producing the weapon, the government-owned Springfield Arsenal, was producing only 160 rifles per week. Even after the army resumed production of the weapon at the Rock Island Arsenal, the amount of hand milling required to manufacture the M1903 limited the mass production of the rifle. Fortunately, when the United States entered the war, the arms manufacturers Winchester and Remington were already mass-producing the Pattern 14 .303 caliber rifle for the British Army. Faced with the inability to produce the number of M1903s required using its own arsenals, and not willing to accept the time that private arms makers would require to retool their factories to make the Springfields, the War Department turned to Winchester and Remington to fill its needs. By slightly rechambering the Pattern 14 rifles in production from the British .303 caliber to the American 30.06 cartridge, these manufacturers were ultimately able to provide most of the rifles that the army required. The new rifle, named the M1917, became the standard U.S. Army rifle of the war, ultimately equipping 75 percent of the American troops.[2]

Like the M1903, the M1917 was a bolt-action rifle with an internal five-round magazine. Although the actions and sights of the two weapons were slightly different (the M1917 cocked on opening the bolt while the M1903 did so on closing the bolt), the loading and firing procedures, the rates of fire, and the effective ranges were essentially the same. The major differences between the two weapons were their weights and lengths. The M1917 was 46.3 inches long and weighed a little over nine pounds. This meant that it was nearly a pound heavier and three inches longer than the M1903, thus making the M1917 the more cumbersome weapon. Left to their own devices, most infantrymen preferred the M1903, not that the army asked their opinions on this matter. Some soldiers, however, took the opportunity to trade their M1917s for M1903s when the opportunity presented itself. One infantryman recalled that when he and his comrades came across Springfields left by the dead and wounded of other units, they avidly picked them up "as we did not like the so called Eddystone [M1917] rifles."[3]

The soldiers armed with the M1903 and M1917 rifles were much more fortunate than the four regiments of African American troops of the disbanded 93rd Division who served with the French army or the soldiers in the North Russian Expeditionary Force. The former were armed with the French M1907–15 Berthier rifle while the latter carried the Russian M1891 Mosin-Nagant rifle, both of which were inferior to the American rifles in all aspects. The soldiers of the American II Corps, which fought with the British Army through most of the war, were armed with the British No 1. MK III Lee Enfield rifles. The key advantage of the Lee Enfield was that its magazine held ten, rather than five, rounds. Although the Lee Enfield was comparable to the M1903 rifles in most areas, the doughboys still preferred the American rifles to the British weapon. Some of this might be tied to the fact that the British issued the Americans worn-out arms. Upon receiving "the hated English Lee-Enfield," Chester Baker claimed that its bore was "so worn it looked like a shotgun." After failing to hit anything with the weapon at the rifle range, the British instructor merely informed Baker, "Well it'll get a Jerry at 100 yards." Some of the Americans' dislike of the British rifle may have been simple chauvinism. Soldiers in the 4th Division claimed that the Enfield was "heavier and clumsier" than their M1903s, even though the weight and length of the weapons were almost identical.[4]

The infantryman's rifle was the source of his individual power, his protector, and his curse. Although eight or nine pounds does not sound like much of a burden, when carried day after day with little sleep and poor rations, the rifle became a ponderous load. The M1903 and M1917 were both well-made and reliable weapons, but they still required constant care and maintenance to keep them in order. Dirt, mud, and accumulations of rust and burnt powder fouled the weapons and prevented cartridges from loading in the chamber and feeding from the magazine or kept the firing pin from making contact with the cartridge's primer. Cleaning the rifle in combat was rudimentary, consisting mainly of removing and cleaning the bolt, wiping down and oiling the chamber, and running a brush and an oiled patch down

Photo 12: The common small arms used by the soldiers of the AEF. From top to bottom: M1903 Springfield rifle, M1917 rifle, British MK III SMLE Lee Enfield rifle, French M1907–15 rifle, M911 automatic pistol (left), and M1917 Colt revolver (right). Source: author's collection.

the bore. Considering how important the rifle was to the soldier, it is interesting to note that the AEF inspector general reported that "great carelessness was displayed in the care of arms" in the fall of 1918. Poor training, especially among replacements, the difficulty in obtaining basic cleaning supplies, and the wet and grimy conditions of the Meuse Argonne certainly contributed to this problem. An inspector of the 91st Division said as much on October 5, 1918. He noted, "much rust visible" on the unit's rifles, but then admitted, "Weather conditions being severe . . . and shortages of oil during [the] march undoubtedly had much to do with this condition."[5]

There is little doubt that the American Army that entered the war in 1917 was a rifle-centric organization. Officers attending the staff college at Fort Leavenworth prior to the war were assured of the American soldier's natural prowess with the rifle and the ability of the weapon to dominate the battlefield. In lectures and textbooks, Charles Crawford, an instructor in the Infantry and Cavalry School, drilled into his students that "the end of all warfare is attained by breaking up and destroying the enemy's forces in battle, and the chief instrument used is the small arm rifle" and that "the casualties inflicted by small arms are from five to fifteen times those inflicted by any other weapon." As has been noted, Pershing certainly held this view and little that had occurred on the Western Front between 1914 and 1917 seemed to shake the Americans' confidence in the efficacy of the rifle and American marksmanship. In fact the 1917 edition of the *Infantry Drill Regulation*, the standard U.S. doctrine for infantry units, continued to state, "Over open ground attack is possible only when the attacking force has a decided [rifle] fire superiority. With such a superiority the attack is not only possible, but success is probable without ruinous losses."[6]

But was this faith in the average American's skill with a rifle and the effectiveness of the weapon justified? There were certainly instances of superior American marksmanship during the war, Sergeant Alvin York and Lieutenant Samuel Woodfill being the finest examples. Although many are aware of York's exploits, Woodfill is much less known. On October 13, 1918, Woodfill, a prewar Regular commissioned from the ranks, killed the crews of five German machine guns in Cunel mostly using his M1903 Springfield (and dispatching others with a pistol and a pickax). In taking out one of the machine guns in a church belfry, Woodfill reportedly killed five machine gunners with five shots at a range of approximately three hundred meters. However, such instances of lethal virtuosity were the exception rather than the rule. Even in the best-trained units, the amount of time dedicated to marksmanship training was not enough to create truly effective combat shooters. As previously noted, during the crisis of 1918 most American training, including marksmanship, tended to be rushed and incomplete. Although it is true that more Americans had experience with firearms prior to entering the service than their European counterparts, this did not parley directly to battlefield effectiveness. It was one thing to shoot targets and stalk game; it was another to stalk and kill another man, especially if that man was shooting back. The doughboys may have been slightly better marksmen than their European peers, but their skills fell short of Pershing's grand expectations.[7]

The other part of the infantryman's weaponry was his bayonet. The bayonet for the M1903 had a sixteen-inch blade while that of the M1917 was one-inch longer. Prior to the war the army had placed as much faith in the bayonet as it did the rifle. The *Infantry Drill Regulation* made clear that rifle firepower would set the conditions for the attack by killing and demoralizing the enemy, but victory would assured by "a short dash and a bayonet combat." "Confidence in their ability to use the bayonet," the manual claimed, "gives the assaulting troops the promise of success." In his program of training for divisions arriving in France, Pershing even went so far as to demand, "An aggressive spirit must be developed until the soldier feels himself, as a bayonet fighter; invincible in battle." Bayonet drill was meant to instill fierceness and a degree of bloodlust into the troops, and the doughboys often went into action with their bayonets fixed.[8]

In training in the United States and France, bayonet practice certainly garnered more than its fair share of time on unit training schedules, but was the time well spent? An idea of the bayonet's continued importance in the Great War can be drawn from the war's casualty statistics. The AEF reported that of the 224,069 wounded doughboys that it treated during the war, only 235 were for bayonet wounds and another 136 were from trench knives or other cutting or piercing weapons. Even though wounds from bayonets and knives may have killed the soldiers before they made it to the hospital, and, as the attacker, the Americans may have killed more Germans with bayonets than the Germans did Americans, we can still be fairly certain that the number of soldiers wounded by bayonets in the war was statistically insignificant. The most important duty that bayonets performed for the doughboys was opening cans and serving as improvised clothing hooks and food skewers.[9]

Bayonets were not the only edged weapons issued to the doughboys. The soldiers also received an array of bolo and trench knives. As the M1917 rifle with fixed bayonet was over sixty-three inches long, it could become unwieldy to use in the close confines of a trench. As the name implied, the various versions of the issued trench knife were for close quarters hand-to-hand fighting as one might encounter in a trench. The first two versions of the American-issued trench knives had wickedly sharp nine-inch triangular blades, wooden grips, and a steel knuckle-duster hand guard that stretched over the fist griping the knife. The blade was specifically designed to easily penetrate the thick wool uniforms and leather equipment worn by the German soldiers. The last model American trench knife was designed to correct some of the flaws identified with the earlier models and had a 6 3/4-inch double-edged flat blade, a brass knuckle handle, and an aptly named "skull crusher" pommel. Each infantry company was to have had forty trench knives for the commander to issue as needed. Although photographs from the period show soldiers carrying trench knives and the troops sometimes discussed having them, accounts of their use in combat are very scarce.[10]

Some soldiers also carried the M1910 or M1917 bolo knife. These were not technically weapons. Their heavy, leaf-shaped blades were intended to be wielded like an ax or machete to clear obstacles or to chop wood for fire, shelter, or improvised litters. However, they could still be used to deadly effect as the situation dictated. The most renowned use of a bolo knife in combat was by Henry Johnson, an African American in the 369th Infantry. While occupying a listening post on May 15, 1918, Johnson and one other soldier were attacked by a raiding party of Germans. After being wounded by a grenade and emptying his rifle into one of the attackers, Johnson used his bolo knife to seriously wound two Germans trying to carry off his comrade.[11]

To meet the demands of trench warfare, the War Department also purchased approximately twenty-five thousand M1897 Winchester 12-gauge pump shotguns. These weapons were converted to "trench guns" by adding a ventilated metal hand guard to protect the firer's hands during rapid firing and by mounting a bayonet attachment for fitting the M1917 rifle bayonet. The shotgun's ability to rapidly fire six rounds and the spread of the weapon's buckshot made the weapon quite deadly in the close confines of a trench. Although the "Trench guns" were reliable and well liked by their users, their shot range limited their overall utility. As the AEF moved out of the trenches to confront the Germans in open terrain, the shotgun's limitations started to tell. An infantry officer reported to the Ordnance Department, "The gun is not suited to open warfare . . . The men much prefer the rifle." Most of the M1897s ended the war arming POW guards.[12]

Officers, senior NCOs, and the regiment's heavy weapons crewmembers carried the seven-shot M1911 automatic pistol or the six-shot M1917 revolver. Both of these pistols fired the powerful .45 Automatic Colt Pistol (ACP) cartridge. The recoil created by the cartridge was prone to take the uninitiated by surprise. One novice noted that the first time that he fired the pistol he lost control of the weapon as it "jumped up" in his hands. His lack of skills encouraged his instructors to remove him from the range and set him to work cleaning weapons. As with the Springfield rifles, the greatest problem with the M1911s was that they were in short supply. To make up this shortage, the army contracted with Colt and Smith and Wesson to convert their existing models of .45 caliber pistols to fire the ACP cartridges. Although the

Colt and Smith and Wesson revolvers were completely different pistols, the Ordnance Department opted to give both models the common name: the M1917 revolver. Pistols were for close-range personal defense and were not all that useful in battle. That being said, both York and Woodfill used pistols during their Medal of Honor–winning exploits.[13]

The doughboys certainly possessed weapons in their arsenal that were much more deadly than rifles, bayonets, pistols, and bolos. While somewhat slow to appreciate the utility of machine guns prior to the war, once in the conflict, the American Army followed the path of their European counterparts and took to the weapons with a vengeance. The machine guns in the American Army's inventory in April 1917 were few in number and mostly obsolete. Faced with the inability of domestic manufacturers to meet its immediate demand for machine guns, the army was forced to turn to the French and British to provide most of these weapons. This meant that the AEF would use four major types of machine guns during the war: the French 8mm M1914 Hotchkiss, the British .303 Vickers gun, the M1915 30.06 Vickers gun (an American copy of the British machine gun), and the American M1917 30.06 Browning. The AEF's first twelve divisions were equipped with the M1914 Hotchkiss guns; the eleven divisions that arrived between May and June 1918 were armed with the M1915 Vickers; and all the divisions arriving after June were issued the M1917 Brownings. Machine gunners in the American II Corps used the British .303 Vickers guns. All of these guns were employed in the same manner in combat, but technical differences between them brought their own advantages and disadvantages to the doughboys.[14]

The most common machine gun used by the AEF in combat was the French M1914 Hotchkiss. Unlike most of its European equivalents, the Hotchkiss was an air-cooled machine gun. The inherent problem of all automatic weapons is the danger of overheating during prolonged rapid fire. Air-cooled guns used ambient air to cool down their barrels and receivers and are thus more prone to overheating than water-cooled guns. The French compensated for this by increasing the weight of the Hotchkiss's barrel and by installing large rings around the barrel and the receiver to increase the surface area for cooling. The advantage of this system was that the crew did not have to carry water to operate the weapon. The major drawback of the Hotchkiss was its great weight. With its heavy barrel, components, and tripod, the M1914 tipped the scales at over 110 pounds.

The M1914 Hotchkiss had a maximum cyclic rate of fire of six hundred rounds a minute, but its awkward system of feeding cartridges into the gun reduced its actual combat rate of fire to approximately two hundred rounds a minute. The gun was fed by inserting a thin rigid metal strip containing twenty-four cartridges into the side of the receiver. These strips were rather flimsy and required a great degree of dexterity on the part of the assistant gunner to keep the gun fed with ammunition. Despite these drawbacks, the Hotchkiss was a reliable weapon in battle. The 3rd Division would earn its nickname, "the Rock of the Marne," for its defense of Château Thierry in July 1918 due largely to the deadliness and tenacity of its machine gun units. Machine gunners fired so many rounds into the ranks of the oncoming Germans that the barrels of their guns glowed red hot. In one short engagement, two Hotchkiss guns from the 9th Machine Gun Battalion fired fifteen thousand rounds to break a German assault.[15]

The British .303 Vickers, American M1915 Vickers, and the American M1917 Browning were all water-cooled machine guns. The barrels of these weapons were encased in a light metal jacket filled with water, which cooled down the weapon during prolonged firing. After approximately seven hundred rounds of continuous fire, however, the water in the water jacket started to boil. At the end of the water jacket, each gun had a water cock valve attached to a rubber hose that fed into a separate condenser can. As the water boiled and turned to steam in the water jacket, the steam travel down the hose to the condenser can where it condensed back to water. After firing approximately 750 rounds, the crew had to stop firing and pour the water from the condenser can back into the machine gun's water jacket. Since some water was lost during the process, the crew had to carry extra cans of water with them in combat.

The British and American Vickers guns differed only in caliber and a few minor technical details. The complete gun with a full water jacket weighed ninety-eight pounds and was fed using 250 round cloth belts. Although the Vickers had a cyclic rate of fire of five hundred rounds per minute, typical rate of fire in combat was approximately 250 rounds per minute. Despite the additional weight and complications to the firing process caused by the gun's water-cooling system, the Vickers was exceptionally reliable and popular with its crews. As a machine gunner in the 129th Infantry proclaimed, "the Vickers couldn't be beat."[16]

The M1917 Browning gun was the brainchild of John Moses Browning, one of the greatest arms inventors in history. The Browning gun was the best weapon of its type fielded during the war. Like that of the Vickers, its cyclic rate of fire was five hundred rounds a minute, but Browning was able to reduce the weight of his machine gun to 84.5 pounds. The Army Ordinance Department planned to make the M1917 Browning gun the sole machine gun in the AEF, but problems with manufacturing and the pace of operations in 1918 meant that only 1,168 of the weapons reached the troops prior to the Armistice.[17]

As with all the war's combatants, the AEF had to contend with the inherent advantages and limitations of the era's machine guns. The greatest drawback of these weapons was the weight of the gun and its accessories. None of the war's machine guns was particularly light, but it is easy to forget that the problem was not just the weight of the gun; the crew also had to wrestle forward its ammunition, repair kit, accessories, and water. A 250-round ammunition box (for one minute of firing) weighed around fifteen pounds and each of the five-gallon condenser cans tipped the scales at twelve to fifteen pounds. Given the extreme weight of the weapon and its ammunition, the era's machine guns were best suited for the defense.

A machine gun squad consisted of one gun, a ten- to twelve-man crew, a mule-drawn cart to carry the gun and another mule cart to carry the squad's ammunition. The carts moved all of the squad's weighty materials on a march. As it was generally impossible to bring the mule carts to the firing lines, the crew brought the carts as far forward to the front as possible before unloading them and carrying the weapons forward by hand. Members of the 3rd Machine Gun Battalion, for example, toted their backbreaking loads over five kilometers during the attack on Cantigny. As two men from the squad had to remain behind with the carts and mules, the rest of the load was distributed among the remaining eight to ten men of the crew. Generally, one man carried the gun, one soldier hauled the gun's traverse and elevation mechanism, another hauled the tripod, and the rest of the crew carried forward the ammunition, water cans, and any remaining accouterments. Even with this distribution, the crew still labored under a ponderous weight. A machine gun officer in the 1st Division estimated that each of his crewmembers carried eighty to one hundred pounds of equipment with them in the Meuse Argonne. To assist the crews and bring up as much ammunition as possible during an attack, infantry commanders sometimes detailed their riflemen to serve as ammunition carriers for the machine gun companies supporting their advance. This seldom worked in practice. After being given four extra riflemen to carry ammunition for each of his machine guns during the Soissons drive, a machine gun company commander discovered that half of these men dumped their ammunition boxes at the first opportunity so they could return to their parent units to fight with their buddies.[18]

Machine guns were important weapons in the Great War. Used in conjunction with artillery, machine guns helped to prolong the trench stalemate by giving tremendous power to the defender. The machine guns also played an important role in the offense when fired from the flanks or even over the heads of the attacking infantry to keep the enemy's heads down while the assault moved forward. Machine guns moved forward with the infantry and were also used to beat back the counterattacks that the Germans inevitably launched to regain important terrain or disrupt the momentum of an Allied success. However, the effective use of these weapons by the Americans was hindered by the innate limitations of the guns, the training of the crews, and the know-how of the commanders employing them.

The major challenge that the Americans faced in using machine guns during the attack was simply that the weapons were cumbersome. As the machine gun squad slouched into combat under the weight of their weapons and ammunition, the less encumbered infantrymen who they were to support left them in their dust. A machine gunner in the 37th Division noted that "it requires every ounce of guts a man possesses to keep pace with the infantry when he is loaded down with fifty pounds of extra weight" and that such an endeavor ultimately stripped them of their "reserves of strength." During the Soissons offensive an officer recalled, "Carrying our machine guns and heavy cases of ammunition we soon fell behind the infantry . . . We could see them up ahead while we were floundering through the shell holes of our barrage with our heavier loads." These problems were exacerbated when the unit moved through mud, shell holes, thick brush, and other difficult terrain. During the opening of the Argonne drive, a machine gunner lamented,

> So deep were the shell holes and mine craters that the ammunition carriers were even unable to carry two small boxes of ammunition, so that the belts had to be removed [from the boxes] and wrapped around the men's necks and waists, and they crawled up and down those slippery banks,

using their fingernails and toes. At times the guns and tripods had to be thrown from the bottom of the crater up to the top to a man waiting to receive it, when the men followed.

One can imagine that after all that grubbing in the muddy shell holes neither the guns nor the ammunition were ready for immediate use.[19]

The AEF's second challenge in using machine guns effectively was the lack of training of the gunners themselves. The shortage of machine guns in the United States meant that most units did not have the chance to conduct any meaningful training with the weapons until after they reached France. The experience of Manton S. Eddy's machine gun company of the 39th Infantry was a case in point. Eddy, who would later rise to command the 9th Division and XII Corps in World War II, trained on four different machine guns during his first year of service. His unit did not receive the weapon he would ultimately use in combat, the Hotchkiss gun, until mid-June 1918. Less than four weeks later, his company was thrown into battle at the Aisne-Marne. Eddy was far from being alone in this dilemma. Charles Minder's unit also trained on the obsolete Colt M1914 and the British Vickers gun before being issued their Hotchkiss guns.

The late issue of these weapons and the crush of events in 1918 hamstrung the effective training of many of the AEF's machine gunners. After being sent to the range in France and ordered to shoot "twenty shots for ranging fire, and thirty for application fire," Minder admitted to his mother his lack of familiarity with the terms and concepts that his instructors were using. "They were all the same to me," he confessed. "I don't know any more what they mean than you do." The machine gun officer Manton Eddy was little better off. Far too much of his unit's training, he later noted, focused narrowly on how the weapons worked, and not enough time was spent on how the guns should be used in battle. He admitted, "The training of the company . . . was almost entirely in technique. A method of extended order drill or how a machine gun squad should advance in an attack seems not to have been thought of; and the only consolation that the company commander could find in hunting an excuse for his apparent stupidity is that no one else seemed to think of it either." The machine gunners' lack of knowledge and skill in using their weapons in combat was not lost on the AEF's more senior leaders. During the Lewis Board, a panel of officers brought together by Pershing in April 1919 to study the army's performance during the war, the commander of a machine gun battalion declared that the automatic weapons "were seldom used to best advantage" because "the personnel was trained in the technical side of the weapons, they were not sufficiently familiar with their tactical employment."[20]

The last reason why the use of machine guns in the AEF was not as effective as might have been hoped was due to the fact that few of the army's infantry battalion, regimental, and brigade commanders knew how to best employ them in battle. Each infantry regiment had its own machine gun company with sixteen guns, and each infantry brigade contained a machine gun battalion armed with sixty-four guns. The machine gun companies were generally put at the disposal of an infantry battalion during an operation and were left with little scope for independent action. How well the infantry commander used his machine guns had much to do with his own tactical expertise and his comfort and familiarity with the weapons. One machine gun officer observed, "The battalion commanders had their hands full with a thousand infantrymen and had neither the time nor the opportunity for any study of the situation as might be applied to the machine guns attached to his command." Busy with their own immediate problems and often unsure of how to use their attached machine guns, infantry commanders frequently gave their machine gunners vague orders or impossible missions. In one such case, after his unit stalled in an attack in the Meuse Argonne, the commander of the 113th Infantry ordered up the machine guns to break the German lines. A nearby lieutenant watched in horror at what came next:

> As I lay in my hole I saw the machine gunners rush forward through the infantry and mount their guns. I do not believe that they fired a shot; the gunners were mowed down before they could pull a trigger. Those that could, dragged themselves into shell holes and abandoned their guns. Our colonel was later criticized by General Morton for the loss of life . . . for he contended that if the infantry could not break the enemy lines, machine gunners who were handicapped with heavy equipment and guns that could only be mounted in exposed positions should not be expected to do so.

A similar failure to understand machine gun tactics by the infantry officers from the 1st Division had previously led to similar results during the Soissons drive. After four days of action one officer estimated that many of the unit's machine gun units had suffered the loss of 80 percent of their personnel and 85 percent of their equipment due to tactical mismanagement. The machine gunners themselves often expressed great frustration at their supporting roles and their fates at the hands of unskilled infantry leaders. The commander of the 16th Infantry's machine gun company later claimed that "during the entire period of this company's existence it was treated as a step child" by the senior officers it served and maintained that as late as the Argonne offensive many commanders were still largely ignorant of how to use his weapons. This observation was also echoed in the observations of AEF inspectors during the operation and by members of the Lewis Board after the war.[21]

The tactical challenges that trench warfare presented also gave rise to a host of other weapons that swelled the arsenal at the infantry commander's disposal. One of the more important of these was the automatic rifle. This weapon was intended to overcome some of the problems of the machine guns by giving the attacking infantry easily mobile firepower to suppress the defenders and break up counterattacks. The automatic rifles were light enough to be moved and operated by a two-man crew while still providing enough automatic fire to keep the enemy's heads down while the riflemen moved forward. The three automatic rifles used by the AEF were the French 8mm M1915 Chauchat gun, the American 30.06 M1918 Browning Automatic Rifle, and the British .303 Lewis gun.

The most common automatic rifle used by the AEF was the French M1915 Chauchat gun. The "Sho-Sho," as most Americans called the gun, weighed twenty pounds and had a cyclic rate of fire of 250 to three hundred rounds a minute, though its actual combat rate of fire was closer to one hundred to 150 rounds a minute due to the weapon's tendency to overheat. In combat it was crewed by two or three soldiers: a gunner and one or two ammunition carriers/assistant gunners responsible for keeping the weapon fed with twenty-round magazines. The Chauchat had the distinction of being many firsts; it was the world's first mass-produced automatic rifle and the first major military firearm to utilize a number of rolled, stamped, and welded parts in its construction. There are of course certain disadvantages in being first. The rushed production of the weapon and poor design of its mechanism and magazine meant that it was a very temperamental firearm. The entire barrel recoiled back inside the weapon during firing before being propelled back into battery by a strong spring. This produced a vicious recoil that gave the unwary gunner what the French soldiers termed *La Gifle* (the slap) and a nice bruise on the cheekbone as well as throwing off the accuracy of the weapon's fire. The weapon itself required a lot of tender love and care from the gunner in the form of constant cleaning and maintenance to keep the gun performing. This was particularly true of the Chauchat's magazine. The weapon's designers had cut "windows" in the side of the Chauchat magazines so the assistant gunner could tell how many rounds remained before he needed to change the magazine out. A small amount of mud or grit in the finicky magazine, or in the gun itself, tended to jam the Chauchat.[22]

Ultimately the Chauchat equipped the first twenty-three American divisions that landed in France. Due to its unreliability and ungainliness, the doughboys tended to heartily dislike the weapon. An officer in the 42nd Division went so far as to call it "a villainous piece of unreliable makeshift." There is much validity to the doughboys' complaints, but it should be kept in mind that the French Army reported many fewer problems with the Chauchat than did the Americans. Much of this had to do with the poor state of the Americans' training. It simply required a lot of patience, skill, and knowledge to keep the weapon functioning, attributes that were at times lacking in the average doughboy. As the commander of the 1st Division reported after Soissons,

> Automatic rifles were fired from the hip without need, and the ammunition was often needlessly expended . . . sometimes the guns were abandoned because the men were tired, or because the ammunition was exhausted. None but the automatic rifle teams had been taught to operate them, and some of these men had only a short period of service and did not know how to prevent or correct jams. In some cases the guns were continuously fired until they became intensely heated.

The AEF made the reliability of the weapons even worse when it attempted to convert the Chauchat from 8mm to the American 30.06 caliber. The rechambering of these weapons was improperly done and the American cartridges proved too powerful for the gun's design. Despite its flaws, in the proper hands the Chauchat was a lethal weapon that provided the doughboys with the mobile firepower that they required. As one Marine later recalled, "That damned Chauchat was a lousy weapon in many ways . . . It was not very accurate, but it usually worked, and this is a great asset in the type of combat we were in. You could use it like a hose!"[23]

The M1918 Browning Automatic Rifle (BAR) was the second most common automatic rifle used in the AEF and was the best of its type of weapon fielded during the war. With a full twenty-round magazine, the BAR weighed over two pounds less than the Chauchat gun and was much more reliable. The rifle also had double the cyclic and combat rate of fire of the French gun. The BAR was to have equipped all of the divisions that arrived in France after June 1918 and all of the earlier-arriving divisions once stocks were on hand, but the pace of the AEF's operations and the shortages of the weapons delayed its combat debut until September 1918. In fact, an automatic rifleman in the 82nd Division noted that he did not have his Chauchat replaced with the BAR until over a month after the Armistice.[24]

Lastly, the doughboys fighting with the British in the American II Corps used the Lewis gun. This weapon weighed slightly over twenty-five pounds without its heavy forty-seven-round magazine. It was reliable and popular with the American and British soldiers who used it during both world wars.

In addition to his small arms, an infantry regimental commander could also call on the firepower of a Stokes mortar platoon equipped with six mortar tubes and a 37mm gun section of three cannons. Although artillery was the king of the Great War battlefield, problems with communications and the difficulty in moving the guns forward during an attack made it unresponsive to the immediate needs of the infantry. By giving each regiment Stokes mortars and 37mm guns, the AEF hoped to give the infantry its own fire-support assets to deal with enemy machine gun nests, strong points, and those other pesky and unforeseen problems that arose on the battlefield.

The AEF obtained 3-inch Stokes mortars from the British to give the American regimental commanders their own "pocket artillery." The mortars had a high angle of fire to drop an eleven-pound high-explosive shell into enemy trenches at a maximum range of approximately eight hundred meters. The biggest drawback to the Stokes was the weight of the gun and its ammunition. Although it could be broken down into its component parts, the weapon's tube, tripod, and base plate collectively weighed 108 pounds.

The 37mm gun, often called the "one pounder" by the doughboys due to the weight of its shell, was intended to give the infantry a long-range flat-trajectory weapon for destroying point targets such as machine guns and pillboxes. While its thousand-meter maximum effective range made it a formidable weapon, the fact that the gun tipped the scale at a robust 170 pounds made it difficult to use in battle.[25]

Both the Stokes mortars and the 37mm guns faced the same problems as the machine gun. The skills of the crew and the knowledge of how to use the weapon to their best advantage were often lacking. Like the machine guns, the Stokes and 37mm guns had to be manhandled to the front, and as such, their crews found it just as difficult as the machine gunners to keep up with the advancing infantry. These weapons also faced one other disadvantage: often the infantrymen did not want them anywhere near them. The mortar men tended to fire off a few rounds and then quickly move to another position. This practice of "shoot and scoot" irritated the infantrymen because they were often left to face the inevitable German artillery retaliation that usually followed the American fire. This also applied to the "one pounders." As one 37mm platoon leader recalled, "Whenever the 37-mm fired it was not long before the Germans would reply with artillery." In fact during the Argonne fighting, an infantry commander shooed the "one pounder" crew away because the gun was drawing fire on his position and wounding the doughboys in the area.[26]

Lastly, the trench stalemate led to a rediscovery of hand grenades. The need for a weapon to clear trenches, dugouts, and bunkers and to disrupt attacking waves of infantry without exposing the soldiers to direct fire had become evident to the European armies by the end of 1914. Grenades seemed to fill this requirement by giving the infantryman a small explosive that he could easily lob into trenches or throw down the stairs of a dugout. While the Americans had learned in their youths how to throw baseballs, they soon discovered that this skill did not transfer readily to hand grenades. The novice grenadier had to forget his fast pitch and knuckleball and learn how to throw his grenade in an arching trajectory to clear the parapet of a trench or to land squarely in a shell hole.

The doughboys used a number of different French, British, and American grenade designs, the most common being the French F1 and 01, the British Mills Bomb, and the American Mark I and Mark II grenades. Of all of these, the French F1 defensive grenade predominated. It weighed 1.3 pounds and came with either a percussion fuse or the Billant automatic fuse. The F1 with percussion fuse was armed by striking the igniter sharply against a solid surface. Although the striker was protected by a removable brass cap until it was time to use the grenade, these caps had a tendency to come off if the grenades were handled carelessly or if bounced around too much in a grenade bag. The ignition system also took some getting used to. As a 2nd Division officer observed,

When the fuse of the egg grenade was tapped on a rock or other hard surface, the fuse started burning and flames and fumes began sputtering out around the tip. When one raw recruit saw the flames and the fumes, he froze with the grenade grasped tightly in his hand. A sergeant standing nearby tore the grenade from his hand and threw it just in time for it to explode in the air about twenty feet in front of the trench.

The F1 with the Billant fuse was a much safer alternative. Following the lead of the British Mills Bomb, the Billant was armed when its nail-like striker pin was released to hit and activate a five-second mechanical fuse. To keep the grenade safe until used, the striker was physically held in place by the grenade's safety spoon, which in turn was secured by a cotter pin with pull ring. To use the grenade, the soldier wrapped his hand around the grenade and its safety spoon, pulled the pull ring, and then threw the grenade. As soon as the grenade left the thrower's hand, the safety spoon flew off, releasing the striker to ignite the fuse. The five-second delay allowed the grenadier to remain outside of the grenade's blast radius but also did not give the enemy any time to pick the grenade up and throw it back. These nasty little devices were very efficient but were as dangerous to friends as to foes in the hands of the stupid and incautious. "A few days ago one of the fellows was trying to show a German family a little more than he knew about hand grenades," one soldier wrote shortly after the Armistice. "It went off, blowing one of his hands off, killing one of the children and seriously wounding the rest of the family."[27]

The major drawback of all hand grenades was that their range was limited by the strength of the thrower. Even a grenadier with a strong arm still had to get quite close to the enemy before using his weapon. The solution to this came with the last major weapon in the infantry's arsenal: the rifle grenade. The French Viven-Bessiere (VB) grenade was the most common rifle grenade used in the AEF. The VB grenades were fired from a cylindrical cup "trombone" grenade discharger mounted to the muzzle of the standard issue M1903 or M1917 rifle. The rifle grenadier slid the VB grenade down the neck of the discharger until it rested firmly on the base of the cup. The grenade was launched and armed when the grenadier fired a standard ball cartridge from the rifle. The gas created by the firing of the rifle cartridge produced enough power to hurl the seventeen-ounce grenade up to two hundred meters and, in theory, create a blasting radius where "any man within 75 yards of an exploding rifle grenade is likely to be wounded or killed." The VB was an effective weapon, but some soldiers, like Private Earl Seaton, were not enthusiastic about carrying the heavy and dangerous sack of grenades that came with being selected to serve as a rifle grenadier. He, however, was smart enough to treat the grenades with due respect. One of his comrades was not so circumspect. His friend was upset at being selected as a VB grenadier and "got disgusted and threw his sack down hard." "It was the last mistake he ever made," Seaton recalled. "His butt was blown clear up to his shoulders."[28]

All of these weapons mattered because they highlighted the new era in warfare that the AEF faced when it landed in France. In its tactics, assumptions about war, organization, and weapons, the U.S. Army of April 1917 was still an army mired in the dogmas of August 1914. The AEF was "thrown into the deep end of the pool" in 1917 and 1918 and had to quickly learn the new weapons, techniques, and rules needed to fight and survive on the modern battlefield. One only has to examine the changing organization of American infantry regiments, companies, and platoons to see these revolutionary changes in action. In 1916 an American infantry regiment consisted of fifty-one officers and fifteen hundred enlisted men. The army had belatedly and grudgingly given the regiment a six-gun provisional machine gun company shortly before the United States entered the war. With the exceptions of these machine guns, all of the unit's other soldiers were armed solely with rifles and pistols. By June 1918, the infantry regiment had ballooned to 112 officers and 3,720 enlisted men and was armed now not only with rifles and pistols but also with sixteen machine guns, six Stokes mortars, three 37mm guns, 390 rifle grenade launchers, and 192 automatic rifles. These changes were also reflected in the infantry companies and platoons. In 1916 the infantry company consisted of five officers and 112 to 122 soldiers with each of its four platoons having one officer and twenty-seven soldiers. In 1918 the infantry company now numbered five or six officers and 255 enlisted men. Each of the company's four platoons held one officer and fifty-eight soldiers. The greatest change can be seen in the organization of the platoon. In 1916 each squad in the platoon was identical and consisted only of riflemen. In 1918 the infantry platoon contained rifles, hand grenades, four automatic rifles, and six rifle grenade launchers. It was organized in half platoons or combat groups consisting of two squads of riflemen, two automatic rifle squads, a hand bomber squad, a rifle grenade squad, and a liaison squad to keep in touch with adjacent units and the company headquarters.[29]

The addition of each new weapon to the unit's arsenal required its soldiers to master not only the technical aspects of the novel system but also how to properly use it in battle to get the best results. This kept the doughboys and their officers scrambling throughout the war to keep abreast of emerging tactics and technology. The army's machine gun pioneer and foremost expert on the weapon, Colonel John Parker, noted the difficulty these changes, and the growing sophistication of warfare, caused the novice doughboys:

> The infantry organization has now reached such a complexity that the infantry regiment in combat is difficult to manage; from the unit command of a platoon leader up to include the regiment as a whole . . . the platoon leader has at least seven different weapons, four of which are organized in teams that lose their efficiency with the loss of a single expert. The company commander has the same problem, and the battalion commander has it in a still greater degree.

Although the doughboys of the AEF would learn all of the ins and outs of modern war, it would be a long and painful process.[30]

11

"Oh, the Army, the Army, the Democratic Army, . . . the Jews, the Wops, the Dutch and Irish Cops"

Ethnic Soldiers and African Americans in the AEF

The divisions that fought in World War I garnered a host of official and unofficial nicknames during the conflict. The monikers of two of these units, the 77th "Melting Pot" Division and the 82nd "All American" Division, stemmed from the simple fact that their enlisted men came largely from immigrant-heavy New York City and the urban northeast. The blend of ethnicities and religions that these soldiers brought to their units made them at once unique but also a representation of the changing face of early-twentieth-century America. To capture the feel and make up of his unit, John Mullin of the 77th Division's 308th Infantry penned a ditty that would become the division's war song.

> Oh the army, the army, the democratic army,
> They clothe you and they feed you
> Because the army needs you. Hash for breakfast,
> Beans for dinner, stew for supper-time.
> Thirty dollars every month, deducting twenty-nine.
> Oh the army, the army, the democratic army,
> The Jews, the Wops, the Dutch and Irish Cops,
> They're all in the army now.[1]

Other divisions were also noted for their racial diversity. The 36th and 90th Divisions, drawn from men from Texas, Oklahoma, Arizona, and New Mexico, contained a mix of Anglo, Native, and Mexican Americans. The 92nd and the four infantry regiments of what would have become the 93rd Division comprised African American enlisted men and an uneasy combination of black and white officers.

To a very great extent large national armies always reflect the societies from which they are drawn. The AEF was no exception. The United States of the Great War era had just experienced the greatest period of immigration in its history and continued to be guided by a legacy of unequal treatment of African, Native, and Mexican Americans. The American Army that fought in France was made up of a mélange of different races and ethnic groups, and the treatment that these soldiers received in the army often reflected the prejudices and attitudes of the larger white Anglo-Saxon Protestant society. The focus of this book is on the life of the common American soldier in the war. As such, it is important to note the commonality of experiences between all the AEF's soldiers: the "Hash for breakfast, beans for dinner, stew for supper-time" that Mullin lamented. In other words, the wool uniforms were just as uncomfortable, the corn beef and hard bread rations were just as unpalatable, and bullet wounds hurt just as badly to an African American or Italian-born soldier as to white, native-born doughboys. With this in mind, this chapter will focus on those times and places where the soldier's race and ethnicity made their experience in the army different from the majority of doughboys.

The flood of the "new immigrants" from southern and eastern Europe into the United States from the 1880s to 1917 dramatically changed the ethnic demographics of the nation. As a result of this influx, first-generation immigrants accounted for some 18 percent of the nation's soldiers or nearly one out of every five doughboys. Although National Guard and National Army divisions were raised regionally, the constant moving of troops between units and the arrival of replacements in combat meant that all of the AEF's divisions contained a fair number of ethic and immigrant soldiers. As this process led to men from a host of different backgrounds being thrown together in a random manner, the wartime army proved to be a much greater "melting" or "mixing" pot of cultures than was experienced in the larger American society. Middle-class, white, native America met the immigrant America of the urban ethnic neighborhoods for the first time on a more or less equal basis. These encounters were not without their moments of humor. One of the most popular jokes of the period was that during one morning roll call a first sergeant sneezed and half the company raised their hands and cried "here." In the multiethnic 82nd Division, one long-service first sergeant overcame the problem of conducting roll calls with soldiers of unpronounceable names by simply translating them into words that more easily tripped off his tongue. Thus, Private Spirigiolosi became Private "Goodwhiskey." Sadly, what Private Spirigiolosi thought of his new name is absent from the record.[2]

The presence of large numbers of foreign soldiers in its ranks created challenges for the army. The wartime fear of possible alien sedition and latent disloyalty led to the public demand for "100% Americanism": the removal of the hyphen from hyphenated Americans by forcing them to conform in all aspects to the norms of the dominant Anglo-Saxon culture. The army thus not only sought to turn the immigrant doughboys into soldiers but also had to work to assimilate them into the larger American society while avoiding the counterproductive excesses of wartime hysteria. The War Department approached these tasks with an unexpected degree of sympathy and understanding and made great efforts to accommodate the special needs of its immigrant soldiers. In September 1918, for example, army commanders coordinated with railroad officials to provide special trains to move three thousand Jewish soldiers at Camp Upton to New York City so they could attend Yom Kippur services. Other units excused Jewish and Greek Orthodox soldiers from duty so they could celebrate religious holidays. In January 1918 the army went so far as to create the Foreign-Speaking Solider Subsection within the Morale Branch to serve as an advocate for these doughboys.[3]

The most pressing challenge presented by the immigrants was that many of them lacked the English-language skills required to undergo training, understand orders, and function as part of a team in combat. Approximately a quarter of these men could not read an American newspaper or write a letter to their families in English. In September 1918 the commanding officer of Camp Dodge, Iowa, reported that his post held 544 soldiers from thirty-five different ethnic groups who "have not a sufficient knowledge of English to readily comprehend commands and read instructions in English." This group included eight American Indians and even five Englishmen. The officer also noted that an additional 271 African Americans and twenty-three white Americans faced the same difficulties in reading. These language problems led to a host of misunderstandings and had an adverse effect on training, morale, and discipline. "The non-English-speaking soldier is not a troublesome problem, but a perplexing one," a morale officer wrote from Camp Devens in September 1918. "His loyalty and patriotism is hidden in the difficulties of making his thoughts and wishes known. He is misunderstood by officers and non-commissioned officers in many cases, so that a thoroughly patriotic and loyal soldier becomes dissatisfied and a problem is created."[4]

In late 1917 and early 1918, the divisions undergoing training attempted to remove the language barrier by establishing post English schools or ad hoc classes that were frequently taught by chaplains, YMCA secretaries, or other service organization personnel. As these classes had to be worked in around the training schedule or were sometimes taught by individuals with scant teaching abilities or a knowledge of their foreign language to connect with the students, the results of these efforts were somewhat mixed. It was not until the late winter of 1918 that officers at Camp Gordon found a more workable and successful approach to solving the problem. Under what became known as the "Camp Gordon Plan," non-English-speaking recruits were assigned to a development battalion upon their arrival in camp. The battalion's companies were grouped by ethnicity and were led by officers and NCOs who spoke the same language as the men. The troops spent three to four hours a day in English lessons and the remainder in military training. The Camp Gordon officials found that having leaders able to speak to the men in their own language improved the soldiers' understanding of their training and made them more amenable to discipline and the service. The post intelligence officer at Camp Gordon reported in July 1918, "Formerly the morale of these soldiers was very low and there was much discontentment among them, but since being placed in separate battalions with officers and non-coms speaking their own language the morale has completely changed, and instead of being discontented all are enthusiastic and content." He went on to boast that while all of these men had previously refused to go overseas, 85 percent were now ready and willing to sail. The Camp Gordon approach worked so well that the War Department mandated it for use at other army posts. In the end, the army got what it needed from the program: immigrants with the motivation and English skills to serve as fighting soldiers. In August 1918 officers at Camp Hancock, Georgia, informed the War Department that 90 percent of the 160 non-English speakers in the post development battalion would be fit for overseas service by the time that their training regime was complete.[5]

Despite the War Department's efforts to integrate ethnic soldiers smoothly within its ranks, it should be kept in mind that the army was still part of a larger American society that was profoundly racist and ethnocentric in its at-

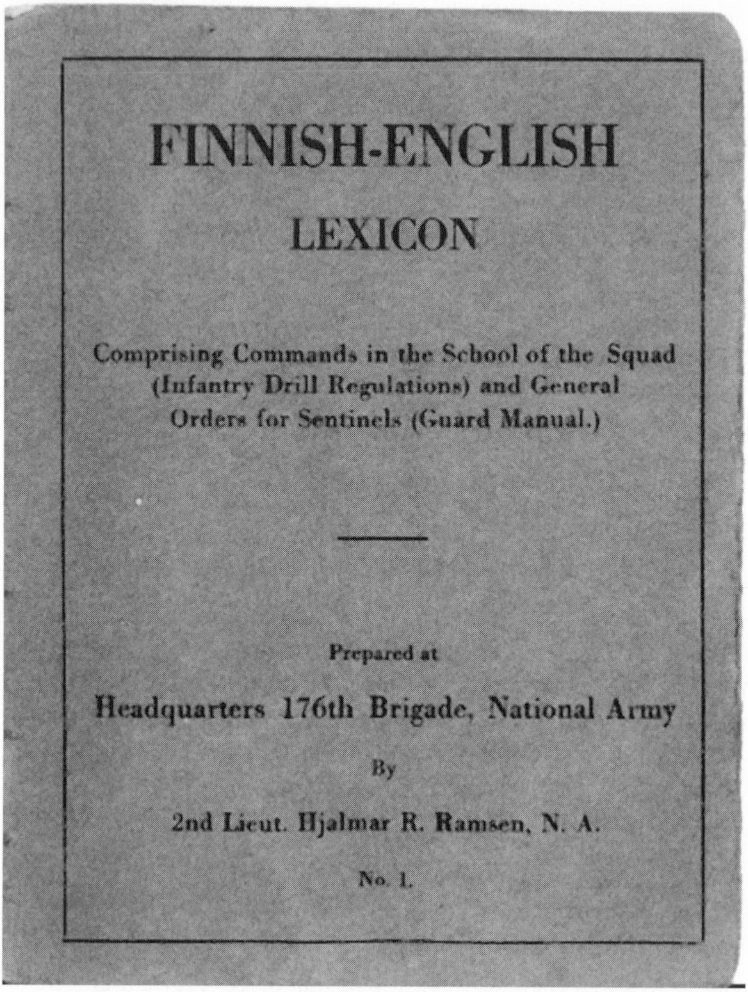

FINNISH-ENGLISH

LEXICON

Comprising Commands in the School of the Squad
(Infantry Drill Regulations) and General
Orders for Sentinels (Guard Manual.)

Prepared at

Headquarters 176th Brigade, National Army

By

2nd Lieut. Hjalmar R. Ramsen, N. A.

No. 1.

Photo 13: Finnish-English phrasebook published at Camp Dodge, Iowa, to help instruct immigrant soldiers in the 88th Division's 176th Brigade. The lexicon includes translations of general orders for sentinels and common orders used in close order drills. I would like to thank Kelton Smith for providing the phrasebook.

titudes and worldviews. This was reflected in the cartoons, ethnic jokes, and letters that peppered official and unofficial publications. The AEF's authorized newspaper, *Stars and Stripes*, frequently contained materials that used images and dialects that poked fun at African Americans and immigrant soldiers. Life could be hard on ethnic soldiers when their Anglo-Saxon, native-born officers and NCOs reflected the bigoted beliefs and prejudice of the nation. A soldier from Brooklyn believed that the mostly southern officers of his unit in the 82nd Division "were shits" because they hated "yankees from the North, Jews and negroes" and seemed to have a particular antipathy for New Yorkers. He recalled that after some of his buddies started singing the old Civil War song "Marching through Georgia" during a hike, his lieutenant subjected the unit to extra close order drill to punish the Yankees and immigrants for their temerity.[6]

The most common form of abuse that the immigrants received was being subjected to the constant use of ethnic slurs and demeaning language. The Camp Devens intelligence officer reported to the Morale Branch that native-born officers and NCOs were not "treating all those of foreign birth with consideration" and that "patriotic and loyal soldiers" were being disheartened by being constantly called "'Guineas,' 'wops,' 'squareheads,' etc." Even at Camp Gordon the morale officer reported that the use of "various epithets such as 'wops,' 'dagoes,' etc." by many of the camp's leaders was causing "trouble and ill feelings" in the ranks of the foreign-born. In a letter to the national headquarters of the American Red Cross in August 1918, a soldier assigned to the 153rd Depot Brigade at Camp Dix, New Jersey, complained that the unit's leaders "talk to us like dogs" and that the leaders cursed the soldiers out when they complained about the poor food and treatment they had received. The practice of using ethnic slurs was slightly curbed after the General Staff ultimately issued directives prohibiting the use of ethnic slurs in the army, but the army as a whole did little to stop the practice.[7]

In some cases the discrimination against immigrant doughboys did not end with verbal abuse. A few officers at Camp Devens resorted to using "personal violence" to get their foreign-born troops "to perform promptly commands which they do not understand." Ethnic soldiers complained that their NCOs "continually humiliated us, put us to work at hard labor and often assaulted and kicked us." They further maintained that "the hardest and dirtiest work was performed by details of us non-English-speaking soldiers. We are a laboring party, instead of soldiers."[8]

As was clear from the previous passages, the attitudes and actions of a unit's leadership set the tone for how well the immigrant soldiers responded to army life and military service. The use of ethnic slurs and violence broke down the trust between the leader and the led and the close bonds of small-group cohesion needed in combat. Where the leaders sympathized with the plight of their immigrant doughboys and treated them with equality and respect, their units benefited. "I felt like hugging and kissing the captain," an Italian-American soldier exclaimed after the officer informed the company "that we Italians were just as good as men as they were, and that we should be regarded as brothers."[9]

Many ethnic doughboys viewed their service as a means of demonstrating loyalty to their adopted country and proving that they were as good Americans as anyone and as worthy of equal treatment as the native born. Like the Irish and German immigrants of the Civil War era, the Italian, Jewish, eastern European, and other "new immigrant" soldiers of the Great War period understood that the uniform was a potent rebuff to those natives who questioned their claim to citizenship and place within the heart of the nation.

Morry Morrison was a case in point. Like with many Russian Jewish immigrants, Czarist pogroms had instilled an antimilitary bias in Morrison's family. The fact that his father had been killed during the Russo-Japanese War made his mother even more leery of his desire to enter the service. Morrison argued with her that "this country was different from Russia; it was worth fighting for" and that he needed to serve to cement his status as an American. At times Jewish and other ethnic soldiers had to physically fight to assert their rights and equality with their more odious comrades. A Jewish soldier from the 77th Division beat up "an embittered anti-Semite" who constantly called into question the bravery and loyalty of his coreligionists. By such actions the immigrants gave the lie to the stereotypes that Jews and Italians were an unmilitary and timid lot of fruit sellers and pasty-faced tailors.[10]

The meeting and mixing of differing ethnic groups together in the ranks and the willingness of the ethnic doughboys to fight against the Germans and if necessary their fellow comrades did break down some of the nation's social barriers. Charles Minder, a 77th Division soldier of old Anglo-Saxon stock, found the organization's cosmopolitan mélange of people refreshing. In a letter home in June 1918, he reported that the "Jewish fellow" in his platoon was "a nice chap," and maintained,

> We have about every nationality you can think of in my company. There sure is some mixture, and I think it about the finest thing in the world for anyone, who like myself, has always suffered from race prejudice, to be mixed up in an outfit like this. The last six months of my life in the army, living and suffering with these fellows, has done more for me to get rid of race-prejudice than anything else could have done.

While a number of other doughboys expressed similar sentiments, it would be wrong to state that the war ushered in a major change in white, native-born attitudes. The Red Scare of 1919–1923 would expose the depth of the country's nativism and xenophobia. Furthermore, it should not be forgotten that scores of returning veterans joined the "new" Ku Klux Klan and embraced its anti–African American, anti-Semite, anti-Catholic, and anti-immigrant agendas.[11]

Immigrants were not the only doughboys who had to fight for equal treatment and their place in American society due to their race or ethnicity. These challenges were also faced by many Native Americans, Latinos, and African Americans. The historians Thomas A. Britten and Susan Krouse have written extensively on how the Great War affected the lives of Native Americans. To Britten, the war was a watershed event in Indian history, for it "fostered a dual pride among Native Americans: pride of Indian heritage and race, and pride of being American." Being essentially special "wards of the state," Native Americans were not subject to being drafted unless they had accepted U.S. citizenship by virtue of having taken fee patents and individual ownership of tribal lands under the provisions of the Dawes Severalty Act of 1887, met citizen competency requirements under the Burke Act of 1906, or had adopted "civilized life" by fully integrating into white society. The Selective Service Act still required all Native American males meeting its general requirements for service to register for the draft. When coupled with the legalistic and contorted definitions of citizenship, this obligation sometimes led to the conscription of Native Americans even though they were not officially required to serve. Despite their exemptions, approximately ten thousand to thirteen thousand Native Americans served in the U.S. military during the war; the majority of them were volunteers. This meant that Indians actually volunteered at a rate disproportionately higher than other American groups.[12]

The Native American doughboys were well aware that they were fighting for a country that had devastated their people and continued to deny them their civil and economic rights. As Sam Thundercloud informed a white interviewer shortly after the war, "I am fighting for the rights of a country that has not done right by my people." Some, however, hoped that their service would change white attitudes and lead to a redress of the Native Americans' complaints. One Oneida soldier believed that he had fought "to give liberty to all people, especially my people." Others shared the desire of other ethnic and racial groups to be accepted as equals by native-born whites. One Native American confessed that he fought because "I felt that no American could be or should be better than the first American." A member of the Kaw tribe, James Wynashe proclaimed, "I thought I ought to be as good as the white boy and have as much right to serve my country." To some extent, their service did lead to a greater expansion of Native American rights after the war. In November 1919, the Congress allowed all Indian veterans to petition for full citizenship, and less than five years later, the Indian Citizenship Act of 1924 removed most of the remaining obstacles to full Native American legal rights as citizens. Full equality was still decades away, but the Great War had certainly cracked the door open for full civil rights.[13]

Some Native Americans were drawn to the military due to the respect that warriors held within their tribes. After being raised on stories and traditions of being a warrior, these Indian doughboys saw the war as a way to emulate the deeds of their forefathers and win esteem and leadership within their societies. While recovering from wounds, the Sioux soldier James Hawk proclaimed proudly, "I wanted to see the old thing through. My grandfather was a chief and was in the Custer battle and the battle of Wounded Knee, but I wanted to be in any battle that would wound the Germans."[14]

This reverence for the warrior had also influenced white views on the fighting qualities of the Native Americans and their place in the army and the larger society. Soon after the United States entered the war, Indian advocates such as Joseph Dixon lobbied the Congress and War Department to raise segregated Indian units. Dixon believed that segregated formations would safeguard native cultures and identities and derail the assimilation policies of the Bureau of Indian Affairs (BIA) while also offering the army whole units of "natural warriors." Citing military necessity and the burdens of keeping such units up to strength, Secretary of War Newton Baker rejected Dixon's argument and decreed that Native Americans would be integrated into white units.[15]

This decision was a double-edged sword for the Indian doughboys. White officers frequently believed Dixon's argument that the Indian soldiers possessed innate tracking, scouting, sniping, navigation, and raiding skills that were lacking in their overcivilized white recruits. The Native American soldiers themselves did little to counter these stereotypes and often enjoyed the status that they brought. Because of these views, Native Americans were often selected to serve as unit messengers, reconnaissance scouts, and snipers. Unfortunately, these jobs also tended to be rather dangerous, and the soldiers doing them often paid dearly to live up to the cultural expectations of their tribes and their white officers and NCOs. However, the Native Americans' willingness to take on these difficult duties, their performance in combat, and the losses that they suffered won the respect of their white comrades and did much to change how Indians were viewed by American society as a whole.[16]

Latino soldiers also faced challenges during the Great War. In addition to facing decades of racial and economic discrimination in Texas and other areas of the Southwest, a string of events in the years prior to the U.S. entry into the war left many Anglos with suspicions about the loyalty of Mexican Americans and Mexican migrants. The Mexican Revolution stoked fears that violence, banditry, and anti-Anglo sentiment would spill north of the all-too-porous border. These fears were borne out in scattered bloodshed along the national boundaries and by Poncho Villa's raid on Columbus, New Mexico, in March 1916. Anger over American meddling in Mexican affairs and constant bigotry against Latinos in Texas led a handful of Tejanos (Texans of Mexican decent) to take matters into their own hands. In January 1915, officials in Duval and Hidalgo County, Texas, uncovered what came to be known as the Plan of San Diego: a reputed plot by disgruntled Latinos to launch a guerrilla war against the Anglos to deprive the Yankees of their ill-gotten gains from the Mexican-American War. The insurgents raided remote ranches, destroyed some property, and killed or wounded approximately sixty whites in Texas. The hysteria created by these limited attacks sparked an orgy of extrajudicial killings in the state that, by conservative estimates, claimed the lives of between one hundred to three hundred Mexicans and Mexican Americans.

White fears and distrust of Hispanics were also fueled by the so-called Zimmerman Telegram, which offered Mexico and Japan vast swaths of U.S. territory if they would declare war on the United States.[17]

Against this backdrop of discrimination and mutual distrust and resentment, the Latino doughboys sought to carve a place for themselves within the army. First they had to contend with the white stereotype that, on the one hand, viewed Latinos as cowardly, lazy, and servile and, on the other, as cruel and bloodthirsty. Although enlistment and conscription patterns led to the grouping of Mexican Americans in units of the 36th, 40th, and 90th Divisions, as with the Native Americans, they were not segregated within the army. This permitted the free intermingling of whites and Hispanics in a more or less equal setting for the first time. To some extent close interactions between soldiers broke down bigotry and stereotypes. For example, Joe Garza reported, "I shared a tent with three Anglos and they treated me like anyone else. Growing up the way I did, I can't describe what this meant to me." As was the case with European immigrants, to further their assimilation into the ranks, the army placed non-English-speaking Latinos into special language classes. The historian José A. Ramírez has pointed out that being in the military "served to break the shell of provincialism" of the Tejanos, and "even the most naïve and uneducated among them had experienced enough to realize that there was much more to life than what went on in the barrios and ranches of their home state."[18]

As with both the immigrant and the Native American soldiers, the Latinos also sought to parlay their service into demands for greater rights and respect from the dominant society. Unfortunately, it seems that Mexican Americans were less successful in overcoming entrenched racism and discrimination than these other groups. The experience of José de la Luz Sáenz was a case in point. He often felt anger over the "egotistical behavior and racial prejudice" of the Anglo soldiers that surrounded him and was once dismissed by an Anglo officer with the cutting remark, "You can't get a thing out of this kind of greaser." In May 1918 he mused,

> It is obvious that the two races, the Anglo Saxon and the Mexican American, misunderstand each other so much. Our military includes soldiers from the north and west that only know our *raza* by what they see in films and hear from journalists who have never seen us or had anything to do with us. Worse still, Texans are especially prejudiced toward us. They do

not know our worth or they chose to overlook our contributions to the United States. They actually deny them.

In April 1918, when the 90th Division sent out directives encouraging its enlisted men to apply for officer training, Sáenz ruefully noted, "The general understanding is that this is not for Mexican soldiers." In the end, he still applied, though presciently believing that his application would "not get anywhere." The absence of other Latino accounts makes it difficult to tell if Sáenz's experiences were typical, but research conducted by José A. Ramírez does reinforce the doughboy's observations.[19]

The plight of the African American soldiers of the Great War has been studied to a greater degree than any of the other ethnic and racial groups discussed in this chapter. The recent works by Chad Williams, Richard Slotkin, John Morrow, and Jeffrey T. Sammons have painted detailed and sensitive portraits of the challenges that black doughboys faced while defending a nation and serving in an army that embraced Jim Crow segregation and the racist assumptions that it rested upon. Those interested in gaining an appreciation of the African American experience in the Great War would also be well served in starting with the classic work *The Unknown Soldiers: Black American Troops in World War I*, by Arthur F. Barbeau and Florette Henri. In all honesty and humility, there is little more that this author can add to these studies in this book. As this work does focus on the life of the common soldier, what follows is an examination of how his race made the black doughboy's experiences differ from those of the average white soldier.

Any discussion of the African American soldier's experience must start with the fact that most white Americans at the time believed that he was inherently inferior to not only native-born whites but also to white immigrants and Native and Mexican Americans. Furthermore the social and economic segregation and subjugation of African Americans were the law of the land in the South and parts of the Midwest and an unofficial reality throughout much of the rest of the country. The desire of whites to keep blacks "in the proper place" had resulted in the lynching of at least 2,833 African Americans between 1882 and 1916. The entrenched bigotry in American society touched nearly every aspect of the black soldier's life. The depth of the nation's racism can be seen in the comments of José de la Luz Sáenz. Although he frequently complained of Anglo prejudice against Mexican Americans, even he was not without the racial prejudice that he often denounced. While on a pass to Paris he complained, "We saw something in a large public area that we did not like. Some Parisian beauties were taking a stroll with two black men," and decried, "Parisian women [who] feel they should associate with black men."[20]

African American society itself was in a state of flux due to economic changes brought by the Great War. Prior to 1914, the majority of blacks lived in the South and the "race question" was generally seen as a sectional issue by nonsouthern whites. By 1917, the wartime boom in industrial production had drawn large numbers of African Americans to the north and west. This increased racial tensions in those areas and was often accompanied by the virulent racism that had heretofore been a southern phenomena. Clashes between white and black workers, police brutality, and endemic racism sparked a violent confrontation in East St. Louis, Illinois, on July 2, 1917, that left as many as 125 African American residents dead.

The decade prior to the U.S. entry into the war had also seen a renewed sense of black empowerment as leaders such as W. E. B. Dubois and Asa Philips Randolph fought against lynching, injustice, and racism. However, any effort by African Americans to rise against their persecutors and the Jim Crow system was all too often met by the full legal and physical force that white local, state, and even federal officials could muster. This was certainly the case in Houston, Texas, in 1917. The beating and jailing of a soldier of the African American 24th Infantry and the constant harassment of the unit's members by the local whites so enraged the troops that on August 23, 1917, they left camp to seek revenge on their tormentors. The violence that followed killed four soldiers, four white policemen, and twelve white civilians. As a result, nineteen African American soldiers were hung without benefit of judicial review and another forty-one were given life sentences for mutiny and assault. The incident was used by the Wilson administration as an excuse to keep the four Regular Army African American regiments from seeing combat in World War I.[21]

Against this setting it is not surprising that the African American community was divided over what support it should give the nation's war effort. In May 1917 W. E. B. DuBois enjoined African Americans to fight, writing, "War: It is an awful thing! It is Hell. It is the end of civilization. Bad as it is, slavery is worse, German domination is worse, the rape of Belgium and France is worse. We fight shoulder to shoulder with the world to gain a world where war shall be no more." By supporting the government, DuBois hoped to demonstrate African American abilities and erode the racial strictures of Jim Crow America. At the Washington Conference of Negro Organizations, he and other black leaders demanded that the United States halt lynching, expand the franchise, abolish Jim Crow train cars, repeal segregation ordinances, and provide "equal rights in all public institutions and movements" but refrained from making the government's acceptance of the demands a prerequisite for African American support for the war effort. In July 1918 he pleaded with aggrieved African Americans, "Let us, while this war lasts, forget our special grievances and close our ranks shoulder to shoulder with our own white fellow citizens and the allied nations that are fighting for democracy." DuBois's desire to "close ranks" was not the only opinion on the matter. Asa Philip Randolph and the writers of the radical black labor monthly *The Messenger* still questioned the relevance of the war to the average African American. Launching a scathing assault on the NAACP's leadership for their support of the war, *The Messenger* thundered, "Let Du Bois, Kelly Miller, Pickens, Grimke, etc., volunteer to go to France, if they are so eager to fight to make the world safe for democracy. We would rather make Georgia safe for the Negro."[22]

Despite the call from Randolph for African Americans to withhold their support for the war until their political and social demands were met, the majority of black doughboys more or less willingly served the very nation that deprived them of their full rights as a citizen. Some of these men were motivated by a desire to give the lie to the white stereotypes about black innate inferiority and cowardice. This was coupled with a belief that their service would lead to a greater equality in the United States. Service outside the South and in France broke down the parochialism of black recruits and allowed them to see that other areas of the world were not bound by Jim Crow or as inclined to view them as inferior beings. Some soldiers became radicalized by their experience and were determined to challenge the status quo upon their return from the war. As one bitter black infantryman warned his Tennessee draft board from France, "Just wait till Uncle Sam puts a gun in the niggers hands and you will be sorry for it." Most did not go to this extreme but still found their time in uniform to be a transformational event in their lives.[23]

No matter how willingly or reluctantly the African Americans served, the army that they joined generally reflected the values and assumptions of the Jim Crow South. There was a common desire within the Wilson administration and the War Department to do nothing that would offend white sensibilities and to not take actions that would raise the embarrassing "color question" of equal rights and social equality. As the historian Chad Williams argues, throughout the war the army demonstrated "a constant willingness to put the racial status quo ahead of sound military logic." This was seen in the organization, officering, and morale-sapping strictures placed upon African American units and their soldiers. Unlike Native and Latino American soldiers, blacks would serve only in segregated units during the war. This allowed army officials to prevent situations that were anathema to many whites: having black officers and NCOs serving over white soldiers and having blacks and whites sharing living, messing, and bathing facilities.[24]

The military's approach to African Americans did not stop with segregation. White commanders also took steps to further ensure that the life of their black soldiers was decidedly separate and unequal. Although Secretary of War Newton Baker appointed the African American reformer Emmett J. Scott to serve as his special assistant to the secretary of war for issues related to black soldiers, most issues that Scott raised during the war received no redress. This was glaringly apparent in the general refusal of white post commanders to prevent discrimination against their men by members of the local community. In one such case, doughboys stationed at Camp Jackson, South Carolina, complained to Scott of their harassment when trying to use the street cars in Columbia and of the fact that they were often hassled by military and civil police while they were on pass in the town, especially when in the company of "decent negro women." In another case, violence and insults against troops of the 369th Infantry by police and residents of Spartanburg, South Carolina, grew so great, and the response by the post leadership to the provocations was so weak, that the regimental commander asked that the unit be moved to New York to complete its training.[25]

When perceived violations of the "color line" by African American soldiers angered the white population in the towns surrounding Camp Funston, Kansas, the commander of the 92nd Division, Major General Charles Ballou, went so far as to blame his troops for the trouble. In one of the most blatant official wartime acts upholding Jim Crow, on March 28, 1918, Ballou issued Bulletin 35, which warned,

It should be well known to all colored officers and men that no useful purpose is served by such acts as will cause the "Color Question" to be raised. It is not a question of legal rights, but a question of policy, and any policy that tends to bring about conflict of races, with its resulting animosities, is prejudicial to the military interests of the 92nd Division, and therefore prejudicial to an important interest of the colored race. To avoid conflicts the Division Commander has repeatedly urged that all colored members of his command, and especially the officers and non-commissioned officers should refrain from going where their presence will be resented. In spite of this injunction, one of the sergeants of the Medical Department has recently precipitated the precise trouble that should be avoided, and then called on the Division Commander to take sides in a row that should never have occurred, and would not have occurred had the sergeant placed the general good above his personal pleasure and convenience. This sergeant entered a theater, as he undoubtedly had the legal right to do, and precipitated trouble by making it possible to allege race discrimination in the seat he was given. He is entirely within his legal rights in the matter, and the theater manager is legally wrong. Nevertheless the sergeant is guilty of the greater wrong in doing anything, no matter how legally correct, that will provoke race animosity. The Division Commander repeats that the success of the Division with all that that success implies, is dependent on the good will of the public. That public is nine-tenths white. White men made the Division, and can break it just as easily as it becomes a trouble maker.

The message to African American soldiers by these actions was clear: the wearing of Uncle Sam's uniform in no way changed their status as second-class citizens outside the gates of the post.[26]

Black doughboys were also subjected to discrimination and harsh treatment inside the army's posts and units. The quality of food, clothing, and shelter given to African American troops, especially in stevedore and labor battalions, was frequently inferior to those of white soldiers. Conditions at Camp Gordon grew so bad that some troops wrote directly to the secretary of war in October 1918 to complain about their plight. The men protested that they never received enough food, that they were worked seven days a week without any hope of receiving passes to nearby Atlanta, that they were forced to labor when sick, and that they were still housed in "tents [with] no flooring in winter clothing just thin blankets no wood to burn." Similar complaints were filed by soldiers at Camp Grant and from the posts around Newport

News. As they were frequently barred from using white-staffed YMCA, Salvation Army, and other social aid society facilities, African Americans in the United States and France generally lacked the degree and range of recreation and entertainment of their white comrades. While some of these facilities were staffed by African American secretaries for the exclusive use of black troops, they were few in number and often given poor facilities. The African American YMCA workers Addie Hunton and Kathryn Johnston noted that they fought an uphill battle throughout their time in France for the proper treatment of the black troops that they served. African American soldiers were also prevented from enjoying the educational opportunities offered to troops from other races. For example, at Camp Sevier, South Carolina, 80 percent of the illiterate white soldiers were sent to school to learn reading and writing, but only 27 percent of the post's illiterate black doughboys were afforded the same schooling.[27]

Much of the discrimination against black doughboys stemmed from the assumptions and attitudes of their white officers. Far too many in the War Department subscribed to the idea that white southerners made the perfect officers for segregated units because their prewar interactions with blacks had given them an innate understanding of what it took to lead African Americans. Unfortunately, these men often viewed leadership as driving or "bossing Negroes," and they were not at all likely to question the Jim Crow strictures of their upbringing. One such officer, the white commander of the 371st Infantry, was described by the African American journalist Monroe Mason as "a southern gentleman with the well-known proclivities of the 'South-in-the-Saddle' in his veins." Not surprisingly, the black troops resented this treatment and worked to make their objections known and their conditions ameliorated. In a complaint that ultimately reached Emmett J. Scott, a soldier at Camp Grant, Illinois, reported,

> They treat us as though we are dogs. We are cursed and dogged around just as though we are not human at all. Every time we are given a command from one of the Cracker officers he has to curse us out. They take us out in the morning after mess, keep us standing in ranks in rain and snow and any kind of bad weather and won't allow us to wear our overcoats. They walk around in the mess hall with a six shooter hanging on his hips and tell you what he will do with it.

This officer was not alone in threatening violence against black soldiers. John Castles, a white officer in the African American 369th Infantry, recalled that as his unit was waiting at Camp Merritt to sail for France in November 1917, he and Hamilton Fish narrowly averted a race riot after an officer from a stevedore regiment drew a pistol on one of their soldiers and called him a "son of a ____ of a nigger" for failing to get out of the white officer's way.[28]

Other white officers were more sympathetic to the physical, social, and psychological needs of their black soldiers. Colonel James Moss, commander of the 367th Infantry, was a case in point. His command philosophy was to "make the colored man feel that you have faith in him, and then, by sympathetic and conscientious training and instruction, help him fit himself in a military way to vindicate that faith, to 'make good.' Be strict with him, but treat him fairly and justly, making him realize that in your dealings with him he will always be given a square deal." A white battalion commander further maintained that "the general attitude of white officers over negro troops is one of desire to educate and help the negro—an attitude almost of pity for his ignorance and hopelessness." The 87th Division morale officer reported that the African American doughboy at Camp Pike, Arkansas, was a "very much satisfied soldier, in so much as he is paid more, clothed better and rationed better than ever before in his life." He went on to note, "The negro is a happy-go-lucky individual, and while at work habitually sings his time worn southern songs, all of which adds to the entertainment of those who happen by." Likewise a white lieutenant wrote home in August 1918 that his five hundred new black recruits were "eager to learn" and took "great pride in being soldiers." This did not stop him from describing them as "a happy bunch of 'children'" who liked nothing more but to "sing and dance." Although these approaches and attitudes were certainly better than threatening troops with pistols, they still betrayed a patronizing and paternalistic kind of racism that assumed that their soldiers were childlike and incapable of action without a guiding white hand. For all of their racist assumptions, the white commanders such as Moss and the commander of the 369th Infantry, William Haywood, still wanted their units to do well and advocated for the welfare, honor, and equal treatment of their men within the overall army.[29]

When white commanders lacked this degree of empathy for their soldiers, the results were predictable. The fate of the 92nd Division was a case in point.

It was the only fully formed African American division of the war and while most of its junior officers were black, nearly all of its field-grade officers were white. The unit's white officers frequently had little faith in the fighting abilities of their men and believed that they could only be led by draconian discipline. The commander of the 2nd U.S. Army, Major General Robert Bullard, a man with his own deep prejudices, admitted that "not one of them believed that the 92nd Division would ever be worth anything as soldiers" and that many of these officers "would have given anything to be transferred to any other duty." The actions of one such man, First Lieutenant Julius Rogovin, were so harsh toward his troops that he was relieved of his command for his "natural dislike for colored troops." He argued that some of his unit's northern officers disagreed with his methods but remained adamant that "after years of intermittent observations in various parts of [the] south" that one had to "rule a negro with a firm hand." Although Rogovin was an extreme case, his underlying disdain for African Americans still seems to have been common in the ranks of the division's white officers. A southern officer in the 92nd Division held such a low opinion of his African American soldiers that he joked with a fellow Virginian, "The thing that I was most afraid of that some of those Germans across No Man's Land would hop up with white sheets on [like the Ku Klux Klan], and start for us. I'd have been trampled to death." After considering the officer's remark, the other officer later mused,

> The negro-race will always be hampered by many restrictions put upon it by the whites, and should never be required to make the supreme sacrifice in the white man's wars. They make good laborers. Let them labor, back of the lines. There are railroads to be built, camps to be drained, highways to be repaired, more than enough work for all. I take this stand in the cause of justice for the negro race. You may say, "But look how negroes fought in the Spanish-American War!" Certainly, that one regiment did. It was the pick of a race numbering in the millions. The draft system got the average of the race.

He argued, "Do not ask them to fight your battles unless you are prepared to give them true equality," but since that was not going to happen, it was best for all parties simply to keep them out of combat.[30]

With the attitudes of officers such as these, it is not surprising that the 92nd Division's combat performance was somewhat lackluster. Robert Ferrell maintains that much of the division's poor reputation stemmed from a single incident in the Argonne where the 368th Infantry broke in battle. As the unit's field artillery and engineer units fought well and the other infantry regiments saw only limited fighting, the division's stigma was ill deserved. Ferrell lays the blame for the collapse of the 368th Infantry squarely at the feet of the unit's white officers. Their lack of skill and faith in their men created a command climate that poisoned the trust and cohesion that units need to face the shocks of combat. Given the attitudes of officers such as Rogovin and the white Virginian, it was little wonder that African American soldiers were unwilling to follow these men or give their all in battle. Unfortunately, the perceived failure of the 92nd Division was used as an excuse by senior white officers to limit the use of black soldiers in combat for the following thirty years.[31]

The African American officers also felt the sting of institutional and societal racism during the war. Under pressure from the National Association for the Advancement of Colored People and other influential African American interest groups, the War Department reluctantly agreed to hold a special Officer Training Camp for black candidates at Camp Des Moines, Iowa, in August 1917. The camp opened with 1,250 candidates; of these, 250 were NCOs or select enlisted men from the Regular Army's 9th and 10th Cavalry and 24th and 25th Infantry, with the remainder being men from what W. E. B. DuBois termed the "talented tenth." This presented an interesting mix of candidates at the course. The black Regulars brought with them a wealth of hands-on experience at soldiering while the other candidates tended to be educated but quite green in military matters. The differences between the two groups created some tension, especially when the undereducated Regulars dominated the handful of commissions to captain and major. The camp ultimately commissioned 639 black officers in October 1917.[32]

Although the army bent to public pressure to allow black officers, this did not change the institution's belief that these men were unsuited for combat leadership. At the outbreak of the war the Regular Army contained only one African American officer, Colonel Charles Young, and even he was quickly shuffled off into retirement in 1917. Throughout the war, white commanders consistently sought ways to remove African American officers from their units so their places could be filled by whites. The 370th Infantry was a case in point. The unit was formed from the 8th Infantry Regiment of the Illinois National Guard and was the only organization whose officers were all African Americans at the start of the war. The unit's chaplain, William Bradden, maintained that the white Regular Army officers sought to purge black officers from the unit's ranks from the moment it was federalized. This effort gained steam when Colonel T. A. Roberts took temporary command of the regiment in July 1918. According to Bradden, Roberts was an "arch enemy, vilifier and traducer of the Negro soldier" and used any possible excuse to relieve black officers of their positions. Racism also seems to have played a part of the removal of Lieutenant Rayford Logan and other officers from the 372nd Infantry. Logan was one of DuBois's "talented tenth" and left college when the war began to seek a commission. Although his white commander stated that Logan was relieved of command for being a disloyal "disturber" in the unit, the young lieutenant countered that the real reason that he was cashiered was because the colonel did not like black officers and wanted them gone from the regiment.[33]

The AEF established an Officer Reclassification Center at Blois, France, in March 1918 to determine the fates of officers who had failed in their duties or to live up to their commander's expectations. The records of the Blois center suggest that African American infantry officers were removed from their units at a greater rate than was the case in white regiments. In the 92nd Division, the commanders of both the 367th and 368th Infantry shed at least 10 percent of their African American officers by sending them to Blois. The 351st Machine Gun Battalion's commander cashiered 20 percent of his black officers. Two of the regiments of the abortive 93rd Division removed their black officers with equal abandon. In Bradden's 370th Infantry, thirteen officers were packed off to Blois, while the 372nd Infantry sent ten. In the case of the 370th Infantry, this accounted for 14 percent of its black officers. Rather than go to the administrative trouble of sending their officers before the reclassification board, some white commanders simply reassigned blacks to staff duties.[34]

African American officers also faced hostility from white enlisted men and officers who refused to recognize their status or even give them the respect due to their rank. A white doughboy wrote to his family in October 1917, "If they bring the negroes here we will have to salute them just the same as the white officers. There is going to be a lot of trouble in camp over this one thing, as many of the boys say they won't salute them." After incidents of disrespect to African American officers by white enlisted men and sporadic fighting between black and white units waiting to sail overseas, Major General J. Franklin Bell promised black doughboys and officers at Camp Upton that they would receive equal treatment and a redress of their complaints. This did not sit well with the post's white southerners. A Georgian thundered,

> There are many negro officers here. They are causing some stir among our Southern enlisted men. Some of the negroes insist on being saluted. They took one colored captain to the hospital this afternoon. He stopped one of our Alabama corporals and demanded a salute. He got it—right smack in the eye . . . General Bell says we can't go overseas if there is any more trouble. Foolish old man. You cannot change a Southerner! We will NOT salute your negroes! War or no war, army discipline or else, it just cannot be done. Better get these colored shavetails away from this place, General, if you want peace.

Despite Bell's rare effort to buck the conventions of Jim Crow, he could not change the attitudes of the large number of other whites who viewed any deference to a black man as going against the natural order of things.[35]

Lieutenant Charles Tibbett discovered that holding a commission and wearing the nation's uniform provided no shield from the Jim Crow attitudes of white civilians. In March 1918, he was pulled from a train and arrested in Chickasha, Oklahoma, for being in a white-only Pullman car. After being jailed for an hour and having his possessions searched by the sheriff for contraband, he was released on a cash bond of $50 and allowed to spend the night in a local African American Red Cross station. The next morning the Yale graduate plead guilty to violating the state's separate coach law, paid a total fine of $24, and was packed off to Fort Sill. The irony of the incident was that all officers, white and black, took an oath to uphold and defend the Constitution. For Tibbett and his comrades, in large swaths of the nation and the army, those Constitutional protections that they were upholding did not apply to them.[36]

Lastly, any discussion of African American soldiers in the Great War must devote special attention to the lives of those soldiers serving in stevedore, labor, and pioneer infantry units.

Approximately 46 percent of the 370,000 African Americans who served in the war never left the United States. The majority of these men were assigned units that performed only hard manual labor. Of the two hundred thousand black men who deployed to France, 80 percent worked in the Service of Supply (SOS) in labor battalions, stevedore units, or pioneer infantry regiments. Although historians have been drawn to the exploits and tribulations of the war's African American combat units, too often this focus ignores the experiences of the majority of black doughboys. It is important to discuss the lives of these noncombat troops because both in the United States and in France they were the most ill-used and mistreated American soldiers of the war.[37]

The fact that so many African Americans were used in hard labor goes back to the racial assumptions of the day and the desire of the Wilson administration to placate white southern fears. The archracist Senator James K. Vardaman and other influential southern politicians were leery of giving large numbers of blacks military training for fear of what such men would do with their newfound skills upon their return home. When these reservations were coupled with the belief that African Americans lacked the courage, motivation, and mentality for combat, setting black soldiers to work at hard labor seemed a rational and politically expeditious solution to the "race question." This policy also ensured that men put to such tasks received almost none of the military training given to white soldiers or those serving in the 92nd and 93rd Divisions. The War Department willingly went along with this solution because using black men in such jobs freed up more whites to serve in combat units. White southerners had fewer objections to seeing African Americans doing menial labor in local army camps and ports because the black doughboys were simply playing the same roles in the military that they had filled in their civilian lives. The morale officer of the Newport News Port of Embarkation fully admitted, "The men have received so little drill and discipline that in only the most technical sense can they be called 'soldiers.' In reality they are simply low grade laborers in uniform, living under quasi-military conditions." To further the illusion that these men were merely "low grade laborers" rather than true soldiers, some African Americans in stevedore and labor units were only issued the army's blue denim fatigue uniform. Their lowly status was also reflected in their living conditions. Stevedores in Camp Hill, Virginia, lived in unheated and unfloored tents during the harsh winter of 1917 and 1918. To make matters worse, most had only one blanket, were often served cold food, and went for four months without any bathing facilities or change of clothing.[38]

Its own policies of sanctioning Jim Crow segregation frequently created self-inflicted personnel policy headaches within the War Department. On the one hand, the commanders wanted white NCOs placed in labor battalions to better "boss" the black soldiers; on the other hand, the army's distaste for having African American officers in combat units meant that it also pushed to use black officers to serve in labor battalions. This created the horror of horrors for ardent segregationists: the possibility that white men would have to work under black men. The outcry forced the War Department to decree that units could not have a mix of races in their NCO corps and that units with black officers could not contain white NCOs. Although black officers serving in labor battalions treated their men with greater sympathy and consideration than most white officers did, their numbers were too small to make a wholesale change to how the African American doughboys were treated in the army.[39]

As with most things in the American Army at the time, the treatment and quality of life that African Americans serving in labor and stevedore battalions received largely depended on the attitudes and proclivity of their officers and NCOs. A morale officer noted, "The *average* officer assigned to such low grade troops is not such as to inspire them or to improve their mental condition." These units tended to be led by southerners or officers who were ejected from other units because they were unfit for overseas service. Charles H. Williams, an African American member of the Army Education Commission, investigated the treatment of black soldiers in early 1919. He reported that these officers tended see themselves "more as foreman and overseers over railroad gangs and plantation" workers than as leaders of true soldiers. Such officers believed that the men in their charge were inherently shiftless and sullen and could only be compelled to work by threats and coercion. A soldier at Camp Humphries, Virginia, reported to Emmett Scott that a white officer in the 551st Service Battalion was heard to direct one of his sergeants to "keep the 'Niggers' afraid of him" and that "its no harm to kill a 'Nigger' or two every once and a while." Shortly thereafter one of the sergeants in the unit shot a black soldier in the leg to get the man "to move along faster and because he did not move off at once." Such attitudes were far from rare and an African American educator observed that in the labor battalions "abusive language, kicks, cuffs and injurious blows were the order of the day in dealing with Negroes impressed into this branch of the service."[40]

Despite having the deck stacked against them, the soldiers in the stevedore and labor battalions did not take this abuse without complaint. As with the doughboy at Camp Humphries, several other men in the posts around New-port News also complained to Emmett Scott and other African American leaders about the abuses they endured. Due to these accusations, the post morale officer was forced to investigate their claims and the general conditions of African American soldiers within the port. Unfortunately, he sided with the white officers and dismissed the complaints as the mere carping of "the culls of the negro draft," whom he dismissed as a pack of syphilitics who lacked the mentality and fitness to serve in labor units overseas. To him, the complainers were those from "a certain class of negroes" who would do anything to get out of work. Ill-housed, ill-clothed, ill-treated, and ill-led, the soldiers who filled these vital yet thankless jobs had unenviable lives. After viewing the poor living and working conditions of the black stevedores at Newport News, Chaplain William Bradden, remarked, "Truly, I would rather be a dog than such a soldier." To him the workers were "the most dejected looking men I ever saw in uniform."[41]

The lives of African American soldiers serving in labor, stevedore, and pioneer infantry units in France were little better than the lives of those serving in similar units in the States. Racism and discrimination did not end at the shores of France. The way that white soldiers and officers continued to view and use black doughboys was still colored by stereotypical assumptions. "They ran a bunch of niggers on us—service battalion men—to work with us," a white engineer soldier from Pennsylvania informed his mother in March 1918. "Well, we can use them. There is a lot of nigger work to be done over here." Lieutenant Edwin Arpin, a Wisconsinite in the 128th Infantry, also showed the depth of racial prejudice that many white doughboys took with them into the service. When his unit was assigned to duty in Bordeaux, his commander offered to aid the local American authorities in dealing with the area's perceived problems with its two regiments of African American stevedores. Arpin's description of how his unit proceeded with the task is worth quoting at length:

> The men were recruited from the waterfronts of New Orleans, Galveston, and other Southern Gulf ports, and needless to say, among them were a large number of the toughest niggers in the U.S. Frequent murders had been occurring on the waterfront, and holdups, hijacking, and things of that sort were quite common at night . . . At the time we took over the area, the suppression of crime seemed to be well-nigh impossible due to the fact that it was almost beyond control. Our first constructive act was to "frisk"

these two regiments of negroes, which took place in a surprise move upon their arrival at the docks in the morning. The result of this operation was about two or three truckloads of razors and knives . . . this move helped somewhat in curbing the unhealthy situation. Nevertheless, each night brought forth a fresh crop of complaints and usually quite a few new prisoners. The American officer in command of the docks co-operated with us wholeheartedly in cleaning up the conditions. It was he who evolved the idea that finally turned the trick. This consisted in the erection of a new "bull-pen" for prisoners, which was paved with fresh-cracked limestone rock in the part where the men slept. In addition to this bed of thorns, the prisoners were further subjected to an ice-cold shower bath at daybreak each morning. There is nothing that a negro hates more than a bath, especially an ice-cold bath. In a short time the news of this treatment spread far and wide and the area became inhabited by an awfully well-behaved bunch of colored boys. From then on our troubles were few.

To Arpin the new regimen put the world back in its proper order and soon the chastised ebony troops were "swinging along in perfect time—big husky rascals, grinning wide and singing away with all their might in excellent harmony."[42]

As in the States, such attitudes and approaches were far from rare in the SOS. Addie W. Hunton and Kathryn M. Johnston, who worked in YMCA huts serving black soldiers assigned to the ports, reported that troops in labor and stevedore units in France were "subjected to a stern discipline; with discriminations, cruel in their intent and execution; long hours of toil; scant recognition for service or hope of promotion." After the 369th Infantry was temporally assigned to stevedore duties upon their arrival in France, an MP in the port beat up one of its black soldiers with no provocation. When a white battalion commander in the regiment complained to the MP's officer about the incident, the policeman countered that the "niggers were feeling their oats a bit" and that he had been given instructions to "take it out of them as quickly, just as soon as they arrived, so as not to have any trouble later on." Given such attitudes, it was little wonder that one black officer reported to Charles Williams in 1919, "The spirit of St. Nazaire is the spirit of the South." Others went even further and argued that black soldiers labored under working conditions and discipline similar to slavery.[43]

African American soldiers serving in AEF labor battalions and pioneer infantry regiments also faced discrimination and harsh working conditions.

Photo 14: Herman Spicer (left) and Irvin Lynch, two engineer soldiers in the AEF, proudly pose for a photo to send home from France, 1918. Source: author's collection.

The fourteen black pioneer infantry regiments that served in France often worked under shell fire right behind the front, repairing roads, removing obstacles, and building infrastructure; however, such work was long on the pioneer and short on the infantry. While white pioneer infantry units were intended to serve as fighting combat engineer organizations, similar black units were used as hard labor and given scant combat training. Like their comrades in the ports, these soldiers worked hard for very little glory or recognition. After the Armistice, they were put to work on the sacred yet distasteful task of recovering the American dead from their scattered battlefields and reinterring them in central cemeteries.[44]

So why did the African American doughboy put up with the discriminations that marred his time in the military and what did he get out of his service? Some, like the AEF's immigrant, Native American, and Mexican American soldiers, believed that their service and sacrifice would validate their demands for equality in American society. As Chaplain William Bradden argued, "By reason of this War this Race, of which we are proud members, will occupy a larger and still larger place in the sun." Perhaps most endured for more prosaic reasons. When faced with such a large and powerful institution with great coercive powers, soldiers of all races and ethnicities generally found it more safe and prudent to "keep one's head down" when faced with the myriad injustices and indignities that were part of army life. When faced with entrenched racism, the African Americans of the Great War fought and used their agency whenever possible to redress their treatment, but when channels of redress were limited, they endured the unendurable as best as they could.[45]

The efforts of black soldiers at times did sway the attitudes and opinions of their white comrades. Just a day before the Armistice, a white doughboy in the 28th Division admitted that the black troops that he had seen had "fought with honor" but had not been given their just due. He mused, "The Negro man is doing his bit . . . willingly, sincerely, faithfully, and well. Have our people at home given him credit for his sacrifices? He left his home, family and loved ones to do his bit for his nation . . . My hat goes off to the colored doughboys who responded to the call of arms." While the acceptance and equality that immigrant, African American, Native American, and Latino American soldiers hoped their service in the Great War would bring proved elusive in the decades that followed the conflict, it was from their small steps that the larger societal changes sprang.[46]

The Ninety-Day Wonders and
Sam Brownes
The Officers and NCOs of the AEF

The doughboys called them "Ninety-Day Wonders" and the "Sam Brownes." Depending on one's outlook, these nicknames could be construed as being relatively positive or decidedly negative. The "Ninety-Day Wonder" moniker came from the fact that, after subtracting physicians, chaplains, and those civilians given direct commissions due to their technical skills, 74 percent of the war's officers were products of three-month-long Officer Training Camps (OTCs). The graduates of these camps also made up the vast majority of the officers in combat units at the battalion level and below. As the army's officer corps grew from 5,791 Regular Army and 3,199 National Guard officers to over two hundred thousand officers by the Armistice, the more optimistically inclined could argue that it was a wonder that the nation could pull off such a miraculous expansion. The more pessimistic doughboy could argue that, given the amount and quality of the training that the OTC officers received, it was a wonder that anyone granted them a commission. The soubriquet "Sam Brownes" came from the leather cross belts that Pershing mandated for wear by officers in the AEF. To some doughboys this nickname was a way to highlight the distance in position and privileges that separated them from their leaders: a visual symbol of the haves and the have-nots. As these two epithets imply, the relationship between the AEF's officers, NCOs, and soldiers was complicated. This intricate interaction was governed by a social contract and expectations of behavior that set the conditions for how all of the parties performed in combat.[1]

The doughboys clearly articulated what they expected from their leaders and were seldom reluctant to criticize those who failed to live up to their expectations. As José de la Luz Sáenz argued, "One who believes the private is only an unthinking robot fools himself . . . We know who lives up to his responsibilities and who does not care." He went on to explain, "Some officers are worthy of respect, while others only deserve contempt. The former are brave and gentlemanly, educated and just. The latter are simply foolish and arrogant, egotistical, vain, haughty, and make full use of the position their wealth secured for them."[2]

To doughboys like Sáenz the social contract between the leader and the led was straightforward. In return for their obedience and willingness to risk life and limb in battle, they expected that their leaders would provide food, clothing, shelter, medical care, and just treatment and, most importantly, would not place the soldiers' lives at unnecessary risk. In return, the officers and NCOs anticipated that the doughboys would unquestioningly obey their orders, stay within the bounds of honorable service established by military law and regulations, and, when necessary, sacrifice their individual needs and lives for the greater good of the group and the cause. Unfortunately, the nation's unpreparedness to fight a modern war, its haphazard mobilization, and the crush of events in 1918 meant that this relatively clear-cut set of mutual expectations was difficult to achieve in practice.

One of the army's greatest challenges in the war was recruiting and training enough officers to lead its rapidly mushrooming units. In April 1917 there were simply no plans for how to accomplish such a major expansion of the officer corps. Furthermore, the army's prewar training for junior officers largely consisted of taking college-educated men from West Point and select universities and having them serve an apprenticeship in their first assignments under the tutelage of long-service officers and NCOs. The idea was that with proper mentoring college-educated men would have the intelligence and drive to learn the technical and tactical knowledge required of a junior combat officer. As there were simply too few experienced officers and NCOs to perform this role during a mass mobilization, the army scrambled to create and implement a new model. In the short term the army graduated the West Point class of 1917 early, gave direct commissions to a few NCOs, recalled retired officers to the colors, and federalized National Guard officers.[3]

The army's long-term solution to its demand for officers was to establish the OTCs and later the Central Officers Training Camps (COTCs). Contrary to popular belief, these camps were not modeled on the Citizen Training Camps held at Plattsburg, New York, and other locations in the summers of 1914, 1915, and 1916 but rather on two three-month training courses held at Fort Leavenworth, Kansas, in the fall of 1916 and winter of 1917. On April 17, 1917, the War Department directed the establishment of sixteen OTCs, each of which would be able to train twenty-five hundred candidates. The camps were to be held at posts where the new divisions were being formed, would follow the three-month schedule established by the Fort Leavenworth courses, and would commission enough officers to fill the ranks of the division at the OTC's location. The plan was for the initial OTCs to graduate in August 1917, just in time for the new officers to be on hand in their units to meet the first levy of draftees. When it became clear that the first OTCs would not provide enough officers for the new divisions, the War Department held three additional iterations of OTCs between August 1917 and July 1918 and then replaced those camps with five branch-specific COTCs in the summer of 1918.[4]

Throughout the war the training of officers at the OTCs and COTCs was hindered by equipment shortages, ill-focused and unrealistic instruction, and a shortage of experienced instructors. All too often the officer candidates were trained in obsolete doctrine and tactics that had long been discredited by the realities of the Western Front. The pressing need for experienced officers led the army to reassign most Regular Army instructors from the OTCs in August 1917. Their places were taken by reserve officers who were often recent graduates of the OTCs themselves. This led to a "blind leading the blind" situation that dogged officer training for the remainder of the war. The army's senior leaders understood the shortcomings of the officer camps and admitted that, given the realities of the time, the military had few other options for expanding the officer corps. The former chief of staff General Hugh Scott confessed, "While these camps did not by any means provide a finished military education to fit an officer for war in the short time possible, they were the utmost that could be provided under the circumstances."

He maintained that despite their flaws, the camps weeded out those most unfit to hold a commission and at least gave the rest "an inkling of discipline and the life of a soldier."[5]

The candidates themselves were more honest in their appraisal of their training. F. L. Miller, for example, characterized his training as "three months spent . . . learning wig-wag and semaphore signaling and reenacting Civil War combat problems through the mosquita filled swamps of Arkansas." When surveyed about his military experience while awaiting discharge, a veteran infantry officer bitterly recalled, "Our army had learned no lessons of modern warfare as developed in Europe in the two years the war had been going on. This was again in evidence in the 1st Training Camp for officers . . . much time [was] wasted in learning methods . . . which were useless in Europe." As the army expected its newly commissioned OTC officers to serve as the primary trainers of its squads, platoons, companies, and battalions, any flaw in their training later manifested itself in the instruction and preparation of their units.[6]

Although the AEF's officers were generally ill trained and ill prepared to face the challenges of modern war, the majority of them were dedicated men who sought to correct their deficiencies and do right by their men. So who were these officers? In 1919 the Morale Branch of the War College, War Plans Division, surveyed two thousand officers awaiting discharge on their attitudes and opinions of their time in the service. As the survey was a random statistical sample of the officer corps and collected information on the men's age, previous military experience, and prewar occupations, it offers insights into the diversity of the backgrounds of the men who sought commissions and indications of their relative social status. As could be expected, the average age of the officers differed somewhat by rank. The average age for lieutenants was twenty-seven, for captain thirty-three, and for majors and lieutenant colonels thirty-five. Nearly 49 percent of the officers stated that they had no previous military service prior to the war and another 18 percent admitted that their military experience had been limited to only military training in school, colleges, or Plattsburg-style Reserve Officer Training Camps. An additional 19 percent noted that they had spent three or fewer years in uniform prior to the war, and thus their actual experience was limited.

Of the officers surveyed, 1,337 listed their occupations at the time that they entered the service. This gives an indication of their social class as well as the kind of man that the army sought for officers. Below is a list of the occupations the officers gave in the survey as well as the number of men claiming each job or profession.

Student 223

Lawyer 136

Civil engineer 132

Salesman 114

Farmer 82

Teacher 59

Banker 47

Railroad employee/worker 47

Clerk 45

Merchant 39

Mining engineer 34

Electrical engineer 33

Accountant 32

Automobile driver/mechanic 32

Construction contractor 32

Engineer 30

Business executive 29

Journalist 27

Bookkeeper 21

Lumberman 21

Manufacturer 21

Real estate/abstractor 21

Insurance agent 18

Electrician 17

Mechanical engineer 17

Broker 15

Cotton trade 15

Mailman 15

Stock breeder 14

Telephone worker 14

Musician 12

Oilman 11

Rancher 11

Telegrapher 11

Architect 10

Miscellaneous 10

Stenographer/typist 10

Structural engineer 10

Advertising 8

Chemical engineer 8

Mechanic 8

Physical director 7

Druggist/pharmacist 6

Foreman 6

Plumber 6

Credit man 5

Machinist 5

Paymaster 5

Surveyor 5

Artist 4

Draftsman 4

Geologist 4

Government clerk 4

Laborer 4

Painter 4

Printer 4

Actor/theatrical 3

Baker 3

Blacksmith 3

Business expert 3

Carpenter 3

Dentist 3

Efficiency engineer 3

Policeman 3

Surgeon 3

Timekeeper 3

Coal operator 2

County/city official 2

Grain dealer 2

Hotel keeper 2

Importer/exporter 2

Meat inspector 2

Publisher 2

YMCA Secretary 2

Auctioneer 1

Auditor 1

Botanist 1

Butcher 1

Chautauqua speaker 1

Clergyman 1

Forrester 1

Histologist 1

Janitor 1

Marine engineer 1

Motorman 1

Municipal engineer 1

Newspaper editor 1

Osteopath 1

Pattern maker 1

Pressman 1

Radio engineer 1

Rubber expert 1

Seaman 1

Soldier 1

Statistician 1

Steam engineer 1

Structural worker 1

Tailor 1

Topographic engineer 1

Valuation engineer 1

Whiskey distiller 1

Although some of the occupations that the officers gave were rather vague, if the students who comprised over 16 percent of the total are factored out, approximately 73 percent of the respondents held professional or white-collar jobs before they were commissioned. This trend was also evident in the statistical information of the candidates from the OTCs and COTCs. Based on the available records, most of the candidates attending the first, second, and fourth series of OTCs were college students, professionals, or white-collar, middle-class workers when they entered training. An estimated 68 to 71 percent of the candidates in these camps were college graduates or had received some college education. Although a policy of drawing more candidates from the enlisted ranks for the third OTCs dropped the number of men with college education to 38 percent, this trend was quickly reversed. The establishment of the Student Army Training Corps (SATC) in September 1918, and its subsequent enlistment of all able-bodied males then enrolled in the nations' colleges and universities, further increased the education levels of officer candidates. Due to the SATC, 91 percent of the candidates in the October Camp Lee Infantry COTS had taken college classes. While the odd automechanic, baker, and janitor managed to make it into the officer ranks, the officer survey and the statistics from the officer camps suggest that during the war the army stuck with its long-standing preference for having gentle educated men as its commissioned leaders.[7]

Officers were only part of the leadership in the army's units. In theory, the AEF's majors, captains, and lieutenants were to be assisted in their tactical, administrative, and disciplinary tasks by their unit NCOs. In old army parlance the NCOs were the "backbone of the army" for they ensured the "good order and discipline" of the troops and directly supervised the execution of their officers' orders. Unfortunately, the selection and training of NCOs during the Great War were even more haphazard than that of officers. In the prewar army, NCOs were selected by company commanders whose long service had given them an eye for seeing leadership talent in their subordinates. The soldiers selected as NCOs then underwent a period of on-the-job training, where the unit's officers and senior sergeants developed and assessed their military knowledge and leadership skills. Long service brought with it experience, and the repeated series of on-the-job training gave the Regular Army NCOs the mastery of technical and tactical skills that were the basis of their credibility and authority with both their officers and their men. The rapid expansion of the army made it impossible to replicate this system. Although some units established NCO schools to train potential corporals and sergeants, most of these courses were poorly focused and too limited in scope to give their students the vital tactical, technical, and leadership skills they needed to succeed.[8]

As the army had no real or coherent system to select and train its wartime cadre of NCOs, it was left to novice junior officers to sort out this problem as best as they could. Regular Army officers did offer some advice on picking potential NCOs. Major Charles Tipps recommended that company commanders seek out "men who have successfully handled six to eight men in civil life as a boss of a group of farm hands, or as the foreman of a small department in some factory," for he believed they already had the basic leadership skills to be NCOs. Another Regular also advised that if the new officers chose "business and professional men, tradesmen, [and] skilled mechanics" as their acting NCOs, the "intelligent and ambitious will rapidly acquire military knowledge superior to that of other recruits in order to measure up to their responsibilities."[9]

As trainloads of draftees began arriving at the training camps in August 1917 the wisdom of Tipps and Wise came up against the realities on the ground. Some officers took the path of least resistance and arbitrarily selected men from the arriving levies to serve as NCOs with the hope of fixing any personnel problems later in training. Upon his arrival at Camp Funston, Private John Nell recalled that his company commander simply went down the line selecting every fourth man to serve as a corporal. Other officers chose to select older or more physically intimidating men to be NCOs in the hope that age or menace would bring natural authority. This ad hoc system for selecting NCOs dogged the army for the reminder of the war. In July 1918 an inspection of the 84th Division revealed, "The noncommissioned officers are as a rule not thoroughly instructed. Many of them are noncommissioned officers simply because there were no others to make." The inspector noted that many of the unit's corporals were recent recruits who had been made their rank after "only a few weeks service." The results were predictable. "Among the so-called noncommissioned officers, who are but the more apt enlisted personnel with chevrons, no high sense of individual obligation to their ill-defined and imperfectly understood responsibilities exists," a lieutenant colonel observed, "and being, like those over whom they have been set, but novices at the game, they are lacking utterly in the confidence which is necessary to force them to the front."[10]

Some of the hastily promoted men were bewildered by the sudden responsibility thrust upon their shoulders. One veteran later confessed, "The confusion was unbelievable—it seemed as if nobody knew anything for sure. I was a corporal within three months and knew very little about the army." Being made a junior NCO also somewhat separated the soldier from his peers and forced him to perform uncomfortable tasks that he was untrained to accomplish. An infantry officer noted the challenge but saw no other option than to force the NCOs to accept the duties and expectations that came with the job:

> Through a lack of material, usually, a Corporal is *chosen* who has never commanded before in his life, and those seven men about his age, fret under restraint. In camp, all sorts of petty requirements are devised to compel the Corporal, against his will, to order the seven unwilling men to perform. In this way he becomes accustomed to command and they to obey, without argument. Then, and only then, will they fight successfully.

Not all of those selected willingly accepted their leadership roles. John Barkley, who would later be awarded the Medal of Honor for his actions in the Argonne, dreaded the prospect of having to "run around after" his squad mates "like their mammies" and went AWOL for a few days to force his commander to demote him.[11]

This lack of a trained NCO corps had immediate and lasting effects on the American Army. As they could not rely on their NCOs to assist them in the training of their units, junior officers tended to take on roles that were normally accomplished by sergeants and corporals. Although officer training had its flaws, it still provided its graduates with a much greater degree of military knowledge than the majority of the army's hastily promoted NCOs. In the Morale Branch officer survey an infantryman admitted, "Training of non-commissioned officers [was] slighted almost to the point of neglect. Officers, from the Company Commander down, [were] obliged to spend fifty percent of their time and energy in doing the work of non-commissioned officers." The tendency of officers to do the work of their sergeants led to a self-defeating cycle whereby the NCOs were seldom able to gain the experience and skills they needed to develop as leaders and gain the respect and authority they needed for their positions. Private D. B. Gallagher observed that it was not unusual for his lieutenant to interrupt his NCOs during drill to correct and lecture them on their performance in front of the men. A major noted that such actions had consequences. "It was often the practice in the formation of the National Army to have a sergeant always supervised by an officer ...Too much supervision [by the officers] was destructive of initiative in the noncommissioned officers, and rather made them dodge than accept responsibility."[12]

The low levels of prestige and responsibility that the doughboy NCOs received were not lost on the Allied officers training the Americans or on many of the American officers themselves. A member of the French Military Mission tried to warn the Americans in January 1918, "The American N.C.O.s have no authority at the present time and consequently no influence over their men. Their situation is scarcely more than that of a corporal in the French army. Nothing has as yet been done to change this situation. Under such conditions, they can neither second the officers efficiently nor replace them." After the war most of the officers surveyed by the Morale Branch concurred with the Frenchman's assessment and agreed that the army had done little to train its NCOs or give them the respect and authority they needed to lead their men. These failings mattered because the realities of the Great War had ushered in a new paradigm in combat leadership. Difficulties with tactical communications, the deadliness of the battlefield, and the subsequent demand to spread out formations and decentralize command required junior officers and NCOs to be able to exercise initiative and make combat decisions. As the battlefield was also particularly lethal for junior officers, the army likewise needed sergeants ready and able to take over command when their captains and lieutenants fell in action. The army's systemic failure to properly select, train, and develop its NCOs later undercut the AEF's combat effectiveness.[13]

Despite the systemic shortcomings of officer and NCO training, the doughboys retained high expectations of their leaders. First of all, the leaders had to "deliver the goods" when it came to meeting the soldiers' bodily, morale, and spiritual needs. The leaders were their unit's conduit for tapping into the army's resources, be it food, medical care, mail delivery, or chaplain services. The soldiers expected their leaders to have the knowledge and skills to accomplish their missions without unnecessary losses. The officers and NCOs had to equally understand the limits of what the soldiers could accomplish and have the moral courage to intervene with the higher headquarters when those limits were reached. In addition to these basic expectations, the doughboys generally wanted their leaders to have a few basic attributes. The leaders had to exhibit physical courage in battle, share the privations and hardships of their men, and treat their soldiers with the justice, consideration, and respect due to fellow citizens of the Republic. Those officers and NCOs who matched these expectations were rewarded with the loyalty of their troops and a greater willingness to sacrifice for the cause. Those who fell short garnered the contempt of their men and the grudging acceptance of their authority.

Upon entering the service, the doughboys became wards of the state and their officers became responsible for their health and welfare. The army had long viewed leadership as a patriarchal and paternalistic endeavor—one where a full belly would lead to full obedience. In fact, in early 1917 Lieutenant Colonel Charles Miller advised the new legion of officers, "With regards to his company the captain stands in the same light as a father to a large family of children. It is his duty to provide for their comfort, sustenance and pleasure; enforce strict rules of obedience, punish the refractory and reward the deserving." Although the doughboys resented being treated like children, they agreed with the good colonel's assessment of their officer's duties. After a stint in combat, Hervey Allen, an infantry officer in the 28th Division, came to the same conclusion. "The men expected to be fed, and they looked to the officers to feed them. To feed, clothe, equip, and pay the men—that is about all a line officer can do anyway . . . Excuses make cold fare." The soldiers respected those leaders who consistently accomplished these basic tasks. Private Albert Ettinger noted that Sergeant Tom FitzSimmons was one of the leaders that his unit could count on to deliver the goods. He claimed that since FitzSimmons "always made certain that his men had dry quarters, plenty to eat, and that their boots and uniforms were in good condition," he was "one of those natural leaders who men would follow anywhere."[14]

Despite the intent of the army's paternalistic ethos, leaders sometimes fell short in looking after the needs of their men. Inspections of the 27th and 30th Divisions in June and July 1918 discovered that officers were not "sufficiently instructed and zealous in providing for the health and comfort of [their] men, especially in matters of rations, bathing, and clothing." Similar complaints would emerge during the fighting in the Meuse Argonne. Although some of these cases stemmed from negligence and lack of concern by the leaders, most came from a simple lack of know-how in coordinating and administering these support functions. The commander of the 52nd Infantry complained that "the greatest difficulty was met with by me in getting officers to properly handle supply and administration." But even he admitted that his officers "had small chance to learn company duties and, in consequence, discipline ran low, kitchens were neglected, equipment and clothing overlooked." Given the pressing needs of the time, training in the OTCs had largely neglected the fine arts of supply and messing. The officers had to acquire this knowledge on their own, and when they fell short, the troops suffered the consequences.[15]

The doughboys realized that their very survival in combat rested upon the technical and tactical skills of their leaders. When their officers and NCOs did not know how to properly employ the unit's weapons, read a map, and match their formations and tactics to the enemy and terrain, the doughboys' lives were at risk. As Major Christian Bach pointed out to the new officers in February 1918, "Men will not have confidence in an officer unless he knows his business . . . If you have a rotten company, it will be because you are a rotten captain." It did not take some soldiers long to realize that the OTCs had fallen short in training their officers to accomplish these vital tasks. After only a few weeks of training, Benson Oakley wrote home that most of his officers were "ignorant" of the tasks assigned them and that they "ought to study up the drill regulations a bit" before subjecting the troops to their misguided instruction. Private John Oechsner was equally scathing in his assessment of his leaders. He later complained that tactics was "all Greek to them," and they "didn't know what the hell it was all about."[16]

The officers themselves were often cognizant of their shortcomings and the best of them actively sought to fill in the gaps of their knowledge. As one captain admitted to a Morale Branch representative in 1919, "It is useless to try to fool the American enlisted man: he soon loses respect for his officers when he observes their lack of experience, gained through the school of hard knocks." As junior officers became the men primarily responsible for training the army's squads, platoons, and companies, they had to scramble not only to expand their knowledge base but also to figure out how to pass their skills on to their soldiers. Many officers reported undergoing last-minute breakneck training sessions to give them just enough know-how to instruct their men. Lieutenant Charles Bolte, who would go on to command the 36th Division in World War II and to serve as the vice chief of staff of the army, recalled, "When it came to teaching the 45 automatic pistol, I had to sit up all night long with a manual just learning how you took it apart and put it together again so the next day I could sit down as if I knew all about it and try to teach this company how to do this very complicated task." Although most officers were like Bolte and worked to master their required skills, the inadequacy of the army's officer training system had still left them woefully unprepared for the challenges that lay before them. This lack of officer and NCO skill, experience, and knowledge contributed to the AEF's high casualties in the summer and fall of 1918.[17]

The doughboys also came to expect that their leaders would serve as a cushion or "heat shield" between them and the demands of their higher headquarters. Officers and NCOs had to be able to gauge the morale and physical state of their troops and be able to communicate to their superiors when their orders were not feasible. As one infantry officer noted, "One of the hardest things for an officer to do is to enforce a stupid order when the men are intelligent enough to know better." This placed the subordinate leaders in a very delicate position. They had to balance the needs of their soldiers with the demands of the mission and their superiors. A failure to promote the interest of the troops led to morale problems, while failing to support the wishes of the higher commander risked the officer being labeled a whiner, a defeatist, or not a team player. As his unit was being demobilized, a captain admitted the difficulty he faced in walking this fine line.

> Now no one knows better than I how many orders you men received, and how it was often beyond human power to obey all of them . . . The Co. Cmdr. is the one man who can't pass the buck on responsibility. We had to take the bushels of orders we received, eliminate those utterly impossible, select those remaining what seemed essential and what we thought the Major and Colonel seemed essential, and then get those things done by the company . . . And then one usually amasses a balling out for something or other that he has left out.

Major Albert Gray and Captain Charles H. Harrington discovered that crossing that fine line had consequences. Gray was removed from his command after arguing with his superior and for coddling his soldiers by "magnifying their troubles or fancied troubles." Harrington was also sacked for disobeying orders to attack the Château du Diable on September 6, 1918, for he believed that the mission "could not be carried out because of the demoralized condition of the men" in his battalion.[18]

Not having the moral courage to apprise the higher headquarters of the limits of the soldiers' endurance also carried penalties. Major Merritt Olmstead argued that the panicked withdrawal from combat of some of the 5th Division's units on October 12 and 13, 1918, stemmed from the failure of commanders from the company to the regimental level to honestly assess and report the poor physical state of their soldiers to the division commander. If pushed beyond their breaking point by their leaders, the doughboys could take matters into their own hands. During the Aisne-Marne offensive, a soldier witnessed doughboys in a neighboring infantry company refuse an order to attack. They did not lack courage, but after days of fighting, "they were so fatigued that there was no strength left in them." While on a short rest from the Argonne fighting, Private John Barkley and his comrades ignored orders from their new replacement officers to drill and clean up their area. The tired doughboys "were all too desperate to be bothered with forms" and told the green newbies that they were not "in the mood for parade ground stuff." When faced with this resistance, the crestfallen officers backed down. Another infantryman believed that many of his unit's stragglers in the Meuse Argonne were due to the fact that leaders "had forgotten that there is a limit to human endurance." Once these men reached their physical and psychological breaking point the social contract between the leader and the led was broken and the stragglers felt free to withhold their willing participation in battle.[19]

When it came to the personal attributes and character that the doughboys expected of their leaders, the most important were physical courage and a willingness of the officer to share the hardships of their men. Despite the massive social, economic, and technological changes that had transformed American society in the fifty years prior to the Great War, most doughboys held to centuries-old conceptions of manliness, honor, and bravery. American officers and NCOs had to prove their fitness to lead and earn the respect of their men by acts of physical courage in battle. Corporal Chester Baker maintained that the example set by the cool courage of his platoon leader during his first assignment in the frontline trenches solidified the officer's high standing with the troops. He recalled, "I noticed that the dugout assigned to Lieutenant Thompson remained empty. During the entire engagement that was to come, I never saw him take advantage of its greater safety; he stayed in the trenches with his men." Shortly after the war, the men of Company E, 107th Infantry, stated that they willingly followed their company commander because of his proven "daring and fearlessness" in battle.[20]

Another component of physical bravery was the leader's ability to keep calm and make rational decisions in times of danger. As combat unleashed a host of unpredictable emotions and behaviors among the troops, an officer exhibiting, or at least appearing to exhibit, coolness and resolve in battle provided the psychological impetus to hold the unit together and direct their energies toward completing the mission. A soldier in the 27th Division noted that his officers gained the respect and loyalty of the company as "they were with the men at times, and their quick decisions, involving as they did all our lives, were such as to steady the men and give them confidence in the success of the operations." Likewise, Hugh Hook praised his company commander because the officer was "calm under fire and quieted the troops by his example." In both cases it was the leaders' personal example of unruffled courage that inspired the trust and confidence of their doughboys.[21]

To the doughboys, if an officer was not willing to undertake the same risk of death and injury as they did, the leader lost the moral suasion and authority to lead. Lieutenant Joseph Lawrence noted that the soldiers in his infantry company contemptuously called their commander "Dugout Pete" because the captain spent much of the unit's time in the Meuse Argonne cowering in his bunker. A similar situation occurred in Horace Baker's company when a green lieutenant was placed in command after the wounding of his veteran officers. While fighting in the Argonne, Baker denounced the fact that "this worthy stayed in the dugout the two days he was with us . . . and I never saw him." Two soldiers in the 42nd Division gave a pusillanimous and obnoxious officer his comeuppance by making him an object of fun and ridicule. The doughboys positioned themselves outside the officer's dugout fired their pistols in the air and yelled out in German to make the panicky officer believe that he was under attack. The failure of all these officers to live up to the doughboys' expected code of behavior negated their ability and power to lead. In these cases they became nonentities within their units, acknowledged by the men as mere objects of derision.[22]

Unfortunately, the doughboys' expectation that their officers exhibit courage and coolness under fire came at a high cost. In terms of percentage of casualties, the most dangerous job in the AEF was to be a lieutenant or captain in an infantry or a machine gun unit. On average nearly fifty-two out of every thousand enlisted infantrymen and machine gunners were killed in action or later died of their wounds during the war. However, eighty out of every thousand infantry and machine gun officers died due to combat wounds. During the 28th Infantry's attack on Cantigny, it lost 60 percent of its lieutenants and captains and 32 percent of its enlisted men. Such high officer losses became a matter of course in the AEF throughout the summer and fall of 1918. For example, after its first four days of fighting in the Meuse Argonne, the 79th Division's 313th Infantry had lost twelve officers killed in action and thirty-three others out of action due to wounds.[23]

The depth of these losses created grave shortages of experienced officers in the AEF and hamstrung efforts to improve the army's combat effectiveness. The army's undertrained NCOs were ill prepared to step into leadership positions, and the often hastily commissioned replacement officers increasingly knew less about combat than the soldiers they led. From the average doughboy's perspective, the loss of their veteran leaders regularly created crises of morale and confidence. One private noted that his battalion commander "was the only officer who was universally liked and admired by the enlisted men," and after his death in the Meuse Argonne, "an instant and serious depression" spread through the unit. The blow to morale in such cases was due not only to the grief created by the loss of good men but also to the breakdown of the vital face-to-face relations between the leader and the led that such losses created. Furthermore, when the fallen leaders were replaced by inexperienced officers the doughboys well understood that their survival was at an increased risk.[24]

Leadership has always been a key component to the cohesion of combat units. When the followers understood that their leaders knew them personally, understood their needs and limits, and were invested in the men's welfare, they were much more willing to follow orders and place themselves in harm's way. The men had to trust their leaders, and the replacement officers were thrust into situations where such credibility with the troops was often sorely lacking. A soldier in the 312th Infantry observed, "The previous days of fighting had depleted the numbers until there were left not more than an average of sixty men in each rifle company. No battalion could boast of more than five line officers, while the lack of non-commissioned officers was a serious handicap . . . No longer did the officer have an intimate personal knowledge of the individuals under his supervision." On October 22, 1918, the 5th Division's inspector general reported that due to the influx of replacement leaders, "in some organizations the officers had been on duty for a very short time, and did not know the men, nor did the men know the officers. Apparently a great many men did not know their officers by sight." He thought that this breakdown in face-to-face relations was a key factor in the precipitous decline in the division's performance in battle. At the end of the day, the doughboys were not willing to risk their lives for officers who they did not know or trust.[25]

Another way officers and NCOs could gain the trust and confidence of their soldiers was to demonstrate an unselfish willingness to share the same hardships in food, shelter, and exertion as their men. Sharing of hardships created a commonality of experience that welded units together and also played to the egalitarian strain in the American soldier. Charles Minder's company commander won the loyalty of his men by walking rather than riding his horse while his troops were marching, sharing his rations and water, and taking turns carrying the packs of soldiers who were worn out by the march. Another soldier remarked that one of the greatest boosts to his company's morale was waking to find their battalion commander "sitting up with his back against a tree, wrapped in a trench coat—no better off than we were"—after a rainy and unpleasant night in the field. By such acts these officers demonstrated to the troops that they were "all in it together" and that their leaders would not ask their men to endure hardships that the officers themselves would not accept.[26]

Of course, those leaders who failed to share their soldiers' hardships often lost the respect and willing obedience of the troops. One MP was particularly incensed by the shenanigans of his company commander. During the Aisne-Marne campaign, when the company was billeted in an open field, the officer detailed some men to dig a dugout and construct a bunk in it of hay bales and boxes for his exclusive use. He then went to sleep with a guard detail over him while snuggled in the unit's only extra blankets. At the time, 75 percent of the company's soldiers shivered with only one blanket and a raincoat to keep them warm at night. To make matters worse, the company mess sergeant was a toady who consistently ensured that the captain's table was well stocked with good food while skimping on the men's chow. In the captain's most insensitive act, he directed the unit's supply sergeant to make room in one of the company's wagons for a portable shower bath that the officer had confiscated for his sole enjoyment. As space was extremely limited in the unit's four wagons, the sergeant opted to leave behind some of the men's rations to make room for the captain's rather extravagant item. In Lieutenant Joseph Lawrence's unhappy unit, the odious company commander "Dugout Pete" compounded his men's hatred in October 1918 by taking the lion's share of the meager rations that managed to reach the front. The captain performed this selfish act despite the fact that his troops had been without food and water for over three days. Although these abuses were the most egregious examples, the belief held by some officers that "rank hath its privileges" certainly encouraged this kind of behavior. A number of officers in the Morale Branch survey decried the failure of some of their peers to share the doughboys' adversities. An infantry officer went so far as to argue that "the tendency of officers to always consider their own comforts and pleasure rather than that of their men" undermined morale in the AEF.[27]

Last, the doughboys expected their leaders to treat them with the justice and respect due to a citizen of the United States. Although the soldiers understood that serving in the army came with restrictions on their freedoms, they were still imbued with a strong sense of egalitarianism and a strong democratic spirit. As such, they generally resented officers and NCOs who acted in a highhanded manner, who were prone to assert their rank and privileges, or who demeaned the troops by word or deed. Soldiers were unwilling to accept that superior rank somehow turned leaders into superior beings. A soldier in the 1st Division complained of "the great gulf" that separated officers and enlisted men. He explained, "The enlisted man could never understand why an officer should have better food, more leave, better quarters than he did. He could not understand why the officer was always the boss when often he did not know what he was talking about." On the other hand, in a letter to his father, Lloyd Short praised his officers because they "don't figure that they are any better than we are at all."[28]

Many officers who participated in the Morale Branch survey also denounced the propensity of their fellows to offend the soldiers' egalitarian sensibilities. An officer who had been commissioned from the ranks condemned the great "gulf between officers and enlisted men" as being "feudal in tendency and undemocratic." He thundered, "It should not be possible for an officer to deal in personalities of a belittling and inhuman kind." Another admitted that "officers failed in many cases to get the best work out of the new men, because they treated them like niggers. No man keeps his self-respect when bullied, ragged and brow-beaten." An infantry lieutenant accused his peers of having "no fair sense of justice" and of treating "their enlisted men like slaves." A further infantryman noted the gross "unfairness" of "officers being able to pull stuff . . . that the same officers would court martial an enlisted man for." The frequency with which these comments popped up in the survey and in doughboy accounts indicates that the officer corps certainly knew that it had problems when it came to officer–men relations.[29]

Outside observers also noted the tensions between the soldiers and their leaders. The most insightful and well connected of these was Raymond B. Fosdick, the director of the Commission on Training Camp Activities and the War Department's special consultant on troop morale. Immediately after the Armistice, Secretary of War Baker sent him to Europe to report on the overall morale of the AEF. Fosdick found that large numbers of doughboys were aggrieved by the attitudes and actions of their officers. He maintained that the draft had led to a lack of any meaningful social, economic, or intellectual differences between the two groups. As the AEF's officers and soldiers came from "a common economic and social reservoir" where there were "plenty of men of superior education and high mental and moral qualities in the ranks," anything that smacked of domineering and swaggering by leaders was "galling to the democratic spirit of the troops." Echoing many of the statements made by officers in the Morale Branch survey, Fosdick asserted,

> The possession of a Sam Browne belt in the A.E.F. has carried with it advantages out of all proportion to disciplinary requirements or the needs of the occasion, and officers have been allowed and encouraged to claim and even monopolize such advantages in ways that have shown a total lack of the spirit of fair play . . . These privileges suggest a caste system which has no sanction in America and against which [the men] instinctively rebel.

Fosdick accurately determined that the problems of the army's leaders were rooted in inadequate officer training and the lack of an institutional program for developing and inculcating solid leadership principles within the officer corps as a whole. He charged that the OTCs "with their hasty training too often turned out officers with no well-developed sense of responsibility, officers to whom the Sam Browne belt and the epaulets were merely the badge of a superior social class, the symbols of rights and privileges jealously to be guarded even at the expense of the welfare and morale of the men of their commands." If Fosdick's observations were accurate, he offered an interesting insight into the attitudes of the American soldiers and a sad indictment of numerous officers.[30]

To be fair to the army's senior commanders, they knew that they had shortcomings within the officer corps and took steps to address the issue. In March 1918 Pershing ordered the establishment of permanent reclassification and efficiency board at Blois, France, to deal with cases of officers accused of being incompetent or unfit for command or commission. Over the course of the war at least 1,682 men, or roughly 2 percent of the AEF's officers, were sent before these boards. The officer overseeing the proceeding estimated that one in forty Regular Army officers and one in eighty National Guard or National Army officers "were found unsuited for the duties they were performing and had to be reclassified." Most officers were sent to Blois because their commanders determined that they were incompetent in military knowledge and skills, lacked leadership abilities, were too unfit for active service, or failed to live up to accepted moral or ethical standards of conduct. The reclassification board had the option of returning the accused back to a combat assignment with another unit, reassigning him to noncombat duties in the SOS, sending him for further training, or revoking the officer's commission and cashiering him from the service. Few of the boarded officers were returned to combat duties, while 882 were reassigned to the SOS.[31]

The Blois reclassification center was a good deal for the AEF. It removed unsuited men from positions that could get doughboys killed but, in the midst of an officer shortage, retained otherwise competent leaders for use elsewhere in the army. The officers who went through the process were less sanguine. To be sent to Blois was to be labeled a failure or a disgrace. The commander of the Blois Officers' Depot, Brigadier General L. M. Nuttman, admitted that the officers "arrived in various states of mind which ranged from extreme anger, through a feeling of injury and a passive acceptance of fate, to an entire loss of self respect." An officer who went through reclassification lamented that it would take him "5 years to get his self respect back" after undergoing the ordeal. In fact, the fear that Blois inspired in the AEF's officer corps led to the term "gone blooey" becoming slang for abject failure. Some of the cashiered officers claimed that their relief from duty resulted from personality clashes with their superiors, from their commanders' desire to pass the blame for failure on to their subordinates, or from appearing to be hardnosed to the notoriously exacting Pershing. Although there was some truth to these allegations, the individual case files from the Blois boards indicate that most of the officers were removed for sound reasons.[32]

Much in the proceeding paragraphs has painted the doughboys' leaders in a negative light. Although it is clear that there were a host of systemic problems with the selection and training of the army's officers and NCOs, it must be noted that most of the AEF's leaders sought to overcome the limitations of their instruction and look after the welfare of their troops. As noted, the doughboy's expectations of their leaders were demanding. This put an enormous physical and psychological strain on their officers and sergeants. The need to be seen by their men as brave and willing to share all adversity took its toll. During his first patrol into No Man's Land, an officer in the 82nd Division was very cognizant of the example he had to set for his men. Despite the fact that he was "badly frightened," the fear of being seen to be afraid forced him to go forward. Even though he was suffering from tonsillitis, Wendell Westover refused to be excused from going into the trenches. He informed his commander, "If I fail to go in the first night the platoon will think I'm yellow." The AEF's high officer casualties were partially a result of the need of leaders to demonstrate their courage in battle to their men and to themselves.[33]

Officers also had to carry the psychological burden of making life and death decisions. "To him first comes responsibility—responsibility for other men's lives," Westover mused. "His the closest contact; his the greatest grief. The Lieutenant is taught that it is necessary to sacrifice men in the attainment of a battlefield objective—then asked to lead those men into battle." Lieutenant F. L. Miller was sobered by requests by his soldiers' mothers that he "look after their boys." He later acknowledged, "Every assurance would be given that I would do my best, but this was a responsibility that weighed heavily on me." These pleadings fell most heavily on National Guard officers. The local and regional basis of the National Guard's recruitment meant that its officers were rooted in their communities and often personally knew the families of their troops. The guard officers

> were looked upon by the thousands of good men and women whose boys were with the troops as the guardians and friends of those lads as well as their leaders in battle. In every case they were daily subjected to a very

heavy and continual pressure, in the form of direct personal appeals, from their own intimate friends, from men of high position and influence, as well as from pathetic hundreds of anxious, proud fathers and mothers, "to look out for my boy," "to bring Joe home safe," "to see that he behaves himself," "to give Bill a chance," and so on.

This link to the communities often built strong cohesion within guard units, but it put an even greater weight on the shoulders of the guard officers. For the guard officers there would be no escape from their wartime performance once they returned home. Regardless of whether the officer was a guardsman, a Regular, or a "Ninety Day Wonder," the leader who could endure these tests, win the loyalty of his men, and make the doughboys more or less willing to risk their lives for the cause was a key element in the AEF's victories.[34]

13

After England Failed
Tommies, Poilus, and the American Soldiers

One of the surest ways that a doughboy could pick a fight with a British soldier was for the American to proclaim that AEF stood for "After England Failed." The Tommies' retort was to observe that the next great war would be "fought between the two yellow races . . . the Japanese and the Americans." Joking like this went far beyond the rough humor that naturally accompanied interactions between soldiers and their allies. When the Americans mocked the Tommies with such taunts they were not only pricking the pretentions of the British but also declaring the ascendance of the United States and the superiority of the doughboys as fighters. As the term "After England Failed" implies, the Americans had a complicated relationship with the soldiers of the Allied nations. On the one hand, the doughboys arriving in France knew that they were as green as grass and lacked the weapons and know-how to wage modern war. On the other hand, they also landed with a faith in American ingenuity, drive, and enthusiasm and a bumptious "can-do" attitude—attributes that were rapidly waning in the Allied armies of 1917—as well as a strong belief that they were the last great hope for the Allied cause. Although at times they were reluctant to admit it, the Tommies, Poilus, and doughboys all needed one another to achieve victory over the Germans. However, this need did not always translate into like or respect. Ultimately, the doughboys' impressions of their Allied comrades tell us as much about how the Americans viewed themselves as they do about the Tommies and Poilus.[1]

Just as propaganda and reporting from Europe had shaped American perceptions of the Allied cause prior to April 1917, they also influenced how the doughboys initially viewed the Allied soldiers. Between 1914 and 1917 scores of Americans volunteered to fight in Allied units or to serve in ambulance companies or other organizations with close ties to the British and French armies. These volunteers often wrote about their experiences, and their works proved quite popular among Americans hungry for news of the war and drawn to tales of daring and adventure. The volunteer-narrators reinforced the romantic view of the war and drove home the themes that the Allies were brave and willing to sacrifice all for ultimate victory. In the volunteers' writings the Allied soldiers became resolute paladins of civilization fighting resolutely against the barbarism of the evil Hun. The American Field Service driver and former Harvard student Henry Sheahan described the average French soldier as "a very fine fellow. He has three very good qualities, endurance, patience, and a willingness to work. Apart from these characteristics, he is an excellent fellow by himself; not jovial, to be sure but solid, self-respecting, and glad to make friends when there is a chance that the friendship will be a real one." Most importantly, Sheahan assured his readers, "Not a single *poilu* wants peace or is ready for peace" until the Germans were defeated. Arthur Guy Empey served in France as an enlisted man in the British Army and made similar observations about the Tommy, describing him as a brave, cheerful, fearless, and ferocious fighter. He informed his countrymen back home,

> To the average American who has not lived and fought with him, the English-man appears to be distant, reserved, a slow thinker, and lacking in humor, but for my associations with the man who inhabits the British Isles, I find that this opinion is unjust. To me Tommy Atkins has proved himself to be the best of mates, a pal, and bubbling over with a fine sense of humor, a man with a just cause who is willing to sacrifice everything but honor in the advancement of the same.

Empey's book about his experiences, *Over the Top*, became a best seller in 1917. From both of these volunteers the message to the doughboys was clear: the soldiers of their allies would be honorable, courageous, and resolute comrades. When face to face with Allied soldiers in France, however, these idealized portraits did not always line up with reality.[2]

Some doughboys gained their initial impressions of their Allied counterparts from their encounters with the French and British officers and NCOs sent to the United States in 1917 to help train the growing American Army. A week after the nation entered the war, the army adjutant general recommended that the chief of staff approach the Allies to obtain men able to teach the novice Americans "those military subjects of the first importance in connection with the character of military operations they are most likely to engage in." He added, "Undoubtedly England and France have hundreds of officers physically disabled but mentally competent, and possessing valuable recent experience in the character of warfare" the Americans would face.[3]

As the Allies had a vested interest in the success of the U.S. Army, they sent over enough officers and NCOs to provide every divisional training camp and many schools with a small cadre to conduct needed technical and tactical training. The 33rd Division received four British officers, five French officers, and several Allied NCOs to assist in their training at Camp Logan. While training at Camp Funston, the 89th Division was assigned three British officers to teach machine gunnery, gas warfare, and bayonet training; five French officers to give instruction on artillery, field maneuver, grenades, automatic rifle, and liaison; and a Canadian officer to teach the Stokes mortar. A member of the division recalled, "These officers were welcome guests. Their opinions on the subjects of their specialties were taken as final." This might have been an overstatement. During the 353rd Infantry's instruction, Captain Bloch of the French advisory mission caused much mirth and confusion when he tried to explain the intricacies of company and platoon maneuver. The Frenchman's orders to "advance in *leetle* columns at twenty paces side by each" left his doughboy pupils exceedingly puzzled.[4]

As the incident with Captain Bloch illustrated, the effectiveness of the Allied instructors and their relationship with the units they taught rested upon their teaching, language, and interpersonal skills. Based on unit histories and soldier accounts, for the most part, the doughboys respected the Allied soldiers and appreciated the "real world" experiences that the men brought to the training camps. A soldier in the 107th Infantry, for example, praised Sergeant Major Tector of the British Army for the physical and bayonet training he gave them. Tector "did splendid work" and "was well known and exceedingly popular among the men." The only problem was that there were simply not enough Allied instructors like Tector to go around. Due to their small numbers, most divisions assigned the Allied instructors to centralized divisional schools. The idea was that the Allied officers would teach select

Americans needed technical skills and these students would return to their regiments to instruct the mass of the troops. This often meant that only a small number of Americans came into contact with any Allied soldiers prior to arriving in France.[5]

It should be noted that almost all of the instruction given by the Allied soldiers in the United States was on technical matters related to the new weapons of the war. From the beginning, the U.S. Army was reluctant to allow the French and British to "interfere" with the Americans' tactical doctrine and training. Part of this was simply pride. One officer on the general staff, Colonel William Johnston, initially argued against employing Allied officers in American training, noting that it would be "a decided reflection upon the ability of officers of the United States Army." In April 1917, six out of the fifteen members of the War College Division staff supported Johnston's stance. The touchiness of senior American officers about the issue was also reflected in the observations of former Chief of Staff Hugh Scott. Upon taking command of a division, he complained that the foreign officers "invariably assumed our total ignorance of everything military, and started their course with the most rudimentary subjects. I had to stop this waste of time, and told them that our regular officers needed only the newest developments as they came up, for they were otherwise as well or better trained than the officers of Europe." Although such opposition by officers such as Johnston and Scott did not halt the use of Allied instructors, it certainly curtailed the extent of what the foreigners would teach the novice Americans.[6]

Another aspect of the Americans' reluctance to take the advice of the Allies on tactical matters and training stemmed from the belief of Pershing and other senior American officers that the French and British were wrong in their approach to the war and that their methods did not match the particular talents of the American soldiers. The AEF's chief of training argued on July 4, 1918,

> In many respects, the tactics and techniques of our allies are not suited to American characteristics or the American mission in this war. The French do not like the rifle, do not know how to use it, and the infantry is consequently too entirely dependent upon a powerful artillery support. Their infantry lacks aggressiveness and discipline. The British infantry lacks initiative and leadership.

The Americans accused the Allies of having become so tied to trench warfare that they had lost the ability and will to return mobility to the battlefield. General Hunter Liggett continued the official mantra that the French were too defensive-minded for "forgetting that they had rifles and bayonets and that trench warfare would not go on forever." In a similar vein, General James Harbord recorded in his diary,

> There is considerable sensitiveness among the French about our not adopting *in toto* their methods of training to the exclusion of and even complete abandonment of our own. Yet, the war can never be won by acting on the defensive, and they now teach nothing but Defensive Warfare. They wished to make us French in teaching, took charge of our programs and had to be resisted with considerable moral force to prevent it . . . They sent us instructions as to how to organize our staff, ignoring our former organization, our history, our peculiarities, our laws, and are a bit sad that in training and organization we have insisted on remaining American.

All of this eventually somewhat coalesced into Pershing's rather nebulous "open warfare" doctrine, and its faith that superior American rifle marksmanship, aggressiveness, and skilled maneuvering could force the Germans from their trenches into open terrain where the Allies' greater resources would then destroy the unprotected enemy army. Pershing's insistence on building an American army employing its own unique doctrine also gave him ammunition to fight off Allied senior officers and politicians who clamored for the amalgamation of the Americans into existing French and British units rather than in an independent American Army.[7]

These stances and perceptions meant that Allied instructors in both the United States and France faced an uphill battle to convince the Americans to adopt what they viewed as tried and true tactical methods. Allied officers were frequently exasperated by the Americans' refusal to heed their advice. At Camp Shelby, Mississippi, Major De Reviers, of the French Military Mission, complained, "When there is a question of drills and maneuvers in which they could readily assist, the American officers are careful not to consult them, preferring to work their own way. Our officers have no part in training except in that of specialties and do not assist at any drills." He claimed that in all of the camps that he inspected, "The word 'specialist' is being deliberately exploited to limit our activity." The Frenchman further found that "false ideas of combat prevail such as antiquated tactical theories of before the war," but that he was "unable to have our infantry combat methods accepted or to have the progressive stages of instruction directed along the lines of modern warfare" because the Americans claimed that they conflicted with "American Methods." In March 1918, the head of the French Military Mission, General Claudon, warned that due to the Americans' intransigence, their training lacked "a programme of exercises in combat in simple but well defined and progressive steps." In the face of Allied complaints, the War Department basically took steps from the spring of 1918 onward to limit the number of Allied officers involved in the training of their troops. Unfortunately, the relegating of the Allies to training only technical skills and the refusal of the Americans to heed the sound tactical advice of their British and French instructors would later contribute to the AEF's high casualties in late 1918.[8]

The doughboys' true interactions with British and French soldiers began upon their arrival in Europe. All of the American divisions sent to the AEF spent some time in training with the Allied armies and occupying sectors of the line under British or French command. Upon landing in France the Allies assigned a small cadre of officers and NCOs to American divisions to serve as instructors, advisors, liaison officers, and interpreters. The 29th Division, for example, reported that it had nineteen French officers and fifty-three NCOs serving in these roles in the summer and fall of 1918. As was the case in the United States, the success of these trainers and advisors rested upon their personalities and ability to impart their knowledge to the neophyte doughboys. One of the more effective of these men was Major "Jimmy" Johnston of the 14th Battalion Highland Light Infantry. When he was assigned to assist the 78th Division's 311th Infantry, he "had been through the mill" at Gallipoli and had served for two years on the Western Front. An American officer noted that Johnston, "always with word of encouragement, to avoid dampening our American energy . . . would help [us] along with quiet hints and canny suggestions that were worth their weight in gold." Albert Ettinger was also charmed by the French NCO assigned to his regiment to teach gas warfare. In the trenches the Frenchman was always full of bonhomie and ready to share his stocks of cheese, bread, and wine with any doughboys that entered his dugout.[9]

The Americans were most impressed by the experience that the Allied soldiers brought to their training and their dedication to properly preparing their units for combat. The commander of the 5th Division's 10th Brigade reported, "The assistance rendered by the French officers attached to our brigade was invaluable. Their greater experience and intimate knowledge of the business of war enabled us to learn a great deal from them even though at times disagreeing with their doctrine and methods." A soldier in the 26th Division was equally impressed with the French and believed that his unit profited from the tactical training it received at their hands. He was taken with the pains that the French officers overseeing the events took in leading the Americans through detailed critiques of their performance. American artillerymen had the most catching up to do when it came to modern warfare and profited the most from the tutelage of the French. Artillery had become the most important player on the battlefield and mastering its new intricacies required an unprecedented degree of mathematical and technical skill. As such, instructors at the French artillery schools did not suffer American fools lightly. One Frenchman told his American charges that their failure to grasp trigonometry left him dumbfounded that they "held commissions in artillery." Despite this criticism, one of the doughboys admitted, "The French know this isn't an Indian war" and redoubled his efforts to master the materials.[10]

Not all of the doughboys were as impressed with the Allied instructors or the things that they were teaching. These men either tended to resent the foreigners' assertions that the Americans knew little to nothing about war or expressed a firm faith in the superiority of all things American. One private noted that it "was somewhat difficult getting use to French instructors" and held that the Americans' own methods and training program was much better than what the French provided. An officer in the 82nd Division denigrated the British training because of its "absolute ignorance of the principles necessary to the development of what we consider effective rifle fire" and haughtily pronounced that only the Americans could "humble the proud autocrats of Prussia." A frustrated Captain Evan Edwards noted of his British instructors, "One could not tell them anything and one could not argue with them. A British non-com does the accustomed thing. He does not think. He dreads anything strange or new. And his always unanswerable reply 'It simply isn't done you know' reduces one to helplessness." Reflecting similar dissatisfaction, the commander of the 29th Division wrote of the Frenchmen assigned to his unit, "The total service rendered by these officers and men may be disregarded. Many of the officers were absolutely incompetent. Many of the alleged interpreters had such an insufficient knowledge of English that they were worthless."[11]

This faith in American exceptionalism and suspicion of Allied methods and motives were given full voice at the highest echelons of the AEF. In July 1918, Brigadier General Harold Fiske, the officer responsible for overseeing the AEF's training program, made a stinging indictment of the Allied officers working with the Americans. He claimed,

> The offensive spirit of the French and British has largely disappeared as a result of their severe losses. Close association with beaten forces lowers the morale of the best troops. Our young officers and men are prone to take the tone and tactics of those with whom they are associated, and whatever they are now learning that is false or unsuited for us will be hard to eradicate later . . . The junior officers of both allied services, with whom our junior officers are most closely associated, are not professional soldiers, know little of the general characteristics of war, and their experience is almost entirely limited to the special phase of the war in the trenches . . . The tutelage of the French and British has hindered the development of responsibility and self-reliance upon the part of our officers of all grades. All our commanders from the division down have constantly at their elbows an Englishman or Frenchman who, when any difficulty arises, immediately offers a solution . . . The assistance of our Allies has become not an asset but a serious handicap in the training of our troops . . . An American army can not be made by Frenchmen or Englishmen.

He concluded by noting, "Berlin cannot be taken by the French or the British armies or by both of them. It can only be taken by a thoroughly trained, entirely homogeneous U.S. Army." As Fiske's views aligned with his own, the next month Pershing directed his commandant of Army Schools to "Americanize the Army Schools in every respect" by purging them of as many Allied instructors as possible. He also worked to limit the number of British and French advisors attached to U.S. units. In order to avoid the effect of the French teaching, Pershing later wrote, "it became necessary gradually to take over and direct all instruction ourselves."[12]

Some American officers realized the shortsightedness of the GHQ's policies toward Allied advisors and the empty promise of Pershing's "open warfare" doctrine. Men, such as the 1st Division's commander, Charles P. Summerall, quietly embraced Allied methods and their strong emphasis on artillery firepower. One of the division's artillery commanders chaffed at "the men who turned from French instruction, from experience gained from four years of war." He was angered by those who touted "American methods" when such methods were merely "the result of experience in the Civil War, the Spanish war and the Philippine war, none of which form any accurate criteria of what the great European war was like . . . The views entertained by our Army," he acidly critiqued, "were crass and ineffective when compared to the tactics developed in four years of actual fighting." The historian Mark Grotrlueschen argues that officers like Summerall who were willing to heed the lessons that the Allied officers offered and adapt them to American realities while gently stiff-arming the AEF GHQ did much to increase the overall capabilities of the American Army.[13]

Of course not all doughboys necessarily agreed that the Allies' methods were the model for the Americans to follow. The British and French track record on the Western Front was not exactly enviable. A soldier from the 89th Division noted of the British that "it took them 500,000 casualties to advance four miles in Flanders" and wondered if they had anything to truly offer the AEF. These kinds of views and a resentment at being treated like dim schoolboys by some Allied soldiers certainly strained relations between the doughboys and the Poilus and Tommies. A Frenchman assisting the 26th Division complained, "It seems to characterize the present attitude of the Americans, who realize that they've got a lot to learn, but don't want anyone to tell them so." Marshal Henri Pétain realized that these attitudes were becoming corrosive to Franco-American affairs and issued a directive on May 1, 1918, to govern how the French should conduct themselves when working with the AEF. "Based on their pride in belonging to one of the greatest nations of the world," Pétain advised his subordinates, the Americans "have an extremely highly developed sense of amour-propre." At all times, the marshal recommended that the Americans should be treated with "patience and tact" and that "an attitude of superiority over them should be assiduously avoided." Those who heeded Pétain's admonitions tended to ameliorate some of the tensions that grew between the Americans and the French.[14]

Regardless of Pershing's or Pétain's desire to shape the interactions between Allied and American soldiers, the doughboys themselves quickly developed their own strong opinions about the Poilus and Tommies. What may be most surprising to modern American and British readers whose perceptions of one another have been shaped by the past seventy-odd years of the "Grand Atlantic Alliance" was the near hatred that many, if not most, dough-boys constantly expressed toward their English comrades. Immediately upon their arrival in France, Lieutenant Colonel Ashby Williams noted, "There was almost without exception among the men an utter contempt for everything that was British." Another American officer stated, "The 35th Division did not get along very well with the British. They did not like the British noncoms, or the British soldiers, or the British officers . . . There were occasional fights between our men and theirs. That did not aid in cementing the entente." On September 11, 1918, an intelligence officer reported that some of the men from the 330th Infantry "expressed themselves bitterly toward the English," and one stated, "if he was put with the British very long he would be fighting them" rather than the Germans.[15]

The depth and virulence of the doughboys' aversion for the British came as a great surprise to many American officers and even some of the American enlisted men. "Coming from the rather Anglophilic part of New England, I was truly shocked by the hostility of the average American doughboy toward the 'Limey,'" Sergeant William Langer recalled, and was stunned that "when word went out that Britishers were billeted in the vicinity, they were positively sought out for a quarrel and a fight." As Langer noted, the South and North-east (especially New England) were bastions of Anglophilia, and many of the nation's economic, intellectual, and political elites had voiced an admiration for Britain and her social institutions since the 1780s. In the 1890s, the admiration of British social order and the need for an ideological justification for colonial expansion culminated in the rise of "Anglo-Saxonism": a faith in the innate superiority of the Anglo-Saxon people and their accomplishments. As most of the AEF's officers came from an educated, upper- and middle-class background and had been schooled in the virtues of "Anglo-Saxonism," it was no surprise that they did not share their men's hatred of the English.[16]

So what were the sources of the doughboys' general dislike of the Tommies? Many of the Americans blamed it on the attitudes that the British exhibited toward them and the Englishmen's haughty assertions of their preeminence in the world and on the battlefield. As one officer observed, "The average Tommy looked upon us as a bunch of greenhorn Yankees, who had made fortunes during the first three years of the war and were now over in France three years late spending them and rising the price of vin rouge and 'oofs.'" A doughboy in the 27th Division, one of the American units that fought with the British 4th Army throughout the war, stated, "Tommy considered himself a superior soldier to the Americans and took no pains to conceal it . . . in fact he took every opportunity to impress upon the mind of the American soldier that such was the case. Our soldiers resented any such attitude and denied it was based on fact."

Ashby Williams came to similar a conclusion when explaining his troop's "violent dislike for anything that was British."

> It was doubtless due in large part to the fact that the British Tommy had been at this game a long time and assured a cocksure attitude towards everything that came his way; perhaps to the fact that most of the Britishers with whom the men came into contact were old soldiers . . . and they looked with contempt on the striplings who had come in to win the war. Perhaps it was due to the fact that on the surface the average Britisher was not after all a very lovable person, especially on first acquaintance.

Such attitudes were not likely to endear the English to "Pershing's Crusaders."[17]

The Tommies further angered the doughboys by expressing their belief that the Americans had waited too long to enter the war and were now only in France to enjoy the fruits of a victory that others had sacrificed to achieve. Lieutenant F. L. Miller noted that immediately upon arriving in France his soldiers got into a fight with British troops after the latter "taunted us by shouting that we delayed coming over until they had won the war." The Americans, however, "were of the opinion that we had come over to save them from defeat." One artilleryman bristled at the fact that "the British soldiers resented the Americans, they said we had come over to steal the glory after they had won the war."[18]

Both the doughboy and the Tommy had been raised and educated in the unshakable belief that their respective societies represented the pinnacle of human development and achievement. This faith was so strong that any other party who questioned its validity or proposed a different contender for the top-seed position was viewed as a foe and heretic. This was certainly how Ashby Williams viewed the matter:

> I think the dislike for the British was a feeling of competition that every strong man feels when he meets another strong man and measures his strength with him, as it were. And this feeling of competition was

aggravated, no doubt, by the inclination of the average Britisher to regard anything that Britain and Britishers do as a little better than can be done by anyone else in the world.

In fairness, if one substituted "American" and "United States" for "Britisher" and "Britain" in the last sentence, one would also have a fair encapsulation of the average doughboy's worldview. In a world where "American exceptionalism" vied with "British exceptionalism," conflicts between the doughboys and the Tommies were bound to arise. That also explains taunts like "After England Failed."[19]

The Americans also resented the Tommies' habit of using tales of woe and other scare tactics to unnerve the new arrivals. Some viewed this as a continued effort by the British troops to lord their superiority over the green doughboys. Soon after landing in France the officers of the 311th Infantry were given a lecture by a British major. One of the Americans recalled, "He cheered us up by telling us that very few ever came back, and narrated several choice tales of sudden death in unusual and gruesome forms." The major was accused of "trying to get the wind up" (British slang for having or showing fear in battle) and removing any misperception that the Americans were "in for a pleasure trip." Likewise during his first encounter with the British, Leslie Baker noted, "They did not lose any opportunities of entertaining us with vivid stories of the dangers of the line." While taking exception to "their efforts to get our 'wind up,'" he still found it "very comforting" that "they knew a lot of the tricks of the game."[20]

When faced with the superior airs and efforts to frighten them, some Americans asserted that the Tommies simply suffered from envy and discontentment with their own lives. In October 1918 a doughboy recovering from wounds in Brest informed an intelligence officer,

> The Tommy is fed up on the war. He sees the Americans and his own colonials getting far more pay than he does. He also has to submit to the strictest discipline such as keeping his equipment and metal parts of his uniform shined up. He sees that he is the only one of the Allied soldiers who must do this. Naturally he becomes dissatisfied with his lot. It is little wonder that he cusses out an American or colonial occasionally.

In a similar vein a soldier from the 82nd Division declared that the British "felt like they were superior to us. They were the highest paid soldiers with $5 per month. When the Americans came over we got $30 per month so

the women considered us millionaires so we were real popular with them."
By placing the blame for their dislike of the British back on the Tommies,
the Americans could absolve themselves from blame in the matter and demonstrate the Americans' superiority in the things that mattered: money and
women.[21]

One of the most important things that shocked the doughboys and helped
to sour their relations with their Albion allies was the belief that the Tommy
had succumbed to pessimism and defeatist attitudes. Time and time again
doughboys noted how by word and gesture the English gave them the impression that they were whipped. One British sergeant informed the newly
arrived Kansans of the 353rd Infantry, "You should have been here long before
this," and then proceeded to proclaim, "We are licked. It was over when the
German drive began. There's no use trying to hold'em. We are licked I tell
you, and you'll be licked too." The doughboys discovered that, despite the
claims of Allied propaganda, their French and British comrades were not all
sure of victory and willing to sacrifice "all save honor" to defeat Germany.
Joseph Lawrence recalled that a despondent English YMCA worker "pointed
to a detail of replacements marching by . . . from England, and said, 'Look
at those old men and young boys. What can you expect of them in Battle?'"
The YMCA worker's comments were mild compared to those of one British
soldier overheard by a doughboy in the 77th Division:

> Here we saw something that really gave us a chill [and] made us wonder
> why we had left old Broadway to come over and try to help these people.
> As we were marching by we saw this Tommy standing on a stump talking
> to a large crowd of British soldiers. "Look at yah," he snarled, "all praying
> each day for a 'blighty.' Yah'd probably trade an arm or a leg to get back
> home. To hell with 'em all. Why don't we just walk away, like they done
> in Russia?" . . . "To hell with the war . . . It don't put any shillings in my
> pocket." . . . Of course, we're [the Americans] all in a kinda shock. We'd
> been hearing all this talk about the gallant Tommies defending poor little
> Belgium. Then we hear this.

Although all of these vignettes came from the spring of 1918 when the Ludendorff offensives had pushed Allied morale to its lowest ebb, the doughboys
who heard them and similar expressions were left with the impression that
the Allies in general, and the British in particular, were a spent force.[22]

These impressions were solidified by other things that the Americans observed. After landing in Liverpool, Thurmond Baccus's unit spent a short time in Winchester awaiting travel to France. Baccus recalled, "There was a large camp of wounded men near by and we visited them to find out about the war. We were told by them to stick up our hands or legs above the trenches and get wounded as that was much better than living in the trench." Likewise, William Triplet and his comrades were shocked when the British troops conducting their training warned their eager pupils that "in six months you'll be bloody well fed up" with the war and then they would willingly stick their hands over the trench parapet in hopes of receiving a "Blighty" wound that would take them out of combat. Such attitudes were materially reflected in the trench lines themselves. A soldier in the 27th Division was surprised how little work the British troops put into maintaining the trenches of their support line: "We learned that the chief reason the Tommies were indifferent in the support line was because they were so 'fed up' with four years of war that they didn't seem to really care whether this particular shanty was blown to smithereens or not." Still, he doubted that the doughboys would ever become as calloused and cynical as the Tommies they encountered. While visiting a British sector on his first tour of the front, an American officer noticed that the English did not put much effort into their defenses because "they know they are outnumbered and seem to feel that they cannot stop the Hun in a good trench any better than in a poor one." A veteran of the 91st Division summed up the opinion of many doughboys when he wrote, "The English and French gave the impression that the war would last for ever [and they] had quit trying." Given these impressions, it is little surprise that on October 19, 1918, the acting inspector general of the American II Corps reported to the AEF GHQ the presence of a "habitual pessimistic attitude of the British soldier toward the outcome of the war" and warned of "this attitude extending even to the officers."[23]

Despite, or perhaps because of, the defeatism that they encountered, the enlisted doughboys often commented that the British soldiers were overdisciplined and too submissive to their superiors. The British Army, the Americans argued, was too tied to class distinctions, which created unimaginative officers and unthinking soldiers fit only for cannon fodder. One American veteran derided British officers for treating "their men like dumb animals," while another noted that he "wouldn't have stood for their discipline." Other doughboys considered British Army discipline "to be a manifestation of meek submission rather than the proud attributes of a trained soldier." The Americans were also inclined to take a rather jaundiced view of English officers. To them, Tommy's officers were too overbearing and "stand-offish" and inclined to stand on strict hierarchical separations of the ranks. The doughboys were mystified by the comforts and privileges that the British officer corps insisted on near the front and the way they would stop everything at half past four for afternoon tea.[24]

These negative opinions of British officers and discipline were not shared by the more Anglophilic American officer corps. American officers in both junior and senior grades praised what they perceived as the unquestioning discipline and loyalty of the British soldier. After training with a British unit, Lieutenant Quincy Mills commented that the English troops and NCOs possessed a soldierly manner "which the American soldier would do well to copy." General Harbord applauded the British technique of training a soldier's "mind, will and body" for "instant response to superior demands." Ashby Williams stated that despite a rocky start, "We soon learned to like the British officers. After you break the outside crust on an Englishman you find inside one of the finest fellows in the world." He went on to claim that the American troops themselves "gained a profound respect, not to say a real affection," for the Tommies after they fought with them on the line. Notwithstanding William's assertions, few doughboys readily shared his faith in any real Anglo-American entente.[25]

It should be noted that the Americans' distain for the English did not extend to all of the soldiers of the British Empire. The doughboys generally held a high opinion of the Scots, Australians, New Zealanders, and Canadians. To the Americans, these Allied soldiers possessed aggressiveness and an attitude toward the war more in line with the American way of thinking. A corporal in the 102nd Infantry noted that most French and British soldiers were "sticklers–solid hunching troops" that had "no dash like the Canucks, Ausies and New Z [ealanders]."An officer explained, "We looked upon the average Tommy as a degenerate, tea drinking, saluting bellyacher. The Australians and Canadians were our sworn buddies, however, and we liked the Scotties." The doughboys saw the British colonial troops as closest to themselves in warlike demeanor, physique, national attitude, and historical and cultural background. While serving in Flanders and Picardy, Rabbi Levinger observed, "The Australians and, in fact, all the British colonial troops, had more in common with the American soldiers than had the British troops themselves. They were like our men, young, hardy, dashing. They had a type of discipline of their own." In short, the Americans liked the colonials and the Scots because they believed that the Australians, Canadians, and New Zealanders were just like them, and therefore far superior to the French and British. This admiration did not stop the Americans from having a bit of fun at their "best comrades" expense. Upon seeing a kilt-clad Scottish sergeant after disembarking in Southampton, England, some wags in the Tank Corps catcalled, "She's going to sleep with me tonight" and "He's going to be my girl tonight." But such humor was still a far cry from what other doughboys' hurled at the English troops.[26]

The doughboys' perceptions and attitudes toward the French soldiers were much more varied and nuanced than those they held of the British. At least until the Armistice, the Americans generally held warmer opinions of the Poilu than the English Tommy. The doughboys often praised the French for their bonhomie, warmth, and willingness to share their experience and limited worldly goods with their American comrades. In a letter to his mother in June 1918, Milton Sweningsen wrote, "We sure haven't met a nicer bunch of fellows than the French soldier . . . [He] is glad and happy to help you out all he can." During his unit's first stint in the trenches, another soldier observed, "The French were swell . . . and their hospitality was sincere and elegant." One of their Poilus won the Americans' high esteem by granting them "free and frequent access to the Pinard supply." During a lull in the fighting near Château Thierry, William Brown remembered that he enjoyed a meal with a group of French soldiers consisting of food and champagne looted from the town of Monneaux. He fondly recalled, "We ate and drank to our heart's content and forgot the war and all its miseries."[27]

Although they noted the great strain that the war had placed on France and its army, fewer doughboys reported hearing defeatist sentiments from the Poilus than from the Tommies. Given the differences in language between the Americans and the French, this might have simply been due to the doughboys failing to grasp the Poilus' discontentment. But whatever the reason, the absence of such open dissent certainly left the Americans with a greater appreciation for the French soldier than for the English. In early October 1918, intelligence officers interviewing men recovering from wounds at Base Hospital 5 found that the doughboys believed that the French were

Photo 15: A group of doughboys pose with French soldiers and *Fusiliers Marins.* The Americans generally respected their French counterparts and sought to learn as much from them as possible during their training and time in the trenches. Source: author's collection.

better fighters than the British because the Tommies were "grumblers" and "not brave." They argued, however, that the French were good trench fighters but not very effective in open warfare because they were cautious and "a bit slow."[28]

The Americans' initial positive reaction to the Poilu also stemmed from the fact that the French Army often assigned some of their best troops to training the doughboys. The doughboys generally praised the training that they received from the elite *Chasseurs d'Alpins*, French Foreign Legionnaires, and French colonial Moroccan troops. The 165th Infantry's Albert Ettinger had nothing but kind words for the French *Chasseurs d'Alpin* who conducted his unit's instruction and accompanied them during their first time into the line. He appreciated their willingness to pass on their hard-won experiences and the kindness with which they received the newcomers. During an unauthorized excursion into Luneville, some of the *Chasseurs* also helped Ettinger and another doughboy slip through a cordon of American MPs by dressing them in French capes and helmets. The Americans also respected (and feared) the combat skills, toughness, and ferocity of the French Senegalese, but were somewhat dismayed by claims (which the Senegalese did nothing to counter) that they collected German ears. As was the case with the Australians, Canadians, and other British imperial troops, the Americans tended to more readily identify with the elite French troops than with the run-of-the-mill Poilus. In fact in a rare moment of magnanimity one doughboy even went so far as to admit that the "French Foreign Legion was almost as good as the American First Division."[29]

While the Americans would later criticize the French for their lack of aggressiveness, at first they were more willing to acknowledge the combat skills and techniques of their Gallic allies than they were of the British. One American officer admitted, "I would much rather go in with the French" than with his own countrymen, because they "are better trained, more experienced, and know trench warfare as the Americans cannot expect to for a long while." He admired the French and wrote to his mother, "It is very amusing to hear the Eng[lish] & Am[ericans] criticism of the Fr[ench] army. According to both the French know nothing, & have no science at all, but when you point out what wonderful fighting they have done they have no answer. It's a funny war, after all." After experiencing combat, some Americans came to realize that the French methods and tactics were much better suited for the modern battlefield than those being pushed by the AEF GHQ. During his unit's first major fighting from May to July 1918, an infantry officer in the 1st Division's 28th Infantry recalled that American formations moved "forward ponderously with heavy losses against hostile fire, with no apparent effort to utilize cover." It was not until his regiment learned from the French Moroccan soldiers how to advance by "moving at a run from shell-hole to shell-hole" in tactics "utilized by the European veterans" that his regiment started to reduce its losses. Such prudence on the battlefield led some of the American wounded who were interviewed in October 1918 to admit "that they would rather go over [the top] with the French than the Americans because the French knew where to go but the Americans 'just went,'" without much thought or preparation.[30]

As part of Pershing's training plan, each newly arrived division was to go through a period of combat seasoning by spending at least a month serving in the Allied trenches on a quiet sector of the front (there will be more about this in chapter 15). Most doughboys spent this phase of their training in the relatively calm French trenches in Alsace or Lorraine. It was during this time that the Americans' attitude toward the French soldier began to change. By 1917 and 1918 the lines in Alsace and Lorraine had become a backwater of the war. They were places where the Germans and French sent their worn-out units to rebuild their strength or where they placed their second rate units to merely hold the line. "The war will not be decided in these hopeless mountains," one French officer explained to an American. "The high command has no desire for a battle here." As such, the contending sides had come to a tacit "live and let live" agreement where aggressive actions by the troops were to be strictly constrained.[31]

The notion of a "live and let live" system during wartime did not sit well with the eager Americans. There was a certain cognitive dissonance in the doughboy being told that the Huns were the great enemy of civilization and then not allowing the Americans to shoot at the Germans. "This ain't a war," a 35th Division doughboy complained. "The Frogs and Krauts got it fixed up between 'em to spend their vacations where their ain't nothin' to bother 'em but scenery." Although he later admitted that at times the "live and let live" system was "practical and appreciated," Levi Hemrick noted that the doughboys' first encounters with the miniarmistices were unsettling to the impatient and combative Americans. The Marine recalled,

> Through the observation slot, I could actually see Germans moving around over there on their side. I could speak very little unreadable French but did manage to ask them why they did not fire on the Germans. Their answer came back to the effect that if they started shooting so would the Germans. While new to the fighting business, we Americans thought that was a strange way to carry on a fighting war.

An officer in the 32nd Division noted that the tacit truce "was something the Yanks couldn't understand," and one of his men stated, "No wonder this war has been going on so long. How is it ever going to end if we don't shoot someone?"[32]

The doughboys' lack of understanding or irritation at the "live and let live" system soon led them to question the resolve and ardor of the Poilus they encountered. Sergeant Elmer Straub complained in his diary that "I am rather disappointed because we can hear only an occasional shot, and things do not seem at all lively." He later caustically wrote of his French allies, "They sure live a soft life and its no wonder they can't win the war." Similarly, a 1st Division infantryman expressed his dislike of the French attitude of "you no shoot, bosh[e] no shoot you," by noting, "you can't win a war that way." One American reduced the tensions between the doughboys and the Poilus over the truce arrangements to the simple fact, "They want to live. We want to fight."[33]

When the Americans broke what they saw as a misguided truce by firing into the German lines, resentments grew between the French and the doughboys. To the French the Americans were screwing up a mutually beneficial and necessary arrangement; to the Americans, they were only doing what they had been sent to do: kill Germans. After American soldiers shot the Germans cutting hay in No Man's Land in the Albertine subsector of Alsace, the French officer in charge of that section of trenches raged at the doughboys for breaking the truce. After the officer expressed his "exasperation, disapproval, and despair" at the American's actions, a doughboy noted, "I began to wonder what side he was working for. The way he carried on about the three Jerries my crew claimed you'd think I ought to send apologies and flowers." A 42nd Division artilleryman disparaged the fact that the French and Germans on their sector in Lorraine "were on terms of love and kisses." The Americans' shelling of a German kitchen set off a week of retaliatory shooting in what heretofore had been a quiet sector. During the shelling, the "French would complain bitterly to Americans for starting it all." The "live and let live" system led many doughboys to the conclusion that the French had lost their vaunted "élan" and were now so worn out that they were suited only for defensive warfare. As the Rainbow Division artillerymen groused after serving alongside the French, "That's a Frog for you. Put them on a safe front and they want to live forever."[34]

The Americans' opinion of the fighting qualities of their Gallic allies was also battered by the battles in the summer of 1918. While fighting beside the Poilu and serving under French command during the fighting around Château Theirry in May and June and during the Champaign-Marne and Aisne-Marne campaigns of July and August, the doughboys often castigated the French for being slow and overcautious, and for their tendency to force the Americans to do "the dirty work" of taking the hardest objectives. To some doughboys the sight of the Poilus retreating back to the Marne in May was proof that the French Army was a spent force; to others, it was a disconcerting tragedy. Upon seeing the fleeing French, a Marine in the 2nd Division recalled, "With their years of experience in warfare, we had admired, almost reverenced the French soldiers. For my own part, I had come to feel that there was a certain invincibility about them . . . Then there met us on the road that day French soldiers retreating, worn-out, haggard, and dejected retreating in disorder from the oncoming Germans." What was worse for him was that "we had regarded a French soldier as worth several Americans . . . It would have been unnatural for the Americans to despair at this turn of affairs." Likewise, when ordered to fall back by a rattled French officer, a Marine entered the AEF's lore by reportedly telling him, "Retreat hell, we just got here." Tales of the French panic were exaggerated and grew with each retelling. An intelligence officer at Brest reported that as late as October 22, 1918, "The story about the French falling back at Château-Theirry" was still being told by wounded Americans. One of the doughboys went so far as to claim "that an American soldier shot a French officer because of the many deaths the falling back of the French caused in American ranks." To the Americans, the verdict was clear; by holding on while the French purportedly crumbled around them, the doughboys had saved Paris and the Allied cause.[35]

During the fighting in the late summer and fall of 1918, the doughboys continued to accuse the French of having the disagreeable habit of leaving the Americans' flanks exposed by prematurely pulling out of defensive lines or by plodding far behind American units during attacks. An infantry company commander believed that Franco-American tension arose during the Soissons drive because the French tended to stop their attacks as soon as they reached their objectives and were prone to retreat "when it might have been best to hold positions gained." The Americans, on the other hand, pushed their attacks whenever they smelled blood and "never stopped until victory crowned their efforts." Caustic and condescending remarks about the Frenchmen's plodding and lack of aggressiveness even reached the highest levels of the AEF. As General James Harbord recorded in his diary,

[The French] do muddle through and get things done in some way. They are not where they say they will be at the time they say they will be there. You find your left flank in the air, the French on whom you depended having concluded to fall back to their soup-kitchens or for some equally important reason, and failed to tell you about it. But the next day the colonel will come out and sob around over "Mes enfants," and they will kiss each other on both cheeks, and go out and die taking the position they gave up the day before. But they are our Allies, God bless 'em, and we have them to get along with until the end of the war.

A Marine merely characterized the Poilu as "old, tired and timid" and likened attacking with the French to "a fast mule teamed with a slow mule in a double harness." As early as June 17, 1918, criticism of the French had grown so great that the AEF GHQ felt it necessary to send a remonstrative to its corps and division commanders warning them and their soldiers against "making rather uncomplimentary remarks about the French," which tended to inhibit "the spirit of fraternity that should exist between the French officers and ourselves."[36]

The GHQ's efforts to stem the poor mouthing of the French were largely in vain. The notion that the French were not carrying their weight while the Americans were winning the war continued to dominate much of the doughboys' narratives of the time. In late September 1918 an intelligence officer noted that veteran doughboys "described the French as fair fighters but blamed them for laying down at times." In fact, "Some of the men said that the Americans had so many casualties at Soissons because the French had laid down and allowed the Boche to flank the Americans." This criticism was also levied by the commander of the 3rd Brigade, 2nd Division, who stated, "The relations between the French and the Americans were not good. When one unit was shot up owing to the failure of another unit to carry its less difficult objective, it naturally follows that relations will be strained between those units." After being assigned to the French XVII Corps during the opening weeks of the Argonne offensive, the officers and men of the 29th Division were especially harsh in their assessment of their Gallic comrades. The commander of the division's 57th Brigade made the following official accusation against the French forces he fought with:

That the French troops did not display aggressive courage. That this lack of morale was the cause of their failure to attain their objective. That because the French attack was so quickly stopped, the Germans were warned of the offensive and were able to bring up reserves to meet the renewal of the attack on favorable ground. That the losses of the brigade were largely increased by the failure of the French to attack when ordered.

He even charged the French with robbing American dead and wounded, a crime, he claimed, that was a "barbarity beneath the standard of honorable soldiers." It is difficult to determine with any certainty the facts behind the American claims and accusations. However, in this case, American perceptions trumped all else. When the doughboys came to believe that actions by the French Army had led to unnecessary American casualties, their impressions of the Poilu soured.[37]

These irritations did not end with the Armistice; in fact, tensions between French and American forces reached a boiling point in December 1918. During the initial occupation of the Rhineland, the doughboys resented French efforts to occupy areas under American control and railed against their harsh treatment of German civilians. When these actions were coupled with the mounting belief that the French people as a whole had grown ungrateful of the American efforts, the doughboys' perceptions of the Poilu reached its ebb. In the winter of 1918–1919, fights between American and French soldiers and other signs of strain demonstrated the enmity between the two groups. The French high command did not want two million Americans to return home with ill feelings toward France and quickly took steps to sooth the doughboys' ruffled feathers.[38]

Although Americans had fought alongside allies and cobelligerents during the American Revolution and the Boxer Rebellion, the First World War was the nation's first large-scale foray into coalition warfare. Whether the doughboy loved or loathed the Tommies and Poilus that they encountered, this first prolonged interaction with foreign soldiers reinforced their faith in the superiority of the American society from which they were drawn. Their contact with the British and French soldiers also forged their belief that they had saved the floundering Allied cause and been the decisive factor in winning the war. In the words of Hervey Allen, the war had demonstrated that the Americans were simply a "bigger race of men" than the Europeans. Decades after the end of the conflict, Philip Foster, a veteran from the 89th Division, claimed, "If it hadn't been for us, they'd [the Germans] have whipped Europe." It became a common occurrence after the Armistice for American units marching past other American units to call out, "Who won the war?" This generally resulted in catcalls or the occasional fistfight as both units proclaimed that it was their organization that could claim pride of place in the answer. When doughboys such as Allen and Foster shouted, "Who won the war?" when passing Allied soldiers, most Americans, regardless of unit, clearly and assertively responded "the United States." These bumptious and bragging doughboys were the opening act of the bumptious, bragging, and assertive "American Century."[39]

14

Harsh Schoolmasters, Devious Huns, and Dejected Prisoners

The Doughboys and the German Soldiers Meet

A picture, it is said, is worth a thousand words. The Great War fell within the great flowering of mass graphic art. In posters, magazine illustrations, and handbills, the populations of the combatants were inundated with a steady stream of images designed to elicit an emotional response and compel them to action. Even before the United States entered the war, art and photographs in popular magazines such as the *Literary Digest, Leslie's Illustrated Weekly,* and the *New York Times Mid-Week Pictorial* were shaping the soon-to-be doughboys' image of their future enemy. From April 1917 to the end of the war, Americans training in the United States were further bombarded with a steady stream of propaganda from the Committee on Public Information and from military sources designed to paint the Germans as a remorseless and barbaric foe.

Some of the most powerful American images of the war came from posters attempting to induce men to enlist, buy Liberty Bonds, or perform the myriad of tasks required of a society engaged in total war. In one of these posters, a hulking and brutal German soldier with eerie green eyes, bloody hands, and a gory bayonet peers menacingly over the destruction of No Man's Land in search of his next victim. The work exhorts the viewer to "Beat Back the Hun." In another, a half-naked woman is shown nailed to the walls of her house with the bodies of her husband and child at her feet. The poster was crowned by the simple and direct slogan "They Crucify" to draw a stark line between "American manhood" and the heartless enemy the Americans would face. One of the war's most iconic posters portrays a massive gorilla wearing a German spiked helmet and a brushy Kaiser Wilhelm mustache stepping onto the shores of America. In one hand the beast carries a ravished woman and in the other a bloody club emblazoned with "Kultur." The poster enjoins the viewer to "Destroy this Mad Brute" by joining the army. These graphics helped to further shape the doughboys' perceptions of the enemy long before they set foot in Europe. The message of all of these images was clear: your enemy has lost their humanity and thus the doughboys' only recourse was to kill them to stop their depredations.

The "thousand words," however, were also important, and the doughboys' perceptions of the German soldiers were likewise formed by what they read. With the outbreak of war in 1914, scores of American journalists flocked to the battle zones to feed the public's demand for news of the events in Europe. Although some of these reporters tried to cover the German side of the war, due to the ease of access or personal predilections the majority attached themselves to the Allied armies. Within the first few months of fighting, the stereotype of the "brutal Hun" was being established in the American mind. Even the American reporters with the German Army tended to further this view. The *New York World*'s special correspondent E. Alexander Powell reported that after the Germans entered a Belgium town,

> The townspeople were shot down in cold blood and . . . when the firing squads could not do the work of slaughter fast enough, the victims were lined up and a machine gun was turned on them. We know that young girls were dragged from their homes and stripped naked and violated by soldiers—many soldiers—in the public square in the presence of their officers. We know that both men and women were unspeakably mutilated, that children were bayoneted.

Although most of the accounts of German brutality were exaggerated by Allied propagandists and came from unverifiable sources, there was enough truth to them to give the reports credibility with American readers. The fact that the Germans themselves admitted and justified the destruction of Louvain, the taking of Belgian hostages, and reprisals against towns and citizens suspected of harboring snipers and saboteurs also tended to allay lingering American doubts on the veracity of the atrocity stories.[1]

Over two years before the United States joined the war, the noted American war journalist Richard Harding Davis had already drawn the ideological lines behind which the doughboys would fight. He reported from Belgium in the wake of the German occupation and had been briefly detained by the German Army. In December 1914, Davis wrote,

> I have seen the war . . . This is not a war against Germans as we know them in America . . . It is a war . . . against the military aristocracy of Germany, men who are six hundred years behind the times; who, to preserve their class against democracy, have perverted to the uses of warfare, to the destruction of life, every invention of modern times. These men are military mad . . . When a mad dog runs amuck in a village it is the duty of every farmer to get his gun and destroy it, not to lock himself indoors and toward the dog and the men who face him preserve a neutral mind.

Davis's belief that Germany's "military mad" rulers had perverted the thoughts and actions of its soldiers was a theme that many other American journalists embraced. In addition to being brutal and uncivilized, the militaristic system in Germany had turned its soldiers into overly disciplined automatons with no independent thoughts of their own. After viewing a German artillery battery in action around Ypres, Arnold Bennett informed his American audience,

> Around the guns were educated men who had spent years—indeed, most of their lives—in the scientific study of destruction . . . These slaves were compelled to carry out any order given them under pain of death. They had, indeed, been explicitly told on the highest earthly authority that, if an order came to destroy their fathers and their brothers, they must destroy their father and their brothers.

He further described a group of German prisoners as having "a brutalized air, no doubt one minor consequence of military ambition in high places." Other narrators described the Germans as an inhuman force of nature or as mere human parts in a crushing "monstrous engine."[2]

The Germans' conduct of the war and their activities in the United States further alienated American opinion. German actions in their occupied territories, the use of poison gas and flamethrowers, acts of sabotage inside the United States, and the sinking of ships such as the American steamer *Gulflight* and the passenger liner *Lusitania* seemed to confirm every negative stereotype that commentators like Davis and Bennett created of the Germans. While the Allies conducted a masterful propaganda campaign in the United States to influence American opinion, the German propaganda operations in the United States were too direct, open, and tactless to appeal to most Americans. The public saw these German activities as cynical attempts to subvert American policies and to enlist German-Americans in disloyal actions. German-Americans, the nation's largest ethnic group at the time, were too divided in their attitudes about Imperial Germany and too fearful about being labeled disloyal to present a counternarrative to the Allied propaganda or to mobilize any meaningful antiwar support.

Germany's resumption of unrestricted submarine warfare in January 1917 and the uncovering of the Zimmerman plot to embroil Mexico in a war with the United States were merely the final acts that pushed the American people and government to war. Before these decisive events, the process of demonizing the Germans had already shaped the public view that Germany was a direct threat to the American way of life and that it was an evil entity capable of any unspeakable act to ensure the perpetuation of its archaic and militaristic society. As was noted in chapter 2, large numbers of American soldiers truly subscribed to the negative image of Germany and its military and believed that the only way to "Make the World Safe for Democracy" was to follow the poster's injunction to "Destroy this Mad Beast."[3]

Although prewar reporting and wartime propaganda had demonized and dehumanized the Germans, once the doughboys came face to face with their foe, many found that their opinions and perceptions of the enemy changed. Some found confirmation of the Germans' alleged barbarity and further hardened their hearts toward the evil Hun. Lieutenant Quincy Sharpe Mills's already negative view of the Germans was deepened by the devastation that he witnessed in France. He sent a steady stream of postcards home showing the wreckage of French towns and reported the outrages that the German occupiers had supposedly inflicted on French women. In a letter dated March 19, 1918, to his mother he wrote, "The more I see what the Germans have done over here, the more I long to kill some of them." On the back of one postcard showing a destroyed village in Lorraine, he penned,

> This card will give you some idea of the sort of Kultur-blasted land we are living in. The more I see of what the Germans have done to this country and the people who live in it—particularly the women and girls—the worse I hate them. They are a race that should be wiped off the face of the earth . . . But you will be thinking that I am too blood-thirsty. Well, so ought you to be, and all American women.

This opinion was shared by an artilleryman in the 32nd Division. During the fighting in the Argonne, he informed his family, "For my part I should like to see Prussia wiped off the map so this so called 'Kultur' would be nix."[4]

Although prior to the Armistice the majority of doughboys never lost their distaste of Germany or ever doubted the righteousness of the Allied cause, some did come to see the humanity of their enemy and developed a more nuanced view of the foe. The doughboys' first encounter with the enemy was often German POWs marching into captivity or in work camps in French ports and towns. These forlorn men tended to erode the stereotype of the German soldier as a deadly and demonic fighting man. Upon seeing German Prisoners of War (POWs) soon after landing in France, one officer mused, "These were the Huns we were taught to hate. They were husky, blond chaps, in faded green uniforms with their little flat caps . . . At any rate I didn't feel any very lusty rage or horror at them, and though one or two of our men cursed at them under their breath, it didn't seem at all convincing, but rather forced." During their first meeting with German POWs, a 33rd Division artilleryman and his comrades were "anxious to see how he fitted in with his press notices." He admitted the Americans

> expected to see stalwart Prussians, fierce of mien and proud of bearing. It was not to be expected that our mysterious targets out there in the blue would prove to be anything like the Heinies we used to know in Milwaukee and St. Louis. Thanks to advertising the soldats had unconsciously endowed this warrior—"the Hun"—with a sort of diabolical personality . . . They were disappointed. In the lead was a young lieutenant . . . As ferocious as a fat contented baby. The haughty demeanor, the pride of position, supposedly so essential to the German officer's well-being, were lacking here.

The soldiers who followed the captured officer were "thin, hollow-eyed and frightened," and had "in their woe-begone faces that hungry-dog look that a man cannot steel himself against."[5]

Other Americans had their stereotypes challenged by more poignant and troubling encounters with the enemy. After his first trench raid in July 1918, the 35th Division infantryman Albert Robinson recorded in his journal,

> We had no fatalities—Fritz left one behind. I looked at him—my first dead foe—and it seemed as though all the glory was struck from war. A mere boy, he was named Opphagedorn . . . he had no head to speak of. A grenade or shell must have done it . . . The identification of the sole victim—which

fell to Lt. Slaughter—was a sad task. He had photographs on him of pretty, homelike women—his folks no doubt. His cap which he had crammed into his pouch at the moment of putting on his helmet, was still wet with perspiration.

After some of his rookie soldiers "declared that they would kill every Bosche they came across in spite of their officers' warnings that all prisoners should be treated kindly," an infantry officer in the 82nd Division noted that the real outcome was much different. Once the boasting doughboys

> saw that the Germans did not have horns or forked tails or anything like that, they decided that he wasn't such a bad enemy after all, and the men at Battalion Headquarters gave the prisoners cigarettes, tobacco, food, and became as chummy as you please in a few minutes although they had declared the day before that the price of crepe was surly going up in Germany after they got a whack at them.

Walter Wolf's interaction with a German POW elicited a similar response. When he encountered a crying sixteen-year-old German soldier in a long line of prisoners he gave the youth a candy bar to calm him. When a German officer snatched the candy away from the boy, Wolf punched the officer in the jaw and moved the boy further back in the line for protection. When faced with dead boys such as Opphagedorn or the lines of dispirited German POWs, some doughboys saw in the Germans not the lethal conquers of Europe, but rather the weak and sad dupes of Kaiserdom or fellow sufferers in war.[6]

Although their encounters with ill-fed, shabbily clothed, and dispirited German prisoners helped to humanize and demystify the enemy, many doughboys retained a healthy respect for the combat skills of his Teutonic foes. The Americans frequently, if grudgingly, acknowledged the Germans' skills at placing their machine guns, concealing their defensive positions, and using artillery and counterattacks to stall American attacks. Some, like Colonel Robert McCormick, even admitted that the Americans were as schooled in war by the Germans as by their Allied instructors.

> The Germans did all they could to assist our training . . . Thus, American indiscretions invariably were punished. Trenches, reserve positions and batteries which were revealed by the least carelessness receive chastisement. Sometimes this came in the form of harassing fire, or fire for destruction, or, in the event of a trench raid by either side, the enemy artillery would fire upon every American position known to it. Thick heads and dull, which

had failed to learn the teachings at school, had the lessons of war pounded into them by the German schoolmasters, whose model was: "he who will not heed must feel."

When later asked if the Germans were well trained and led, a soldier simply replied, "You're damn right they were. They were the greatest trained soldiers in the world."[7]

For their part, the Germans did not always share a respect for the fighting abilities of the Americans. The doughboys were certainly fresh, youthful, and enthusiastic, the Germans noted, but the lack of experience and the poor training of American officers and men hindered their performance in battle. "In the opinion of German troops opposite them," a Bavarian division commander reported, "the individual American soldier is very brave but the troops as a whole lack a sense of unity and consequently their attacks break up quickly." Likewise, the commander of Infantry Regiment 102 informed his superior, "The American soldier is brave and bold, lacks the proper junior leadership and often shows himself to be improperly trained. If our artillery and machine gun fire comes into effect properly, the opponent is thrown into confusion and the attack comes to a halt." The Germans' critique of the Americans usually focused on the doughboys' tendency to move forward in clumsy mass formations, their inability to match their tactics to the terrain, poor cooperation between the infantry and artillery, and a lack of skilled and imaginative leadership. Another German commander observed,

> Even when deployed the enemy suffered bloody losses. The separate and isolated groups coming in carelessly at first, were at once subjected to the withering concentrated fire of light and heavy machine guns . . . Gaping holes were torn in the lines of riflemen, entire columns being mowed down . . . They were visible at great distances and offered excellent targets . . . One could plainly observe that the unrest in the ranks grew every minute. Lone individuals and frequently entire detachments ran aimlessly about.

This criticism was justified and the American attacks were too often ham-fisted and amateurish. But, for all of their harsh appraisals of the doughboys' skills, the German accounts also betrayed an underlying tone of dread and apprehension. On October 26, 1918, the commander of Infantry Regiment 111 reported that the "Americans conduct themselves rather boldly, indicating their inexperience," and that their tactics denoted "A certain naïveté." He

explained that the Americans were "effective solely on account of its mass action and its freshness." But it was the Americans' ability to use their freshness
and mass that was the trouble, for those were traits that the German Army
could no longer hope to match.[8]

The doughboy's face-to-face encounters with Germans came in three
forms: as an active combatant seeking to do him ill, as a dead man, or as a
prisoner. Of these it was the Americans' treatment of prisoners that tells us
the most about how they viewed their enemies and perhaps also gives us insights into how they viewed themselves and their war. Through the comments
made by German POWs about their captors, it is also possible to get the other
party's view of the Americans. In September 1918 the chief AEF base censor
assumed the responsibility for censoring the incoming and outgoing mail of
German POWs held by American forces to ensure that no information that
could damage the Allies would be leaked to German authorities. The section responsible for censoring POW mail also reported any information that
they deemed to be of military value to the Intelligence Division of the AEF
GHQ. On December 6, 1918, the section further began sending translated and
transcribed passages of the prisoners' mail to GHQ that offered any insights
into the attitudes of the POWs and their correspondents in Germany about
captivity under the Americans, their general attitude toward the Americans,
and general feelings about the outcome of the war. These reports offer unique
views of the Americans from the perspective of the German POWs and their
families back home.[9]

For both sides in a war, combat is the realm of violent emotions, fear,
and uncertainty. The Hague Convention and army regulations required the
doughboys to accept the surrender of enemy soldiers who were unwilling or
unable to continue fighting. Once the enemy ceased being an active combatant, his captor was prohibited from killing him and took on the obligation
of safeguarding the captive and providing for his welfare. Unfortunately, the
strictures made by the dispassionate, humanitarian, and comfortable diplomats around a conference table were not always easily imposed upon tired,
excited, and angry men on the battlefield. For both the would-be captor and
the would-be captive, the first seconds and minutes of their initial encounter
were fraught with apprehension and doubt.

The first split-second decision that the captor must make is whether or
not at that moment he is willing to take prisoners. It is not difficult to find

instances where doughboys chose not to take prisoners in letters and diaries from the period and in postwar accounts. This is not to say that the killing of German prisoners or potential prisoners was widespread; rather, it is to acknowledge that such acts do happen in war and that the Americans were not immune to this fact. The would-be captor's mental and emotional state at the time that he came into contact with the enemy shaped much of the outcome. On September 30, 1918, Private Gilbert Max of the 307th Infantry recorded in his diary, "After a 2 hour barrage we made an attempt to break thru. We did & got 16 prisoners. We saw one of our sergeants get killed and we decided to kill the 16 prisoners." A Marine reported that after his company had taken four German prisoners after a tough fight in the Meuse Argonne, "One of the Germans did something trivial that met with Captain McClure's displeasure and he told his orderly to shoot them." The orderly followed the order without question. The high emotions, desire for revenge, or the simple blood lust that sometimes came with close combat made Max and McClure willing to commit "crimes of passion" that would not have sat well with the high-minded gentlemen of the Hague.[10]

The process of making the sudden life-and-death decisions of taking German prisoners can be found in the accounts of two sergeants assigned to Company L, 325th Infantry of the 82nd Division. The regiment suffered heavy losses during its attacks near St. Juvin on October 11–13, 1918. In fact, the unit went into the battle with one hundred officers and 3,273 soldiers, but when it came out of the line less than two weeks later on October 23, it had been reduced to twenty-three officers and 513 enlisted men. These loses may have contributed to the actions and attitudes of the company's First Sergeant John Grove and Sergeant F. J. Hawke. When asked to chronicle his combat experiences shortly after the Armistice, Hawke informed his commander unapologetically that "My motto was take no prisoners." He readily admitted, "the first one I saw I started out to kill, but luck was against me" when the man surrendered to another soldier. Later, while leading a patrol to eliminate a German machine gun, his "luck" changed. The three-man machine gun crew did not see Hawke until it was too late and fled as soon as his presence was revealed. Without giving them much of a chance, Hawke shot two of the Germans and "convinced them that I held the winning hand." He was disgusted that upon stopping "the miserable curs even dropped on their knees" to beg for their lives and he "used his hob nails [boots on] one of them." The incident left one German dead, another mortally wounded, and the third a very battered prisoner. In a separate incident during the battle, First Sergeant Grove recounted,

> I happened to look over and saw two Germans going like hell for Germany. I got one through the head with my Springfield and the other man [ran] back where they started from. At this stage the excitement was great. I went around some bushes to get the other one and even within five yards of them I could not see him. He was hiding behind some bushes, so I called for him to come out. After I called twice I heard him start to cry for mercy. I knew I had him then, so I went after him (on guard) with my mind made up to stick him, but when I got to him I could not carry out my intentions, for I never saw such a sight in all my life. His eyes were as big as silver dollars—easy—and his hair was standing right up straight. I have seen men scared, but never had I ever seen a sight like this. I had a man cover him, while I looked for any weapon he might have on him, and, after satisfying myself that he had none I sent him back a prisoner.

We will never know why one of the sergeants gave vent to his passions and why the other did not. Was Hawke a sadist who viewed his cringing enemies as mere dogs while Grove was more inclined to see the humanity of his foe? Or was it that much of war takes place in ethical grey space? In both cases it was a razor-thin snap decision that led two Germans to the prisoner cage while three others went to the grave.[11]

Like many of the infantrymen of the war's other combatants, some doughboys developed a code of acceptable behavior when it came to taking prisoners. To them, Germans who fought to the last minute and then attempted to surrender as the Americans closed in on them had put themselves beyond the bounds of mercy or honorable treatment. These cases of "situational ethics" particularly seemed to be true for those banes to the doughboys' existence: German snipers and machine gunners. As one wounded American indignantly explained to a military policeman after killing a group of Germans trying to surrender, "You see they figure it is alright to kill until they are about to be killed and then play the coward's part . . . not with me." Although the doughboys had admitted to a violation of the laws of war, the MP's only response was, "This is a pretty rough war." William Brown recalled,

> The German sniper was the one we had to watch out for—for he was the trickiest soldier the Germans had and an absolutely dead shot. When he shot—he shot to kill and rarely missed his mark . . . But once we located

him, that was the end for Her[r] Sniper, for we sent out a small patrol, flanked him on all sides—so as to make escape impossible and proceeded to remove him from this earthly sphere. A sniper never was taken prisoner.

One American patrol caught a German machine gun crew in a building and "paid them back" for their murderous effectiveness in mowing down their fellow doughboys. A patrol member noted, "They tried the 'Kamerad' stuff, but we threw them out the window and when they got through falling 150 feet, they didn't man any more machine guns." It is interesting that none of the men who provided these accounts had any qualms over their actions. In fact, the statements that Brown made in his postwar memoir were rather boastful of the killing of Germans. They believed that their actions were fully justified and seemed to have assumed that their readers would also see the logic of their "situational ethics."[12]

The "situational ethics" also excused killing POWs due to military necessity. If a unit was unable to secure, move, or care for the POWs or if the military circumstances made taking prisoners inconvenient, some soldiers were told it was OK to ignore the rules. While he was attending the 3rd Corps Intelligence School, one of Sergeant Albert Robinson's instructors informed the students, "If you are out for prisoners and identification and you get more prisoners than you need—or they don't feel inclined to return with you— bring back identification"; in other words, killing prisoners was acceptable in certain cases. An infantry officer had similar experiences while training with the Allies. He decried the fact that both British and French instructors tried to instill in the Americans the military wisdom of taking no prisoners. To his credit Allen believed that it was a "stupid policy" that would cause undue resistance from the enemy and thus cause more friendly casualties. Allen's justification, however, was based more on the long-term consequences of killing POWs than on its immorality or identification with the enemy.[13]

Some of the doughboys who refused to accept capitulations or shot POWs were influenced by the belief that the Germans were a treacherous enemy who often faked surrender, made false use of Allied uniforms and Red Cross insignia, and used other underhanded methods to lure unwary Americans to their death. Propaganda at home, tales told by Allied soldiers, and stories in *Stars and Stripes* painted the picture of an enemy who would use any form of deceit and dirty trickery to gain an advantage. "The Germans came out of the woods 3 times today and we slaughtered them like pigs," William Phillips noted in his diary on September 29, 1918. "We take no prisoners. They are so tricky we can't trust them when they show the white flag—so we shoot them." On hearing word of a possible armistice, a soldier wrote to his mother on October 16, 1918,

> I don't know what this peace move will amount to but however much we would like a peace we know that we can't trust these Germans and there never was a time when they needed to play for time as just now. We have them worried. I think the Kaiser would like a rest for the winter. Whenever a nation sends their men over the top with French overcoats on and Red Cross emblems on their sleeves, but with grenades in their hands and machine guns hidden and shouting "Kamerad la France," meaning "Brothers of France" they are not fit to trust for a minute.

After hearing of German soldiers faking surrender to ensnare Americans into deadly traps, William Graham took a page from Philip Sheridan and stated, "The sooner our men wake up to the fact that it is more dangerous to take prisoners than fight the Hun in ambush, the better for them. The slogan should be 'No Prisoners.' The best Hun soldier I've seen was a dead one." Those doughboys who subscribed to Philips's and Graham's view of the enemy ultimately believed that self-preservation was more important than the risks of taking potentially perfidious prisoners. In most of the accounts of soldiers who took this view, it should be noted, proof of the enemy's evil actions came from what they read or heard rather than what they had personally experienced.[14]

We will never know how many Germans were killed by Americans during or after the act of surrendering, but the killing of POWs was the exception rather than the rule. Most doughboys, it seems, were rather benevolent toward their prisoners. A soldier in the 32nd Division steadfastly maintained, "I never saw any prisoners ill-treated by combat troops, though ill-treatment may have occurred in the rear. The men who fought and exposed their lives usually seemed to feel no great personal rancor." Similarly an infantry in the 1st Division later recalled, "We held no animosity toward them. I think prisoners were well treated. We took watches, knives, money from them, but gave them no ill treatment." This claim was backed up by some of the prisoners themselves. Rudolf Gordun wrote to his family that he felt himself lucky to be captured by doughboys. He noted, "The American combat troops as could be expected, were very decent. They pointed their revolver at me, but did not shoot immediately, when I hesitated about surrendering. The French would not have acted that way, they would have cut the matter short with a shot."[15]

Although having their surrender accepted was the most important trial for the German prisoner, their tribulations were far from over. Before being moved to the rear, they were first searched for weapons and items of military usefulness. As the 1st Division soldier noted earlier, in the process of these searches the doughboys took personal items from their captives. This plundering of POWs was widespread among all of the war's soldiers. By American Army regulation and policy, enemy prisoners were not to be deprived of their personal effects and valuables or of photographs and letters of a nonmilitary nature. Officially, the AEF frowned on the stealing of these items and required its corps and division inspectors to report on the treatment of POWs within their units. On September 30, 1918, for example, the inspector general of the 26th Division reported, "Some of the Prisoners of War were robbed of personal effects at the time of capture and during the time they were being marched by details from the line to the rear." He noted that "Much of the property is now being recovered, and every effort is being made to identify and punish the guilty persons." On October 28 a German aviator named Max Kluforth accused doughboys of depriving him of several of his personal items after he had been shot down behind American lines near Exermont. After American officials investigated the incident, an American artilleryman was found in possession of the pilot's seal ring and was arrested. The artilleryman in this case was unlucky as few doughboys were ever prosecuted for robbing POWs. The AEF's own inspector general was wise enough to understand why. At the end of the Meuse Argonne campaign he admitted, "At the beginning of the operations pilfering of personal effects from prisoners, especially officer prisoners, was almost universal. This was excused by the officers of the divisions as the American soldiers' natural tendency to get souvenirs." The fact that doughboys and their officers viewed the plundering of POWs as legitimate spoils of war undercut any real effort to curb the practice. Relatively few Germans complained of the practice. Either they also accepted it as a reality of war or they were just too happy to be alive to protest.[16]

Although the doughboys frequently robbed German prisoners, incidents of the physical abuse of POWs were rare in American accounts. Inspector general officers reported no serious incidents of mistreatment of POWs during the Argonne drive. In fact, despite his unit's recent heavy casualties, on October 15, 1918, the 82nd Division inspector general admitted that he "was impressed with the consideration shown the captured enemy." This is not to say that the Germans were not at times subject to physical violence to cow them or to speed their movement to the rear. William Brown recalled an incident when a captured German lieutenant "objected strenuously" to being searched and manhandled by the doughboys. The officer's objections were cut short by a punch in the jaw that then rendered him "as timid as a hare." Although doughboys were required to safeguard their prisoners by quickly removing them from the dangers of the battlefield, this was not always carried out. Upon capturing a number of Germans, Thurmond Baccus noted, "The prisoners were given something to eat and stretchers to carry wounded to the rear . . . they were under shell fire all day carrying back wounded." As this practice was common in all the era's armies, it elicited little comment from the doughboys or the Germans.[17]

Accounts of doughboys' brutality against POWs are also largely absent from German accounts. The prisoners themselves generally praised their treatment at the hands of the Americans. In a Christmas Eve letter home in 1918, a POW informed his family,

> There can be nothing worse, than to be continuously in the front lines with rain pouring down, standing up to the knees in mud, and treatment getting worse. That is why neither officer nor soldier, even though defending themselves when the American drum-fire buried us up; everyone threw away his arms. We were well received by the [American] soldiers, many of whom spoke German. They had much tobacco, gave us all we wanted, and we lit our pipes of peace.

"As I have said before and must again repeat the treatment of [German POWs by] the Americans is unsurpassable," Otto Teubel assured his father. "How awful on the other hand is the hatred of the French towards us defenseless prisoners." As he was being marched through French villages, one German officer was especially glad to be held by the Americans, for his guards prevented the French locals from doing any harm to him other than hurling verbal abuse.[18]

From the letters opened by the American censors, it is clear that German prisoners like Teubel were relieved that they were captives of the Americans. Although the Germans knew that their mail was being read, thus opening the possibility that the writers were currying favor with their captors, it does seem that their opinions were genuine. Some believed that they were better off in American hands because the doughboys lacked the hatred and desire for revenge that they felt were common among the other Allies. One German lieutenant found a marked improvement in his treatment when he was transferred from French to American captivity. He claimed that the French were "mad with hatred" and thus withheld food and proper shelter from their POWs. In a letter home dated January 21, 1919, Lieutenant F. Clausen admitted, "I must thank God that I fell in the hands of the Americans, for, even though there is much that could be improved here, they are the ones of all our enemies for whom I have the greatest liking; in spite of the fact that they are the ones responsible for the outcome of the war." Paul Lucus expressed similar thoughts, noting, "By all means I am glad that I am in American captivity, for I would not have been able to stand it with the French or English. I would have preferred death. The American on the other hand, treats us honorably, and respects in us, the old soldier who has done his duty."[19]

The friends and family of German prisoners being held by the AEF generally agreed that it was good that their men folk were in American hands. They often commented not only that the Americans were more humane than the British and French but also that they expected the United States to be more fair to Germany during the upcoming peace conference. One civilian noted, "You were fortunate to fall into the hands of the Americans; they are a smart set of boys, and I am sure you are being treated well. I cannot imagine otherwise, for I have always known them to be gentlemen. Here in Germany, we have great hopes in Wilson, that he will get us a fair Peace, for at present, things look very bad for us." From Berlin, another German wrote his relative in an American POW camp, "We are more or less relieved knowing that you are in American captivity for the Americans have our deepest sympathies, and are considered the most humane among our enemies; they do not mean to do evil towards us Germans." Herr Harris wrote to his son in March 1918, "We thank God that you are with the Americans and not with the French, by whom our people, in spite of all protests will probably be held for years, for the purpose of reconstruction of their devastated provinces." These feelings were so strong that one doughboy claimed that his young prisoner had been told by his mother that he should surrender to the Americans if the opportunity arose because she even hoped that he would be sent to the United States and have the chance to become a citizen.[20]

As with their family members, many POWs thought that the Americans respected Germany and were willing to lay the blame for the war on the Kaiser and his militarists rather than on the German people. One jaded German POW even reported home to a friend in January 1919, "Oh, this infamous war. Let us forget it, for I am full of hatred that I should have been obliged to take part in such a criminal act . . . I joyfully greeted America's entering into the war, for it was the best for the German people. America conducted the war against the German government and not against the German people." Another observed, "The Kaiser had to go, otherwise, it would have been impossible to make peace. The American believes to have freed the German people from its tyrants . . . For the German people it is better that the hated is concentrated on one individual." Because of these views, the German soldiers also placed great hope in Woodrow Wilson's ability to rein in Allied revanchism and give Germany a just peace. "Let us hope that Wilson will bring about Peace in accordance with his fourteen points, and not be influenced by France and England; then things will not be bad for us," one hopeful POW wrote home.[21]

The letters examined by the AEF censor office tend to paint the Americans as relatively fair and benign jailers. The Germans generally reported that their captors treated them justly and honorably and did everything possible to ensure their comfort and well-being. Given the scarcity of food in the German Army in late 1918, it was not surprising that some POWs focused on the material benefits of being held by the Americans. Sergeant Richard Obersigner wrote his wife,

> That we are prisoners we have as yet not felt, so to speak, for the Americans treat us just like they do their own men. We might almost say this is also the case with regard to our food. We have thoroughly recuperated from the strains of war. Some of us have already developed quite a little belly. It is a pity only that one cannot get beer, but in place of that we get pure bean coffee and real marmalade. At noon to-day we had goulash and soup. For supper we had hamburger steak and soup. At each meal we have coffee and white bread—like cake. For breakfast coffee, white bread and bacon.

The sergeant was so taken with his captors that he admitted, "If I were not married I would not return to Germany, but go right away to America, as much money is earned there in my trade."

A German officer was more satisfied with the moral aspects of his confinement and the Americans' willingness to treat POWs as honorable men and soldiers. On November 12, 1918, he wrote,

> Yesterday, the Armistice was signed, but under different circumstances than I calculated. My conscience is clear; the loafers who have spent the time at home will now be able to sleep quietly at night . . . Our feelings are naturally depressed, but the Americans are reserved in expressing their joy over the victory and are very considerate not to injure our feelings. I especially esteem the Americans; they are a quiet, thoughtful, industrious, and sympathetic Nation . . . We are permitted to take a walk outside the enclosure. For this period, we fifty officers give our word of honor not to attempt an escape and walk around the vicinity for an hour or two. This is very pleasant because one can see the world directly and not through a barbed wire fence. Our escort on these occasions is but a single American officer. All of them are very fine and neat people and at times one can converse with them.

As with Sergeant Obersigner, the officer's view of the doughboys was so positive that he added, "Very often I think of going to America for a few years. Most assuredly one can learn a good deal there."[22]

These upbeat assessments of the Americans also had the advantage of tempering criticism that the POWs had of the conditions of their captivity. As with so many things, in the summer and fall of 1918, the AEF was woefully unprepared to guard and care for large numbers of German prisoners. In 1917 the U.S. Army even lacked a standing military police corps or a plan for administering POWs. Thus, the AEF had to improvise both under the duress of wartime. By the time of the Armistice the AEF had hastily constructed ten large POW camps and seventy-six smaller POW labor camps to house its 48,280 German prisoners. The AEF barely accomplished this difficult task while also coping with the massive logistical headaches of feeding, clothing, moving, and supplying its own troops. During the Argonne offensive, the AEF captured an average of twenty-six hundred Germans per week. The historian Richard Speed argues that under the stress of these mounting numbers, if it were not for the fortuitous arrival of the Armistice, the American POW system would have been overwhelmed. The ad hoc nature of the American camps and their administration led to complaints from the prisoners about poor drainage in the sites, poorly constructed barracks, lack of firewood, and a monotonous diet. Due to the general American benevolence toward the POWs, however, many of the Germans took a more philosophical view of these poor conditions or blamed the French for the situation. Lieutenant I. R. Fredrich complained of the mud in the camp and that "the barracks it is normally very cold, because we have no flooring and the ground is damp and cold," but he noted, "The Americans do everything to better conditions, but they have to contend with all sorts of difficulties." "There is no doubt that the Americans show their good intentions," another officer maintained, "and if conditions are not such as one would like to have them, it is because of the tremendous difficulties they are confronted with."[23]

Some of the Germans took the friendliness of their American captors and the doughboy's negative comments about their Allies as further signs of hope for their nation. A few prisoners even expressed dismay over how Germany found itself at war with the United States and hoped that the American attitudes boded well for the future. A POW admitted to a family member in February 1919, "Germany made an error in 1917 when the trouble started with America . . . I have already written you that the American soldier prefers us to those he is aiding. In the next war the sides will be drawn differently." His interaction with the doughboys had also made Walter Mattes optimistic of the future:

> As I said at the time, it is even today a conundrum to me how America happened to enter the war on the other side. Ninety-nine out of every hundred Americans are friendly toward us, and wish us a speedy return home, in order that they too can get out of this country. How fortunate it is that Americans got a chance to go to Germany. You should hear these people talk about Germany, all are enthusiastic. One thing is clear to me, even today, should we ever again have a war with France . . . not one American would come over here. Any American will tell you that, face to face.

Although both prisoners were overly sanguine in their views on the Americans, their comments, and those in the proceeding paragraphs, reinforce the argument that American captivity was relatively benign and that the doughboys held little lingering animosity against their foes.[24]

Of course not all of the German prisoners were happy with their captors and the conditions inside the American camps. Some railed against the Americans' sanctimonious attitudes about Germany and the war. One German officer was outraged that the Americans showed the POWs in his camp a film titled *The German Atrocities in Dixmude*. He noted, "In this manner, outrageous lies are being shown the Americans, and finally they too, who up to now were fairly reasonable, believe such stuff." Lieutenant D. R. Klopter was even more scathing in his assessments of the doughboys and their war aims. First he was incensed that his camp was guarded by African American troops. "You probably know that the Americans have four classes of people," he seethed to his father. "Being given a colored guard means that they class us a few grades lower in scale, about sixth or seventh class." What angered him the most was the American faith that they had the solution to Germany's problems. "America wants to present Germany with a panacea for all troubles: Democracy. They always talk Liberty, Equality and Fraternity, but acting in accordance there is another thing. They are always in the tow of France . . . If this is the freedom they wish to give us, I would express my thanks and decline." Despite his resentment, he did retain some optimism for the future, noting that since "the Americans and French are like cats and dogs among themselves . . . it does not seem impossible that some day these noble brothers will be at logger heads, and then we will have a chance to stand by, as a neutral third party, and skim off the cream."[25]

Other prisoners were merely discontented with the physical discomforts of their confinement and the conditions and nature of the work they were forced to do. All of the combatants used POW labor to perform menial tasks. The contending powers agreed that such work would not be conducted within artillery range of the front and that the tasks that the prisoners performed would not directly be related to killing their countrymen. The Americans put their POWs to work for nine hours a day (including transportation time), six days a week, repairing roads, unloading ships, performing minor construction tasks, and disposing of old or dud munitions. The work was not easy and was performed in all types of weather. This caused one to grumble, "Here we have rain, and again rain, in fact one never gets dry. I am disgusted in having to work out in this weather. We surely work enough, but they are not satisfied with this, and we are continuously driven to work more. This is what they call 'Kulture,' they, who would want to make us free. Our prisoners were not subjected to such things." Some POWs had much more to complain about than did this man. After the Armistice the Americans assigned some German POWs the hard and dangerous task of disposing of surplus munitions. The POWs dreaded this work, and some complained that forcing them to perform this task was a violation of international treaties intended to safeguard captives. This point was driven home on July 9, 1919, when twenty-five POWs and one American guard were killed when surplus crates containing gun cotton and cordite that the prisoners were destroying set off a massive explosion at St. Loubes. Afterward, prisoners in several labor companies staged work stoppages to protest the practice. The American officials were unmoved by their actions, and after being confined to camp on a diet of bread and water, the protestors returned to work.[26]

Whether the doughboy viewed his German enemy as a lethal, harsh schoolmaster, a devious and deluded Hun, or a pitiful and dejected prisoner, he should be commended for his ability to overcome the vicious and dehumanizing propaganda of the era to treat his foe with humanity. Although the Americans sometimes gave into stereotypes and the passions of war, it seems that these incidents were rather limited and not unique in the experiences of the war's other combatants. The best indictors of the doughboys' generally fair and humane treatment of his foes come from the accounts of the Germans themselves and from the fact that the rates of escapes, sickness, and death in American POW camps were lower than those of the other powers.[27]

Training and Trenches in France

Tom Carroll was with the first contingent of Americans to arrive in France in late June 1917 and his unit, the 16th Infantry, was selected by Pershing to march in the Fourth of July parade in Paris. Although the AEF's senior officers often recalled the excitement with which the Parisians greeted the neophyte doughboys, Carroll's reminisces of the event were much more pedestrian. His unit assembled for inspection at 6:30 AM and then moved to the Invalides where they "stood, hot and sweaty, at attention mostly, for hours in the hot sun while all the big shots made speeches." Carroll and comrades then proceeded to march through the cheering crowds of Paris with the unmeasured gait of green troops.[1]

John J. Pershing was a serious, no-nonsense professional. He was well aware that two-thirds of the marchers were basically raw recruits and to him they presented an "untrained, awkward appearance." As he watched the green doughboys of the 16th Infantry amble through Paris, it was clear to him that his army had much work and learning to do. As more American units arrived over the next fourteen months, it became ever more obvious to the Iron Commander that the training they received in the United States had failed to prepare them for the challenges ahead. To correct this problem, Pershing and the AEF staff attempted to craft a standard training regimen for his army and to build from the ground up a school system and training infrastructure to complete the doughboys' preparation for battle. Pershing envisioned that it would take approximately a year for the AEF to be completely formed, trained, and able to play a major role in the war. The preparation of the Americans would be critical, for once he saw the condition of the Allied armies in 1917, he came to believe that the AEF would be *the* army of 1919: the only force in the Allied ranks with the strength and morale to see the war to a victorious conclusion.[2]

For the most part the training of the divisions in the United States had been wildly uneven and woefully incomplete. To "secure a certain uniformity in standards" of the AEF and "give the troops the advantage of the latest tactical and technical developments and make up for the defects of training at home," Pershing ordered that all arriving divisions undergo a uniform three-month training period upon their arrival in France. He realized that the stateside training had been hamstrung by equipment shortages so the first month's training would focus on teaching individual doughboys and their squads, platoons, and companies the intricacies of the new weapons and small-unit tactics of the war. This phase of training was to be conducted by the French and British. During this period American NCOs and officers would also spend one or two days touring the frontlines to give them a brief introduction to trench warfare and combat. The second month of training was to instruct the Americans in trench warfare and to give units from the platoon to the regiment some degree of combat seasoning. This consisted of progressively larger American units under Allied command occupying trenches on the quiet sectors of the front. The last month of training was to prepare the AEF's regiments and brigades to fight open warfare and focused on how to maneuver, control, and supply large units while integrating all of the new supporting weapons in the AEF's inventory into their operations. Following completion of the initial three-month program, a further three to four weeks of training would center on division operations. In theory, once the divisions had gone through the entire sixteen-week regimen they were ready for active operations.[3]

Pershing's plan was logical and practical and ultimately irrelevant. The Ludendorff offensives in the spring and summer of 1918 threw the AEF's well-laid plans into confusion. To free up experienced Allied units and provide the coalition with a reserve of fresh American troops, the AEF GHQ and the Allies truncated the doughboys' training and rushed them into quiet sectors of the front. When it became clear in August 1918 that the tide was turning against the Germans, the training of the American divisions arriving in the summer and fall was further shortened. Unexpected heavy American casualties and the need for an unrelenting effort against the Germans meant that these divisions were thrust into combat with two or fewer months of additional training. In the end only the 1st, 2nd, 27th, and 42nd Divisions completed most of Pershing's training scheme. The press of events and military necessity destined all other divisions to enter battle with lesser degrees of readiness. Just as had been the case with stateside training, none of the divisions that arrived in France from March through October 1918 followed a comprehensive or full training regimen. The training of no two of these units would be the same. Like all premature births, the AEF's "army of 1919" faced a struggle for life.

The soldiers of the AEF's first four divisions were generally content with their training and believed that the Allies had done everything possible to tutor them in modern war. Their training had also accomplished Pershing's other goal of hardening them to the realities of the life of a soldier. Leslie Martin, an infantryman in the 1st Division, had very little training from the time he enlisted on May 9 and his arrival in France on June 26, 1917. His unit immediately began a rigorous course of training under elite veteran French troops. One thing that stood out to him was the toughness of the routine:

> We hiked about three miles out to the drill ground every morning, carried our full field packs out there, then we would unsling the packs, drill until about 11 o'clock, swing our packs, and start for dinner . . . those packs, one's rifle, everything the infantryman carried, weighed 63 lbs. when they were dry. But it rained a lot in France, then they really were heavy . . . I used to wonder why we always had to carry those packs. Well, they were muscle builders.

During this time, another green soldier in Martin's regiment learned a further important lesson in soldiering: never volunteer for anything. This became clear after he responded to his sergeant's offer of free tobacco and cigarettes, only to discover that it was a ruse to gather a detail to unload machine gun carts from a boxcar. Despite this lesson in "old soldiering," the soldier also admitted that his time training with the French provided him with the vital skills he needed to survive.[4]

The soldiers of the 42nd Division found their early instruction in France to be particularly arduous. The division's units arrived in France in late November and December 1917 and conducted their training during the bitter winter of 1917–1918. Working through heavy snows and freezing temperatures led some in the division to compare their plight to that of their revolutionary forefathers at Valley Forge. Faced with a shortage of firewood in his camp around Rimaucort, an Iowan of the 168th Infantry snapped, "At Valley Forge at least they had fire." The division's combat regiments culminated their two months of preliminary preparation with an extended march to billets near Rolampont. The 168th Infantry, for example, marched fifty-four kilometers in freezing weather. The misery of this march would go down in the division's lore. At times during the march the temperatures were below zero and drifts covered the road with three or more feet of snow. Brief breaks in the freezing temperature turned the tracks into gelatinous rivers of mud. While bad enough on the infantry, ice and mud made the routes particularly treacherous for wagons and horses. Upon reaching their campsites at the end of a hard day's march, the Rainbow doughboys often went to sleep hungry as their mess wagons were hopelessly mired on the roads. An officer in the division claimed that since there were no spare boots in the unit, when the hike wore out the soldiers' shoes some men completed the march with their feet wrapped in rags and sandbags. He also asserted that the shared hardships of the march built a deep esprit de corps and hardiness in the division that later paid dividends in battle.[5]

As was the case with the other early-arriving divisions, the doughboys of the 42nd benefited from realistic and relatively unhurried instruction given by the hands of experienced French soldiers. Martin Hogan, of the 165th Infantry, recalled, "We trained hard and earnestly. Proficiency meant life; it meant an earlier end to the gruesome game." Of his training another soldier likewise observed, "Gradually novices learned to use their weapons, acquiring the knowledge necessary to fit soldiers to the exacting demands of the front." At times the training also suddenly brought to the soldiers the ugly realities of their endeavors. On January 17, 1918, Lieutenant Scott McCormick was instantly killed when a bag of grenades that he was carrying during a trench raid exercise exploded. The event made clear to the onlookers that the "gruesome game" was played for high stakes.[6]

These 1st and 42nd Division doughboys were more fortunate than those who came after them. Given the idiosyncratic nature of the AEF's training in Europe, it is not surprising that the doughboys in the later-arriving divisions had a more varied critique of their final preparation than those who landed in 1917. The soldiers who arrived in France from the spring of 1918 onward were often harsh critics of their training in France. They noted that much of

this time was spent in weapons training, bayonet fighting, and very basic soldier skills rather than on needed advanced instruction on modern tactics and
techniques. The Americans were sometimes irritated that the Allied trainers
viewed them as rank amateurs who had to be taken in hand like raw recruits
even though some of the doughboys had been in the ranks for some time.[7]

Approximately half of the American divisions were instructed by the British during their initial phase of training. The first thing that the British did
was to have the doughboys turn in all of their American weapons so they
could be reissued with British rifles, Lewis Guns, and Vickers machine guns.
Two things irked the Americans about this process. First, the British tended
to assume that the Americans had little previous training and thus tended to
pitch their classes at a rather rudimentary level. As such, a great deal of the
weapons training focused on the age-old British technique of the "naming
of the parts": striping the guns down to their components and learning their
proper nomenclature by rote memorization. Little time was spent learning
the vital task of how to employ those weapons properly in battle. The other
complaint was that as soon as the doughboys completed their training, they
turned the British weapons in and never saw their kind again while in France.
In other words, the doughboys spent their first period of training learning the
excruciating details of weapons that most would never use in combat.[8]

Other training during this phase consisted of practice marches, instruction in gas warfare, and even more bayonet practice. Although an officer in
the 28th Division claimed that under the British tutelage his unit "made surprisingly rapid progress," many doughboys found this training to be stultifying and unproductive. One of the division's soldiers asserted that his time
with the English merely "consisted of six-mile hikes each day to a hillside
drill field where we practiced throwing dummy hand grenades and listened
to lectures." Another member of the division stated that his comrades found
that this was "one of the most trying periods of their long probation," as they
"whiled away the long, warm days, drilling and hiking, doing much bayonet
work, polishing and cleaning rifles and other equipment and putting in time
as best they could." It was not that the Americans were not willing and eager
to learn; they had some inkling of what was in store for them and just expected more from their instruction.[9]

The only commonality that existed in the training of the divisions that
arrived in France in 1918 was that their schooling was hurried. The need to

rotate the Allied units conducting the instruction to the line or to have the American units undergoing training moved to be in position to backstop the front often meant that the American divisions spent the time intended to complete their preparations shuttling between different Allied formations and sectors of the front. The experience of the 33rd Division's 131st Infantry was a case in point. It spent only thirty days in training before it was ordered to occupy a quiet sector of the British trenches. During this time, the regiment was trained by two different British units in two different regions and had used up much space on the calendar simply marching from one location to another.[10]

Even when the instruction was sound, the sheer amount of information that the green doughboys had to absorb was daunting. An infantry officer lamented the fact that "neither the training schedule nor the drill ground afforded the opportunity for training the personnel selected. The training schedule already included more than could be accomplished." This fact, however, did not stop his unit from packing as much instruction as possible into the day. The officer noted that in July 1918 the 353rd Infantry followed a breakneck daily schedule:

5:15: Reveille followed by breakfast at 5:45 and then clean up and
   inspections until 7:45
8:30 to 8:45: Close order drill by platoon
8:45 to 9:15: Company in the attack
9:15 to 10:30: Training of company specialists and bayonet and grenade
   training
10:30 to 11:00: Close order drill and battalion training on alternate days
11:00 to 11:30: Gas defense
11:30 to 1:00 PM: March to camp for lunch and then return to drill fields
1:30 to 2:45: Organization of a company strong point
2:45 to 4:45: Preparation and occupation of a center of resistance
4:45 to 5:30: Training on outpost, advance, and rear guards on Monday–
   Wednesday with test by the battalion commander on attack and
   defense on Thursday and Friday
5:30 to 7:30: Return to camp for dinner
7:30 to 8:00: NCO School
8:00 to 9:00: School for company commanders

Given the pace and subject matter of this schedule, one wonders how much the troops actually got out of their training period. After following a similar routine, an engineer complained, "Our training was something like a meal in which one swallows one food after another, still digesting the first while swallowing the last. In this respect, at least, it was not designed that we should front the Huns with empty stomachs."[11]

The situation was even worse for those divisions that arrived in the late summer of 1918. Captain Clarence Minick of the 91st Division's 361st Infantry kept a detailed diary of his unit's activities from the time he landed in France on July 20 until the Armistice. His record offers insights into the frenetic pace of the doughboys' training in France and some of the shortcomings of the system. After a week of unloading their ship and reconditioning the soldiers after their sea voyage, on July 29 Minick's company began its training with the French. Although he noted that the French drill was a repeat of what they had learned at Camp Lewis, the troops did "have more spirit," for they knew "we are going to get into a fight before many months." The French support had its limits and Minick and his comrades were forced to improvise to complete their instruction. On August 9 he wrote, "This morning I went out and fixed up a target range, used cans and everything else for targets."

The pace for Minick's regiment for the remainder of August was grueling and gives an indication of the atmosphere in the Allied ranks in late 1918, the frenetic efforts that were made to get the 91st Division ready for battle, and the shortcuts and risks that the AEF was willing to accept in the training of its forces. Minick recorded the following training events for August 3–31:

3 August—Battalion field problem
7 August—Company all day hike
9 August—Brigade maneuvers with a total march of 20 kilometers
13 August—12 kilometer hike
16 August—Brigade field problem
17 August—Brigade field problem in the morning and a Regimental field problem in the Afternoon, focused on "how to take German machine guns"
20 August—Regimental field problem
21 August—Regimental field meet with competitions on gas mask donning and semaphore signaling and shooting matches for rifles, pistols, and automatic rifles

22 August—Brigade field problem
25 August—Regimental maneuvers
26 August—Night maneuvers
27 August—Overnight 20 kilometer hike
31 August—Brigade field problem

Although the pace of this training was unrelenting, it is difficult to determine how realistic it was or how well it actually prepared Minick's soldiers for combat. While he noted that all the soldiers wore gas masks for the regimental field problem on August 20, some of his other entries indicate that the field exercises were more akin to route marches than authentic tactical maneuvers. Whatever the 361st Infantry got out of its training in August would have to do, for the whirlwind series of unit moves in September 1918 made further instruction all but impossible. During the entire month of September, Minick recorded only four days spent in training.[12]

Although the later divisions such as the 4th, 7th, 36th, and 91st suffered the most from the frequent moves and hectic tempo of their training, all of the divisions that arrived from the spring of 1918 onward had their instruction and readiness hindered by this vagabond existence. Troops needing specialty instruction on machine guns, mortars, and the other weapons that had been in short supply in the States suffered the most from these disruptions. An inspection of machine gun units in the 27th, 30th, and 78th Divisions in early July 1918 uncovered that their frequent changes of station had stymied any efforts to give their machine gunners a coherent and complete plan of training. The ability of the crews to master their machine guns was also hampered by frequent changes in weaponry. A lieutenant admitted, "You might say our men were a little confused" after they had been issued four different types of machine guns in less than a year of service. The soldiers muddled through these distractions as best they could. Charles Minder's battalion received their Hotchkiss guns only a few weeks before the unit went into battle. To make up for time, he recalled they were frantically studying, "night and day, learning all we can about the new French machine gun." He acknowledged that their training was far from complete when they went into the line.[13]

The AEF's artillerymen were the least likely troops in the AEF to have their training in France shorted or hand waved. The war had brought massive changes to the use and science of artillery. The development of indirect fire and the need to deliver a mass amount of shells in intricate creeping or box barrages had fundamentally changed the skill sets of the war's cannoneers. Artillery became *the* weapon of the Great War. In the words of Henri Petain, it conquered while the infantry merely occupied. Given the importance of this weapon, the French were not going to allow the callow Americans to fritter away its power with lackluster training plans. Unlike many AEF units, American artillery regiments almost always completed the two and a half to three months of training prescribed by the AEF GHQ and the French. Much of this instruction was done in French artillery schools using French instructors. This suited the green doughboys like Private Dewitt McIntyre just fine. "I am still in school and will likely be there for some weeks to come," he wrote his folks. "We are having a very fine school. The instruction is much better that what I received in the U.S.A. for our instructors have all had experience at the front."[14]

As McIntyre alluded to, due to stateside shortages of guns and instructors, many doughboy redlegs had their first real introduction to cannons only upon reaching the French artillery schools. Upon being issued his French 75mm guns, an overjoyed officer in the 304th Field Artillery proclaimed, "At last we have real matériel to work with, and should be compelled no more to the 'simulation' which had characterized our training at Camp Upton." His unit spent over two months at the Camp de Sourge artillery school where everyone in the unit, from cannoneers to signalmen, caisson drivers, and supply soldiers, were put through "the hard grind of the artillery school" until they were proficient on their specific duties. Leland Linman, an artilleryman in the 35th Division, recorded in his diary that his first month in France was spent learning the intricacies of his 75mm gun and in ceaseless "gun drills" mastering the intricate ballet of operating the piece. After that, his unit moved to the Camp Coet artillery camp for another month and a half of instruction focusing on actually firing the cannons and learning how to operate them as part of a larger unit. From there Linman's 129th Field Artillery spent two weeks firing barrages for the division in an inactive sector of Alsace front. The importance that the French (and the American converts to firepower-centric warfare) placed on the proper training of artillerymen ultimately made the doughboy cannoneers the most skilled soldiers in the AEF.[15]

Unfortunately, the only way that this degree of training was possible was for the AEF to strip the arriving divisions of their artillery regiments so that the cannoneers could be trained separately from their parent unit. The great downside to this approach was that most American infantry units were never able to train with their supporting artillery and that brigade and division staffs had little opportunity to learn or practice how to incorporate fires into their plans of operation. This later led to major troubles with infantry–artillery coordination during all of the AEF's operations.

The second phase of the doughboys' European education was to do a stint in the Allied trenches. The intensity of this introduction to war varied from unit to unit depending on the parameters set by the Allied commanders with whom the American served, the sector of the front they occupied, and the period of the war when the stint took place. When the 168th Infantry did its first tour in the trenches in late February and early March 1918, the commander of the French brigade in which they were assigned opted to pair each doughboy with a Poilu. This ensured the safety of the French lines while also allowing the doughboys to learn by watching and mimicking the actions of veterans. As the war progressed, such one-on-one attention proved harder to accomplish. By the time that the 82nd and 89th Divisions reached the front in July and August, their units went into the line as whole battalions under the command of a French regimental or brigade commander. Later, when entire American regiments went into the line, two of the American units were put into the lines at a time with a French regiment inserted between them. The French regimental commander controlled both his and the American units.[16]

The intensity of the aggressiveness between the German and Allied troops in the sector where the doughboys served their time in the trenches determined how much the Americans got out of their experience. Pershing and the Allies hoped that sending the Americans to less active sectors would give the novices a needed tutorial on modern trench warfare without subjecting them to the human "wastage" that would sap the AEF of its strength and morale. This required a balancing act that often proved difficult to negotiate. Many doughboys complained that their service in the trenches was too quiet and uneventful to offer any real combat seasoning or did not give them the right experiences for the kind of combat they later faced.

As was noted in chapter 13, the Americans often found themselves occupying trenches in Alsace and Lorraine. Much to the doughboy's chagrin, the daily routines in these sectors were frequently governed by the "live and let live" system. The Germans and French had worked out tacit truces that were a good deal for both parties. Neither side had wanted to see the bellicose doughboys screwing up their pacific arrangements. This led the doughboys to decry the lack of warlike aggressiveness in these sectors and their inability to truly experience battle. From the Colette Sector in July 1918 one soldier wrote, "No-Man's Land here is ridiculously safe. I wish we had Ford cars to carry our patrols to the German wire. [On patrol] we don't crawl—just stroll over and back." The area occupied by the 325th Infantry was so tranquil that an officer even claimed to have gathered fruit and shot quail in No Man's Land. A sergeant in the same regiment recalled his stint as "a dull period as men sat for days in the trenches gazing intently at the enemy lines but seeing nothing to shoot at." Although his company sent out patrols after dark, none ever made contact with their elusive enemy. The 35th Division's William Triplet went so far as to claim that his unit's time in the sleepy and dull French trenches was a "vacation from our previous grueling experience" of training behind the lines with the British.[17]

Other soldiers rightly claimed that the training Americans received in the Allied trenches did little to prepare them for what they eventually faced in the battles of the summer and fall of 1918. One doughboy stated that "what the infantry learned of trench warfare was of no practical value to it in carrying on open warfare in the Argonne." He went on to note that what the division's artillerymen, signalers, and medical personnel learned in the Vosges they had to "pretty nearly to unlearn in the days to come." This opinion was shared by the commander of the 77th Division, Major General Robert Alexander. He maintained that for his soldiers in the Vosges, "an occasional trench raid and routine gun fire had been the limit of their warlike activity" and that this in no way prepared the division for the ugly and unrelenting combat it faced shortly thereafter in the Oise-Aisne offensive.[18]

Although the American experience of training in the Allied trenches often failed to meet their expectations of war, the proceeding accounts were too quick to downplay the benefits that the doughboys gained from this time. While service in the trenches was certainly more tranquil and less sanguinary than what came later, this time was far from bloodless. When American aggressiveness broke the rules of the "live and let live" system, the Germans were quick to punish the neophytes' transgressions. After units from the 29th Division began to launch raids and use machine guns and artillery to harass the foe, the Germans responded in kind, and the "quiet" sector became quite active. Though William Triplet found the trenches to be "a kindergarten rather than the first grade in the school of war," he noted that the German schoolmasters were happy to administer a "stinging slap on the wrists" when their American pupils got out of line. The Germans also attempted to take the starch out of the newcomers with trench raids and gas attacks.

On the night of April 20, 1918, the Germans launched a massive raid against units of the 26th Division in trenches around Seicheprey that killed eighty, wounded 195 more, and led to the capture of over 130 American prisoners. While much less dramatic, soon after the men of the 168th Infantry occupied the French trenches, an abortive German raid, and the punishing artillery barrage that accompanied it, killed twenty-one soldiers and wounded twenty-two others. No matter how light these casualties or how calm the sector, the fact that the enemy was able to inflict harm on the doughboys made their time in the trenches an eye-opening experience.[19]

If some doughboys downplayed the intensity of their experiences in the trenches, others freely admitted that their first encounters with war left lasting impressions. In even the most tranquil of sectors, the situation forced the troops to come to grips with the seriousness of their situation and their own morality. Looking back on his first spell in the line, an infantryman in the 42nd Division recalled, "One learned later to laugh at the caution and discretion with which one went about his duties those first few days, but at the time war was a thing to be treated with respect, and not taken lightly . . . We felt rather queer and empty at the stomach when we actually realized for the first time that there was a need to kill or be killed." As the troops reached the front, the enemy went from being an abstraction or a passing encounter with harmless POWs to a palatable incarnation of menace. As could have been expected, the Germans did everything in their power to disconcert the new arrivals. Upon settling into their segment of trenches, the men of the 127th Infantry were rattled when they found a banner strung above the German lines announcing "Welcome 32nd Division." Other units recorded similar experiences. To the upstart American warriors the messages on the banners were clear: if, despite wartime security measures, the Germans already knew the Allied plans for rotating units through the trenches, what other dangerous information might the enemy know?[20]

It was during their first nights in the trenches when the realities of war and the fear of the unknown first came home to the doughboys. Men standing sentry duty in the trenches or occupying listening and observation posts in No Man's Land often did so alone. This isolation, the innate human fear of the dark, and the presence of an all-seeing and unseen enemy capable of all forms of evil and mischief played on the soldiers' minds. After being sent to man a listening post in No Man's Land, Duncan Kemerer admitted, "I was never so scared in my life, as all was so quiet, and the least noise or movement of shrubbery in darkness made you have all kinds of imaginations." He further confessed that "I was never so relieved in my life" as when his four-hour vigil came to an end. The need to stay alert also troubled the soldiers' leaders. "From the worried look he always wore," Frank Tiebout observed of his lieutenant, "one would think that the fate of the army, the safety of democracy and the political freedom of the next generation depended upon our staying up all night."[21]

Kemerer's and Tiebout's experiences were quite common. Doughboy letters, diaries, and postwar accounts frequently commented on the trepidation and the weight of responsibilities that the soldiers felt when standing guard in the darkness. One soldier recalled,

A sentry on post at first spent most of his watch fighting down fear, and as the night wore on the tensions began to tell, his eyes and ears to play him false. Gazing out into a blackness so intense that it seemed to have physical body, he created for himself a thousand imaginary dangers—posts seemed suddenly to transform themselves into crouching Germans waiting to rush upon him and chop him into mincemeat.

During their tour in the trenches, members of the 140th Infantry became convinced that a "phantom sniper" was stalking the unit's soldiers. The fear of this "phantom sniper" put the troops on edge:

The men on lonely sentry posts saw the sniper all night long. Who could blame them? Was it the wind that rustled or did a stealthy footfall press the dead leaves? Did a twig snap or was it the click of a rifle bolt drawn back. Were those dancing shadows among the moonbeams—or did something sinister move there—something menacing, silent, invisible. The voices that challenged in the night were tense as tight bow strings . . . for it was not the known and actual danger that causes flesh to creep—but the unknown, lurking, unseen in the shadows and taking every imaginable form.

This fear of the unknown also affected officers. For Lieutenant John Castle the nights and early morning hours in the trenches were the worst part of the tour. He recalled, "The nervous strain of these nights is terrible and they are years long, especially the hours of dawn. During those hours of stand-to, I used to wander up and down the trenches, talking to the men and trying to instill a confidence that I did not have myself."[22]

When the fear and imagination of these soldiers finally got the best of them, they tended to shoot first and ask questions later. Corporal Frank Faulkner's company defended a set of trenches located in a shell-torn woods. He recorded that the splintered trees "looked much like the forms of men, so we spent the first night shooting up stumps." An infantry officer noted that his men were so untrained and jumpy that they often "fired wildly at every shadow, and threw grenades when rats scuttled along" during their first tour. Such actions frequently sparked an orgy of shooting all along the lines as units in adjacent trenches believed that the shots and grenades indicated a German raid. After a sound in No Man's Land spooked Sergeant William Triplet's squad, they responded by firing rifles and Chauchats, throwing fifteen hand grenades and launching twenty-one flares (a month's allocation) into the darkness. Daylight revealed that the enemy body count consisted of a single rat. Not all such tales came with happy endings. Nervous sentries with itchy trigger fingers often caused friendly fire casualties during a unit's first stint at the front.[23]

The most dangerous aspect of life in the trenches was the constant threat of enemy shellfire. Most units suffered their first casualties of the war from artillery while they were serving in the Allied trenches. As will be examined in chapter 20, enemy artillery was generally the most feared weapon in the German arsenal. Shelling brought with it the possibility of sudden death. This came home to Lieutenant Edward Hardin during his tour of the French trenches in Alsace. As he explained to his mother on August 5, 1918:

I have had an experience tonight which I don't care to repeat any time soon, for it was the narrowest escape from death I have ever had. Capt. Gause and I were in our dugout getting up some reports and were just about ready to start out on our nightly tour of all our Company's gun positions, when we realized that the Boche was strafeing all around our dugout. You see we have gotten so used to hearing shells burst all during the day and night that we pay no attention to them unless they are unusually close. When we looked outside we found that shells were bursting . . . so we decided that the position was growing unhealthy and went back inside to

put on our coats to move off to another place. We had hardly gotten inside
when a most terrific explosion knocked us both off our feet. The candle
was blown out, and the sheet iron on our roof rattled and banged, the floor
buckled up in the center and dirt and rocks rained in on us through gaps in
the roof. Gosh! I thought my last minute had come. Everything was in total
darkness in our tiny hole and when I reached out instinctively for my gas
mask, it was covered with tomato ketchup, a bottle of which was sitting on
a shelf in the dugout. My first thought was that the Capt. had been killed
and that it was his blood on my mask. That brought me to full consciousness so I called out and asked him if he was hurt. From way over in the corner where he had been knocked came the answer. No! but let's get the hell
out of here! I then struck a match and locating the candle, lit it, and such
a scene as met my eyes—everything turned upside down . . . and our only
exit blocked by dirt. By this time we were both well aware of our danger,
for another shell might come over any minute, so we started out, and any
rabbit or chip-munk which would have seen us dig our way out with our
bare hands would have turned green with envy. We came through that wall
of dirt in nothing flat! And right at our door, not six feet from us, was the
cause of the trouble—a hole about twenty feet deep and at least thirty feet
wide—a crater such as is made by the Boche 9 inch shell.

Like Hardin, infantrymen in the trenches feared and hated artillery because
they were powerless to respond to the threat and could merely scramble for
dugouts in hopes of sheltering from its pulverizing rage.[24]

Close calls and the sudden snuffing out of lives from artillery became the
stuff of unit lore and legend. Sometimes, the soldiers' first brush with shellfire
provided fleeting moments of absurdity and humor. Company M of the 325th
Infantry's first night in the trenches on June 30, 1918, was warm and pleasant.
The company commander and many of the unit's soldiers had opted to sleep
in the open trench rather than in their fetid and damp dugouts. Before bedding down on the fire step, and contrary to standing orders, the officer made
himself comfortable by removing his boots. When the Germans shelled the
trench, the officer and the other sleepers bowled one another over in a mad
dash for shelter. "When the first shell came over," the company first sergeant
later recalled, the commander "opened his eyes and on the second he sat up in
bed and on the third he jumped out of bed and started putting on his shoes,
but as he could only get one on in the excitement he threw it off and took his
helmet in one hand and his Bull Durham in the other and beat it for the dugout." In the dugout, the one-shoed and shamefaced lieutenant realized that

he had left his gasmask topside but was fortunate that one of his soldiers had recovered and returned it to its disheveled owner. It must be stated that most of the soldiers' experience with artillery did not end so merrily. Even during Company M's seemingly funny episode, two of the company's soldiers were wounded in the bombardment.[25]

In addition to defending the trenches and enduring artillery barrages, some Americans also had the opportunity to hone their combat skills by patrolling No Man's Land and launching trench raids into the German lines. American commanders generally subscribed to the British belief that trench raids were good for maintaining the aggressiveness of the troops, giving them confidence through their ability to dominate No Man's Land and providing needed intelligence of enemy units and activities. As these raids required the soldiers to leave the relative safety of their trenches, cross the cratered and barbwired wilderness of No Man's Land, and operate in the terra incognita of the enemy defenses, they were particularly hazardous undertakings. A misstep or making too much noise risked alerting the enemy and the patrol being caught in the open under a hail of gun and artillery fire. These operations were usually conducted at night, which not only compounded the fear of the unknown but also required the patrol leaders to have strong navigation skills. The patrols were scheduled to leave at exact times from exact places and were to return to friendly lines through specific points. Errors in navigation risked not only blundering into German positions but also the danger of getting lost between the lines and returning the patrol to the wrong checkpoint. With nervous Americans on guard in the Allied trenches, the latter mistake could become very deadly.

Patrols and raids required more courage and placed more psychological strain on the participants than waiting passively in the trenches. Despite this fact, many of these activities were undertaken by volunteers. Warren Jackson speculated that what drove him and his comrades to sign on to these perilous missions were curiosity, boredom, and "the fear of being called a coward" if one did not step forward. Jackson found the experience to be terrifying. He and a few Marines went out on a night patrol with some veteran French soldiers, whose whispered instruction in French he did not understand. He felt that "half the Prussian Guards" were "about to swoop down on us," and he dreaded being left behind when his clothes became entangled in barbwire.

He later made two more trips into No Man's Land but admitted that since he "was not one of those heroic souls that crave a large share of hazardous adventure," the duty was never very appealing to him.[26]

The pull on young men like Jackson to demonstrate their courage to themselves and their peers by stepping forward for these missions placed them under an enormous psychological strain. This was evident in the case of Captain Charles Clement, the commander of E Company, 328th Infantry. He certainly felt the need to live up to the high expectations of being a brave and competent soldier and officer. As soon as his unit first entered the trenches in late June 1918, he pestered his battalion commander to allow him to send a patrol into No Man's Land. When the battalion commander relented, Clement led his patrol out on the evening of July 1. After being out only a brief period of time, the patrol hastily returned to friendly lines. One of the sergeants on the patrol claimed that the captain had created so much noise in No Man's Land by cracking pecans, talking loudly, and poking at rocks with his cane that the NCO feared for the lives of the men on the detail. The sergeant had to restrain the officer and carry him back to the trenches. A court martial later found that Clement had consumed a quantity of Scotch before the patrol to steady his nerves and had led the mission while intoxicated. After an emotional plea to the court to be allowed to clear his name, the panel allowed Clement to return to duty in his regiment as a private. On October 8 he was killed by a German sniper during his regiment's attack on Champrocher Ridge.[27]

Most of the raids and patrols never encountered the enemy. Some led to long remembered tragic-comic episodes. During a trench raid in March 1918, one of Tom Carroll's boots was caught on German barbwire as his raiding party beat a hasty retreat from the enemy lines. When a flare went up signaling for a protective artillery barrage, the panicked Carroll quickly divested himself of the fast-held boot and "ran back in sock foot thru mud and water" to safety. After returning from his anticlimactic first patrol on July 17, 1918, another soldier humorously admitted, "We expected to win the war that night but didn't." When one of his unit's patrols did make contact with the enemy, the Americans "offered the Germans what grenades they had and had sauntered home at a brisk clip." Not all of these endeavors ended so drolly. In fact, some officers and soldiers denounced the missions as pointless diversions that generally failed in their intent while causing needless casualties.

On August 31, 1918, a trench raid by 125 doughboys from K Company, 115th Infantry, managed to reach the German trenches and kill some of its defenders but failed to produce the hoped-for intelligence on the enemy. Unfortunately, as the Americans were returning to friendly lines, the Germans killed or wounded half of the raiders with machine gun and artillery fire.[28]

As with most things in war, much of the doughboys' time in the trenches was spent in the mundane, boring, and mindless routines of army life. For the most part, trench warfare in the Great War consisted of defending what one held and waiting for things that never happened. This was doubly true on the quiet sectors of the front. Private Albert Dahinden wrote to a friend in May 1918, "A fellow does not mind being up to his knees in mud and water so much if he really thinks he is really doing something than the utter uselessness of it all, that gets on a fellow's nerves." But the "utter uselessness" of waiting for attacks that never came still required the soldiers to be ready for the possibility of action. For example, soldiers on the front line were ordered to wear their full uniforms at all times and to have their equipment and weapons readily at hand to react at a moment's notice.[29]

The troops actually spent very little time in the frontline trenches. A stint in the front for a unit was generally around three or four weeks in duration. During those weeks, an average infantry company would spend five to fourteen days occupying the forward combat trenches, where they had to be constantly at the ready for battle. Another week would be spent in the reserve trenches, able to respond to an enemy attack and still within artillery range, but at a lesser degree of readiness. In a letter home in August 1918, Edward Hardin wrote that he was happy to be rotated to the reserve trenches after fourteen days on the front lines and losing one man killed, one wounded, and two "who lost their minds from shell shock." He informed his mother, "We are not shelled here but very little ... and best of all, we can sleep at night, which is quite a relief ... It's a great life, and a hard life, and yet where life is held so lightly, it seems particularly dear to us all." The last week would be spent in an ironically named "rest" period immediately behind the lines. This period was anything but restful. The soldiers at "rest" were put to work bringing up the supplies and building materials needed to keep the trenches functioning and labored at whatever other tasks or training they were set to. As the infantryman Paul Andrews wrote his uncle on July 18, 1918,

I have had one trick in the trenches and am now back of the lines having a rest for a while, before going back for another trick. I might add that rest in the army is more work than in the front line, as we are on the go most of the time, drilling or doing other fatigue duty. Such as the job I was on the other day, cleaning the streets of this town, or like this morning when they woke us up at half past four to fall out with full equipment and practice open formation work with airplanes directing us, etc.

Although Andrews was miffed at the army's concept of "rest," he noted philosophically, "This is sure a great life, one thing about it, you get variety, as you never know what or when the next order will be."[30]

Another of the soldiers' irritations was that no matter the combat situation, the army bureaucracy had to be served. It took a lot of supplies and equipment to adequately defend, maintain, and live in the trenches. The defenses required constant hard labor to keep the earth from reclaiming its own and to keep the troops fed and armed. As it was impractical to have the units rotating in and out of the line to carry in all the impedimenta required of these tasks, the Allied armies stacked the front lines with "trench stores" that remained in place when the units left. When a company relieved another unit, the newly arrived officers were required to inventory the items and account for any shortages. This accounting not only tied up a lot of the officers' time but also ensnared them in the endless flow of paperwork that was the fodder of distant staffs. The AEF GHQ mandated that American trenches be constantly stocked with a bewildering quantity and variety of items. The official trench stores for an infantry company consisted of:

256 boxes of solidified alcohol for heating rations	1,024 emergency reserve rations
	31 metal washbasins
12 large marmite and 12 small milk ration cans	500 blankets
	2 trench pumps
250 bed sacks	250 sets of fatigue clothing
15 trench stoves	250 Arctic overshoes
40 pairs of barbwire gloves	24 buckets for carrying grenades
256 leather jerkins	235 rifle breech covers
10 flashlights with batteries	1 large 12 power magnifying
30 brass rifle cleaning rods	periscope

4 trench periscopes	1 sniper scope
16 rifle periscopes	4 Bellsar gas alarm triangles
4 sniper spotting/observer scopes	4 Klaxon gas alarms
2 Strombos gas alarm air horns with 6 cylinders	17 trench fans to remove gas from trenches
4 gas alarm rattles	28 yards of blanket cloth for
1 wind vane	gas proofing shelters

Additionally, the units could obtain engineer tools and materials from the division or regimental engineer stores, such as lumber, duckboards, sandbags, barbwire, and barbwire pickets for the upkeep of the shelters and trenches. Few trenches were ultimately equipped with all of the items on the list, but officious staff and supply officers could and did make life hard on the line officers when hungry soldiers ate the emergency rations or the inventory of blankets came up short.[31]

Life in the trenches brought with it its own miseries. In fact, during their time in the trenches, the doughboys were as much at war with nature (if not more so) than they were with the Germans. Depending on the season and the geography, the trenches could be cold, wet, and uncomfortable places to live. The dugout shelters were often poorly ventilated. The odor of unwashed bodies and rotting food and the haze from cigarette smoke and wood- or coal-burning stoves left the occupants half-asphyxiated. Rain or melting snow led to rivers of mud and posed the danger of sodden trench walls collapsing in on the occupants. For most modern Western people today, mud is an inconvenience; something to gingerly scrape from ones' shoes or grudgingly wash from ones' children. Mud to the doughboys was a Jobian curse. It slowed the progress of troops and supplies to and from the front by making these efforts mass tests of strength and endurance. Despite their best efforts, mud clung to every item the doughboys possessed, doubling the weight of their uniforms and equipment and jamming weapons. Mud increased exposure to trench foot and, given the shortage of washing facilities in the line, was a thing to be endured rather than overcome.

To add to their unease and misery, the doughboys also found that they were far from being the sole occupants of their trenches and dugouts. The prevalence of food, dead bodies, and other unsavory things to feed on in and around the trenches led to a massive explosion of the rat population. The abundance and audacity of the vermin came as a shock to the Americans. An artilleryman noted that his shelter "was full of rats, addicted to creeping across faces or chewing up shoes while the city slept." Likewise William Graham recalled,

> At 1:30 a.m., I awoke from my sleep to such a noise I never heard before under my bunk. I moved quietly ... to look over the edge toward the floor and lo and behold two of the finest well-fed rats I have ever seen were having a splendid time with my hobnail shoes. First one rat would go into my shoe, explore the interior and then come out ... look at his or her mate then the second rat took a look around inside the shoe. I came to the conclusion it was time for me to call a halt on this acrobatic feat of the said rats. The only weapon I had handy was my "overseas" cap and I threw it at the rats who made a hasty retreat down a hole which was in the floor nearby.

A lieutenant wrote home that his soldiers constantly marveled at the size of the rats in their trenches. One soldier joked that he woke to find a rat in the process of putting on his boots and walking off with them, while others declared that "all trench rats are equipped with rubber boots—size 10's—and gas masks."[32]

Before giving up the effort as a lost cause, the doughboys often attempted to rid themselves of the rat infestation. An officer stated that his men on night duty constantly worked to develop ingenious devices to kill or capture the rodents. Most of these endeavors failed. The "better mousetrap" invented by the soldiers of the 140th Infantry was to put a piece of bread on the end of a bayonet attached to a rifle. When the rat boldly moved forward to claim the food, the soldier pulled the trigger and killed the pest with rifle fire. Some soldiers resorted to the more mundane approach of trying to roust the rats from their lairs so they could be trapped, stomped, or beaten to death as they scurried for cover in the open trench or shelter bay. After their first fitful night sharing their dugout with their rodent roommates, Thurmond Baccus and his comrades managed to trap seventeen rats the next morning. The doughboys soon found that the successful killing of some rats put but a small dint in the legions that remained. Sometimes gas attacks would kill a multitude, but, as the dugouts were generally gas-proofed, many rats still survived. The rats became, like the mud, something to be endured rather than conquered.[33]

In the final analysis, the doughboys' training with the Allies and experience in the trenches were a mixed bag. It gave the troops a taste of combat, but this was at best a snack rather than a meal. Although the quiet sectors imparted few tangible tactical lessons and skills to the doughboys, the experience did boost the novices' self-assurance and inured them to hardships. One officer claimed that serving in the trenches "helped the confidence of our men a great deal" and mentally prepared them for what was to come. Another maintained that the experience was vital because "The civilian mind, even with a year of training, does not easily adapt itself to the requirements of a soldier at war." To him, the most important aspect of his unit's time in the Vosges was the hardening that came with the reality that "feather beds and waffles for breakfast" were not a part of war. Private Paul Andrew agreed with this assessment. After spending time training, marching to the front, and living out in the open, he wrote his aunt,

> There is no question, this is some life we have over here, everything is crude and rough, but it agrees with me and I feel fine. It is funny to think back on city life and compare it with what I am now doing . . . The best part of it is that it all seems like camping out to me, and I don't mind it a bit, am perfectly happy and contented. It is surprising what a fellow can do without when he can't get it. This life sure does put you in great condition tho, I can hike eight or nine miles, anytime now, with full equipment on my back, which weighs around sixty or seventy pounds.

The soldier-historian of the 29th Division was more circumspect in his appraisal of his unit's introduction to combat. "While it gave the individual soldier the exalted morale so valued by military leaders," he noted, "it also inclined to give him a careless disregard for the future and a contempt for enemy power" that would later come back to haunt him.[34]

Before leaving the subject of the doughboy's training in France, it is also important to discuss the other efforts that the AEF GHQ made to prepare the Americans for battle. To address the Americans' lack of technical and tactical skills, the GHQ created a vast network of schools and courses. This put the AEF in a double bind. There was a crying need to school the troops in modern war, but the education system required to accomplish this task would itself require a huge outlay of instructors, administrators, support troops, and other resources. The GHQ also had to balance the need for officers, NCOs, and specialist troops to have time to attend the schools against the combat unit's need to have those same soldiers available to lead and train their organizations. Despite its good intentions, the AEF GHQ was never able to properly thread this needle during the war.

To fill its schools with students and instructors, the GHQ resorted to the simple bureaucratic expedient of issuing quotas to its divisions. These quotas were enforced regardless of the unit's situation. It was not unusual for units to be scalped of key junior officers and NCOs during important periods of training, or even in the midst of combat. During a postwar review of the AEF's performance, the commander of the 7th Division complained,

> Every organization after its arrival in France was to a great extent disorganized by the system of instruction adopted by the G.H.Q., in constantly withdrawing officers and noncommissioned officers to send them to school; thus leaving the organizations entirely without their complement of instructors. While these officers and noncommissioned officers were benefited . . . the organization itself lost by their absence more than was gained by the individuals that attended the schools . . . The action of superior authorities in taking away large numbers of officers of all grades, and enlisted men, to attend school and receive instruction absolutely destroyed all results in the way of instruction in the companies and battalions, and I consider these two organizations to be the very best schools for both soldiers and junior officers.

This fact was not lost on the junior leaders themselves. In the Morale Branch survey an infantry officer denounced the situation wherein "somebody's obsession regarding the necessity for schools kept about 50% of officers away from their units all the time, when they ought to have been giving their time to their men."[35]

The students attending the schools often complained that the courses were too long and that many of their instructors were ill prepared for their duties. The GHQ intended that the schools be thorough enough so that the graduates could return to their units with the knowledge to adequately train their troops. However, this gave zealous school commandants license to add all manner of minutia into their curriculums and to lengthen the time of their courses. Corporal Fred Takes spent a month in a course on the Chauchat gun. After all that time, he knew the ins and outs of the weapon's technical aspects but had only spent one day of the course learning the tactics for using it in combat. Of the AEF's schools, an infantry officer trenchantly observed, "Three weeks courses were given in courses that any reasonable man ought to learn in three days. If he couldn't learn grenade throwing, for instance, in three days, he ought not be an officer." The commander of the 77th Division was also outraged at the "waste of invaluable time" in having to send his soldiers to a six-week course on the bayonet that should have been no more than two weeks long.[36]

The problems with the AEF school system did not stop there. The school commandants often resorted to reassigning the best students from graduating classes to their organizations to serve as instructors. These actions had major consequences. Combat units were robbed of some of their most apt leaders and lost the knowledge that these students turned instructors could have returned to the organization. The practice may have also been counterproductive, as one student later admitted that he and his comrades "feared to make good grades in school because of the danger of becoming an instructor." Furthermore, the use of instructors who had themselves just graduated the course ensured that the schools would never rise above an elementary level. As an engineer officer complained, "The instructors were 2nd Lts, who had finished the previous course. It was not their fault that they didn't know [the material], but it was a joke." Another officer groused that his teachers "were officers who never had active service at the front and their theories were sometimes complexing to the veterans just in from the line."[37]

Despite the best intentions of Pershing and his staff, enemy actions, the press of events, and the systemic problems of creating the AEF's training infrastructure worked to stymie their efforts to properly prepare the AEF for combat. Although the AEF schools, training with the Allies, and time in the trenches eroded some of the Americans' ignorance of modern war and gave the doughboys some seasoning for combat, on the whole these efforts fell far short of Pershing's expectations. With the exception of those units that arrived in France in 1917 and early 1918, the training of most of Pershing's divisions was incomplete and short on realism. Their unforgiving finishing school of war would be held along the Marne, Aisne, and Vesle and in St. Mihiel and the Argonne.

16

"Mother, Take Down Your Service Flag, Your Son's in the S.O.S."

Life in the Services of Supply and the Rear Area

In later wars combat soldiers would call them pogues, chair-borne rangers, Rear Echelon Motherfuckers (REMFs), People Other Than Grunts (POGs), and Fobbits. The objects of this derision were the vast number and variety of troops who spent their war behind the lines supplying, directing, and administering the fighting men and building and staffing the ponderous infrastructure that modern armies need to function. As the derogatory names imply, the combat soldiers saw these men not as comrades in arms but as slackers who whiled away their time in the safety of the rear enjoying good food and comfortable billets. The grunts also complained that these troops also took or pilfered the lion's share of the comfort items, such as candy and tobacco, which the folks at home and the army had provided for all the nation's soldiers. Although there have always been tensions between those at the "teeth" of an army and those at the "tail," the material demands of total industrial war meant that for the first time in American history the division between these two groups grew from a crack to a chasm.

Nothing captured this new disdain more than a letter sent from Lieutenant Edward Hardin to his mother in February 1919. Hardin was a member of the 29th Division's 111th Machine Gun Battalion, a unit that had recently been bloodied in the Meuse Argonne. It was his sad duty to inform her of the battalion's fall from grace.

> I wonder if the following parody on "Where do we go from here" has become popular in the States yet—"O, Mother take down your Service Flag, your son's in the S.O.S." . . . This is what the

combat troops used to sing to the Quartermaster, Ordnance and other troops stationed behind the lines in the S.O.S. (Service of Supplies) and now, Irony and Fate!—we are transferred to the S.O.S. . . . Our Division, as you know, has seen some mighty tough fighting and we all resent being classed now with the "Boulevard Soldiers" or the "Back Area Heroes" as the S.O.S. is generally known or called.

The song that he referred to originated in the workshops, warehouses, and offices of the SOS headquarters at Tours. Although Hardin claims that the combat troops originated the ditty to poke fun at the rear-area soldiers, it was in fact a combined lament and song of pride crafted by the doughboys of the SOS themselves.

> Mother, Take Down Your Service Flag, Your Son's in the S.O.S.
> He's S.O.L., but what the hell,
> He never suffered less.
> He may be thin, but that's from gin,
> Or else I missed my guess.
> Mother, Take Down Your Service Flag, Your Son's in the S.O.S.

The term "SOL," Shit out of Luck, was one of the more popular of the war. Those who served behind the lines understood that the combat soldiers thought of them as lesser beings and may have viewed themselves as being SOL for their assignments, but they also knew that without the work in the rear, those at the front would founder.[1]

It is interesting to note that the "rear" of an army is always relative to the beholder. To the infantry private at the front, the rear-area personnel began with "those bastards at company headquarters" and then proceeded upward and rearward. Even when it came to noncombatant soldiers, there was a pecking order that separated them from those supposedly enjoying the greater comforts of the rear. Thus the doughboys working in the regimental and division supply, ammunition, and sanitary trains, whose duties often subjected them to shellfire and the hardships of the front, looked down on those slightly further to the rear in the depots of the Advance Section of the SOS. Of course, the troops in the Advance Section of the SOS resented the easy life of those timid souls working in the SOS Intermediate and Base Sections, while the personnel in those sections looked askance at the troops still in the United States.

Moving, feeding, supplying, paying, healing, and administering a two-million-man army in France was an inherently complicated, labor intensive, and wasteful effort. As France was already stretched to the breaking point to provide services for the French and British armies, the AEF took what it could from the French while also constructing its own barracks, berths, warehouses, and railroads. All of this required the Americans to devote a huge outlay of manpower to accomplish work that would never directly kill, wound, or capture a German but that made those combat tasks possible.

There is some uncertainty surrounding what percentage of the AEF's personnel strength was devoted to noncombatant duties. Based upon the experience of the Allies, in the fall of 1917, the AEF GHQ estimated that "just under one man in three was necessary [to be] in the S.O.S." to keep the fighting men in the field. From the beginning, the AEF had difficulty in raising the manpower to reach even this woefully inadequate ratio. Major General James Harbord, the commander of the SOS, maintained that the London Agreement of April 27, 1918, undermined the AEF's ability to create the robust support and supply infrastructure that it needed to conduct sustained operations. Under this shortsighted arrangement the British would only assist the United States in transporting American infantry, machine gun, engineer, and signal units to France until the crisis of the Ludendorff offensives passed. This, Harbord claimed, deprived the SOS of the manpower it needed to function efficiently and ultimately led to some combat divisions being skeletonized so their soldiers could be reassigned to noncombatant duties. "At the end of August [1918]," Harbord complained, "we had in France 61,061 officers and 1,354,067 enlisted men, of whom less than 300,000 were in the S.O.S. . . . We were long on bayonets [that is, combat troops] and short on stevedores, railroad operating men, engineers and the like."[2]

Although the London Agreement and the earlier-than-anticipated commitment of the AEF to combat certainly complicated the development of the SOS, the army was far from being as starved of noncombatant manpower as Harbord suggested. Major William Haseltine estimated that 30 percent of the American Army was working in the SOS in November 1918, but soldiers in the SOS comprised only part of the noncombat troops required to keep the army functioning.

According to the AEF GHQ Personnel Division, on November 11, 1918, the AEF had 546,596 soldiers assigned to the SOS and another 173,008 troops working in noncombatant jobs in the supply trains, headquarters, and hospitals assigned to large combat formations. By these figures, nearly 37 percent of the AEF's personnel were employed in vital noncombat roles. More recently, the army historian John McGrath estimated that when one considers soldiers assigned to headquarters, as well as medical and logistics units assigned to duties outside of the SOS, combat troops comprised only 53 percent of the AEF's manpower. The complications arise when one tries to define what it means to be a combat soldier. As they seldom pulled triggers but were constantly under small arms and artillery fire while laying and maintaining phone lines, were the soldiers in divisional field signal battalions combat or noncombat troops? Even accepting the lower estimate that 37 percent of the AEF's strength was devoted to noncombat tasks, these numbers still represented a dramatic and historical shift from previous American military practices. By the Armistice there were nearly twice as many soldiers serving in the SOS as Ulysses Grant and William Sherman had in their combined armies in 1864.[3]

Although it is possible to describe some commonalities in the experiences of infantrymen, machine gunners, and artillerymen, the vast array and conditions of work performed by those behind the lines make it impossible to depict the life of the average soldier in the SOS and rear area. The life of a black stevedore in St. Nazaire was fundamentally different from the truck driver in a divisional ammunition train, a logger in the 20th Forestry Engineer Regiment, a headquarters clerk at Chaumont, a railway construction soldier, or a soldier-farmer working for the Quartermaster Corps Garden Service at Versailles. Even soldiers in the same branch or occupational specialty had radically different lives depending on what type of unit they were assigned to. Thus the life of a medical orderly in a divisional field hospital was fundamentally different from that of a medical orderly serving in a base hospital in Paris. Given this multiplicity of experiences, this chapter can offer only the barest glimpse of the lives of those who waged the Great War behind the line.

As previously noted, in the minds of the combat doughboys the "boulevard soldiers" of the rear area lived a charmed life of relative ease, and they were seldom reticent about showering SOS troops with their hearty scorn. World War I witnessed a great flowering of bitter and ironic song parodies penned by soldiers to express their dissatisfaction with their plight, their commanders, and the world in general. In one such song, the Marines compared their existence to those in the SOS:

They brought us rations once or twice a week,
Is it any wonder we're not fat and sleek,
But the people in the rear,
Eat with plates and silver gear,
Oh, it's a stay in the S.O.S. if you're a Sheik

There is little doubt that the life of the AEF's combat soldiers was more glum and difficult than those in the rear and that scores of troops in the SOS experienced what at the time was termed a "good war." But the daily life of the majority of soldiers working behind the front was one of unremitting hard labor under difficult conditions. Fighting occupied only a small slice of a combat soldier's time in France. Although the rest of the time was spent in marches, drills, and fatigue duties, the combat troops did enjoy periods of rest, refit, and recuperation. Combat soldiers at rest still required food, supplies, and the labor of the rest of the AEF to keep them in the field. As Clarence Mahan, a truck driver in the 1st Division Supply Train, explained, "Our rest periods were few and far between as there were always troops to be moved and rations to deliver." "Surely the life of a supply man was no bed of roses," the teamster Carl Noble later lamented. "We were on the go most of the time, day and night." As Mahan and Noble could attest, the work of the great machine of the SOS and the rear services never stopped.[4]

This ceaseless exertion was also driven by Allied and AEF regulations. Because GHQ and French law mandated that railcars had to be unloaded within twenty-four hours of their arrival, doughboys working in various depots often started work at four in the morning to get the job done within the allotted time. This also meant that the soldiers performing that job generally worked seven days a week. The fact that it was not until January 1919 that General Harbord allowed units in the SOS to cease work on Sundays and holidays is an indication of how much effort was required by those in the rear to keep the AEF functioning.[5]

The hard work of the doughboys in the rear services was also seen in the AEF's logistical statistics. The army's ill-used stevedores unloaded over 1.3 million tons of supplies in French ports. AEF railroad construction engineers laid 1,002 miles of track and placed into operation 1,667 American locomotives. Railroad construction units built 19,697 railcars and other rolling stock from parts shipped from the United States to Europe. One of these regiments worked in shifts to meet this demand with eighteen hundred men laboring during the day and four hundred at night. By the end of October 1918, the unit was assembling an average of ninety-six complete cars a day. Doughboy carpenters built over sixteen thousand buildings. To meet the army's insatiable demand for lumber, the 20th Forestry Engineers grew to become the largest regiment in American history. By the Armistice it contained over five hundred officers and thirty thousand enlisted men and had logged and cut over 222 million board feet of lumber, 3.4 million railroad ties, and 1.2 million cords of firewood.

The work of the SOS and rear services did not stop there. The doughboys were prodigious consumers of food, clothing, and ammunition and keeping them supplied with these items alone required supply troops to receive, warehouse, move, and distribute mountains of material. By the Armistice, the SOS Headquarters estimated that the AEF was consuming 51.22 pounds of supplies per soldier per day to keep the army in the field. Between June 1917 and May 1, 1919, the troops in France consumed over 2.3 billion pounds of food with the individual soldier being issued an average 4.3 pounds of food per day. In hard numbers, during the same period the AEF ate 620 million pounds of potatoes (its largest single food item), 581 million pounds of meat, and 464 million pounds of flour. On average each doughboy went through 14.6 pairs of heavy wool socks, 8.8 winter undershirts, 8.3 pairs of winter drawers, six pairs of wool breeches, five pairs of shoes, and 3.8 wool service coats per year. At the Armistice, the AEF had also expended 8.5 million artillery rounds, over 2.9 million grenades, and 608 million rounds of small arms ammunition.[6]

The men serving in the rear area had mixed views about their assignments. While there was much hard work, there was very little glory. The AEF awarded 4,324 Distinguished Service Crosses, the nation's second-highest award at the time, during the course of the war. As could be expected, over 75 percent of these awards went to infantrymen. Only 368 of the medals were given to noncombat troops, with the bulk of these (250) going to medical personnel assigned to combat units. The AEF's own ambivalence over the large number of men in the SOS was also reflected in the award of the service chevron. The service chevron was a small gold stripe worn on the left cuff of the uniform coat. As a chevron was awarded to the soldier for every six months overseas, it was valued by the soldiers as a visible indication that the man was a veteran who had done his bit. When the AEF first instituted the award in February

1918, however, it was only to be given to soldiers in the Zone of the Advance: the area forward of the SOS Intermediate Section. This made most of the soldiers in the SOS ineligible for the award. In the face of growing complaints from SOS troops and pressure from Washington, in April 1918 the AEF GHQ allowed all doughboys to wear the service chevrons who served in the European theater of operations. Although the GHQ had corrected the problem, its initial policy on the chevrons had made it clear to the soldiers in the SOS that the army's senior leaders viewed them as second-class troops. This was also reinforced by other AEF policies. After complaints by frontline soldiers that the troops in the SOS were sponging up too much of the army's comfort items to the detriment of the fighters, in July 1918 the YMCA directed that 70 percent of its supplies would be reserved for the doughboys in the line.[7]

Given these jaundiced views of the combat troops and the AEF GHQ, it is not surprising that many SOS and rear-area soldiers were not happy with being noncombatants. Lieutenant Reginald Thompson was upset when the army sent him to serve as a supply officer in a depot unit. He complained in a letter home, "I joined the army to fight the Dutch, and I thought that I had left the mercantile business far behind, but at present my war consists of issuing uniforms, fitting shoes, book keeping and quarreling with the battalion supply officer." He added sarcastically that his life was "all very glorious and thrilling." Thompson was far from alone in this opinion. When the essayist Carty Rank visited the AEF in 1918 he recalled, "On the way to headquarters I passed many doughboys who looked well fed and happy, although they assured me that they would much rather be in the front lines taking a shot at a boche than doing quartermaster work. They preferred the Springfield to the packing crate." Later he observed,

> Many would-be fighters were assigned to S.O.S. work much to their disgust . . . one husky doughboy that I met [said,] "Look at me, standing six-foot-two in my socks and stationed here in a warehouse telling a bunch of French girls how to check up trainloads of coffee, flour and bacon when they arrive. Gee, but I would like to get up where I could have a whack at Fritz!"

But even that fellow admitted philosophically that "it is all part of the big game over here" and understood that his part was important to the war.[8]

While the combat doughboys were happy to make fun of the rear-area types, the SOS men were also willing to lampoon themselves and their lack of military glory. In April 1918, shortly before the GHQ lifted the restrictions on the service chevrons, a SOS doughboy sent the following song to *Stars and Stripes*:

> When this cruel war is over, and the boys go marching home,
> I'm afraid I'll be an outcast, and forever have to roam;
> When wound chevrons they exhibit, and their service stripes of gold,
> And they tell admiring lassies, of their doughty deeds and bold,
> I'll be missing from the circle, and nobody there will hear,
> How I—I was but a hero, in the SERVICES OF THE REAR.
>
> Chorus:
> For I'm a S.O.R. boy—also an S.O.L.
> I never pulled a trigger, or sent a Boche to hell;
> I never saw a dugout, in fact was never near—For I performed my duty in the SERVICES OF THE REAR.

For some soldiers, their assignment to noncombat units was no laughing matter. After washing out of officer's training and being posted to Intermediate Ordnance Depot #2, Benson Oakley was despondent. He wrote his wife, "How I wish I were a Captain! It makes me sick sometimes dear to think I'm not an officer because I want to be something, rather someone you will be proud of when I return." He added self-pityingly, "I . . . wonder if you ever feel ashamed because I'm not an officer." Without a commission and the ability to see combat, Oakley believed that he would be a lesser man in the eyes of his spouse.[9]

Other troops were more concerned about their lack of training to perform their noncombatant job rather than an absence of honor and excitement. In many rear-area positions, the army simply expected the troops to learn by on-the-job training. One such soldier was trained for only three days in France before he was selected to care for his infantry regiment's horses. His instruction in France was limited to "a little gun practice and bayonet practice" and "about 15 minutes of relaying messages as a runner and a little training with a hand grenade." Private Edgar Ferrill of the 2nd Ammunition Train admitted that he "had little training for front line handling [of] ammunition." He did not, in fact, believe that he needed much instruction, noting, "If you got through the shellfire you went with another load"—that was that. Although troops assigned to tasks such as Ferrill's could get by on brawn and observation, other jobs in the rear required more technical training than the army offered. Another private lamented that he "had no actual hospital experience in the states" and struggled to learn the ropes of caring for the wounded when he was assigned to an ambulance company in the 3rd Division. When the 29th Division landed in France, its quartermasters had difficulty finding qualified drivers for their newly issued trucks and had to ask for volunteers to fill the seats. The supply officers discovered that the volunteer drivers' lack of training led to delays in getting supplies delivered, increased breakdowns, and a spate of accidents.[10]

Not everyone sought combat duty, and some practically avoided it. Benjamin Heath was a fit and intelligent soldier who rose to the rank of sergeant major before the war ended. Heath was quite happy working on the staff of the 82nd Division. Although his qualities could have made him a good candidate for officer training, he avoided that possibility, noting to his sister, "I feel that I would be of more service to Uncle Sam in a quiet way just where I am." Being in the division headquarters certainly had it perks. As the fighting picked up in the summer of 1918, he wrote home, "I am still playing little Jack Horner in my own little corner and hoping that the boys that are in the fighting will show what the Americans can really do." Despite Heath's relatively safe position behind the fighting lines, he felt free to lord over the lesser lights of the SOS. He wrote his mother that the troops in the SOS "live comparatively comfortable and it is easy to make their lives back there where there are no dangers." Without any hint of irony, however, he then went on to note, "I feel like a slacker, but I am satisfied to stay right where I am rather than try for a commission in [the] infantry."[11]

Other doughboys were not quite as happy as Heath in being in the rear but grew to accept and even like their assignments. Just as the 18th Infantry was marching to the front for its first stint in the trenches, Lieutenant William Haselton received orders for duty on the 1st Division staff. The young infantryman recorded in his diary that the assignment was a "great surprise" and admitted that he was "a bit disappointed" at the noncombat assignment. He did confess, however, that "things looked brighter after getting on the job." Unlike Haselton, Sergeant Joe Scheck was positively giddy over escaping infantry life. After being pulled from serving as an infantry trainer, he wrote a friend expressing his joy in a new assignment: "I'm working as an entertainer on the AEF entertainment circuit with another soldier and our act is a success. We are living under the best army conditions and are traveling around France in good style." Eight days later he informed his sister, "Still in Le Mans but [I am] getting along better than ever. I'm living in a nicely furnished room and eating first class meals at the new Y.M.C.A. Expenses paid by the entertainment dept of the AEF." Few army assignments could have been better than having an all-expense-paid tour of France with good food, comfortable billets, and a nontaxing job.[12]

Some in the SOS had no problem at all living and working far from the front. One song popular with the rear troops boasted,

> And when they ask us how dangerous it was,
> Oh, we'll never tell them, No, we'll never tell them.
> We spent our pay in some café, and fought wild women night and day.
> 'Twas the goddamndest job we ever had
> And when they ask us, and they're surely going to ask us,
> Why we didn't win the Croix de Guerre,
> We'll never tell them, No, we'll never tell them.
> There was a Front, but damned if we knew where.
> 'Twas the goddamndest job we ever had.

Other doughboys were happy to be away from danger for the sake of their families. A private tried to assure his aunt that her son would be safe during the war by noting, "Take courage from the fact that even the most advanced Base Hospitals are always at least fifteen to twenty five miles back of the lines, and there is only the occasional shelling or air raids, no cause for worry."[13]

Contrary to the beliefs of the combat doughboys and some of the rear-area troops themselves, assignment to noncombatant duty was not always free from danger. In fact, divisional supply soldiers and some troops in the SOS Advance Section frequently came under enemy shellfire and air attacks. This reality came as a shock to Clarence Mahan after he was reassigned from an infantry regiment to the 1st Supply Train. He was happy to be out of the trenches, but later admitted, "I thought that this would be a safe place. Little did I know for I was actually 'out of the frying pan and into the fire.'" While driving in a convoy under shellfire, he discovered his unit "could not stop and dig fox holes" like other doughboys, "as we had to keep moving for ammunition and food had to be delivered." Those bringing up ammunition faced the constant danger that a shell or accident would set off their loads and blow them to Kingdom Come. Another driver recalled,

Hauling ammunition at night had some hazards. In the first place, you could have no lights of any kind, as they would likely draw enemy fire . . . One time we had to pass a crossroad on which the "Heinies" were dropping a shell every so many minutes. The "game" was to wait, back aways, until a shell hit and then guess how many rigs could gallop across before the next hit.

In this game, guessing wrong had immediate and spectacular consequences. There were other dangers also associated with these jobs. Gasoline-powered vehicles also brought explosive possibilities. This fact was not helped by the carelessness of some troops. Mahan wrote that three drivers in his unit used gasoline from their trucks to clean the floors and kill the lice in their billets. When one of them lit a cigarette, the building burst into flames, killing one, seriously burning another, and completely destroying the structure.[14]

Supplying the combat troops should be a very straightforward operation. Logistics units simply had to get the right item, be it ammunition, food, medical support, or replacements, to the right place, at the right time, into the right hands. Yet, as with nearly everything in war, this seemingly easy process was always beset by a multitude of obstacles that the logisticians had to overcome. Under the best conditions, keeping the troops supplied as they moved forward in battle was a complex and difficult undertaking. The situation in the Meuse Argonne region fell far short of the best conditions. Much of the American First Army's rear area had been the front lines of the Battle of Verdun in 1916. The region's already underdeveloped road network had been devastated by over a year of artillery fire and belts of trenches and barbwire further canalized movement. The hilly and wooded terrain of the area and the narrow, obstacle-strewn streets of its towns and villages only added to the woes of the Americans traveling to and from battle. On September 27, 1918, one artilleryman reported,

All the wheeled materials in the A.E.F. is on the road out of Avocourt and all of it bound toward the Front. Ambulances are stalled in ditches. They can't get back and men who might have had a chance for their lives are dying because nothing can be done for them . . . What to do? Not much of anything. The road through Avocourt is paved with vehicles—a double column of them stretching for infinite miles forward and back—locked hopelessly end to end and hub to hub. It was hopeless to attempt the

hairpin curve through Avocourt . . . An M.P. colonel making a futile effort to straighten out the tangle raged back and forth in front of us. He
was swearing like an insane man and tears were rolling down his cheeks
unchecked.

The conditions in the Argonne described by the artilleryman were far from
unique. Similar problems had arisen in the Americans' previous campaigns,
albeit on a smaller scale.[15]

Although Henry Ford and other American manufacturers had pioneered
the mass production of automobiles, most of the AEF artillery, field kitchens, and supply trains continued to be moved by mule and horsepower. This
age-old system of conveyance brought with it its own challenges for the
doughboys. By the Armistice the AEF had received 67,985 horses and mules
from the United States and had purchased another 175,635 from European
sources. Even these numbers outpaced demands. Difficulty in obtaining harness animals led the AEF GHQ to reduce the number of horses and mules in
its divisions from 7,701 in January 1918 to 6,663 by June of that year. Although
the influx of trucks somewhat helped to offset the loss of these animals, the
shortages of mules and horses forced the rear-area soldiers to do more with
less and contributed to the army's supply problems throughout the war.[16]

For the doughboys, pack and harness animals often proved to be finicky
and fragile creatures. Those soldiers assigned to duties with horses and mules
quickly discovered that the army expected that the animal's care and feeding
took precedence over that of their doughboy-masters. In other words, the
horse was to be groomed, watered, fed, and bedded down before the soldier
went through a similar process. The great disadvantage of using horses in
war was that they were prodigious consumers of fodder and water. As the
war had left the French countryside, especially in the battle areas, denuded
of natural fodder, the AEF had to obtain, package, and transport most of its
own animal feed when operating in Europe. In May 1918 the AEF mandated
that draft horses weighing twelve hundred pounds and over would be fed
fourteen pounds of hay and twelve pounds of grain, and mules would receive
twelve pounds of hay and eight pounds of grain. The regulation allowed field
commanders to slightly increase the fodder when the animals "continuously
perform heavy work for at least eight hours per day." Under the stress of
battle, these allocations proved unrealistic, and in October 1918 GHQ reduced
the ration to ten pounds of hay and nine of oats for draft horses and eight

pounds of hay and seven of oats for mules. Even at these reduced rates a large percentage of the AEF's animal-drawn wagons were carrying the fodder to feed the animals pulling the other animal-drawn wagons. As the fodder was heavy and bulky, feeding the AEF's horses and mules was a ceaseless and backbreaking chore for the army's teamsters. As twenty to twenty-six pounds of fodder ultimately created twenty to twenty-six pounds of manure, the troops assigned to horse duty also had to contend with the laborious and odiferous chore of "mucking out" the stables and horse lines.[17]

Under the strains of combat, draft animals quickly began to show their inherent fragility. A team driver in the 2nd Division explained,

> Horses are a serious problem in warfare. At best, the army did not feed them too well and, at the front, forage got through only after most other supplies. It seemed that a horse would wear out, from work and lack of sufficient rest and food, quicker than a man and take much longer to recover. Often roads were muddy with mireholes that necessitated doubling up weakened teams to get through them. Sometimes horses would go down from fatigue and not be able to get up again. Whenever we got back from a drive, quite a few horses had to be replaced.

Carl Noble had a similar experience and after just a few days of campaigning he noted that "the animals were showing the strain." As campaigning wore down the strength of horses, unit supply trains faced increasing difficulties in delivering the goods. The unit received new horses to replace those horses that had died or had become lame, but many were poorly broken and refused to work. As a number of Noble's wagon drivers were equally inexperienced, it was difficult to keep the supply column moving. It got so bad that the commander of Noble's infantry regiment temporarily assigned eighty infantrymen to his supply company to help it push and pull its twenty wagons through the axle-deep mud of the roads. The infantrymen were incensed at the assignment: "They said they had to do all the fighting, and now they had to work like hell and do the work of horses for a bunch of supply company men who had never seen a shell explode." Noble admitted, "I felt sorry for the men, but without supplies they couldn't eat in the morning and our animals were exhausted."[18]

Being assigned to horse duty brought with it other discomforts and dangers for the riders. Those doughboys who believed that they would escape the hardships of the infantry by riding in comfort through the war were quickly disabused of that notion. Soon after entering the army, George O'Brien admitted to his mother that after five and a half hours of mounted drill, "Gee, am I sore. I split my buttocks right. They certainly are sore." Things did not get much better, for a few weeks later he wrote, "As luck would have it, it fell to my lot to ride a rawboned old 1300 Lb. plowhorse . . . It's backbone was as sharp as a cleaver . . . Well my south end was as raw as a piece of beef . . . and to make it worse [we had] no bridles and it was ride on, fall off, get on, bleed a while, walk, ride, etc." The combination of half-broken horses and half-trained men was always a dangerous one. As H. W. Carver informed his wife,

> This a.m. we went out for horse exercises and were given the command to gallop—when a big truck passed us and as the horses were most all out of control anyway—they stampeded—I have never seen such a mess . . . Several men were thrown and one Armstrong was dragged a quarter of a mile . . . He was taken to the hospital by a passing car and I rode by to see him. I hardly think that he will live . . . he never will be able bodied—he sure was a wreck.

Even the best-trained and most docile of horses and mules could give their riders unexpected bites and kicks. All of this was just part of the life of being a teamster in the AEF.[19]

Operating motor vehicles brought other challenges and tribulations. Over the course of the war, the AEF received 51,693 trucks and several thousand other motor vehicles from the United States. The demand for automobiles and the ad hoc nature of American mobilization meant that the AEF ultimately contained over two hundred different types of motor vehicles. This created a nightmare for drivers and supply officers because each of these vehicles often required unique repair parts, tires, and mechanical know-how to keep them running. If the right part was not on hand, it could take weeks before a broken truck returned to operation. Although gasoline was dangerous, it was somewhat easier to move, and, unlike horses, trucks only consumed fuel when they were running.[20]

This was not to say that motor vehicles did not come with a price. To the supply officer for the 29th Division's 111th Machine Gun Battalion, replacing horses and mules with trucks was a mixed blessing. His efforts to move his twelve-truck supply convoy to the front in late September 1918 were plagued by mechanical breakdowns, bad weather, and horrendous roads. After moving only fifteen miles, the convoy ground to a halt when the forward drive shaft of one of his four-wheel-drive trucks shattered. Fortunately, the truck's driver had enough skill and mechanical knowledge to completely disconnect the forward drive and rig the truck so it could move on the rear drive alone. The problems did not end there. In the midst of a "driving rain," the officer noted,

> It grew dark early, making the road impossible to see, and finally three forward trucks slipped into a ditch on the side of the road in spite of the drivers' desperate effort to prevent it. After all efforts to get these trucks back on the road had failed, the loads were removed but the trucks were hopelessly mired, and it was decided to lay up for the night ... During the night further complications arose as the road was used by three divisions to move their wagon transportation forward, and by daylight the road was jammed and traffic was at a standstill both ways.

The supply officer narrowly averted having his mired trucks being pushed over on their sides to clear them off the road when the crew of a passing artillery tractor graciously agreed to pull the vehicles from the ditch.

In the coming days, the supply officer met with other obstacles. Heavy enemy shelling of the roads necessitated long detours and forced his convoys to limit their moves to hours of darkness. Upon arriving at his unit's supply point in one small town, the village major gave the supply officer only ten minutes to bring in the convoy, unload the trucks, and leave the location. The convoy's nighttime excursions often took them through a tangle of artillery batteries firing on enemy positions. The gun flashes blinded the drivers and disrupted their night vision. Given the road congestion, weather conditions, and fatigue of the drivers, accidents were bound to happen. The officer lamented, "The roads were so slippery that, in slowing down for a turn, one of the rear trucks hit the one in front. The truck continued to slide after the brakes were applied, the radiator was smashed and it was rendered useless." A truck driver for the 1st Division shared these experiences and often found that bringing supplies up at night was dangerous and nerve-racking. During the Soissons drive he recalled, "As always it was difficult to drive without lights ... as we had to keep up with the truck ahead. Otherwise we would have gotten lost which would have been a disaster." He further noted that when he lost contact with the convoy, his assistant driver would have to get out of the cab and "feel the road" for ruts created by the trucks ahead of them to ensure that they were still on the path.[21]

Although the need to keep troops fed and supplied required moving a constant stream of materials around France, any intensification of the fighting led to busts of activity as the rear-area troops worked to push forward ammunition and other expendable supplies and to care for the surge of wounded and prisoners of war returning from the front. Working at a base hospital as an X-ray technician, Evan Miller's life reflected this dynamic. His hospital received its first trainload of wounded from the fighting around Château Thierry at 2:00 in the morning on June 2, 1918. He informed his sister, "Believe me it was some job getting them brought up from the station and then taken to the proper wards." He worked until 5:00 PM carrying stretcher cases to their rooms. This was good practice, for two days later another train carrying four hundred patients arrived at the hospital. He and his comrades worked from 6:39 AM until 10:00 in the evening to sort, bed, and treat the troops. Over the next few days he X-rayed twenty-five to thirty patients per day. August 8 brought another rush of wounded and Miller processed six dozen X-ray plates and another five dental films.

As busy as these times were, a number of soldiers in the SOS still enjoyed the many benefits of living in the rear. For example, Miller was able to convert an empty room in the hospital into his own private bedroom, using an unneeded X-ray bed at his bunk. He noted that he was able to watch the frequent movies shown at the facility. The hospital also offered the benefit of having a well-stocked mess hall. On January 17, 1918, Miller's dinner consisted of creamed salmon, boiled potatoes, asparagus, bread, butter, cocoa, and canned pineapple. Every Sunday, he and his comrades enjoyed a chicken dinner. Despite the fact that Bernard Bockemuehl was assigned to a base hospital outside Paris and found the City of Light to be a "great town," he was not happy with his assignment. He complained to his sister in September 1918, "They work me pretty hard at times. I generally get an hour or two off every night." Although Miller and Bockemuehl endured some trying periods and bouts of hard labor, one wonders if most combat doughboys would have willingly traded places with them.[22]

Before leaving the subject of life behind the lines, it is also necessary to discuss two groups that were often maligned by soldiers: staff officers and senior commanders. As the changing nature of battle also took senior officers further away from the front lines, they were accused of being "château generals." According to this charge, generals whiled away their hours in the comfort and safety of the rear, detached from the realities of combat, yet were all too willing to callously and blindly send their troops to their deaths. One junior infantry officer complained, "In battle, General and Field Officers remained far to the rear, but after the battle they come and bitterly criticize the work of the combatants, when if the higher officers had been in their proper places they could have personally directed the fighting." Without other recourse for expressing their discontentment with distant commanders, the doughboys vented their bitterness or lampooned their superiors in song. One line from the ever-popular "The Mademoiselle from Armentières" quipped,

> Our General, he got the Croix de Guerre.
> But the son of a bitch was never there

Another song groused,

> The Admirals of Paris, the Crillon Generals and such,
> Are always telling others how to lick the bloody Dutch,
> But if they had to shoulder a gun or look the Boche in the eye,
> They'd never leave the troop train 'cause they'd lay right down and die.
> Oh it's drive the general's car my boy, if you want to come out whole,
> For a tin hat never takes a chance with his immortal soul.
> They always sleep between the sheets and eat three squares a day,
> While the doughboy's up to his neck in mud for thirty-three dollars pay.

Although the doughboys had much cause for their resentment, their criticism was sometimes misplaced. The dominance of the artillery during the war, and the lack of any viable system to allow commanders to communicate with their subordinates while on the move, meant that generals and other senior officers were tied to their command posts by the telephone lines they depended on to receive and give orders. If the commanders attempted to move closer to the fighting, they would risk losing any sense of the larger battle and would find themselves actually commanding only their drivers and immediate staff officers.[23]

The other bane of the doughboy's existence was the staff officer. The vast expanse, depth, and scope of the AEF required the army to field a small army of staff officers to plan operations, run logistics, ensure the smooth operation of the army, and serve as Pershing's eyes and ears in all corners of his far-flung command. They were vital to the running of the army. However, their officiousness, prying, and predilection for making seemingly nonsensical demands without having to either take responsibility or suffer the consequences for their actions made them the bane of the combat soldier. The phenomenal growth of armies during the Great War and the mountains of goods that they consumed led to unending demands from higher headquarters for information and statistics from their subordinates. One company commander complained that staff officers bombarded his regiment with

> reports on how many men we had; how many shirts each man had; how many extrashoe-laces were in our possession; how many men had W[ar]. R[isk]. insurance; how many were yet to be inoculated and how many times. Twice a day that I have to report for officers meetings; twice a day would the Colonel hold forth on the reports the general wanted, which company commanders would prepare at once, personally, in writing; then the adjutant would begin on the reports the colonel wanted; the supply officer would chime in with a few more that he had to have by six o'clock at the latest. Life was a veritable nightmare of typewritten figures . . . the men, quite naturally, looked upon the officers as a set of lunatics who didn't know their own minds for 10 minutes at a time.

Sometimes the senselessness of the staff officers' requests could be a source of great humor. While his unit was under heavy shellfire in the trenches, John Stringfellow received a message from his divisional headquarters ordering him to send three tenors to the rear for duty entertaining the troops. Although the request left him flabbergasted, Stringfellow admitted that when the soldiers in the lines were polled as to their musical ability, he found that "every man that day sang tenor."[24]

Few things were worse to the combat veteran than having clueless beings from headquarters tell them about the realities of combat or how they should be fighting. An infantry officer noted that being subjected to enduring lectures by the staff was "worse than a German offensive." He groused, "I spent several hours listening to staff officers who have never had even an ambush patrol beyond our own wire, tell how an enemy machine gun nest should be cleared out." Another officer was irritated by having to endure the raft of unrealistic exercises that the staff put together and then foisted upon the troops. He sardonically noted that the exercises were "the only opportunity the staff officers have of demonstrating to you how much they know about war. Perhaps the best thing about these problems is that they are easy to forget when you go to meet a real enemy and have to use common sense."[25]

The soldiers' anger at staff officers often stemmed from the perception that the staff members were out of touch with reality or were strict pettifoggers of ridiculous rules. Lieutenant Hugh Thompson was quite irritated that a senior staff officer inspecting the front trenches exhibited a complete lack of understanding about the tactics and procedures in the trenches. The defending infantry were only to fire a signal flare in the event of an attack by the enemy. The flare was to signal the artillery to fire an immediate protective barrage into No Man's Land. Despite the lieutenant's insistence that the flares were only for real emergencies, the staff officer still insisted that one be set off to "see if the artillery was on the job." Once the artillery began their frantic firing, the staff officer ordered it stopped and was then "dumbfounded to learn that no one could halt the whiz-bangs once the signal for the barrage had been given." As the officer's "parade ground antics" had given away the barrage lines and gun positions of the American artillery, the gunners had to redo their plans and move their guns. Jeremiah Ewarts's run-in with a staff officer while returning from Cantigny in late May 1918 was even more exasperating. Upon discovering that his unit's route to the rear area was under enemy observation and artillery fire, he made the snap decision to detour from his given course to find a safer path to his destination. Unfortunately, this common-sense decision was a violation of his orders. Upon safely reaching his destination, Ewarts was hauled before a division staff officer and reprimanded for his actions. In the face of such impregnable inanity, it is little wonder that some troops sang of the staff,

> At the Chaumont G.H.Q., they say,
> Time is quietly idled away,
> Addin' up the roster sheets and figgerin' out soldiers pay.
> They never have to make the war,
> Nor fall out for reveille,
> If I ever do a hitch again,
> Chaumont is the place for me.

Who could blame them for such musical rebellion?

As long as there are armies, it is safe to say that the combat soldier will believe that anyone not directly fighting and sharing his privations is somehow getting over on the system. The Great War, however, was the dawn of a unique

American contribution to warfare. The Americans' unparalleled ability to project and sustain power halfway across the globe made it a major player in World War I and foreshadowed the strengths that the nation would bring to bear in all of its subsequent conflicts. As such, the advent of this unique "American Way of War" meant that the men laboring in the SOS and working in the staffs proved as vital to the AEF's victory as those fighting at the front.[26]

17

"How 'Ya Gonna Keep 'Em Down on the Farm, after They've Seen Paree?"
Sex, Sin, and Temptation in the AEF

In 1918, Joe Young, Sam M. Lewis, and Walter Donaldson penned a song that would become one of the top hits of 1919. In a humorous way it asked a serious question that was in the minds of many American parents, wives, and girlfriends as the doughboys were returning home:

> How ya gonna keep 'em down on the farm
> After they've seen Paree'
> How ya gonna keep 'em away from Broadway
> Jazzin' around and paintin' the town
> How ya gonna keep 'em away from harm, that's a mystery

As the folks back home realized, wars had often led to a loosening of morals and being far away from home sometimes led soldiers to sow their wild oats and experiment with things that would have brought familial and communal censure in peacetime America. As the old farmer in the song explains to his wife,

> Mother Reuben, I'm not fakin
> Tho you may think it strange
> But wine and women play the mischief
> With a boy who's loose with change.

Even the AEF's senior leadership agreed with this view. In August 1918, the GHQ issued Bulletin 54, which started by admitting, "The disturbances of normal social conditions caused by war tends to a breakdown of moral standards and an increase of immorality and venereal disease." The parent's fear expressed in the song and in Bulletin 54 was somewhat justified. The doughboys' exposure to sex,

alcohol, gambling, and free and easy cursing did present a stark contrast between Pareé and the crabbed and repressed realities of small-town America so
eloquently depicted in Sinclair Lewis's book *Main Street*, published in 1920.[1]

Army life had long been seen by Americans as a path of sin and dissipation. Efforts by army and civilian Progressive Era reformers to "humble the
conditions" of the hard-living Regulars had met with some success in the decade prior to World War I and had resulted in a marked decline in the rates of
alcoholism and venereal disease among the troops. This being said, Rudyard
Kipling was still correct in noting that "single men in barracks don't grow
into plaster saints." Despite the best efforts of the reformers, the areas around
the Regular Army's camps and forts were still studded with the gin joints,
gambling dens, and bordellos that catered to the proclivities of an often bored
and restless soldiery. Much to the outrage of the public, the mobilization
and stationing of the National Guard and much of the Regular Army on the
Mexican border in 1916 had led to an uptick of these traditional soldier vices
in the camps of Texas, Arizona, and New Mexico.

With the American entry into the Great War, the mothers, fathers, and religious leaders of the nation were bound and determined to keep the scandalous temptations of wine, women, and song from soiling those called to serve
in the ranks. In June 1917 a group of concerned citizens from Fowler, Illinois,
petitioned the president to "keep our boys clean; not only from the ravages of
the liquor traffic, but the scarlot women as well." Their demands were echoed
by family members from across the United States. The message to the army
and the Wilson administration was clear: America expected its young soldiers
to be returned home from the war free from moral corruption.[2]

Pushed by parents, religious groups, and progressive organizations, the
army sought to create as wholesome an environment as possible in its posts
and training camps. Under Sections 12 and 13 of the Selective Service Act of
1917, the War Department was authorized to suppress prostitution, the sale of
alcohol, and other vices around its camps. In April 1917, the War Department
formed the Commission on Training Camp Activities (CTCA) to head off the
problems that had occurred in the camps on the Mexican border in 1916 and
to reassure the mothers and fathers of America that the army would look out
for the moral, ethical, spiritual, and physical well-being of their boys. Secretary Newton Baker selected Raymond Fosdick, a noted Progressive reformer
who had previously tackled the social ills of New York City, to serve as the

chairman of the committee. Fosdick was uniquely suited for the position and had formerly worked with Baker to investigate the vices in the border camps. He summarized the goals of the CTCA as supplying "the normalities of life to nearly a million and a half young men in training camps, and to keep the environs of those camps clean and wholesome." In accomplishing the latter aim the CTCA took it upon itself "to prevent and suppress certain vicious conditions traditionally associated with armies and training camps."[3]

The CTCA mobilized local, state, and national political, religious, and law enforcement officials, social reformers, and the American Social Hygiene Association to suppress the sex, gambling, and alcohol trade around the nation's training camps. Backed by the support of the War Department, public opinion, and the weight of the Selective Service Act, post commanders and the CTCA went after vice with a passion. When it came to prostitution the CTCA and the War Department followed a policy of "absolute repression." Communities anxious to attract training camps to their areas readily consented to the suppression of vice. The leaders of some larger cities, such as New Orleans, were more reticent in shuttering the bars and brothels, but eventually even they were brought to heel. The committee was successful in getting Montgomery, Alabama; Douglas, Arizona; Louisville, Kentucky; Savannah, Georgia; Deming, New Mexico; Jacksonville, Florida; and Hattiesburg, Mississippi to close their red light districts. These areas were also shuttered in El Paso, Waco, San Antonio, Fort Worth, and Houston, Texas; Alexandria and New Orleans, Louisiana; Norfolk and Petersburg, Virginia; and Charleston, Spartanburg, Columbia, and Greenville, South Carolina. The CTCA further used its might to force other cities without established red light districts to close their open houses of prostitution.[4]

For the first time in the nation's history, the War Department also established a Morale Branch as part of the general staff and assigned morale officers in every large unit and post. One of the responsibilities of the morale officers was to monitor the moral climate of their organizations and to provide advice and training to unit officers on maintaining a morally upright unit. The army made clear that part of the officer's paternalistic duty to care for his men was to further the goals of the CTCA. At Fort Sheridan, for example, the morale officer Myron Adams went so far as to publish *Officer's Responsibility for His Men*, a pamphlet intended to explain to novice leaders their obligations of moral uplift. Adams made clear that "the leisure hours of the men can be made valuable or dangerous . . . An unwise use of leisure hours results in destroying the good spirit of the company, multiplying delinquencies and discrediting the character of the army among civilians." To live up to their responsibilities, the officers were expected to eradicate gambling and drinking and to take "social measures to diminish sexual temptations." Similar publications were published by the army, the YMCA, and other social welfare agencies.[5]

Although the army and CTCA were generally successful in suppressing illicit sex in the United States, the crusade against "John Barleycorn and Demon Rum" proved much more of an uphill battle. Prior to the war, the Women's Christian Temperance Union and the Anti-Saloon League had succeeded in passing prohibition in nineteen states. These organizations allied with other reform groups to argue that the wartime needs to protect soldiers and society from temptations and to prevent the diversion of important food grains to alcohol production made prohibition a national priority. Ultimately, their efforts would lead to the passing of the Eighteenth Amendment in 1919. Efforts to keep alcohol away from soldiers in the United States were mixed, and in France, they were, to use the temperance term, a "Teetotal" failure.

Section 12 of the Selective Service Act of 1917 made it a misdemeanor punishable by a $1,000 fine or twelve months in jail for any "person, corporation, partnership, or association" to "sell, supply, or have in his or its possession any intoxicating or spirituous liquors at any military station, cantonment, camp, fort, post." It further made it illegal to "sell any intoxicating liquor, including beer, ale, or wine, to any officer or member of the military forces while in uniform."

These provisions did little to prevent those well-wishers wanting to provide the troops some merriment before going overseas, or those hoping to make a buck off the troops from offering alcohol to the doughboys in the United States.[6]

As we have seen, the train trips to the stateside training camps often resembled drunken frat parties, and army efforts to provide order and discipline on the journey met with little success. Notwithstanding the labors of military authorities and the CTCA to halt the use of alcohol by soldiers, those seeking liquor while undergoing training could generally find it if they were willing to run some risks. While waiting to sail for France, Mervyn Burke recalled that "liquor was readily obtainable in any bar in any town." Although saloons in New York refused to serve men in uniform, he discovered that they willingly dispensed their libations at the "side doors." Adept soldier smugglers evaded guards and regulations to bring in liquor for themselves and their comrades. A Kentuckian in the 22nd Infantry maintained a contented buzz while stationed at Governor's Island, New York, after he successfully smuggled in "a good supply of 'white lightening'" after returning from leave at home. Henry Schulz informed his brother that the soldiers at Camp Dix, New Jersey, were not allowed to bring any form of civilian luggage into the barracks because men returning from leave often snuck whiskey back into camp in the bags.[7]

The operation of the iron laws of supply and demand further allowed bootlegging to flourish in camps across the United States despite the best efforts of army and local officials to stop their activities. A 32nd Division infantryman observed that imbibers in Texas could find liquor peddlers to supply their need just a short walk off post. The morale officer for the 91st Division at Camp Lewis frequently informed his superiors of the military police's attempts to halt the flow of alcohol to the post from Tacoma and Seattle. The MP's believed that bootlegging and other vices flourished because at least 5 percent of the camp's soldiers left post on pass in search of "meretricious adventure" rather than a "quest of healthful amusement and entertainment."[8]

A lack of money or ready access to liquor still did not prevent soldiers from seeking alcohol. Richard McBride's first sergeant was a Regular with twelve years of service. Although McBride stated that the sergeant knew his job, "he had a tendency for the 'grape'" and would drink "anything with an alcohol content, like vanilla extract when the normal commodity was not available." A Marine wrote home in January 1918 that one of his companions died after going on a binge and drinking "bay rum which had a lot of poisonous stuff in it." The crackdown on alcohol consumption also did not stop the army dentist Clifford Bogan. While stationed at Camp Funston, he was charged with stealing medicinal alcohol from the 341st Field Artillery infirmary and proceeding to get riotously drunk while on duty. Due to their easy access to intoxicants, doctors and other medical professionals (such as Bogan) seemed to be at particular risk for substance abuse. A greater percentage of doctors were removed from their jobs and sent to the Blois Reclassification Center for alcohol and drug problems than any other group of officers in the AEF. First Lieutenant David S. Carey, for example, was removed from medical duty at

Base Section 3 "due to his habitual use of alcohol and drugs which made him inefficient in the performance of his duties." The lengths that all of these men went to obtain alcohol pointed to their having drinking problems. They were far from being alone. Between April 1, 1917, and December 31, 1919, the army treated 4,374 soldiers for acute or chronic alcoholism and 2,507 were admitted to the hospital for drug addiction. Of these men, 441 alcoholics and 1,179 drug addicts were discharged from the military due to disability, while another fifty alcoholics and ten addicts died as a result of their affliction.[9]

The army was concerned not only with the health and readiness implications of alcohol abuse but also with its effect on discipline. Between April 6, 1917, and July 1, 1919, the army tried 577 officers and 2,862 soldiers for being drunk on duty or other offenses related to alcohol. During the same period another ninety-nine soldiers were convicted of possession or use of narcotics. Despite the prohibitions against liquor enumerated in the Selective Service Act, commanders generally turned a blind eye to drinking and let miscreants off with relatively light punishments unless the drinking resulted in a breakdown of the good order and discipline within the unit. This was doubly true for officers. Captain Frank Tullidge discovered that the army had little patience for officers who failed to live up to its moral code, especially if the man's failings became open and public. While stationed at Camp Sherman, Ohio, in November 1917, Tullidge went on a monumental bender. He went AWOL from camp, checked into a hotel under an assumed name, and brought a "woman not his wife" into his room for "immoral purposes." When the captain was apprehended by authorities, he was "so drunk while in uniform, in public, as to disgrace the military service." The court martial found him guilty of all charges and Tullidge was cashiered from the army. Captain Robert Igoe of the 139th Machine Gun Battalion had a drinking problem but was otherwise a competent officer. He had been found drunk in October 1917, but following an oral pledge "to absolutely abstain from the use of intoxicating liquor in any form," his commander had given Igoe a second chance. In January 1918, however, Igoe borrowed $50 from one of his soldiers, went AWOL to New Orleans, and proceeded to get drunk in violation of his pledge. For this a court martial sentenced him to be dismissed from the service and a year of hard labor at the disciplinary barracks at Fort Leavenworth.[10]

The doughboys' access to and use of alcohol increased dramatically upon their arrival in France. In keeping with stateside policies, on December 18,

1917, General Orders 77 stated flatly, "Soldiers are forbidden either to buy or accept gifts from inhabitants, whiskey, brandy, champagne, liquors or other alcoholic beverages other than light wine or beers." Furthermore, it mandated that any soldier returning to camp intoxicated would be seized by the guards and forced to undergo a round of VD prophylactic treatment. The major problem with this policy was that it was completely unenforceable. Soon after the issue of General Orders 77, the AEF chief surgeon reported to the AEF chief of staff, "Insomuch as wine is sold in France not only in hotels, inns, bars and grocery stores, but generally in almost every type of store, it has been found obviously impracticable to prohibit its use." This fact was no surprise to the troops themselves. In a letter to his girlfriend from July 1918, one officer explained, "I . . . find that regardless of the sign over the door, any or every place sells wine or beers."[11]

Despite official sanctions against drinking, the soldiers were quick to take advantage of the impossibility of enforcing Pershing's rules. Even an officer, a man charged with enforcing the unenforceable, joked in a letter home, "Here I am at last in the land of wine and absinthe . . . Am learning the language rapidly, 'Biere,' 'Blank vin,' and 'rouge vin' are some of the more important words." Although William Roper limited himself to an occasional sip of wine, he noted that since alcohol "was easily available at inns and dram-shops . . . some of the men would get drunk at every opportunity." Despite the belief that the French were fleecing the troops, some doughboys were amazed how cheap alcohol was in France. As a soldier from the dry state of Kansas wrote his father in October 1918,

> I think [the French] have made more money in the towns where the American soldiers are stationed than they have had for the last 10 years . . . White and red wine can be bought for 1.50 [francs] a bottle (30 cents). Some of the soldiers get tanked up on it . . . French people have it with every meal. Champagne can be bought for 9.00 [francs] a bottle $1.75 this is extra dry [which] costs about $7.00 in the U.S. Beer costs .30 centimes a bottle [or] 10 cents.

Given the European armies' acceptance of troops drinking and the availability of alcohol in France, some soldiers were irritated at the Americans' continued parochial attitudes toward a little imbibing. A veteran of the 1st Division who arrived with the first contingent of American soldiers was somewhat disappointed to discover that when his unit served with the French, it was not given all the components of the Gallic soldier's rations. He recalled, "We were well aware that their rations included wine but that was not part of what we got, as the good people of the W[omen's] C[hristian] T[emperance] U[nion] and others who were advocating Prohibition at home had sufficient clout then & didn't want their men 'demoralized' by the Demon Rum."[12]

The bounty of booze in France of course led to problems. The Americans were often criticized by French officials for being obnoxious, belligerent, and blusterous when drunk. This fact was not lost on the doughboys themselves. Soon after arriving in France, Knud Olsen quickly found the drinking habits of the Americans and the French differed greatly. He recalled,

> We could buy any amount, anyplace. They didn't have saloons or bars like we did. You went to a house and they would bring your bottle of whatever you wanted and you just sit there and drink it. The French handle their liquor much better than the Americans did. They would sit at the table and drink all day, be drunk by the evening, but they never made any trouble, they just get up and quietly find their way home. When the Americans came in they just went wild. Got drunk and wanted everyone to know it. It kind of scared the Frenchman at first.

Likewise, a soldier in the 32nd Division believed that drinking was a problem in his unit and that "American soldiers could take lessons on handling their liquor from observing how the French civilian made a bottle of wine last for an evening of pleasure."[13]

The inability of some soldiers to follow the French example contributed to the AEF's crime and discipline problems. In the last four months of 1918, the MPs assigned to the 2nd Army and its attached divisions made 249 arrests for drunkenness. It should be kept in mind that these numbers only reflected the men who were apprehended by the MPs. Most drunk soldiers were discovered by their unit officers and their cases were handled within their organizations using company punishments. Drunkenness and the bad behavior it encouraged were not limited to the troops. As in the States, officers in the AEF exhibited their fair share of drunken buffoonery and likewise garnered the punishments due to those failing to uphold the dignity expected of officers and gentlemen. Lieutenant Thomas Hazzard was sent to Blois and cashiered after groping a woman in the company of another officer and getting into a fight while intoxicated. In August 1918, four officers were involved in a drunken brawl with three other officers on the streets of Langres. When

Photo 16: The doughboys often commented on the ready availability of cheap alcohol in France. With each sporting their own bottle of wine, these soldiers seemed primed for a drink-induced good time. Source: author's collection.

confronted by the MPs, two of the tipsy officers became belligerent, and one, Captain Ambrose Gains, pulled a knife on a policeman and told him, "I have a notion to run this through you." With the assistance of the French police, the MPs managed to hustle the resisting officers into custody. Young drunk men with guns and other weapons always posed potentially dangerous situations. This was borne out in the actions of Private George Orange. After becoming riotously intoxicated in a French café in December 1918, Orange pulled out his pistol and started firing. Fortunately, MP Sergeant John Martin was quickly on the scene, removed the frightened café patrons, and managed to disarm and arrest Orange without any bloodshed.[14]

Although many, if not most, doughboys sampled the alcoholic pleasures of Europe at some point during their time overseas, few got into the kinds of trouble exhibited in the previous examples. Some had no desire to imbibe or did not like what they were served. Sergeant Elmer Lewis informed the folks back home, "We don't paint very many towns red over here as there are not very many to paint and besides the wine here is not very good for a person to drink about all you get is sour wine and it makes you sick if you drink very much of it, besides I don't like the taste of it." Similarly, in a statement that would have broken the hearts of French brewers and vintners, Lieutenant C. F. Watson observed, "The wines are not worth monkeying with but the beer isn't so bad. I would still like to have someone line me up in front of a few Schlitz in brown bottles." A sergeant claimed that he abstained from drinking during his first ten months in the army. His teetotaling ended on the night of the Armistice when he accepted two glasses of wine from a Frenchman. House admitted that this small amount of alcohol was enough to get him "loaded," and after embarrassing himself during the escapade, he was so mortified that it was his "last drink for a while."[15]

Most soldiers, it seems, generally saw drinking and even the occasional bender as a harmless diversion and a low-order vice. Charles Minder echoed the thoughts of many of his comrades when he admitted that he had taken to drinking because "when you are tired out, a glass of wine or ale braces us up, and makes us feel better right away. For a little while, we forget all about the darn army and the war and the unreasonable officers." Likewise, a 3rd Division machine gunner spoke for countless of his fellow combat veterans when he defiantly wrote in bold, large, block, all-capitalized letters, on the back of an envelope containing a letter home to a friend in April 1919, "DONT LET THE STATES GO DRY."[16]

One of the other, less than wholesome activities common with the doughboys was gambling. Long before Roman legionnaires cast lots for Christ's meager possessions, soldiers were drawn to games of chance. The men who responded to the U.S. Army Military History Institute's veteran survey frequently stated that gambling was a popular off-duty recreation in their units. Corporal Edmund Grossman recalled that in the 139th Infantry "the men liked to gamble" and their time was taken up with "lots of poker-playing and shake dice." Gambling was popular because it was a communal activity that brought together comrades, offered the possibility of riches to bankroll other insalubrious activities, and was a diversion that consumed some of the long and boring hours of soldering. Furthermore, for soldiers overburdened with gear that left precious little room for personal items, a deck of cards and a pair of dice took up little space and weight. These games also modeled a life often governed by the luck and randomness of the battlefield.[17]

The most popular games of chance in the AEF were poker and craps, with blackjack being a distant third. Although most games were for small stakes, they could sometimes bring in big money for the skilled and lucky. One soldier called poker the army's "national indoor pastime," and in one four-hour session he won a thousand francs. This was equivalent to $200 at the time, or over six times the amount of a private's monthly pay. James Lindsey observed a blackjack game on his voyage to France that held a pot of over $1,500. Sergeant Webb Ayres admitted, "We had a few addicted Crap Shoot-ers," and claimed, "One told me he sent $19,000 home to have a garage ready when he returned. He would only take out one dollar from [his] paycheck [and] send the rest home for [the] business savings. Then from that dollar he would shoot crap." The draft brought into the ranks a handful of men with considerable skill at gambling and, perhaps, cheating. These sharps made quick work of their novice comrades. A 1st Division soldier recalled, "Games, usually dice, began immediately after pay call. The unskilled or unlucky, were quickly eliminated and most of the money wound up in the hands of the more experienced or lucky gamblers. Strangely enough, these were usually the same individuals month after month."[18]

Soldiers caught gambling could be charged with violating the 96th Article of War, but few doughboys were called on the carpet for the offense. In fact, between April 6, 1917, and June 30, 1919, only eleven officers of the eighteen tried and twenty-six of the forty-one enlisted men tried were convicted of gambling. Although the commanders condemned gambling, they generally turned a blind eye to it unless it caused disruptions to the good order and discipline of the service. This was particularly true in the case of friendly card games between officers. Lieutenant Thomas Lynch broke these unspoken rules when he cheated at a game with fellow officers from the 360th Infantry at Camp Travis, Texas, in February 1918 by using a deck of marked cards. He was cashiered after the court found him guilty of conduct unbecoming an officer and a gentleman. Lieutenant Thomas E. Jones likewise ran afoul of the authorities for borrowing money from his soldiers and then using that money to gamble with the troops. Although the board sentenced Jones to be dismissed from the service, President Wilson commuted the sentence to a reprimand from the division commander.[19]

Despite the tacit acceptance of gambling in the ranks, the practice was still viewed by the doughboys, including some of the gamblers themselves, as a disreputable activity. A soldier in the 42nd Division recalled that during a lull in the action he and his comrades were passing the time shooting craps. But

Photo 17: A group of soldiers in the Services of Supply enjoy a poker game in the barracks. Source: author's collection.

as soon as enemy shells began "falling like meteors," the group was caught in a dilemma. "Most of us were the sons of God-fearing parents, and you can't go to heaven with a pair of dice in your hand. Nor would it do to get right with God on the spot, in front of everybody." Rather than putting away the dice and losing some of their tough guy mystique, they played on, but he ruefully admitted that they were now "shaking the bones with no effort of our own."[20]

The greatest hindrance to doughboy gambling (and other vices) was not necessarily the moral strictures against the activity as much as a pure lack of money. As Private Ralph Williams explained, "Eighty percent allotments were suggested and since we only received $30.00 per month as private soldiers, not much was left for Poker or Crap Games." A private in the 1st Division admitted that as he and his comrades were not paid for over three months, there was simply nothing to gamble with. These complaints were widespread and the AEF's pay system was notoriously ineffectual. In May 1918, an article in *Stars and Stripes* reported that Private A. E. Scerth had been in the army for a year before he was paid. While Scerth's case was extreme, it was far from rare. Although Luther Grover had been in France since October 1917, in September 1918 he thanked his sister for sending him a dollar because "it was the first piece of good american money I have had all the time I had been in france." On August 4, 1918, Bernard Bockemuehl wrote his mother, "I got paid yesterday the first time in three months got a whole hat full of French money."[21]

Bockemuehl's statement about receiving a "hat full of French money" illustrated the problem. The army had no other way of paying the troops their nonallotted money than giving them cash. This required a unit pay officer with an armed guard to draw, count, and complete the accounting for enough currency to pay every member of his organization from a central pay office, move these bags of money back to the unit, and then disburse it to the troops while always maintaining the strictest of accounting. At the pay table, company officers had to verify the payroll and work with the pay officer to reconcile any pay discrepancies due to stoppages, forfeitures due to legal actions, or additional allotments for things such as Liberty Bonds. As units were constantly on the move or going in or out of action, this process was doomed to failure. If a soldier missed the infrequent pay calls because he was away from the unit due to sickness, schools, or details, he was out of luck for that month. The AEF GHQ attempted to fix this problem by issuing every soldier an individual pay book in the fall of 1918. In theory, a soldier could use the book to draw pay from any disbursing officer if they were away from their units. In reality, pay remained sporadic until after the Armistice for troops not assigned to stable and stationary posts.

All of this was enough to make the average soldier curse—which they did. Of all the doughboys' venial sins, cursing was perhaps the most common and least harmful. Soldiers from even the most religious and upright upbringing readily admitted to cursing while in the army. An artilleryman confessed that he and his comrades grew adroit at "fluent profanity": "Any operation, from firing a battery to tying a shoestring, generally called forth some sulphurous remarks, delivered with amusing and sometimes artistic vehemence. The very picturesqueness of the blasphemy was engaging, and some of our men were adepts who could curse, without repeating themselves, till they ran out of breath and had to stop from sheer exhaustion." Doughboys cursed for a host of reasons. When his fellow Marines were hit by falling equipment during their odious train trips across France, Warren Jackson noted, "following such an accident there would follow a volley of oaths at the pack and its owner, with some extra cussing for the Marine Corps, the French, and the war in general." For these men, and others in the AEF, cursing provided some limited means for the powerless to vent against the unfairness and privations of military army life. Most importantly, in times of stress and fear it gave the soldier-swearer a relatively harmless path of expelling some of their pent-up emotions and striking back at a world they did not control.[22]

For whatever reason that doughboys resorted to profanities, it is interesting to note that some were even willing to share their newfound vocabulary with polite society. A female friend of Private Andy Magnus asked him, "Say what do you mean by 'S.O.L.' If you shouldn't remember what you wrote I will quote it. You said in regard to the newspapers, 'Newspapers were never transferred so that leaves me S.O.L.' Be sure and let me know what that means in United States language." Soon after entering the army another soldier wrote home to his sister, "I got my uniform. We all get in a row and get a Barracks Bag, and they look at you and pick up a pair of pants and throw them in a bag if they fit alright O.K. if they don't you are shit of luck S.O.L. I will have lots of new words when I get home." It is not much of a stretch to argue that "shit out of luck," or the more commonly used acronym "SOL," was one of the most popular phrases and uses of vulgarity in the army. It neatly encapsulated the randomness and impotence of the doughboys' lives. However, the free use of the term, and other profanities, in letters and conversations points to another reason for the prevalence of cursing. The troops viewed cussing as a sign of manliness and it created a soldierly persona that separated them from those in the buttoned-down, gentle civilian world.[23]

Of course not everyone in the army used profanities or were tolerant of those that did. To some, it was simply not wise in the midst of battle to tempt the wrath of God by taking His name in vain or uttering other dangerous oaths. Commanders, chaplains, and the staffers of morale and recreation centers (often run by religious organizations such as the YMCA) sometimes attempted to bridle the loose and profane tongues of the rough soldiery. A sign posted in one YMCA hut carried the admonishment, "SWEAR; if you can't think of anything else to say, but do it softly—very, very softly, so no one else but yourself will hear you." The Yankee Division's Chaplain Michael O'Connor took a more direct approach and fought fire with fire. During a service near the front, he surprised the doughboy congregation by "ripping out at them a string of their favorite oaths and epithets." One in the audience recorded, "The boys almost curled up in horror. Then he said, 'It doesn't sound very well to you does it, to hear such words from a man in priestly garments? It doesn't sound one bit better to me to hear them coming from you dressed in the uniform of Uncle Sam.' And he proceeded with an anti-profanity sermon that bit straight through the toughest hide." When Corporal Paul Maxwell's class arrived at the Central Machine Gun Officers Training School in September 1918, their new commander explained that he intended to make officers and gentlemen out of them. "His first act," Maxwell recalled, "was the ban of most soldiers two favorite words, namely, disparaging reference to ones ancestry and a four letter word denoting erotic pleasure but never in polite society."[24]

These efforts, as with most others to rein in the soldiers' language, met with very little success. Far too many troops saw a bit of cussing as not only harmless but also practically beneficial. Sometimes, to the soldiers at least, it was downright funny. One fondly remembered, "Marching through small French towns at route step, some men would break ranks and teach the french obscene and vulgar expressions which the french knowing no English would wave and shout to passing troops, thinking they were expressing a proper english greeting." Poor Chaplain O'Connor would have been appalled.[25]

Of all of the things that worried those back home about keeping the boys down on the farm "after they've seen Paree,'" sex took top billing. Sex, both premarital and extramarital, was a sin in all of the dominant faiths in America, and indulging in it carried not only the connotations of immorality but also a lack of proper self-control. Doughboys engaging in sex also risked contracting diseases and fathering children out of wedlock. As noted earlier in the chapter, the public's concern over the risks of sexual immorality in the ranks drove the military and the Wilson administration to take drastic steps to remove temptations from the areas around the nation's cantonments. Section 13 of the Selective Service Act of 1917 gave the secretary of war the power to "do everything by him deemed necessary to suppress and prevent the keeping or setting up of houses of ill fame, brothels, or bawdy houses within such distance as he may deem needful of any military camp." Anyone the military or local authorities found guilty of establishing a place of "lewdness, assignation, or prostitution" or engaged in "immoral purposes" at those locations could be fined $1,000 and sentenced to a year in jail.[26]

Although it took some time to get the system of suppressing prostitution operating, most post commanders took this responsibility very seriously. Under orders of the commander of the 91st Division, the division surgeon took an active role in stamping out immorality around Camp Lewis. The division surgeon strong-armed officials in nearby Tacoma to establish a "women's detention station" for confining prostitutes and checking and treating them for venereal disease. To aid in this effort, any soldier who contracted VD was ordered to provide the name of the woman who gave him the disease. After the camp leaders became convinced that the National Dance Pavilion that abutted the post was a mere cover for illicit assignations, they had members of the Justice Department raid the establishment, arrest ten women dancers, and carry them off to the new Tacoma detention station. In April 1918, Camp Lewis authorities redoubled their attacks against "fallen women" after receiving reports that local prostitutes had tricked soldiers into marriage to obtain the men's allotments and insurance benefits. This concern was not completely overblown. Second Lieutenant Arthur Fortinberry married a woman shortly before leaving for France after a whirlwind courtship. Soon after, Fortinberry's soldiers provided evidence that the woman had been a prostitute at the time of the marriage. As this led to the young officer becoming an object of mockery within the unit, he was dismissed from the service because the Blois board concluded that his "influence and usefulness as an officer is at an end."[27]

Similar efforts to stem the sex trade were made by officials at other posts. Although these endeavors were much more effective than those taken by the army in France, federal, state, and local authorities never completely ended prostitution around army camps in the United States. For example, when he arrived at Fort Sam Huston in San Antonio, Texas, in November 1917, Earle Poorbaugh found that the town contained a thriving red light district. George O'Brian found a similar situation around Camp MacArthur, Texas, the following month. He wrote to his mother that a "great many" women around the camp "make their living following army camps. That sure is a hard old life for such people. I can't see where anyone who thinks anything of themselves could ever have anything to do with them." But such hedonism did not last. A few weeks later, he reported, "They are certainly getting after the immoral women here. One day they arrested eleven and the next day eighteen were taken. When arrested they are sent out of town. Sometimes it looks as tho some of them are up against it. If it keeps up they will be interned and if they have any diseases they will be cared for, then made to work." Despite the crackdown on prostitution, he admitted that it was only partially successful for "there are many of the soldiers who are even anxious to spend their money that way."[28]

When it came to soldiers having sex in France, the environment was completely different from that in the States, and the AEF's leaders were presented with multiple dilemmas. Experience had taught many Regular Army officers that a percentage of soldiers would always seek and find sexual gratification regardless of orders designed to limit these endeavors. On the other hand, the moral and political climate in America would not allow for a free and liberal approach to the matter. The AEF also had a vested interest in protecting its manpower from the ravages of venereal disease. This fact was driven home to the leadership when VD rates among the first-arriving Americans at St. Nazaire skyrocketed to 240 cases per every thousand white soldiers and 625 for every thousand African American soldiers in the summer of 1917.[29]

The relative importance of the matter was evident in the fact that one of Pershing's first orders issued in France was devoted to the matter. On July 2, 1917, General Orders 6 warned, "A soldier who contracts venereal disease not only suffers permanent injury, but renders himself inefficient as a soldier and becomes an encumbrance to the Army. He fails in his duty to his country and his comrades." Men contacting the disease were basically "damaging important government property," so Pershing directed commanders to court martial those who became infected. Pershing also understood human nature and the fact that the army could never stop illicit sex. As such, he further directed that commanders conduct bimonthly medical inspections and periodic briefings on the dangers of VD. Lastly he ordered commanders to establish prophylactic treatment stations in troop concentration areas, and soldiers were required to seek treatment within three hours of any possible exposure to the disease.[30]

Five months later the AEF GHQ issued further orders reasserting and clarifying General Orders 6 and further attempting to limit the risk of VD exposure by forbidding doughboys from entering bordellos or other "habitations, rooms or apartments" used for prostitution. This last restriction caused considerable tension between the AEF and French authorities. As one American medical officer noted, the French attitude was "if a man and a woman wanted to sleep together it was no one's business and no one should interfere with them." As such, the French Army believed that it was far better to establish official brothels and insist on the medical inspection of prostitutes within its area of operation so the soldiers could have a sexual outlet while the army maintained some control over the VD rate. The French argued that the American approach was illogical and dangerous. George Clemenceau himself warned Pershing that placing brothels off-limits to Americans would drive prostitution underground, and thus increase the risk of VD, and lust-driven doughboys would start to prey on the honest women of France. The French premier reportedly offered to set up brothels for the exclusive use of the Americans. Understanding American realities better than Clemenceau, Pershing flatly rejected the scandalous offer and refused to rescind his orders.[31]

About the time that Pershing was forbidding soldiers from frequenting prostitutes, some officers at Blois ran afoul of the AEF's emerging policy by sanctioning the opening of a brothel for the sole use of the doughboys. The process was to be efficient, safe, orderly, and quite French. The women of the *maison tolereé* were inspected by an American medical officer twice a week to prevent infection, and a section of MPs guarded the premises to ensure order and that only soldiers with authorized passes were allowed inside. The hours for enlisted men were from 4:00 to 9:30 in the evening and officers were allowed in after 10:00 at night. The soldiers were charged ten francs per night, five for the room and five for the girl. Everything seemed to be running smooth until an MP on duty shot a drunken French soldier in the leg when he tried to force his way into the establishment. Once the AEF GHQ found out about the bordello, it was quickly shuttered and its organizers disciplined. However, these stateside-like crackdowns were ineffective in denying the doughboys' access to sex. Despite Pershing's injunctions, French officials at St. Nazaire claimed that in only ten days, sixty prostitutes working in four different bordellos serviced fifteen thousand American soldiers: an average of twenty-five men per prostitute per day.[32]

The French were often befuddled by the Americans' official stance on sex. Madam Moindroit, the proprietor of a brothel in Langres, was quite irritated when the American authorities in the town had placed her establishment off-limits to doughboys. On April 30, 1918, she sent a complaint through the town mayor to the general commanding the region's American troops stating that her house operated "under the cover of French law" and that she was "licensed for her commerce and am paying very heavy taxes owing to the particular nature of my business." Madam Moindroit maintained that when the French Army turned the town over to American control, "I thought then I had a right to expect to benefit from the American patronage under the shelter and regulation of French law." She pointed out that her prostitutes were inspected twice a week by a French military and civilian doctor and that when demanded, she had "hastened to facilitate" inspections of her girls by American military physicians. She offered to reserve part of her brothel for an American-run prophylactic station so that any soldier using her services would run "a minimum risk." She closed by pleading, "Under the circumstances, I appeal to your goodwill and clear-sightedness, not only in my interest, but also in that of the troops under your orders. My experience permits [me] to state that the closing of my establishment will favor clandestine prostitution, to the great detriment of public health and morality." Although there is no record of the general's response to Madam Moindroit, it is doubtful that he would have explicitly given permission for her business to remain open. What is interesting is that her prediction proved all too true. On July 9, 1918, an American military doctor, Captain Henry Young, reported to the Langres commandant that there had been a dramatic spike in venereal disease infections in the area, mostly contracted from "women picked up in the park." The doctor recommended that the MPs step up their inspection of nighttime passes, that the army require soldiers to be back in their quarters by 9:30 PM, and that "all parks, woods and secluded places in and about town be out of bounds after 9:00 P.M."[33]

To combat soldiers picking up women on the streets, some commanders tried to place other restrictions on their off-duty activities. On February 10, 1918, Captain George S. Patton, then overseeing the AEF Tank School, ordered, "In order to keep up the high moral standard of the United States Army, officers and men of the Tank Corps will not be seen publically walking or talking to women of doubtful character." Likewise, to control VD rates in Brest, the commander of the port ordered that his soldiers were forbidden to be on the streets of the town with any French woman, noting that such females were bound to be prostitutes as "no decent girl would go out alone with a man." After several embarrassing incidents of mistaken identity, he quietly let the matter die.[34]

Ultimately education proved the most important tool at the army's disposal for dealing with doughboy sexuality and VD exposure. Under the auspices of the Army Medical Department, the YMCA, and the American Social Hygiene Association, the U.S. Army embarked upon the first widespread effort at sex education in the nation's history. Through frank lectures, graphic photos, movies, and an endless variety of pamphlets, these organizations warned the soldiers of the dangers of sex to their health, the security of the Republic, and future generations. The quality and content of this "sexual hygiene" education varied greatly depending upon the views, agendas, and the predilection of the individual instructors. Many line and medical officers took a pragmatic "boys will be boys" approach to sex and stressed prophylaxis and the fact that catching VD would remove vital manpower from the war effort and result in the culprit facing military punishment. Not surprisingly, the tack taken by YMCA secretaries and chaplains was often of the "thou shalt not" variety. They tended to maintain that unsanctioned copulation led to immorality, personal degradation, and the risk of the indulger's immortal soul. Still others stressed that inconstant soldiers risked bringing venereal diseases back home that would endanger wives and future generations.[35]

The anti–venereal disease pamphlets used in these education efforts offer interesting insights into the state of sexual thought in America during the war and, to some extent, the perceptions about sex held by the doughboys. The American Social Hygiene Association's tract *Keeping Fit to Fight* informed its readers that "many men go all their lives with wrong ideas about sex picked up when they were boys from bad companions and smutty stories." It set out to give the men "the right idea" about sex by providing expert wisdom such as "masturbation does not necessarily make a man insane, but it may weaken both body and willpower." It also posited that "it is not true that use of the sexual organs makes them stronger," and in fact, too much sex or masturbation could lead a youth to be "sexually dead before he reaches full manhood." The author stressed that the only true protection against VD was abstinence. This theme was also pushed by the AEF's senior leaders. AEF Bulletin 54 stated that "sexual continence is the plain duty of members of the A.E.F., both for the vigorous conduct of the war and for the clean health of the American people after the war." Echoing the position in *Keeping Fit to Fight*, it maintained, "Sexual intercourse is not necessary for good health, and complete continence is wholly possible." Following the adage that idle hands (and active penises) were the devil's workshop, the bulletin enjoined commanders to keep their troops occupied with "work, drill, athletics and amusements."

The main focus of *Keeping Fit to Fight* and similar pamphlets was to caution the soldier on the dangers of VD. It warned, "Women who solicit soldiers are usually diseased" and "All loose women are dangerous, and any man who goes with one, no matter how clean she may look, or whatever she may say, runs the risk of getting a terrible disease." After these admonitions, it then cataloged the various forms of VD, their cures (or lack of cures), and their long-term consequences to the soldier and their loved ones. To drive the last point home, the cover of one of the editions of the booklet has an illustration of a soldier looking over the shoulder of his wife at their newborn baby. *Keeping Fit to Fight* made little effort at subtlety and ends with the bold font warning "KEEP AWAY FROM THE WHORES."[36]

These education endeavors, and the fears that they inspired, paid off in some cases. A soldier in the 35th Division noted that after his unit "had been taught about the dangers of contracting venereal disease," few men were willing to risk having sex. He confessed that "as many of those in my company were naïve country boys" most of their relations with French women remained of a "boy meets girl type." Similarly, there was "not a lot" of sexual conquest for the men in Corporal Edmund Grossman's infantry company because they "were afraid of disease." This was also reflected in a letter Paul Rhodes wrote home from France in December 1917. He swore to the home folks, "You can be sure that your Big Brother is going to keep clean and pure for his loved ones at Home."[37]

There were other disincentives for those seeking carnal pleasures. Both in the United States and France, the doughboys were subjected to periodic "short arm" medical inspections to ensure that they were free of VD. Those doughboys who recorded these examinations were generally mortified by the experience. A soldier in the 26th Infantry believed that "the indignity of indignities was 'short arm inspections.'" In the pre-Internet age of the Great War, one's genitalia was still considered to be a "private matter." The "inspections were unannounced and all personnel undergoing inspection were required to strip from the waist down and stand on his footlocker at the front of his bed to be inspected by the medical officer." This usually entailed the inspector lifting and holding the penis with a pencil or similar object while searching for the telltale signs of infection. This process continued in Europe.

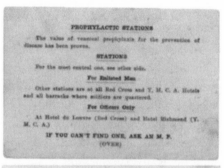

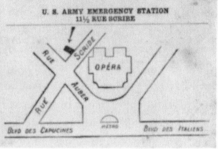

Photo 18: These illustrate the AEF's two approaches to controlling venereal disease. The pamphlet on the left warns of the dire consequences of consorting with women of "easy virtue." On the more pragmatic side, the card on the right (shown front and back), which gives the locations of the AEF's prophylactic stations, was issued by the army to doughboys on leave in Paris. Source: author's collection.

While temporarily stationed in Southampton, England, awaiting transport to France, Earl Cave in his diary noted that he and his comrades had the run of the town. However, the price for their freedom was undergoing a "short arm examination" every night at six o'clock. In June 1918 a doughboy at Camp Meade informed his friend, "We just had a short arm inspection. I guess you know what that is. One fellow had crabbies and another a dose & some are ruptured." As was clear to Cave and this doughboy, the troops needed to be careful while out on the town because sooner or later the army would catch those who had been careless in their sexual activities.[38]

Those found with VD paid a hefty price. In the army's eyes a soldier that caught VD was guilty of dereliction of duty and other offensives and should justly pay the price for his transgressions. "If a soldier was found with VD," Sergeant Earle Poorbaugh recalled, "he was hospitalized until cured, then court-martialed for having willfully contracted VD. [The] usual sentence by court-martial was three months confinement at hard labor [and] loss of two-thirds of pay for this period." The army was especially intolerant of officers who contracted VD, believing that these men should have known better than to have become infected and that they failed to set a better example for their soldiers in their personal conduct. Lieutenant Earnest W. Chase was sent to Blois for reclassification after contracting the disease. His commander criticized him for not keeping "his mind on his work" and for a failure "to render adequate service to his country without selfish concern for himself." The fear of judicial punishment certainly swayed some soldiers. As one wrote his girlfriend in March 1919,

> You surely are true blue Sweetheart, and I am true blue too, as I have strong will power and believe me a man needs that in France as women are easy to get over here, but not for me. A soldier who contracts any disease over here is court martialed and has to stay over here until cured. Believe me the biggest majority of women over here are rotten.

The object lesson provided by a comrade was enough to stifle the libido of the men in a machine gun company in the 82nd Division. After one of the men in his company was sent to the AEF venereal camp, never to return to the unit after contracting VD, Henry House pointed out "some of the soldiers bothered" to chase women, "but not many."[39]

As House noted, during the war, the AEF established a venereal disease isolation and treatment camp at St. Aignan. Fear of being sent to the camp was another deterrent to promiscuity. As the army had no intention of returning infected men to the United States, after the Armistice all men underwent repeated inspections for VD while waiting to embark. Those found with the disease were yanked from their homebound units and sent to one of the four new venereal camps the AEF set up at Bordeaux, Le Mans, St. Nazaire, and Brest. To ensure that assignment to these camps was to be as unpleasant as possible, camp commanders set the soldiers undergoing treatment to as much hard, dirty, and disagreeable labor as their medical condition allowed.

These punitive measures were also accompanied by a realistic understanding of the urges of young men far away from home. Pershing and his senior medical officers wisely acknowledged that their efforts to control VD had to have an element of prevention that went beyond lectures and judicial punishments. Within a month of the first arrival of Americans in France, the AEF ordered local commanders to establish as many prophylactic stations as were necessary in their areas to cater to those doughboys that had still persisted in having sex. Although some doctors balked at staffing such stations as being beneath their dignity, on the whole the system worked as well as could have been expected at the time. Soldiers on leave in Paris were even issued a small business card containing a map to the city's prophylactic facilities.

The fear of the treatment itself, or the embarrassment of seeking it, also provided some doughboys with a further reason for abstinence. "The rule was if you were with a woman you had to go to a certain place and get a shot," Knud Olsen remembered. "The only thing was you had to wonder if the shot was worth the woman." The AEF experimented with issuing doughboys individual prophylactic kits containing an ointment consisting mostly of calomel, but these efforts were limited by shortages of the packets and the belief by some officers that giving the soldiers the kits would promote promiscuity.[40]

As previously noted Americans had long viewed France as a place of inconstant and unsteady morals and many arriving doughboys expected to find legions of "wild women" awaiting them. These prejudices reached the senior ranks of the AEF. In October 1917, the AEF chief surgeon reported, "As a result of the ravages of war, the long-continued absence of the male population from their homes and the great number of women bereft of their husbands and fathers, a veritable demoralization of the female population has occurred . . . A large proportion of the thousands of women in ammunition plants were said to be loose and disease is extremely prevalent among them." Given this situation, these officers maintained that they were duty bound to protect their naive doughboys from the onslaught of these wanton women.[41]

Some doughboys were shocked by the open sexuality they encountered in France. A New Yorker informed his new wife, "The French women are wild, wild women and no doubt they are making wild wild men out of some of the boys. They stop one right on the street anywhere and after talking with a Sammy walk away with him—poor fool." The soldier hastened to add, however, that he "wouldn't be led away from his little wife" and "won't have

anything to do with a 'Frenchie.'" Perhaps to make his wife jealous, after a trip
to Tours he wrote,

> The city is filled with wild, wild women who "shake a wicked hip" right at
> an American. One accosted Willet and I and said "will you go with me?"
> and I said, "No I will not go with you" and she beat it away. Willet said he
> told one to go to Hades one night when he was stopped and she chased
> him two blocks. Can you imagine that?

A lieutenant was quick to tell his would-be American girlfriend, "The girls
here are not at all what you expect." After reassuring her that he had "not
seen a pretty one yet," he confessed, "One of them embarrassed me greatly
however. I walked past two of them on the street and one said, 'Oh la-la-la
chicken.' What do you know about that. I gave her a dignified look that I
guess she will remember and walked over nearer a policeman." It is clear that
few doughboys understood how the war had disrupted society or the changing morays that governed European sexuality. Chaplain Lee Levinger pointed
out, "In France, the daughter of a good family went out only with a man she
knew, and then strictly chaperoned . . . This seclusion of respectable French
girls and the conspicuousness of the loose element made many soldiers hold
light opinion of the virtue of French women generally."[42]

What the doughboys saw in Europe tended to confirm their belief that it
was a den of loose morals and sexual license. After thumbing through French
books and magazines, one puritanical doughboy confessed, "Talk about pictures and cartoons—they're some of the most obscene I've seen but that is
the way of the French, nothing fazes them." The Americans frequently expressed disgust over the prevalence of prostitution in French, British, and
German cities—though this aversion did not stop some from sampling the
wares. The Americans were also amazed by the apparent willingness of some
European women to trade their virtue for the soldiers' extra food, clothing,
and luxury items. Charles MacArthur wrote that his cook used his easy access to army rations to make many amorous conquests, and ruefully noted,
"It was a rare virtue that could resist a quarter of beef." These exchanges grew
greater during the occupation of Germany. MacArthur observed, "German
ladies had been without soap for several years and to obtain a bar would do
almost anything. Some would do anything." A soldier billeted with a German
family boasted to his friend in April 1919,

You ought to see the two dutch girls here where I am staying, one 18 and the other 23 . . . I told her that I was going to take her back home and she thinks it is so . . . say chocolate and then you can see her come up to my room, for a couple of marks you can get them to do anything. I get my washing done for a bar of soap and some places you can get a piece of hide for soap.

Some doughboys went so far as to assume that all European women were wanton. One soldier remembered, "We had this guy in Company C who simply walked up to this nice-looking lady in Nancy and asked her for it. She just smiled and told him no, she didn't do that type of thing." The perception that European women were "easy" became so entrenched that soldiers sometimes mistook innocent encounters with the local women for sexual solicitation. Helene Lamberger wrote the *Stars and Stripes* that "the 'street system' of doughboys and wild women will make a lady shrink all the way back into her shell for fear of being misunderstood."[43]

The songs that the doughboys sang give some indication of their attitudes toward sex and their perceptions of European women and societies. Like cursing, the songs were a vocal release from the constraints of normal life. They gave the troops a way to thumb their noses at convention and to boast of their manliness and sexual prowess. The lyrics often reflected the callousness and carousing that accompanied war and displayed a deep misogynistic attitude and lack of respect for women. Some of the more popular and bawdy songs in the AEF were "The Mademoiselle from Armentières," "Bang Away on Lulu," and "Bon soir, ma Cherie." A few of the endless varieties of obscene lyrics to "The Mademoiselle from Armentières" include

The mademoiselle is on the Marne, *Parlez-vous?* Fucking horses in the barn.
The mademoiselle from Bar-le-Duc, *Parlez-vous?* She'll fuck you in a chicken coop.
The mademoiselle from Is-sur-Tille, *Parlez-vous?* She can zig-zig like a spinning wheel.
The mademoiselle from gay Paree, *Parlez-vous?* She had the clap and gave it to me.

"Bang Away on Lulu" was an old cowboy and Appalachian song that chronicled the sexual proclivities of the tune's heroine. Despite many of Lulu's moral failings, as the song's chorus proclaims, her departure left the soldiers mightily disappointed.

Bang away on Lulu
Lulu's gone away
Who am I gonna bang bang
Now Lulu's gone away

Captain John Thompson admitted that while his Marines were proud of the Corps' stirring hymn, they seemed most moved by "a brazen-throated gunnery sergeant . . . roaring out: 'Bang away, Lulu.'" "To say that our songs were risqué would be putting it mildly," recalled Albert Ettinger. "They were as bawdy as the collective imagination of 3,000 horny men could conceive." Despite their admiration for Chaplain Francis Duffy, as Ettinger and his comrades in the 165th Infantry were receiving his benediction while marching to battle near Exermont, they were lustily singing "Bang Away on Lulu." "Bon soir, ma Cherie" chronicled a doughboy's efforts to win, or at least rent, the affections of a French girl.

Bon soir, ma Cherie, comment allez-vous?	Good evening my dear, how are you?
Bon soir, ma Cherie, je vous aime beaucoup.	Good evening my dear, I love you very much.
Avez-vous un fiancé, ça ne fait rien	Do you have a boyfriend, it does not matter
Voulez-vous couches avec moi ce soir	Would you sleep with me tonight?
Oui. Combine?	Yes, How much?[44]

Other doughboy songs made light of the natural consequences that came from French women being too free with the Americans. One version of "The Mademoiselle from Armentières" told of the peril of succumbing to a doughboy's charms:

Oh landlord have you a daughter fair, *Parlez-vous?*
With lily white tits and golden hair,
Hinkey Dinkey, *Parlez-vous?*
Oh yes I have but she's far too young, *Parlez-vous?*
She's never been scroughed by anyone,
Hinkey Dinkey, *Parlez-vous?*
Six months after when she did try, *Parlez-vous?*
Her apron strings she could not tie,
Hinkey Dinkey, *Parlez-vous?*
Nine months later it came to pass, *Parlez-vous?*

That an American soldier jumped out her ass,
Hinkey Dinkey, *Parlez-vous?*

Another song joked,

Aprés la guerre fini,	After the war is over
Les Americans partis	And the Americans leave
Mademoiselle seul au lit,	Mademoiselle is sleeping all alone
Bouncing the new baby	Bouncing the new baby
Quand la guerre est finis	When the war is over
Les Americans partis	And the Americans leave
Laissez les pauvres Françaises	Leaving the poor French girls
Un souvenir Bébe	With a souvenir baby.

All of these songs show that the doughboys were often willing to boast and joke about sex in a way that would have been all but impossible at home. They also reflect the soldiers' smug faith in American moral superiority over the Europeans. In fact European morals were held in such low esteem that the doughboys registered great surprise whenever they encountered a French woman of "pure" reputation. W. A. Sirmon noted that one girl in Landremont, France, was called "Joan of Arc" for the "remarkable achievement" of "having gone through the four years of the war; and still retaining her virtue."[45]

So to what extent did the doughboys enjoy the hedonistic pleasures of the "wild women" of France? Based on prophylaxis records and soldier surveys, George Walker, a doctor and Medical Corps lieutenant colonel, estimated that 71 percent of the AEF's troops had sex while serving overseas. Walker was the AEF's leading expert on venereal disease and was also its proto–Alfred Kinsey. His work *Venereal Disease in the American Expeditionary Forces* chronicled the army's efforts to control the diseases and was a somewhat voyeuristic look at the sexuality of the American soldier of the Great War.[46]

Based on venereal disease records, it is clear that a number of American soldiers had active sex lives. During the war, 357,969 soldiers were treated for VD, which accounted for just under 10 percent of the army's total admission for all diseases. VD alone resulted in the loss of 6.8 million duty days. There was a notable difference between the rates of infection in the United States and Europe: 127 cases per thousand men versus thirty-four per thousand. The difference was due to the number of men who entered the service already infected with the disease and the army's efforts to heal or discharge them prior to them being shipped overseas. The infection rates in the States and AEF still fell far short of those troops stationed in the Philippines. Since the Spanish-American War the rate in the Philippines had consistently held at around 192 per thousand men.[47]

This being said, Walker's estimates of the doughboys' promiscuity were perhaps too high. When it came to sex and the doughboy, the rules of real estate applied; it was all about location, location, location. Beginning in the fall of 1918, the AEF chief surgeon required all large unit medical officers to provide the number of soldiers in their units who had contracted VD or had received prophylactic treatments in their monthly sanitation reports. Assuming that the VD and prophylaxis numbers indicate at least one sex act, it is evident from these reports that troops assigned to the camps and ports of the SOS were much more likely to have sex than those assigned to combat units. In November 1918, for example, Camp 4 of Base Section 1, with a strength of 7,759 soldiers, reported forty-six new cases of VD and 2,060 soldiers had been given prophylaxis during the month. That same month, Camp St. Sulpice reported that forty-seven of its 9,299 men had contracted VD and another 795 had undergone prophylactic care. Despite Pershing's strong stand against illicit sex, among the roughly three thousand men assigned to his headquarters at Chaumont in December 1918, 401 had sought prophylactic care while another eighteen contracted VD.[48]

The figures given in the sanitation reports are raw numbers, so it is impossible to state that they are a complete indicator of sexual activity among the troops. For example, fifty prophylactic treatments could indicate that fifty soldiers had sex in the month or that one soldier sought treatment fifty times during the month. However, they do indicate that some soldiers in the rear area seem to have had markedly better access to sex than all other troops in the AEF. In October 1918 the surgeon assigned to the headquarters of Base Section 5 at Cherbourg reported that five soldiers had VD and 174 had undergone preventive care for the disease out of a strength of 250 men. The month prior, the Convalescent Camp at the Limoges Hospital Center, with a staff of fifty-five doughboys had three cases of VD and forty-two prophylactic treatments. Although there were no VD cases in November among the three hundred soldiers assigned to the Garden Service Company at Versailles, there were 244 prophylactic treatments given during the month. Given these numbers, had Marie Antoinette still been in residence, she would have had to change her famous phrase to "let them have sex."

As a point of comparison, the 3rd Division, with a strength that ranged between sixteen thousand and twenty-eight thousand in the fall of 1918, reported only five cases of VD and forty prophylactic treatments in September and nine cases of VD and no instances of prophylactic care in October. The division surgeon claimed that even these infected men were replacements who had contracted the disease while en route to the unit. Similarly, the 77th Division had four cases of VD in September and ten in November. The total number of VD preventive care for the two months was six. In October and November the 80th Division had only five new cases of VD and approximately thirty prophylactic treatments. In October 1918, the SOS headquarters at Tours, which held fifteen thousand soldiers, or roughly the same number as a depleted combat division coming out of the line, had eighty-three new cases of VD and 5,071 soldier had received prophylaxis during the month.[49]

It should be noted that when the requirement to report these statistics began, all of the combat divisions were actively involved in battle. Moving to the front and fighting certainly cramped the style of any combat doughboy lothario. However, other VD and prophylactic statistics in the AEF covering the entirety of a unit's time in France also highlight the disparity of sexual activities between combat units and those in the rear. Walker noted that 15 percent of men assigned to the AEF's base sections underwent prophylaxis and over 52 percent of the doughboys stationed in the District of Paris also sought the treatment. Although the annual rate for VD infections in the AEF was thirty-five infections for every thousand soldiers, twenty-six of the twenty-nine combat divisions had rates of less than thirty per thousand and thirteen of these divisions had infection rates of less than twenty soldiers per thousand. The 77th and 90th Divisions, both of which were in France for approximately a year, were the "good boys" of the AEF. Their rates of infection were less than ten out of a thousand. Although there were more infantrymen in the AEF than soldiers in any other branch, they had the army's lowest rates of infection at roughly seventeen men per thousand. Artillerymen had the next lowest rate at just fewer than thirty per thousand. The difference was due to the artillerymen's training. As much of their early time in France was spent in artillery schools close by French towns, they simply had better access to sex than did their ground pounding brethren. In November 1918, the Saumur Artillery School, with a population of 3,508 men, reported eleven cases of VD and 389 prophylaxes. Noncombat troops and members of the Air Service had rates that averaged between fifty and sixty-two per thousand men.[50]

The combat doughboys often made it clear that the chief cause of their continence was a lack of opportunity. As one Marine recalled,

> We were soon to learn that our idea of a warm France with lots of beautiful French girls was a fantastic dream that didn't in any way approach reality for a long time. At first one wondered where all the girls had gone. Apparently the only women folk left in the dozens of small villages were old, weather-beaten, field-worked, tired and worn-out women that had as much romantic appeal to us young fellows as an old shoe.

Robert Bressler assured his parents, "We have been in the woods for over a month now and have not seen a girl for that length of time. In fact I have seen very few during all the time we have been over here so that you need not worry about me falling in love with any." Similarly, a Kansas doughboy wrote home in August 1918,

> You asked me if I had ever seen the pretty French girls that you hear about in the states. So far I haven't seen enough that I would look at a second time, to be counted on one hand. There is to be sure plenty in Paris, or several of the large cities but except for my short time in Paris I have yet to see them, let alone talk to them. This part of the army, so far, has spent its time in tiny little country villages miles away from anywhere or anything. A good part of the time we have been at deserted towns where you see nothing but soldiers.

Lastly, an officer lamented that in the villages where he stayed "young women are as scare[d] as young men over here" and that it was impossible to find any females between the ages of "3 and 83."[51]

Although many doughboys complained about the easy virtue of French women, some combat troops stated that their romantic intentions were sidelined by the old-fashioned values and courting rituals of the few remaining young women they encountered. Following a tradition that prohibited them from interacting with men without first being properly introduced, proper women declined to date Americans. During a briefing given while he was training in Texas, José de la Luz Sáenz recalled, "The French officer called our attention to a French custom among the women. He told us that we should not expect them to accept us without first securing permission from parents and grandparents." After striking up a friendship with one French girl, W. A. Sirmon was dumbfounded that the relationship stalled at small talk. The young officer wrote: "These peculiar customs get me—I have never been introduced to her and can't get introduced properly because we have no friends in common." Along the same lines, Frank Holden remembered, "I could not put those two things together—a young girl of 19 could not go out with a boy unless her mother went with her, but could sit in her house with the boys and smoke cigarettes." Another doughboy remembered, "The peasant girls seem to be very much afraid of the American soldiers. We found later that they had been warned to stay away from us as we were terrible dangerous men."[52]

Not all combat soldiers were as unsuccessful in love as these men and the rates of VD in certain combat units rivaled those of the rear-area troops. Venereal disease in the 32nd and 42nd Divisions was much greater than in other divisions, with just under sixty and forty infections respectively for every thousand of their troops. The 32nd Division's rate was understandable. Upon arriving in France in February 1918 the AEF GHQ turned it into a replacement division and sent many of its subunits to work in the SOS. Once it was reconstituted as a combat division in mid-April the "soft life and high living" in the rear had already taken its toll. The case of the 42nd Division was harder to sort. Although it was the second-longest-serving division in France, its infection rate was more than double that of the longest-serving unit, the 1st Division. Perhaps the Regular Army discipline within the Big Red One made the difference.[53]

The American divisions serving with the British Army under the II Corps also had elevated rates of infection and prophylaxes. The number of soldiers seeking prophylaxes in the II Corps far exceeded other AEF combat units. This was perhaps due to the fact that the British Army's leaders had a more tolerant "boys will be boys" view of sex and turned a blind eye to the Americans who patronized brothels within their sector.[54]

Ironically, military policemen had the highest rates of VD in the AEF, with just under 130 men infected out of every thousand. Prior to the war, the army had no standing MP units and Pershing had to create an MP corps from scratch. This often meant that soldiers were assigned to these units without training, knowledge of the law, or any real selection criteria. Their assignment to cities and towns and the power that their positions bestowed gave them access to prostitutes and made them subject to corruption. Some MPs developed close relations with brothel keepers and provided security and cover for these assignments in return for free sex or kickbacks. In one town the policemen were shaking down doughboy johns for five francs before allowing them to enter the brothels. The mayor of another town stated to an American officer, "Your police run the other boys away from the girls and then take them for themselves."[55]

Not surprisingly, despite the best efforts of the AEF's social welfare agencies to provide the doughboys with wholesome entertainment while they were on pass, many soldiers visiting the army's sixteen official leave areas sought out intimate companionship. On average nearly 30 percent of soldiers in the leave areas received prophylactic care per week. Nîmes must have been a particularly randy town, as its average weekly rate of preventive VD care was 104 percent. In November 1918, of the 3,870 soldiers at the Savoie Leave Area, 2,406 sought prophylaxes. Paris was the great sin city of the doughboys' imagination and was a particularly popular location for assignation. "Gee i had the pleasure of seeing Paris," Private Fey Neff gushed to his brother-in-law in January 1919, "Gee lots of wine and French gash." Although Neff did not directly admit to indulging in these temptations, he simply hinted, "You know me."[56]

There were also periods of greater sexual activity among the troops. The average rate of VD infections per month in the AEF in 1918 was thirty-five out of every thousand men. However, there was a major spike in infections between October 30 and November 20, to between fifty and fifty-seven infections per thousand. This was due to the large influx of replacements and casuals moving through the country and the celebrations that accompanied the Armistice. There was also an increase in VD and prophylaxes with the initial occupation of Germany. Mervyn Burke noted that prior to the Armistice his unit was "rarely in a location where there were any women" and opportunities for sex were limited. This changed during his service in the Army of Occupation when, despite orders against fraternization, such contacts became widespread. An officer noted the irony of a directive issued shortly after the fraternization edict that stated, "Applying for prophylactic treatment against venereal disease will not be considered evidence of having fraternized with the enemy." The biggest increase in the AEF's VD rates occurred in the last weeks of June 1919 as men sought one last chance to sow their wild oats before returning home. During those weeks the infection rates soared to between eighty-three to ninety-three infections per thousand troops.

A 32nd Division doughboy recalled, "In Brest . . . men coming from the front who had no contact with the female sex went foolish, houses on our beat that held these women were busy." He stated that at this time it was a "frequent sight" in Brest for lines "of men numbering 40 or more waiting to have sexual intercourse at a house where there was but one prostitute."[57]

For racial, health, and discipline reasons, senior officers in the AEF were particularly concerned about the sex lives of African American soldiers. Many white soldiers, especially southerners, were outraged by the willingness of European women to have sex with African Americans and viewed such activities as further evidence of European debasement.

Charles MacArthur remarked that an officer in his unit "canceled all Franco-American relations, and even let on that we were fighting on the wrong side" after he saw a black man leave the room of a white prostitute. Many white Americans feared that contact with the morally degraded French would cause African American doughboys to develop a "taste" for white women while serving overseas. The archracist Mississippi senator James K. Vardaman thundered warnings of "French-women-ruined Negro soldiers" descending on the fair white daughters of the South. Vardaman would have been shocked to know the total number of "French-women-ruined" soldiers, both black and white, in the AEF. Like their white countrymen, the African American doughboys liberally sampled the carnal fruits of France. When his unit entered the French town of Britchwiller, Melville T. Miller recalled, "The women seemed to be very much excited, that was something, they had never seen black people. . . . and the men had a ball." Experience with French sexual freedom even prompted one soldier to remark, "Sex in Harlem is in its infancy."[58]

As previously noted, white officers took many measures to restrict the black doughboys' social interactions with the French. Not all of these efforts were strictly racist. The initial high incidents of VD infections among the African American troops in the SOS threatened to slow the buildup of the American Army. These high rates were generally due to the fact that soldiers in black units generally received much less training and sex education than their white comrades. White commanders in the SOS sought to bring down the VD rates among African American troops by finally providing the needed education and, in the fall of 1917, forcing black soldiers returning to camp after leaves and passes to submit to compulsory prophylaxis. That draconian measure was not imposed upon white SOS soldiers. Although humiliating and unfair, these measures did lead to a drop in the VD infection rate from seventy-six to thirty-five men per thousand. This can be seen in the records of the 1,650 men assigned to the Stevedore Division at Camp Foreston Creil. In November 1918 while its men had been given 1,650 prophylactic treatments, the unit had only five cases of the disease.

The monthly sanitary reports also counter the contention of whites that the African American soldiers had overactive sex drives. For example, in October 1918, the 324th Labor Battalion had no new VD infections and only six of its members had sought prophylaxes. Likewise, the following month the 321st Labor Battalion also had no cases of the diseases and merely five of its 108 soldiers had received preventive treatment. These figures might also indicate that the commanders of these units, following a common practice in the United States, simply did not allow the black soldiers to have passes and leaves.[59]

On the whole, the doughboys experienced a degree of sexual freedom, exposure, and education unknown in prewar America. These first steps in the American sexual revolution were of deep concern to a number of American moralists and social reformers. George Walker and some of his fellow doctors also took an interest in how the war had changed the sexual practices of the doughboys. In typical Progressive era fashion, they attempted to statistically and scientifically study what the troops were up to in bed and what it meant for American society.

Walker conducted a detailed survey of 3,069 doughboys that had contracted VD to gain insights into the circumstances of their infection and their sexual activities. Nearly 42 percent of the men admitted that they had been drinking prior to the act, with half of them claiming that they were completely intoxicated. When it came to finding sex, 46 percent stated that they met the girl on the streets, 29 percent met them in a café, and only 16 percent stated that they had been infected in a bordello. This perhaps highlights the AEF's mistake in trying to shut down rather than regulate the sex trade. Although the average amount the soldiers paid for sex in these encounters was 14.84 francs (roughly $2.95 at the time), 37 percent of the infected soldiers boasted that they had paid nothing for intercourse. The compiler of the study found the last claim to be questionable, noting that it was at odds with what he witnessed and that "it is an amusing disposition on the men's part to give the impression that his general attractiveness is sufficient to cause conquest without the payment of money." This last statement was too ungenerous. Some doughboys claimed that they were offered free admission into the beds of lonely French women whose husbands and lovers had been killed or were long absent from home. The medic James Lindsey recalled that he was once pulled off the street by a French woman who just wanted some fleeting companionship.[60]

Walker and his compatriots wanted to dig even further into the doughboys' intimate lives. They chose a man to clandestinely interview French prostitutes to gauge the Americans' changing sexual proclivities. After interviewing 237 soiled doves, the operative reported some disquieting news. He determined that

> perversion is common in France; that it is preferred to the normal method and that it is by no means confined to prostitutes and their associates but it practiced in other grades of society . . . A striking and disturbing feature of the evidence gathered by the investigator was that the Americans in a very short time were indulging in perversions almost as willingly and as frequently as the French.

One of the women told the agent that the "Americans were very different from French when they first landed; but now they have changed, they have been to school in France, to the school of love . . . and now they can make love like the French, and perversion is just as common among them as with the French." Another likewise opined that when the doughboys arrived they "would make love in only one way. Later they learned much about love in France and now they are generally willing to make love, in several fashions." Due to this learning process she concluded now, "They are all perverts." Walker never defined what was meant by "perversion" and "normal" sex and thus leaves it to the puerile imagination of the readers to reach their own conclusions. We can at least assume that "normal" in this case was good old-fashioned missionary position sex and that any deviation from this approved method of coupling was "perversion." Other sources do note that the war introduced many Americans to oral sex and other positions that would have also landed on Walker's naughty list of forbidden pleasures.[61]

Although the AEF's leaders were generally willing to turn a blind eye to doughboys having sex as long as it did not hinder military operations or the military's reputation, this grudging tolerance did not extend to homosexuality. The judge advocate general reported that between April 6, 1917, and June 30, 1919, eleven officers and 142 enlisted men were convicted of sodomy, and another four officers and thirty enlisted men were convicted of assault with intent to commit sodomy. Under the 93rd Article of War, sodomy was defined as a "detestable" crime where there was any forced or consensual sexual penetration of the anus of a man or a woman. In the case of consensual sodomy, if one of the participants was a "boy of tender age," he would not be liable while the adult would be charged with forcible assault. Oral sex was not part of the sodomy offense. Between April 6 and June 30, 1918, two officers and fifty-five soldiers were convicted for "Buccal coitus," giving or receiving oral sex. For some reason, this offense was not listed in the summary of July 1, 1918, to June 30, 1919. The records for sodomy and "Buccal coitus" did not specify the genders involved in these cases, but the evidence suggests that a fair number were linked to homosexual acts.[62]

Reflecting the opinions of the time, the soldiers themselves believed that homosexuality was beyond the pale. Tom Carroll was happy that his company first sergeant was relieved from duty after a rumor spread that the NCO had been caught in bed with a young boy. Second Lieutenant John W. Royer, a machine gun officer in the 29th Division, was tried in August 1918 for making "advances and invitations of an unnatural and immoral nature" to three of his soldiers while sailing to France and of sodomizing another soldier on numerous occasions. Major John English was packed off to Blois after engaging in "sexual perversion" with two of his orderlies while assigned as a medical officer for the 60th Coast Artillery. He was found sleeping naked with one man and one of the orderlies accused him of "improper advances" and of attempting "to fondle him, hugging him and playing with his private organs." Although the reclassification board recommended that English face a court martial, the reviewing authority directed that the army quietly accept the major's resignation "in view of the injury to the service that will result from a trial."[63]

It is difficult to state with any accuracy how much of the doughboys' wartime experiences with alcohol, gambling, cursing, and sex changed American morals and mores. Some attitudes remained entrenched. For example, after a major charged with "immoral conduct" committed suicide, George Patton wrote in his diary that since the man had a family, the officer "did a good thing" to spare them from humiliation. Some veterans embraced and furthered the alcohol and sexual liberality of the Jazz Age or at least enjoyed the occasional opportunity for a binger at the odd American Legion or Veteran of Foreign Wars convention. Most of the soldiers who indulged in the various pleasures of the flesh seemed to have put their experiences down to a youthful sowing of wild oats and quietly returned to the buttoned-down realities of postwar America. They often fondly recalled the indiscretions of their youth. The most vivid memory ex-Private James Lindsey had was the time that he and his buddies stole a bottle of champagne from a Frenchman's cellar and got riotously drunk. Despite the fact that he became hung up on a fence while trying to sneak back into camp, and his frantic efforts at freeing himself only resulted in throwing up the ill-gotten booze, at age one hundred he still laughed and boasted of the incident.[64]

18

"Sky Pilots," "Holy Joes," and the Doughboy's Religion

While sheltering with a group of soldiers in a cave during a heavy shelling, Sergeant Richard McBride remembered that the huddled and scared masses instinctively sought comfort and assurance. In the midst of the incessant pounding, "One of the men asked if anyone knew of a prayer to say. They looked at one another for the answer, then at me. I suggested we recite the Lord's Prayer. We did, in unison. A short time later the shelling stopped, giving us an opportunity to leave our cave of supplication and hope and go on our separate ways." At that moment in the cave McBride and his fellow sufferers felt a deep need for divine intervention and took comfort in faith. But what happened when the danger was past and the soldiers left their "cave of supplication"? Did the troops continue to embrace this spirituality or was it put on hold until the next occasion presented itself for holy help? This was one of the few instances where Mc-Bride inferred anything about his religious beliefs, so it is difficult to answer this question for him. Religion was part of the doughboy's worldview, but the depth of feeling behind it and its importance to the individual differed greatly within the ranks.[1]

During the Great War, American society remained overwhelmingly Christian in its religious orientation. However, successive waves of immigrants and generations of relative religious toleration had created a great diversity of American religious denominations, beliefs, and practices. This diversity was reflected in the ranks of the army. This was evident in a survey of the religious affiliations of 25,607 soldiers at Camp Devens taken in August 1918. As the camp drew most of its men from the immigrant-heavy and cosmopolitan Northeast, it is not surprising that Catholics made up 46 percent of the troops and that the camp contained a multiplicity of other faiths. The total number of soldiers who stated their religious preferences is as follows:

Catholic: 11,731	Christian, non-denom.: 133	Atheist: 5
Baptist: 3,517	Unitarian: 126	Dunkers: 5
Methodist: 3,058	Protestant, non-denom.: 89	Progressive
Congregational: 1,710	Mormon: 60	Brethren: 4
		Russian Protestant: 4
Jewish: 931	Adventist: 36	Dursi: 3
Lutheran: 848	Islam: 30	Agnostic: 2
Episcopalian: 837	Quaker: 25	Church of God: 2
Greek Orthodox: 676	Reformed: 20	Free Thinkers: 2
Presbyterian: 604	United Brethren: 16	Gregorian: 2
No preference: 594	Evangelical: 14	Nazerine: 2
Christian Science: 261	Holiness "Holy Rollers": 7	Plymouth Brethren: 2
Universalist: 230	Spiritualist: 7	Swedish Mission: 2

Additionally, Russellities, Janhers, Mennonite, Mission, Church of Christ, Pentecostal, Polish, Theosophist, Universal, Armenian Apostolic, Christian Apostolic, and Hilieterestis all could claim one soldier each from the ranks of Camp Devens. To a lesser extent, this diversity was also seen in the 5th Division. In July 1918, G. C. Stull, the chief chaplain of the 5th Division's 11th Infantry, gave the following religious affiliations for the 3,564 men in his regiment:

Catholic: 1,034	Presbyterian: 157	Congregational: 17
No church affiliation: 689	Jewish: 82	Russian Orthodox: 14
Methodist: 540	Reformed: 73	Quaker: 5
Baptist: 434	Episcopalian: 53	Dunkers: 4
Lutheran: 257	United Brethren: 34	Christian Science: 2
Christian, non-denom.: 163		

The regiment also had one soldier each claiming membership in the Swedish, Adventist, Universalist, Salvation Army, Mormon, and Mennonite churches.[2]

As National Guard and National Army divisions were initially raised on a regional basis, these units often reflected sectional variations in creeds. In the New England–raised 26th Division, roughly half the unit was Protestant, 49 percent was Catholic, and less than 1 percent was Jewish. A survey of 10,034 soldiers in the 36th Division, drawn from Texas, Oklahoma, and the Southwest, found that 87 percent of the soldiers were Protestants, that 15 percent were Catholics, and that there was only "an infinitesimal amount of Jewish personnel." There were many more soldiers from evangelical sects in the division than was evident in the Camp Devens sample. Most of the division's Catholics tended to be from the unit's Mexican American population. The actual breakdown of the denominations in the division was:

Baptist: 3,925	Episcopalian: 170	Adventist: 17
Methodist: 3,102	Church of Christ: 107	Mormon: 14
Catholic: 1,260	Holiness: 23	Holy Ghost: 9
Presbyterian: 818	Apostolic: 20	Salvation Army: 9
Lutheran: 314	Christian Science: 20	Evangelical: 8
Jewish: 190	Congregational: 20	Universalist: 8

In October 1918, chaplains in the African American 92nd Division reported that with the exception of 520 Catholics, all of the division's remaining soldiers were Protestants, with the majority of these being Baptists or African Methodist Episcopalians.[3]

Although there were a handful of atheists, agnostics, and "free thinkers" in the ranks, the statistics show that the majority of the troops in all these units self-identified with some denomination or faith. What is impossible to glean from the numbers was the depth of the soldier's beliefs or how important religion was in their daily lives. It is interesting to note that a significant number of men in the 11th Infantry and at Camp Devens stated that they had no religious preference or were nondenominational Christians or Protestants. Sadly, the numbers alone do not explain what the soldiers meant by this appellation. Were these men doubters unwilling to embrace the socially loaded labels of atheist and agnostic, ecumenical in their personal beliefs, or merely lukewarm in their convictions? The soldiers' letters, diaries, and memoirs only somewhat clarify the question of their commitment to faith. In some of these records soldiers expressed deep religious convictions and wrote of the important role that faith played in their lives. Other soldiers only mentioned prayer and other religious practices in passing while even larger numbers made no mention of anything hinting of religiosity at all.[4]

However, there are some indicators that the average doughboy took more than a passing interest in religion. In the late summer of 1918 the statistics-hungry AEF GHQ devised a standard monthly report for chaplains that detailed their pastoral and religious work as well as any additional educational or entertainment efforts that the Sky Pilots had undertaken in their units. These reports give some, albeit limited and unconfirmed, indications of the soldiers' participation in unit religious activities. Chaplain John O'Leary of the 7th Infantry, for example, reported in August 1918 that while the regiment was out of the line he held services every weekday morning and twelve times on Sunday for an average of one hundred men per service, held twelve communion services for an additional four hundred soldiers, gave two Bible classes, and heard the confessions of 420 doughboys. If O'Leary's estimates are correct, then roughly half of the regiment's soldiers attended his Sunday services and many others participated in his other religious activities. Chaplains from other units reported similar figures. In November 1918 the chaplains of the 92nd Division held 176 services with a total attendance of 25,344 while those of the 81st Division held ninety-five services for 14,175 doughboys. Although combat cut down the number of services that chaplains could perform, in the midst of the Meuse Argonne fighting in October 1918, the padres of the 82nd Division still conducted forty-nine services for 9,840 doughboys. As these services were voluntary, the statistics point to the fact that large numbers of doughboys were seeking some degree of religious participation.[5]

For the most part, the men who entered the army with a strong religious faith tended to retain their convictions during their time in service. For many of these soldiers their religion was a comfort in times of hardship, and they often found their faith strengthened by the ordeal of battle. This was certainly the case for Alvin York. In January 1915, after going through a long period of dissipation, York underwent a shattering conversion experience that led him to completely renounce his sinful ways. He joined the fundamentalist Church of Christ in Christian Union and embraced its literal interpretation of the Bible. When the war and the draft came, York's faith presented him with a dilemma. He was forced to reconcile the biblical injunction "Thou shalt not kill" with the demands of compulsory military service. He recalled that it was a most awful thing when the wishes of your God and your country sorter get mixed up and go against each other . . . I wanted to do what was right. I wanted to be a good Christian and a good American too . . . If I went away to war and fought and killed, according to my reading of the Bible, I weren't a good Christian. And if I didn't go to war and do these things, according to Uncle Sam, I weren't a good American.

After the local and district draft boards repeatedly rejected his request to be granted conscientious objector status due to his religious convictions because the government did not recognize his church as a valid pacifist denomination, York dutifully reported to Camp Gordon. However, he could still not resolve the demands of the sacred with those of the secular. York's company and battalion commanders were also religious men and used Bible passages to assure him that combat service was not incompatible with his religious obligations. They even granted him a leave to return home so he could think through his ethical dilemma. After considerable prayer a "great peace" and "a great calm" came into York's soul and he believed that God had pointed him toward a decision to fight. Throughout the war his faith sustained and comforted him. "I believed in God and in his promise," he maintained, "and I knowed as long as I did that He would believe in and watch over me." York credited God for the feat that won him the Medal of Honor and maintained that he went into battle with God's assurance that "so long as I believed in Him not one hair on my head would be harmed."[6]

York was far from being alone in trusting to divine providence to bring him safely through battle. An infantryman reassured his sister in December 1917, "I don't mind being here a bit as long as the Lord is with me and which I hope he always is." Edwin Arpin discovered that heavy shellfire tended to refuel his religiosity. He recalled,

> On occasions of this sort one sometimes felt an overpowering need for help beyond anything in the material world. Something wherein to be carried away into an atmosphere of mental peace beyond the reach of the awful present . . . The simple prayers of childhood took on a profound meaning never before appreciated. From the storehouse of my limited memory the Lord's Prayer and the Twenty-third and Ninety-first Psalms were an unfailing source of comfort.

In the midst of death and destruction, both men took deep comfort in their belief that their faith had provided them with spiritual body armor.[7]

For others, close calls in combat strengthened their faith and gave them the comfort that they benefited from otherworldly protection. One such doughboy, Thurmond Baccus, became more reverent after a shell fell on a spot that he had just left. The shell killed and wounded several surrounding soldiers and left him uninjured despite the fact that a fragment from the shell ignited a grenade that he was carrying in his pocket. He marveled, "That was the second time The Great Power from above directed me and many more times protected me." A 35th Division doughboy admitted to his mother that when he entered his first real combat in the Meuse Argonne, "I prayed and I am not afraid to admit it to anyone. I know it helped. Fear really never entered my mind, altho perhaps many things stared glumly and blackly at me. Yet my faith that everything would be alright for your sake never failed me. Believe me, I prayed often." After a very close call on the second day of the battle when a spent shell fragment struck him in the back of the neck, he saw proof that "my prayers must have worked."[8]

Although the randomness of death in combat drove some soldiers to give into a pessimistic fatalism, others saw in these events the hand of God and took consolation in their denomination's tenets of predestination. Alvin York's simple faith certainly helped him to reconcile some of the irreconcilable facts of war and religion. He later wrote,

> I know, of course, that some people will say that if He protected me, why didn't he protect the other American boys who were killed, and the Germans too? He was their God as well as mine, and if He was a just and righteous God, why didn't he protect them? I can't answer that. I ain't a-going to try to. I Don't understand the way in which he works . . . I jes accept them and bow my head and bless His holy name, and believe in Him more'n ever.

York explained, "There is no use worrying a Bout Shells for you cant keep them from bursting in your trench. So what is the use of worrying if you cant alter things . . . just ask God to help you and accept them and make the best of them by the help of God." Shortly after coming out of the line, Harry Callison pleaded with his mother, "I don't want any of you to worry. Life is too short for that and our well-being is in the hands of One who is wiser and more just than we can expect to be an don't think He wishes us to worry about it but just go on and live our lives as we can see it." "Battles bring out fear in some soldiers—fear of death," a soldier in the 18th Infantry later admitted, but "my

Protestant Religion taught me to have faith and that life was destined, what is to happen will happen."[9]

The arbitrary nature of the battlefield and the possibility of sudden death or grave injury drove some men to embrace faith for the first time or more readily than they had before. Infantryman Lunie McCarly's experience in combat led him down a path of soul-searching and self-reflection. In September 1918, he informed his sister, "you know i have been a Bad Boy all my life But i have changed some and am going to live a different life." He also admitted to a newfound spirituality and beseeched her, "i want you and Rob to get near to our good lord." McCarly's conversion would not have surprised Chaplain Lee Levinger. He observed,

> At the front, even the most thoughtless desired some sort of personal religion. In the midst of the constant danger to life and limb, seeing their comrades about them dead and wounded, with life reduced to the minimum of necessity and the few elemental problems, men were forced to think of the realities of life and death. With these internal questions forced upon them, the great majority must always turn to religion. The men prayed at the front. They wanted safety and they felt the need of God. After battle they were eager to offer thanks for their own safety and to say the memorial prayers for their friends who had just laid down their lives.

The chaplain for the 30th Infantry also commented on this reality. After weeks of hard fighting in the Meuse Argonne, he reported, "I noticed that the men of my regiment are more *religious* than I have ever known them to be." Ministering to troops during the battle led another padre to conclude. "Despite what may be said, the American soldier is not hostile to religion and on the contrary, he feels lost without it."[10]

Some soldiers certainly gave proof to the old adage "There are no atheists in a foxhole." One Marine observed that for one of his comrades, "Bibles always seemed the subject furtherest removed from his mind," yet during heavy shelling at Belleau Woods, he noticed that the man "was extremely busy in a nervous perusal of his Testament." A sergeant in the 77th Division noted that it was often the men who "were always so tough and foul-mouthed back in Camp Upton" that became the most reverent prayers in the line. But the close proximity to death did not change the attitudes of some nonbelievers. To the newly religious, one atheist retorted,

What the hell good is all of this praying going to do for you? If your name is on one of those shells, you are going to get it no matter how much you pray. Don't you think that the men who have been killed already in this war for the past four years prayed? Don't you think their wives and mothers prayed for them? What the hell good did it do them?

Although his arguments were logical, war itself is an illogical undertaking and few doughboys were willing to turn their backs on the possibility of divine protection. In fact battlefield conversions often took the form of bargaining with the Almighty. An artilleryman in the 82nd Division admitted that in battle, "I asked God to spare my life and I would try to be a better person when I got home." Some chaplains understood the realities of sudden battlefield faith. During the Argonne fighting, one fervently hoped, "May they not forget Him to whom they prayed in the recent crisis!"[11]

Not all soldiers found their faith unscathed by war. Charles Minder, a particularly sensitive and religious machine gunner from New York, found that his early excitement about the war had quickly turned into a crisis of faith and confidence. In a letter home from May 1918 he confessed,

> Mother, I don't like the idea [of going into action] at all. I am utterly helpless. I don't feel that I am a coward . . . I have no desire to harm anyone, I don't want to kill. I am being forced to do something against my will, that's what bothers me. They may be our enemies but I know that many of them are being forced to kill, just as I am . . . If there is a God, why doesn't he put a stop to this mother? Surely, even tho he is of "too pure of eyes to see evil," he must be aware that his children are slaughtering one another against their wills. Is this evil force, War, more powerful than God? I can't believe it, nor can I understand it.

Although he continued to wrestle with these issues of faith for the remainder of his time in the service, Minder was still unwilling to fundamentally question his religious upbringing. While he admitted to feeling blue and homesick due to his ethical dilemma, he still acknowledged, "All I can do is carry on and trust in God."[12]

Others shared Minder's difficulty in reconciling the ugliness of war with their religious convictions. After attending "a good, old fashioned, restful, soul-satisfying church service," Lieutenant Reginald Thomson confessed, "I am still interested in speculation upon the ultimate realities of life, of the relation of mind and matter, and other kindred subjects, in spite of the fact that

I have been rather busy during the past months learning the most scientific methods of killing fellow men." To a very great extent, the army's chaplains and other religious figures worked hard to convince men like Minder and Thomson that they were involved in a just and religiously sanctioned war. During a prayer service a YMCA worker informed Private Thomas Marshall and the other attendees "that this cruel war is because God in his generosity gave man free will, which man abused more and more until it has been so overdone that we are called on to bring the world back to its senses again." After the YMCA man's sermon, Marshall left convinced that "there is a greater cause than killing Germans" at issue in the war. We can hope that the YMCA secretary was correct in his biblical interpretations, for Marshall would later die of wounds that he received during the Meuse Argonne campaign.[13]

It must be stated that much written in the proceeding passages came from soldiers who were deeply religious or at least very conscious of the role of faith in their lives. The record suggests that the 82nd Division infantryman, Fred Takes, perhaps represented the "average" doughboy's typical religious experience. He was a Roman Catholic who took his faith seriously but not too seriously. Takes was not always consistent in attending church services. Soon after arriving in France, on one Sunday he made confession at 8:30 AM, attended Mass and received communion at 9:00 AM, listened to another Mass at 10:00 AM, attended High Mass at 11:00AM, and then stayed on to attend Vespers at 3:00 PM and a benediction at 7:00 PM. On another occasion, he went to a local French priest for confession but found the experience "rather funny, because the priest spoke no English." To minister to the American, the priest "had a card printed in English and on this card you would point out your 'tricks'" and then the padre assigned the proper penitence. However, these two events were the highpoint of Takes's religious efforts during the war. Although he sometimes attended other church services, he admitted that he skipped religious gatherings frequently because he did not want to make the trip or would rather spend his time resting. That being said, his diary records that he did spend much time in private prayer.[14]

The men who the army expected would minister to the religious needs of Takes and his comrades, and would aid them in dealing with their spiritual and ethical struggles, were the chaplains. When the United States entered the war, the Regular Army had fewer than seventy chaplains in its ranks, and the National Guard could boast only a handful more. As with so many other things in its mobilization, the army was caught flatfooted when it came to providing religious services to the troops. In the summer and fall of 1917 it muddled through as best it could by using the limited number of chaplains it had on hand and by occasionally calling upon local clergy and members of religious organizations such as the YMCA and Knights of Columbus to minister to the troops in training. A bill from September 1917 that would provide one chaplain for every twelve hundred soldiers painfully made its way through the legislative and executive branches before finally being signed into law on June 23, 1918. This bureaucratic foot-dragging left the army woefully short of chaplains throughout the war.[15]

To aid the military in finding and vetting those seeking to become chaplains, the War Department and Navy Department turned to the General Committee on Army and Navy Chaplains of the Federal Council of the Churches of Christ in America for Protestant preachers and to Reverend Lewis O'Hern and the National Catholic War Council for Catholic priests. The two groups established standard procedures for bringing clergy into the ranks. The applicants had to be sponsored by a recognized denomination and submit an application with documentation of their religious work and education and letters of recommendations from those familiar with the candidate's character and qualifications to serve. The recommenders were sent a standard form that asked about the candidate's loyalty "to Christ and the Church and our Country," his personality, and his ability to cooperate with "other social and religious leaders and agencies."

They were also asked, "Has his ministry to men shown force and influence distinctly on religious and spiritual lines?" and "Has he shown initiative and capacity in what is termed welfare work among men, using alert and wholesome methods for their social and interest and betterment?" The candidate's packet was then reviewed by a committee of noted religious leaders. If he was selected to be a chaplain, the candidate then attended a five-week chaplain school at Fort Monroe, Virginia (which later moved to Camp Zachary Taylor, Kentucky), to provide him with a basic knowledge of military service and rudimentary military training before he was formally commissioned.[16]

In late 1918, the 2nd Army's Senior Chaplain tasked the Senior Chaplain of the 79th Division to submit biographies of all the chaplains in his organization, detailing their education, military service, work with the YMCA, and previous teaching and athletic experience. Twenty of the division's twenty-one chaplains complied with the request and their responses offer an insight into what type of man served in the AEF's chaplain corps. When it came to denominations, seven of the chaplains were Roman Catholic priests, five were Methodists, two Presbyterians, two Episcopalians, two Baptists, and one each from the Church of Christ and United Brethren of Christ. Nineteen had graduated from college in addition to their seminary studies. Sixteen had graduated from seminary schools and of the remaining four, two had attended seminary school for at least one year and the other two had only studied theology as part of their regular undergraduate education. All except one of the officers was native-born. The Roman Catholic chaplain of the 315th Infantry, First Lieutenant Joseph E. Camerman, was born in Doel, Belgium, and attended seminary school in Louvain before immigrating to the United States in 1906.

Although four of the 79th Division's chaplains had some military training as cadets while in high school or college, only two had any real military service prior to the war. Elijah Arthur, a Presbyterian chaplain in the 313th Infantry, had served briefly during the Spanish-American War and had been an officer in the Indiana National Guard since 1913. William T. Willis graduated from the Virginia Military Institute before entering seminary school. After ordination, he returned to VMI to teach mathematics and military tactics. He was commissioned in the Regular Army in June 1916. Twelve of the eighteen remaining chaplains had been in uniform less than ten months at the time of the Armistice. Chaplain Conrad Goodwin had only received his commission on September 25, 1918.

The average age of the 79th Division's chaplains was thirty-six. The oldest was Elijah Arthur, age forty-eight. The youngest, at twenty-eight, was the chaplain of the 304th Ammunition Train, Ernest L. Loomis. The chaplain's average age was considerably older than the average age of the army's line officers and soldiers. This perhaps better positioned the "Holy Joes" to serve as the "Big Brothers" to the rank and file that the AEF senior chaplain envisioned.

The range of experience of these officers as clergymen varied greatly. Elijah Arthur and Charles Frick had served as ministers for over eighteen years, while Zenas C. Staples had only been ordained as a Methodist preacher in June 1918. The group's average experience was eight years of service as ordained clergymen. Additionally, eleven of the twenty had served as high school or college teachers or administrators before they entered the army, and many noted that they had continued to take an active role in educating their unit's soldiers since being in uniform. Reflecting the era's concept of "muscular Christianity," it is not surprising that fifteen of the chaplains had played high school or college sports. Many also noted that they had experience in coaching or running school athletic programs prior to entering the army.

One 79th Division chaplain, First Lieutenant Oscar Whitfield Reynolds, can serve as a character sketch of an "average" AEF chaplain. Reynolds was born on September 1, 1880, in Nebraska and was thirty-eight years old when the war ended. He graduated from the University of Nebraska before entering the Boston University School of Theology. While at college he was active in the YMCA, served two years as a cadet, and had played baseball and football. At university he had also been elected president of the college athletic association and vice president of college athletic board. His religious career started in 1907 when he became a Methodist Episcopalian pastor. He was elevated to deacon in 1911 and rose to full minister in March 1916. Due to his educational background and one year of experience teaching college, his commander appointed him to serve as his regiment's educational officer where Reynolds oversaw four schools with a total of 225 soldier-students. Reynolds must have found military service agreeable, for in 1920 he accepted a Regular Army commission. He served as an army chaplain until he retired in September 1944 at the rank of lieutenant colonel.[17]

Although the army had developed a logical and thorough process to commission chaplains such as Reynolds and his fellow padres, it could not keep pace with the growing army's demand for clergy. These shortfalls were obvious to Pershing. On May 1, 1918, General Orders 66 established the AEF GHQ Chaplains' Office to coordinate religious matters within the American Army and appointed Bishop Charles H. Brent as the AEF Senior Chaplain. The following month, Brent opened a chaplain school in Neuilly-sur-Suize to educate newly arriving or appointed chaplains on their duties in France. The short course consisted of a series of lectures on practical soldiering—such as gas training and what to wear at the front—and on the duties expected of the chaplain, from burying the dead to pastoral care. The Capuchin monk turned Catholic chaplain Celestine Bittle recalled that the parting word of wisdom to the novice chaplains from their chief instructor was a "plea to grasp the spirit of the great movement with heart and soul," and to "Be a Christian gentleman at all times."[18]

The shortage of military clergy in the AEF led Pershing to direct Brent to hold boards to select those doughboys and welfare agency workers with the "necessary educational, ecclesiastical and physical requirements" to be commissioned as chaplains. The candidate was required to submit an application and letters of recommendation from his commander to a board of senior AEF chaplains. The board evaluated the candidates on their pastoral work as a clergyman and ability to teach and their knowledge of English grammar and composition, arithmetic, geography, and history.

Private Oliver Enselman became a chaplain through this route. Although he had graduated from the University of Michigan and the Garrett Biblical Institute and had served as a Methodist Episcopal minister, he had chosen to enter the ranks as an enlisted man. When he discovered that the AEF was actively seeking chaplains, in October 1918 he sent his application to the board. Citing his coolness under fire and his high moral character, Enselman's company and battalion commanders in the 138th Infantry strongly recommended him for a chaplain commission. Based on his background and service record, the AEF Chaplain Board approved his application on November 11, 1918.[19]

Despite these measures, the AEF never came close to having one chaplain for every twelve hundred men during its war. In fact on October 11, 1918, the AEF senior chaplain reported that there were 789 chaplains on duty in France. The arrival of a large number of chaplains in November and December 1918 increased the number to approximately 1,250 but even this rise left the army short of padres. With two million men in Europe, the AEF was still short roughly 420 chaplains. The AEF tried to get close to the target ratio by assigning twenty-one chaplains per division. Unfortunately, even this proved hard to maintain. In September 1918 the 2nd Division reported that it had eighteen chaplains on hand, but of these, four had been evacuated due to sickness and one other had been gassed. The division chaplain begged the GHQ Chaplain's Office for two more Navy padres to minister to the 5th and 6th Marine regiments. The following month the 89th Division had fourteen chaplains while the 92nd Division could boast only thirteen.[20]

Some units attempted to make up their shortage of clergy by using the civilians working for the YMCA, Salvation Army, Jewish Welfare Board, and Knights of Columbus. For example, in September 1918 the 3rd Division had its full complement of twenty-one chaplains but had only accomplished this by assigning Father J. M. Blaise of the Knights of Columbus to serve as the padre for the 4th Infantry. The division's chief chaplain commended Blaise for "doing splendid work and [being] greatly loved by the men." The work kept Blaise busy, for in August he reported holding on average fifteen services on Sundays and twenty more during the week with an attendance of approximately two hundred men per service. He also heard the confessions of 150 men, visited the unit's men in the infirmary daily, and corresponded with thirteen soldier family members or friends during the period. The fifty-year-old Baptist YMCA secretary who served as the acting chaplain for the 103rd Military Police Battalion likewise earned the respect of his flock by sharing the soldiers' hardships. He marched with them with full pack and ministered to the troops so close to the action that he was once gassed while serving as a stretcher bearer.[21]

The AEF senior chaplain's October 1918 list of clergy serving in France provides a relatively complete record of the theological background of the army's chaplains as well as information on where the men were assigned. From this record it is possible to gain insights into the army's efforts to provide proper religious support to its diverse population as well as into where the army believed that religious comfort was most needed. The number of chaplains, as listed by denominations given in the chief of chaplains report, was:

231 Roman Catholic	7 Southern Methodist	3 Christian Science
82 Episcopalian	Episcopalian	2 Dutch Reformed
81 None Listed	5 Jewish	2 Unitarian
79 Methodist Episcopalian	5 African Methodist	2 Evangelical
76 Baptist	Episcopalian	2 Universalist
71 Presbyterian	4 Northern Baptist	1 Salvation Army
31 Lutheran	3 Reformed	1 Evangelical
31 Congregational	3 Mormon/Latter	Association
25 Methodist	Day Saints	1 Campbellite
15 Disciples of Christ	3 Northern Methodist	1 United Evangelical
11 Church of Christ	Episcopalian	
8 Southern Baptist	3 United Brethren	

Prior to World War I the army drew most of its chaplains from the mainline Protestant denominations and the Catholic Church. Although chaplains in the prewar National Guard tended to be more reflective of the religious affiliations of their local members, the Guard, as a whole, still generally followed the Regular Army practice. While Catholic and mainline Protestant chaplains still occupied the bulk of the wartime chaplain ranks, the October report indicates that the army made great efforts to minister to the varied religious needs of the doughboys. The admission of Jewish rabbis and men from a variety of evangelical sects, the Mormon Church, the African Methodist Episcopalian Church, and even nontraditional faiths such as Christian Science and the Salvation Army demonstrates that the army was quite progressive in its religious outlook and attuned to the needs of a largely draftee army.

From the assignments of these 789 chaplains, it is also clear that the army believed that it was most important to have these limited spiritual resources posted to combat units. Nearly 47 percent of the AEF's chaplains were assigned to infantry regiments and machine gun battalions. The AEF posted another 15 percent to artillery units and 9 percent to the engineers. Altogether, over 86 percent of the army's chaplains served in combat or divisional units. Only 105 chaplains ministered to all of the remaining soldiers serving in the AEF's higher headquarters, hospitals, and the massive bulk of the SOS.[22]

Few chaplains quibbled with this assignment pattern as most seemed to have sought out assignments to combat units because they also believed that they would do the most good in those positions. Like other men, some chaplains also sought combat assignments to prove their courage and manhood. This was certainly the case with Arthur Hicks, who hoped that his assignment as a chaplain for the 53rd Artillery would be an opportunity to test his bravery. Shortly after the Armistice, he wrote to his wife, "I really wanted to know just what the sensations are that a man experiences when he goes with the soldiers over the top." He was disappointed that he saw little action besides watching the American guns fire and lamented, "You will never know whether or not I am a coward." Those not selected for combat duties were often disappointed. When Celestine Bittle expressed distress at not being sent to a combat unit at the end of his chaplain's course, the senior instructor gently chided, "There are hospitals and camps in the Base and Intermediate Sections which have no chaplains. These men have souls, too, need you, and are waiting for you."[23]

Despite the shortage of clergy, the GHQ Chaplain's Office did all it could to assign chaplains based on the density of given denominations within the divisions and regiments. The 89th Division drew its draftees from Missouri, Kansas, Nebraska, Colorado, Arizona, and New Mexico. As such, in October 1918 it held four Baptist, four Catholic, two Presbyterian, and one chaplain each from the Methodist, Episcopal, Disciples of Christ, and Mormon denominations. The 82nd Division's chaplains were even more diverse. This reflected the circumstances of the unit's mobilization. At first the 82nd was manned by officers and draftees from Georgia, Tennessee, and Alabama. However, in October 1918, most of the southern draftees were transferred to other divisions and their places filled by draftees coming mostly from New York and New England. Reflecting this residual southern and mostly northern mix, in October 1918 the 82nd Division's chaplaincy consisted of eight Catholics, six Methodists, three Baptists, a Jewish rabbi, a nondenominational Christian, a Unitarian, and a Salvation Army secretary.[24]

What is notable about the army's approach to religion in World War I was the ecumenical spirit that it sought to nurture in its chaplain corps. The size and diversity of the soldiers' beliefs and the difficulty in raising enough chaplains to meet demands meant that it was impossible to always have a specific clergyman on hand to minister to the individual beliefs of all the members of a unit. As such, the army demanded that all chaplains treat all denominations and faiths with equal respect and whenever possible learn the religious rituals and services needed by their doughboy flocks. While attending the AEF chaplain orientation course, one Rabbi was pleased that the assembled chaplains willingly exchanged information on important rituals and prayers that were unique to their faiths. He believed that this allowed him to minister to most of the soldiers he encountered and give them the comfort that they needed at the time of their greatest troubles. He observed, "These men did not go out to convert others to their own views of truth and life; they were ready to serve pious souls and bring God's presence near to all." On September 10, 1918, the 82nd Division's senior chaplain reported,

> The chaplains in the Division are working together in wonderful harmony. This is indicated in the fact that Roman Catholic and Protestant chaplains have learned from the Hebrew chaplain how to administer comfort to a dying Jewish soldier. Each Jewish and Protestant chaplain carries a crucifix and has been taught by a Roman Catholic chaplain to administer comfort to a dying Roman Catholic; likewise, the Roman Catholics and the Jewish

chaplain have been instructed to administer consolation to a dying Protestant soldier.

It is noteworthy that similar comments pepper the correspondence of other AEF chaplains.[25]

The doughboys appreciated this ecumenical approach. William Graham praised his Baptist chaplain for ministering to all the unit's denominations without any hint of narrow sectarianism. The chaplain always carried handfuls of Catholic rosaries and generated such devotion that volunteers from several faiths once spent three hours cleaning up a shell-damaged French church on the Marne so he could conduct services. Those religious leaders who failed to live up to this expected religious tolerance were often disliked by the men. This seems to have been particularly true of the YMCA secretaries who manned the AEF's recreation huts and often filled in as ad hoc unit chaplains. Many of these men exhibited a prejudice against anything not white, Anglo-Saxon, and Protestant. Judge Ben Lindsey found that there was a deep cultural divide between the soldiers and the YMCA workers and chaplains. This was due to the fact that in the training of their workers, the YMCA had placed their greatest emphasis on "the importance of saving soldiers from sin and getting them to 'accept and follow Jesus Christ.'" Furthermore, he noted, "Some of the Y workers arrived in France with an evangelical Sunday-school attitude of superior virtue . . . And their assumption of evangelical superiority seemed to convict them of the soldier's third cardinal sin—snobbishness, lack of humility, boastfulness." These men, Lindsey maintained, failed in their ministerial roles and were denounced as "Holier-than-thou's" by the troops.[26]

Despite the religious tolerance that the AEF Chaplin's Office sought to instill in its Holy Joes, it found that some men were not suitable to be chaplains for theological reasons. In August 1918 the senior chaplain for the 89th Division tried to get the Christian Science chaplain Walter Cross removed from the unit. He argued that the number of Christian Scientists in the division was "too small to justify the presence in the division of a man whom I have found of no value in the larger work of the chaplain." He found Cross a poor worker and, because of the tenants of his faith, ill suited to minister to his unit's sick and wounded. This was also the case of another Christian Scientist known to Lee Levinger. "He was handicapped for the necessary work of caring for the sick and wounded," Levinger recalled, "by a unique attitude towards physical suffering, different from the rest of us and different from that of most of the soldiers themselves." The man could not give the prayers that most doughboys needed for their spiritual comfort.[27]

In a nation that was still wrestling with latent, and sometimes overt, anti-Semitism, the army also took pains to accommodate the religious needs of Jewish soldiers. In September 1918 the 37th Division's senior chaplain reported that his office had done everything possible to allow the unit's Jewish soldiers to celebrate their High Holy Days. As the unit lacked a Jewish chaplain, he turned to a French Army rabbi to hold the services and arranged to transport interested soldiers to the synagogue in Luneville for the Day of Atonement ceremonies. Lee Levinger claimed that "the tendency of the American Army during the World War was definitely against prejudice of any kind" and that "in all my experience abroad I have never seen a clear case of anti-Semitism among higher officers and only seldom in the ranks." He was pleased when many Christian soldiers asked to sit in on his services, and he eagerly answered their questions on the Jewish faith. After receiving complaints from Jewish soldiers and family members about the army's policy for marking graves, on July 29, 1918, Pershing directed that the graves of all Jewish soldiers be marked with the Star of David rather than a cross. But sometimes identifying the religious preference of the dead was difficult. The soldier's identification tags were supposed to be marked with a "C" for Catholics, "P" for Protestants, and "H" for Hebrews. However, these distinctions were not always made and even Levinger admitted that his dog tags never had his religious affiliation. Because of these oversights, it ultimately took over three months to verify the Jewish dead of the 27th Division.[28]

Despite the army's best efforts, Levinger confessed, "It was hard to be a good Jew in the Army." He found the "Sabbath could not be kept at all, even in rest areas where there was no immediate danger to life. No soldier could disobey an order to work on the Sabbath; if the work was there, the soldier had to do it." The rabbi also observed that keeping kosher in the ranks was a chore. Faced with the reality that pork was a staple in the AEF's diet, one Jewish soldier from a strict Orthodox family admitted, "I just had to bend a few rules for the duration." Sometimes Levinger even had difficulty ministering to all of his Jewish flock. One Orthodox soldier was upset that he only conducted half of his service in Hebrew. The soldier was pacified only when

Levinger pointed out that over half of the men at the service could not speak the language. The Jewish soldiers' greatest complaint was that there were simply not enough Jewish chaplains to meet their needs. One rabbi lamented the fact that while there were over fifty thousand Jewish soldiers in the AEF they were served by only twelve Jewish chaplains (a ratio of one chaplain per 4,166 Jewish soldiers). Because of this shortfall, Leo Simons complained in *Stars and Stripes* that it had taken nearly a year for the army to provide a religious service for the 150 to two hundred Jewish soldiers stationed at Chaumont, and he feared that this service would be a unique event.[29]

Regardless of their faith or denominations, the role of the chaplain within a unit was somewhat nebulous. "The work of a Chaplain," a Sky Pilot observed, "has never been handicapped by over-precise definition." In an effort to better codify the role of chaplains within the army, in the fall of 1918 the AEF Chaplain's Office requested that select chaplains in field assignments submit short essays explaining how they saw their roles within their units. Their responses offer insight into how the chaplaincy viewed itself and its function in the AEF. Many responded that they were the "big brother" or "sympathetic parent" who guided the doughboys toward spiritual enlightenment and away from sin. One claimed a more expansive purview for the chaplaincy, proclaiming, "The Chaplain is the leader of leaders in all that pertains to the preservation and development of true manhood." The varied duties of the chaplains were reflected in the responses of two of the essayists. A chaplain from an artillery regiment described his focus as

> *First*; To minister directly to the spiritual needs of all of the men of his regiment systematically and to all other soldiers, as the opportunity affords. *Second*; To minister indirectly to such spiritual needs by endeavoring to give the men enjoyment and by showing friendliness. *Third*; To promote the development of character among the men by wholesome recreation and remedying all conditions that tend to break down character. *Fourth*; To do everything possible to improve the spirit and morale of the regiment.

Likewise, another chaplain explained, "First, he must be the Religious guide and Spiritual inspiration of all of the men in his unit; secondly, he must minister as far as possible to their material comfort; thirdly, his duties include the care of the dead and keeping of records and forwarding of reports as specified in general orders." As both men admitted, they were expected to be the spiritual mentors of their soldiers, but the army expected much more than religion from them. Unit commanders often expanded the function of their chaplains to include serving as their unit morale, athletic, education, and burial officers.[30]

In whatever role they were playing in their units, the more successful of the AEF's chaplains were those who could cultivate human connections between themselves and their flocks. The 26th Division's Michael O'Connor advised novice chaplains,

> The chaplain who associates with his men as a big brother, a human be-
> ing, conversant with human frailties, a man not severe in his reprimands
> for either language or conduct, a man who can reprove without causing
> resentment, will have an influence that will rather attract than repel the
> representative of religion and cause it to be loved rather than hated or
> burdensome.

The chaplain of the 166th Infantry cautioned the novices to always "keep the soldier's point of view" in mind in their interactions with the troops. The soldiers, he opined, wanted their chaplains to be direct and to present issues in a "matter-of-fact" manner. "He has neither the time nor inclination in his thought process to deal with the abstract and demands truth garbed in simplicity." Last he enjoined the padres to be cheerful and to "let them know that someone is interested in them."[31]

The doughboys generally revered chaplains, such as the 42nd Division's Francis Duffy and the 26th Division's Lyman Rollins, who shared the dangers and hardships of the front and avoided sanctimonious judgments of the troops' foibles. The doughboys also expected the Holy Joes to play the part of a man among men and exhibit the characteristics of "muscular Christianity." Lyman Rollins was certainly part of the "church militant" and waged a constant battle against sin, the devil, and the Germans. He never shirked from danger. When his 101st Infantry launched the first large-scale American raid of the war on the night of May 30, he went over the top with the raiders. Rollins was gassed during the attack and was cited for his bravery in battle.[32]

Those chaplains and other religious figures who failed to live up to the doughboys' expectations quickly lost any moral suasion with the soldiery. Bob Casey developed a decidedly negative view of the chaplain serving his unit. He described the padre as merely "a face at the mess table, a whining voice droning at public exercises, an empty pated authority on all subjects be-

tween abacus and xylophone." The soldier's chief complaint against the chaplain was that he made little effort to visit the troops either in the field or in the
barracks. In fact, one company commander went so far as to request that the
chaplain come to his location to attend to a death in his unit without telling
the "Sky Pilot" that the dearly departed was merely a dead battery horse. Both
the commander and the attending troops got a good laugh at the chaplain's
sputtering indignation once he discovered that he had been hoodwinked. At
the end of the episode, the artilleryman turned more philosophical:

> What good is a chaplain? All the good in the world if he fits but it seems safe
> to guess that a leader in a man's world ought to be a man ... Men ... are
> not irreligious. They probably are willing to listen to vital philosophies.
> But religion must be at least as vital as the lives they lead ... preached to
> them by a man who lives that life with them and understands their necessi-
> ties by comparison with his own. The drool of platitude and the intonation
> of the mortuary chapel leave them half amused, half angered.

One chaplain discovered that it was pointless to preach to most soldiers and
found that talking to them informally and directly was the best way to proceed: "The strongest hatred of the fighting man was directed against sham
of whatever type ... he was certain to prick the bubble of a poseur at once,
and was more than suspicious of anything which even tended at pose or pre-
tense." There was a fine line in this approach. Horatio Rogers, the son of
an Episcopal minister, remained unimpressed by the religious mentoring he
received throughout the war. He railed against his chaplain because "he tried
to lower himself to what he considered was the soldier's level, and he put it
quite low."[33]

The soldiers showed little sympathy for ministers who did not meet their
exacting demands of conduct and bravery. In the Argonne, the padre who
the troops in Bob Casey's unit derisively called "Charlie Chaplain" further
alienated the troops by drawing enemy artillery fire after he carelessly drove
a wagon down an exposed road under enemy observation. When the inevitable enemy response caused the chaplain to move with undignified haste to
a muck-filled ditch, he lost the last shred of moral authority with his flock.
As Casey noted, "That an officer should show signs of nerves was unthink-
able." The chaplain assigned to the 8th Field Signal Battalion, John "Holy Joe"
Keplinger, was stationed with the unit's forward aid post during a period of
heavy shelling in the Argonne. The medical officer noted that the chaplain

became so panicked that he "rushed to the opposite corner of the cellar and squeezed himself as far down in the corner as he could and sat there with an expression of terror on his face." The exasperated surgeon yelled at him, "Goddam you Joe, come out of that corner and give us some help here." This outburst shook the chaplain out of his paralysis, and after retorting to the medico, "Don't take the name of thy God in vain," he returned to his duties helping with the wounded. When a YMCA chaplain notorious for harping on "the dangers of booze, women and gambling" visited some troops in a rest area, one of the soldiers greeted him with "Well! Well! Here comes Old Wine, Women, and Song again! . . . That sissified son of a gun is using up gasoline over here to warn us fellows against skirts, when he ought to be down in the trenches where he belongs or get to blazes out o' here."[34]

Not all of the AEF's chaplains were well suited to meet the doughboys' expectations, the demands of their position, or the physical and mental hardships of their duties. Many of the chaplains were much older than their flocks and found the exigencies of serving on or near the front to be too taxing. Although the 37th Division's senior chaplain found A. J. Funnell to be "a good man" who had "done faithful and efficient service," he recommended that Funnell be removed from the 147th Infantry and sent to minister at a base section because serving as a chaplain with an infantry unit was "beyond his strength" and his health was not up to the "strenuous work incidental to the active sectors" where his regiment operated. Some of the chaplains' duties were emotionally draining. After working at a mobile hospital, a padre noted, "A chaplain's work is not like that of any other soldier. He sees the soldier more in his hours of trouble and real need, often after the doctors have decided they can do nothing more for them." Even the well-respected Francis Duffy had his breaking point. After a week of frontline ministering during the brutal fighting along the Ourcq River in July and August 1918, Duffy's regimental commander believed that the padre was on the brink of a physical and mental breakdown. The unit took very heavy casualties, including Duffy's friend Joyce Kilmer, and Duffy had spent days encouraging the troops, comforting the wounded, and burying the dead. He later admitted that burying the battle's dead was "the saddest day in my life" for "I knew these men so well and loved them as if they were my younger brothers."[35]

The doughboys sometimes forgot that their chaplains were flawed humans governed by the emotions, passions, and temptations that came with war. While observing Chaplain John de Valles working at an aid post during an attack, an officer in the 26th Division recalled:

> I had never in all my life heard a priest swear, but I heard Father de Valles, after he had seen the mangled bodies during the attack say, "kill the bastards!" When I talked to him about it later in the day, he said he really didn't mean to swear, but before he knew it he had said it, and he knew that under the circumstances he would be forgiven.

Some of the chaplains themselves were lacking a bit in "Christian charity" and humility when it came to the failings of their peers. In February 1919, Chaplain Arthur Hicks wrote home,

> I must confess that I work harder both mentally and physically than most of the chaplains I have seen. One that I have in mind spends his nights in poker playing and was said by officers of his regiment to be the only officer on the ship who had a set of poker chips with him. Another spends his time loafing about with a little troop of actors who are giving a mighty poor show. He drinks with the officers and smokes cigarettes constantly. Then he is so often away on Sunday that he cannot care for his work.

Despite Hick's carping, in general the men who volunteered to serve as chaplains during the war worked diligently and selflessly to bring physical, mental, and spiritual comfort and guidance to the doughboys that they served.[36]

As the doughboys began returning home in 1919, Chaplain Gibson Mosher mused upon the state of the troops' spirituality. Mosher had served his time in a base hospital and had seen his share of suffering. He had also found comfort in his faith when his son Cyril was killed in action at Belleau Woods on June 18, 1918. Based upon his interactions with the doughboys he maintained,

> They are not coming back home eager to become identified with churches or to make a very loud profession of Religion. They are coming back with a clearer conception of the mission of the church, and of the practical application of Christianity to humanity. They are coming back with a broader vision, and a keener knowledge of world conditions: a deepening sense of the injustice of wrong, and the sovereignty of right . . . and with an exalted conception of the Home, the flag, and the Cross.

It is difficult to state with any certainty the degree to which Mosher's hopes were realized or if the doughboys returned from combat with a greater or diminished religious faith. For some, such as Roy Burkhart, the war encouraged the search for deeper religious understanding and meaning. While waiting to sail for home, he informed his cousin, "I am still studying for more truth which will establish a closer and keener relationship between my God and me. It is the source of my contentment, happiness and joy." Their wartime experiences certainly led other veterans to embrace the secular cynicism and hedonism of the Roaring Twenties. It is possible that most soldiers simply passed through the war without having their faith greatly altered by the experience at all. Unlike much else in the record of the doughboys' experiences, the record of their religious beliefs is too idiosyncratic and incomplete to make too many bold declarations on their spirituality.[37]

19

The Longest Hours
Preparing for Battle

In many ways combat in World War I was dependent on the ticking hands of a watch. Artillery, the war's signature weapon, and the relative lack of effective tactical communications meant that going into battle was governed by the ironclad and unbending rule of the clock. If the attacker had any hope of overcoming the innate power of the defense, artillery fires and the movement of a tidal wave mass of assaulters had to work in perfect harmony and synchronization. This demand for faultless timing had even changed men's fashion. Prior to the Great War men carried pocket watches tethered to them by chains. Wristwatches were affectations of women and a man daring to wear one was considered effeminate. Now, however, in the last minutes before going over the top, no officer wanted to fumble through his pockets to retrieve a watch or to have his hands encumbered by a timepiece. They kept vigil on their wristwatches as they toll the time remaining to the artillery barrage and the moment when they would have, by their commands and example, to get the doughboys that huddled around them to break from the safety of cover and face a cruel world.

Time, as the soldier waited for battle, was an oppressive thing. Some troops compulsively checked and rechecked their weapons; others tried to maintain half-hearted conversations though some of their peers remained silent and lost in their thoughts. Some men prayed. Many were wary of showing the external signs of the fear and nervousness that were natural to their situation. Even when surrounded by comrades, waiting for combat was a lonesome period for the doughboys; for war was waged as much in the mind of the individual as it was on the battlefield. With the soldiers standing alone with their worries and anticipations, the period immediately before battle made this time the longest hours of many a doughboy's life.

Although Pershing had intended that the AEF would receive a seasoning to war while serving in quiet sectors of the front, the uneven nature of this experience and the whirlwind events of 1918 meant that most American combat soldiers did not get their first real introduction into the realities of war until the summer and fall of that year. Preparing to go into combat presented soldiers with mental and physical strains that actually differed from those that came with the fighting itself. Green troops faced the fear and stress of dealing with the unknowns of battle. Conversely, veterans returning to battle had to cope with knowing what lay before them. While their perspectives were different, both the green soldier and the veteran had to undergo a psychological preparation for what was to come. Both also experienced the physical rituals that prepared them and their units to go over the top: units had to move into position; individuals had to take on or shed equipment and supplies; and the leaders and the led had to make sense of their orders and missions and understand their roles within the larger framework of the operational plan.

Preparing for battle started with the frenetic movement of troops. In theory, soldiers launching an attack were to be fully rested and supplied. They were to go over the top with full bellies and vigor to better prepare them to face the shocks of battle. In practice, this rarely happened. The Allied crises of the spring of 1918, the fluid nature of the Allied response to the strategic situation in the summer, and Foch's demand that Pershing launch a major attack in the Meuse Argonne only days after the conclusion of the St. Mihiel offensive meant that the doughboys were constantly on the move through most of 1918. As we will see in the next chapter, part of the nature of combat is exertion and exhaustion. Unfortunately, this process of exertion and exhaustion started well before the doughboys took their first steps in battle.

World War I was a war fought by the watch and the railroad timetable. The movement of hundreds of thousands of men to ensure that they were at the right place at the right time to accomplish their assigned combat mission required an intricate ballet of planning and synchronization. Getting the troops into their attack positions in time for zero hour, the codename generally used for the exact moment of the attack, required days or weeks of movement by train, truck, and foot marches. These movements followed the mind- and body-numbing practice that the later GI generation would term "hurry up and wait": bursts of frenetic activity punctuated by hours of nervous idleness while awaiting orders or delayed transportation.

Long-distance troop movements were generally done by rail. Train travel in France brought the doughboys into contact with the infamous "40–8" cars. Each of these small boxcars was designed to accomplish the rapid movement of the largest possible number of soldiers with the shortest amount of trains and time. The "40–8" gained its name from the ubiquitous "40 Hommes, 8 Cheveau" stenciled on their outsides, indicating that they were to carry either forty fully equipped men or eight horses. Some soldiers claimed that as many as sixty soldiers at times were packed into the tight eight and a half foot wide by twenty and a half foot long space. The cars were often dirty, especially if the eight *cheveau* had occupied them prior to the forty *hommes*. Adding to the discomfort was the fact that there were no accommodations in the cars other than rows of nails or pegs to suspend rifles and packs. At stated capacity there was just enough room for a man to sit if he bent his knees or squatted on his pack. Sleeping was another matter. A Marine recalled,

> With two men where there were hardly room for one, the inevitable result was a troubled night with bumped heads, cramped legs, and air that savored of Limburger, though no cheese was there. I waked several times in the night to find someone's foot or leg had pressed against my head. And in that crowded place, where else was there to put it! A pack might lose its moorings on the wall . . . and tumble heavily upon some unlucky fellow.

At first some found riding in the French cars to be novel and entertaining. A 77th Division soldier reported home that he "felt like a hobo" and that the car's "wheels must have been square, instead of round, the way the car did bounce and jump. We sure had a lot of fun over it." For most soldiers this novelty quickly wore out.[1]

Soldiers sometimes tried to escape the cramped and fetid confines of the "40–8" cars by hanging out the door or even climbing on the top of the wagons while the train was moving. To warn lollygagging soldiers of the dangers of rail travel in France, the army printed signs warning, "YOUR HEAD MAY BE HARD. But it is not as hard as bridges and tunnel arches. Only six inches clearance. Don't ride on tops or sides of cars." It added humorously, "The railway

Photo 19: Doughboys waiting to travel to the front in a "40–8" boxcar on a siding in France. These doughboys were somewhat fortunate in the fact that their cars contained straw to cushion these notoriously uncomfortable floors. Source: author's collection.

co. will hold you responsible for damages to bridges and tunnels and signal towers. They are not insured. KEEP YOUR BLOCK INSIDE." While playful, this warning was deadly serious. After Private Rippney failed to appear for roll call the morning after his company arrived by rail at Meru, France, on April 10, 1918, his company searched the area for him but came up empty. Nine days later, his body was discovered along the rail tracks some thirty miles from Meru. Rippney had been riding on top of the railcar when he fell or was knocked off.[2]

Although train travel was trying for the infantry, it was even more arduous for artillerymen and other soldiers whose units contained a large number of horses, wagons, and other heavy equipment. Loading an artillery regiment onto a train was a frustrating and laborious event. The unit's cannons, caissons, and wagons had to be loaded onto flatcars by hand and secured so that nothing projected from the sides of the cars or shifted during the move.

Anything sticking from the sides of the trains risked striking bridges, tunnels, passing trains, or any other human, animal, or material thing in their paths. The more difficult task was loading the unit's horses and mules, which often "required blindfolds, ropes, prayers, and curses to get them onboard" the narrow "40–8" boxcars. Once the eight horses were in the boxcar, one unfortunate driver had to ride in the narrow and dangerous space between the horses to see to their needs and to keep them calm. This often resulted in injuries to the drivers and occasionally in their deaths.[3]

The sheer number of trains on the French rails and the natural deterioration of the rail system under wartime conditions made train movements very slow. Although troop trains were to have been given priority of movement, doughboys frequently found themselves wiling away the hours on rail sidings in the middle of nowhere as other trains with supposedly greater precedence slowly passed by. For those heeding the call of nature while the train was moving, sometimes the cars had a bucket, or the soldier could attempt to relieve himself out of the side door. Having a bucket filled with human waste in an overcrowded and rocking boxcar presented its own problems. For anyone who has been worn out by the forced idleness of an airplane sitting on the tarmac for hours without air conditioning, access to a bathroom, or food service in the close confines of a modern airliner (keeping in mind that the passenger cabin in a Boeing 767 is almost twice as wide and a bit more comfortable than a "40–8" car) seated next to a guy who has not bathed or changed his clothes for three days, you have some limited appreciation of the doughboys' experience with French rail travel in 1918. After the war, some soldiers took their experience of riding the French rails as a badge of honor and celebrated their travels and tribulations by forming a club inside the American Legion known as the Society of Forty Men and Eight Horses. In tribute to the society's philanthropic efforts, in the 1940s France sent forty-nine of the World War I boxcars to the United States to be displayed in each of the existing states and the District of Columbia.

Upon detraining, some doughboys had the mixed blessing of boarding trucks for their trip to the front. The French and American trucks that hauled American troops generally had a row of benches on both sides and in the center of the bed. As with the "40–8" railcars, they were not designed for comfort. The inadequately maintained and war-torn roads of France made travel in even the trucks with the best suspension systems a bone-jarring experience. The 82nd Division infantryman Fred Takes noted that the roads and the seeping of the trucks' exhaust into the troop compartment left him and his comrades "white with dust" and with "sore eyes and headaches." But it was still better than walking, and each vehicle could transport 16–19 fully equipped infantrymen to the front.[4]

Ultimately, the autoroutes and the rails ended, and all troop movements to the front concluded with a foot march. Although the soldiers were conditioned to route marches during their training, these hikes often lacked the intensity and the relentless pace of those in the combat zone when units were racing against time to get into position for an actual attack. While the troops often shed equipment prior to going into battle, the marches to the battle zones were still conducted wearing full packs and weapons weighing fifty to seventy pounds. This weight, when combined with a lack of sleep, short rations, and an unremitting rate of march, wore the troops out well before the fighting began. Warren Jackson and his comrades pronounced their unit's march to the Soissons battle to be "the worst hike we had ever taken." "Mile upon mile we labored on," he recalled, "almost to exhaustion, yet very little rest." When the unit halted to stock up on ammunition, Jackson was dismayed to be burdened with additional bandoliers containing 240 rounds. When this was added to the existing weight of his pack and the one hundred rounds of ammunition that he already carried in his cartridge belt, the ponderous and ill-balanced load made his unit's march to the front even more miserable. The march was so arduous that many men fell by the wayside due to fatigue. Jackson's experience was far from unique. During one particularly grueling march, a doughboy recalled, "Man after man pitched drunkenly onto his hands and knees . . . and rolled like a log into the ditch at the side of the road, while the tortured column, looking neither to right or left, blindly and unceasingly reeled ahead, leaving the fallen to lie wherever they had chanced to drop."[5]

Captain Clarence Minick's diary entries for September 1918 offer insights into the hurried pace of the 361st Infantry's preparations and movements prior to entering battle in the Meuse Argonne. On September 3 and 4, the regiment marched to the railhead at Chillendry to begin its move to the front. Most of the regiment's marches were made at night to conceal the Americans' movements from the Germans. These night marches added to the doughboys' woes. In the darkness, as men punch-drunk from a lack of sleep tripped and stumbled their way forward, marchers often lost contact with those in front of them. This led to a frantic search for the lost column and a wearing "accordion" effect when the march alternated between slow prodding, sudden sprints, and troops smashing together as the column came to unexpected dead stops. The rest of September was a blur of activity for the regiment:

September 6–7—Rail move to De Mauges
September 10—Fourteen-kilometer march to billets outside of Vacon
September 11—March to reserve trenches at Void near St. Mihiel
September 13–14—Rail movement followed by fourteen-kilometer march to
    Marats la Petite
September 16–17—Sixteen-kilometer night march to Neubecourt
September 17–18—Night march to Bois de Couté
September 18—Night march to Bois de Hesse
September 19–20—Remain all day "under cover" in the woods

From September 21 to 23, the regiment's soldiers set to work repairing roads and buildings immediately behind the front. This hard labor sapped much of their reserves of strength and left them with little rest before the battle. On September 24 and 25, the unit completed the last phase of their movement to the front with a forced march to their jump-off point for the Meuse Argonne attack: the support trenches around Hermont. When Captain Minick's doughboys went over the top on September 26, nearly half of the sixty-eight days that they had served in France had been spent just moving from one place to another.[6]

Although the Great War was run by timetables, the inherent friction and uncertainty of warfare led the best laid plans of mice and men to go astray. When unforeseen events or staff missteps disrupted the steady flow of troops to their precombat positions, the doughboys suffered. During the opening of the Soissons drive, Captain Malcolm Helms encountered great difficulty in getting his unit organized and moving. He later wrote,

Upon unloading at night, we found ourselves in a dense wood. It was pitch dark and a steady drizzle was falling. We started down a road with orders to jump off for the attack on the other side of the woods at daybreak. The road was choked with every type of vehicle used in warfare, ration carts, ammunition, trains, and every kind of military supplies, and lines of infantry were weaving in and around them and crossing each other. I ordered each man in single file to grasp the clothing or equipment of the man in front of him to keep other units from cutting through and separating parts of our column. It seemed hours that we struggled through mud and water and when our artillery barrage opened up we had to run the last hundred yards or so to reach our position on time.

During the same battle, a 2nd Division Marine recalled that his unit nearly had to sprint to their jump-off locations in time for zero hour. "They growled at the pace the major set" during the quick march, and the doughboys' "bodies cried for rest, for food, and for water. Tempers flared and men lashed out viciously against the other, cursing those who stumbled, who cursed in quick retort." For these men, exhaustion had set in before the first shots of the battle were fired.[7]

Upon receiving orders for battle, units and individuals underwent a series of physical preparations for combat. According to AEF GHQ policies, an infantry company was to go into combat with a total of six hundred hand grenades, 240 VB rifle grenades, and 320 magazines and 10,368 rounds of ammunition for the Chauchat automatic rifles. As the grenadiers and automatic riflemen with these weapons could not possibly carry this weight themselves, the grenades and magazines were spread out among the members of their squad. When added to the wire cutters, flares, trench knives, weapons, rations, and other gear the men were supposed to carry into battle, the soldiers were in danger of becoming slow, waddling targets for the enemy. Veteran units and soldiers generally went through a prebattle ritual of shedding much of this encumbrance. During preparations for St. Mihiel, Marines in one company threw away most of their newly issued grenades because they did not want to carry the extra weight and because of their belief in the rumors that the nasty devices would easily explode if rattled or hit by rifle or shellfire. Prior to going into action at Soissons, a veteran 1st Infantry Division infantryman lightened his load to ease his mobility in combat. "As was my usual custom," he later recorded, "I had discarded my pack, retaining only my cartridge belt, gas mask and pistol, knowing that I could always find an entrenching tool carried by some unfortunate comrade who would have no further use for it." An artilleryman was amazed at how much equipment some infantrymen were willing to discard when going into battle. He observed that a passing group of doughboys "had flung all unnecessary equipment aside, preserving rifles, rations, and a single blanket apiece. They looked like wash-women, each with a blanket over his head, shawl style." The "live for today" attitude that these troops exhibited later led to hardships in the Argonne when the overly hasty discarders were left with little to protect themselves from the elements.[8]

For artillerymen and other heavy weapons crewmen, preparation for battle also entailed the moving and stockpiling of heavy and dangerous ammunition for the opening bombardments. A single round of fixed ammunition for the French 75mm gun weighed twenty to twenty-five pounds while those for the French 155mm gun tipped the scales at ninety-five pounds. Each of these projectiles had to be manhandled into caissons and ammunition bunkers to be ready for action. Furthermore, keeping the guns fed with shells during the preparatory barrage was a backbreaking effort. The same was also true for the crews of Stokes mortars. William Langer's unit, the 1st Gas Regiment, was responsible for setting up the Stokes mortars and Liven's projectors to fire gas, thermite, or smoke shells to aid the infantry in taking their objectives. Both these weapons and their ammunition were very heavy and difficult to maneuver in the close confines of a trench. In moving forward to set their weapons to support an attack by the 90th Division at St. Mihiel, Langer recalled that with their equipment and the four bombs that each man carried, he and his comrades were weighed down with 105 pounds of gear. After this endeavor, he mused, "Modern warfare is indeed at least 90 per cent hard labor."[9]

While units were undergoing these prebattle preparations, individual doughboys engaged in their own mental, physical, and spiritual rituals to ready themselves psychologically for battle. As they were involved in lethal pursuits where many of the variables of life and death were beyond their control, it is not surprising that some doughboys turned to superstitious prebattle rites and customs. Faith in a lucky talisman or ritualistic practices that had supposedly brought protection in previous combats was not uncommon in the ranks. Some, like Horace Baker, steeled themselves for combat by a compulsive reading of their Bible or by attending religious services. In what was one of the more common precombat rituals, Charles MacArthur noted, many soldiers wrote "solemn letters," which they "surreptitiously handed to the chaplain for transmission in case of sudden death." Ironically, these letters often brought more comfort to the writers than perhaps they ever would to the reader. In writing a final letter the soldiers had to accept their possible fate and mortality. It offered the doughboys a means for unburdening and resting their souls before facing death and brought some degree of peace of mind to the writer. Some of these last missives were nothing more than inscriptions left on diaries or books in the soldier's meager possessions. On the flyleaf of his diary, Private Clee B. Baugler simply wrote, "To my mother this little book is a diary of what I done in Eng. and France before I was Gone to My Resting Place above. May god be with you until you are gone home also . . . Good By to ALL." Fortunately for Baugler and his mother there was no need for this post mortem missive.[10]

The problem for green troops in facing battle was the unknown. There has always been a delta between what a soldier imagines war will be like and the realities that he actually encounters during the fighting itself. Large numbers of doughboys went to France with overly glorified views of war and were impatient to get into the fray. In 1917, one young officer was certain that the Americans would transform the situation on the Western Front into "the warfare of the old days, the warfare of our own West and South, when sabers flashed to the beats of galloping horses, and men went miles over the top instead of yards." Another envisioned that he would have "the chance to charge with thousands of other horsemen" in an attack that would send the Germans reeling back to Berlin. These romantic visions were sorely tested when the soldiers encountered the industrial scale of killing and destruction of the real war.[11]

For many doughboys, the hope for glory and the desire to participate in great events made waiting to sail for France, and the excitement that would follow, a nerve-wracking experience. A soldier in the 28th Division griped in December 1917, "We have just received the bad news this week, we are to be given another 16 weeks of training down here. This makes us mad, we thought that we would get to France soon, now I doubt we will ever get across." Likewise, after he was not selected for a levy of troops bound for service in France, one Marine wrote home from Galveston, Texas, "You should have seen and heard the noise from the lucky ones [selected to go] and the sorry looking faces on those who lost out . . . every single fellow just wild to brave the waters and battlefields of Europe." He tried to explain to his folks, "We know you at home wish we could stay here all the time and we are just as anxious to go in spite of all that are left behind." Many impatient doughboys shared Mike Scheck's concern "that the show will be over before we get there and I hardly think we will see any fighting."[12]

Photo 20: Having completed their training, this cannon crew from the 79th Division's 312th Field Artillery prepare to enter their first combat in the Meuse Argonne, September 1918. The faces of these young soldiers express a range of emotion from confidence to apprehension of what was to come. Source: author's collection.

The excitement for battle did not end when the troops reached France. For some, the anticipation—the desire for something to happen—could build up to a palpable degree of nervous energy. As Private James Miller grumbled to his mother in early March 1918, "It's been so quiet and unwarlike over here that lots of the boys are doubting the existence of the war and are [hoping] for a chance to rush up front." He concluded, "The greatest wish of a soldier seems to be where he ain't." Some soldiers found their first minor brushes with war to be exciting, especially when viewed from a distance. In a letter home in April 1918, soon after arriving in France, Charles Minder fairly gushed,

> We can hear the bombarding going on all the time. Tonight we can see the flashes of artillery very plainly. It is all very interesting. I don't know where to start. It was just like I read about, but when I read the war stories a couple of years ago, I never thought that some day I would be in it. And here I am now, a soldier, and I guess there will be just as much adventure ahead of me as the other soldiers went thru who have gone ahead.

His ardor was not shaken a few days later when his unit passed through a bomb-damaged French town that reminded him of photos of the destruction caused by the San Francisco earthquake. He still reported, "This is all too thrilling for words, I guess before long we will be in the more exciting spots also." Even as they waited as the division reserve for the Argonne battle, a sergeant in the 82nd Division claimed that his soldiers believed that if they "did not get into it soon, it would be all over and we would be cheated out of our chance to see the 'real thing.'" As would be the case with many of their fellow doughboys, Miller's and Minder's initial enthusiasm faded the closer they moved to the actual fighting and the more they witnessed the cost of war.[13]

Having been brought up to see war as the ultimate test of manhood, the greatest source of anxiety for many doughboys was whether they had the courage to face down their fears and meet the challenges of combat. Scores of soldiers had doubtlessly read Stephen Crane's *The Red Badge of Courage* and perhaps identified with its main character, Henry Fleming, and his efforts to prove himself in battle. In fact, the book went through four publishing runs in 1917 alone. One pensive officer confided to his commander shortly after the war the thoughts he had just before going into battle. He admitted, "It had always been a matter of conjecture to me for long, long years just how one would feel when under fire in the face of the enemy, and I remember that during the next two or three hours, I again turned that question over and over in my mind and wondered how I would feel the next morning." The fear of showing fear or failing to live up to the expectations of others, he confessed, "furnished an interesting laboratory experiment, so to speak, in psychology in the way of introspection." Like many green troops, the young officer found that the waiting and anticipation of action was the worst part of his experience though he had no regrets about going into combat.[14]

For novice soldiers it was often the sight of the devastation just behind the front that eroded their romantic visions of war and offered a sobering prelude to what they were about to face. In describing the scenes of desolation he witnessed, the California native C. E. Rebendale noted, "The ground in the villages fields and forest is nothing but craters, all the cities in range of the German guns are leveled like San Francisco was [in 1906], grate [*sic*] trees are twisted to pulp." The destruction in the Meuse Argonne sector left a lasting and depressing impression for green and veteran doughboys alike. One long-serving soldier found the region to be "dreary and desolate." He observed,

"This is the worst I have seen during all my time over here. This has been a battlefield for a very long time and everything in every direction is wholly demolished." As his company marched across the old Verdun battlefield en route to its assault positions in the Argonne, one of its officers described the area as "a mass of ashes, torn trenches, barbed wire piled high from shell fire." Even more disconcerting was the mass of "bones on the ground from old graves which had been disturbed by fire." Passing through the desolation, one of the company's sergeants was heard to mutter, "Sherman didn't say half of it," when the Civil War general stated, "War is hell." When faced with such massive ruin and an appreciation of the artillery fire that had caused it, a doughboy did not have to have much of an imagination to conjure up what was in store for him.[15]

If a soldier's imagination was still lacking, other sights offered further food for thought as they closed in on the front. If the soldiers had not been well bloodied while serving in the Allied trenches, their move to an active battle area brought the sudden realization that at its core, war was essentially about death, dying, and injury. An artilleryman was shaken by what he encountered while moving to the fighting at night:

> The yellow light cast distorted shadows down the slopes, and over the huddled heaps here and there in the wheat stubble. I paid no attention to them till I noticed the horses swerving nervously away from them. German and American dead were flung about thickly. The sickly light added an unnatural note of horror to the twisted masses of bodies, giving some of them a semblance of life and almost imperceptible motion, while the eyes and teeth of the dead faces glittered coldly in the moonlight.

A soldier in the 35th Division admitted to his wife that he was rattled at seeing "Amer., French and Hun graves, in many places there were groups of them, many in number" as he marched to the Meuse Argonne front. The reality of war was brought home to another infantryman when he tripped over something in the dark. "I reached down and picked up a bleached thigh-bone," he mused in his journal, and confessed, "That didn't add to the gayety of the situation."[16]

The sight of all this death and devastation certainly preyed on the mind of many a doughboy. Horace Baker had previously expressed that he had no qualms about seeing his first action. He even admitted, "I had a curious war-horse feeling that I wanted to get into the fray." His attitudes changed somewhat as his unit marched through the devastation behind the front lines. "For the life of me," he noted, "I could not imagine how any could escape that awful place. And then there was a realization that in a short time I too would be where blood ran freest." When encountering the unavoidable presence of the dead, for soldiers like Baker, war was no longer a source of academic speculation or romantic notions. When looking at the dead, it took little imagination for the doughboys to envisage themselves as the lifeless mass that lay before them.[17]

If these sights were not enough to disquiet those going into battle, the words and actions of those around them often added to the doughboys' apprehensions. Numerous veterans of the 2nd and 3rd Divisions were rattled by seeing veteran French troops hastily retreating and offering pessimistic assessments of the situation at the front as the Americans moved into battle around Château Thierry. A Marine preparing to go into action at Belleau Wood was uneasy after hearing a rumor that a neighboring company had just returned from action with only eight unwounded men on its rolls. Soldiers from the 82nd Division marching into action in the Argonne met with similarly gloomy assessments. When Thurmond Baccus crossed paths with a disheveled soldier from the 28th Division, he asked, "Does it treat you that rough up there, Buddy?" The Iron Division doughboy's laconic reply was "You will look a lot worse than I do when you get relieved." The men of the 325th Infantry's machine gun company encountered similarly cheerless greetings as they moved into position in the Argonne. A soldier from the unit they were relieving called to them, "You are going in looking like a division; will come out looking like a platoon," while another shouted to the company bugler, "You won't need that horn up there. You'll only blow one call and that will be taps."[18]

Watching the steady stream of wounded coming back from the front also undermined the soldiers' enthusiasm for war. As with viewing the dead, it did not take much for doughboys to see their future in the maimed men who passed by them. The grievous and mutilating wounds caused by the war's artillery shells and high-velocity bullets led some to contemplate what end they would prefer if they were injured in the upcoming battle. After witnessing British wounded being evacuated from the front, a previously eager 77th Division soldier's thoughts grew morbid. He informed his mother,

It's an awful sight and gets on my nerves. I can't stand seeing anybody suffering. I think instantaneous death is better than this long drawn out suffering you endure when you get wounded. I don't fear death as much as I fear suffering. These sights make me feel like a dumb animal ready for slaughter . . . I only hope and pray that if I have to go in this war, that it will be instantaneous, I would like to be sniffed out as quickly as you would snuff out a candle.

After one of his comrades had his arm blown off by shellfire as his unit awaited action, another soldier confessed, "After that I would pray if I was to get hit—Please God kill me immediately." In the same vein, Lieutenant Herman Daccus mused, "I felt that I would rather be killed outright than lose arms or legs or suffer brain damage."[19]

The emotions and attitudes of veteran soldiers returning to battle were somewhat different from those of green troops. Their fears and anticipations were shaped by the tangible realities of what they already knew about combat. Not all veterans were created equally and their attitudes upon reentering battle depended much on their previous combat experiences. Some veterans marched into a new battle with the confidence that came with previously surviving and succeeding in combat and the faith that they now possessed the skills to survive and prosper on another battlefield. Others, particularly those who had seen the hard and costly fighting at Cantigny, Château Thierry, and Soissons, tended to be more circumspect than those whose experiences were limited to the more tame actions at St. Mihiel. In fact, some of the soldiers who received their first blooding at St. Mihiel were later shocked by what followed in the Meuse Argonne. An officer in the 5th Division recalled the shattering of illusions and the confidence of the unit's supposed veterans upon attacking Cunel on October 11, 1918. He recalled, "The men still remembered the victorious rush at St. Mihiel and dashed forward impetuously. But it was a different enemy here, one who was sticking till the last and fighting for every foot of ground."[20]

Despite having, in the words of their Civil War ancestors, "seen the elephant," the veterans were not immune from speculating about what lay ahead for them as they returned to battle. Warren Jackson, a veteran of Belleau Wood and the Aisne-Marne fighting, admitted, "Before we went over at St. Mihiel I formed vivid pictures of the kind of things that we would experience in making the attack." Jackson felt more apprehensive as he prepared for that battle than he had been in his previous actions. The troops had heard of the strength of the German defenses and knew of the previous bloody French failures to reduce the salient. He later confessed, "We expected this to be the hottest thing we had gotten into. Numerous jesting remarks were made about So-and-So not coming back, with an accompanying smile that was somewhat forced." Just before the battle he sent twenty dollars home to his mother because "Somehow, I had a feeling that if I did not send the money home, within a few days some stranger would take it from my corpse."[21]

Despite their prebattle jitters, few doughboys seemed to have doubted the righteousness of their cause or the necessity of sacrifice to achieve victory. In a letter to his mother from June 1918, for example, Lieutenant John Castles wrote, "War is not all bad & some great results are going to come from this one to us as a nation even tho' we pay for it dearly." But this knowledge was still cold comfort to the veteran doughboys moving into a new battle. Going into the Argonne, one battle-hardened Marine became quite morose. He recalled that before launching the attack,

> It was time for sober thinking. A seldom-spoken thought lay in the mind of every man, as always in such times as this. Is this my last time in? You dare not dwell too long on thoughts about yourself, nor dare to think of home . . . Your thoughts go out to the fellows around you, marching close at hand, and you wonder which of them, these pals and friends of yours, will die.

Just as with the green soldier, for the veteran these hours were a time of introspection and questioning. The only difference was that the veteran had an inkling of what was coming and what it might mean for themselves and their comrades.[22]

With all the preparations complete, and while all the individuals' emotions and thoughts of the future were still coursing through their minds and bodies, in the final countdown to zero hour the tensions grew to a high pitch. The sights, in these last hours and minutes could be awe-inspiring. The artilleryman June Smith described the opening of the Argonne campaign to his mother: "The big guns opened up and all the others followed they kept this up for several hours and you never heard such a roar in your life. There were about 500 big guns in a space about a mile. You could sit and read a paper most any where by the light of the gun flashes." At such times, the infantrymen found it much harder to maintain such a clinical detachment about a battle's opening moments. In the time just before Zero Hour at Belleau Woods on June 6, 1918, Elton Mackin observed,

> Hushed commands brought the chilled, sleepy men to their feet . . . There were last-minute instructions and bits of advice flung here and there. Careless of cover, the men in the first wave stood in the wheat, adjusting belts and hitching combat packs to easier positions . . . There were half-heard murmurs of conversation among the men, and, at times, a spurt of nervous laughter, quickly stilled.

He recalled that when zero hour arrived, there were "No bugles. No wild yells," just the shrill notes of his sergeants whistle, and then "the spell was broken." As his unit stepped off, it occurred to him, "Suddenly we didn't want to die," but now there was no going back. Discipline, the fear of punishment, patriotism, comradeship, the burden of expected behavior, and a host of other factors drove Mackin and the war's other doughboys over the top and into battle.[23]

20

The Big Show
The Doughboy in Combat

Lieutenant Wendell Westover was transfixed by the small drama he observed during the 2nd Division's attack on Blanc Mount Ridge in early October 1918. To his front an infantry platoon was maneuvering to destroy a German machine gun that was holding up the American advance. As he looked on, a few of the platoon's soldiers on one flank stood up and rushed forward a few yards, drawing the fire of the German gun. With the machine gun crew's attention drawn to that flank, "those on the other end would make a quick advance." Westover admitted that while their tactic "was no parade ground demonstration," the doughboy's "flanks were creeping outward and the line developing into an arc . . . would eventually envelop the gun position." He quickly added, however, "that is if a sufficient number of survivors was left to reach it." As the platoon's assault continued,

> Already five men lay still on the ground over which they had come. The right squad sprang up and forward. One, two, four men dropped; staggering, slumping forward to the ground. The rest threw themselves into shellholes and paused. They were close now, but where there had been thirty men a few moments before, only nine were still able to move. Of these, two more fell in the final assault.

When the platoon's survivors killed or captured the German crew, "there was a pause at the gun," Westover observed, and the doughboys "spread out and continued to advance—carrying on the attack under a newly appointed leader." And there, in a microcosm, was the doughboys' experience in combat. Their tactics, often lacking in refinement and skillful execution, resulted in heavy casualties, but, despite this ham-handed approach, the doughboys still managed to overcome the Germans they encountered.[1]

In one of the most famous passages from *Leviathan*, Thomas Hobbes warns the readers of a dystopian society where there is "continual fear and danger of violent death: and the life of man, solitary, poor, nasty, brutish and short." To a very great extent, what Hobbes described was the reality lived by the combat doughboys during the Great War. Paired down to its essential core, combat is about killing and dying and the confusion, exertion, and privation that are inseparable from those lethal acts. It is also about getting relatively rational people to do and endure seemingly irrational things. Combat is an environment where the senses are bombarded by a host of sights, sounds, and smells. The soldier's brain is confronted with perceptions from these inputs that unleash emotions and responses that range from fearful paralysis, to brave selfless sacrifice, to murderous rage and bloodlust. Even the most thorough and realistic training falls short in preparing troops for these realities. Unfortunately, the doughboys entering combat in 1918 were far from thoroughly and realistically trained. Furthermore, they faced an experienced enemy who skillfully sought to make the doughboy's life in battle "short," or at least one of "continual fear and danger of violent death."

The average doughboy's life in combat was governed by the intersection of four things: the fellow soldiers of his unit, the environment, the Germans, and the vital Maslovian issues of food, clothing, sleep, and shelter. The infantryman's world was first bound by the units in which he served. Most important to him were the seven or eight men in his squad. His circle of support and obligation then expanded to include the fifty-nine men in his platoon and the 261 men in his company. Although the soldier might come into contact with other officers and men from the battalion, the regiment, or outside organizations, his life, especially in combat, was lived at the company level and below. In these small units the doughboys developed the ties that provided the physical and mental support that they needed to cope with the stresses of combat. The degree of comradeship and cohesion, and the skills and abilities of the NCOs and officers within these small units, determined the degree to which the individual soldier's daily existence was "solitary, poor, nasty, brutish and short." Although I will expand on this issue in both this chapter and in chapter 22, it must be kept in mind that even the most cohesive and best-trained companies still faced the ugly attritional realties that Westover described so well.

The limitations and capabilities of the war's weapons and the sheer density of troops on the Western Front meant that the tactical advantage generally lay with the defender. Despite the time they spent in the trenches, fighting off German counterattacks, or in the AEF's limited defensive battles (such as those fought around Château Thierry), most of the doughboys' actual time in combat was spent as the attacker. Unfortunately for the attacking Americans, their German foes had learned much about defensive warfare since 1914. Despite their losses in the Ludendorff offensives, the Germans remained masters at wringing the last drop of advantage out of the terrain they defended and the weapons they possessed. This was made clear to the commander of the 320th Infantry during his early attacks in the Argonne. He found that the German machine guns that flayed his troops "could be seen only at rare intervals" during the American assault. To make matters worse, "The enemy intrenchments afforded every advantage in position, concealment and for enfilade fire. Time and again rushes were made from the front and flank against the nests only to be met by a curtain of lead that was absolutely impassable . . . Here lives were needlessly lost in trying to rush through this curtain of lead."

During his unit's first real taste of combat in the opening hours of the Meuse Argonne offensive, the 79th Division's Major Charles DuPuy had a similar epiphany. He found that trying to attack the German positions from the flanks only led the attackers into the path of another well-concealed enemy machine gun. In the end, he admitted, "it was necessary a great many times to simply charge a gun from the front and both flanks, and take it regardless of our losses, which, per gun captured, averaged ten to twenty men." After a few such encounters with the wily Hun, DuPuy concluded, "The tactics which we had learned, proved to be of little value."[2]

Although the American tactics may have been "of little value," even with the best doctrine and preparation, the doughboys still would have faced serious difficulties in overcoming the German defenses. The Germans generally defended terrain of their own choosing and possessed ample time to site and camouflage their earthworks and position their machine guns to cover the most likely routes that the Americans would take. When the situation allowed, the Germans further took the time to position their cannons, register their artillery targets, and dig in their telephone lines to give the defenders the most responsive and accurate artillery fires possible. Even under the best of circumstances the deck was stacked against the attackers. As the 3rd Division commander, Major General Beaumont Buck, mused in his diary on October 14, 1918, "We have to take the ground from him foot by foot, and the taking is very costly as he has machine guns everywhere most skillfully installed."[3]

The doughboys' attacks generally followed a rather simple formula. At a certain hour the Allied artillery would fire a barrage to kill as many of the German defenders as possible, or at least create a volume of shells that would keep the enemy from firing as the infantry moved forward. If time and resources were available, the doughboys then launched the attack following closely behind a creeping barrage intended to keep the Germans' heads down right up to the moment that the Americans were upon them. The American infantry would maneuver in their assigned sectors to predetermined objectives, taking ground and killing and capturing the Germans that they encountered on the way. While simple in concept, this formula proved devilishly difficult to pull off in practice.

The infantry put much hope in the artillery's ability to kill or suppress the defenders. Unfortunately, the war's primitive tactical communications systems led to complex and inflexible artillery plans. This meant that the infantry had little way to get support from their artillery once an attack began. If, as so often happened, the artillery barrage did not go off as planned or the infantry failed to keep up with the creeping barrage, the doughboys faced the dreaded prospect of attacking the entrenched German positions with only the light weapons they carried or with the support of the limited number of machine guns, 37mm cannons, and mortars owned by their regiments. The failure of an expected artillery barrage to materialize seldom stopped an American attack from going forward.

Once the doughboys reached their objectives or faced so much resistance that they could make no further headway, they dug in to hold what they had gained and to protect themselves against the inevitable German artillery and infantry counterattacks. The soldier's hasty fortifications were quite primitive and mainly consisted of digging individual one- to three-man foxholes. Digging in under fire was a particularly harrowing experience. Doughboys scrambled to find the best natural cover and pile up enough dirt to protect them from enemy bullets and shells. During this process, life and limb depended on the soldiers accomplishing the task quickly while exposing their bodies as little as possible as they dug. One soldier was amazed to see that when a soldier was caught in the open he would "literally lay down behind his helmet" and "extend the body in a straight line, so as to keep the whole person as much as possible within the narrow space of protection provided by the helmet," while they attempted to dig in. Although the helmet offered little real protection, he still claimed, "Our iron headgear was a psychological as well as a utilitarian advantage." Lieutenant A. L. Slattery further noted, "It is wonderful how quickly a man can with any kind of implement dig a hole for his head and shoulders" when encouragement is provided by enemy fire. In fact during a particularly harrowing barrage of German machine gun and shellfire, a desperate doughboy in his company was seen trying to "dig in with a pen knife." This soldier was not the only one to regret throwing away his shovel. After discarding his entrenching tool prior to going over the top, Earle Poorbaugh was left with only the lid of his mess kit for digging in. When faced with heavy enemy fire, he recalled, "I was really making the dirt fly with this improvised shovel."[4]

The ubiquitous fox and shell holes became the sole form of shelter for most infantrymen in battle. When properly dug, they provided protection from enemy small arms and some shellfire. Their only protection from the elements was provided by the shelter halves, blankets, or raincoats the soldiers could erect over the holes. If, as was so often the case, those items had been thrown away by the troops, life in these holes could become quite uncomfortable. This was particularly true in the Meuse Argonne when the weather in October and November turned cold and rainy.

As Carl von Clausewitz perceptively observed, war has always been the realm of chance, probability, friction, and confusion. Even with the best planning and preparations, few American attacks played out as the commanders envisioned. When the barrage failed to materialize, when the weather prevented supplies from moving up, when the enemy was not where they were supposed to be, and when the troops were dead tired, the junior officers and soldiers had no other option but to improvise on the fly. Unfortunately, this "making do" often came at a price. During the Meuse Argonne fighting, the troops of the 3rd Battalion, 26th Infantry, had to lie under heavy German artillery fire for forty-five minutes while waiting for their supporting barrage to begin. Their objective was a series of German positions located on high ground that could only be reached by crossing an open valley without much cover. The Americans relied on the barrage to keep the enemy's head down long enough for them to scramble across the deadly ground. The artillery was to land on the enemy positions for fifteen minutes and then creep forward at a rate of one hundred yards every three minutes. Unfortunately, the American barrage "was scattered" and failed to suppress the Germans. As soon as the doughboys moved forward, they were hit by German fire from their front and flanks. To the American battalion commander, "It became clear that there was but one thing to do and that was to rush across the valley and close with the enemy on the opposite side." The doughboys ran across as fast as they could and gained the high ground, killing German artillery and machine gun crews as they went. But during the thirty-five-minute attack, the battalion lost a third of its strength with nine officers and 150 soldiers killed.[5]

The rate of casualties in such attacks was truly staggering. During its capture and defense of Cantigny in May 1918, the 28th Infantry lost fifteen officers and 130 soldiers killed and thirty officers and 690 soldiers wounded. Altogether, the regiment lost 60 percent of its company officers and 32 percent of its enlisted men in five days of fighting. These losses were on top of the average loss of fifty men per day that the 2nd Brigade, 1st Division, suffered in the month prior to the Cantigny assault. During the Asine-Marne offensive, the brigade commander estimated that in eight days of fighting, his unit's total casualties were 126 officers and twenty-one hundred soldiers. Roughly 20 percent of these casualties died as a result of the action. On October 8, 1918, alone, an attack by the 36th Division's 71st Infantry Brigade resulted in the loss of 33 percent of its officers and 23 percent of its enlisted men. Fred Takes's company went into the Meuse Argonne campaign with 250 men. After nine days of continuous combat, the company had been reduced to three five-man squads. Another soldier in Takes's regiment called these days of fighting, "the worst piece of wholesale murder I saw in the whole war." Given the unalterable attritional nature of warfare and the Americans' sketchy and incomplete training, this level of loss was the rule rather than the exception in the AEF's combat operations.[6]

From the soldier's perspective, such attacks were quite confusing, ugly, and personal. To the soldiers, each of the losses enumerated earlier represented the loss of a buddy or important leader in their lives. Elton Mackin's unit suffered its first casualty soon after beginning the advance on Belleau Woods. This loss stunned some of the attacking Marines and they stood wondering what to do. The halted party was hustled forward by their first sergeant's harsh word, "C'mon, goddamnit! He ain't the last man who's gonna be hit today." At that moment the realities became crystal clear to Mackin and his comrades. All combat doughboys faced the stark realization that the war that they imagined and trained for seldom matched the actualities they encountered. After an attack near Vaux on July 21, 1918, Private Willard Thompson recorded in his diary:

> By misunderstood orders [we] went Over the Top in the face of a machine gun nest. We got 100 ft and though men were falling fast we kept on until ordered to cover. Another runner and I formed a left flank out post where we fired 100 shots a piece at the machine gunners that is whenever they gave us a shower. We ran out of ammunition and went back for more, believe me with our packs on it was some job, but my pack saved my life, 3 bullets found their way there instead of my back.

After crossing an open roadway near Exermont under intense fire on October 11, 1918, an 82nd Division infantryman found himself at the base of a low hill defended by a strong party of Germans. He recalled, "I crawled about 100 yards when a German machine gunner opened fire on me. I kept on crawling but the faster I crawled the more bullets were hitting around me. I stopped and lay very still like [I was] dead." The tactic seemed to work, "For a few moments the bullets still came very heavy throwing dirt on me as they struck the ground. Finally he quit. I jumped up and crossed the road on the other side which was more protected by a bank." After another failed attempt to storm the enemy positions in which his officer and several of his comrades were killed and more were wounded, his unit pulled back and dug in for the night.[7]

Duncan Kemerer had a similar experience when his unit ran into unexpected enemy resistance while probing German defenses in the Theacourt sector in November 1918. Crossing an open valley, his unit was hit unexpectedly by German machine gun, rifle, and mortar fire. Worse still, the Germans expertly laid an artillery barrage behind the startled Americans to keep the doughboys in the killing zone by preventing their retreat. The American formation broke up as the troops scrambled to find any possible cover. After a mad dash, Kemerer ended up sheltering with another soldier behind a railroad embankment. With the enemy's fire coming in hot and heavy, the two doughboys' first thoughts were to rid themselves of the numerous grenades they were carrying as they were "afraid of a bullet hitting them and setting them off." Kemerer remembered being startled after "a bullet hit my helmet a glancing blow, leaving a crease in it." In the face of such heavy resistance, Kemerer's commander ordered the unit to withdraw. Given the confusion and the state of the troops at the time, the unit quickly lost its cohesion and discipline. The retreat, he noted, "came to resemble a rout as everybody started to run to get away from the rifle and machine gun fire and to get through the shell fire that was to impede our retreat to the rear." It was clear to these Americans that this was not the war portrayed in their manuals or the one envisioned in their training.[8]

As Kemerer could attest, the World War I battlefield was a fearsome place. Its sights, sounds, and smells confronted the doughboys with a host of overpowering sensations. More than anything else, these sensory inputs imprinted in the doughboys' minds their understanding of life in combat. It was the noise of battle that left the most lasting impression on one artilleryman:

> The deep muffled booming of the howitzers sounded like thunder coming from a Cyclops' cave. Waves of sound seemed as material waves of water. We were engulfed in them. They surged, and washed, and echoed from crest to crest in volcanic ones. The great forged-steel bolts passed with a rushing noise like a huge wind. Trees along the slopes of our hill bent heavily, with their branches waving and shaking, and their heads bowing as if a tornado were blowing above them, and little ripples ran along the grass tops as volley after volley raged past.

For the 5th Marine's Burt Richardson, two noises stuck with him in combat. One was that made by the German machine guns. "Their Maxims have a different sound than our machine guns; it is a steely, metallic note like hitting an anvil with a hammer," he recalled. "When a number of them open up together, there is something fiendish and cruel and pitiless about the sound." The other sound was even harder to forget. After a failed attack in June 1918, the wounded left untended between the lines cried out in "weak plaintive voices, calling for help, begging for water; and some bitter from vain pleading, cursing: 'Oh God, I'm dying! If you are white men, why don't you come help me? I'm wounded, I tell you! . . . Help me you yellow devils.'"[9]

For other doughboys it was the smell of battle that long disturbed their memories. After treating a wounded comrade, one soldier was unable to escape the feel and odor of his act of mercy. He later wrote, "My hands were sticky with blood and my nose was full of the smell of it." Some men could not shake the stench of death that permeated the battlefield. The smell of rotting and burned human flesh has a particular lingering quality to it. It seems to almost cling to the clothing and skin of the living. It was an odor that presented the soldiers with an unavoidable reminder of what the future might hold for them. In some cases one horror of the battlefield helped to cancel out the others. As one 82nd Division soldier recalled, "The smell of gas killed all other odors. I had rather smell gas than the odor of dead men and horses."[10]

For most doughboys, it was what they saw in battle that most stuck with them. The sight of horribly mutilated dead and wounded men and the destruction caused by the war peppered the writings of the American soldiers. Two months after the end of the war, Sergeant Major Paul Landis's lingering memory of combat came from what he saw during the 3rd Division's defense at Château Thierry:

> There was a broad meadow on the southern bank of the Marne sowed with wheat which the Germans had to cross in their attack on the night of 14–15th [July 1918]. We just fairly rained shells and machine gun bullets over this field and after the battle it resembled nothing more or less than wheatfields at home during harvest time, but instead of sheaves of wheat, the field contained hundreds of Germans and some Americans who fell in the battle.

The sights and other experiences of battle so startled some doughboys that they bucked the censors to warn those at home about what they had seen. In March 1918, Walter Shaw informed his mother, "I read some papers from the States, some of the junk they have in them is shure a joke. No one ever knows how it is until he gets here and see it all." An engineer tried to caution his family, "If Addie thinks of trying this thing [military service] he'd better think well. There is no romance or heroics over here that I can find. It's downright dirty work." Clarence Hackett likewise said of a friend still in the States, "I hope he never has to come to France *for this war sure is hell.*" Unfortunately, Hackett was closer to the mark than he knew. He died of a gunshot wound to his right hip on July 27, 1918.[11]

One aspect of the "downright dirty work" that the combat doughboys had to face was the killing. Through religious, legal, and cultural norms, the killing of a fellow human has been rightly stigmatized in society. War, however, required the doughboys to go against this deeply ingrained stricture to actively bring on the demise of their enemy counterparts. Wartime propaganda and training were meant to demonize the Germans and reduce the barriers that the civilians turned soldiers had in killing them. Even though he had little contact with the enemy, Frank Town had little compunction about proclaiming to his sister, "Being over here for a while makes one care less about killing a Hun." Infantryman Fay Neff admitted to his sister while training in the United States that he was "getting hardened to this life" and the idea of "one man killing another," and that as he was sailing for France he hoped to "get one Hun before he gets me." His training and mental preparation for killing must have paid off, for he later bragged,

> Can you picture me in a trench and [a] Hun in another trench only about 3000 ft away from us. Those were the Happy days just as soon as they try and take a peep one of the Boys would take [a] shot at him and put em out of the world. Gee sis we had no heart [and] kill them left and right. That's one thing we taught never let a wounded Hun behind us put em out of misery because they were so tricky.

He felt no guilt at his work and noted that when the Germans launched an attack, "how we did mow them down." Not all doughboys took to slaying as readily as did Neff. After his machine gun crew killed a number of Germans, Charles Minder lamented, "Oh, I pray God that I will be delivered from this some way. Somehow I don't want to carry on. I would much rather get hit myself than ever have to shoot another man again."[12]

Chaplain Lee Levinger claimed that the doughboys did not succumb to the brutalization that many feared naturally came with combat. To him, Neff would have been an anomaly and Minder more the rule. The chaplain, however, seemed to have been overly optimistic in his assessments. Although few soldiers became remorseless killers, many, if not most, grew desensitized to killing or at least came to view it as a hard reality of life. Notwithstanding Levinger's hopeful beliefs, the doughboys followed the inflexible logic of combat that has forever guided and dogged the steps of soldiers through the centuries—kill or be killed and the less thinking about it the better. This was certainly the case with Clarence Mahan and Knud Olsen. During Olsen's first encounter with the enemy, he discovered three Germans in the open. As he was getting ready to fire on them, he admitted, "I was hesitating because I didn't really know if I wanted to kill someone." In that moment, however, a German bullet whistled over his head and altered his resolve. "Getting shot at by them," he admitted, "changed my whole feelings about being able to kill someone," and he fired on the party. Mahan, a veteran of the 1st Division, acknowledged,

> We were scared but we had to develop a numbness and unfeeling attitude toward it all. Otherwise we would have lost our minds. I have not dealt on the heart of it all, but war does something to a person. To see blood and carnage everywhere as men horses and mules are blown to bits, developed in us a certain savagery and hate that pushed us on toward a terrible enemy with a willingness to see him destroyed.

This is not to say that killing did not leave a mark on the soldiers. Long after the war another 1st Division combat veteran, Sergeant Donald Kyler, stated flatly, "Military life (particularly combat experiences) had molded and stiffened my character. But it had lessened my sensitivity to the value of human life. That rigidity was detrimental to my career in industry and in my personal life."[13]

Of course not all soldiers had qualms about killing or even put it down to being an unfortunate necessity of war. One of the dirty little secrets of war is that sometimes combat and the act of killing are a pleasurable experience for the soldier. Those in modern Western societies have been conditioned to view war as a soul-crushing evil and soldiers as victims and unwilling participants of unspeakable, humanity-stripping horrors. Yet, there has always been something in war that is alluring to humans, something that taps into a primal nature that the modern society never wants to admit. This desire to hunt and kill one's enemies has been termed bloodlust or, more poetically, "combat euphoria." It is clear from the record that despite the popular view that the soldiers of the Great War were mere sufferers and "closet pacifists," some of the soldiers enjoyed their time in battle. At the conclusion of the Oise-Aisne offensive, one doughboy reported, "Life has no thrill more maddening or intoxicating than that of a great winning battle. It is worth a lifetime, to have the feeling for a day. It runs the whole scale of emotion. It beggars description." He admitted that combat brought "incessant excitement and endless thrills, and there was something new every day." Sometimes the emotions and excitement of fighting unleashed a torrent of bloodlust. During a successful assault on the German trenches at Blanc Mont, one doughboy became a remorseless killer. "Carried on a crest of hysteria, fear, and a choking urge of exaltation," he came upon two Germans fleeing from his advance. In that moment, said one observer, "The beast was loosed. The thin veneer of civilization was scratched and broken, the caveman in him revealed. It was a race—short, swift and deadly—between two who ran in fear, and one who followed after in fearing passion." Sensing that they were losing the race, the Germans turned and tried to surrender. Their pursuer, however, was too far gone to grant quarter and quickly dispatched both men. Afterward the victorious doughboy stood grinning over his prey as if waiting for someone to praise him for his work. Private Fay Neff even bragged to his sister on October 30, 1918, "Well sis i had the pleasure of getting a few Huns when we were on our last front." Knud Olsen, who at first was hesitant to fire on the enemy, confessed that later he "enjoyed shooting at them." None of these men seemed to have been psychopaths or sociopaths; they were, however, proud of their skills and accomplishments against the enemy and did not appear to have any guilt in their killings.[14]

It is impossible to uncover how many doughboys experienced "combat euphoria" or took pride or pleasure in the slaying of their enemy. Few dough-boys were as open about discussing killing as Neff and Olsen. Perhaps the mores of society discouraged doughboys from discussing these events in their letters and memoirs. However, an untold number of doughboys cer-tainly experienced the feeling of the "beast being loosed" and the "pleasure of getting a few Huns" as did Neff and the soldier at Blanc Mont.

Regardless of whether a soldier was attracted or repelled by killing, when confronted with all of the battlefield's ugly realties and impressions, it was natural that most doughboys had to cope with fear. Fear is an instinctual response to the environmental stimuli of danger. As has been the case with soldiers throughout history, the doughboys experienced fear in a multitude of forms. The most prevalent source of fear was the soldiers' knowledge that they faced death, maiming, and serious injury in combat. Fear was a natural reaction to their desire for self-preservation in the face of these facts. When initially confronted with the knowledge that he was facing men who were actively trying to kill him, Sergeant Donald Kyler freely admitted, "During the first few days in combat, I was very much afraid." This was also the experi-ence of the 102nd Infantry's Private Albert Dahinden. In a letter from August 2, 1918, to a family friend he laid bare his feeling upon entering combat for the first time:

Your delightful letter received after ten days of the most strenuous and hair-raising experiences I ever had or fear to have had. Notice I said fear, for that is correct. In times past I thought I had seen the Grim Reaper but a while ago I could almost hear him sharpening his scythe . . . A description of my felling as I ducked and dodged the big ones is beyond my limits. One thing I know is that my nerves are still quivering, and I have been out of direct fire for nearly a week. . . . The day they shelled us and gassed us I thought my chances of seeing little old Seymour were mighty slim.

This incident and the fear it inspired proved to be enough excitement for him. After the friend suggested that home was going to be too quiet for him upon his return, Dahinden quipped, "If anyone so much as shoots a cap pistol off when I am around I'll choke him to death. No more shooting for yours truly if I do get back."[15]

The doughboys' other sources of fear were the anxiety of letting down one's comrades and, often, simply the fear of being afraid. Pride, specifically the desire to retain one's status and respect in the group, was a terrible and powerful motivation for the soldier to suppress his nervousness. Being labeled a coward remained an unforgivable stigma in the AEF. Most doughboys seemed to acknowledge that fear was a reality of combat; the litmus test for them was whether or not an individual was governed by his fears and failed to meet his obligations to their comrades in battle. In other words, it was OK to be afraid as long as your fears did not prevent you from doing your job and carrying your weight within the unit. Even after Albert Dahinden confessed his fears, he remained committed to the cause and willing to face the dangers of battle again and again. He rationalized this by noting, "Someone has to do it and it might as well be me as some poor fellow back home."

The doughboys had good reasons to experience fear on the battlefield. Regardless of whether the doughboys were attacking across an open field or defending from their foxholes, the bane of their existence was the German artillery. Artillery was the war's greatest killer and was responsible for approximately 70 percent of the conflict's casualties. A barrage assaulted all the body's senses and was most hated by the soldiers because they were absolutely powerless to do anything against it other than to huddle in the scant recesses of Mother Earth. While repairing a break in a telephone line, Horatio Rogers and five other soldiers were caught in the open by German artillery fire. He later recalled, "I flopped flat on my face in the mud and pulled my helmet over my eyes ... There is no way to express on paper the sound a shell makes. It begins as a whine, and then, rising to a terrifying crescendo shriek it ends in a shattering crash." Their close escape provided an unexpected burst of cathartic laughter. It was made even funnier by the fact that one of their number had wet himself during the experience. However, Rogers sheepishly admitted, "As a matter of fact we had all experienced that interesting sphincteric phenomenon." Shellfire also brought other physical responses to its victims. As one soldier recalled, "Some instinct sent the shoulder blades together with a bang and the most thoughtless heroes rolled up like armadillos," as they cowered in foxholes to escape the bursting shells. For George O'Brian, mimicking an armadillo was insufficient. After having "a taste of what it is to be under heavy shellfire," he informed his mother, it was "enough to make me wish I was as small as an ant and crawling into some might small crevice further underground."[16]

Death and injury from artillery often came quickly, sometimes with little to no warning, and the effects of shell fragments and shrapnel on the human body were horrifying and sobering to those witnessing a bombardment. In his first experience with shellfire during the Aisne-Marne push, the artilleryman L. V. Jacks was appalled by the destruction of a nearby kitchen wagon and its crew. As soon as the first shell hit, one of the men started to flee:

> The explosion lifted him from the earth, hurtling him forward like a sack of meal for twelve or fifteen feet. He fell on his face in the mud and, rising himself on his hands, tried to crawl along. He actually did move two or three feet, with his face turned up toward the sky and his legs trailing helplessly, for he was mangled almost beyond recognition. He threw back his head and screamed and screamed, as he struggled along leaving a red trail in the mud. His agony seemed to last hours, though it was not more than two or three seconds till he sank down on his face and died. A second man standing in front of me fell straight over dead, with a piece of shell in his heart. He was lucky and died quickly. A third near by was terribly torn, his chest shattered so that one could see his heart beating, and he, too, died in a few moments ... That first shell was a shock to say the least.

Although Jacks would be shelled frequently over the course of the war, he never overcame the discomfort and mental unease that came from being bombarded. Most disquieting for him was that "death fell from nowhere. A man was alive and active one instant, limp and dead the next. It was a nightmare, life-in-death feeling that was produced."[17]

Time and time again, doughboys echoed Jack's observations and wrote that the worst aspect of the shelling was their absolute impotence against the enemy artillery. This helplessness in the face of obliterating and mutilating death eroded the doughboys' morale and resiliency more than any other factor in combat. Private Paul Andrews, who would be killed while fighting in the "Lost Battalion" pocket on October 6, 1918, informed his uncle in August, "That's the hell of the thing, no action, just staying in one spot all the time, waiting for the shells to drop, day and night, it seems as if it would never stop . . . take it from me we are under some strain." After enduring the shelling with no chance of retaliation he groused, "All I want now is to just get in sight of the enemy, and have a chance to fight face to face with a few of them." Another 77th Division doughboy wrote, "We never know when a shell is going to drop on us and snuff us out. We feel like it's coming, and [it] makes us uneasy, just like a doomed prisoner feels in the death-house, knowing he is going to be electrocuted. The torture of waiting for it is the real punishment." Although German machine guns, the other great killer of Americans, also elicited great fear in the soldier, it was at least a weapon that could be destroyed using the weapons and tactics at the doughboy's disposal. After being constantly shelled in Belleau Wood, a 2nd Division Marine noted,

> A thousand machine guns could not give one that helpless feeling brought on by the approach of the overawing, merciless shells. They carry him instantly to oblivion by covering him in his hole or with their terrible force blow him to atoms . . . It would have seemed a thousand times better to face an army of machine guns with my bayoneted rifle in hand and a chance—though a shadow of a chance—to act, to *do* something, to be opposed by an enemy where there was a chance to fight back.

In the end, he maintained, "merciless shellfire tears the nerves to pieces."[18]

Walter Shaw constantly discussed his experiences with enemy bombardments in his letters home. Unlike most doughboys, he did not self-censor his correspondence to keep the folks at home from worrying about him and generally exhibited a willingness to discuss what he had seen and felt in battle. His sentiments about shellfire were typical of many doughboys. After his first tour at the front, he confessed to his mother, "Well I was scared the first shell . . . It seems as if you can't be missed." After this experience, he informed her, "I took $5000.00 govt. life insurance out in behalf of you," and half-joked, "I am worth more dead than alive maybe." Shaw never grew accustomed to shellfire and told the folks at home that "I will admit I was afraid of the shells" and that he "didn't get very used to them even if they don't come within 200 yards of you." A few close calls under shellfire only reinforced his aversion to bombardments. After days of heavy shelling Shaw declared, "They wreck ones nerves."[19]

Unlike Shaw, some doughboys claimed that over time they became inured to shellfire. As they grew more experienced, many doughboys became adept at predicting where a shell would fall based on the sound it made in flight. James Dalgren mused to his girlfriend on October 16, 1918, "It's real fascinating to sit here and hear the shells whistle and burst for you wonder if you will hear the next one whistle for they say you never hear the one that gets you whistle." After days of being under enemy fire, one artilleryman admitted, "Funny how quickly you get used to such things. A week ago Don and I were jumping because a lone shell had burst in the next county. Now we can tell the direction by the screech and we don't bother to flop unless it's coming right at us." He casually stated, "It seems as if we have always been under fire." Lloyd Short likewise informed his sister of his growing indifference to artillery fire. "It sure does not take a fellow long to get used to dodging them when you hear them coming toward you like a train at a crossing," he wrote on July 15, 1918. "We hit the dirt and lay face downward until the shrapnel quits falling which is only a few seconds and go on about our work whatever it is. It is quite fascinating at times." But such skills were no guarantee of survival. The doughboys remained wary of German mortars, for example, as the shells from these weapons arrived with little warning and thus afforded the doughboys scant opportunity to seek cover. Ironically, Lloyd Short's "fascination" was cut short when he was killed in action only four days after writing his sister the letter.[20]

Artillery also tended to reinforce to the soldiers the inherent uncertainty and randomness of war. This manifested itself in the close calls, miraculous escapes, freak accidents, and deaths that surrounded them. Shellfire could obliterate one man while leaving another only a few feet away completely unscathed. Fred Parker wrote his girlfriend that he "got scratched up a bit" after a shell landed next to the wagon where he and a comrade were sleeping. The shell blew in the side of the wagon and covered the men with bricks and other debris. While the shell "didn't do us any damages to speak of," he was rattled by the fact that it did kill nineteen other soldiers resting nearby.

Another soldier discovered a comrade staring in "fascinated horror" at a shell that had landed less than three feet from where the man was sitting, but had failed to explode. After the near escape, the lucky doughboy "was so shaky that he was useless for the rest of the day."[21]

If being shelled by the Germans was not bad enough, battlefield confusion and worn-out cannon barrels sometimes resulted in American soldiers being shelled by their own artillery. An officer in the 35th Division complained, "Our artillery gave little support" during his time in the Argonne, "and on several occasions fired short as much as a kilometer, causing losses to our troops." During one attack near St. Juvin, a battalion of the 325th Infantry had the misfortune of simultaneously being bombarded by both German and American artillery. The poor state of communications meant that a message from the battalion commander to stop the American artillery sent at 11:00 AM did not reach the offending cannoneers until the late afternoon. An infantry officer at the scene angrily informed his superior that such friendly fire "injures the morale of troops more than anything that could possibly happen."[22]

Although they caused many fewer casualties than artillery, the doughboys also feared poison gas and being attacked by enemy aircraft. The reason for this loathing was similar to that of being shelled; there was little that the troops could do to respond to these forms of attack. Nearly 9 percent of the AEF's combat deaths (1,221 soldiers) resulted from poison gas. An additional 70,552 doughboys were hospitalized for gas poisoning, which accounted for over 31 percent of the army's total combat casualties. Many of these casualties can be traced back to the poor training that the doughboys received in gas warfare. A single gas attack in March 1918 against the 42nd Division's 165th Infantry resulted in the gassing of nineteen officers and 405 soldiers. Lieutenant Colonel H. L. Gilchrist, a medical officer who investigated the incident, discovered that "many soldiers and officers were found without proper gas protection, that is, respirators either not in the alert position (mounted on the soldier's chest ready to be donned) or no respirators [being worn] at all."[23]

The fear of being gassed and the discomfort of wearing gasmasks placed a physical and psychological burden on the soldiers that was far greater than the actual effectiveness of the weapon itself. Captain John Stringfellow noted, "That intangible substance, that one could not fight, but only ward against when wakened in time, wrecked the nerves of the men through fear and as a constant threat accomplished more in breaking the morale than in actually disabling the soldier." Units in the line posted "gas guards" to look for the early signs of a gas attack and to provide timely warning for the soldiers to don their masks. Depending on the concentration of the gas, the soldiers had roughly thirty to forty-five seconds to put on their gasmasks before they received a casualty-causing dose. The gas guard looked for gas clouds, the distinctive light plopping that a gas shell made when it ruptured (as opposed to the violent explosion of high-explosive shells), and the telltale smell of poison gas: new-mown hay for phosgene and garlic for mustard gas. The dread of being gassed became so prevalent in his unit that Stringfellow only used experienced men as gas guards because the newer soldiers tended to overact at the slightest hint of a possible attack. A Marine noted that being a gas guard was such a weighty responsibility that it preyed on the nerves and minds of those assigned to the duty. For the gas guard, with his senses straining to detect an attack, "The more he meditates, the more he is inclined to feel that a deadly gas attack has come to snuff out the lives of all it was his duty to protect." It was not at all unusual for a panicked gas guard to sound a false alarm that would send his comrades scrambling out of their sleep or other activities to don their masks. As the gas guards used large clacker rattles, claxons, and gongs made out of artillery shell casing to rouse their comrades to actions, these loud alarms tended to set off a chain reaction as other units up and down the line picked up the original gas guard's warning and set their own men into action.[24]

The effects of the gas were horrifying enough to give the soldiers ample reason for their fears. The two most common poison gases that the doughboys encountered were phosgene and mustard. Phosgene is a pulmonary irritant that kills and injures by causing such inflammation in the respiratory passage and lungs that the body produces a wave of oedemic fluid in an effort to protect the tissue and wash the agent from the body. The buildup of the fluid fills the lungs to the point that the soldier drowns. Men exposed to a lethal concentration of phosgene died a painful death; their last minutes filled with futile and labored gasping for air like a fish floundering after being removed from water. No glorious or heroic passing here.

Mustard gas was a vesicant agent that caused large, painful, and incapacitating blisters to form on the surfaces of the body on which it came into contact. Mustard tended to do the most damage to the moist areas of the soldier's body—the eyes, nose, mouth, armpits, and crotch. Depending on the concentration of the gas, it could cause temporary or permanent blindness. If the soldier breathed in mustard gas, the blisters formed on his windpipe and lungs, destroying the lining of the mucus membrane and the bronchioles. Mustard killed by inhibiting the soldier's ability to breathe or by drowning as the blisters erupted and filled his lungs with fluid. Mustard, which was actually a liquid rather than a gas, was an exceptionally persistent agent that could linger in an area long after the initial attack. When the air was cool, mustard tended to collect in shell holes, trenches, and other low-lying areas and would be absorbed into the ground. If the temperature warmed up, the mustard gas again atomized and rose into the air, poisoning unsuspecting and unwary people. Of the patients where the exact type of gas that poisoned them could be identified, 76.1 percent fell to mustard gas, 18.7 to phosgene, 5 percent to chlorine, and the remainder was injured by arsine.[25]

Being gassed was an exceptionally traumatic experience. Humans will naturally start to panic when they cannot breathe or see or if they feel intense burning sensations. Gas exposure could quickly sap the soldiers' ability and will to fight. In June 1918, Earl Seaton and several of his comrades were hit with a mustard gas bombardment. He later recalled,

> Our eyes were watering and we could feel burning where we sweat . . . We got a bath at a field hospital and French clothes . . . When we got the bath we had bandages on our eyes and they really hurt . . . Most of the bad burns were around the testicles, underarms and wherever there was moisture. They used a clear substance like Vaseline on the burns. The eyes healed first. Grease had to be kept on the penis to keep the channel open . . . Two new artillery men came in badly burned. Their faces and eyes were okay but they had worked all night at a battery and sweat a lot. Their private parts were like beefsteak.

Being gassed was particularly hard on the musician Walter Shaw. While serving as a stretcher-bearer in the 1st Division, he had taken his mask off in a rainstorm so he could see to find a wounded officer in the dark. While searching for the officer, he fell into a shell hole filled with mustard gas. "The first breath of gas was the worst of all," he explained to his mother from a field hospital, "it almost took my breath." He was blind for two days and afterward he confessed that his eyes were still so weak that he could not write a letter home. Shaw was despondent over his future, writing, "I can't say when I will be able to play clarinet again as my lungs are weak and I can't talk much above a whisper. I don't know when it will wear off."[26]

Seeing the effect that gas had on men like Seaton and Shaw rattled many doughboys. In the summer and fall of 1918, AEF medical officers noted a dramatic uptick in what they termed "gas hysteria" and "gas neurosis": men fervently claiming that they had been gassed and demanding treatment. For exposure to anything other than mustard gas, it was hard for doctors to gauge the accuracy of the soldiers' claims. Often the symptoms of gas poisoning were the same as those for pneumonia, influenza, exhaustion, or a respiratory infection. However, the number of "gas hysteria" cases does point to the deep psychological effect that the weapon had on the doughboys. This was also seen in other areas. During an attack in the Argonne one private was in the act of putting on his gasmask when he made the unfortunate discovery that it had been shredded by shrapnel. In a panic, the man ran to a German prisoner and forcefully snatched away the German's gasmask. Fear and the survival instinct quickly drained the American's reservoir of human kindness.[27]

Wearing gasmasks was far from a pleasurable experience for the doughboys. The standard-issued masks in the AEF were the French M2 and the Corrected English Model mask (CEM), an American version of the British Small Box Respirator. The M2 was used by troops outside the main battle area and as a backup mask for some combat troops. The CEM and its variants were the most common masks used by the AEF in combat. It consisted of a rubberized cloth faceplate with built-in goggles and elastic straps to fit the mask to the wearer's head. Unlike modern gasmasks, the CEM was not completely airtight. To compensate for this fact, the mask contained a spring clip that closed the wearer's nose to force him to breathe through his mouth. The soldier breathed in and out of a tube while clinching a mouth guard, much like one on a modern swimming snorkel, between his teeth. The tube was connected to a hose that ran to the mask's filter, which was held in a canvas pouch worn around the neck and resting on the soldier's chest. As one veteran recounted, "The flat mask and goggle eyes give the owner an ape-like look too grotesque for words."[28]

Wearing the masks was uncomfortable on the best of days, and combat seldom occurred on the best of days. On rainy, hot, or tense days, the soldier's discomfort with the masks was magnified. The small eyepieces on the mask severely restricted the soldier's peripheral vision and made it even more dif-

Photo 21: Soldiers practicing donning their gasmasks. Getting the clumsy masks on in less than thirty seconds could mean the difference among life, death, and serious injury. Source: author's collection.

ficult to locate the enemy on the battlefield. The mask's faceplate was baggy and frequently sagged under the weight of the hose, making it tricky for the soldier to keep the eyepieces properly aligned with the soldier's eyes. Although the army provided the soldiers with an "anti-dim" compound to keep the mask's eyepieces from fogging up, it was only marginally effective. On hot days, or when the soldiers were engaged in anything other than moderate physical activity, sweat and condensation ran down the eyepieces and reduced the wearer's already limited field of view. The same problem occurred if it was raining. As the soldier's air supply had to pass through the thick canvas of the bag and over six inches of decontamination granules in the filter, simply breathing was a chore. As Private Fey Neff informed his sister, "Gee sis i did hate those gas masks. The first time i put one on i thought i would die for the want of air." To add to the discomfort, after wearing the mask for only a few minutes, the soldiers' jaws began to ache from clinching the rubber mouthpiece between their teeth. Lastly, the clumsy masks made spoken communications all but impossible. Warren Jackson noted, "While the mask was on, the rubber mouthpiece could be removed and with one 'lung' of air a fellow could hastily say a few words. Following the remarks, which in all probability were not understood by anyone, the speaker had to hurriedly thrust the rubber tube into his mouth for a breath of fresh air." The longest that he had to wear his mask at one time was three hours. "The discomfort was so great when kept on for very long," Jackson admitted, "it was a common thing for a man to remove the mask in sheer desperation, little knowing, and sometimes not caring much what the consequences might be." Despite the inherent problems with the masks, the soldiers had no other options but to endure wearing them. Soon after the Armistice, a doughboy stated somewhat philosophically, "You can imagine now how it is to fight with a gas mask on with the alternative of making fertilizer for the Future Farmers of Northern France."[29]

To a much lesser extent, the doughboys were also leery of German airplanes. Long before the United States entered the war, American newspapers and magazines were filled with stories about the brave pilots battling in a new form of warfare in the skies of Europe. As few Americans had much experience with aviation, at first the doughboys expressed their fascination at the novelty and excitement of war in the air. As one 32nd Division soldier wrote to his mother in December 1917, "We see all the biplanes in the air every day. Five or six in the air at once. It seems nice to see all those things . . . we used to pay 50 [cents] to see." When the Americans were on the receiving end of German aviation, their enthusiasm for flying machines quickly waned. As with artillery and poison gas, the doughboys were galled by their inability to keep the Germans from attacking them or from reporting their locations to the enemy artillery. "The German pilots liked to straff [sic] troops in the trenches," F. L. Miller complained. "We lost but few men because of this but it had considerable psychological effect. One feels so defenseless with an enemy plane turning on its nose and flying down a trench with machine guns blazing."

During the Meuse Argonne offensive, an officer in the 82nd Division was frustrated when "those damned Boche planes flew right on our necks and dropped little lights and the Boche artillery put their shells just where they wanted them." Likewise, Bob Casey maintained that artillerymen feared the enemy's air observation because, he joked, it "divines your innermost thoughts, discloses to the enemy your morale, age, weight, and attitude toward the income tax."

The ground pounders' efforts to retaliate against the offending enemy fly-ers resulted mostly in wasting ammunition as the Germans were flying too low and fast or too high for the unskilled doughboys to hit them. As Miller observed, "We shot rifles at low flying planes, they should have been easy to hit, but I never saw a plane brought down by ground rifle fire." This impotent firing only added to the soldiers' feelings of powerlessness in the face of air attacks. An infantry officer during the Soissons offensive decried the fact that "Germany mastered the air as far as the doughboy was concerned."[30]

The American ground troops generally blamed their vulnerability to the German air force on the American Air Service. The doughboys had little re-spect for American aviators and believed that they lacked the courage to fight the Germans in the air and yet lived high on the hog while on the ground. In a parody of the song "Homeward Bound" the ground pounders lashed out at the flyboys,

> Way back in the rear, where no guns they hear,
> Our aviators tune up their planes,
> Then they go out and flirt with the Janes.
> But when dangers hovering around
> You bet your elbow they're never found.
>
> Because they're homeward bound,
> They're flying fast and near the ground.
> And while the shot and shells are flying
> For the S.O. S. they're sighing.
> It's good they get high pay
>
> To buy champagne 'most every day.
> But if you want to hear our aero-planes sound
> Don't come near when Fritzie's around.
> Because they're homeward bound.
> It's a hell of a, hell of a sound.

Although some of this was the natural grousing of the infantry's perceived relative depredation, much of the doughboys' discontentment was justified. An infantry officer explained the frustration that he and his soldiers felt dur-ing the Meuse Argonne:

> Our own planes were again careful not to come out, as usual. The moral ef-fect of the presence of one of our own Planes is wonderful, until of course

the men see him get away at break-neck speed when the enemy Plane appears on the scene. The men feel that when *they* take almost impossible chances, walking into Machine Gun Nests ETC., that our Planes ought to at least take a little chance.

To the infantry, the inability of the American aviators to keep the German flyers off their backs was just another indication that they were suffering the casualties and enduring the hardships while other members of the AEF were enjoying glory and having a "good war."[31]

The doughboy's fear of German artillery, poison gas, air attacks, machine guns, and all the other implements of his destruction made combat a daunting endeavor. Although he was wrong about a great many things, the World War I veteran turned military historian S. L. A. Marshall was right when it came to understanding many of the human dynamics of combat. He observed, "The battlefield is cold. It is the lonesomest place that men share together." To face the isolation and fear that came with combat, the doughboys naturally turned to their comrades for support and reassurance. One Marine believed that the comradeship of soldiers was "not a friendship of the soft and slushy kind . . . but a friendship based on the realization of the little human fears we, man for man, try so hard to conceal." To him, the faith in one's buddies rested upon this: "Respect and liking, common ground for common men, a mutual trust learned at risky work and during weary marches, made us conscious of the qualities that each carried in his heart and soldiered by. There were a hundred of little things that each one did, which served to make the other fellow understand."

Sergeant Albert Robinson was heartened by the fact that he served with "as glorious a bunch of fellows as ever trod at the heels of Sir Lancelot or Capt. Kidd." This intense identification with comrades and their units was key to the soldiers' will and ability to suppress their fears and face the shocks and privations of combat. One soldier swore that it gave him great comfort upon going into battle for the first time knowing "on my right and left lay my buddies who would do anything to protect me. There is no place you rely so much on your buddies as on the field of battle."[32]

The bonds of comradeship also placed a burden of mutual obligation on all of the parties. A soldier's buddies consciously or unconsciously imposed on the doughboy the harshest and most unforgiving form of peer pressure. Most doughboys would run extraordinary risks and make extraordinary

Photo 22: Kendal Rauch (far left) and his infantry squad mates from the 4th Division. The doughboys often noted that the greatest source of their morale, support, and survival in battle was their comrades. Source: author's collection.

sacrifices to not let their buddies down in battle and to remain a member in good standing of the squad. To suffer one's share of risks and hardship was also tied to the soldiers' sense of manhood. Private Thurmond Baccus proclaimed that one of the great things that kept him soldiering on was that "you feel like a man among men" in his squad. This adherence to manliness did sometimes come at a cost. Elton Mackin felt particularly sorry for a green replacement officer that was assigned to his company during the fighting at Blanc Mont. He recalled, "He was young and desperately anxious to hold his place in the ranks of hard-bitten men who played a wicked, vicious game. Boy-like, he wanted a place among them; sought their recognition." Mackin observed that the officer tried hard to cover his nervousness in his first action by displays of bravado. The man was "the type who leads a desperate charge and cannot tell you why," but did so mostly because "his manhood ordered it so." After the officer was mortally wounded the toughness of manhood departed and the boy's last cry was for his mother.[33]

Within the small group, to fail in one's duties or the test of manhood was to risk ostracism and the withdrawal of support that was vital to the soldier's physical and mental well-being. To remain in the good graces of the small group sometimes meant doing things that the soldier would rather not do. After their officer called for volunteers for a particularly dangerous mission at St. Mihiel, all of the men of his unit stepped forward. One of the men later recalled, "That's the worst part of a call for volunteers. It takes more courage to say No than Yes." Comradeship thus served two purposes: it provided the individuals and groups a means for meeting their vital needs, and it also gave the army the ability to get those same individuals and groups to do vital things in battle—killing, dying, and persevering—that common sense and instinct might not otherwise incline them to do. Pride is a son of a bitch.[34]

This reliance on comradeship and small-unit norms had a built-in weakness. For one, soldiers, especially green ones, tended to huddle together when moving forward in battle. An artilleryman witnessed this phenomenon while observing a company of American infantry attacking in the Meuse Argonne. The attacking troops were within the range and observation of the German guns, yet despite the efforts of their officers to get the men to spread out, "They were evidently coming together for comfort and sympathy, forgetting that in their situation the best comfort lay in keeping far apart and offering enemy gunners the smallest possible target."

He noted that the company's progress could be traced by the "little circles" of dead troops caused by enemy shells landing in the middle of the unit's jumbled masses. Other doughboys and their German foes reported seeing the bodies of American infantrymen laying in closely grouped formations as if the men had been shot down while marching in a parade.[35]

Furthermore, even though the small unit's norms of behavior generally motivated its soldiers to fight, those same dynamics could have the opposite effect. Major General Hanson Ely once observed a regimental commander order a sergeant to make another attack on the German positions near Bantheville in October 1918, despite the fact that previous assaults had been bloody failures. Although the sergeant told the colonel that his men would "quit" if pushed forward again, the commander would not relent. Shortly after launching the attack, the NCO's prediction came true. Ely was sensitive to the attacker's plight, noting, "Those men practically agreed among themselves that they were not going to stay in those woods and within half an hour they began to come back. That was not mutiny . . . It was just a feeling among the men that they had stood all they losses they could stand, compared with other organizations in that particular outfit; and they quit." As illustrated, if the small group "stuck," its men tended to "stick"; if the members of the small unit determined that they had given enough, then all tended to give way. The trick for commanders was knowing exactly where that breaking point was with their units. This was a difficult task because it varied wildly from small unit to small unit.[36]

The attritional nature of the battlefield also all but assured that at some point the doughboys in a combat unit would lose friends and comrades. These casualties could shake the cohesion of a unit and encourage fear and hesitation in the ranks. Fred Parker wrote home that his worst experience in the war came when "the two best friends I ever had, and I don't think I ever had any real ones until I came in the army, were sent West [that is, killed] right along side of me at St. Quentin." After that he was glad to be gassed and wounded to see the end of his combat duties, admitting, "Believe me that is enough war for [me]." Seeing a friend killed beside him broke the spirit of one Marine, and "the damn of his false fortitude broke and he cried." The man's sergeant spun him around and spat, "You'd think that you were the only guy in this man's war to lose a pal. We've all lost 'em up here an' we want *men* in their places—not babies! Now, dig in!" The sergeant's comments were heartless, unsympathetic, and exactly what the Marine needed to hear. Given the situation that the squad faced, the sergeant realized that the squad could ill afford any of its members to be unfocused on the tasks at hand and refused to allow the man to wallow in self-pity and thoughts of death. Over time, necessity forced the doughboys to psychologically isolate themselves as best as possible from the loss of friends. Later the crying Marine admitted, "We learned to close our minds to the memory of men who fell. We took the way of living day to day, and braced our inward fears toward some vivid time and place when we in turn would fall, and be, we knew, forgotten in the column." Despite the Marine's admission, the winnowing away of comrades in battle certainly eroded the trust and confidence that were central to small-unit cohesion.[37]

Although the presence of comrades and small-unit peer pressures certainly encouraged a soldier to be resolute, ultimately the individual had to resolve his internal struggle with his fears. Some soldiers steeled themselves for battle by constantly talking to their buddies, others by praying, or cursing, or singing, or anything that would take their minds off of thinking about their impending mortality. Many soldiers reported that they or their comrades started chain smoking in an effort to calm their fears and to appear calm and collected in action. A machine gunner found combat to be "a terrible strain on your nerves and, unconsciously, you are continually rolling cigarettes. I smoke two or three packs of Bull Durham a day." The effort to seem unruffled by smoking did not always work as intended. During a heavy bombardment Warren Jackson recalled,

> Bergeman and I sat facing each other at opposite ends of a grave-like hole. His hands shook as he rolled cigarette after cigarette. No sooner did he get one lighted, than he was rolling another, his hands trembling so that half the tobacco might be shaken from the paper before he got it rolled. Even now I can see his big eyes roll at the fall of each shell. If I looked as scared as he did, I presented a picture.

The hardest part of combat is sometimes simply waiting for the next event, such as the end of a shelling or the start of the next attack to begin. The act of smoking during such periods gave the men something to do with their hands and to keep their minds occupied with something other than contemplating the future. An artilleryman later wrote, "I saw the leading driver jerk out a package of cigarettes. He was going through the fiction of smoking to steady his nerves. In less than a minute he had lit and thrown away five cigarettes, nervously inhaling perhaps two or three puffs from each." This method of coping with fear only lasted as long as the soldier's tobacco supply. Although the doughboys were supposed to receive an issue of tobacco as part of their rations, constant problems with the distribution of supplies meant that the troops often went without smoking materials. One soldier recorded that one week he received "one box of matches and 3 packs of cigarettes," and the next "one pack of cigarettes, [a] can of Prince Albert and a sack of Velvet."[38]

Whether due to small-unit norms of behavior, the need to prove their manhood, or the fear of being punished by the army for cowardice, the majority of combat doughboys were able to find the courage and resolve to keep fighting regardless of their doubts and worries. Some gained more mastery over their fears after surviving their first combat actions. For all its fearsomeness, actually being in combat provided a counterpoint to the more dire conceptions of battle that many soldiers held prior to going into action. Lieutenant John Castles found his first time under fire to be disconcerting.

He discovered that combat had "a Yale-Harvard football game feeling, only magnified many times," but also admitted to experiencing a fear that was "a terrible thing and hard to define." Having survived a bombardment, his confidence was restored and his anxieties were assuaged. Castle recalled that his fear "only lasted a fraction of a second, and I did not feel panicky or forget what to do, but during that fraction of a second, I just hurt physically all over, especially [in] my mouth." The soldiers were also better able to handle their fears when their leaders seemed to be calm and composed. "I didn't feel so lion hearted with those shells cracking and bullets whizzing just above" a young officer confessed shortly after the Armistice. But, upon seeing his company commander under fire, "walking around like it was a May Day celebration, I was cooled down considerably, and proceeded to do a little walking around on my own hook thinking to myself that they didn't have any more nerve than I did."[39]

The absurdities that occur in war at times provided something to break the tensions that the soldiers felt in battle. Often the irrationality of war gave way to bursts of gallows humor that would have shocked and befuddled the uncomprehending folks back home. A Marine remembered that after a shell killed a nearby group of French officers pouring over a map, he was surprised to find one of his buddies "rolling in the wheat in an uncontrollable spasm of mirth." Although the situation was far from funny, the other men of the squad quickly joined into this uncontrollable laughter. As the group laughter slowly subsided, the Marine asked his buddy what had caused the outburst. The man pointed to the dead Frenchmen and gushed, "Oh, Jesus, I bet they were surprised." Another doughboy noted passing the corpse of a German soldier who had been blown in and out of his grave three times during the fighting on the Ourcq River. Some doughboy had hung a sign on the corpse's chest stating, "For the love of God, leave me alone. I got appendicitis." For these men, laughing at death somehow took away its sting and their gallows humor allowed them to somewhat conceal their own apprehensions.[40]

Captain Herman Ulmer was also able to see the humor of combat. On October 13, 1918, he was expecting a German counterattack on his positions but had instructed his soldiers not to fire on some hazy forms approaching for fear that they would hit a patrol that he had sent out earlier in the afternoon. Thinking that the forms were Americans, he "beckoned the men to hurry on in." Afterward, he recalled, "It struck me as exceedingly ridiculous that, when the enemy was coming over to attack us, I should get up and wave them a wel-come. The Germans, as they proved to be, refused my hospitable invitation, and were evidently somewhat peeved at my attempt to fraternize with them, for when I waved, they raised their rifles and fired." The event would have been even funnier except the German fusillade wounded the officer's orderly in the leg and one of his sergeants in the shoulder. Later in the action, Ulmer informed his regimental commander, "I remember noticing a particular old Bosche whose suspenders had either been shot away, or had been broken by his efforts to make his withdrawal as speedy as possible—at least, his breeches were hanging down his back. The sight of that white rotundity waddling hastily up the hill was so ludicrous that I refrained from shooting, although it did make an admirable target." But even Ulmer, who had such a knack for recording the absurd and amusing realities of military life, admitted, "It may be that many more humorous incidents occurred, but after that first three days [in the Argonne], I was unable to appreciate humor in any form, and they escaped my notice."[41]

After a long spell in combat, fear and absurdity simply gave way to fatal-ism. Constant exposure to death, random chance on the battlefield, fatigue, and privation led to a deep lassitude in many doughboys. By the time that the Americans entered the war, the French Army had come to call this profound soldier melancholy the "cafard." In some ways fatalism was an antidote to fear. Once the doughboys became inured to death and accepted the possibil-ity of their own demise, or reached the point of mental and physical exhaus-tion that they no longer cared what happen to them, their fear of battle often waned. As his unit moved into the Argonne fighting, a soldier in the 32nd Division noticed, "A feeling akin to absolute despair possessed some as we lined up. They judged that certain death was ahead. Others, who had now been through two great battles and survived, felt satisfied that the law of aver-ages would not permit them to escape much longer, and they set themselves with quite a reasonable show of coolness to face what they considered their probable and approaching end." Sergeant Donald Kyler, who had previously admitted that he was "very much afraid" of going into battle, explained that over time "gradually a sort of stoical numbness came" where he no longer feared what lay ahead.[42]

Such a rapid decent into fatalism could be alarming to members of the unit. During the grinding drive in the Meuse Argonne, one officer grew concerned after noticing that "the men aren't talking. They don't seem to give a damn what happens to them." The ever-observant Chaplain Lee Levinger was quick to catch on to the changing mood of his flock in combat. He explained that despite their

> deep yearning for personal religion, the men adopted fatalism as their prevalent philosophy. For one thing, it seemed to answer the immediate facts the best. When five men are together in a shell hole and a bursting shell kills three of them and leaves the two unharmed, all our theories seem worthless . . . And when they must face conditions like this day after day, never knowing their own fate from minute to minute, only sure that they are certain to be killed if they stay at the front long enough, they become fatalists sooner or later.

The chaplain confessed, "I argued against fatalism many times with the soldiers, but I found when it came my own turn to live under fire day after day that a fatalistic attitude was the most convenient for doing one's duty under the constant roaring menace." After this epiphany, Levinger admitted, "for the time being, I was much of a fatalist as the rest."[43]

If left unchecked, however, stoic fatalism sometimes led to morbid thoughts, inordinate risk taking, and premonitions of death. Such was the case with C. D. Grant. After the death of one of his friends, he wrote in his diary on August 13, 1918, "I wish it could happen to me and have it over, it sure is terrible." When another comrade broke his arm three days later, he called him a "Lucky devil" for escaping the fighting. Edwin Arpin told of his last encounter with his friend Orville "Andy" Anderson during the fighting in the Meuse Argonne,

> I came upon "Andy" entirely alone, sitting on a huge log wrapped in an atmosphere of almost un-natural gloom. Rather grimly he motioned me to take a seat by his side. Needless to say I was only too glad to find him alone so we might better enjoy these few moments together. And although he appeared anxious to have me near, at the same time he seemed to be entirely disinclined towards conversation . . . He seemed entirely oblivious to my rather clumsy efforts to break the spell. My first impression that he was merely suffering from an overdose of lonesomeness eventually gave way to the realization that it was something of a much deeper nature. Something which I never before encountered, the disheartening specter of fatal premonition.

When Anderson was duly killed the next day, Arpin's beliefs in premonition seemed to have been confirmed. Many of these premonitions were most likely due to the creeping sense of powerlessness that entered the lives of many combat troops. At some point, perhaps, fatalism turned premonitions of death into self-fulfilling prophecies. As the reporting of events that did not happen did not make it into the doughboys' narratives, we will never know how many soldiers had premonitions that never came to pass. However, the frequency with which the doughboys mentioned premonitions and morose thoughts indicates the hopelessness that their experience of modern war left them with.[44]

Another way that some doughboys dealt with fear and the hardships of combat was to simply remove themselves from the possibility of death. This took the form of self-inflicted wounds (SIW) and straggling. Straggling will be covered in chapter 22, but this is a good place to discuss the problem of SIWs. Some doughboys sought to avoid the front altogether by injuring or otherwise making themselves unfit for duty. The number of SIWs increased dramatically as the AEF entered combat in the summer of 1918. In July alone, the 1st Division reported seventy-two cases of self-injury. After the AEF's adjutant general, Brigadier General Robert Davis, warned that "unless this tendency is checked it may become prevalent at times when morale is weakened by great strain," Pershing ordered division inspector generals to report and investigate all suspected cases of SIWs in their units. In August, fourteen divisions reported a total of 179 cases of self-inflicted wounds, of which, 131 were deemed accidental, thirteen were intentional, and in the remaining cases the inspectors could reach no definite conclusion. In all but fifteen of the 179 cases, the soldiers were in infantry or machine gun units. The 6th Division's inspector general reported that between September 6 and October 18 his unit had forty-four cases of SIWs and determined that fifteen of these cases were accidental while the remaining twenty-nine were "intentionally inflicted, with a desire to evade and avoid further active service." All of these wounds occurred after the division began its movement into the combat zone, not while the division was in training.

The 6th Division inspector also complained that a lack of time and manpower made it "absolutely impossible . . . to investigate each of these cases properly." As this was also true in other divisions, one can assume that some number of the cases labeled accidental were in fact deliberate self-injury. The difficulty in determining motive in such cases led the 6th Division inspector to recommend to the AEF GHQ that when any soldier was hospitalized with wounds to the hand, arm, or lower leg, "the evidence is *prima facie* that the wound was intentionally inflicted," unless the soldier could definitively prove otherwise. The justification that the officer gave for this "guilty until proven innocent" approach was that any other approach would not do "justice to the Government, nor to the comrades of a man guilty of a self-inflicted wound."[45]

The inspector general's rationale for this harsh measure had some merit with the doughboys. The doughboys themselves had little tolerance for fellow soldiers who shirked their responsibilities. After one of his soldiers shot himself in the foot to get out of the line on October 31, 1918, his officer admitted that he "felt a twinge of sympathy for him." His comrades, however, were not so forgiving. As soon as the soldier shot himself, "none of his companions seemed interested in him." His erstwhile comrades refused to assist in bandaging or evacuating the wounded man, and he was forced to "look for help on his own account." Private Tom Carroll witnessed a fellow soldier shoot himself through the right hand on March 25, 1918, while the 16th Infantry occupied a sector of French trenches. As the wounded man left for the rear, he proclaimed, "Out of the trenches, no more trenches for me." Just before his unit attacked Cantigny, another man in Carroll's company "lost" his false teeth. This was after the man discovered that he could not be sent to the front lines because, without teeth, he would be unable to hold the mouthpiece of his gasmask. The company commander had no option but to reassign the shirker to the unit kitchen until the company was pulled from the line and the man was refitted with a new dentures. Others simply "lost" their gasmasks on the way to the front to avoid combat. In most of these cases, the offenders were shunned from then on by their compatriots for breaking the cardinal rules of the military pack: do your part, share the dangers, and never leave your comrades in a lurch.[46]

Along with coping with their fears, the doughboys had to contend with the confusion, sense of isolation, and privations that were part and parcel of combat. Many of the proceeding passages in this chapter have pointed to the battlefield confusion the doughboys faced and to their efforts to make sense of what was going on around them. Part of this confusion was due to the fact that the troops seldom had a clear knowledge of their unit's missions or the terrain and enemy that they would encounter. "I guess the officers knew [the plan]," a soldier in the 35th Division recalled, "but privates were given no such information." This was also the experience of Private John Nell. He complained, "We enlisted men never knew much about our movements, only what we were told and what we could see and hear. The woods were so thick; our vision was only in and around where we were standing or walking. We did not know what day of the week or day of the month it was the entire time." Although the troops were always aware that the enemy was somewhere to their front, actually making contact with the Germans often came as a shock and a surprise. While attacking, contact often came in the form of sudden bursts of machine gun and rifle fire, sometimes from unexpected directions.[47]

Having such a lack of information in the ranks caused endless problems for the AEF. In one of the more egregious examples, an infantryman in the 2nd Division knew so little about the situation at Soissons that he believed that the French Moroccan soldiers attacking on his unit's flanks were enemy Turks. When his mistake was brought to his attention, he sheepishly confessed, "Well, I got a few of them anyway!" While few doughboys were as clueless as this man, the ponderous size of the American units and the nature of the terrain over which they advanced left many soldiers physically and mentally isolated in battle. During the Soissons drive a veteran Marine was taken by the surreal and compartmentalized nature of the battlefield;

> The senses ceased to function normally. Only a vague sort of way did I comprehend that the ranks to the left were being shot to pieces. However, as my eyes chanced to be in that direction, something caught my gaze with an almost paralyzing reality. A shell made a direct hit on the line, and a pack and helmet went spinning high into the air. Yet there were minutes such that had all the world, more than a dozen steps away, ceased to exist, we would not have realized it.

A machine gunner wrote of a similar sense of isolation, pointing out, "About all we see of the war are the few hundred soldiers we see about us, and at times you get the impression that your squad is fighting the war all alone."[48]

In the tangled terrain of the Argonne region and some of the AEF's other battlefields, it was easy for the doughboys to become separated from their comrades. Few things were more disconcerting to the soldiers than being lost and alone somewhere in enemy territory. As he struggled through the hills and thickets of the Argonne, Private Milton Sweningsen recalled that he only saw glimpses of the other men of his company as he navigated through the undergrowth. Upon emerging into an opening in the woods, he was startled to discover that he was absolutely alone. All at once Sweningsen was deprived of the physical and mental support structure of his small unit. Furthermore, he had little concept of his unit's mission and was without a map. "What to do?" he recalled thinking. "It did not make sense to me to start attacking alone. This was not a one-man war. I knew that there were no soldiers anywhere I could see, so I guess I started for the rear." The doughboys who found themselves isolated on a chaotic battlefield had to determine what they would do next. Some, like Sweningsen, straggled toward the rear; others, as Private Ray Johnson recalled, "wandered helplessly about or attached themselves to other advancing units." The later course was chosen by Private Vernon Nichols and two of his other lost comrades from the 91st Division. For three days, this leaderless band crisscrossed their area of the front, temporarily attaching themselves to the American units they encountered and fighting and resting as they saw fit. The key difference between Sweningsen's actions and those of Nichols was that Nichols was still bound to his two comrades and thus retained some semblance of their small-unit norms of behavior while Sweningsen was truly isolated from both comrades and the collective rules that bonded them together.[49]

In addition to the confusion and isolation of combat, the doughboys also had to cope with the hardship and privations of life at the front. Ground combat is a tale of exertion. It constantly demands a taxing degree of physical and mental effort from its acolytes. A month after the Armistice, Lieutenant William Haselton summed up his life as "wet feet and sniffles, trudging thought the snow and slush and mud for hours." Marine Frank Merrill offered a similar lament: "No training could have prepared me for the exposure to bad weather and hunger from slim rations and missed meals. This was part of a dog's life." War is never just about fighting the enemy. In fact, actually engaging the enemy and being under fire occupied only a fraction of the doughboys' time, even when they were "in combat." The most persistent and unrelenting "foes" that the soldiers faced during active operations were the weather, lack of sleep, shortages of rations, lice, and other environmental factors that steadily wore down their strength and will. Combat for the doughboy was about exhaustion, privation, and, occasionally, the Germans.[50]

For the majority of combat doughboys, their time at the front was spent living in the open. As shelter and the ability to stay warm and dry at the front usually depended upon what they could improvise and the meager items the soldiers could carry, the weather played an outsized role in their daily lives. Slight changes in precipitation and temperature determined if the troops were miserable or contented. Although the AEF was fortunate to fight its early battles in the spring and summer of 1918 in relatively temperate conditions, by the fall the weather offered the doughboys much more reason for misery than for contentment.

The doughboys, especially those fighting in the Meuse Argonne, frequently complained about the weather in France. Prewar tourist publications touting "Sunny France" provided an ample source for the doughboys' sarcasm. An artilleryman joked to his would-be girlfriend on November 1, 1918, "We are having a fine lot of weather now, it rains about 8 days out of a week." Most doughboys believed that the rain was no laughing matter for it brought with it increased sickness, trench foot, and, most importantly, major and constant discomfort. Private Joe Romedahl groused, "The hardest thing to put up with at the last was the cold, wet, rainy weather." The troops in his unit fought for days wearing wet uniforms. Wearing clammy wool uniforms grown heavier by their inability to shed water undermined the soldiers' spirits. As an infantry battalion commander reported in the Meuse Argonne, a "cold misty rain had been continually falling for practically 72 hours and the rain more than anything else seemed to lower the morale of the men." Anyone who has ever been cold and wet for an extended period of time can sympathize with these soldiers' plight. An infantryman in the 35th Division complained to his mother on October 2, 1918, that his unit only seemed to march, camp, and fight in the rain. Worse still, he was miserable because the brief periods of clear weather were "not long enuf to dry out our tents, clothes and blankets." Under these conditions, the doughboys' despondency arose from the fact that getting warm and dry seemed a remote possibility.[51]

In the Meuse Argonne, the rain was accompanied by a drop in temperatures that placed additional strains on the soldiers. Although the Americans' wool uniforms were intended to retain their warming properties even when wet, they became so saturated and dirty from living in foxholes that the cold of October and November easily penetrated to the men's skins. As noted previously, the troops themselves added to their misery by discarding the clothing that would have eased their suffering. Just before he was killed in action on October 5, 1918, Paul Anderson informed his family that when his unit attacked, the soldiers left behind their blankets and other cold weather items and moved forward with only their combat gear, overcoats, and basic toiletries. He lamented, "I sure do miss my things these last few nights. It has been cold as the devil [at] night and to save my life I can't make a knee-length overcoat cover me up from head to toe." As lighting fires for warmth would have drawn enemy artillery fire, the men flailed their arms, stamped their feet, and huddled together as best they could to eke out what precious little heat they could muster. Under these conditions, one Marine found each new morning to be particularly trying. After spending the night in a water-filled foxhole in the Argonne, he observed,

> The most painful part of such a situation is the necessity of getting up to face another day. Even the balmy breeze of a June morning can feel cold then, whereas the steady knife-edge wind of November is pure agony. It drives inside to meet the chills deep in your bones and makes you shake. Your lower jaw trembles like a loose-hinged gate until you can lash it fast with your helmet strap, pulling your face together to stop the chatter of your teeth.

He discovered that his only remedy for these chills was deeply inhaling a hastily rolled cigarette.[52]

As previously noted in chapter 5, the soldiers' misery was further compounded by shortages of clean water and food. In early October 1918, Paul Andrews claimed that all he had to eat for three days was a "can of corn beef, a can of salmon, and a small can of hard tac." Although he had the ingredients, he could not make a fire to brew his coffee. For him, the worst part was that "the only water we had to drink was what we got out of a dirty river and it was filled with gas but we had to drink it." This meant that his total caloric intake for the three days combined was only 1,670–1,700 calories. The doughboys, especially those fighting at Soissons and in the Meuse Argonne, frequently complained of fighting on short rations. For example, only three days before the Armistice, Gilbert Max recorded in his diary that he had "nothing to eat for 3 days except bully beef and hard tack." Like many other doughboys, Max was surviving on roughly 2,000–2,500 calories per day. As a point of comparison, if a soldier in World War II ate all three of his daily K Ration meals, he consumed 2,830–3,000 calories per day. Even then, army nutritionists argued that the K Rations were still too low in calories. The current U.S. Army estimates that the average soldier in active combat requires 4,000–4,600 calories per day, while the U.S. Department of Agriculture recommends that a male aged twenty-one to twenty-five engaged in moderate to active labor should consume 2,800–3,000 calories a day. Although most Americans today are taller and heavier than those of the World War I era, it is fair to argue that large numbers of doughboys were not consuming enough calories or eating the proper balance of proteins, carbohydrates, and fats to sustain their strength, endurance, and health in battle. The troops did the best that they could under the circumstances. After being on short rations for six days of fighting in the Argonne, an infantry company was overjoyed at capturing a German cabbage patch. One of its members noted, "There was a mad rush for eats and every one of us ate the Hun cabbage as though we had captured Hindenburg or was indulging in beef-stake." But windfalls like this were few and far between and most doughboys had little option other than tightening their belts and making do with the scanty rations they received or straggling from the lines to beg, borrow, or steal food.[53]

The unavoidable byproduct of the rain and the digging and the movement of thousands of troops was mud. Simply put, mud compounded the misery of every one of the soldiers' other miseries. It further weighed down already heavy uniforms and equipment; it clung to boots, dogging each footfall, and hindered efforts to dry out shoes; it clogged equipment, and mud made it harder for units to do routine things such as run supply operations. The mess undermined the Americans' combat capabilities and operations. After being in the line for only six days, a battalion commander reported that "the men had difficulty keeping mud from the bores of their rifles" and none of the unit's automatic rifles was functioning. The muddy conditions in the Meuse Argonne made it difficult to move wagons and trucks cross-country. As this tended to keep wheeled transportation bound to the area's limited road network, it hamstrung the AEF's logistics operations. This was one of the reasons that the troops on the line often went short of food and other Maslovian necessities.

Under combat conditions it was almost impossible for the doughboys to rid themselves of mud or to keep clean. As their tour in the lines wore on, cleanliness often fell further and further down in the soldier's vital "to do" list. When faced with the realities of the front, one officer informed his family,

"To wash was not so important." Combat reduced his dressing and cleaning up to merely "putting on my shoes and inhaling a cigarette." Being clean was not only important for sanitary and health reasons; it also had a psychological effect on the soldiers. The inability to have clean clothing reinforced the soldiers' lack of control over their environment and fueled fatalism. As one dirty doughboy expressed to his family in the midst of the Argonne fighting, "The way I feel now I don't ever think I will get or feel clean again, but what the hell is the use."[54]

With no facilities for washing themselves or their clothing, the doughboys improvised as best as they could. But even these improvisations seldom added much to their cleanliness. Francis Byrne wrote his father that during a pause in the fighting in the Argonne,

> We had a little over half an hour to wait and several of us decided to try and wash some of the mud and grime which had been caked on us for the last week and while I was bending over the bank of the canal, I slipped and in I went, heels over head with every stitch of my clothes on and a howling November gale blowing. There was a great yell and laugh sent up by the whole company when I hit the water and you can imagine the miserable way I looked when they pulled me out. There was no way of drying off and nothing left [for] me to do but run around in a circle to keep from freezing.

A Marine recalled that during his time at the front, twenty men tried their best to get clean using one gallon of water brought up in an old molasses bucket. The water was so nasty by the time that it was his turn to wash that he decided that it was pointless to try. At the first opportunity he hiked back to a spring a mile behind the lines for his much needed wash. Given these facts, it was little wonder that an officer from the 1st Army's inspector general's office discovered that most of the doughboys that he encountered at the front were dirty and grubby. When questioned, a man from the 168th Infantry stated that he was wearing no underwear because "he threw it away three or four weeks before as it was filthy" and that thirty or forty other members of his company were in the same condition.[55]

The doughboys' wet, cold, hungry, and unsanitary life led to dramatic spikes in illnesses. This was borne out in the monthly reports submitted by division surgeons and sanitary officers. In October 1918, the 26th Division's sanitary officer reported that it was so difficult to get fresh water to the front-line troops that many soldiers were seeking water from shell holes, puddles,

Photo 23: Two doughboys getting shaves from their buddies in a bombed-out French building in 1918. Getting cleaned up was one of the first steps in restoring mind and body for most doughboys after coming out of the line. Source: author's collection.

and other unsafe sources. As a result, he noted that "diarrhea will prevail in some measure until battle conditions are so much relieved as to allow treated water to near the front lines." To make matters worse, heavy German shelling prevented field kitchens from operating close to their units in combat, thus reducing the soldiers to one meal a day. The commander of the 1st Battalion, 325th Infantry, stated that by October 15, 1918, "The men were cold and hungry, not having had anything to eat but a small amount of hard-tack and corned beef since Oct. 9 . . . They were all suffering from diarrhea," because "the only water obtainable was from a ditch." The situation was the same in the division as a whole. During the month of October the 82nd Division's chief surgeon reported that an average of seven hundred soldiers per day were being hospitalized due to influenza, diarrhea, or exhaustion.[56]

The lack of cleanliness and the wet and cold weather led to one of the war's signature ailments: trench foot. Trench foot developed when the soldier's feet were wet and cold over a prolonged period of time. As a result, the feet swelled and interfered with the circulation of blood to the area, leading to blisters, open wounds, and necrosis of the feet and toes. In advanced cases, gangrene set in, which often led to amputations. The spike in trench foot cases during the Argonne campaign led the 1st Army inspector general to warn the AEF GHQ that it "was liable to become a menace unless preventative steps are taken at once." After inspecting soldiers from a number of divisions, he reported, "Some of these men have not had a change of socks during a tour of 18 days at the front and many have not removed their shoes or rubbed their feet more frequently than once in from three to five days." A private in the veteran 42nd Division told the inspector that he had not taken off his boots and changed his socks in two weeks. Many of the soldiers that the inspector queried stated that they had not received whale oil and foot powder before going into action. Most also claimed that "they had received no special instruction as to care of their feet" during their time in the service. As the AEF's infantrymen fought the war on their feet, even mild trench foot made life a trial, and in more serious cases it rendered the soldier unfit for duty.[57]

If this was not bad enough, the doughboys' inability to keep clean quickly led to one of the other great banes of the troops' existence: infestations of lice. Lice, or "cooties" as the soldiers sometimes called them, grew fruitful and multiplied as they sucked blood from the doughboys' unwashed bodies and found perfect nurseries for their eggs in the rough seams of the soldiers' dirty uniforms. Like many other frontline doughboys, Thurmond Baccus claimed that he was lice-ridden for most of his time at the front. Of course it did not help that he had no change of clothing from September 25 to December 3, 1918. Another joked to his sister that he and his comrades were so covered with lice that "every night we took off our shirt we would have to nail them on the floor or the shirt would walk away." The constant and inescapable itching caused by the pest drove the troops to distraction. A soldier in the 77th Division complained to his folks,

I don't mind being under shell fire, or in the front line, but these damn cooties are driving me nutty. I itch and scratch from head to foot, and every day I "police" my shirt and kill them by the hundreds but they still bite. I had to throw my undershirt away it was so bad, but they were right back again on my other shirt and if I don't get rid of them soon your youngest is going to lose his good nature and get real mad. This is a hell of a life we are living anyway at its best, but with those pests added to it, gee whiz but they are fierce.

The worst part of the infestation for him was that "they wake you up in the night and keep you busy all day, it is just scratch, scratch, scratch until you wish you could jump out of your skin."[58]

As the soldiers attested, catching lice was easy; the difficult part was getting rid of them. The army did issue small tins of insecticide and the soldiers could purchase louse powder in some of the French shops they frequented. Unfortunately, these remedies seldom killed all of the men's lice and their eggs, or if they did, the men were soon reinfested as the powder wore away in the grimy conditions of the front. Like the Civil War soldiers who proceeded them, the doughboys whiled away some of their time "reading" their shirt for lice. During the "reading," the lice and their eggs were killed by running one's thumbs or a candle flame up the seams of the uniform to crush or fry the vermin's' bodies. These efforts were largely fruitless, as one soldier complained, "No more than you kill off a few you find, you find it is only a short time after when a new flock of eggs seem to hatch out and you have dozens more over you." Thurmond Baccus and his buddies tried to deal with lice by improvising a boiler from an old bacon can and washing their shirts, pants and underclothing in boiling water. But, like insecticide and "reading" the uniforms, the result was short-lived. One soldier grew so irritated by his cooties that he took the drastic action of dousing the seams of his clothing and his skin with kerosene in hopes of killing his unwelcome guests. Although he succeeded in irritating his skin to the point that it "burned like fire," the lice survived the ordeal. Some soldiers tried to make the best of the situation. One first sergeant noted that during a lull in the Argonne fighting, "We had a little board and raced cooties, making little bets on the side." He confessed, "I had some pretty fast ones and won a few francs on them. The only trouble was I hated to kill them after winning for me." The only real solution was to send the soldiers and their uniforms through a detailed delousing session when they were pulled from the line. But even this process only offered a temporary solution, as the troops were again lice-ridden soon after returning to the front.[59]

To top off all of the privations of the doughboys in combat was a lack of sleep. In premodern wars soldiers generally fought campaigns of marching culminating in one to three days of battle. This rhythm gave soldiers periods of rest and refit during the campaign. Between 1864 and 1918 battles had given way to combat. The size and resiliency of modern armies meant that a few days of battle no longer settled armed struggles. Combat was an all-

Photo 24. Doughboys "reading their shirts" to kill "cooties" after coming out of the line. Source: author's collection.

encompassing environment where armies fought long, wearing campaigns and soldiers were in close contact with the enemy for weeks on end. One of the first things to be affected by the shift from battle to combat was the soldiers' ability to rest and sleep. The unrelenting pace of operations and the nearness of the enemy required soldiers to always be on guard or on the move. Because of this, the troops survived on the snatches of sleep that they could muster during lulls in the fighting. One soldier noted that "for five long weeks" in the Meuse Argonne "rarely did I even get a whole nights rest." Corporal Francis J. Byrne wrote his father that during the 1st Division's advance toward Sedan in November 1918 his unit "had been in the line for five or six days and for four days and three nights previously none of us had had a wink of sleep."

The soldiers adapted as best as they could to the situation. Left with no other option, the doughboys followed the old soldier maxim that advises: Why stand when you can sit? Why sit when you can lay? Why wake when you can sleep? The troops made due by snatching what sleep they could. An infantryman confessed in a letter to a family friend, "We are so tired that at every opportunity we would fall down. I'll tell you a fellow is tired when he can sleep with it raining like mad, no blankets or protection and machine gun bullets cutting the grass and bushes all around." After some time in the line, a 35th Division infantryman quipped, "I am getting so I can sleep in most any posture of the body and upon most any kind of surface. Have not tried standing up yet but I expect that will come with practice." This joking masked a serious problem. After the 3rd Division spent twenty days fighting and marching, Major General Beaumont Buck recorded in his diary on October 15, 1918, that "men fall asleep while creeping forward- officers have dropped in their tracks from exhaustion." Sleep deprivation not only impaired the judgment of officers and soldiers, but it also slowly wore away their ability to cope with the physical and mental stresses of war.[60]

There were limits to what even the best-trained and disciplined doughboys could endure. The breaking point of American units varied considerably from unit to unit. This point was unpredictable, as it was governed by the level of training and the quality of leadership within the units and uncontrollable variables such as the intensity of the enemy's resistance and the terrain and weather. Some units, such as the 35th and 79th Divisions, reached the limits of their endurance after relatively brief periods of fighting in the

Meuse Argonne. Others, such as the 1st, 2nd, 3rd, 42nd, and 82nd Divisions, were able to stay at the front longer and take harder knocks. But even these veteran organizations had their thresholds of pain and suffering. The 3rd Division and its 38th Infantry Regiment had won the nickname "Rock of the Marne" for their stalwart defense of Château Thierry in July 1918. They had the reputation for being crack units in the AEF. Yet, after a week of bloody assaults near Cunel, the 3rd Division inspector general reported on October 15, "Although I am inexperienced in judging men under battle conditions, I wish to state that those officers and men whom I saw of the 38th Infantry appeared to me, to use a slang term, 'all in.'" Even "Pershing's Pets," the storied 1st Division, was not immune from exhaustion. During its first two weeks in the line in the Argonne in October 1918, the unit suffered over nine thousand casualties prompting the division inspector general to note, "The morale of the unit is not nearly as high as it formerly was. This is shown by the general demeanor of the men and the lack of snap and spirit which formerly prevailed in this unit."[61]

The amount of time that a combat unit spent in battle before being relieved was governed by the situation at the front, its number of casualties, and the overall condition of its troops. The AEF's huge divisions were intended to have staying power in battle, but few in the AEF envisioned the degree of losses that the units would suffer in its campaigns. Corps and division commanders generally determined when it was time for a unit to be relived from the line and sent to the rear for rest and refit. The soldiers coming out of combat often presented a frightful appearance. One infantry company commander stated of his unit's time in the Argonne, "The inclement weather and lack of food brought an added disgust. Save a few Irish dispositions there was not a cheerful aspect during those twelve days [at the front]." As they "trailed back out of the battle area into a land of life and rest," the company was "represented by 53 lousy worn out human beings." Charles MacArthur's impression of his battery's move to the rear was equally grim: "Everybody was sick, everybody was filthy, everybody was hungry and underweight. Sunken eyes peered out of deep tangled whiskers, and everybody was fidgety and cross. You could get a fight out of anyone with a dirty look."[62]

What these troops needed was to be taken away from the sound of the gun for physical and mental recuperation. For the doughboys, rest meant sleep in some degree of comfortable shelter, baths and clean clothes, nutritious and plentiful food, time to acclimate their replacements to the unit's norms, and a period to mourn their losses. If the war situation allowed, the AEF was able to meet some of these requirements. After their harrowing experiences of the Soissons drive, the men of the 26th Division were pulled out of the line for a week to rest and refit. For Horatio Rogers, this time was bittersweet:

> We stripped to the skin, bathed vigorously, threw away all of our old clothes, and drew a complete new outfit. It was a relief to be free from the burning itch of lice, even for a few days. Our duties for this week in Mèry were light. A formation morning and evening, grooming horses, leading to water, that was all. The rest was eating, sleeping, and swimming in the Marne. An attempt was made to revive discipline which at the front had grown very sketchy. We were reminded that officers were to be saluted and certain other formalities observed. As for food, Joe Wilmer and the cooks outdid themselves. There was milk and sugar in the coffee and seconds at every meal. We supplemented our rations with eggs, wine, and butter from the shops in the town.

The regimental band played every night as the men "loafed around on the grass and smoked." Rogers's unit was even entertained by "the Sweetheart of the AEF": the Broadway actress and singer Elsie Janis. Despite all of the frivolity, the troops could still not shake off the effects of their recent time in combat. As Rogers recalled, "I don't remember seeing any enthusiasm among the men who went through it, or feeling any myself. We all were indifferent to everything except food and sleep." After having a photo of himself taken in town and sending it home, he was shocked to find that its arrival greatly scared his family because he "looked like someone in the last stages of consumption."[63]

As Rogers noted, getting the troops deloused was a priority when coming off the line. Although the AEF stood up mobile bath and laundry units, much of this work was done in improvised facilities that the division sanitation officers established behind the lines. After six weeks without a bath or change of clothes, Fred Takes admitted that he and his comrades "were as lousy as a Coo coo." His company was deloused in a captured German bathhouse and they received all new uniforms except for their overseas caps and overcoats. When there was no new clothing on hand for an exchange, the AEF used mobile steam sterilizers to wash and delouse the men's clothing. This process sometimes did not turn out as intended. As one soldier explained to his father,

This morning we went to a sawmill and had our cooties killed. That is a queer place to slaughter "seam-squirrels" isn't it? But if you could have seen the mill yourself, you would probably have fun of the opinion that it might serve the purpose of a delousing machine as anything else; it's a joke of a mill . . . we hiked over to the mill, carrying all of our clothing and equipment and striped outside, and you may take my word for it the air felt pretty chilly . . . They had a big box in which we put our clothing and blankets and left them in for forty-five minutes while live steam was turned on them. One of the men put in his leather vest and when it came out you would have died laughing to look at it. It had shrunk to about one forth of its original size and the lining which did not shrink was all puffed out around the edges. It had the appearance of a piece of burned liver.

This was far from a unique experience. Another private complained that he was unhappy with the delousing, for his uniforms tended to shrink during the process. Despite these annoyances most doughboys would have agreed with Fred Takes's observation: "We sure did enjoy that bath and change of clothes."[64]

Unfortunately, the doughboys' definitions of "rest" did not always match the AEF GHQ's definition of "rest." If the pace of operations was hectic or rest facilities and delousing stations were unavailable, the soldier's "rest" period could be far from restful. After a week in the lines in the Argonne fighting, the 325th Infantry's machine gun company was pulled out of combat for a mere twenty-four-hour period of rest. After occupying their rest stop in the remnants of the town of Fleville, one of the soldiers expressed his view that whoever sent them there "ought to be court-martiled." The accommodations in the ruined town were poor; the location was still within the sound of the battle; and the chance of real rest was scant. One of the unit's officers complained to the regimental commander that the soldiers were "glad to get back up front," as "there was just as much rest up there" as there had been in Fleville.[65]

The soldiers found it equally irksome when their periods of rest were punctuated by training and work details. As the AEF entered combat in the summer and fall of 1918, the GHQ issued a steady stream of "Notes on Recent Operations" and other reports and directions intended to help the army profit from its hard-won experiences. This often meant that units coming out of the line were presented with new weapons, drills, or procedures that the AEF GHQ expected them to master before returning to battle. Worn out from their recent endeavors, made somewhat cocky by their veteran status, and naturally hesitant to heed the advice of a distant and safe authority, the doughboys often resented these training demands and the officers who tried to impose them. They were even more irritated if their rest periods were consumed by cleaning up the mangy towns in which they were billeted or if they were set to labor at any of the myriad of tasks not actually involving fighting that the AEF needed to keep running. The last thing that prevented the rest periods from being restful was that it was always in the back of the soldiers' minds that they would soon return to battle. For most of the AEF's combat units, from the St. Mihiel offensive onward, true rest did not occur until after the Armistice.[66]

21

"The Cavalry, the Artillery, the Lousy Engineers"

The Artillerymen, Tankers, Combat Engineers, and Signalmen in Battle

One of the favorite marching songs of the AEF's infantrymen proclaimed the superiority and toughness of their arm of service over all of the other branches of the army. They tended to sing it with the greatest gusto when passing noninfantry units:

> The infantry, the infantry with dirt behind their ears,
> They can whip their weight in wildcats and drink their weight in beer,
> The cavalry, the artillery, the lousy engineers,
> They can't lick the infantry in a hundred thousand years.

If the AEF's casualty figures were any indication, the infantrymen earned the right to be boastful. As previously noted, out of every thousand infantry officers in the AEF, eighty-eight would be killed in action or would die of their wounds. Nearly fifty-two out of every thousand enlisted infantrymen shared the same fate. This was the highest rate of casualties of any branch of the service. Although the infantry was also the largest arm in the AEF, its losses were still proportionally higher than the army's other branches. As a point of comparison, the artillery lost eight officers and six soldiers out of every thousand of their officers and enlisted men, while the engineers averaged ten officers and six soldiers killed out of a thousand of their officer and enlisted ranks. For the much smaller Tank Corps, the figures were sixteen officers and seven enlisted men killed out of every thousand tankers. Contrary to the doughboys' belief that American fliers shied away from combat and danger, the air service still lost thirty-one officers (but only .6 enlisted men) per thousand air corps officers during the war. When not busy whipping their weight in wildcats, the infantry also garnered most of the war's top medals. Of the 122 Medals of Honor awarded in the conflict, ninety went to army or Marine riflemen. Infantrymen were also awarded over 75 percent of the AEF's Distinguished Service Crosses.[1]

The last chapter discussed the general combat experiences of all of the AEF's soldiers, but it was heavily weighted toward the infantryman's life in battle. Despite the losses and hardships that were part and parcel of the infantrymen's experiences, they could not accomplish their missions without the support of the other combat branches of the AEF. All of the AEF's combat troops faced fear, death, hardships, and privations. However, the roles, missions, and equipment of the artillery, Tank Corps, engineers, and field signal units presented them with unique challenges that made the lives of their soldiers in combat differ from those of the infantry.

Infantrymen rightfully complained about the physical exertions they endured, but the life of an artilleryman also contained its share of hard manual labor. Much of the artilleryman's unremitting toil was dedicated to the care and feeding of his unit's draft animals. When it came to horses and mules, the problem for the artillerymen was one of scale. At full strength, an infantry regiment contained sixty-five horses and 325 mules while a field artillery regiment had 1,163 horses and 162 mules. For the infantry, this equaled one draft animal for roughly every ten soldiers in the regiment, while a light field artillery regiment (with 75mm guns) had one horse or mule for every 1.2 men. Furthermore, the infantrymen could still perform their missions if their units grew short of draft animals, but this was not the case for the artillery. Having this many animals meant that the care and feeding of horses and mules occupied much of the artillerymen's lives in and out of battle. For the most part, the infantryman looked after himself, his personal equipment, and his small arms. The artillerymen were stuck in a steady cycle of hauling forage and water, grooming the animals, mucking out the horse line, maintaining the tack, saddles, guns, and caissons, and then taking care of himself, his personal equipment, and small arms. By regulation, the needs of the draft animals came before those of the soldiers. After artillery units were pulled from the line for rest and refit, the care of their animals still remained a top priority for the troops. When one doughboy asked why the animals took precedence over the soldiers, he was told that horses could not take care of themselves, and "if a man was lost another could take his place, but horses were scarce." The AEF's heavy artillery regiments replaced draft horses with tractors, but mechanization and the finicky nature of the war's motor vehicles brought their own headaches. For one, the AEF was perennially short of tractors and trucks and the replacement parts to keep them running. In the Argonne, the 55th and the 158th Artillery Brigade reported that they only had twenty-four and twenty-eight trucks respectively for hauling shells (with many of these broken down), when each should have had 105 trucks on hand.[2]

Merely moving artillery around the front often presented difficulties. Under the best conditions, it required a lot of effort for the draft animals to pull the guns, caissons, and crews. Unfortunately, wartime conditions were generally far from optimal. It was difficult to maneuver a team of six horses with a caisson and cannon through the narrow roads, rubble, and shell-torn ground that tended to characterize the terrain of the front. When the horse team grew so weak that it could not move the guns, human muscle power had to take over. The crews of a four-gun battery from the 101st Field Artillery discovered this the hard way after they tried to maneuver their teams off a crowded road at night. As soon as they left the road, the cannons sank up to their hubs in mud. The horses strained to pull the guns out of the muck but soon lost their forward momentum and "gave up on pulling on what became an immovable load." By now the guns were mired up to their breechblocks. At first a crowd of cannoneers took hold of the wheels and tried to get them started while the drivers whipped their horses forward, but it was soon apparent that nothing could be accomplished in that way. The mud was too deep for the men to get a foothold and, as soon as the guns settled lower, the frightened horses refused to bruise their necks against the unyielding collars. Dawn was fast approaching and with it came the fear that the Germans would soon find the helpless section trapped in the open. Desperation, diggings, and seven extra teams of horses managed to free one of the guns, but the remaining three remained hopelessly stuck. After freeing all of the remaining horses from the morass, the artillerymen camouflaged the mired cannons and made a hasty retreat to their new firing position. Fortunately, the Germans did not spot the pinned guns and after another night of digging, pushing, and hauling, they too were freed and put into their proper place. Both crews and horses, however, were much worse for the wear. On another occasion the men in the same battery spent a night in the Argonne engaged in the near-Sisyphean task of manhandling four of their guns up to the top of a hill whose grade was too steep for the horse teams to navigate.[3]

Just like the doughboys, the strength and health of the horses and mules waned over the course of the campaign. It was not unusual for a six-horse team to shrink to a four-horse team due to wounds and sickness. This attrition, of course, put more strain on the remaining horses and hastened their decline. Private Earl Tesca believed, "It seemed that a horse would wear out, from work and lack of sufficient rest and food, quicker than a man and take much longer to recover." He noted, "Often roads were muddy with mireholes that necessitated doubling up weakened teams to get through them. Sometimes horses would go down from fatigue and not be able to get up again. Whenever we got back from a drive, quite a few horses had to be replaced." A soldier in the 306th Field Artillery recalled that shortly before the Armistice, the surviving horses in his battery "looked like scarecrows," and added, "If the war would have gone on longer, we would have been pulling those 75's by hand."[4]

Given their close interaction, it is not surprising that the artillerymen developed a "love–hate" relationship with their horses and mules. The animals could be quite cantankerous at times, causing no end of problems for their harried teamsters. When cursing and pulling on reins failed to get their unwilling beasts to move, tired and exasperated drivers made free use of their whips to prod them forward. This sometimes led to rebukes of the guilty teamsters by their officers. In one case the commander of the 26th Division, Major General Clarence Edwards, chastised an artillery driver for hitting a reluctant horse, shouting, "I would rather have you hit this long nose of mine, than hit that horse over the head." Drivers found that performing other seemingly easy tasks with their animals was equally trying. Just like the soldiers, horses wore gasmasks at the front. As horses do not breath through their mouths, and will still work if blind, their masks were simply large, chemically treated flannel bags that fit only over their nostrils. Unfortunately, fitting the masks to a skittish horse in combat was far from an easy task. John O'Brien narrowly avoided a vicious kick from a horse that he tried to mask while under fire. After many failed attempts, he threw the mask down and yelled, "All right, you idiots, put them on yourselves!"[5]

Despite these irritations, many crewmembers became quite attached to their animals and mourned their loss. The Great War was hard on horses and mules. On August 1, 1918, a battery of the 102nd Field Artillery had sixteen of its horses killed in an enemy bombardment. Seeing their animals cruelly injured or wounded left lasting impressions on their riders. Horatio Rogers was deeply saddened when his horse Peanuts went lame during the St. Mihiel drive and was sent to the rear, even though Rogers claimed that the animal often "made life miserable for me." He was further distressed when another of the unit's horses was "standing with its head down between its knees and bloody froth coming out of his side at every breath" after being hit in the lung by a shell fragment. Despite all the death that surrounded him, another soldier remembered that "one of my most painful memories at the front was seeing a shell drop near two artillery horses." After the shell cut through one of the horse's abdomens, it walked around dragging its intestines until its feet became so entangled in the mess that it stumbled and fell. After the incident the man mused, "It isn't fair to take poor dumb animals and force them to work and die in the fighting."[6]

The war's artillery pieces were heavy and complex pieces of machinery that operated under the iron and unforgiving laws of physics. When gun tubes recoiled and heavy breechblocks swung in and out of operation, the combination of weight and impulsion created a deadly environment for the incautious or unlucky gunner. During a heavy bombardment in the Argonne, one such man failed to move his hand away from the gun after pulling the lanyard. As the gun recoiled back into battery, his hand was caught under the rollers and became stuck fast in the mechanism. One of the other members of the crew noted that they "had a devil of a time getting him out" because of the gun's elevation and the fact that it was "so hot that nobody could stand near it, let alone handle it." To free the man, his crew placed a wooden duckboard over the gun's muzzle and ten soldiers pulled down on the board to push the barrel far enough out of battery to remove the mangled hand.[7]

Serving in the artillery also came with other occupational hazards. Over time, cannon barrels tended to wear out due to continual firing. A badly worn barrel, faulty shell, or other mechanical breakdown could lead to the explosion of a gun. One such accident occurred when a cannon in the 101st Field Artillery exploded during firing, killing one of its crewmembers when the gun's flying seventy-pound breechblock smashed into his back. Furthermore, the firing of artillery produced a loud blast and a pocket of overpressure that deafened the artillerymen and constantly buffeted their other senses. As one cannoneer joked, "Deafness was a blessing in the field artillery. It came in ten minutes' fire and lasted a week—excepting in a few cases, when it was permanent."[8]

At certain times, being an artilleryman offered moments of great excitement. While in the trench lines or during defensive lulls in the fighting, artillery units had to be prepared to execute a "Normal Barrage" to support the infantry. This barrage was emergency artillery fire initiated by the infantry when they were under immediate threat. The connotation was that the fire would only be given when the doughboys were in extreme danger from an enemy raid or sudden attack. Each artillery battery was assigned a specific section of the line that they were required to cover to protect the infantry. After registering some of their guns to fire on predetermined coordinates in that area, an artilleryman from the battery constantly scanned that sector for distress rockets from the American infantry. At a moment's notice a call or a distress rocket from the infantry sent the gunners scurrying from their dugouts to fire round after round into the preset coordinates. To quicken their response, some artillery units even kept one man at each gun with a round in the breach ready to pull the lanyard at the first sign of trouble. "Later in the war I grew blasé to most of the familiar sights and sounds," a cannoneer admitted, "but the cry of 'Normal Barrage' never quite lost its pulse-quickening quality."[9]

Unless they were firing these emergency barrages or were being bombarded themselves, the excitement of the artillerymen with firing quickly gave way to the industrial monotony of the factory floor. Once the gun was sighted for the fire mission, it became a process of feeding the gun shells with occasional pauses to shift fires or to recheck the gun's sights. All firing began with the gun captain or battery commander's prescribed fire command, a specific incantation that informed the gunners of the range, angle of fire, and type of shell and fuse to be used for the bombardment. After the order to fire was given, the crew banged away at the target until they were ordered to cease fire. Bob Casey, an artilleryman in the 33rd Division, described the excitement and drama as his battery fired its first shots in the Meuse Argonne: "A dozen guns turned loose at once with a detonation that took one in the pit of the stomach. In thirty seconds hell was loose once more and tons of shell were screaming over the hill toward No Man's Land." But Casey admitted that after five minutes, "the firing settled down to a steady business like the operation of a boiler factory," and the crew's initial enthusiasm and excitement faded. The battery periodically increased the range of their firing to keep pace with the advancing infantry, with the monotony of firing broken only by orders to move to another position to start the process over again. This firing drill became rather routine. Day after day the artillerymen's lives consisted of hard work getting the guns into place, hard work in the weightlifter's ballet of muscling heavy shells to the guns, hard work getting the guns ready to move again, and waiting. It was business as usual, as long as the Germans were not retaliating.[10]

Given the importance of artillery in the war, both sides played a deadly cat-and-mouse game of locating and destroying their foe's cannons and ammunition dumps. The enemy's counterbattery fire was thus the artilleryman's greatest source of death and fear in combat. A cannoneer in the 26th Division noted that his unit's first experience with counterbattery fire came as a bolt from the blue and shattered the otherwise workaday firing of the battery. He recalled,

> There was a heavy explosion followed by cries of "Stretcher-bearer," and when I looked across I saw the first section gun pit enveloped in smoke. I joined several men who were running towards the place, and when I got there the sight made me sick to my stomach. A German 150-millimeter shell had exploded between the wheels of the gun, reducing it to junk and turning the gun pit into a shamble. Storer and Ben James lay on the ground a little way down the hill. The remains of the others were in the gun pit. Rigby was still alive and conscious, but died on the stretcher before he could be put in the ambulance at the foot of the hill. There was a wire camouflage net above the pit, and from its meshes hung bits of bloody flesh and rags. I took one look inside and turned away.

While observing German shells fall on a nearby battery, another artilleryman admitted that it was disconcerting being on the receiving end of artillery fire after his "entire experience with shells had hitherto been on the sending side." He and his comrades were sobered by the incident: "We did not speak of it but each of us knew what the other was thinking. We pictured ourselves in the same situation—fixed targets for the painstaking Boche—unable to move—or to return a shot." In these cases the artillerymen got a taste of the powerlessness felt by the infantry while they were being bombarded.

The fear of being found by the Germans and shelled drove the American gunners to be nocturnal animals. They moved and resupplied their guns as much as possible under the cloak of darkness and the iron press of time. As one gunner put it, "Stowage of shells had now become not so much a matter of weight verses brawn as a race with daylight." As the guns were still required to be ready to fire at any time of day, this constant nighttime activity deprived the artillerymen of sleep and slowly wore down their reserves of strength.[11]

Any empathy that an artilleryman felt for his comrades undergoing a bombardment did not extend to the enemy. The chance to eliminate the Germans' guns brought great satisfaction to the American cannoneers, who had their own unique form of bloodlust. It seemed to them to be somehow more sporting to target enemy artillery than to engage in other forms of firing. On September 29, 1918, one artillery battery from the 33rd Division located and destroyed three enemy batteries over the course of the day. One of the officers assigned to the American battery later gushed, "Sniping is a much better game than barrage firing anyway. You are shooting at someone who's shooting at you—which seems to be a fifty-fifty proposition—and you jolly well know whether you are ahead or behind in scoring." It must be kept in mind, however, that this form of bloodlust was something new on the battlefield. As indirect fire became the norm in the Great War, the gunners targeted enemy troops and guns that they could seldom see. The success that this battery boasted of in "sniping" the German artillery was relayed to them by forward or aerial observers. The artillerymen only saw the results of their work if they moved forward and passed the locations that they targeted. Even then, the artilleryman could never be sure if it was his gun that wrought the damage. This allowed the gunners to distance themselves somewhat from the killing act in a manner unknown to the rifleman or the tanker.[12]

Being in the artillery also brought other advantages. While artillerymen often reported being short on rations in combat like their infantry comrades, they were better positioned on the battlefield to ease their hunger. The artillery emplacements behind the lines were closer to the supply trains than was the infantry and were often set up astride major roads and supply routes. The artillerymen also had the space on their caissons to carry extra food when they came across ration dumps. Division inspector generals frequently denounced crews for adding extra weight in food and packs to caissons, but this proved ineffective in changing the cannoneers' habits.[13]

When the U.S. Army entered the war, it had seventeen Regular Army cavalry regiments and viewed cavalry as a major arm in battle. During the war, the army raised twenty-four new cavalry regiments. The intense firepower and the strength of the defenses on the Western Front, however, meant that the use of cavalry in combat was strictly circumscribed. Bowing to this reality, the army ultimately converted all of the National Guard and new Regular Army cavalry regiments to field artillery. In the end, the army sent only four cavalry regiments to France (the 2nd, 3rd, 6th, and 15th Cavalry). Although these units saw some combat at St. Mihiel and the Meuse Argonne, they spent most of their time serving as liaison elements between corps and acting as mounted MPs and straggler-control troops during the war. Their place as the mobile arm of war was being eroded by a new weapon: the tank.[14]

Being a tanker in the AEF brought its own unique challenges. Cut down to its essence, a tank is mobile, protected firepower. The idea was to provide a weapon that could cross shell-torn ground, crushing barbwire and other obstacles as it went, and destroy machine guns and other pockets of enemy resistance that would otherwise have held up the infantry attack. When the Americans obtained their first tanks from the French and the British, the weapon still had a number of bugs to work out. The primary tanks used by the AEF in combat were the French FT-17 in its light-tank battalions and the British MK V in its heavy-tank battalions. The MK V had an eight-man crew consisting of a commander, driver, and six gunners, with one or two of these gunners also serving as an onboard mechanic. Its "male" version was armed with two six-pound cannons and four machine guns while the "female" variant was armed with six machine guns. As the engine and transmission of the tank were in the crew compartment, the MK V tended to be a noisy, suffocating, and hot environment. The internal temperature of these tanks could easily rise to ninety or one hundred degrees. These factors, a British tank officer explained, rapidly wore out the crews:

> The scorching sun outside, and the terrific temperatures inside, made the Mark V tank almost unbearable after three hours of action. The ventilation was bad, the fumes of petrol and cordite soon impregnated the close atmosphere, drivers collapsed in their seats, gunners fainted at their guns; many vomited and grew delirious. Often the heat and fumes became so overpowering that the crew were forced to get out and take cover underneath.

Although the MK Vs were a formidable weapon, it was certainly no picnic to man one.[15]

The French FT-17 tank had a crew of two: a driver and a commander/gunner. It was equipped with a rotating turret, which mounted either a 37mm cannon or a Hotchkiss M1914 machine gun. The small size of the FT-17 made it faster and more maneuverable than the MK V. As the engine was separated from the crew compartment, the FT-17 was also somewhat more comfortable to crew. The light tank did have its drawbacks. The commander of a British MK V tank sat next to the driver and could easily pass on instructions for directing the tank. The remaining crewmen of the MK V could also focus on one task at a time: either driving, firing the guns, or maintaining the engine during operation. In the FT-17, however, the tank commander had to perform many tasks simultaneously. He stood or sat suspended on a swing set–like seat behind the driver with his head and shoulders sticking up inside the turret. As the inside noise usually hindered oral communications, the commander communicated with the driver by a standard set of taps and kicks to the driver's shoulders and head. While directing the driver, the commander also had to locate targets, manhandle the turret and gun to bear on the enemy, fire, and reload without any assistance. More Americans served in combat with the FT-17 than any other tank of the war.[16]

Both tanks suffered from limited visibility for the crew. Once the tank's hatches were closed for battle, the crew's field of vision was severely restricted, and they were only able to get fleeting glimpses of the terrain and enemy as they moved forward using the tanks' small armored vision ports. The crew's relative blindness was exacerbated when they donned their gasmasks. Of the thirty-four tanks of the 301st Tank Battalion that supported an attack by the 27th Division on September 28, 1918, nine of them became stuck in trenches, shell holes, or sunken roads. One of the battalion's officers claimed that these losses were caused by the "inability of the driver to see and could have been avoided with proper vision." To further complicate the matter, the Germans had learned of the tanks' vulnerability and tried to fire on the vision slits to disorient or blind the Allied tank crewmen.[17]

As the Allies were still working out the kinks in the designs of the tanks, it is no surprise that the vehicles required much maintenance to keep the temperamental beasts working. The 301st Tank Battalion lost 15 percent of its tanks to mechanical breakdown before the unit even reached the front in late September 1918. One five-tank platoon alone lost a tank to an engine problem and another to a broken track. The movement from the muscle age to the machine age also brought with it a vastly increased logistical burden. While men and horses can stumble through a campaign on short rations, a tank without gas simply stops, and no amount of spurring, cursing, or inspirational leadership will change that dynamic. At the front, the refueling itself was done manually with the crew pouring gas into the tank using three- to five-gallon cans. Gasoline proved to be bulky and dangerous to move forward for refueling the tanks in battle. Going into the attack on St. Mihiel, an officer in the 345th Tank Battalion had the bright idea of extending the cruising range of the unit's tanks by sending them into battle with between twenty and sixty gallons of gasoline strapped to the outside of the vehicles in cans. Soon after going into action, enemy fire ignited the gas cans and resulted in several vehicles trailing sheets of flame as they advanced. Fortunately, no one was injured by the experiment, but during both the St. Mihiel and the Argonne offensives, American tanks often ground to a halt due to a lack of fuel. If that was not enough, just moving the tanks to the front could be a difficult operation. An officer in the 326th Tank Battalion recalled that rail loading his tanks in preparation for the St. Mihiel attack turned into an all-night affair. Loading the flatcars was done under a driving rainstorm and the ramps became so slippery that the tanks kept sliding off, often damaging the ramps in the process.[18]

As noted earlier, the first tanks were also prone to becoming "ditched" in trenches or large shell holes or hung up on stumps. As Lieutenant John Castles attempted to move his FT-17 Renault tank across a German trench during the St. Mihiel drive, he found, "The heavy rains had undercut the walls and as the trench was not revetted, the weight of the tank just caved it in and over we went . . . as I stood there helplessly watching the tractors revolve, merely digging themselves in further." When the tank became ditched or mired in the mud, the crew had to dig out the machine by hand or hope that another tank could help to pull it out. This process could be maddeningly slow and backbreaking, especially if the crew was under fire. In some cases the ditching of a tank proved deadly even without enemy action. The 345th Tank Battalion lost one of its soldiers when the tank that he was driving slipped into a deep,

water-filled shell hole. The tank overturned, submerging the crew compartment in the water. The weight of the water prevented the driver from opening
the tank's heavy armored doors and the man drowned.[19]

Despite these problems, many of the AEF's tankers were excited by the
prospect of crewing the novel weapon. Upon his arrival in France in April
1918, Lieutenant Harvey Harris was assigned as a supply officer in the Provost
Marshal Department. He quickly grew bored of this mundane assignment
and sought a more exciting posting. After transferring to the Tank Corps,
Harris admitted in a letter home that with the new job he would "get what
I've always secretly wanted . . . In perfect safety to playfully swing a machine
gun back-and-forth at a row of advancing Boche, and see them go down like
trees in a big wind." Harris liked the idea that "two men in a tank have a fire
superiority over 100 infantry." He claimed to have joined the tanks because he
saw "the wonderful possibilities of the tank," because of a "desire for blood,"
and because of "the romance of such a service which is a combination of all
branches." To assuage any trepidation his parents might have at his new posting, or in a fit of self-delusion, he assured them, "We go out in an armored
car, along with and usually in the rear of the doughboys. So you can see how
safe it is. Further there is no dugout life but we live back in billets and fair
comfort." His last prediction proved to be somewhat true. During the fighting in the Argonne, the tankers of the 1st Brigade tended to pull back into
assembly areas behind the lines to conduct resupply and maintenance of their
tanks. This meant that the tankers were relatively better fed than their infantry counterparts. One tank officer believed that this was a bad practice for it
led to "a rear echelon complex" in the minds of the tankers that "makes them
soft and unwilling to move forward to assault positions in the very early hour
of the morning." It is doubtful that many of his men agreed with this assessment that they were living in the "comparative luxury and quiet" of the rear.[20]

Despite Harvey Harris's assurance or romantic misconceptions, life in a
tank in combat was far from the idyllic life that he initially envisioned. With
their large loads of gasoline and ammunition, the tanks could be death traps
when hit. After a nearby tank was smashed by a German shell, a doughboy
observed that the crew had no chance to escape: "The dead driver, burnt
to a crisp, sat bolt upright and rigid, his mouth open, and his white teeth
gleaming from the blackened face in a terrible grin, his hands still firmly
grasping [the controls]." Harris himself witnessed what happened when a

German 77mm shell penetrated the turret of a tank and ignited the vehicle's ammunition. The only things that were left of its commander were pieces of flesh and the metal identification tag that the man had worn on his wrist. Losses could be high in both men and machines. In two days of fighting to break the Hindenburg Line, the 301st Tank Battalion lost a third of its men (112 soldiers). Of the thirty-four tanks involved in the action, the battalion lost sixteen destroyed by enemy fire and two more destroyed in an unmarked British minefield. Between September 26 and October 4, 1918, the 304th Tank Brigade lost 53 percent of its officers and 25 percent of its soldiers.[21]

Given the crew's restricted visibility and the difficulty that tank officers had with passing orders to their other tanks, sometimes the tank commanders were forced to exit their vehicles to confer with the infantry, direct their units, or guide their drivers around obstacles. George Patton was seriously wounded in the Meuse Argonne while on such a mission. During the war, the American tanks were committed to supporting the infantry. One of the greatest challenges that the tankers faced was a general lack of understanding in the infantry and the American Army as a whole about how to best utilize tanks. The tankers and infantry seldom trained together and had no real conception about how the other branch operated or its strengths and weaknesses. After supporting the infantry of the 35th Division, one tank officer wrote, "It surprising what they asked us to do. Doughboys to Generals have sent us against places a battleship couldn't capture."[22]

When sent to assist the infantry in these situations, combat for the tankers became deadly and disorienting. At close range, enemy machine gun bullets caused small pieces of the interior armor of the tank to flake off, and bullet fragments penetrated the vehicle's vision ports and points where the armor plates came together. John Castle found this phenomenon to be particularly disconcerting, and this rare account of U.S. tankers in battle is worth quoting at length:

> The bullets beat a continuous tit-tat all over the tank as we got to close range, and the hot lead began seeping through, thousands of small globes of fire. Slowly we pull down the center of the draw, I vainly searching through my sights for the guns. They were certainly well hidden, but finally I spotted one and let them have it. When about 50 yards down the draw at least 15 guns must have opened up on [my] tank, and the noise of the bullets, a good many of them explosive ones, rattled off the tank, was

indescribable. One gun couldn't have been more than thirty yards away, for its hail against the turret slit was terrific in its force and the red hot lead poured through almost in a stream, but I couldn't find it. The seepage now became terrible and as neither one of us had [antisplinter] masks it was a wonder we weren't blinded. Our hands and clothes were burned all over, and Donald had his tin hat so tilted to protect his eyes that he could hardly see, while I kept mine glued to the .37 site. The Boches were shooting at the slits and I wouldn't have put my eye to one of them for a cool million. Suddenly something hit me with a force of a steam hammer in the ribs . . . It was a little more than half of a bullet that had come through one of the slits on the right side of the driver, glanced up and walloped me in the right side in the ribs. I couldn't imagine what it was at first, for it felt as though someone had hit me with a baseball bat. I assured Call I wasn't killed and climbed back [into the turret] and back we went.

After knocking out two of the offending machine guns, Castle's luck ran out. In the shuttered confines of the tank, he had failed to see a German cannon waiting in ambush. As he recalled,

crash! bang! The lights flared up all around and then went out. I came to momentarily in a shell hole about 30 yards from the tank. The blood was pouring out of my nose and mouth and I could hardly breathe. The old tank . . . was about 30 yards away and I could dimly see about half the turret was gone. Even as I looked at her, crash! they hit her again and a big cloud of black smoke hung over her like a pall.

In one sense Castle was fortunate. When the tank was hit, his driver had sought cover in a nearby shell hole. When he realized that Castle had not followed him, he returned to the tank and pulled the wounded officer to safety. Although the combat life of a tanker was a far cry from that of the infantryman, it was far from being staid and safe.[23]

The life of the AEF's engineers in combat was also not a pleasant one. In addition to picks, shovels, and the other tools of the engineer's trade, they generally carried the same rifles and equipment as the infantry and faced very similar degrees of privation at the front. In fact, the army's "pioneer infantry" regiments were intended to serve the dual role of engineers and infantry in battle. During the course of the war, the army raised thirty-six pioneer infantry regiments, of which twenty-six made it to France before the Armistice. The majority did not arrive until August, September, and October 1918, and senior army commanders were often at a loss to know what to do with these units. Few pioneer infantry units ever fought as true combat units. As fourteen of the twenty-six regiments in France were manned with African Americans, senior commanders believed that they were only fit for road repair and the salvage of equipment left on the battlefield. In fairness, the troops in white pioneer infantry regiments also saw very little combat. As one officer observed, the pioneer infantryman was saddled with "everything that the infantry was too proud to do and the engineers too lazy to do."[24]

In addition to the pioneer infantry units assigned to the corps, each division had a regiment of engineers to perform light construction, fortification digging, bridge building, and obstacle clearance in support of the unit's infantry, artillery, and supply trains. In combat, the divisional engineers could be assigned to clear barbwire and other obstacles to open the way for an infantry assault, could follow the infantry and assist them in building defensive works on their final objective, or could open paths to allow for the forward movement of reinforcements and artillery. These tasks often subjected the engineers to the same dangers from shell and small arms fire as the infantry. At times, the engineers ran even greater risks. Prior to a large trench raid conducted by the 26th Division at Seicheprey on May 30, 1918, four squads of men from the 101st Engineers moved into No Man's Land with tools and Bangalore torpedoes to create gaps in the German wire for the raiding parties. At forty feet in length, the torpedoes were too long to maneuver through the twisting Allied trenches, so the squads had to move to the front by walking exposed over the top of the trench works. Once the first belt of wire was blown, the engineers led the infantry through the gaps and destroyed the second belt of wire with smaller explosives that they had carried in their haversacks. While four of the engineers were gassed during the dangerous operation, the party was fortunate to suffer no other casualties. The 2nd Engineers won the respect of the Marines for building defenses and fighting alongside them as infantry during the battle of Belleau Wood. Seeing the sappers in action prompted the Marine John Thomason to exclaim, "If I ever get a drink, a 2nd Engineer can have half of it!—Boy they dig trenches and mend roads all night, and they fight all day!" As the engineers lost nearly 27 percent of their soldiers during the battle, the Marines' admiration came at a cost.[25]

Few engineers experienced this level of excitement. Both division engineers and pioneer infantry regiments spent most of their time on the vital mission of repairing and maintaining the transportation routes to the front.

This included building or repairing bridges and roads damaged by shellfire, the elements, and German sabotage. This was particularly true during the Meuse Argonne campaign. Company E, 101st Engineers, spent October 15 to November 9 repairing a two-kilometer section of road between Champ and Marre. This included spending days to fill in a massive forty-foot-wide and eighteen-feet-deep crater made by a German mine at a key crossroad. Between October 6 and November 18, seven companies of the African American 805th Pioneer Infantry were each given a one- to two-kilometer segment of road around Claremont and Charpentry to mend and keep open. The regiment's five other companies worked building ammunition dumps, laying light-rail lines, and keeping the railheads at Varrennes, Auzeville, and Aubreville up and running.[26]

As the roads and bridges around the front were well known to the enemy, they drew an abundance of artillery fire. Crossroads and choke points within enemy observation required constant work by the engineers to fill shell holes and clear away rubble to keep traffic moving. For the engineers, it was a constant scramble to accomplish this work in between the enemy barrages. In his first major action with B Company, 117th Engineers, Alphonse Bloemer recorded in his diary that enemy shelling on August 9 and 10, 1918, killed one and wounded four other soldiers in his platoon as they were mending a road near Château Thierry. The shelling left another man shell-shocked. The incident led Bloemer to record laconically in his diary that he had "seen some real war lately." Roads were also particularly vulnerable to air attack. With trucks, wagons, and troops lined up like "ducks in a row" on a road, a German aviator simply had to align his craft with the roadbed and fire down its length. On November 9, 1918, Alphonse Bloemer reported that his unit had suffered four casualties in an air attack as they were working on a path in the Argonne. The work of the engineers at the front was arduous, tedious, ceaseless, and essential to maintaining the rest of the army in the field. However, little honor or glory was attached to this thankless job by the AEF as a whole.[27]

Lastly, the AEF's field signalmen, runners, and messengers endured their own hardships and risks. Without reliable communications to and from the front, the AEF's already overburdened command, fire support, and logistics systems quickly descended into confusion and inertia. The most common combat communications device during the war was the field phone. It allowed instant voice and Morse code communications between stations, but this technology had its own limitations. The phones and wire were heavy and it required much labor to string and maintain the lines as a unit moved forward. This proved a daunting task for the signalmen during the AEF's offensives. In the Soissons attack, the men of the 2nd Signal Battalion were broken into five-man wiring parties that moved forward carrying forty pounds of wire along with their issued packs and weapons. The parties were required to lay five hundred yards of wire and maintain a relay station to make repairs on their segment of line. The weight of their equipment and the task of laying the wire often meant that the signalers lagged behind the advance. At St. Mihiel a harried signal officer lamented,

> After the first jump-off we were advancing so rapidly that it was nearly impossible to maintain communications; and at no time was it more important. We would advance to a new position, and just about the time we had communication we would advance again. It kept up this way for five days and nights. We would lose men and equipment so fast that I wonder we did anything at all.

The situation only became worse when the AEF entered the Meuse Argonne. The other problem with field phones was that they could only link command posts to other command posts. They were relatively effective at connecting infantry battalion headquarters to the regimental headquarters, but lateral communications to adjoining units and supporting artillery at the battalion level and below were nearly nonexistent. The system was completely useless for allowing command and control of troops at the sharp end of battle at the company level or below. Although the AEF had a radio "spark" set, their weight and small numbers meant that they were not used forward of the regimental and, more usually, the brigade level.[28]

The bane of the signalman's existence was the fact that the fragile telephone wire that connected the army's field phones was easily broken by enemy fire and the careless footfalls of inattentive doughboys. A lineman stated that the "universal lament" of the signalman was that "artillery, with their heavy gun carriages and cumbersome equipment, were everlastingly ripping up their field wire and imposing upon the already overburdened signal troops a never-ending task of maintenance." When the connection was cut, the signalman had to trace the line back to the break and fix it, often under enemy fire. As the lines were continually severed, the linemen were incessantly out in the open repairing the breaks. In a single night in the Argonne, the lone-serving signalman in a 32nd Division artillery battalion went out four times under shellfire to repair broken lines. After the last trip, "he was so weak from exhaustion and strain that he could hardly stand." As a result of their efforts to keep the lines open as far forward in the line as possible, casualties among signalmen mirrored or exceeded those of the units they supported.[29]

The AEF also tried to ease its communications problems by using carrier pigeons. During the war, the War Department purchased over ten thousand pigeons at two dollars apiece. Each division contained a pigeon company consisting of nine officers, 324 soldiers, and truck-mounted pigeon coops. The company was responsible for the training, care, and issuing of the division's birds. Before an operation the division signal officer allocated pigeons to the unit's brigades or regiments depending upon the subordinates' needs and missions. Using the same criteria, the brigades and regiments in turn further issued pigeons to their battalions and companies. During the St. Mihiel offensive the army issued 597 pigeons, and in the Meuse Argonne 442.[30]

Although the army claimed that pigeons delivered 95 percent of the messages sent, they were hardly an efficient means of communications. The doughboys who were ultimately entrusted with the pigeons at the front were seldom Signal Corps soldiers. They had little knowledge of how to feed and care for the birds and often resented having the responsibility for the animals dropped upon them just before going into battle. The pigeons arrived at the front in large wicker baskets, which not only were difficult to carry in combat, but also made their bearers conspicuous on the battlefield. Attacking infantrymen were more concerned with their own safety than those of the birds, and the fragile baskets and their equally delicate contents were often battered as the men jumped from shell hole to shell hole. While the divisional pigeon coops protected the birds from poison gas, there were no such safeguards for the birds at the front. Ashby Williams reported that after going for days on short rations, pigeons became a welcome addition to the hungry infantrymen's provisions.[31]

Furthermore, despite the Signal Corps' claims, pigeons were not all that effective in delivering communications. The birds needed time to acclimate to new locations before being used (a problem during the 1st Army's rapid shift from St. Mihiel to the Meuse Argonne), would not fly at night, and became disoriented in bad weather and shelling. While the signalers touted one pigeon's success in carrying a message over forty kilometers in the Argonne in only twenty-five minutes, few birds seemed to be this prompt. This was the case with the "Lost Battalion" and its famous pigeon, Cher Ami. The bird was hailed for carrying a message that stopped an American barrage that was unknowingly killing the men in the pocket. Cher Ami was awarded medals for "bravery" and ended up being stuffed and displayed in the Smithsonian. However, it took Cher Ami over an hour to return with its message to the divisional loft and it took the men at the loft another eighteen minutes to relay the message to the division message center for action. In the hour and twenty-two minutes it required to deliver and disseminate the message, the barrage had already ceased.[32]

When the field phones and all other forms of communications failed, commanders were left with no other option but to send runners and messengers out to deliver the vital orders and reports they required to keep their operations on track. Although this sometimes fell to Signal Corps soldiers, in most cases the messengers came from doughboys within the units themselves. Runners and messengers endured some of the greatest stresses and dangers on the battlefield. They had to be brave, determined, and able to work without close supervision. Their mission required them to go out alone or in a very small party, leave the safety of cover and protection, and cross the deadly ground over which their units had just crossed to deliver their messages. Once they delivered their reports, they had to go through the entire process once again to return replies from headquarters back to their commanders.

Being a messenger on the battlefields of the Great War was a serious matter. As one doughboy put it, "Runners didn't last. Everyone knew that." Given the chance of survival, for important reports commanders often sent out multiple runners in the hope that at least one of them would survive the sprinting odyssey back to headquarters. During fighting near Fismes in August 1918 an infantry captain had to send three runners back at short intervals to deliver one message. After witnessing his two predecessors fall, the last runner "took the note and, cursing as fast and freely as his breath would permit, set off at top speed along the fatal path," through a German bombardment. The last runner was himself wounded by shellfire, but he still managed to deliver the message. In many cases, the attributes needed for the job and the dangerous nature of the mission meant that messengers were volunteers. But the peer pressure of the service made refusing the task difficult. When asked to be a runner by a long-service NCO, one soldier recalled, "Could any man who had pride refuse and let that stern old soldier see the coward inside?" After the Aisne-Marne campaign, the commander of the 1st Division, Major General Charles Summerall, complained that runners were too "slow and uncertain and the casualties among them are out of proportion to the service that they render." His efforts to stop his subordinates from using messengers in combat were futile, because, in the end, they were often a commander's only means of communication in battle.[33]

22

Restless Young Men with Guns
Morale and Discipline

At different times in history large numbers of restless young men have been a boon or a curse to the societies from which they were drawn. When properly channeled, the passions and energies of youth could build cities and further agriculture, the arts, and science. Restless young men could also turn to crime or coalesce into violent mobs that sought to tear down the structures of their social orders. Most challenging of all to a society is when it has hordes of restless young men with guns, for given on to them is the terrifying power of life and death cut loose from the wisdom and restraint that come with maturity. An army is essentially a collection of restless young men with guns straining under the control of supposedly more mature and experienced NCOs and officers. As with other armies throughout history, the thing that kept the AEF from becoming an amoral Hobbesian mob was morale and discipline.

Going into the war, the American Army was well aware of the importance and codependence of morale and discipline in warfare. Many Regular Army officers were familiar with the new science of psychology and with emerging theories such as Gustave LeBon's discourse on the "mass man" and mob mentality. In 1906, the army reformer J. Franklin Bell went so far as to lecture a group of Leavenworth students that "the military commander who contemptuously disregards the psychological equation of his soldiers will never succeed on earth." Likewise, Lincoln Andrews warned the army's new officers, "In a command of soldiers on the battlefield, you have a crowd subjected to the strongest emotions, the ideal conditions for developing a mob." The army relied on two main pillars to give its soldiers the psychological discipline to fight and die. First, it sought to instill high morale within the individual soldiers and their units to create the esprit de corps and unit cohesion so vital to battlefield survival and performance. Second, the army could draw upon its judicial system to impose discipline by punishing offenders of military order and making them object lessons for their peers.[1]

Simply stated, morale was the unit's and its soldiers' collective ability to more or less willingly accept the hardships that came with military service and the mental and moral shocks of battle. Morale provided individuals and units the resiliency and fortitude to endure privations and casualties while staying focused on achieving their missions. The first component of the individual doughboy's morale was his faith in the righteousness of the nation's cause and the belief that the people at home were committed to the war effort. The military also attempted to create morale by smoothing the transition of the individual from being a civilian to being a soldier.[2]

For the first time in American history, the War Department made a concerted effort to instill and maintain high morale within the ranks. It created a Morale Branch within the general staff to monitor and encourage the systematic creation of morale within army units. Although this was a step forward, the Morale Branch's dual role as an intelligence gatherer on conscientious objectors, aliens, and possible radicals within the ranks often diverted its attention from its primary goals. The War Department understood that easing the transition from civilian to soldier rested somewhat on its ability to provide healthy outlets for the recruits' angst and irritations through recreation and entertainment while the men were training in the United States and France. Unfortunately, the army lacked the know-how and resources to accomplish these tasks on such a monumental scale. The solution was to outsource many of these morale-producing diversions to civilian aid and welfare organizations.

In April 1917, the War Department turned to Raymond Fosdick to organize the Commission on Training Camp Activities (CTCA) with the goal of suppressing vice around the camps while simultaneously offering the recruits wholesome, morale-building pastimes such as movies, athletic activities, and recreation huts and canteens that served as refuges from the daily military grind. The CTCA gathered together a constellation of new and existing social welfare organizations, most notably the Young Men's Christian Association

(YMCA), Knights of Columbus (K of C), Salvation Army, Jewish Welfare Board (JWB), and American Red Cross (ARC), to accomplish its objectives.[3]

On the whole, the CTCA's "public–private" endeavors worked quite well in the training camps and embarkation ports in the United States. Most camps boasted a large recreation hall constructed, manned, and supplied by one of the major welfare agencies as well as smaller-sized YMCA, Salvation Army, or K of C huts and canteens scattered throughout the post. These halls and huts tended to be very popular with the troops. They offered snacks and drinks, billiards, phonographs, and other amusements, and, most importantly, a quiet place to write letters and find what Fosdick termed "the normalities of life" away from the realities of the barracks and drill fields. One recruit exclaimed, "The Y.M.C.A. here is the most human institution in this big, rawly human community . . . because the men feel at home and have a real time, and can smoke and put their feet on the table." The Marine Lloyd Short heartily agreed. "The Y.M.C.A. here is a fine place for the boys to spend their time," he wrote his father from Mare Island, California, in April 1918. "There is either a lecture or show here every nite also have a library full of books and magazines of all kinds."[4]

The CTCA and its member organizations further sought to enlighten and entertain the doughboys by organizing lectures and other educational activities as well as showing movies and bringing shows and entertainers to the camps. The CTCA endeavored to build theaters capable of seating three thousand soldiers in each training camp and sought the aid of the entertainment firm of Klaw and Erlanger to procure the acts and talents who would perform in them. Marc Klaw formed a committee of noted entertainers, including Irving Berlin and George M. Cohan, and organizations, such as The Friars, Actor's Equity, and the National Vaudeville Club, to assist him in organizing tours. The admission to the events was to be minimal: fifteen, twenty, or twenty-five cents, just enough to cover the expenses involved. The commission encouraged family members and the public to purchase "Smileage" coupon books for soldiers that would enable the troops to gain "free" admission into the various theatrical events offered in camp. As with the recreation huts, the doughboys were generally enthusiastic about the entertainments the CTCA provided.[5]

To maintain the vital linkage between the soldiers and the folks at home, the Young Women's Christian Association, YMCA, ARC, and Salvation Army also constructed a number of hostess huts and inns in the major training camps and ports. These were intended to provide the soldiers a quiet place to meet with family members and friends. They were also designed to tamp down sin and temptation by giving the troops a chaperoned environment to interact with "respectable" lady friends. Many of these huts and inns had inexpensive accommodations where distant visitors could stay while meeting with their service members. The Salvation Army's Red Shield Inn at Camp Lewis, for example, originally contained nineteen guest rooms as well as a lunch counter, reading rooms, and a visitor parlor. When the demand for the guest rooms grew too great, the Salvation Army built a new structure with 150 rooms. Appropriately, the Red Shield Inn survives today as the Fort Lewis Museum.[6]

Although the War Department and CTCA did an admirable job at building a robust morale infrastructure in the United States, the AEF was hard-pressed to duplicate this success in France. The AEF was even more ill prepared to establish and maintain the recreation huts, the canteens, the entertainments, and the rest of the physical architecture of morale than was the stateside army. Pershing quickly followed the precedent of the training camps by farming out these requirements to the same organizations that had supported the army's morale and welfare work in the United States. In late August 1918 the AEF GHQ issued General Orders 26, which made the Red Cross responsible for "welfare work" in the AEF while the YMCA (and later the Salvation Army and K of C) would "provide for the amusement and recreation by the means of its social, educational, physical and religious activities." This would be a tall order for the organizations. Not only would they have to wrangle shipping space for their workers, entertainers, and goods on the army's overburdened sea transportation, but they would also have to coordinate with French authorities and the AEF for real estate and labor to construct their required huts, warehouses, and other facilities.[7]

It is not much of an exaggeration to state that the three most hated institutions for soldiers serving in the AEF were the German Army, the American military police corps, and the Young Men's Christian Association. In fact, the soldiers' criticism of the YMCA grew so great that the secretary of war directed Pershing to investigate its wartime activities and those of the other major civilian service agencies operating within the AEF. The report of the investigation ultimately ran to 1,271 pages in six volumes. All but 160 of those pages were dedicated to the work and efficiency of the YMCA and the dough-boys' opinions of the agency.

As the AEF had no ability to operate canteens and stores to sell its soldiers refreshments and the small sundries, cigarettes, and other comfort items desired by the troops, the YMCA volunteered to serve as the U.S. Army Quartermaster agent for those sales. Although the YMCA eagerly embraced this sales role as a means of getting the doughboys into its huts, where they could be introduced to the organization's teachings, it was not prepared to take on the logistics, planning, transportation, and staffing required of this mission. As the YMCA focused on operating the canteens as a business, it set itself up for failure and the undying enmity of many a doughboy.[8]

The doughboys were not privy to the agreement between the Quartermaster Corps and the YMCA. They did not know that the army's quartermasters had purchased cigarettes and other sundries with the intent to have the YMCA sell them at cost plus a small service charge. What the doughboys did know was that the folks back home had donated money to the various service agencies to buy cigarettes and other small comfort items for free issue to the boys in France. The "Damn Y," as the troops often referred to the YMCA, was also the largest and most successful of these fund-raisers. The troops were thus surprised and outraged when they were seemingly charged for those same items in the YMCA canteens. It did not help that some of the organization's ill-trained workers sometimes mixed up items for free issue with those for sale. Few things irritated a doughboy more than paying for a package of cigarettes from the YMCA only to open the carton and find a note from some civic organization in the States expressing their hopes that he would enjoy his free gift. Captain Carrol Missimer pointed out, "Despite the fact that the YMCA had more funds than any other Welfare organization over here, they gave less than any. What the Red Cross, Salvation Army and K of C had, they gave freely at all times and gave it gratis. The YMCA did not."[9]

The troops were not only angered by having to pay for what they thought should be free; they also accused the YMCA of gouging them on the prices of the items the agency sold. An investigator from the 1st Division stated that he found instances where the YMCA charged five times as much for tobacco as was allowed by the commissary and quartermaster departments and their prices for chocolate were double those in French stores. Some soldiers went so far as to label the YMCA workers out-and-out crooks. As with unit chaplains, soldiers sometimes deposited money with the YMCA workers or had them send money back to the States before going into action. In some cases, this led to abuse. After his family failed to receive $294 that he had sent home via the YMCA, Harry Callison mused, "I haven't much to kick about as I ought to have known better in the first place but when I get home, I want YMCA's among a few others to keep out of my sight. If they don't I might be tempted to hurt their feelings or something."[10]

There were other points of friction between the YMCA and the dough-boys. For one the organization had a very effective publicity campaign in the States that informed the folks back home that the YMCA was "giving away millions of dollars worth of free supplies in its front line trench work, or while the men were going into action or coming out of action." Besides the absence of the organization's largesse, the troops greatly resented the as-sertion that the YMCA workers were anywhere close to the front. The troops were outraged when YMCA workers took posed photographs to make it seem to the home audience that they were close to the fighting while doing their work. In one particularly egregious case, a YMCA secretary filmed another of the organization's workers handing out hot chocolate to wounded men at the front. In reality, the "wounded" were members of a hospital staff who had been bandaged to appear to be injured. One soldier was so incensed by this kind of behavior that he wrote his mother in December 1918, "Don't ever give the Y.M.C.A. another cent . . . All their talk in the papers we get from home about the wonderful work of the Y.M.C.A. in the front is absolutely wrong. I have been on the front since August 14 and we seen one Y.M.C.A. man once. He gave us one cigarette to the man."

The 3rd Division inspector general reported that the Red Cross was popu-lar with the soldiers because, in contrast to the YMCA, "they did what they did quietly without a lot of noise and advertising—and did it generously and sincerely."[11]

The perception that the YMCA men were shirkers also rubbed many sol-diers the wrong way. In the pages of *Stars and Stripes*, one doughboy de-nounced "the spectacle" of a YMCA worker, "of draft age, undeniably healthy and fit for active service, cosily situated behind a counter during working hours," while wearing an officer's uniform and enjoying officer privileges in food and accommodations. Another trooper told a visiting dignitary, "What is that dolled-up guy doing behind the counter, selling cigarette and living in the best billets in town, when he ought to be soaking with the rest of us? He's a fake. That's what he is—a fake!" There were certainly grounds for the soldiers' complaints. The YMCA was the largest agency in France that catered to the doughboys' comfort and recreation. By the time of the Armistice, the YMCA had 4,444 workers in Europe (which would rise to 6,430 by April 1919); the Knights of Columbus had 1,019; Salvation Army had 134; and the Jewish Welfare Board maintained 129 workers. Although the American Red Cross had 5,601 personnel in Europe, many of them were assigned to duties outside of the AEF. The troops' anger ultimately led the YMCA to stop enrolling men who were eligible for service in the ranks.[12]

Lastly, the pompous "holier than thou" manner of many of the YMCA secretaries and their propensity to cater to officers rather than the troops also soured their relations with the average soldier. A lieutenant stationed at Langres complained, "The personnel of the Y.M.C.A. has been very poorly chosen. The attitude seems to be a little too much religion and not enough practical Christianity. Our men did not go to the Y.M.C.A. because as a rule they always had religion thrown at them." Soldiers in the 29th Division reported that some YMCA workers even forced them to participate in the prayer sessions that they held between reels of movies and that some men had been refused the sale of canteen goods because they had not attended church. If that were not enough, the troops alleged that the worker's allowed officers to cut in line ahead of the troops and to buy larger quantities of goods than were permitted to the men. In some cases officers bought the store out of high-demand items before the troops even had the chance to buy them. It is interesting to note that while male YMCA secretaries were often reviled by the troops, the doughboys had very favorable opinions of the organization's women workers. "The women as a rule were more aggressive and hard working than the men," an officer reported, "and did not become so irritable under strain as did the men."[13]

As the AEF inspector general office investigated the YMCA, it also dug into the activities of the army's other social welfare organizations. What stands out in these investigations was the doughboy's near-universal condemnation of the YMCA and their near universal praise for the Salvation Army, K of C, JWB, and ARC. Most of this praise stemmed from three major observations by the troops: the other agencies served all comers equally and at little to no charge; their workers were gracious and dedicated; and, most importantly, the soldiers could count on the members of those organizations to be where they were needed most—close to the front and in forward aid stations and hospitals.

This was all in stark contrast to the doughboys' perceptions of the YMCA. The Knights of Columbus, for example, took great pride in advertising to the soldiers, "Everything Free," and then absolutely following through on that promise. The Knights of Columbus workers had a reputation for "endearing themselves to the enlisted men." The fact that the organization did not have the personnel to operate many fixed huts meant that their workers were free to mingle with the troops as far forward in the line as they were allowed and personally gave out their wares. Few things tickled the soldiers or boosted their morale more than hearing stories of how "their" elderly and mischievous K of C or Salvation Army men were caught by senior officers sneaking to the front lines to deliver their goods. While his unit was moving to Château Thierry, Martin Hogan recalled that a K of C worker in a dugout near the front flagged down the passing trucks and "handed out to us their last reserves of chocolate and cigarettes." He confessed that the items "are mightily welcome on the eve of a 'go' at the front." What moved Hogan most, however, was that the workers were obviously and sincerely disappointed that their meager stock ran out before all the boys could be served.[14]

The Salvation Army and ARC were also popular with the troops. The 42nd Division's inspector reported that in his unit, "Nothing but praise is heard of the Red Cross and its personnel." An officer in the 112th Infantry noted that while the Salvation Army charged a nominal 50 centime fee for the warm drinks, doughnuts, and cakes that they served, no soldier was ever turned away empty-handed if he did not have money. During the Argonne fighting they were very close to the front and "any hour of the day or night that a wet, cold, hungry soldier called on the Salvation Army they were glad to get out of their beds, make a fire, warm the soldier and furnish him with something hot to eat or drink." The AEF's chief inspector singled out the work of the Salvation Army's doughnut "Lassies" as being particularly inspiring to the troops. Throughout the AEF's major battles, "the sight of the never-tiring, enthusiastic Salvation Army girl frying donuts and cooking chocolate right up near as near to the enemy as it was possible to get became a most familiar sight to those soldiers who can boast of front line service."[15]

Although the work of the service agencies, including the much maligned

YMCA, to provide the doughboys' with goods, services, and comforts certainly boosted morale, the most important contribution to the soldiers' spirit was the fact that their efforts represented a tangible link between the troops and the home front. Horace Baker admitted that he and his comrades "did not like the taste" of the cigarettes handed out by a welfare worker as they marched to the front, but "we appreciated them and the spirit that gave them, even though I did not smoke." Another observer noted of the comfort items the troops were issued, "It was good to have the sense of greeting from home however disguised." The cigarettes and chocolate were proof to Baker and his comrades that the folks at home remembered and appreciated the troops.[16]

The work of the welfare agencies also provided an escape from their daily grind and a fleeting taste of home and their civilian selves. Private Albert Dahinden wrote home in May 1918 that soon after coming out of the line, "I immediately made tracks for a French town which sheltered a Salvation Army [hut]. There I had two pieces of real American made pie. I'll tell you the pie sure was good and well worth the four mile hike." Some agencies consciously endeavored to bring this feeling of home and normalcy to the troops in France. The ARC's chairman, Henry Davidson, was proud of the fact that

> the American soldier interpreted "Rest Station" . . . as something more or less like home and the good old dishes of childhood. Home, therefore, became the keynote in all the buildings and furnishing of the Red Cross way-stations on the road to war. There was home flavoring in the seasoning of the food, and the home atmosphere in the chintzes and various commodities at hand, such as soap, towels, reading matter, and phonograph records.

In many ways, the popularity of the various agencies' female workers with the boys was because they personified home to the troops. A *Stars and Stripes* writer spoke for many doughboys when he observed, "In an army of young men three to six thousand miles from home, there are times when there is nothing better in the world a soldier needs and wants quite so much as just to sit and talk with the kind of girl he used to call on in his home town." Doughboy letters and diaries frequently noted the soldier's pleasure in interacting with the American women working for the American Red Cross, YMCA, or Salvation Army. In fact, these women were frequently referred to as "real girls" in the soldiers' correspondence to separate them from their less perfect European cousins. All of this also bolstered the soldiers' morale, for their connections to home reminded them of what they were fighting for.[17]

The time that it took to build up the AEF's morale infrastructure and the army's unexpected early commitment to battle meant that few soldiers had the opportunity to enjoy leaves or entertainments prior to the Armistice. It was not necessarily due to a lack of trying. In February 1918 a group of patriotic performers gathered to form the Over There Theater League and worked with the army and the YMCA to bring quality acts to the troops in France. While these professional acts, especially Elsie Janis, were generally well received by the troops, the lecturers, Chautauqua speakers, and amateur performers that the YMCA placed on tour met a more negative response. An officer in the 4th Division noted of the lecturers his unit received, "One devoted himself to the labor question, and the other to sex morality. One of the lecturers started with a full house. He finished on his third night with 5 people present, three of whom were janitors."[18]

When entertainments were not forthcoming, sometimes soldiers took matters into their own hands. Although amateur theater did not seem to have been as popular in the AEF as it was in the British Army, troops in some units did put on shows to entertain their comrades. One such effort in March 1918 consisted of burlesque routines titled "The Rumors That Run through Camp," "The Supply Sergeant," and "Oo La La" and netted two thousand francs for one company's unit fund. The show was well received by the troops, but a reviewer did note that "a burlesque show without chorus girls is one of the horrors of war." The coming of the Armistice gave the troops the time and the boredom to unleash their pent-up muses. In March 1919 alone, units around Coblenz, Germany, put on six soldier shows, which led one officer to report, "The results obtained have been most admirable, and have provided surprisingly good shows for the soldiers." Another officer observed, "The entertainment which seems to have caused the army the greatest amount of enjoyment has been the soldier show."[19]

A few lucky soldiers also had the opportunity to see movies sent from the States. Like most of the entertainment in the AEF, however, the opportunity to see a film was rather slim for the troops prior to the Armistice. In general, soldiers serving in large towns and fixed SOS camps had much greater access to all forms of entertainment than those in combat divisions. From August 1917 to April 1918, only 372 movies reached France, and many of these were "poor in content and in physical condition." A year later, the number of films had increased and the YMCA reported 4,392 film showings in April

Photo 25: Doughboy minstrel show *Somewhere in France*. Such shows helped to ease the monotony that was a natural part of military service, especially while the soldiers waited to sail for home after the Armistice. Source: author's collection.

1919. Those who watched the movies seemed to enjoy them. As Private Paul Rhodes wrote home, "We had movies here in a barn last night and they were good. We had one reel of Universal Cartoons and Current Events and a three reel picture by the Kalem Company entitled 'Kerry Gow,' and Irish Love Story and it certainly made me think of my courting days."[20]

In January 1918, the AEF GHQ issued General Orders 6, which permitted commanders to grant seven days of leave every four months for officers and men "of good standing" in their units. Working with the YMCA, the AEF established nineteen leave areas in the French Alps, the Riviera, the Côte d'Or, and other popular tourist areas. The YMCA contracted with hotels, resorts, and casinos in those areas for lodging and provided a host of activities and recreations for the troops on leave. Soldiers going on leave were given an extra dollar per day to cover food and incidentals. Although the Ludendorff offensives and the subsequent Allied counterattacks curtailed the number of Americans able to take leave just as the leave areas were getting up and running, a few fortunate doughboys were still able to enjoy them before the end of the war. One of these lucky souls, Private Harold Lane, wrote home that the best part of his and his buddy's leave at the St. Malo Recreation Center was his ability to "live like civilians for a little more than a week." He noted, "Every morning we could have our breakfast served in bed if we wanted it or we could get up just as we like. All of our expenses, that is, car fare both ways and hotel bills were paid by the government so all we had to spend money for was when we went on little excursions there or bought our meals out side of our regular hotel."

The granting of leaves picked up dramatically after the Armistice. In a letter home from the Nice leave area in May 1919, one soldier proclaimed, "I am on furlough and having the best time of my life." The end of the war also brought with it a liberalization of leaves and passes to Paris. From January 18 to March 15, 1919, alone, 118,920 soldiers participated in YMCA sightseeing excursions in the City of Light. Excursions to Paris and the AEF's leave areas proved to be the highlights of thousands of doughboys' existence and were the last chance for many to sow their wild oats before returning to their buttoned-down civilian lives.[21]

While movies and leave areas were nice amusements, the most common diversions and recreation in the AEF came from sports and reading. The army had long viewed sports as a means of maintaining the health of the troops, building aggressiveness, and keeping idle hands busy and out of trouble. The YMCA and Knights of Columbus also took the lead in providing sports equipment to the AEF. Unfortunately, the AEF's sports program suffered an early setback when $30,000 in sports equipment was lost when the SS *Oronsa* was torpedoed by a U-Boat in April 1918. To offset these losses, the YMCA contracted with French companies to make baseball bats and gloves. The range of the soldiers' interest in sports was reflected in the equipment issued to the 2nd Division: 177 baseballs, 696 bats, 886 mitts, 176 basketballs, 301 footballs, 277 soccer balls, 146 volleyballs, and ninety-three sets of boxing gloves. Like many other pastimes, athletics in the AEF dramatically increased after the Armistice. This push culminated in the Inter-Allied Games held in and around the American-built Pershing Stadium on the outskirts of Paris from June 22 to July 6, 1919. Twenty-eight Allied nations participated in the event. The games had twenty-four events ranging from baseball, football, soccer, and rugby to marksmanship, grenade throwing, swimming, and equestrian contests. Beginning in March 1919, soldiers and units from across the AEF participated in championship games to determine the American team for the Inter-Allied competition. In the end, the doughboys made a good showing in the Inter-Allied Games, taking first place in twelve of the twenty-four separate events and coming in second in seven other events.[22]

In the decades prior to the Great War, free public education had dramatically expanded literacy in the United States. The constant desire for information from home and news of the war and home fronts, as well as the desire to escape the boredom of soldiering, made the doughboys great letter writers and readers and devourers of books and newspapers. The American Library Association (ALA) supplied around five million books to the armed forces during the war. Roughly half of these volumes were sent to the AEF, where they were available for free check out for the soldiers. In fact, when the ALA discovered that some YMCA workers were charging a deposit from soldiers when they checked out books, it refused to furnish more volumes until the practice was ceased. Knowing that the soldiers would pass their books around, the ALA was not very concerned when the doughboys failed to return the works that they borrowed. As such, more than half of the books that they had brought to France disappeared into the ranks.[23]

The doughboys appreciated the books offered by the ALA, and the respite that the volumes offered from their daily grind turned some men into avid readers. L.V. Jacks recalled that books were passed between the men in his unit until they were "literally worn out by handling." He noted that "the A.E.F. was an education in itself to any one who was alert to seize it, for in the vast force there was always an amusing interchange of ideas, experiences, theories, and information." He was astounded by an afternoon he spent "listening to a vigorous dissertation on 'Taras Bulba' by an ex-cowboy who had somewhere chanced on the book." The refined Jacks admitted to carrying copies of Thomas á Kempis and Sophocles's *Antigone* while his comrades read Winston Churchill's *A Far Country* (by the American author, not the British politician) and Hall Caine's *The Woman That Thou Gavest Me*. The doughboys seemed most drawn to adventure novels and other light reading.[24]

The doughboys were always hungry for news. They wanted to know what was going on in the war, in the AEF, in the United States, and in their hometowns. Some of this news was readily available from sources in Europe. The Paris editions of the *Chicago Tribune* and the *New York Herald* and the *Continental Daily Mail* were the main civilian newspapers available to those in

the AEF. The primary military news source was *Stars and Stripes*. This weekly
paper ran from February 8, 1918, to June 13, 1919, and provided its readers with
summaries of what was going on in the States, news from around the AEF,
and notices of changes in army policies. Its editorials, cartoons, and letters
to the editor allowed the soldiers to vent their anger at the petty injustices of
army life and gently mock their officers and other tormentors. As such, it was
popular with the troops. In late February 1918, a soldier from the 1st Division
wrote to a relative, noting that he had just received the second edition of the
new *Stars and Stripes* and opined that it was "surely worth the cost," for it
was "a scream from start to finish." At its peak the paper was being read by
526,000 troops in the AEF. When *Stars and Stripes* closed shop, it was replaced
by the *AMAROC News* for troops serving in the occupation of Germany in
the 3rd Army.[25]

   In addition to *Stars and Stripes*, some units also published their own local
newspapers. Censorship regulation and the hurried pace of the AEF's training and operations meant that the American Army never truly saw the burst
of "trench journalism" enjoyed by the British Army. In fact, as late as February 1919, the AEF chief censor had only given official sanction to nineteen
newspapers, only two of which were published by combat units. An unknown
number of other publications were printed without the blessing of the censors, but the frequent moves of the AEF's combat organizations certainly curtailed these efforts. With the relaxing of censorship rules after the Armistice
and the troops settling into occupation duties, many more units began publishing their own newssheets.[26]

   It is clear that the Red Cross and other support agencies made great efforts
to get newspapers and periodicals to the troops during the war. In fact, in
the fall of 1918, the 2nd Division reported receiving and distributing around
one thousand magazines a week. One doughboy even noted, "I remember on
the Argonne front, the Red Cross would bring newspapers up each morning,
and that was greatly appreciated by the boys." But this soldier's experience
seems to have been the exception, as other combat troops often complained
that news of any kind was slow in reaching the front. Charles Minder noted
that he was fortunate to get a copy of the edition of the *New York Times* from
July 20, 1918, on September 1, 1918. Although the paper looked "as if the whole
77th Division had been reading it," he was still thankful that it provided him
with the "big picture" of what was happening in the war. To the troops, old

news was still better than no news. A military policeman admitted that he was "always glad to see a paper, no matter how old it may be." The same was true for local papers sent to the doughboys by the people at home. These local publications were more dear to the soldiers than any other news source, as they provided the troops a fleeting glimpse of home. They could also, however, bring the soldiers a bittersweet reminder of what they were missing and how things were changing. After reading some of his hometown rags, Harry Callison mused, "The old town seems to have lots doing in our absence."[27]

Home was constantly on the minds of most doughboys. As such, mail from friends and family members in the United States served as the greatest prop to maintaining the individual soldier's morale. At the same time, bad news from home or a lack of mail from the States could also undercut the doughboy's spirits. It is interesting to note the subjects that the doughboys wrote about in their letters and what they omitted. Generally speaking, those seeking great and vivid descriptions of the war in the soldiers' correspondence would be disappointed. Due to censorship rules and a desire not to worry those at home, the troops tended to self-censor and focus on the mundane realities of their lives. What they universally wanted to know was how the folks at home were fairing and what was happening in and around the old homestead. The doughboys exhibited an almost pathological need to stay connected with their former lives and attachments.

In addition to letters, the doughboys were also thankful for packages from home. With limited pay and problems with the YMCA serving as the quartermaster store, these packages often contained important comfort and hygiene items that could be hard to come by in France. Like the letters, the packages were also a tangible link to home. In January 1918, Corporal Francis Byrne thanked his mother for sending a box "containing the cakes, towels, soap, writing paper, gum & etc." He noted that "four or five of us frontally attacked the daintys which disappeared in a surprisingly short time. You know that it doesn't take much time for a bunch of hungry boys to make away with anything like that, especially when it comes from home."[28]

Such linkages to home came at a price. With shipping space at a premium, the AEF GHQ constantly worked to limit the flow of unnecessary goods to France. One of the GHQ's concerns was the number of packages being sent from the States to the soldiers of the AEF. In April 1918 the GHQ ordered that packages could only be sent from home at the soldier's request. The soldier was to get his commander's approval to request a package and specify exactly what was to be sent to them. Authorities in New York would open France-bound packages to check their contents against the soldier's approved list. This system collapsed under the protest of the folks back home and its own bureaucratic weight. With Christmas approaching, in the early fall of 1918 the AEF GHQ again worried that a flood of packages from home would overwhelm the army's hard-pressed sea and rail transportation system. To deal with this potential problem, the AEF restricted its soldiers to receiving only one Christmas package from home. Soldiers were issued a single printed Christmas Package Coupon, which they mailed to whomever they wished to receive a parcel from. The stateside sender could mail the package free to Hoboken, but it had to have the official coupon pasted to the outside of the box and the package itself could not weigh more than three pounds or be larger than "9 by 4 by 3 inches." With his Christmas package coupon, one soldier enclosed a request for Hershey's milk chocolate (plain and with nuts), Wrigley's gum, nonperishable hard candy, a dozen Gillette safety razor blades, a stag or bone-handled pocket knife, and a pair of woolen wristlettes.[29]

When sending mail the doughboys had to contend with censorship. The AEF GHQ was so concerned that American troops could send sensitive information through the mail that might aid the enemy that it established the army's censorship policies in AEF General Orders 3 within weeks of Pershing's arrival in France. This order laid out what the troops could send through the mail and made regimental or unit officers responsible for censoring their soldiers' correspondence. The Intelligence Section of the AEF General Staff also printed a folder for all arriving soldiers outlining the censorship and operational security rules that applied to those serving in France. The card informed the soldiers who they could write to and what was and was not permitted to be sent. Specifically they were warned not to disclose their locations (hence the "Somewhere in France" that heads many soldiers' letters) or "the movements of troops, their condition, the effects of hostile fire upon them, nor their losses." When it came to informing those on the home front of how the war was going, the soldiers were directed to not express their "opinion on military matters," to trust their leaders, and to "avoid in any way giving the impression of pessimism." If all this weren't enough, in the wake of the Mata Hari scandal, doughboys were enjoined, "Always look with suspicion on strangers, and never tell anything of a confidential nature to women, as women are the most successful of enemy spies." The soldiers were prohibited from sending mail through the French postal system or using codes, ciphers, or other means of avoiding censorship.[30]

Although most doughboys understood the need for censorship, they still chaffed at having it imposed on them. As one exasperated 26th Division artilleryman wrote his sister in February 1918, "I cannot tell you where I am or what we are doing or nothing like that . . . so you see I cannot write much only that we are well and getting along good and hope to be back to the US soon." As much of the censoring was done by the soldiers' own junior officers, many doughboys were reluctant to delve too deeply into personal matters. For their part, the officers were far from thrilled at having to read their troops' correspondence. First of all it took up a lot of the officers' time. Captain Clarence Minick observed that censoring his company's mail "keeps 4 officers busy about a hour each evening." Furthermore, few officers relished their "peeping Tom-like" snooping into the intimate lives of the men they had to lead.[31]

Despite the AEF's policies and threats, many doughboys still tried to get information past the censors as best they could. Private Harold Lane got around the censors in August 1917 by sending a letter detailing his first weeks in France with a soldier returning to the United States.

Others tried to get around the censors by using oblique references to standing questions or hints from previous discussions or correspondence. Such tactics perhaps led to more confusion than enlightenment to the folks at home. For example, a soldier in the 79th Division informed his parents, "In reference to [the] other question. Cannot say, I do not know if you know what I mean but that is all I am allowed to say." If the soldiers could not get past the prying eyes of the censor, at least they could try to have a laugh at the official's expense. Private Knud Olsen wrote in a letter home to "look under the stamp." If the censor went through the laborious process of steaming or soaking off the stamp, he would have found printed under it, "was it hard to get off?"[32]

To keep the mail flowing and the troops happy, the AEF had to establish a complex postal distribution network in Europe. The goal of the Military Postal Express service was to have letters to the soldiers in France within sixteen to twenty days of their mail being received at the New York central post office. Getting mail to units scattered and moving across France in a timely matter was no easy task. The military post claimed that their work was made more difficult by mistakes made by the senders. One-third of the six million letters the military postal service received in the last week of August 1918 were improperly addressed. Despite these problems, in the last four months of the war, the Military Postal Express delivered 103 million letters from the States and processed fifty-six million letters from the soldiers to the folks back home.[33]

Regardless of the Herculean efforts of the Military Postal Express, few doughboys were satisfied with the timeliness of the mail. Although he was happy to finally hear from his sister, one private railed against the post office in March 1919 because her letter dated October 1918 was the first mail he had received from home in five months. Corporal Paul Rhodes was only somewhat better off. On January 31, 1919, he wrote his sister that he had just received the letter that she had sent to him on November 25, 1918, and that her letter was the first that he had gotten since October 1, 1918. This lack of communication weighed heavy on the soldiers' minds. Some were worried that the people at home were hiding bad news from them or had forgotten about them.

In a fit of self-pity, Private E. F. Satterwhite wrote home,

It is hard for me to write for I think that no one cares for me anymore as I get no letters and I write all the time but you all don't seem to ans[wer] . . . I think I ought to quit writing but I have nothing to do and I think I will write once in a while and if people I write don't want to hear from me I wish they would write and tell me to quit writing. . . . After one is gone from home so long he is forgotten.

Such sad thoughts usually dissipated with the arrival of the delayed mail. As one wagoner declared upon receiving his long-tardy letters, "It did me a lot of good to think that every body had not forgotten me."[34]

Although they were quick to chastise those in the States for failing to correspond, many doughboys sheepishly admitted that they had been delinquent in keeping those at home informed of their doings in France. The troops often complained that they simply lacked the time and stationary to write home. A corporal in the 1st Division advised his mother to "take into consideration the fact that writing by candle light & a great many times in the cold is not a very comfortable thing." A few doughboys acknowledged that a lack of mail from the front could cause consternation among their family members. To try to ease the worries of his mother, George McLaughlin wrote her in September 1918, "From now on you must remember that no news is good news." It is doubtful that this statement comforted or mollified his mother.[35]

Although the doughboys did not want their families to worry about them, their correspondence was peppered with their concerns about what was happening in the States. Their most common worries were over the health of their family members and the financial state of those on the home front. The troops expressed these concerns even while they were locked in combat and their minds should have perhaps been focused on more pressing matters. Captain Clarence Minick had left a pregnant wife behind when he sailed for France and constantly fretted over the health of his spouse. On October 22, 1918, as his unit was returning to battle, he finally received word that his wife had given birth to an eight-pound baby girl on September 30 while the new father had been fighting in the Argonne. The outbreak of influenza in the United States in the summer of 1918 dramatically increased the anxiety of many of those serving in France. Even though he was recovering from gas poisoning, George O'Brien's greatest worries were about the flu epidemic back home. After one of his comrades received notice of a death at home, he wrote to his mother, "It is the tho[ught] of such things that make all of us here anxious. Hope nothing of that kind has happened."[36]

What comes across in the doughboys' letters home is their sense of powerlessness to control or help with their family's problems in the United States. After the death of his infant daughter to pneumonia, Paul Rhodes was troubled over the health and mental state of his wife. He informed his sister that he had urged his wife to move in with their mother and that "I hope she does for she is so lonesome now that the baby has been taken to heaven." Although his unit was about to enter the fighting in the Meuse Argonne, the thoughts of a soldier in the 26th Division were firmly fixed on the plight of his family. The sudden death of his father had left the family's finances in disarray. From thousands of miles from home, he cajoled his sister, "Well don't you think it would be wise for Ma to get that house off her hands and not put in another cold winter in Attleboro for pretty soon it will need painting and the roof needs much fixing." Existing family tensions could also frustrate the faraway doughboys and worsen their sense of helplessness. One of Ira Wilkenson's greatest concerns was what the folks in the States were doing with the money that he had sent home. He warned his sister on May 13, 1918, that if anyone had taken his savings, "When I return home, someone is going to regret it,"

Photo 26: The soldier with his sweetheart and the father with his children illustrate the bittersweet draw of hearth, home, and heart. The doughboys went to great lengths to keep in touch with those at home and were frustrated at any delays in the mail. News, or the lack of news, from home could quickly raise or lower the soldier's morale. Source: author's collection.

and he complained, "I guess they think they can take advantage of me since I have got away over here."[37]

When it came to romance, correspondence between the doughboy and his sweetheart could either reinforce his morale or send it spiraling downward. Maintaining a long-distance relationship was hard and a number of soldiers expressed their fears over the continued love and fidelity of the girls back home. The dreaded "Dear John" letters of World War II had a number of antecedents in the Great War. Private Frank Graves recalled that one of his comrades was devastated when he received a letter from his girlfriend stating, "Don't write to me anymore. I'm getting married." Likewise, after receiving only sporadic letters from his girlfriend, a soldier in the 78th Division asked his sister, "Do you think Elizabeth has some one else. Let me know your idea of it. If she has then i wont look for her when i come home . . . I don't know if she cares for me or not. To Hell with her if i thought she was untrue." He then added melodramatically, "If she is not waiting for me i am going to reenlist in the army for four years more." Although he and his wife Helen had a strong and loving marriage, Corporal Benson Oakley was not above indulging in a bit of long-range jealousy. When Helen began corresponding with an old flame, the despondent doughboy wrote home, "I was mad because he had done so. I'm trusting you dearest and do not want you to be corresponding with him and I know you won't—because I don't want you to." Fortunately for the Bensons, the correspondence was harmless and the couple enjoyed a happy reunion at the end of the war.[38]

Despite the risk of heartache, many doughboys relished writing to their beloveds. In their romantic letters, the soldiers were free to seek affection, to grasp at a bit of normalcy, and to hope for a better and more full life when the war was over. This was evident in the correspondence that flowed between Goldie Little and Elmer Lewis during the war. Elmer met Goldie while he was training at Camp Lewis, Washington. He was so smitten with the girl that he proposed to her after a very brief acquaintance. Although Goldie turned him down by noting that she did not love anyone at the present, Lewis was not to be denied. They maintained an affectionate correspondence during Lewis's time in France. It is clear from his letters that her writing did wonders for his morale. "I get a lot of peace thinking about you," he wrote in August 1918, "I like to think of the good times we used to have and dream of the good times to come when I get home again." He even claimed that her love made him a better and more disciplined soldier, noting in February 1919,

> I am afraid that some one else will make my sweet girl love them and I don't want to come back and find that I have lost her for dear if you were gone I don't think I would be a good soldier very long. The thoughts of you dear have made me be a good boy. I have not been with any French girl or been drinking since I have been in France, for dear I told you that I would be good and will [even if] it breaks my neck.

Although Goldie's letters sustained him throughout the conflict, their relationship does not seem to have long survived his return to the United States. However, their correspondence highlights the powerful effects that such romantic connections had on the spirit and resiliency of many dough boys.[39]

It is clear that the army and the nation made great efforts to build and sustain the individual soldier's general morale during the war through recreation, entertainments, and keeping the mail from home flowing. The army's attempts to create combat morale, however, were much more of a mixed bag. On the one hand, the military understood and tried to foster esprit de corps within its combat units. On the other hand, the army's personnel and replacement policies undermined the maintenance of a strong small-unit cohesion in the AEF. Combat morale is the individual soldier's and his unit's collective ability to endure the physical and psychological shocks of battle while trying to accomplish the unit's mission. At the company level and below, the differences between combat morale and small-unit cohesion were so closely entwined as to make them basically indistinguishable. Combat morale and unit cohesion are created or destroyed by the individual and his unit's confidence in their training, their faith in their leaders, and the degree of mutual trust and confidence between members of the unit.

Esprit de corps is a powerful military tool. Given the attritional nature of the Great War, the AEF's commanders needed their soldiers to take such a deep pride in their units that it pushed them to great feats of courage and sacrifice in battle. Whether playing to their vanity and ego, pointing to the superiority of their masculinity, or sanctifying and justifying their losses, the doughboys generally needed to take pride in their units and its feats. This psychological need was not lost on the ever-perceptive Chaplain Levinger:

> The good soldier thinks that he belongs to the best company in the best division in any army and the world; that his officers are the ablest, his comrades the most loyal, his own soldierly qualities at least on par with the best. Each division was firmly convinced that its own battles won the war, while the others merely helped. None of them would give the French and British credit for more than adequate assistance.

Even soldiers in units whose performance in combat had been lackluster, such as the 35th and 79th Divisions, were quick to blame any shortcomings on "other" units within their organization, the impossible tasks given them, or the malignant influence of outside agents.[40]

It is interesting to note that much of the esprit de corps in the American Army in the first months of the war was built upon a negative base. The Regular Army troops looked down on the amateur "Tin Soldiers" of the National Guard. The National Guard detested the pretentions of the Regulars and looked down on the dissolute mercenaries that filled its ranks, and both the Regulars and the guardsmen scorned the timid-soul conscripts of the National Army. Each group thus initially built their sense of identity on what they weren't. When such rivalries pushed soldiers and units to better themselves, they served an important military purpose. One Midwest guardsman thundered in his journal, "The regular army used to sneer at the National Guard. We used to have to swallow it in the old armory days. But we never claimed to be more than emergency soldiers. And now that the emergency is here let us see what had happened . . . I am tired of being scorned by the regular army."[41] Such unfettered tribalism could also erode the faith and confidence that the AEF as a whole needed to operate smoothly.

At first the Regulars and guardsman were unsure if the draftees had the guts and dedication to make reliable soldiers. One Kansas volunteer could not contain his displeasure when his National Guard unit received their first batch of conscripts. As he informed his mother, "Believe me I sure would hate to be so low down as a drafted man in classed by the volunteers. Everyone that inlisted hates them like poison and you can't blame us at all when you put your self in our place." In a similar vein a doughboy in the regular 10th Engineers wrote home, "I'd like to see a list of the men drafted. They are preparing for quite a bunch of them here and from the Regular army men and officers, they need not expect much consideration . . . They are considered slackers already."[42]

While such sentiments peppered the letters and diaries of many Regulars and guardsmen, their opposition flew in the face of reality. The transfers of large numbers of troops among the divisions in the stateside training camps, and the influx of draftees to refill the ranks or to later replace losses in combat, tended to dilute regional unit identities and homogenize the army as a whole. This is not to say that units did not try to imprint their pride and rituals on the newcomers. A 32nd Division soldier boasted that he and his comrades took "a monstrous pride in the combat power" of his unit and that new men joining the unit were told, "You belong to the 32nd now. You have to live up to it." Slowly all the "tribes" in the American Army had to build a new esprit de corps more on what they were and what they had done in the war, rather than on what they had been. Sometimes during this process the draftees even surprised them. In a letter home from October 1918, Francis Byrne enclosed a clipping announcing the award of the Distinguished Service Cross to Private William McLoughlin. He noted that the draftee McLoughlin had been a conscientious objector who "didn't give us anything but trouble from the time we got him." Byrne was astonished that as soon as the conscript got into battle, "he turned into a rip-snorting devil and Lord help the Bosch he got his hands on."[43]

Like boys on a schoolyard, doughboys were quick to boast about the exploits of their units while denigrating those unfortunates in other, lesser units. One of the popular taunts thrown by passing units was "Who won the war?" Depending on the tone, context, or degree of sarcasm used when asking this question, the soldiers could tout their successes or run down the accomplishments of the opposing unit. Epic rivalries grew up between the AEF's divisions. Doughboys passing men of the 42nd Division could always get a rise from their opponents by stating that yellow was "the biggest color in the Rainbow" or stating that the Rainbow only "comes out after a storm." One Marine proudly wrote home that his 2nd Division was "the highest and most honored of Uncle Sam's divisions," and dismissed the 42nd Division as merely "another outfit that claim they won the war and aren't afraid to make their point known, when there aren't any 1st or 2nd Division men around." For their part, the men of the 42nd gave as well as they got. Charles MacArthur noted that few in the 42nd were fond of the Marines. After being catcalled by a group of Leathernecks, the men in his unit responded with "Go home and tell your mother you have seen the soldiers." As to the vaunted reputation of the Marines, he noted, "Those Germans had pet names for the Rainbow besides which Devil Dog sounds like Sissy," and added cattily, "The Marines made up Devil Dog themselves." These encounters did not end just in boasting and insults. As one doughboys observed, "There are fierce scrapes when men of the different divisions get together and start arguing."[44]

Living in a sea of uniformity, the troops were especially proud of wearing their distinctive unit shoulder patches and other insignia that showed their veteran status. Like the British Army, the AEF slowly came around to the idea of providing every one of its major units a unique patch to help to identify at a glance the affiliation of each member of the army. These patches were designed to highlight some part of the unit's lineage and often came in a variety of styles or colors that could allow the observer to discover not only the soldier's division but also his brigade of regiment. For example, the patch of the 42nd Division was a rainbow, denoting the fact that its units were drawn from National Guard organizations from across the United States, while the pine tree insignia of the 91st Division denoted that its draftees came from the woods of the Pacific Northwest. The 81st Division's insignia, a black wildcat, is credited with being the first shoulder patch worn in the AEF. Most of the AEF's other divisions followed suit, but as most of their insignias were not approved by the AEF until the fall of 1918, few doughboys actually wore them until after the Armistice.

The shoulder patches quickly became popular with the troops and served as an intense focus of their pride and esprit de corps. When he was informed on October 30, 1918, that the 26th Division's shoulder patch was to be "a light blue YD," for the Yankee Division, an artilleryman went so far as to steal a pair of horizon blue French army pants he found hanging on a line so he could cut them up to make patches for his battery. The symbolic power of these insignia was so great that the troops resented anything that deprived them of the honor of wearing their patches. When he and his comrades were transferred to the 88th Division from their veteran 32nd Division in the winter of 1919, George O'Brien lamented, "We had to sew on their insignia on our sleeves. For a while no one made a move to do so but now we have to. We certainly prefer the cross arrow [insignia of the 32nd]."[45]

The doughboys' other source of sartorial pride was their overseas and wound stripes. In February 1918 the AEF GHQ authorized soldiers to wear a small, gold chevron on the left cuff of their uniforms for every six months that the soldier served overseas and a similar stripe on their right cuff to denote that the soldier had received a combat wound. Soldiers who served overseas for less than six months were authorized to wear a blue chevron on their left cuff. The overseas stripes were popular with the troops because they served as a visual testimony to the degree of the individual's veteran status. As one soldier boasted to his father upon receiving his first chevron, "I think they are rather pretty . . . they give an idea about how long a person has been over here." When the troops returned home, it also quickly separated the half of the army that had served "over there" from the other half who had spent the war safely in the States. The wound stripes were also an explicit testimony of the soldier's saltiness. They were awarded for a single incident where the soldier was wounded or gassed in combat. If a soldier was wounded at roughly the same time in two different parts of the body, he only received a single wound stripe for the event. For the doughboys, seeing a soldier with two or more wound stripes singled the man out as one who had truly seen war.[46]

Photo 27: Two veterans of the 81st Division proudly wear their unit shoulder patches and overseas stripes. The 81st Division is credited with introducing the shoulder patch (in this case a wildcat on a circular background) to the AEF. The patches and the overseas stripes (the small chevron on the soldier's lower left sleeve) were some of the greatest visible sources of esprit de corps in the U.S. Army. Source: author's collection.

Another source of esprit de corps and morale in the AEF was the animal mascots and pets that the doughboys picked up in their travels. Pets were both a link to normalcy and a source of entertainment and affection. Although dogs and cats were the most common pets among doughboys in the AEF, sometimes the selection of animals could be quite eclectic. One artillery battery kept "Two rabbits, a crow, a cat and a dog, named Teddy." The soldiers would go to great lengths to keep and protect their animals. The soldiers in one aero squadron managed to sneak its goat mascot to France by carrying it in a sack while boarding their ship and by hiding the animal's smell by constantly dousing it with toilet water and talcum powder during the voyage.

A company of Marines adopted a mixed-breed Irish setter and named it Verdun Belle and kept their faithful companion safe in the line by fashioning a gasmask for the dog from a cut-down French gasmask. A unit's love for its mascots, however, could prove troublesome. When their dog and her puppies ran in front of their artillery battery while it was firing during the Champagne fighting, the unit momentarily ceased shooting so one of its members could run forward of the gun, dodging enemy shells, to rescue its dogs from danger. Despite troubles such as these, at least one soldier maintained that there was a more practical reason to keep pets. He claimed that one of his mates had obtained a rabbit, who always accompanied the unit into the trenches. When the rabbit "heard a shell his little ears would go up": "If the shell was going to go over us he'd just stand there. If he scooted down into the trench we knew we'd better take cover too because a shell was going to land close by. He was a real lifesaver." In recognition of the close bond between the doughboys and their pets, at the end of the war the army allowed units to bring back their animal mascots to the United States, but the Department of Agriculture required that some returning animals had to be quarantined for ten to twelve days.[47]

Despite all of these official and unofficial methods for building and sustaining combat morale, the War Department often issued decrees that hamstrung the most important source of morale in the army: the development of close bonds between soldiers and between soldiers and their leaders. As noted in chapter 20, the soldier's survival, sense of well-being, and combat motivation generally stemmed from how well he was integrated into his squad and platoon. An enlisted man noted the importance of this relationship and stated, "The life in the Army is much more intimate than even the most affectionate family . . . There could be no closer intimacy than is in the barracks of a company under the conditions we had in France." The strength of this "family" rested upon how much its members trusted one another and its leaders, but the War Department and the AEF GHQ's personnel policies consistently harmed the development of this vital small-group cohesion.[48]

While the majority of its divisions were still training in the United States, the War Department began moving large numbers of soldiers from one camp to another to meet its demands for men with certain specialty training, to remove enemy aliens from its ranks, and to bring units slated for early departure for France up to their full strength before sailing. In reality, the willy-nilly migrations of troops seldom accomplished these goals and merely served to constantly disrupt training in the divisions and the creation of unit identity and cohesion. Seventeen of the forty-one divisions that reached France lost at least ten thousand men each to transfers between the time they were raised and the time that they sailed. The remaining divisions suffered lesser but still significant transfers of their soldiers. The 86th Division suffered the most disruption from these levees. Between January and April 1918, over one hundred thousand men were sent to the division and during the same period the War Department ordered that eighty thousand of the unit's soldiers be sent elsewhere. By the end of April 1918, the unit was left with only ten thousand men, roughly a third of its authorized strength. It was perhaps a small mercy that the AEF GHQ broke up this ill-starred unit upon its arrival in France and sent its soldiers to fill other places in the army.[49]

The trust that was essential to small-group cohesion came from the creation of long-term familiarity between soldiers and from the hardships that they shared in training and combat. This was difficult to maintain when a doughboy never knew with any certainty if he would be torn from his buddies and hurried off to a new unit of strangers while he was training in the States. As the morale officer of the 89th Division reported in July 1918, "Many friendships are no sooner made than broken. No man knows from one day to the next whether he will be in Camp Funston or sent to fill up another division." Charles Dienst, a captain in one of the division's infantry regiments, maintained that the transfer of large numbers of troops "seemed at the time to be striking at the progress and efficiency of the organization." As one of his soldiers departed for parts unknown, Dienst observed this parting of two buddies: "I'm ready to go," said the transferred man, "but I should like to go with my old outfit." The man who was left behind answered, "We're going to be filled up with strangers. I don't like it either." The results of these transfers were generally negative for the unit losing the soldier, the unit gaining the soldier, and the soldier himself. As the War Department tended to accelerate the movement of new troops to a division as their time to sail grew closer, the men that the gaining unit received were often poorly trained. An infantry officer in the 89th Division denounced the fact that his unit was brought up to strength by a "large contingent of newly drafted men" with no training when his regiment was only two weeks away from sailing. He scrambled to give the new troops their inoculations and the rudiments of drill and marksmanship. After facing similar personnel disruptions before his unit sailed, an officer of the 307th Infantry confessed that the regiment "never really found itself" before entering battle.[50]

Personnel disruptions did not end when the units arrived in France. To close the wide chasm in the doughboys' stateside training, the AEF GHQ established a large number of specialty schools and imposed attendance quotas on its subordinate units to fill the new courses.

Although the training in modern weapons and tactics was needed, the length and scheduling of the courses tended to strip combat battalions and companies of their junior officers and NCOs during key periods of their units' training. The absence of these leaders during their units' final preparations for combat often prevented them from building the trust that was so essential to small-group cohesion. To make matters worse, many of the officers and NCOs sent to the AEF's schools never returned to their units. The GHQ allowed its schools to retain some of their best students to serve as instructors. For example, between March 5 and November 11, 1918, the Infantry Specialist School requisitioned around 9 percent of the officers sent to its courses. This meant that the AEF's infantry regiments were deprived of 504 officers exactly at the time when they needed them the most.[51]

To provide officer replacements in France, on October 10, 1917, Pershing ordered the creation of the AEF Army Candidate School to select, train, and commission the army's suitable enlisted men. While noble in intent, the Candidate School proved to be a major hindrance to the morale and effectiveness of the AEF's combat units. Like other AEF schools, the Candidate School was filled by giving the divisions a quota to fill. For example, on September 18, 1918, the GHQ tasked each division to send twenty-five soldiers from each of their infantry regiments and six more from their machine gun battalions for officer training. In the three months prior to the Meuse Argonne, the 107th Infantry alone sent seventy-five soldiers to the Candidate School. The effect of these directives was to strip the combat units of many of their most promising NCOs. All but twenty-six of the 847 of the soldiers who graduated from the Candidate School on October 31, 1918, had been NCOs when they entered the course. One hundred and ninety-five of these men had even been company first sergeants when they enrolled in the course. An infantry company commander in the 308th Infantry noted that sending such large numbers of NCOs for officer training "proved a great loss to the regiment" and undercut the overall morale and combat readiness of the organization.[52]

The loss of friends to combat and transfer further eroded morale and cohesion in the AEF's combat units by breaking the bonds of trust and identification that bound soldiers together in combat. Reflecting these psychological blows, Corporal Francis Byrne went so far as to advise a recently drafted friend, "Don't make 'too many friends.' It doesn't pay to have too many of them I have found out to my sorrow." Many doughboys reported that the loss of familiar officers and buddies left them feeling estranged from their units. "The old battery has changed so much since I left the states that I wanted to get out," an artilleryman in the 35th Division lamented in a letter to his mother in September 1918, for the unit "has been filled up with drafted men three times and all the officers are new men and that makes quite a difference."[53]

Soldiers returning to their units after recovering from wounds seemed to feel particularly alienated from their organizations. A 28th Division infantryman recalled that there were "very few of my old buddies left" upon his return to his company after spending a month in the hospital. After recovering for forty-five days from wounds that he received in the Aisne-Marne drive, Irving Abrahams observed, "In my old company I felt like a stranger, for so many of the old crowd had been killed at the time that I got mine." A private in the 121st Field Artillery was dismayed to find that "it doesn't look like the old outfit now ... A person does not feel quite at home for some time."[54]

The AEF's personnel replacement policies did much to fuel the estrangement felt by both these soldiers and the replacements themselves. The unexpectedly high casualties of the summer and fall of 1918 forced the AEF GHQ to scramble to refill the depleted ranks of its divisions. Following the precedent used in the United States, the GHQ sometimes simply stripped soldiers from newly arrived divisions undergoing their initial training to bring more seasoned units back up to strength. In late August 1918, for example, the GHQ ordered the 7th Division to transfer eighty men per company in the regiments of the 13th Brigade to the 4th and 26th Divisions. Similar shortsighted policies sometimes diverted soldiers who had recovered from wounds to new units rather than returning them to their old companies. During the Argonne battle, the 80th Division's 320th Infantry received seven hundred replacements, drawn mostly from men from other units who had been released from the hospital following their convalescence for their wounds. Neither party was happy with this arrangement. One of the regiment's officers recalled,

> The men wanted to return to their old organizations, where their friends were. Each felt an affection for his old outfit and thought no other equal to it. Their wishes weren't consulted, nor ours . . . At once esprit de corps crashed. Instead we had "esprit de malcontent." No one should blame these men. They had been treated like cattle. They thought they had been sold to the highest bidder.

As had been the case with the men taken from the 7th Division, the AEF's policy of "robbing Peter to pay Paul" when it came to replacements created morale problems for both the gaining and the losing unit.[55]

The situation with men coming directly from the United States to serve as replacements was even worse. By the late summer of 1918 the ceaseless demand to fill the battered ranks of the AEF meant that the training of new draftees in the United States had all but broken down. In fact, complaints over the poor training of the new arrivals were a constant refrain from the units in the field. Officers frequently reported that their new replacements had received little to no tactical training prior to their arrival in France and far too many had very scant instruction on firing their rifles and using other basic weapons. One lieutenant recalled that twelve of the replacements that his company received on the eve of its attack at St. Mihiel had never been given any rifle training. Without time to correct this deficiency, their sole combat training consisted of firing five rounds into the dirt at their feet just before going over the top. The commander of the 307th Infantry informed the 1st Army's inspector general in October 1918 that 90 percent of the 850–900 replacements that his unit received just before going into the Argonne had never fired a rifle or thrown a grenade.[56]

This lack of training should have come as no surprise to the army's senior leaders. Inspectors in both the United States and France had warned the

Army General Staff and the AEF GHQ of the deplorable state of instruction given to the draftees entering the ranks in the summer and fall of 1918. The intelligence officers and operatives of the 2nd Depot Division (formerly the 83rd Division) interviewed soldiers from each new shipload of troops arriving in France to gauge their morale, loyalty, and state of training. On August 12, 1918, one agent reported that the twenty-five hundred replacements sent from Camps Hancock and Gordon were wholly untrained, with most having "been in the service only a few weeks" before sailing to France. The 597 draftees from Camps Gordon, Pike, and MacArthur who landed in France on September 16, 1918, "had all been in the army less than a month and have had little or no training." The intelligence operatives frequently noted that the replacements who arrived between August and October had scant training in gas defense and were fortunate if they had more than a day or two of rifle instruction or had spent more than a day on the rifle range. These shortcomings had also been noted by inspectors in the United States. After examining the basic training in several camps, an officer of the Army General Staff Training and Instruction Branch reported on October 2, 1918, that "men do not remain in the replacement camp long enough" to receive adequate training and observed that the seventeen hundred men preparing to leave Camp Gordon for France had received "no instruction in gas, rifle practice, and bayonet." At Camp Greenleaf he found that "during their fourteen days in the receiving camp they are given infantry training which is a joke," mostly due to the fact that "they are drilled by a few noncommissioned officers who know nothing, and by doctors who have had three or four days military training themselves." He was shocked to discover the general practice where "enlisted men have had to be placed in overseas units before being trained; many of them receive only three weeks' training," which included one week spent in the detention camp for quarantine.[57]

The life of a "casual" or replacement in the AEF was far from enviable. Few had had the time to build ties with any comrades before they were counted off, lined up, and hastily marched off from an AEF casual company to replace the dead and wounded of some distant and unknown unit at the front. A veteran infantry NCO admitted that the "replacements get the end of dirty things in the Army. They are shoved from pillar to post and back again . . . They acquire buddies one day to have them leave the next day . . . Their A[rmy] P[ost] O[ffice] number is changed before they receive mail from the folks at home." One such soldier described his life as a "casual" as being an end-less cycle of moves from one location to another in a vain search of his new unit, "with only a boot and a shove to help him on his dreary way." A war correspondent noted of the newly arrived replacements, "We could always recognize them on the roads of the battle area. They were paler, slighter, than the men who had had their proper hardening and had not just come from crowded transports, and they looked about nervously."[58]

The reception that the new men received at their new unit depended much on the mood and depth of fatalism of the veterans they first encountered. Oftentimes, if the unit was out of the lines for training or rest, the newbies would be teased, tested, and gradually integrated into the collective. Captain Fred Jankoska and his first sergeant, Harold C. Woehl, did their best to prepare their replacements for battle by pairing them up with veterans who would show the new men the ropes. Those arriving in the midst of battle, on the other hand, had to complete their instruction by a rough and deadly version of on-the-job training. As one Marine recalled, "Replacements always had a devil of a time when they first reached the firing line. They either learned fast, along with having lots of luck, or they didn't learn at all." He noted that their option was to emulate the "old timers," who "even though they may not have always known what to do next, they at least seldom betrayed that fact to us."[59]

It is little surprise that these exceptionally green and unprepared dough-boys often became casualties before puzzling out the survival skills of war. "Men who do not know the rudiments of soldiering," the AEF Inspector General noted, "soon become either 'cannon fodder' or skulkers."

An infantry regimental commander in the 77th Division complained in October 1918, "It was practically impossible to handle these men over the present terrain. They had no idea what it meant to extend [the formation] and would have to be led around from place to place." The fact that their new leaders "were practically strangers to them . . . made them very difficult to handle them . . . They were continually getting lost and straggling."[60]

Who could blame the replacements if they did straggle or prove difficult to handle? They certainly understood their plight and were painfully aware of how unprepared they were for battle. Milton B. Sweningsen had only been in the army for thirty-five days before sailing to France. In that brief period he was given very little relevant training. His training in France consisted of a bit of close order drill and one day on the firing range before being sent as a replacement to the 35th Division. He arrived in his new infantry company as they were entering the Argonne fighting. As he had been given no training in basic infantry tactics, when his officers ordered the unit to "deploy as skirmishers" and "advance in squad column," he had no clue what those commands meant. He later recalled thinking, "Now here I was, at the bottom of a hill, in a pit of fog and on the attack," without any idea of what he was supposed to do. He made it through the ordeal by sticking close to his squad leader and mimicking the NCO's movements and actions.[61]

The replacements were not the only doughboys whose morale and resolve were shaken by their incomplete training, ill-prepared leaders, and heavy casualties. One of the key indicators of the doughboys' combat morale was the large number of stragglers absent from their units in the Meuse Argonne. Major General Hunter Liggett later estimated that approximately one hundred thousand soldiers, or roughly one out of ten doughboys, had straggled from their units in the first month of the Argonne drive. This phenomenon was nothing new. Major General Robert Bullard stated that during the fighting around Château Thierry and during Aisne-Marne campaign, "Far back behind our lines and camps my provost marshal now began to gather large numbers of American soldiers" who were absent from the battle lines.[62]

It is impossible to know if Liggett's estimation of the number of stragglers was correct. However, reports by MP detachments and divisional inspectors general suggest that his figures were not far off. On October 8, 1918, the military mayor of Raucourt informed his superior that his MPs had apprehended "between 600 and 700" stragglers from the veteran 1st Division. Four days later the MPs of the 36th Division claimed to have rounded up another five hundred stragglers. In mid-October one division reported that its frontline strength was only sixteen hundred men, yet when it was pulled from the lines 6,818 soldiers suddenly reappeared in the unit's infantry regiments alone. The 1st Army's inspector general believed that the majority of these men were stragglers who had hidden out until the fighting was over.[63]

The scale of the straggler problem forced the AEF's corps and divisional commanders to take immediate and drastic actions. This was far from an easy undertaking. The region of the Meuse Argonne attack was blanketed with forests, dotted with small villages, and honeycombed with abandoned French and German bunkers and shelters. All of these were perfect hiding places for doughboys seeking to avoid combat. In fact, in early October, MPs from the 32nd Division discovered ninety soldiers hiding out in a large German dugout. To stem the tide of wayward soldiers, units formed "Hobo barrages" of MPs and troops drawn from the reserve to comb through their rear areas, round up all soldiers absent from their organizations, and herd them back to the front. By October 18, 1918, the V Corps had diverted forty-five hundred of its troops to deal with its straggler problem. As the AEF's casualties mounted, it had neither the time nor the manpower to bring the stragglers to justice. In the majority of cases when stragglers were apprehended, they were simply returned to their units without charges being filed against them. The 1st Corps commander attempted to punish stragglers by giving them "the most disagreeable work that could be found" and by forcing the offenders to wear "a large white placard . . . upon which was printed in conspicuous black letters 'straggler from the front line,'" but these efforts did little to prevent soldiers from leaving the front. In fact, straggling remained a problem to the end of the war. Between October 28, 1918, and November 1, 1918, the MP companies operating in the 1st Army's sector rounded up 613 stragglers. Just two days before the Armistice, the 2nd Army Provost Marshal noted that "straggling has been allowed to become a menace to the success of operations" and ordered the unit's MPs to "take such definite, immediate, and aggressive steps" to check the still growing problem.[64]

The question that remains is, what caused these doughboys to straggle from the front? As noted in the last chapter, the terrain and confusion of the Meuse Argonne led to a large number of "accidental stragglers" as men became separated from their units due to the natural fog and friction of war. Others left the line because of the breakdown of the social contract between the leader and the led. As noted in chapter 5, after fighting for days on scant rations, many doughboys left the lines to find food. Most of these "accidental" stragglers and food seekers returned to their units on their own as soon as they could, but those men found hiding out in the woods and shelters far from the fighting made deliberate choices to absent themselves from the fighting. Unfortunately, as few of these soldiers ever discussed why they avoided combat (or even admitted the act), the historical record is largely silent on their motivations. Perhaps they were all too aware of their own sketchy training, and the lack of combat skills of their leaders, to hazard life and limb at the front. Some of the veterans may have reached their limits of endurance and felt that it was now time for the newly arrived doughboys to do their share of sacrifice.[65]

The number of stragglers certainly points to problems of morale in the AEF, yet despite these issues, it must be kept in mind that the majority of doughboys continued to soldier on until the end of the war. Those who stayed were held in place by the bonds of comradeship, the need to show courage and prove their manhood, their faith in the American cause, and a host of other factors. For the most part, their combat leaders also attempted to set a good example for the men. Although the AEF's junior officers and NCOs were far from ready to face modern war, the majority took their jobs seriously and often sacrificed themselves as they led their troops forward. When the officers and NCOs displayed courage and endurance, the troops tended to follow. As one doughboy recalled, "The sergeants and older members formed the rallying-points that held the outfit together," when losses and privations began to erode the endurance of the troops.[66]

It is also interesting to note that despite all the blows to morale, from shortsighted personnel policies, heavy casualties, problems with supply, and the privations of the front, the Germans' efforts to corrode the Americans' spirits and induce the doughboys to surrender fell largely on deaf ears. A German surrender leaflet dropped on the American lines stated,

Never say die!

Don't die till you have to! **What business have you to die for France, or Alsace-Lorraine or for England in France?** Isn't it better anyhow to live than to die, no matter for how "glorious" a cause? Isn't it better to live and come back to the old folks at home, than to rot in the shell holes and trenches of France? You have heard many high falutin words about "liberty" and "humanity" and "making the world safe for Democracy" but honest now, aren't these catch words merely sugar coating to the bitter pill of making you spend wretched months far from home? Do you really believe those German soldier boys in their faded grey uniforms on the other side of "No Man's Land" are hot on the trail of your liberties? Just like you, they want the war to end with honor so that they can go back to their home folks. All they want is a chance to live and let live. And so, if it should happen to you to fall into their hands you will find that they will treat you fair enough on the principle of "**live and let live.**" Why run anymore chances than you have to, you might as well be a free boarder in Germany till the war is over. **You don't want to die till you have to!**

During the fighting in the Argonne, Germans showered the 32nd Division with leaflets that touted the fact that while the doughboys were suffering, "corporation heads at home were growing fabulously wealthy at the expense of the rest of the country." The leaflets, one artilleryman observed, "roused only loud derision among the hopelessly skeptical Americans." He explained, "Since the days of Peter the Hermit and Bernard of Clairvaux there has not been an army so blindly devoted in general to its ideals, so little given to counting the cost, and so little affected to adverse propaganda as the A.E.F." If he was right, then the doughboys truly did see themselves as "Pershing's Crusaders."[67]

When esprit de corps, small-group peer pressure, and the individual's sense of duty were not enough to encourage the doughboy to be a well-behaved, obedient, and reliable soldier, his officers could always turn to the military justice system to get him back on the straight and narrow path. The overriding purpose of this system was to ensure that those restless young men with guns stayed firmly under the control of their leaders and that the doughboys would more or less willingly put themselves in harm's way and kill the enemy. The focus of military law was ultimately to ensure perfect discipline and obedience in the ranks through a rigid enforcement of the Articles of War. Military justice was intended to not only punish reprobates but also make object lessons of them for their peers. To accomplish these goals, the military evolved a tiered system of judicial procedures that would hear a soldier's case based upon the seriousness of his offense and the degree of punishment he could receive.

A soldier could be tried by a general, special, or summary court-martial. The general court-martial consisted of a panel of five to thirteen officers and heard cases that constituted serious breaches of the Articles of War. This court had wide latitude in assigning punishments and could impose life sentences and the death penalty. All military death penalties had to be certified by the president. A special court-martial consisted of a three- to five-officer panel and judged noncapital crimes and offenses of the Articles of War. Its punishments were limited to dishonorable discharge, confinement, and forfeiture of pay for not more than six months. In a summary court-martial, the soldier was judged by a senior officer, most typically his regimental commander. These courts were for minor violations of the Articles of War and were limited to imposing dishonorable discharge and not more than three months' confinement and three months' forfeiture of pay. To ensure that a doughboy's misdeeds would not cause undue hardship on their families, the AEF GHQ ordered that any forfeiture from a soldier's pay would come from only what was left after deductions had been made for his mandatory family allowance, War Risk Insurance, and Liberty Loan payments.

Although the courts had wide latitude in their sentencing, the *Manual for Courts-Martial* did provide the maximum possible sentences for an array of crimes. For example, a soldier convicted of arson could get up to a twenty-year imprisonment at hard labor, while one found guilty of assault and battery could be sentenced to serve six months hard labor and lose up to six months of pay. In cases where the soldier was found guilty of murder or rape, the mandatory sentence was death or life imprisonment. Soldiers guilty of serious crimes or sentenced to long terms of imprisonment could be sent to federal penitentiaries or to the military Disciplinary Barracks at Fort Leavenworth, Kansas, Alcatraz Island, California, or Fort Jay on Governor's Island, New York. The Disciplinary Barracks had the reputation of being particularly harsh places to serve out one's sentence due to their rigid enforcement of a host of petty rules and for putting the hard in hard labor. When ordered confined, 40.7 percent of convicts served out their sentences in their post guardhouses, 52.8 percent were sent to one of the Disciplinary Barracks, and 6.5 percent were confined in federal penitentiaries.[68]

Battalion and company commanders also had the power to impose punishments on their soldiers for minor breaches of good order and discipline that fell beneath the threshold of a court-martial. Punishments in such cases were generally limited to assigning the soldier to extra and onerous work details, confinement in the guardhouse for up to a month, and the loss of up to one month's pay. To encourage the offender to mend his ways and to set an example for his comrades, the army intended that it be seen that the prisoner's plight was as disagreeable, dishonorable, and humiliating as possible. The prisoner only left the guardhouse under armed guard to do hard and unpleasant work around the camp, such as cutting wood, cleaning the streets, or serving as the kitchen police. He was denied the honor of being a soldier by being forced to wear a fatigue work suit instead of a uniform, was not allowed to wear any insignia such as the branch-colored cords on the campaign hat, and was denied the right to perform any military honors. These punishments hit the soldiers where it hurt most: in their pride, in their pocketbook, and in their free time.

Unlike with courts-martial, there were no records kept of company and battalion punishments. As such, we will never know how many soldiers were disciplined under those proceedings. However, based on the doughboys' narratives, such punishments were common. They also seemed to accomplish the purpose of imposing discipline or at least making the doughboys understand that the military forces that controlled their lives were very different from those of civilian society. One Marine wrote home, "Discipline is more than you could ever imagine. Everything is business here and no more foolishness goes." After one of his barracks mates was caught stealing an egg from the messhall, he reported home that "he got off very easy at that with a fine of $20.00. That is $20.00 for one egg so you see they are pretty costly here when obtained in that way." Private Luther Grover found out that the army frowned upon sleeping in on duty days. After failing to rise at six one morning, he was sentenced by his commander to get up at five in the morning for two weeks to feed his artillery battery's horses. Sometimes company punishments were more physically demanding and creative. Soon after landing in France, Marines who ran afoul of the rules in Warren Jackson's unit were submitted to a grueling regimen. For hours at a time the recalcitrant troops trotted around their makeshift brig with a heavy sandbag strapped to their back, urged on in their labors by the bellowing of a particularly odious sergeant.[69]

There were, however, limits to the commander's ability to impose company punishments indiscriminately. Upon being brought up on charges, the soldier could opt for a court-martial rather than submitting to the justice of his company or battalion commander. Paul Maxwell described his company commander as "a martinet with a sadistic complex." When this officer brought charges against him for having a small piece of lint next to his bunk during an inspection, Maxwell rejected the commander's offer of company punishment for the offense and chose to be tried by a court-martial. The company commander was livid at Maxwell's maneuver but did not want to risk having his imperious treatment of his soldiers exposed before his superiors. Having had his bluff called, the captain dropped the charges against Maxwell.[70]

Despite the legal limitations of these nonjudicial proceedings, company punishments flourished in France because the AEF GHQ did not want to be burdened by a large number of courts-martial or to have numerous soldiers sent back to the States for imprisonment or dishonorable discharge. In April 1918, General Orders 56 urged commanders to limit their number of courts-martial and greatly restricted the cases where soldiers could be returned to the United States to only those situations where the men's crimes merited hard labor in a penitentiary. The following month, General Orders 78 gave division commanders the power to assign soldiers sentenced to confinement by courts-martial to "provisional disciplinary detachments." These detachments would put the troublemakers to hard labor until such time as they were needed for combat, and then they were to be returned to their companies. Although few of these penal units seemed to have been formed, they did seek to strike the balance between giving commanders the ability to maintain discipline and the AEF GHQ's desire to maintain the army's personnel strength.[71]

There has always been a criminal element within any organization or society containing a large and diverse group of people; the American Army in the Great War was no exception. Given the nature of its mandate, the military judicial system dealt with offenses that mirrored those of civilian society, such as murder and rape, as well as crimes such as misbehavior before the enemy and disobeying a superior officer that were purely military in nature. Between April 6, 1917, and June 30, 1919, 36,248 soldiers (2,711 officers and 33,537 enlisted men) were tried by general courts-martial. During the same period, 39,285 soldiers were tried by special courts, and 438,361 men were tried by summary courts-martial. Although these figures sound high, the army's crime rate actually declined during the war. Between 1909 and 1916, an average 5.4 percent of the Regular Army's enlisted men were brought before a general court-martial. Only .73 percent of wartime enlisted men faced a similar trial, despite the fact that the army had grown from 133,000 Regulars to a force of four million men.[72]

For having such a large number of "restless young men with guns," violent crimes were rather rare in the American Army of the Great War. The judge advocate general reported that between April 6, 1917, and June 30, 1919, six officers and 137 soldiers were convicted of manslaughter, two officers and eighty-eight soldiers were convicted of murder, two officers and sixty-five enlisted men were convicted of rape, and another 130 enlisted men were convicted of assault with intent to commit rape. One officer and forty-eight soldiers were also convicted of mayhem: an ancient crime where the perpetrator caused injury to any part of another man's body that rendered him less able to fight or defend himself. The most common violent crime was assault. During the war, fifty-four officers and 1,687 soldiers were convicted of the various offenses (simple assault, assaulting a superior officer, and the like) related to assault.[73]

The Articles of War permitted the death penalty in cases of extreme violence and for military offenses in a time of war that undercut the discipline, effectiveness, and safety of the army. From the time that the United States entered the war until June 30, 1919, general courts-martial sentenced 145 men to death. Military offenses (desertion, disobedience of orders, misbehavior before the enemy, sleeping on guard post, and spying) accounted for 44 percent of these capital offenses. In the end, only thirty-five soldiers were actually executed, with twenty-five of these men being put to death in the United States and ten in the AEF (one additional soldier was executed in the AEF after June 30, 1919). No soldiers were executed for purely military offenses.[74]

President Wilson and Secretary of War Baker were generally inclined to see the doughboys as citizens who were only temporarily in uniform, citizens who still retained their rights and legal protections. As such, the two tended to show mercy in death sentence cases, especially when the offenses were purely military in nature. For example, on the night of November 3, 1917, Privates Forrest Sabastian and Jeff Cook of the 16th Infantry were discovered by their corporal sleeping while on guard duty while serving in the French trenches in Lorraine "in the face of the enemy." Both men were found guilty by general courts-martial and sentenced to be executed by firing squad. As they were the first soldiers in the AEF condemned to death for military offenses, the severity of their sentences raised questions in the War Department. On May 4, 1918, President Wilson granted the two full and unconditional pardons based on their youth and the fact that their "offense seems to have been wholly free from disloyalty or conscious disregard" of their duties. Likewise, after Private Albert Beauregard was found guilty of going AWOL "in the face of the enemy" from October 31 to November 19, 1917, he was also sentenced to be executed. However, the president commuted the sentence to life imprisonment, dishonorable discharge, and the forfeiture of all pay and allowances.[75]

This is not to claim that the wartime justice system was fair. Mirroring the norms of the times, African American soldiers were much more likely to have their death sentences carried out than their white comrades. Of the eleven soldiers executed in the AEF, eight were African Americans and one other, it was claimed at the time, was a Native American. Also reflecting the realities of Jim Crow America, five of these black soldiers were convicted of rape while the other three were convicted of murder and rape or murder and attempted rape. Furthermore, the military justice system tended to move swiftly and decisively against accused African Americans. Privates John Mann and Walter Matthews, both African Americans, were accused of "with malice aforethought willfully, deliberately, feloniously, unlawfully and with premeditation" killing Private Ralph Foley by beating and stabbing him on February 13, 1918, at Camp Logan, Texas. At the time of his death, Foley had been guarding Mann and Mathews while they were picking up refuse on the post. The very next day the two assailants were tried by a general court-martial. After a short period of deliberation, they were found guilty of murder and sentenced to be "hanged from the neck until dead." The death sentence was confirmed by President Wilson on March 22 and the pair were duly executed on April 5, 1918.[76]

Most offenses committed in the American Army fell far below the threshold of capital crimes. For example, in February 1918, the military police of the 29th Division at Camp McClellan, Alabama, made 399 arrests. The most common offenses were for AWOL (132 cases or 33 percent of the total) and being caught in a restricted area on post or in town (121 cases or 32 percent of the total). MPs cited fifty-one soldiers for being in improper uniforms, thirty-seven for being in town without a pass, thirty-seven others for being drunk, nine for altering their passes, nine more for associating with prostitutes, and one each for disorderly conduct, showing "insolence to M.P. on duty," and speeding in an automobile. These arrests reflected an overall trend in the army. The most common offenses for officers during the war was being AWOL (525 cases), offenses where the officer was drunk (515 cases), and conduct unbecoming an officer (334 cases). The most common offenses for enlisted men were being AWOL (6,660 cases), desertion (3,607 cases), larceny (2,290 cases), and offenses while serving as a sentinel, such as sleeping on guard duty (1,996 cases). These numbers do not tell the whole story. Although the number of desertions appears high, in the seven years prior to the war desertions in the Regular Army averaged 3,692 per year: a figure greater than that of the wartime army that was roughly thirty times its size.[77]

The question that remains is, how did the soldiers themselves view the military justice system? To some extent, the success of the army's wartime justice system could be judged by the flurry of newspaper reports and congressional investigations that hit soon after the Armistice. The returning doughboys showed little reticence in informing their elected officials of the abuses and injustices that they endured or witnessed. Senator George E. Chamberlain, a member of the powerful Committee on Military Affairs, became the veterans' champion for addressing these alleged misuses of power and led the charge to reform military justice. The former Oregon governor and attorney general and his allies charged that "the military Criminal Code itself is not modern and enlightened, but is an archaic code which systematically belongs to medieval times."

The critics of the military judicial system specifically charged that commanding officers had too much influence on the members of court-martial boards and that this led to an arbitrary execution of justice based upon the whims and predilections of the commander. Chamberlain and some of the experts testifying during the subcommittee hearings on his military justice reform bill also denounced the widespread charges brought against doughboys for violating the Ninety-Sixth Article of War. This "devil's article," as one witness testified, was a "catch-all for everything that nobody had thought of putting specifically among the offenses triable by a court." Under Article 96, if a commander could not charge a soldier for any other misdeed, he could still try the man for the rather nebulous offense of acting in a manner that was "prejudicial to good order and military discipline."

When Chamberlain and his supporters proposed that enlisted men should be included on court-martial boards and that an army lawyer had to be present during general courts-martial, the Army Judge Adjutant General Enoch Crowder launched into a spirited defense of the military's judicial system. Crowder and many other senior officers opposed including enlisted men on trial boards because they believed that such a measure too closely resembled the soldiers' soviet councils established during the Russian Revolution. Taking away some of the judicial powers of commanders, who "know much about discipline and something about military law," and placing it into the hands of lawyers, who "know much about law but little of soldiering, or of the discipline indispensable to successful soldiers," would lead to a state where officers could issue orders but have no power to enforce them.[78]

Although the army was largely successful in turning back the reformist tide, many doughboys agreed with Chamberlain's critique of military law. To them, the military justice system seemed arbitrary, unfair, vindictive, and counter to their democratic sensibilities and their rights as American citizens. A veteran testifying before Chamberlain's subcommittee stated flatly, "The very fact that some officer put charges against a man was sufficient to have the man convicted." Corporal Vincent Gianatasio also believed that there was "no chance to ever win at Summary Court, you're guilty as soon as the case starts." Even some officers agreed with this indictment of the judicial system. In a survey of returning officers conducted shortly after the armistice, several officers claimed that "the courts-martial system at present does not give a man a fair chance," with one noting, "It's hard to make human beings perfect. Some officers however have no fair sense of justice and treat their enlisted men like slaves." The army's courts-martial statistics confirm that these accusations had a lack of impartiality. Nearly 86 percent of soldiers tried by general courts-martial and 85 percent of those sent before special courts-martial were found guilty during the war. A whopping 94 percent of soldiers tried by a summary court-martial were convicted of their offenses.[79]

Chamberlain's other accusations also seem to have had merit, for example, the lack of any meaningful investigation of the charges before a soldier went to trial, the tendency of commanding officers to "put on trial a needlessly large number of trivial charges," the harshness of some sentences, and the fact that officers had little understanding of the law or proper judicial proceeding when serving as councils for the defense, prosecutors, or members of the court-martial. Noting the high number of soldiers court-martialed, the head of the American Legion's National Legislative Committee, Thomas W. Miller, thundered, "A system that practically brings 10 per cent of your force during a war before a court is obviously wrong." An officer returning from France admitted, "I do not believe that many officers who sit on the courts-martial are efficient enough or well enough versed in the matter of law to be on a courts-martial," while another confessed, "The average officer defending the accused does not devote enough time to the case." These accusations were true. During the war, men graduating from officer training courses had received only six to thirteen hours of instruction on military law and the *Manual for Courts Martial.* This was far too little education for men judging or defending others.[80]

The doughboys themselves also viewed the system as too rigid and harsh. One soldier missed loading a train with his unit because his officer had given him permission to have breakfast at the train station's café. While the man was eating, that same officer managed to wrangle passage for his unit on an earlier train without informing the soldier. When the man duly reported in to the local provost marshal soon after finding that he had been left behind, he was arrested. After being court-martialed the unfortunate soldier was sentenced to three years in prison and received a dishonorable discharge. George Loukides was sentenced to ten days in the guardhouse after going AWOL to celebrate Greek Orthodox Christmas. He felt that he had been punished because the court officers were unwilling to listen to his defense that his officers did not understand the fact that Christmas for the Greek Orthodox fell thirteen days after the Protestant and Catholic observation. His experience with the court left him with a lasting mistrust of the military justice system.[81]

Given what they perceived as an arbitrary justice structure, it is not surprising that many doughboys sought to buck the system and get away with petty offenses as much as possible. After going AWOL to visit his home in Pasadena, California, Floyd Sosey boasted to his mother, "I outwitted the M.P.s all the way down and got clear into camp with out being caught." When cornered by one of his sergeants and accused of the offense, Sosey was even slick enough to convince the NCO that he had seen and talked to Sosey while the wily doughboy was out of camp. Such actions came as no surprise to Chaplain Lee Levinger. He perceptively observed,

> These men were not trained soldiers, accustomed to such a system; they were healthy American boys and whom this constant subjugation to external control meant the immediate seeds of revolt. Autonomy meant then the evasion of the law . . . the test of manly independence came to be simply "getting away with it." If a man was caught in an infraction of the rules he had to take his punishment; if he was not detected or not convicted he was a successful soldier.

However, "getting away with it" did not extend to infractions against one's comrades. While it was OK to steal from the army or break minor rules, stealing or otherwise harming a fellow soldier often brought harsh barracks room justice. An infantryman stated, "It is interesting to note that the punishment imposed on a thief by official authority . . . was often was less severe than that imposed by his comrades. The life of a petty thief in a unit might be, and often was, made so miserable that he would want to transfer out."[82]

Some doughboys even charged that numerous Americans soldiers were executed in France without any form of trial. In 1923, after some of these charges were published in the press, the Senate ordered a special committee to probe the allegations. After reviewing the testimony of over one hundred veterans who claimed to have witnessed the brutal treatment of American soldiers or summary executions, the committee found that their claims were unsubstantiated. In one of the cases, the committee investigated Major Hierome P. Opie, of the 116th Infantry, who was accused of shooting a soldier who was retreating from battle on October 9, 1918. The committee concluded that Opie had merely fired shots in the air and in front of a group of fleeing soldiers to halt their retreat and to prevent a general rout of his unit. However, the committee did substantiate two cases of summary executions in the AEF. In one of these cases, a conscientious objector was bayoneted to death by a guard who had orders to make the man put on his pack and march with his unit to the front. In the second case Lieutenant Emmet S. Cochran shot and killed Private Edward Whitaker, an African American soldier in the 369th Infantry. Cochran claimed that Whitaker attempted to stop him from quelling a riot of black soldiers in the town of Dommartin la Plachette and that he shot the private after Whitaker aimed a rifle at him. In both cases, courts-martial acquitted the accused killers of any wrongdoing.[83]

Although cases of summary justice of doughboys were rare, they still occurred. In fact George Patton boasted to his wife of just such an occurrence in the Argonne in late September 1918. When his tanks became stuck in German trenches on the second day of the offensive, George Patton became enraged when the infantrymen his unit was supporting were not doing "a damned thing to kill Bosch" and remained in nearby ditches refusing to move forward. As he was the only officer on site, he ordered the cowering doughboys to help free his tanks by clearing a passage through the trench walls. He wrote his wife on September 28, 1918, "I think I killed one man here. He would not work so I hit him over the head with a shovel." In another case, a soldier in the 16th Infantry refused an order to go over the top with his company. Despite strict prohibitions on striking subordinates, the soldier's company commander noted with approval, "two black eyes and threats of more delivered by his platoon sergeant got him forward."[84]

It must be noted that not all doughboys objected to the military's disciplinary and justice system or even the dealing out of summary punishments when the situation dictated. Alonzo LaVanture for one found the discipline in his unit to be very strict, but as soon as he was promoted to sergeant he saw the merit of the system and came to believe "the stricter the discipline the better for the recruits." After serving as a witness during a court-martial, an 82nd Division doughboy admitted that he found the military legal procedures "more fair than the civil courts at home." None of the members of the 16th Infantry seemed bothered by their platoon sergeant's beating of one of their comrades when the man refused to go forward. In that case, the man's greatest crime was not disobeying an order but rather, in their eyes, failing to live up to his obligations to the group.[85]

The members of the AEF specifically tasked with suppressing crime and maintaining law and order were the members of the military police. There was no standing military police corps in the army when the United States entered the war. As such, the AEF had to improvise one by using manpower from its depot divisions and with replacements arriving in France. Unfortunately, the AEF never had enough MPs to accomplish the multitude of tasks assigned to them. The divisional MP companies had the mission of traffic control in the division's rear area, the apprehension of stragglers, the temporary holding and transfer of enemy POWs, the maintenance of discipline, and the suppression of crime within the division. Other MP companies were assigned to escort POWs from the front and to guard POW camps and to ensure discipline and fight crime in the AEF's ports, camps, and bases. To add to the problem of being overtasked, the men transferred to the AEF provost marshal's department to fill its MP companies had very little police training.

Although the AEF's crime rate was relatively low, the army did have its fair share of thugs and criminals that kept the MPs busy. In fact, the head of the AEF Division of Criminal Investigation claimed that "some of the cleverest and most desperate crooks in the United States were caught in the draft and lost no time in starting operations in France." One gang of nine deserters conducted at least thirty-two major crimes, including robbery, assault and battery, and attempted rape, in Paris before they were captured by the AEF Criminal Division in January 1919. In one instance, four of these outlaws beat the owner of a cafe senseless and robbed her of 1,860 francs. During the raid on the deserters' lair, the MPs recovered large sums of stolen money and other loot, several firearms, and a Red Cross ambulance.[86]

Despite such valiant efforts, MPs remained patently unpopular with their fellow doughboys. One officer lamented "the way in which life overseas was made miserable by Military Police when our allies allowed no such petty annoyances." The MPs made themselves odious by their rigid enforcement of pettifogging rules, their highhanded treatment of their fellow troops, and the fact that they were generally far removed from combat. A soldier complained in *Stars and Stripes* that he was grabbed off the streets of Tours with a large number of other doughboys by the MPs for failing to salute. After being lectured by the MPs' commander for their poor discipline, the man tried to explain that he was unable to salute because of a recent wound. The unsympathetic officer dismissed his explanation as a poor excuse. Doughboys seem to have particularly hated Marines serving as military policemen. One recalled,

> They patrolled the railroads, hid in the bushes, lined the streets, and came out of the floor and every café and coeducational centre. Always they wanted to know who we were, where we were going, what we were doing, and were we looking for trouble? It was pretty hot, and we had shed a few clothes, so they yapped: "Where the hell's your blouse?" The answer to this one was easy and immediate "I left it up at the front where their ain't no Marines."

The same man gleefully recalled that when one of these "S.O.S. cowboys," as he termed the MPs, pulled a pistol on a wisecracking comrade, his friend disarmed the policeman and proceeded to beat him senseless with the weapon.[87]

The actions of the MPs themselves often brought them into disrepute. As previously noted, MPs had the highest VD rates of any group in the AEF. With scant training in policing or ethics, a number of MPs stationed in the towns occupied by the AEF succumbed to graft, corruption, and the strongarming of French civilians and their fellow doughboys. In Le Mans, an MP sergeant formed his own "strong-arm squad" that randomly raided the city's hotels and cafés to enforce his version of army regulations. Over time, the sergeant started to harass women who refused his advances, assaulted business owners who attempted to halt his depredations, and was accused of shaking down prostitutes for protection money. The local American intelligence officer that reported the sergeant's actions was angered that the NCO's officers were unwilling to stop the "strong-arm squad's" activities or to address other MP failings in the area.[88]

Perhaps the most hated and feared MP in the AEF was the former Phoenix, Arizona, policeman Lieutenant Frank "Hard Boiled" Smith, the commandant of Prison Farm Number 2. Smith's camp on the outskirts of Paris earned a reputation for being a particularly harsh, unjust, and violent place. Over the course of its existence, the camp housed between five hundred and twelve hundred prisoners. Its demographics were described as "twenty-five per cent the scum of the American Expeditionary Forces; 25 per cent would be if they had the chance; and 50 per cent good soldiers gone bad." Most of the prisoners were men caught being AWOL while visiting Paris. One such soldier, John Forbes, was arrested by the MPs in Paris for a minor infraction. He claimed that an MP detachment under Smith's command subjected him to "the roughest form of treatment" during his four days in their custody. This consisted of being manhandled, thrown to the ground, and forced to endure harsh drill and exercise sessions that brought the prisoners to the brink of collapse.

Smith was a man of inflated ego and violent emotion who once described himself to a group of newly arrived prisoners as "the man with the brass knockers on around this place" and warned them that if they did not behave themselves, "we will kill you and send you out in a box." Smith's methods were so brutal and vindictive that army and congressional investigators later accused him of abusing both his authority and his prisoners while in charge of the camp. At least nine soldiers accused him of striking them in November and December 1918 alone. Smith was also charged with stealing his prisoners' money and possessions and deliberately depriving the men of adequate food, clothing, and shelter. After being court-martialed for abuse of prisoners and larceny, Smith was sentenced to be dismissed from the service after serving three years' (later reduced to eighteen months') hard labor. In a case of poetic justice, Smith later claimed that he was himself beaten and doused with fire extinguishers while in custody at St. Nazaire while he was waiting to sail to the Disciplinary Barracks at Governor's Island, New York, to serve out his sentence.[89]

Although incidents of mass straggling, the inequities of the military justice system, and the depredation of officers such as "Hard Boiled" Smith highlight the challenges the AEF had in maintaining discipline in its ranks, the American Army remained a relatively well-ordered force throughout it service. Despite heavy casualties, generally inadequate training, and unprepared leaders, the morale in the AEF withstood these hammer blows to its overall morale. In the end, the restless young men with guns proved to be a greater threat to the Germans than to themselves or to the people of France.

23

CC Pills, Going West, and the Hen-Flew-End-Ways

The Sick, the Wounded, and the Dead

There has always been a fundamental truth about war: sometimes it gets its participants sick, hurt, or killed. The sixty-odd years prior to the Great War pitted medical science against weapons science in a race to see if the healers or the killers could save or carry off the greatest number of people. To a very great extent, the soldiers of World War I lived in an age of medical miracles. More medical advances had occurred between 1840 and 1910 than in all of previous human history combined. During those years the momentous breakthroughs in anesthesia, antisepsis, asepsis, bacteriology, and immunology revolutionized medical care and offered solutions to heretofore intractable health problems. At the same time, however, that same human inventiveness was put to work developing weapons that would complicate the healers' work by the scale of human wreckage the implements of destruction created and the new medical challenges that they posed. It is a great irony that war itself often pushed forward medical science by forcing doctors to make a virtue of necessity. During the Great War procedures that had been pioneered prior to the war, such as triage, psychological care, and blood transfusions, became common or accepted practices by the war's end. Experiences during the war with gas gangrene, trench fever, massive wounds, and gas poisoning forced doctors to innovate to save the lives of their patients. As one American doctor ruefully admitted of his military experience, "I learned more medicine than in any recent two-year period of my medical life."[1]

As previously noted, the doughboys' encounters with military medicine began at the very moment of their induction with their physicals and inoculations. Many took away from these assembly-line procedures the belief that the army's medical personnel were a rather imperious and unfeeling lot. As part of their indoctrination, the new civilian turned military doctors were warned that the ranks were filled with malingerers seeking to avoid work and training by faking a variety of medical complaints. One soldier reported that of the twenty men who appeared with him at sick call, only two actually received any real medical care. To most of the ailing, the doctor simply gave a "malicious grin" and prescribed "two hours of strenuous exercise" before returning the men back to their units as fit for duty. Another trainee recalled, "The doctor, who is usually a pleasant sort of fellow, asks what your ailment is, and you explain your troubles to him. No liquid preparations outside of castor oil are to be had, although thirty-eight different drugs are used. Nine times out of ten you are given pills. The doctor's orders are: Keep your head cool, your feet warm, and your bowels open." As the passage highlights, the standard complaint of many soldiers was that the medicos simply gave soldiers a dose of the ubiquitous "CC pills," an aspirin-like concoction, regardless of the soldiers' symptoms and without any real examination and sent them back as ready for duty. Private Knud Olsen complained, "At Camp Dodge they either gave you an aspirin or painted with Iodine and marked you fit for duty." This practice was so widespread that the terms "pill-roller" and "pill-pushers" became doughboy slang for all medical personnel. As medics and doctors were not directly assigned to combat companies and battalions, few soldiers were able to develop the close bonds with their corpsmen that later American soldiers enjoyed. As such, many doughboys never overcame their cynical view of army medicine. When his company was pulled out of the line after nine days of fighting in the Argonne, an 82nd Division infantryman noted that most of the unit's survivors were sick and exhausted. He recorded that he and his buddies did not seek medical attention because "we didn't like the idea of walking 4 or 5 miles and maybe then not getting any care."[2]

This is not to say that the troops did not appreciate the care that they were later given when they were seriously sick and wounded. Many doughboys were effusive in their praise of the doctors and nurses who treated them. Major Martin Tinker was so admired by his patients that some wrote to him after the war to thank him for his skills and sympathetic treatment. Tinker operated on William Stout after he had been hit in the arm and hand by a machine gun bullet in October 1918. Although the surgery was unable to return full function to Stout's hand, in July 1920, he wrote Tinker,

> I desire to write you and express my thanks to you for what you sincerely tried to do . . . I always admired you and loved you very much for your kindness toward me. Your kind hearted nature, your cheerfulness, your words of encouragement were always a source of pleasure for me and I can sincerely say that I had more respect for you than any other officer with whom I came in contact. While others were haughty and arrogant, cold hearted and apparently unsympathetic toward those who suffered with pain and anguish, I found you to be a ray of sun shine in a cold and heartless world.

Another former patient promised Tinker, "I am mighty proud of the operation and will at any time give my very best recommendation to any one who is so lucky to have you perform the operation on them." He closed by stating that he was "ready at any time to assist you in any way that is possible for me." These were ringing endorsements indeed.[3]

Being inducted into the army also brought many soldiers into their first contact with dentistry. While many soldiers had a jaundiced view of military doctors, they were even more damning in their opinions of dentists. In fact, until 1901, most dental care in the army was performed by enlisted hospital stewards. While the army brought in its first contract dental surgeon in 1901, it was not until 1911 that it commissioned its first dental officer. It seems that both the army and its soldiers viewed dentistry as a lesser handmaiden to "real" medicine. In some cases, the actions of the dentists themselves did little to help their cause. A Missourian wrote home to his sister in December 1917,

> Well I have lost 3 teeth in this horrible war. I was a fool for letting them pull my teeth, makes me sick every time I think about it—two of them at least could have been crowned. They don't do anything but pull and fill in the army. Those that can't be filled they yank them out—talk about hurt they could not have done worse if they had used a pick and shovel on me.

Charles Minder also had a bad experience with army dentistry. After reporting in with a toothache, "the dentist took one look at it, reached for a pair of pliers, gave it a yank, and before you could say 'Jack Rabbit!' it was out, and I was on my way back to the line. He didn't use anything to deaden the pain, no antiseptic, nothing at all." Minder was so incensed by his treatment that he swore that if he were to meet the dentist after the war, he would throw a brick through his window.[4]

Whatever the virtues or shortcomings of the military's doctors and dentists, their skills were vital to the smooth running of the military machine. The war created a staggering number of sick, injured, and wounded soldiers. As official army reports varied considerably in their accounting of casualties, the most accurate source for pinning down the exact figures for how many doughboys received medical treatment during the war is the meticulous multivolume history *The Medical Department of the United States Army in the World War*. According to the volume on medical statistics, over 3.5 million soldiers were admitted for treatment of a disease, 299,069 were seen for nonbattle injuries, and 224,089 received care for battlefield wounds between April 1, 1917, and December 31, 1919. When it came to disease, nearly 43 percent of admissions came from five maladies: influenza (791,907 cases), venereal disease (357,969), mumps (230,356), measles (98,225), and tuberculosis (38,607). With the exception of VD, the spread of these diseases was a direct result of bringing large numbers of men together into the close confines of training camps, transports, and trenches.[5]

During the war, just under 14 percent of the AEF's doughboys were battle casualties: those who were killed in action, those who later died of their wounds, and those who suffered nonfatal combat wounds (including gas poisoning). The ratio of killed to wounded in the AEF was 1 to 4.2. Roughly one in ten of the AEF's doughboys (210,398 men) received nonfatal combat wounds. Although gas casualties accounted for 31 percent of the wounded, the greatest source of combat injuries was from projectiles fired by artillery or small arms weapons. In half of these cases, the surgeons could not or did not specify the type of projectile that caused the wounds. When the projectile could be identified, 28 percent were caused by machine gun or rifle bullets and 70 percent were due to artillery shell fragments and shrapnel.[6]

Modern artillery shells caused horribly mutilating wounds. The effects of shellfire even gave rise to lurid postwar tales that the army had secreted away hundreds of "basket case" soldiers in isolated wards in hospitals across the nation. A "basket case" was a soldier who had lost all of his limbs during the war and thus had to be carried around in a basket or litter. Although the army surgeon general, Merritte Ireland, stated categorically in March 1919 that no doughboys had suffered such wounds, the myth died hard. The idea remained in the public mind largely due to Dalton Trumbo's novel *Johnny Got His Gun* (1938), the movie based on the book from 1971, and the song "One" by the band Metallica, released in 1989. In the novel, the doughboy Joe Bonham suffers the trauma of losing his limbs, face, eyesight, hearing, and ability to speak, and yet is fully conscious and aware of his situation. Although no soldiers were recorded as actually enduring such injuries during the war, the reality of the grievous wounds that the doughboys suffered were nearly as nightmarish as any that could be created in the mind of a novelist.[7]

Beyond the statistics and the myths, it should be kept in mind that military medicine served three major purposes in the Great War. One was humanitarian: to preserve life and restore, as much as possible, the heath of the sick and wounded. Another was linked to morale. It was of vital importance to the soldiers to know that if they were wounded, the army would make every effort to preserve their life and limb. The last was practical: to conserve the fighting power of the army by healing the soldier so he could return to battle as soon as possible. To accomplish these goals, the central tenants of the AEF's treatment of battle casualties were to treat the wounded as far forward as was feasible, to return the lightly wounded back to combat as quickly as possible, and to steadily evacuate the more severely wounded back through various levels of treatment facilities until they reached the hospital that best provided the care that the soldier required.

The wounded man's first level of care came from himself or his comrades. Each soldier carried a first aid bandage in a small, sealed copper case. When wounded, the man, or his comrade, was to apply the bandage to stop bleeding until the injured soldier could be carried to the battalion aid station. Although the average doughboy's medical training was rather sketchy, they did the best that they could for their buddies as the combat situation allowed. After being shelled in the Argonne, Horatio Rogers discovered a wounded member of his company as the unit moved forward:

> His face was the color of ivory, his coat was soaked in blood, and there was a hole the size of my fist in the right side of his chest below the shoulder, from which blood was pouring. I ripped open his first-aid packet and plugged the hole with gauze. It didn't stop bleeding, so I used my own packet and then tied my belt around his chest to keep the packing in.

Having expended all of his meager medical supplies and unable to linger longer with the wounded man, Rogers pushed him into a shell hole to protect him from further injury and then moved forward, hoping that the company medical detachment would soon discover the man.[8]

To avoid being separated from their comrades, some of the slightly wounded opted to forgo anything other than bandaging themselves or receiving first aid from their buddies. A 91st Division infantryman was hit in the forehead by a shell fragment that cut the top of his helmet. He informed his girlfriend that the fragment "cut my right eye brow open and cracked my skull, but it did not do much damage and it seems to be all right again now except a slight head ache once in a while." He continued to soldier on, perhaps oblivious to the fact that in addition to his wounds, he had also suffered a concussion. In the heat of battle, some men did not even realize that they had been wounded. It was not until a lull in his company's fighting in the Argonne that Lieutenant John Stringfellow felt a lump or bruise though his uniform near his shoulder. After removing his tunic, he discovered that a spent rifle bullet had entered his arm at his elbow, traveled just under his skin, and lodged in his shoulder muscle. He had been wounded sometime during the day's action but had never felt it.[9]

Medical personnel at the company level were scant. Each infantry company generally had two medics (called sanitation men at the time) assigned to them from the battalion aid station before going into battle. These medics were only equipped with a belt or pouch containing a number of bandages and a hatchet or bolo knife for improvising splints. Their main role was to provide emergency care to stop bleeding and stabilize the wounded long enough for stretcher-bearers to pick the soldier up and move him to the battalion aid station.

The next level of care for the wounded was at the battalion aid station. After assigning eight medics to the companies, the battalion aid station was left with a stretcher squad consisting of four two-man litter teams and an aid station squad made up of two medical officers, three NCOs, and three sanitation men. The aid station itself was located one hundred meters to a kilometer behind the front lines depending on the combat situation. While the battalion aid station was the first place where the wounded would see a doctor, the medical care that the officers provided was rather basic, consisting mostly of reapplying or adjusting bandages, basic splinting, and other stabilizing care that prepared the patient for further movement to the rear. The only triage at this level was to weed out the slightly wounded and send them back to the front and to direct the walking wounded to proceed to the dressing station under their own power. The medical officers also had a limited supply of antitetanus serum and morphine for pain. Although the widespread use of antitetanus was another of the war's life-saving innovations, receiving the shot was a far-from-pleasant experience for the patient. One soldier went so far as to argue that the shot was more painful than his wound. He claimed that the hypodermic seemed to be "about the size of a twenty-penny nail" and that the "ministration raised a welt about half the size of a tea cup with an accompanying sensation unpleasant to an extreme extent." To ensure that the soldier was not given an overdose of morphine or the tetanus serum, the medical officer was to use iodine to mark the wounded soldier's forehead with an "M" or "T" to indicate to others in the chain of treatment that the man had been given shots of those drugs.[10]

With only two medical officers and nineteen total enlisted men providing care for a thousand-man infantry battalion, heavy casualties could quickly overwhelm the aid station's limited capacity. This was particularly true for the stretcher squad. They had to scour the battalion's front for the wounded and bring their heavy loads back to the aid station, often through difficult terrain and enemy fire. As one Marine recalled, "Carrying the limp form of a wounded man three-quarters of a mile is an undertaking to say the least." In the opening days of the Argonne offensive blocked roads forced litter carriers in the 79th Division to carry their wounded over five miles to the divisional dressing stations. Regiments attempted to increase their number of stretcher-bearers by assigning members of the regimental band to the duty or by using captured Germans for the task. At times, the divisional ambulance companies also provided extra litter teams to the combat regiments. Even with these expedients, casualties among the litter teams and the unexpected numbers of wounded during the bloody actions at Soissons and the Meuse Argonne often left infantry units woefully short of personnel to move the injured to the rear. A private in the 2nd Division nearly bled to death a few days before the Armistice because his regiment had lost many of their stretcher-bearers. He was fortunate that a passing friend recognized him and stopped his bleeding by applying a tourniquet made from a leather bootlace above the wound.[11]

Although the majority of stretcher-bearers were courageous and dedicated, not all lived up to the life-and-death responsibilities of their positions. On the opening day of the Argonne attack, the inspector general of the 79th

Division discovered a severely wounded man laying on a litter in the middle of a road while the four men who should have been carrying him to the dressing station lounged in a ditch beside the road. When the inspector asked the bearers why they had stopped, they replied that the way to the station was under shellfire. Not being satisfied by this response, the officer drew his pistol and threatened to shoot one of the party if they did not pick up the litter and carry the wounded man. He then escorted the party to the rear. Two weeks later, the inspector general of the 82nd Division reported that "stretcher bearers are frequently selected from men believed to be less valuable as fighting men." He argued, "It is a mistake to choose stupid men, men with an imperfect understanding of English or men of faint resolution" for such an important job. While some combat units assigned their infantrymen to augment the litter carriers, this practice was frowned upon by the AEF GHQ. Senior AEF commanders did not want to dilute the fighting power of their combat units to perform this task. This, however, did not stop the troops from aiding their injured comrades. At Soissons, Warren Jackson and a buddy improvised a litter from a blanket wrapped around two rifles to remove their wounded friends from the front. Jackson's actions were certainly altruistic, but others used aiding the wounded as an excuse to straggle from the front.[12]

From the battalion aid station the wounded proceeded to the divisional dressing station. Each division manned two or three of these stations at locations one to six kilometers from the front depending on the combat situation. The dressing stations were run by the four divisional ambulance companies (one horse-drawn and three motorized). Whenever possible, the ambulance companies sent their litter parties forward to the battalion or regimental aid stations to carry the wounded back to the dressing stations. The dressing stations were more than just what the name implied. They were in fact minihospitals where emergency surgeries could be performed to stop major hemorrhages and to close sucking chest wounds. One of the stations' other major functions was to apply splints to immobilize fractures. This was vital to stopping more damage to the body as the broken ends of the bone continued to lacerate the wound and to easing the pain of those bouncing through the torn roads of the front during the ambulance ride to the field hospital. The stations also contained kitchens and wards where the wounded were treated for shock by warming their bodies and giving them hot drinks and food. This practice represented one of the war's major medical breakthroughs. Treating soldiers for shock greatly improved their survival chances by strengthening their constitutions and stabilizing them for later surgery or evacuation to receive a higher level of care.[13]

The last mission of the dressing station was to evacuate the wounded to the field hospital or other treatment facility. At full strength each division had thirty-six motor ambulances and twelve horse-drawn ambulances. As these resources could quickly be overtaxed, it was common practice to move the walking and slightly wounded in empty supply trucks returning from the front. As the ambulances frequently operated within the range of German artillery, it was not unusual for patients to receive additional wounds during their evacuation. The amount of time that it took to evacuate the wounded depended on the extent and condition of the sector's roads and the amount of traffic operating on them. During the St. Mihiel operation, ambulance drivers in the 2nd Division managed to have their patients delivered to the field hospital within twenty minutes of the men being wounded, but the 5th Division's drivers required four to six hours to perform this mission. The poor transportation infrastructure and crowded roads at Soissons and the Meuse Argonne greatly hindered the evacuation of the wounded. On average at Soissons, it took seven or eight hours for the injured to reach the field hospitals. During the Meuse Argonne, it was even worse. The AEF inspector general reported that it took five to six hours for the wounded to reach the field hospitals and another ten to sixteen hours for them to arrive at the evacuation hospitals. Medical personnel were more pessimistic and later estimated that it took ten to twelve hours for the wounded to arrive at the field hospitals. Their higher estimates may be closer to the mark. Ambulance drivers informed the 79th Division's inspector general that it took them fifteen hours to make the five-kilometer trip to the unit's field hospitals. The inspector believed that the delay resulted in "hundreds" of unnecessary deaths. To solve this problem, some medical officers took matters into their own hands and took the risk of moving their treatment facilities closer to the fighting to better serve the wounded. In the Argonne, the commander of the 4th Sanitary Train moved his unit forward because it was taking his ambulances twelve hours to make the round trip to and from the front lines and the wounded "were accumulating in great numbers without receiving proper medical attention or first aid." His actions certainly saved lives or at least provided more comfort to the wounded.[14]

The process of being wounded and evacuated to the rear was harrowing for most soldiers. Instantly those suffering serious wounds went from being an active agent on the battlefield to a near-helpless encumbrance to those around them. The man's sense of dread and powerlessness was compounded when the fighting moved on, leaving them alone on the field. Then he began to worry that his wounds would not be tended before his life ebbed away. Charles P. Darby, a soldier in the 321st Infantry, explained these fears in a letter to his mother he wrote while recovering from the wounds that he received in the Meuse Argonne:

> I contracted pneumonia from lying on the wet ground for so long after I was wounded and a lot of bad blood and corruption formed around my lungs. Well this had to be taken out right away and so I was operated on and part of one of my ribs is gone. The gunshot wound on the knee was painful but luckily the kneecap wasn't fractured. It hit me and then bounced out . . . The firing position of a soldier in battle is lying flat on his stomach keeping as low as possible. The first bullet that struck me went in between my two shoulder blades and came out my right side about the ninth rib. Well this knocked me about five yards . . . I rolled over on my right side and just at that moment I was hit in the right knee.

The severely wounded man crawled to a shell hole and "prayed for an ambulance to come there and take me to a hospital and also made up my mind there that if I lived thru that I would be a better man in the future." He laid in the hole for several hours before hearing the approach of a number of Germans. The helpless man feared what would come next and "wondered what they would do to me if they found me. I could not run or make a fight and I heard they were very cruel to their prisoners." Fortunately for Darby, the Germans only wanted to surrender and one of the German prisoners dressed Darby's wounds and helped him to the rear. This, however, was not the end of the doughboy's ordeal. The ambulance trip to the rear "was a rough ride, and one poor fellow who had been shot in the head, groaned and screamed all the way to the hospital and kept crying for water." Darby informed his mother that he hoped to return to work in a steel plant upon his return home but noted that after his wounding, "I am not as good a man physically as I was before the war."[15]

Darby was far from alone in experiencing a long and painful trip to the hospital. Lieutenant F. L. Miller was wounded in the leg by a machine gun while trying to clear the Bois de Septsarge in October 1918. The bullet fractured his thighbone, leaving a wound so extensive that he believed that the Germans had used "dum-dum" bullets. His ambulance trip from the front was horrible. Not only did its bouncing through shell holes and rutted roads constantly jar his fractured leg, but also the wounded man lying on the stretcher above his head died during the journey, an experience that he recalled "didn't do much to improve my spirits." As with the stretcher-bearers, the quality of care that the wounded received was dependent on the fortitude and skills of the ambulance drivers. While he was being evacuated, Edwin Arpin's ambulance came under shellfire and the driver abandoned his vehicle and its mostly helpless passengers to seek cover. To get the feckless driver to return to his duties, Arpin pulled out a Luger pistol that he had captured and threatened to shoot him. Although his trip was harrowing, life improved greatly for the wounded doughboy upon reaching the hospital. After being washed, warmed, and deloused, Arpin admitted, "I lay stretched out on my cot actually giggling with sheer joy."[16]

The next stop on the casualty's travels was to one of the division's four field hospitals. These hospitals were located three to eight miles from the front and were equipped to care for and temporarily hold 216 patients each. It was usually at the field hospitals where the first true triage of the wounded occurred. Given the relatively limited holding and treatment capacity of these hospitals, it was important for their medical personnel to quickly and efficiently separate out those men who required immediate life-saving care from those whose wounds allowed them to safely move on to an evacuation hospital and those whose injuries were so extensive that it made little sense to evacuate them or devote critical time and manpower to their care. Although this process sounds rather cold-blooded, in a hospital filled with wounded, it was simply illogical to devote efforts to try to save a horribly wounded man whose likely chances of survival were slim when the same amount of care and time could be used to perhaps save a score of others.

The field hospitals were equipped to perform nonspecialist surgery and had mobile X-ray machines, laboratories, electric light sets, and large steam sterilizers. To keep the flow of patients moving so as to not overburden any of the links in the evacuation chain, during the Meuse Argonne the 1st Army's chief surgeon directed that the field hospitals perform only minimal operations and have most of their casualties transported to the evacuation hospitals within fifteen hours of their arrival. Although this sounded good on paper, the 1st Army's directive proved to be impractical in execution. Large numbers of the wounded who arrived at the field hospitals were "nontransportable": men who were likely to die if moved any further until they received extensive medical care. During active operations, the 2nd Division's hospitals handled on average 120 wounded men per hour and performed fifty operations per day. Ninety percent of these operations were on nontransportable casualties. On average these men remained in the hospital for four days. In the 89th Division, nontransportables remained in the field hospitals for five to eight days before the staff felt that it was safe to send them onward.[17]

During the highs of the fighting, working in a field hospital was a grim and grueling process. During the fighting along the Marne from July 15 to 20, 1918, the surgeons in the hospitals "operated continuously on head, chest, abdominal, and thigh cases." During the Meuse Argonne the 42nd Division's field hospitals each employed six operating teams and four shock-treatment teams working in shifts to give their patients around-the-clock care. The sights and fevered pace of activity in the hospitals often shocked the uninitiated. After visiting a field hospital near Fleury in late September 1918, an MP later wrote, "What a sorrowful looking place this was!" He was stunned by the large pile of bloody and torn clothing that had been removed from the wounded before they could be treated and was amazed at the ability of the staff to operate on ten to twenty of the wounded at one time. Another soldier was sobered by the sight of the seemingly endless stream of ambulances arriving at the hospital he marched past and by the number of freshly dug graves for those who had not survived on the outskirt of the facility.[18]

If it was traumatic to view the hospitals, it was certainly no bed of roses to be treated in one either. Knud Olsen, an infantryman in the 82nd Division, was wounded in the hand on October 14, 1918. Upon reaching the field hospital early the next morning, he was put on a stretcher on the bare ground in a corner of the operating tent. He recalled,

> The doctors would take care of the most severely wounded first. One doctor was in a dark room with the X-ray equipment. He'd tell the doctor operating on a soldier where to operate. I laid on a stretcher on the floor all day long waiting for my turn. They put me to sleep with ether then they operated. Then they took me to a ward of 50 beds in a wooden building. When I came to at midnight there was a doctor by my bed.

As he had gone for forty hours without food, his first thought was for something to eat. Fortunately the hospital's mess hall was still open, and Olsen was delighted when the doctor sent over roast beef, mashed potatoes, and gravy.[19]

The wounded man's next stop in his chain of treatment was to one of the AEF's thirty-seven evacuation hospitals. These semifixed sites were located nine to fifteen miles from the front and each had a one-thousand-bed capacity. The evacuation hospitals were intended to give life-saving care to the severely wounded and to provide ten to fourteen days of recovery time to the doughboys to strengthen their constitutions before sending them on to base hospitals for follow-up care and convalescence. During active operations, the evacuation hospitals could also quickly become overwhelmed by the influx of casualties. On October 10, 1918, for example, Evacuation Hospital 9 was inundated with over fourteen hundred men needing care. Between September 26 and November 11, 1918, this hospital alone cared for over thirty-two thousand sick and wounded doughboys. In times of stress, the AEF GHQ could reinforce the evacuation hospitals by assigning additional surgical teams to them or by sending a mobile surgical hospital to their location. As the name implied, the AEF's twelve mobile surgical hospitals were designed to move rapidly around the Zone of Advance to respond to the army's medical needs. As such, all of the mobile hospital's operating theaters and support equipment was mounted on trucks. Even with the addition of these surgical teams, life in an evacuation hospital could be grueling. A surgeon from Evacuation Hospital 6 wrote to a fellow doctor on November 3, 1918, "There are twelve operating teams here at present. Six teams work from 8 AM to 8 PM while the other six work from 8 PM to 8 AM. There are 18 tables in the operating room, so each team runs 3 tables. We have been very busy during the last few days." This surgeon was somewhat fortunate, for from October 4 to 11, 1918, the surgical teams of Evacuation Hospital 15 worked eighteen-hour shifts to keep pace with the number of wounded arriving from the Argonne fighting.[20]

The final link in the chain of the doughboys' medical care was the base hospital. The AEF operated eighty-three base hospitals and five convalescence camps prior to the Armistice. The army also sent patients to nineteen other hospitals operated by the American Red Cross. Additionally, the AEF established sixty-three camp hospitals to provide medical care for soldiers assigned to the SOS's ports and fixed bases and camps. All of these hospitals were intended to provide the final surgical, medical, and convalescence care that the seriously sick or wounded soldiers required. Each base hospital provided general surgical and medical care and also included specialists in orthopedic, urological, neurological, maxillofacial, psychiatric, and ear, nose, and throat surgery and treatment. Although this line-up of doctors and surgeons generally contained enough knowledge and skills to handle most cases, the AEF also provided additional resources to some of its base hospitals to have them serve as specialist centers for doughboys requiring specific expert treatment. For example, Base Hospital 117 specialized in treating the AEF's severe war neurosis or shell-shock cases while Base Hospital 115 was focused on treating head wounds, facial reconstruction, and ear, nose, and throat cases. The hospital's focus on facial reconstruction is worthy of note. It is not much of a stretch to state that the Great War gave rise to modern plastic surgery. Soldiers in the AEF suffered 8,603 facial wounds, leaving many men with horribly torn and disfigured features. Using innovative techniques in bone and skin grafting, the army's maxillofacial surgeons were able to return functionality to scores of soldiers' faces while also working to restore the men's visages as much as possible to their prewound state.[21]

As with the other elements of the AEF's medical system, the base hospitals were also swamped by the high casualties of the summer and fall of 1918. Base Hospital 6 is a case in point. Although it cared for 24,122 patients during its fifteen-month existence, over half of them, 12,988 soldiers, were hospitalized between July and October 1918. During that four-month period, the unit's surgeons performed 2,090 operations, or on average seventeen surgeries per day.

On November 11, 1918, the hospital was caring for 4,319 sick and wounded men in its overcrowded wards. A doctor recalled, "There was little celebration of the Armistice . . . until several weeks after, simply because everyone was so rushed with work that there was no time."[22]

Base Hospital 52 did not begin its operations until September 4, 1918, and as many of its surgical teams were sent to reinforce hospitals coping with the flood of casualties closer to the front, it never had as many patients as Base Hospital 6. However, Base Hospital 52 still cared for 6,388 patients between September 4, 1918, and January 23, 1919. Of these patients, 36 percent were gas cases, 33 percent were general medical cases (mostly influenza), 17 percent were combat wounded, and the remaining 14 percent of patients were for non-combat-related surgeries. Reflecting the major medical breakthroughs of the era, the combat-wounded soldiers' chances of survival were markedly improved once they reached the base hospitals. Only 6 percent of the combat casualties who reached Base Hospital 52 died of their wounds. In its fifteen months of operation only 434 of Base Hospital 6's patients (1.9 percent) died while being treated. Of these dead, 283 succumbed to pneumonia during the influenza outbreak.[23]

For the men undergoing treatment, their arrival at the hospital could be unnerving. After he was wounded in the Argonne, Lieutenant F. L. Miller's serious wounds quickly landed him in Base Hospital 7. He later recounted,

> I was wheeled into a waiting room with a thin wall between me and where a patient was undergoing surgery. The sound from the room was disquieting as I could hear a tap, tap, tapping of the surgeon's chisel against bone, a prelude as to what was soon to happen to me. The anesthetist, a young Medical Corps lieutenant, was out of sorts, as his contemplated trip to Paris for the weekend was being delayed by this duty. As a result he poured ether into the cone over my face by the bucket-full which gagged me unmercifully.

Although Miller's initial surgery was uneventful, the tissue became dangerously infected with gas gangrene: a virulent form of infection caused by the well-manured soil of Northern France entering the wound. Fortunately for the young officer, two British doctors, Alexis Carrel and Henry Dakin, had discovered the best treatment for gas gangrene earlier in the war. First, the wound was thoroughly cleaned and debrided (the cutting out of dead flesh until the surgeon reached healthy tissue), and then the wound was left open and steadily flushed with a solution of hypochlorous acid (commonly known as Carrel-Dankin solution) to wash out and slowly kill off the bacteria that caused gas gangrene. During his treatment, Miller was confined to bed with his leg suspended by a Balkan Frame traction device while Carrel-Dankin solution constantly dripped into the open wound. As the Carrel-Dankin solution was somewhat caustic, the treatment was far from comfortable. His condition grew so dire that the staff moved him to the ward for patients who "were not long for this world," and his mail from home was returned marked "Deceased-Verified-Statistical Department." Although Miller beat the odds and was returned to the United States in 1919, he was not discharged from the army hospital at Fort Sheridan until September 1920.[24]

Lieutenant Russell Warner's interaction with the medical system was more positive. He was wounded by a sniper on June 6, 1918. The sniper's bullet passed through his gas mask, a notebook in his pocket, and his dog tags before entering his chest above his ribs: "It was a bad shock and much bleeding and as I staggered back towards my men, I fell down." After directing one of his sergeants to take over the command of the unit, Warner passed out and did not regain consciousness until he was in the hospital. At first Warner believed that he must have been captured, but "Then came a voice, a female voice, with a Kentucky accent, which said 'Lt. do you want some cocoa?'" "That was," he recalled, "the sweetest music I ever heard." As with Miller, Warner's wound developed gas gangrene and he was treated using Carrel-Dankin solution, which cleared up the infection. While he was recovering, he periodically "scratched out a few small scabs of iron or steel just under the surface of the skin."[25]

Warner's reference to being woken by a "female voice" needs elaboration. During the war, at least 10,600 women who had enlisted to serve in uniform in the U.S. Army worked in France. The greatest number of them, approximately ten thousand, were members of the Army Nurse Corps. The corps was established in 1901, and during the war 19,222 women served in its ranks. At least six hundred other women served in the army in France as telephone operators (the famous "Hello Girls") and Quartermaster Corps clerks, or as bacteriologists, laboratory technicians, or physical therapists. Several thousand other women served out of army uniform as Red Cross nurses, as relief workers, and as members of the social organizations working to provide for the morale, welfare, and entertainment of the doughboys.

Doctors, doughboys, and army inspectors were uniformly warm in their praise of the skills and attitudes of the women in the army. The wounded believed that the women who treated them were generally more attentive and caring than male attendants. Their efforts were also vital to the success of the army's overstretched medical system. By the start of the Argonne offensive, Base Hospital 6 had 106 nurses on staff from the Army Nurse Corps. With the arrival of the flu, one doctor noted, "for several weeks many of the nurses kept on duty who should have been in bed, and all were suffering from overwork and nerve strain," yet "there seemed never a time when the nurses were too tired or busy to do extra kindnesses for the patients." Shortly before the Armistice, a senior army inspector reported to the secretary of war, "Every nurse performed her work uncomplainingly and with a fine, cheerful sprit."[26]

Despite the nurses' obvious capabilities, the army's males were not above taking a rather patronizing attitude toward the women who treated them.

While recovering in a hospital, Lieutenant Warner claimed to have witnessed a rather humorous incident:

> There was the old sergeant brought into the hospital dirty, bloody and apparently unconscious who had a wound near his privates. A new and embarrassed nurse was supposed to be helping a doctor who said to her, "Nurse, take hold of the man's penis and hold it up out of the way so I can see what I am doing." The nurse obeyed timidly and about that time the old sergeant opened one eye and took a look. Shortly thereafter the doctor said to the nurse, "You may let go. It will stand alone now."

If the incident did occur, like the penis in question, it certainly grew in the telling. Army nurses, even the "new and embarrassed" ones, had received training on anatomy and usually served their apprenticeship in hospitals by undressing and cleaning the wounded before they would have been allowed to assist a doctor in surgical care.[27]

Although some doughboys went AWOL from their medical treatment to return to their comrades, most seem to have been thankful for the release from the privation and dangers that their recuperation brought them. The average time for hospital recovery from a wound was 102 days, while wounds with resulting fractures took the longest to heal, requiring on average 225 days of hospitalization. While recovering from a wound, one infantryman enjoyed nature and the continuation of life on a glorious fall day. His romp through this "fairyland," he wrote to his mother, "made me feel that even war with all its gruesomeness, with all its barbarity and relics of past age brought up to the advanced standard of modern warfare, that even that could be forgotten and replaced again by nature's own beautifulness." Continuing his nature analogy, he believed that Germany would soon be defeated, "and then will come Spring again with everything glad and happy." He did find that the worst part of his hospital stay was boredom. The recovering doughboy spent most of his time reading, playing solitaire, and worrying "about what we are going to eat for the next meal."[28]

Although this infantryman spent a relatively comfortable time during his recovery, few wounded soldiers were as fortunate as Private Lloyd Richmond. He suffered several wounds in October 1918. His father, Lieutenant Thomas Richmond, was serving as a doctor at Base Hospital 27 and used his connections to ascertain his son's condition and to have the wounded boy transferred to Thomas's care. While he confessed to his wife, "I had a hard time getting him," as he "had to get permission from the head cheese," on December 2, 1918, the good doctor was able to retrieve his son. The only hitch came on their train ride to Base Hospital 27. While traveling on the train, Dr. Richmond was called away to another car, leaving his son asleep on a seat. The doctor returned to find an MP shaking his son and ordering him off the train. When the irate doctor confronted the MP, the policeman lamely offered that it was against regulations for an enlisted man to sit while officers stood. Upon arriving at Base Hospital 27, Lloyd was given a private room and a thorough medical inspection from his father "from head to foot." Afterward, he reported to his concerned wife, "I am pleased at the way he is doing—& think that he is going to come right along."[29]

Not all of the war's wounds were physical. In fact, while the Great War added new, idiomatic medical terms, such as "trench foot" and "trench mouth," to the nation's vocabulary, "shell shock" continues to thrive in the popular imagination as one of the signature maladies of the conflict. Mental trauma in soldiers is as old as war itself, but the nature of combat in World War I made "shell shock" a major medical and military challenge for the first time in history. From the war's very beginning, doctors noted a marked increase in the number of men being brought in for treatment without apparent physical wounds but "with staring eyes, violent tremors, a look of terror, and blue, cold extremities. Some were deaf and some were dumb; others were blind or paralyzed." After first labeling this phenomena "shell shock" in the belief that these symptoms were caused by the soldier being concussed by an exploding shell, military doctors quickly turned to the new science of psychiatry to explain why increasing numbers of men with these strange manifestations were filling army hospitals. Although the term "shell shock" continued to be used throughout the war by soldiers and doctors alike, soldiers suffering from mental trauma were increasingly labeled as having "Not Yet Diagnosed-Nervous" or "war neurosis."[30]

It is impossible to state with any accuracy how many doughboys suffered from post-traumatic stress or war-induced neurosis for the simple fact that the definitions used by doctors at the time to classify patients with mental health issues were broad and inexact. The AEF reported that 27,657 soldiers were admitted to hospitals for "neuropsychiatric diseases" between April 1, 1917, and December 31, 1919. These diagnoses ranged from encephalitis to apoplexy, mental deficiency, and malingering. Over 45 percent of these cases were diagnosed under four rather indistinct categories that tended to be associated with what today we would term post-traumatic stress: "neurasthenia," "shell shock," "hysteria," and "psychoneurosis." In fact, the army psychiatrist John Rhein maintained that approximately 10 percent of the AEF's casualties were due to combat-related mental health issues.[31]

In trying to explain the sharp rise in psychiatric casualties in modern warfare, Lord Moran (Charles Wilson), a frontline military doctor in World War I who rose to become Winston Churchill's personal physician during the Second World War, postulated that each soldier had a reservoir of courage that was slowly drained by the experience of combat. The depth of the reservoir varied greatly from man to man, but when it ran dry, the man was no longer an effective soldier and often succumbed to mental breakdown. Although Moran's assertions were deeply rooted in Victorian and Edwardian class and racial assumptions, his instincts were confirmed by further studies conducted in World War II. Using extensive records collected by the U.S. Army Research Branch during the Second World War, Samuel Stouffer and seven other prominent sociologists and psychologists concluded that the most effective period of combat performance for American infantrymen peaked at 3.5 to 3.9 months in combat for privates and at seven months for NCOs. After those peaks, the soldiers rapidly lost their combat edge and were more likely to suffer combat fatigue, neurosis, or wounds. Although an absence of records and the limited length of the American's time in combat in the Great War make it impossible to confirm Stouffer's finding for the AEF, surviving accounts seem to confirm these later conclusions.[32]

It is important to note that most doughboys, officers, and medical personnel were rather understanding of those comrades who suffered from a mental breakdown in battle. A postwar study observed, "The average American soldier's attitude toward 'shell shock' had a large proportion of tolerance and curiosity in it." However, coming face to face with the affliction could itself be unnerving for the onlookers. An artilleryman recalled that during the Aisne-Marne drive,

> The nights were continually disturbed by . . . the cries of shell-shocked men. Most of these outbursts began with a howling peal of laughter, a laugh to make one's skin creep and his hair rise, and ended in a shuttering wail, frequently followed by tears. The shell-shocked men seemed to laugh and to cry almost interchangeably, and some of whose faces were

drawn up as if in a great merriment had tears running down their cheeks, at the height of the convulsion. These men had become insane, and some of them caused no little trouble to their comrades trying to care for them.

Perhaps the doughboys' sympathy for their shell-shocked comrades stemmed from the fact that they understood the fine line that separated them from those who had broken under the strain of battle. Like Moran, the doughboys seem to have accepted the fact that each man had a breaking point.[33]

One such man was Duncan Kemerer, an infantryman in the 28th Division. His company had taken heavy casualties in the Champagne-Marne and Aisne-Marne fighting in July and August 1918 before being assigned to the Fismes sector. While fighting near Fismette, he survived a number of close calls from German artillery and had become weakened by days of going short of food and water. But after two incidents where shells killed soldiers standing close to him, Kemerer could take no more. As he recalled, "Shell shock is terrible . . . when I came to I was lying on the dirt floor of the cellar, and when a shell burst overhead, I would yell and try to dig a hole in the ground with my fingers for protection." After being evacuated to a hospital at Chaumont, he admitted, "It was tough for a while as every time someone dropped something on the floor, like for instance a spoon, or [I heard] an unusually loud noise, I would holler and either try to hide under the sheets or get under the bed." Fortunately for him, after three weeks of treatment "plus rest and good food," he was considered well enough to return to his unit.[34]

Kemerer's treatment reflected the state of the art of medical thought for caring for those suffering from combat fatigue and war neurosis. Building on the experiences of the French and British, American doctors rightly noted that most of the doughboys being treated for "shell shock" were in fact victims of combat fatigue: the cumulative wearing down of their ability to cope with battle due to a lack of sleep, poor food and water, exposure to the elements, and the nervous strain caused by fear and death. The field hospitals served as the first stop for shell-shock casualties. Doctors claimed that the best treatment for combat fatigue "war neurosis" cases was to give the patient a bath, clean clothes, hot food, and a chance to sleep. One noted that it was not unusual for the soldier to "fall into a profound slumber which lasted for thirty-six to forty-eight hours." Unfortunately, shortages of beds at the forward hospitals often meant that men who could have been rapidly returned to duty after such treatment were evacuated to base hospitals to make room for other casualties. Rhein maintained that upward of 65 percent of the AEF's psychological casualties could have been returned to duty within ten days if they would have received proper treatment at the front rather than being sent for care further to the rear. Despite this problem, 60 to 70 percent of the "war neurosis" cases still returned to combat duty after twelve to fourteen days of treatment under a trained psychiatrist.[35]

Of course not all shell-shocked doughboys recovered so rapidly. On June 16, 1918, the AEF designated Base Hospital 117 as its primary care facility for soldiers suffering from mental illness. During its existence, the hospital treated 2,973 neuropsychiatric cases. The majority of the hospital's patients fell into three major categories: hysteria (28 percent); concussion neurosis— mental problems brought on by being near an explosion (22 percent); and neurasthenia—an indistinct diagnosis based upon the apparent nervousness and depression of the patient (12 percent). Psychiatric care in the hospital was directed by its chief clinician, Captain Sidney Schwab, who "followed the Freudian mechanism in everything except their dependence upon the sex element" to get at the root cause of the soldier's neurosis. The regimen at the facility also included carpentry, basket weaving, and other crafts and working on the hospital's farm and military drill to remind the patients that they remained soldiers while undergoing treatment. The treatment further included a degree of emotional blackmail as the men were gently reminded that while they were at the hospital they were letting down their comrades and perhaps missing out on finishing off the German empire. For the most part, these treatments were successful. The readmittance rate in the hospital was relatively low, with 126 men being twice admitted and four returning three times for further neuropsychiatric care.[36]

Faced with an unexpectedly high number of psychological cases in the Soissons and the early days of the Meuse Argonne and the limited capacity of Hospital 117 to accept more patients, the AEF stood up three other neurological hospitals. These hospitals were positioned closer to the front with the intent that they could more rapidly treat and return soldiers to the fighting. Between September and November 1918, these three facilities treated 2,296 neuropsychiatric cases. Although the treatment in Base Hospital 117 and the three other neurological hospitals reflected an admirable and cutting-edge approach to combat-induced mental illness, they still only saw a small number of these cases. Most doughboys with psychiatric problems were treated at evacuation and nonspecialist base hospitals. While these facilities generally had at least one psychiatrist on their staffs, they were often overwhelmed by the influx of mental cases. Doctors treating mental casualties were under pressure from their military superiors to quickly return their patients to the front, though the soldiers sometimes required a more long-term treatment to address the underlying causes of their psychosis. The medical community touted its success in treating mental illness and its ability to preserve fighting power, but at times, this short-term focus was detrimental to the soldier's long-term mental health. In 1919, mental casualties accounted for 38 percent of all hospitalized American veterans. Uncounted more lived with the recurring psychological trauma of the Great War for the rest of their lives.[37]

One cannot leave the doughboys' medical experiences without discussing the great influenza pandemic of 1918. The numbers of influenza cases and deaths will never be known with any exactness. The nature of the disease and how it killed were responsible for the confusion. The outbreak was particularly shocking because it tended to be more virulent among the young and healthy rather than carrying off the very young or old. This was caused by the robust immune system in the healthy overreacting to the influenza virus, which killed them by flooding their lungs with fluids. On the other hand, those who survived the influenza itself had their constitutions so weakened that they were very vulnerable to the other great killer: pneumonia. In fact, the AEF did not instruct medical officers to make influenza a reportable disease until October 7, 1918. After the war, the Medical Department estimated that 798,509 soldiers contracted influenza during the war, or roughly one in four doughboys. It was by far the greatest single killer of American soldiers of the war, with perhaps as many as forty-four thousand being carried off by the disease itself or the pneumonia that followed. Ironically, had it not been for the influenza outbreak, the Great War could have been the first American conflict where combat deaths exceeded those caused by disease.[38]

The military medical community was certainly caught off guard by the virulence, rapid spread, and degree of mortality of the disease. As a doctor at Base Hospital 6 lamented, "During the influenza epidemic we all learned a good deal about the disease . . . although in the end we came out knowing as little about its bacteriology and cause as in the beginning." He later confessed, "Such barriers that we tried to throw in the way of the spread were swept away as chaff before a mighty tempest. This frightful epidemic seemed to know no bounds, and before its advance we stood helpless." The historian Carol Byerly notes that the doctors themselves bore some responsibility for the problem. Given the tremendous breakthroughs of their era, the doctors' hubristic faith in medical science and their own skills initially led them to downplay the seriousness of the influenza outbreak. As crowded training camps, troop ships, and frontline trenches allowed the virulent strain of influenza to spread rapidly through the ranks, the demoralized doctors were left shaken by their failure to control the disease and hesitant to question the health-related decisions of their line-officer superiors.[39]

The doughboys themselves were equally demoralized by the disease and their letters in the fall of 1918 are often filled with news of influenza in camp and concern for those at home. Camp doctors frantically tried to stem the disease by strict quarantines and by imposing rules that forced cots to be laid head to foot and requiring soldiers to wear masks. The epidemic played havoc with the soldiers' training, sailing schedule, and peace of mind. A nearly illiterate Indianan wrote to his grandmother on October 8, 1918:

> Was Supposed to leve here the 5th But the HEN-FLEW-END-WAYS [influenza]—Caught us. We are under cornteen [quarantine] at present But will leave Soon as the Cornteen is Lifted . . . the Hospitals is all full Here and they are using some Barreks to put the sick soldiers in[.]the Anfluesy [influenza] is sure taking [unintelligible]fast they go there at the rate of one a minute and they are dying one Ever Hour they take Nemonia [pneumonia] and all Doctors is Buisy Examinions us and Spraying our nose's and throuts Every night.

George Hetrich, who worked in the Camp Sherman base hospital laboratory, was appalled by the toll the influenza epidemic took on the camp. He informed a friend in October 1918 that the medical officers had been forced to open a whole new hospital annex to handle the deluge of patients and that the camp was undergoing a strict three-week-long quarantine. He noted, "We lost 942 men in these three weeks and as high as 170 men a day. The men died like flies." Hetrich himself came down with the flu and spent five days in the hospital with a 102-degree temperature. As a laboratory technician, he also had the mournful task of assisting with autopsies, a task that often required him to work from early morning to 10 PM.[40]

For those who contracted influenza, their suffering left a lasting impression. Paul Maxwell caught the disease while training in Camp Hancock, Georgia, in November 1918. The number of infected was so great that he and fifteen other men from his unit spent most of their first day on sick call lying on the bare ground, waiting for a mule-drawn ambulance to take them to the base hospital. He recalled that once he arrived, "I laid for several hours on a stretcher in a huge room filled with other men on stretchers, checked out by a Doctor and Nurse then removed to a tent colony occupied by hundreds of overflow patients." The tent he was placed in had a dirt floor, one electric light bulb, folding cots, and a zinc bucket to serve as the patients' toilet. When an orderly brought him a cup of oyster stew, Maxwell "promptly vomited up" and the orderly merely "kicked dirt over it and left." Due to his fever he remembered little of his eight days in the hospital other than the fact that one of his tent mates died during the ordeal.[41]

Death, whether from diseases like influenza or from enemy action, was an inescapable reality in the Great War. The AEF lost 36,694 soldiers killed in action while another 13,691 later died of the wounds that they received in combat while undergoing medical care. Roughly 2.5 percent of the soldiers in the AEF died as a result of enemy action. In the American Army as a whole, disease carried off 58,119 doughboys while an additional 5,591 died of nonbattle injuries. In the AEF alone, 1,799 men died from accidents, 268 were drowned (not including those lost at sea in transport sinkings), and 240 more committed suicide. These nonbattle deaths often were as troubling to the soldiers as combat losses because they seemed particularly ironic or pointless. For example, in one incident in March 1918, ten soldiers were killed and two more were severely injured after a dud shell that they were toying around with exploded. A similar needless loss occurred in Charles Minder's company. He and his comrades were swimming and washing up in a canal after being relieved from a particularly harrowing stint at the front. Unfortunately, one of the men could not swim and he drowned after inadvertently stepping into the deep part of the channel. After surviving weeks of shelling in the line, the demise of this combat veteran in such a manner was particularly disheartening to his buddies.[42]

Thanks to the ever-increasing ingenuity of the human mind, death on the battlefields of the Great War came in a wide variety of forms. The most common was being horribly mutilated or atomized by a shell. Others were killed by being incinerated by flamethrowers, being choked to death by poison gas, having one's head staved in by a trench club, or being riddled with machine gun bullets. Sometimes the killing was mercifully quick, but at other times, the man lived out his last moments in physical and mental agony. As a medic in the 79th Division lamented to a friend at home, "I have seen men die . . . in such pain that it seemed merciful when their Maker called them." It was a harrowing experience for those who watched their buddies endure such an end. After a popular man in their platoon was shot in the stomach by a sniper, his comrades knew that his wounds were fatal and that they were helpless to do anything about it. Most troubling, the injured man himself understood his fate. "His eyes were clear and fully open, surveying every place and motion," one of the man's friends recalled, but "sometimes there was a trace of wonderment, of questioning, a man's eyes asking 'Why?'" His powerless pals gathered around the stricken man, made him as comfortable as possible, and then sat "motionless as they watched their comrade die." Often, the press of battle and the numbness and fatalism that came to govern many veterans' outlooks left no time or place for such morning of the dead. Warren Jackson recalled,

> Looking over my shoulder, I saw Rosenow—who had been scarcely an arm's length away—sink to the ground with an almost inarticulate "Oh, God!" The little shell had made almost a sieve of the lower part of his body. From his waist downward at least fifty shell fragments must have penetrated. I started to take out an emergency kit, but I saw he was dead . . . Anywhere else I would have been appalled by the so sudden passage of a friend, but in the anguish and stir of battle one was not affected so. Perhaps a fellow had become somewhat inured to death. With all respect I say that his passing was to me, at that moment, as under other circumstances, as at another time, seeing a dumb animal die.

It is one of the myriad of sad things in war that this was the case. Like many doughboys, Jackson hardened his heart to death as a necessary mental survival mechanism.[43]

This is not to say that the doughboys became totally inured and desensitized to the death that surrounded them. When time and combat allowed, soldiers could be quite sensitive to the need to honor their fallen comrades and to see them decently buried. When the 28th Division's John Flynn was killed by gas on November 5, 1918, his comrades built him a coffin of pine boards lined with cheesecloth stuffed with sugar sacks and made a pillow for his head. The soldiers washed the body and dressed it with new under-clothing, shirt, and shoes. He was laid to rest in the yard of a French church, with a local priest celebrating the mass. At the playing of taps, one of Flynn's comrades admitted, "Between sobs and tears, I almost broke." When a popu-lar member of their battery was killed in the Argonne, his fellow cannoneers constructed a wooden coffin for the man out of ammunition boxes, rever-ently buried him themselves, and hammered the man's name on a mess kit lid that they nailed to the cross they had built to mark the grave.[44]

It was important to the doughboy to know that if he was killed, his body would receive proper burial and that his next of kin would be informed of his passing. Despite any callousness that the soldiers developed toward death, they also wanted to ensure that their comrades received like treatment. In October 1918, a First Army inspector strongly recommended that the AEF as-sign rear-area troops the task of removing the dead from the front during ac-tive operations. He noted, "Men who are fighting should not be called upon for this duty; nor should the bodies of the dead be allowed to remain lying around the front line. This is a great source of loss of morale ... It takes the heart out of a man to have the body of his chum lying around unburied for three or four days." Unfortunately, during the army's fierce periods of fight-ing few of the AEF's dead could hope for such careful and reverent treatment. In fact another inspector discovered that during the fighting around Château Thierry, "very little attention was paid to the burial of the dead," and that bodies lay on the field for days before being interred. In many cases, the dead were simply partially buried in shell holes with no attempt made to identify the fallen. Despite AEF directives for the proper collection, identification, and recording of the fallen, the pace of operations and the number of dead often overrode these concerns. The AEF had established grave registration units, but by the Armistice the total number of soldiers in these units was only forty-eight officers and 872 men, far too few to keep up with the grim demand.[45]

The AEF GHQ required that each combat regiment designate a unit burial officer to oversee the interment of the unit's dead. This sad but necessary task often fell to the regimental chaplain. During and immediately after the fighting, the chaplain and a small detail of men would comb the battlefield searching for and collecting the dead. One chaplain later recalled, "If we had allowed ourselves to dwell on it, we would have been incapable of carrying on with the work: it was so ghastly, so full of pathetic and horrible details." The work also kept the burial officers quite busy. In the last week of October 1918, the chaplain for the 8th Machine Gun Battalion reported that he had only conducted two services during the week and one on Sunday but that he had overseen the burials of 125 men. During the same week, the 30th Infantry's chaplain admitted that while conditions at the front made it impossible for him to hold services, he had buried twenty men for the regiment and 186 more from other units.[46]

The burial party was to ascertain the identity of the dead and to properly mark the grave with something that could easily identify the spot to follow-on grave registration personnel. Each soldier was issued with two-round aluminum identification tags. One of these tags was to remain with the body while the other was to be affixed to the grave marker. The burial officer was required to report the location of the grave, the name, serial number, and unit of the deceased, the date of the death and burial, a description of the grave marker used, and if the man's identification tags were with the body and attached to the marker. If possible, the burial party was also to gather the dead man's personal effects so that they could be returned to the soldier's next of kin. These meager items showed not only how much combat encouraged soldiers to pare their belongings down to the bare level but also what they valued. When Sergeant James B. Newcomer of Company B, 328th Infantry, was killed in action on September 17, 1918, at Pont a Mousson, the burial party recovered "142 francs, One match, One fountain pen, Two pocket books, Bunch of photographs, One notebook, Two pocket mirrors, A bunch of letters." Although these items had little intrinsic value, having an item that was last held by a loved one was often priceless to those he left behind.[47]

The elaborate process required of the burial officer was intended to aid in the later collection of the body and to prevent a repeat of the mistakes of the Civil War, where huge numbers of men were buried without any identification. Unfortunately, this system often broke down under the pressures of war. Although units were often very careful in caring for their own dead, the fluid nature of some of the AEF's battles, the high number of dead they created, and the mixing of units across the same terrain often led burial parties to be rather hasty in their efforts. If an engagement had resulted in a large number of dead, after the battle the task became simply to get the decaying flesh under the ground as quickly as possible. Such work was certainly no joy, and time and necessity hardened those associated with the work. One lieutenant assigned to the unpleasant duty informed an associate that after the battles of Château Thierry,

> [There were] Dead Krauts and dead Yanks all over the place . . . and not enough men to do the job decently . . . It was pretty warm out there in the sun . . . and there were some of them that we didn't get to for nearly a week. A corpse should never be left in the sun. It just plumb spoils. About the end of the week the decedents were all swelled up and gassy and it was certainly a rotten job putting them away. You get used to it after a while though. You put on your gas mask and stick the corpse in the belly with a bayonet. That lets the gas out so you can roll him into a normal grave.

Grim reality and practicality thus end talk of noble sacrifice and the honored dead. Under such conditions, few in the burial party took the time to search the corpse for their identity tags or effects.[48]

The passing of a soldier also set into motion a process for informing the doughboy's next of kin of his death. Once a unit verified the death of one of its soldiers, a report of the man's passing eventually landed in the AEF Central Records Office. The Central Records Office then notified the War Department of the death, and it in turn sent a telegram to the next of kin. The family was thus informed of the loss of its loved one by a terse message delivered by a random messenger boy. On September 16, 1918, the mother of Lloyd Short received a telegram that simply stated, "Deeply regret to inform you cablegram from abroad advises that Private Lloyd Short Marine Corps was killed in action July Nineteenth. Body will be interned abroad until end of war. Accept my heartfelt sympathy in your great loss. Your son nobly gave his life to the service of his country." These few lines set off not only a wave of grief but also quests by family members to find out more about the passing of their kin. One mother admitted, "At first, I thought that I should go mad at the meager information in that bare, bald telegram from the War Department announcing Harold's death."[49]

In a sad and small mercy, details of the fallen's demise from the man's friends, chaplain, or officers often followed the official notification. Private Walter Shaw was born in Leavenworth, Kansas, on January 13, 1896, and over his short life developed a great love of music, ultimately becoming an accomplished violinist and clarinet player. Walter joined the army at the outbreak of the war and was assigned as a musician and stretcher-bearer in the 18th

Infantry. His wartime letters were peppered with reference to his music and he even insisted on paying for his sister's music lessons while serving overseas. Walter hoped to return to Europe after the war to continue his study of music. He was killed in action on October 2, 1918, in the Argonne. The 18th Infantry's bandmaster wrote Shaw's father in January 1919 to provide details of Walter's passing. He noted,

> Walter met his death in the town of Charpentry—near the Argonne Forest, during a night bombardment—& is buried near this same town. Walter alone was instantly killed by the shell but many comrades were severely injured by the same shell. . . . Your son Walter was a steady reliable boy—and very studious. He was exceptionally popular among the band boys and his genial spirit & peculiar sense of humor gained him a host of friends in the Regiment, who keenly felt his loss. You may justly feel proud, Mr. Shaw, in being the father of one of the bravest boys I have ever seen in action. He has been with us a number of times when we were exposed to extreme danger . . . We, his comrades, can well understand your grief & I assure you have our sincere sympathy—yet it must be a source of [unintelligible] satisfaction to know your son met his end fighting a just fight—& met it courageously.

Likewise, Paul Andrews's company commander reported to his family that when he was killed while serving as a member of the "Lost Battalion," "he defended his position fearlessly . . . through his coolness and cheerfulness under the most distressing circumstances helped steady the men in his platoon and keep them nerved to fight." The captain went on to note, "It was a privilege to serve with a man of his character. The men of the company feel his death very keenly as he was among the most popular in the company. He was known as 'smiling Andrews.'"[50]

In an effort to comfort the survivors, in such letters the departed were invariably brave and dedicated to the cause and died quick and painless deaths. Despite this, it should be kept in mind that these were far from being form letters. In fact, writing condolence letters took a toll on those carrying out the sad duty. One chaplain reported, "I always found these personal letters very difficult to write. It meant the infliction of a very severe suffering upon loving hearts that were looking forward with fondest hope to the happy return of one they loved most dearly and who would now never come back to their welcoming embrace." The few lines in these letters, however, brought some comfort and closure to the families of the fallen.[51]

Photo 28: Private William Roberts of Provence, Oklahoma, poses with his mother while training at Camp Travis, Texas, in 1917. Roberts, who served in Company H, 59th Infantry, 4th Division, was killed in action on September 1, 1918. The American Red Cross provided free photographs of soldiers' graves to their next of kin to provide some closure to their grieving families. Source: author's collection.

Given the inevitable confusion of war, sometimes families received false notifications of the deaths of their soldiers. Although these cases had happy endings, they often sparked frantic efforts by the all-too-alive doughboys to ease the minds of their kinfolks. One such unfortunate wrote his sister, "I met a guy from Chi[cago] the other day and from what he told me Im suppose to be dead . . . They said my mugg was in the paper and my name as killed in action." Despite the seriousness of the situation, he was still able to joke, "The only time Im dead is when theres some work to do." A 79th Division doughboy informed his parents in December 1918, "George just received a letter from his folks saying you received a letter from Washington saying that I was missing. Well I'm very much alive and am with the old company." Private Duncan Kemerer's parents were notified by the government that he was killed in action in Fismette in August 1918. Fortunately, they received a letter from him from the hospital three days after the government's belated and inaccurate notification. However, the army still carried him as missing in action until 1938, when he finally convinced them that he was still very much among the found and living.[52] Regrettably, in the vast majority of cases the War Department's death notices had few such happy endings.

At the end of the war, doughboys were buried in over twenty-three hundred temporary military cemeteries in France. Another eighty-five cemeteries were in Britain and there was a smattering of smaller burial grounds in Belgium, Italy, Germany, and Russia. Some 9,120 hastily dug graves remained scattered across the AEF's battlefield. All told, some seventy-five thousand American soldiers were initially buried overseas. The War Department's policy was to return the remains of the dead to their family members if they so requested and to consolidate the bodies of those who were to remain in Europe into nine large cemeteries built in locations close to where the soldiers fell. This required a monumental effort. To collect, identify, and reinter the American dead, the AEF expanded the Graves Registration Service (GRS) to 14,300 troops, mostly drawn from African American pioneer infantry regiments and labor battalions. This task was arduous and extremely horrid. The African American soldiers of Reginald Thomson's 813th Pioneer Infantry were assigned to recovering the hastily buried dead of the Belleau Woods and Château Thierry battlefields and to construct a permanent cemetery for the region. Thomson was surprised to find the sites overrun with American sightseers and noted, "Our guards have great difficulty in keeping them away from our work—which you may imagine is far, far from pleasant." GRS officers used the reports of unit burial officers to locate gravesites, but as these records were often incomplete or the graves had been lost due to shelling or other disturbances, the GRS had to resort to dividing the former battlefields (comprising around nine thousand square kilometers) into zones and methodically combing through the areas to find the fallen. Although it took several years and thirty million dollars, the government eventually returned 45,588 remains to families in the United States and another 764 bodies were dug up and sent to next of kin living in Europe. The remaining 30,922 American dead from the Great War rest in France and England in cemeteries administered by the American Battle Monuments Commission.[53]

The army went to unprecedented lengths to identify its dead. It did not want a repeat of the Civil War, where over 150,000 soldiers were buried without any form of identification. The requirement that all doughboys wear identification tags went a long way toward solving this problem. This measure, however, was not completely foolproof. The 6th Division's Inspector General reported on October 17, 1918, that many of the soldiers in his unit were without dog tags because they had lost them through carelessness. The dog tags were hung around the soldier's neck by a thin cotton tape that was easily broken, potentially leading to the loss of the disks. To fix this problem, he suggested replacing the tags with an aluminum band that would be riveted or crimped around the soldier's wrist. When the GRS soldiers uncovered a grave, their first action was to recover the dead man's dog tags. If this was not successful, the body with all of its grave goods was turned over to an examiner, who would comb through the man's remains and possessions in search of letters, diaries, or any inscriptions that could point to the fallen's identity. Through this process, the GRS claimed to have accurately identified over 95 percent of the AEF's dead. As they operated in the days before dental records and DNA analysis, the GRS's assertions may be somewhat exaggerated, but the organization should be credited with making the first concerted effort to give name to as many of the nation's war dead as possible. There are still 1,644 American World War I service men buried in graves marked only with the inscription "Here rests in honored glory an American soldier known but to God." Following the example of the British and French, one of these men became the first to be buried in the Tomb of the Unknown Soldiers in Arlington National Cemetery on November 11, 1921.[54]

Four thousand four hundred and fifty-two service members of the Great War are still missing. This includes those lost at sea, those whose bodies were obliterated by shells, and those whose grave sites were lost to history. These grave-less men are commemorated only by inscriptions on the walls of the American cemeteries in France and Britain. Perhaps 37 percent of those missing are residing in the graves marked unknown. Unlike those service members who are unaccounted for from World War II, Korea, and Vietnam, the American government has not actively searched for the missing from World War I since 1919. Sometimes, however, luck rescues long-absent doughboys from oblivion. In 2006 a party of people searching for relics of the Great War using metal detectors discovered the remains of a group of doughboys killed during the battle of St. Mihiel. A team from the Department of Defense Joint POW/MIA Accounting Command recovered three bodies from the site and, using DNA analysis and artifacts from the location, managed to identify and return to their surviving family members the bodies of Henry Weikel, Thomas Cotello, and Carl Willing. The men, all from the 60th Infantry, had been killed in action near Jaulny on September 16, 1918, and buried in a forgotten common grave. Sadly, the body of another soldier, Sergeant William Wood, who was also reported to have been buried in the grave, was never found. It is hoped that at some point, Wood, and the other missing Pershing's Crusaders, will be discovered and properly honored.

24

"And We'll All Go Back 'Cause It's Over, Over Here"

The Armistice, Occupation Duty, and Returning Home

On September 19, 1918, Sergeant Walter Snider wrote to his wife, "All of the news at late looks encouraging and I trust the enemy will concede their defeat by Spring or sooner." Despite this optimistic outlook, he confessed, "They cannot win and it puzzles me to think of a reason why they want to continue the great sacrifices which are daily being suffered by both sides."

After hearing that the Germans were ready to discuss peace terms, he even became hopeful of an early return home, penning, "Wouldn't it be great dear to be there by Xmas?" As the Allies began their series of coordinated hammer blows against the Germans in the late summer and fall of 1918, doughboys like Snider could nearly feel it in their bones that their enemy's strength and will was waning. That being said, in the fall of 1918 there was still a lot of killing and dying to do as the Americans' foes fought hard and skillfully to the end. In fact, the AEF lost most of its casualties in the last six weeks of the war, and October 1918 holds the dubious honor of being the bloodiest month in American military history.[1]

The steady, if costly, taking of enemy-held territory, the increasing number of German POWs, the capitulation of other nations of the Central Powers, and rumors of unrest in Germany all pointed to an impending Allied victory. In early November, several rumors of an armistice circulated in the United States and France, prompting premature celebrations of the end of the war. These rumors placed the doughboys in a difficult position. On the one hand, the troops were eager to bring the war to a successful conclusion; on the other hand, no one relished the idea of dying in the waning days of the conflict. A soldier recovering from wounds in Base Hospital 7 reported that at the first of these rumors, a number of men threw away their crutches or jumped out of beds even though they had previously claimed to have been completely crippled. He noted, "Some had been 'goldbricking' for a long time as they were not at all interested in being sent back to the front. There were some red faces when it was learned that the battles were still on."[2]

Some doughboys closer to the front sought to hedge their bets of survival by reining in their aggression and taking fewer chances on the battlefield. George Dongarra was to turn twenty-three on November 11 and "didn't want to be killed before that date." When his truck carrying ammunition broke down two days before the Armistice, he admitted, "I convinced the other driver to linger on the troubled motor, we took our time, we slept, and so on until 11 A.M. on Nov. 11th."

Other cases of moderating aggressiveness carried graver consequences. On November 5, an officer from a neighboring division discovered that soldiers from the 26th Division's 103rd Infantry and 104th Infantry had established an informal truce with the German units in the Bois d' Haumont. The Germans in the area had informed the Americans that they were unable to surrender for fear of what would happen to their families if they were reported as deserters but would not fire on the doughboys if the doughboys would not fire at them. With peace fast approaching, this arrangement seemed sensible and agreeable to both parties. The tacit truce also bound the two groups to fire high if ordered to shoot by their superiors, to give one another advanced warning of any attacks, and to direct artillery to fire into empty space. An investigation by the AEF GHQ charged that officers in both American regiments had turned a blind eye to their soldiers' pacific inactions. Ultimately, the commanders of the 103rd Infantry and the 52nd Infantry Brigade were relieved of command because of the incident, which provided Pershing with the final reason for removing Major General Clarence Edwards from the command of the 26th Division.[3]

Although some doughboys declined to risk their lives in the lingering days of the war, orders were still orders, and Pershing demanded that the Americans push their attacks and capture as much territory and as many Germans as possible before the conflict closed. Some commanders, such as the 89th

Division's Major General William M. Wright, enthusiastically followed Pershing's guidance and drove their men in all-out attacks on the Germans until the very stroke of 11 AM on November 11. Wright ordered an assault crossing of the Meuse River on November 10 and 11 that would end up costing his division several hundred casualties before the Armistice went into effect. One of these was Major Mark Hanna, the commander of the 2nd Battalion, 356th Infantry. He was killed by a shell only hours before the ceasefire. One of his soldiers later wrote his wife, "Major Mark Hanna was a man to the core . . . If it were not for him with his cool way, I have my doubts whether I would be here to write you tonight. He went through hell twice that night . . . and met his death after accomplishing the job he was assigned to do." It is hoped that Hanna's widow took comfort in these words, but her husband's death was rather pointless at that place and time of the war.[4]

The artillerymen of both sides seem to have taken a particular joy in banging away until the last possible minute of the fighting. Perhaps this deadly schadenfreude stemmed from a relative detachment from the killing and the dying that was simply impossible for those much closer to the firing line. C. D. Grant, an ambulance driver operating just behind the forward troops, recorded in his diary on November 10: It "seems both sides are trying to kill as many as possible. Never saw such shelling and firing, trying to kill us all." A number of American artillerymen also relished the idea of firing the last shots of the war, and many batteries claimed this distinction in their postwar histories. Artillerymen in one unit ignored their officers' orders to cease firing at 10:40 and sent shells screaming into the German lines until exactly 10:59 AM. One of their officers noted, "To them peace approaches as a regrettable interruption." The intensity of their firing was so great in the last moments of the war that the paint on their barrels melted and bubbled as the cannons overheated. The enemy, however, had also responded in kind by shelling the roads near the artillerymen's positions. In the final twenty-three minutes of the war, the officer noted that thirty-four men died and another thirty-nine were wounded in his vicinity due to the enemy's retaliation.[5]

Then, it was over. The thing that often struck the doughboys in the moments after the firing ended was the strange silence. In his Armistice Day diary entry, C. D. Grant simply recorded "ALL OVER! Impossible to believe that it can be so quiet after the awful shelling." An infantryman in the 1st Division remembered,

At the front our days & nights were filled with the sounds & smells of the bombardment. Never were we free of it & we had to learn to live with it. On Nov. 11 at 11:00 A.M. those sounds and vibrations abruptly stopped. The quietness that followed was awesome; you could feel it—almost smell & taste it. There was no singing, no shouting, no laughter; we just stood around & looked & listened.

Even the bellicose artillerymen seemed awed by the sudden change. One noted, "The silence is oppressive. It weighs in on one's eardrums . . . There seems to be something uncanny—unnatural in the all-enveloping lack of sound." The first thing he recalled hearing as the cacophony of war ended was the sound of a bird singing, shortly followed by a group of nearby engineers crooning, "And we'll all go back 'cause it's over, over here," in parody of the song "Over There."[6]

What these engineers had so quickly grasped and celebrated was that they had survived the greatest war in human history. For the combat doughboys, the Armistice was a reprieve from the very real possibility of a death sentence. What the troops did in the hours following the Armistice depended on where they were located and what their units were doing at the end of the war. The infantrymen who were actively fighting the Germans when the ceasefire went into effect often relished being able to do those little things that being in combat had prevented. They stood fully erect, pulled themselves from waterlogged foxholes, shucked off their weighty equipment, and looked to their personal comforts as much as possible. In William Graves's company the officers gave permission for the men to build heretofore forbidden fires to dry themselves and their clothes and to boil up coffee. After that welcome development, Graves recalled, "We, my buddy and I, sat up & quietly drank and talked in our pup tent until 2:00 A.M." Troops who were resting out of the line tended to celebrate in a more animated manner. A private in the 310th Infantry wrote his sister, "We had a great time when we received the news [of the Armistice]. We was in a big woods where the Huns had made dugouts. We shot off our rifles and had sky rockets and flares . . . why it was some noise." As other units also reported joyous weapons firing, it is a wonder that there were few reports of injuries or deaths due to the revelry. Some doughboys were more contemplative at the war's end than their bullet-slinging comrades. Paul Rhodes informed a family friend, "You asked me what I did when I heard there was no more fighting. Well I'll tell you. I just sat down and cried with joy. I said to myself 'At last our prayers are answered!'"[7]

Those doughboys who ended the war in the towns and villages further from the front were often caught up in the emotional outpouring of the French people who surrounded them. On November 12 a Marine wrote his mother, "France is literally wild over the signing of the Armistice. They have much reason for rejoicing as they have stood up under four years of this and then to realize that it is over is something to rejoice over." The following day, Harold Lane reported, "They have been celebrating over here and every one seems happy. We had passes yesterday afternoon and last night and it certainly was amusing to see how the people acted. Almost every Frenchman wanted to hug and kiss the American boys and we had to be on our guard or they would have smothered us." Far from the front, the wine flowed, the kisses rained, the bells tolled, and, occasionally, somber ceremonies and masses were held to remember the shared losses of the two great republics.[8]

For some, the Armistice had come too soon. Lieutenant Reginald Thomson, for one, felt rather let down by the quick end of the war and was embarrassed by the kind treatment shown to him by the French. As he informed a female relation, "It is all over now and even tho' I still don't feel like a regular soldier. I can be thankful that I have been as fortunate as I have—so far as my own life is concerned." Although he quipped that "by the time I get home to Kansas perhaps I can have a few fairly satisfactory stories manufactured," he admitted that in the presence of French soldiers, "I feel rather cheap at times when some of these old veterans salute me." As an officer in the 813th Pioneer Infantry, Thomson may have regretted spending the war repairing roads rather than fighting at the front. Perhaps Thomson was one of the many youths who hoped that war would be his great testing of courage and manhood and felt unfulfilled after having few opportunities to prove his mettle. An untold number of doughboys regretted the end of the fighting because they relished the danger and excitement that the war brought. The reader may find it strange that every war creates "adrenaline junkies": soldiers who thrive on the inherent action and risk of battle. These American versions of the German Ernest Junger were somewhat rare, but many doughboys, when later safe at home, did miss the exhilaration of war. Few things make one feel more alive than to have survived close encounters with death.[9]

Regardless of whether the soldiers rejoiced or regretted the coming of the Armistice, the peace initiated an ambiguous situation between the doughboys and their German counterparts. The Armistice itself was merely a ceasefire in a war that was still officially ongoing. The terms of the ceasefire gave the

Photo 29: Doughboys and French civilians celebrate the Armistice on the evening of November 11, 1918. Source: author's collection.

German Army only fourteen days to remove all of its soldiers from Belgium, France, Luxembourg, and the areas of the Rhineland that would be occupied by the Allies. During this period, however, many American units would be in very close proximity to the enemy. Although the doughboys were reminded that they were still at war with the Germans and were ordered not to let their guards down or to fraternize with the foe, this guidance was not always followed. On November 12 and 13, inspectors from the 2nd Army and the IV Corps discovered that troops from the 28th, 33rd, 7th, and 92nd Divisions and their German counterparts were actively crisscrossing the former frontline to socialize. One of the inspectors was outraged to find a group of seventy-five Germans and forty Americans from the 110th Infantry "all laughing, talking and fraternizing" while the doughboys who were manning an outpost nearby went about their duties without their rifles. Another discovered that there were explosions and "promiscuous firing . . . all along the front" as curious doughboys avidly tried out the grenades and other weapons in the enemy's arsenal.[10]

Much of the post-Armistice interaction between the Americans and the Germans centered on the exchange of souvenirs. In fact, the 2nd Army inspector uncovered that doughboys in the 28th Division were enthusiastically trading their raincoats to the Germans for Luger pistols on November 12. This should not have surprised him for the Americans were notorious for their ceaseless search for war booty. A common joke at the time quipped that while the French fought for glory, and the British fought for king, country, and empire, the Americans fought for souvenirs. Carrying back home a war trophy was the ultimate proof that the soldier had, in modern military parlance, "been there, done that." It was a testament to friends and family that the man had been tested and his foe bested. Some soldiers even copied a British practice of creating a souvenir "hate belt" consisting of a German Army belt decorated with insignia that were supposedly taken from Germans that the doughboy had killed or captured. Although many doughboys shed their booty along the way to lighten the load in their packs, others doggedly clung to them as powerful reminders or totems of their triumphs and tragedies. After being wounded and evacuated to a hospital, Edwin Arpin was determined to hold on to his hard-won Lugers. He was angered when a hospital supply sergeant took his pistols without giving him the proper receipt documenting his valid ownership of the weapons. Arpin believed, probably correctly, that the sergeant intended to keep or sell the guns. When he was being transferred to another hospital, the supply sergeant was conveniently nowhere to be found. This was not going to deter Arpin, and he broke into the sergeant's storeroom to retrieve his cherished pistols.[11]

Arpin was far from being alone in his attachment to his captured prizes. The Americans had avidly collected war booty throughout the AEF's campaigns, with the most popular souvenirs being the German spiked *pickelhaube* helmets, the steel "coalscuttle" helmets, Iron Cross medals, German belt buckles, and Luger pistols. One artilleryman recorded that after St. Mihiel he encountered a number of infantrymen returning from the front "hung all over with souvenirs . . . Some carried German helmets in a bunch, like carrots, and some had several pairs of German field glasses hung around their shoulders." Luther Grover sent home "a German helmet picked up from the battlefield," which "still carried the mud from the field and is decorated in the camouflage colors," along with "straps from a German's uniform, buttons from a dead soldier's coat and the cap worn inside the helmet." Some of the American souvenir hunters sought to turn their countrymen's thirst for collectables into money. In one of the few perks of their job, some infantrymen turned handsome profits by selling captured German items to YMCA secretaries, MPs, and members of the SOS far removed from the fighting. Even the artilleryman just mentioned could not resist buying one of the Luger pistols proffered by a passing souvenir-laden doughboy.[12]

For one very large group of American soldiers there would be no souvenirs. Approximately half of the soldiers mobilized for the war, some two million men, never made it closer to France than Camp Upton, New York. Those doughboys were still undergoing training or were involved in a myriad of stateside missions such as running port facilities, guarding the Mexican border, and protecting the northwestern lumber industry from the supposed machinations of the Industrial Workers of the World. The stateside soldiers' attitudes about not having the opportunity to serve in the AEF varied. Major General Leonard Wood, a man who was himself greatly frustrated by his inability to secure a command in France, informed the soldiers being discharged from Camp Funston, Kansas,

> Although I appreciate how keenly you feel the disappointment of your failure to secure duty overseas in the actual battle area, I know you rejoice together with all Americans in the prospect of a righteous and just peace imposed upon the enemy and the termination of the terrible conflict which has involved the whole civilized world. You have done your best. You have cheerfully and loyally discharged the clear duty of every citizen in time of war and your work has been part of the great National effort which has aided in securing a victorious peace.

Many soldiers certainly shared Wood's regrets. As early as August 1918, Charles Mitchell, a soldier assigned to the Quartermaster General's office in Washington, DC, complained, "I like my work, but wish they'd let me go to France. I hate to think that all my pals have gone and I lay at home." At first Oliver Van Camp seemed satisfied that he would spend the war at Camp Merritt, New Jersey. In April 1918 he wrote his mother, "I guess I am going to stay here for good from the way things look now. I'll be perfectly satisfied if I do." But as he spent more time in the service, he began to feel that he was missing out by not going to France. By July, he observed, "Well the war news is certainly of a most encouraging tone . . . I sure would like to be there and put my two cents worth in," and the next month he lamented, "I would also like to get over with the rest of the boys but I guess I'll have to stay here and do my bit as best I can." Perhaps he was one of the troops at Camp Merritt, who, after the

When the 91st Comes Home

Photo 30: This cartoon from the Camp Lewis newspaper, *The Bugle*, expresses the disappointment that some of the doughboys felt at never getting the chance to serve overseas. It shows the 91st Division "big brother" coming home from the AEF with medals and souvenirs to tower over those of the camp's depot brigade and 13th Division, who never sailed for France. Source: *The Bugle: A Camp Lewis Weekly Newspaper*, December 6, 1918.

Armistice, dug a false grave with a marker inscribed, "Sacred to the memories of our hopes of going over which died here November 11, 1918."[13]

To Wood, Mitchell, and Van Camp, their inability to get overseas left a hollow feeling. They had been left out of a chance to test themselves in the greatest event of their generation. Like those poor souls in Shakespeare's *Henry V*, many stateside soldiers feared that in the years to come they would "think themselves accurs'd ... and hold their manhoods cheap," as the returning heroes of the AEF boasted of their exploits overseas. Not all of the stateside soldiers were so disappointed by their plight. Long after the war, Hershie Mowrey admitted,

> I'm sure I was the luckiest soldier in WWI. I never missed a meal, I never suffered an injury or a wound or an illness and I have countless pleasant memories of the most rewarding years of my early life. And the beauty of it—I was paid well and my clothing, a place to sleep and 3 meals a day as an enlisted man are what we know today as fringe benefits.

Without a doubt, many nondeploying doughboys shared Mowrey's sentiments. It was perhaps easier for soldiers like Mitchell and Van Camp to meet the popular wartime expectations by writing that they were disappointed at not going to France than to buck the trend and admit that they were happy to have remained safe and content in the States.[14]

The troops in the AEF certainly had little sympathy for their stateside brethren. The combat veterans took a perverse pride in the privations that they had endured and their correspondence oozed with the near contempt that they felt for those who sat out the war at home. Two weeks after the Armistice, June Smith informed his mother,

> We sure feel sorry for the poor boys in the schools and training camps that have such hard times in their warm barracks. If they would get out and sleep in a mud hole for two or three nights [and go] on a hike for three weeks [covering] about 20 miles a night in the mud and rain with fifty pounds on their back, and get two meals a day of coffee, hard tack and corned beef cold then land on one of the hundred fronts in France and loose more men in a half hour than your hot house plants loose in five years that is a few of the hardships you have to go through on the front.

Similarly, another penned, "Well i bet there was a lot of Boys sorry that they did not come across ... It was a living hell on the last front ... the Boys at home don't know what hard ships we had to go through. We have earned our gold stripe and all the glory of a Yank." Pete Scheck found the gloating of his fellow combat veterans and the complaints of the stateside doughboys to both be misplaced. He wrote his sister in March 1919, "If you hear any of those fellows who couldn't come over and are making a kick about not having a chance tell them their crazy."[15]

Although the vast majority of doughboys in France welcomed the end of the war, the troops who most rejoiced at the Armistice were the 4,460 Americans being held prisoner by the Germans. Most of the American POWs were fortunate to have been in captivity for a relatively short period of time. The Germans took their first doughboys captive during a trench raid on November 3, 1917, but it was not until their attack on Seicheprey on April 20, 1918, that they bagged a large number of Americans (183 men). Most of the war's American POWs were held for less than six months. This is not to suggest that the POWs did not suffer from danger and privation during their captivity. The first moments of being captured were particularly harrowing for the doughboys. As many of the POWs were taken in quick German raids or counterattacks, the transition from being a fighting doughboy to a helpless prisoner could be bewilderingly abrupt. On October 15, 1918, this was brought home to Lieutenant Thomas Walker and the men of his platoon. His first indication that his unit was about to be overrun was when his sergeant "jumped up and called out 'Good God, Lieutenant, look what's coming.'" Moments later his outpost was surrounded by forty Germans and forced to surrender. A party from the 308th Infantry suffered a similar change in fortune when they mistook an advancing German patrol for a group of Americans and were likewise swamped by the enemy. Their case highlighted the inherent dangers that came with the first moments of captivity. When one of the Americans failed to get the word of the surrender, he continued firing and wounded one of the German captors. The enraged Germans threatened to kill all of the American POWs if they did not identify the shooter. Fortunately, a German officer intervened and hustled the doughboys to the rear.[16]

Following their capture, most doughboy POWs marched several days from the front to temporary holding pens before being transferred to camps in Germany. For many, this phase of their incarceration was the worst. Along the way, the captives were dragooned into performing whatever labor that the Germans needed at that moment. Some American POWs in Walker's vicinity were forced to haul cannons while the lieutenant himself carried a wounded

Die ersten gefangenen Amerikaner.

Photo 31: Propaganda photograph of the first Americans captured by the Germans in November 1917. The photo, which was intended to show the German public that the Americans were not much of a threat, backfired on the propagandist as the doughboys were noticeably younger, taller, and better clothed than their captives. Source: author's collection.

man on a stretcher for about six kilometers. Many Americans complained about the quality and quantity of rations that they were given on their march to the holding pens. Private Julius Lombardi received no food during his first three days in custody, and after that only a small quality of "very poor" coffee and "sickening" adulterated bread. In fairness, given the food situation in Germany at the time, the food doled out to the POWs was not much different from that being served to their German captors. During their time in the pens, the doughboys were also interrogated by German intelligence officers. Although these officers sometimes made threats against the Americans if they failed to divulge information, in the vast majority of cases, the process was harmless.[17]

Approximately two-thirds of the American-enlisted POWs ended up in the prisoner camp in Rastatt in Baden, Germany. Most of the American officers were held in camps in Villingen, Karlsruhe, and Landshut, Germany. The prisoners arriving in these camps were in various states of privation and disarray. POWs complained of being robbed of their boots, coats, personal items, and toiletries en route to the camps. Fortunately, the American Red Cross, working through Swiss authorities, had devised a system for providing needed clothing, food, and sundries to the arriving Americans and for supplying a weekly package of rations and necessities to the POWs during their captivity. Although there were slight variations from week to week, the average weekly Red Cross ration per soldier was four pounds of hard bread; two pounds of corned beef hash; a pound each of canned corned beef, salt pork, salmon, tomatoes, butter, sugar, and prunes, raisins, or figs; two cans each of corn and peas, a bar of soap, and eighty cigarettes. Once a month, the POW also received a pound of chocolate or candy. While there was some looting and pilfering of the POW packages by hungry German civilians and soldiers, on the whole the Americans fared much better than captives from Italy and Russia who received no outside support from their nations during the war. However, those doughboys who were not in the large American camps, and thus escaped being registered for packages from the Red Cross, often suffered privations. After being wounded and captured at Château Thierry in June 1918, Philip Rosen ended up in Camp Boval, Belgium. As he was the only American in a camp of fifteen hundred soldiers, he never received Red Cross packages. His daily fare was five hundred grams of sour black bread or 250 grams of hard bread, very watery vegetable soup, "muddy synthetized coffee," one hundred grams of meat (which was mostly bone), and sometimes fifty grams of marmalade.[18]

On the whole, the Americans' captivity was relatively benign. Some soldiers complained of being manhandled, struck, or dealt petty humiliations during their transit to, and time in, the camps. For the most part, however, mistreatment was uncommon. In fact, Carl Dennett, the American Red Cross commissioner who oversaw the care of American POWs, concluded, "The American Prisoners in Germany were not subject to any systematic or authorized physical abuse. Their clothing and personal effects were stolen and it is doubtless true that they would have starved and suffered for proper clothing, had it not been for the relief packages . . . but they were not physically abused, except in rare instances." This was further verified by neutral observers sent to inspect the camps. This is not to say that the POW experience was pleasant. Vermin-ridden bedding, shortages of heating and cooking fuel, and the natural restlessness and boredom that came with being confined made life behind bars physically and mentally trying. To ease some of these burdens, the Red

Cross did provide the POWs sports and recreation equipment, books, and musical instruments. At Rastatt, the Americans put on vaudeville shows and concerts and even published their own newspaper, *The Barbed Wireless*. Life for captive officers could be better still. They were allowed enlisted POW orderlies to clean up their quarters and were sometimes paroled to roam the local towns if they pledged to not escape. All this aside, the doughboy POWs were happy to see the Armistice and the return of their freedom.[19]

As the first POWs were returning to American hands, the AEF itself was moving into its sector of the Rhineland for occupation duty. Under the provisions of the Armistice, the Allies were to occupy bridgeheads east of the Rhine River. If the Armistice was to break down, these bridgeheads were intended to provide the Allies with a forward jump-off point for further military action against the Germans. The American zone was centered on Coblenz, and doughboys were garrisoned throughout the zone to keep the peace, enforce the Armistice, and prepare to resume the war if necessary. It was that last provision that grated on the doughboys. Within six days of the Armistice, the AEF GHQ directed its units to begin a rigorous training regimen designed to both keep the Americans at a fighting trim and ensure that idle hands did not turn into the devil's workshop. For combat veterans fresh from the Argonne fighting, this training scheme was irksome and unnecessary. They chaffed against what they saw as a resumption of petty West Point–style discipline and the inanity of peacetime soldiering. As one soldier wrote his mother, "They are trying to make soldiers of us now that the war is over but they began too late on me."[20]

As the Americans marched into the Rhineland, Pershing had to balance a number of competing concerns. He wanted the doughboys to treat the German population with respect to both encourage the acceptance of American ideas of liberal democracy and siphon away the resentments of the population that could lead to resistance. On the other hand, as the resumption of the war was still a possibility, Pershing wanted to prevent the doughboys from becoming overly friendly toward the locals. In an order issued on November 28, 1918, Pershing cautioned the American soldiers of the Army of Occupation, "You have not come as despoilers or oppressors, but simply as the instruments of a strong, free government whose purposes towards the people of Germany are beneficent," and "While you appear among them as a conquering army, you will exhibit no ill will toward the inhabitants." He went on to direct, however, that "Germany remains enemy territory, and there must be no intimate personal association with its inhabitants."[21]

Despite Pershing's admonitions to remain aloof with the Germans, most doughboys developed cordial relations with the locals. In fact, the American occupation of the Rhineland was accomplished with much more curiosity than hostility by both sides. As they entered Germany, a soldier in the 42nd Division recalled, "Hospitality was offered in each village through which we passed. Everyone seemed delighted that the war was over . . . It was difficult to be formal and correct conquerors when confronted by smiling children and frauleins. The men even enjoyed swapping lies with the German veterans who still wore their uniforms." The Germans' friendly attitude greatly accelerated the doughboys' shedding of their wartime perceptions of the enemy and furthered the process of "humanizing" the German people. General Henry Allen, the commander of the Army of Occupation, noted of the doughboys, "By the time the soldiers had reached their permanent stations their mental attitude had changed. They learned that a great deal of what they had heard about the innate viciousness of all Germans was not true and their war memories began to fade." Reflecting this new attitude, the infantryman Charles Hill admitted that the Germans were "ordinary people" whom he liked, "even though [I was] taught to hate them."[22]

The AEF's policy of billeting the doughboys on German families until proper barracks could be procured all but assured that Pershing's antifraternization policies would fail. Unlike the French practice of billeting the American in local barns, in Germany the doughboys shared rooms in German homes. This intimacy prompted many Americans to comment that while the French had treated the soldiers well, the Germans had treated them as part of the family. Frank Town recalled that the family he lived with wanted to "do little favors for us always," and accepted the Americans with the greatest hospitality that they could muster. These encounters were symbiotic. The Americans received all the physical and psychological comforts of home, while the Germans gained access to the doughboy's largesse. Charles Holbrook and four other doughboys were billeted in the house of Frau Huaptsman and her three young children. She had lost her husband in the war and the Americans stole chocolate and soap from army stores to help her out.[23]

It is interesting to note that as the Americans' opinions of the Allies, particularly the French, declined, their attitudes toward the Germans improved.

Considering the earlier American acceptance of the Allied claims of German barbarism, the shift in the doughboys' attitudes was remarkable. As noted in chapter 9, a cooling of relations between the French and the Americans in the waning months of the war had fueled the doughboys' discontent with their Gallic allies. Things had grown so bad that the American liaison officer to the French Army in Germany reported the growth of "almost hatred of the [American] enlisted man for the French" within the Army of Occupation. The average American soldier gave voice to his frustrations with the French with a host of unflattering post-Armistice comparisons between France and Germany. One of the more telling indicators of the doughboys' dissatisfaction with their erstwhile allies was the frequency with which the Americans criticized the French for failing to meet German standards of sanitation, honesty, diligence, and intelligence. The doughboys even paid the Germans their highest possible compliment by favorably comparing Germany with the United States. Using the same terms that early-twentieth-century Americans often used to describe themselves, one soldier stated that the Germans were "very progressive, clean, industrious and patriotic." The doughboys' growing affection for the Germans and disillusionment with the Allies even prompted some soldiers to question the United States' support for the Allies in the war. A soldier in the 82nd Division wrote, "In my opinion we whipped the best people over there." After serving in the Army of Occupation, another soldier laconically observed, "We was fighting on the wrong side." Less than a decade after the war, Elizabeth White asserted, "The returned soldier was wont to state with firmness that he would never fight in France or for France again." Though it is hard to say how many doughboys took these positions, a majority of the Americans who served in both Germany and France would have agreed that the former was cleaner, more progressive, more advanced, and more like the United States than the latter.[24]

The average doughboys' preference for Germany outraged and concerned some Americans. Editorials in the *Stars and Stripes* and the *Amaroc News* reproached the American soldiers for their fraternization with German women, for praising their enemies, and for criticizing their Allies. An editorial called "Those Frogs" in the *Amaroc News* from May 16, 1919, shamed the doughboys for speaking ill of the French. The writer noted,

> When you recall your exploits and you recall his, remember: that in proportion to every soldier we lost, France lost ten ... That you lost three or

four of the best pals in the world up in the Argonne, but the French soldier lost 30 or 40 just like them. That you had 75 days of hell—he had four years. That you have been away from home—a vine clad cozy affair, but it's there and your mother is there and sister, your wife just as sweet as they were nine months ago, while his home may be a pile of rocks, and his wife and sister have been hungry, and they have lived in an armed camp, and may not be like they were in the Spring-time of 1914. Then—remembering these things, think before you criticize the "Frog." His faith has cost him more than you have paid.

Likewise, officers in the 167th Infantry tried to convince their soldiers that the Germans' friendliness was all a show and that the Huns only seemed more clean and orderly than the French because they had not endured the physical ravages of war.[25]

Few doughboys listened to the sentimental appeals for Allied comradeship and forgot the past wrongs and slights done to them in France. However, fears that the Americans soldiers' shift in attitude heralded a dangerous informal "alliance" between the doughboys and the Germans were unfounded. While the Americans may have been more impressed with the Germans than with the French or English, the Teutonic nation still fell far short of the Yanks' idealized America. Even given the doughboys' assertions that the Germans were "just like" Americans, their loud pronouncements of American social and cultural superiority left no doubt that the Germans occupied an inferior position in their American exceptionalist worldview. The editor of the *Amaroc News* acknowledged this American perception and wrote that the soldiers held "a fairly general conviction that Germans, as a people, in many respects fall short of American ideas and ideals." Ultimately, the praise and preference for Germany over the Allies only reflected the American soldiers' rating of the relative social and cultural development of the various European states. While Germany outranked France in the doughboys' estimation of social advancement, both fell far short in comparison to the United States.[26]

For their part, the German population generally viewed the American occupation as benign and even beneficial. The U.S. Army routinely censored the incoming and outgoing mail of its German prisoners of war. While the Base Censor office had always passed on any information that they deemed to be of value to the Army's intelligence service, on December 6, 1918, the office began a systematic program of collecting and reporting passages of POW correspondence that "throw any light whatever on their condition of mind—

whether they are resigned to their captivity under the circumstances—what their opinion is of the Americans, particularly opinions that are expressed by their people in Germany in regard to the outcome of the war." The Base Censor office gave their inspectors further guidance to report on correspondence related to the demobilization of German troops, attitudes of the German people toward Allied occupation forces, and information regarding the political, economic, industrial, social, and religious conditions inside Germany. For the most part, the letters to POWs from German civilians in the American zone were complimentary of the doughboys' behavior and their lack of any lingering bitterness over the war. A citizen of American-occupied Trier reported on January 9, 1919, "We in no way suffer here because of the change. On the contrary, I feel much safer now that we have American troops here. I hear everyone is glad that things turned out the way things did, because the Americans are so agreeable here." Another wrote to his POW son,

> We have American troops in Coblenz, and let me tell you dear boy, that the American is a fine, noble minded person. We associate like comrades. Up to now there has not been the slightest occurrence of any kind. On Christmas the Americans had an electric lighted Christmas tree on the border of the Rhine. The same was beautiful. Much has been done for the civil population on the part of the Americans. They have found a hearty reception everywhere.

"The Americans are all very polite and amiable people," Herr Allerodder observed. "One would not believe that they were our enemies, and here for the purpose of Occupation."[27]

Although local German officials urged their citizens to cooperate with the Americans, the warm German welcome that the people gave the doughboys reflected a great deal of self-interest. Many were relieved to be occupied by the Americans rather than the justifiably vengeful French and Belgians. The Germans also retained great faith in Woodrow Wilson and the hope that the United States would prevent France and England from imposing a harsh peace on Germany. Large numbers of people in the American-occupied Rhineland were also thankful for the economic and political order that the doughboys brought. In March 1919, one admitted, "We have protection and can carry on our business unmolested, whereas the Sparticists are keeping other places in constant agitation." Anna Fink's interest in the Americans was more pecuniary: "In the taverns the price of a glass of wine has been reduced from one

Mark fifty to thirty Pfennig; also meat has become cheaper, and other things will follow. If it continues things will not be so bad; at least the usury will stop. It had become so bad that one could not buy anything anymore." To paraphrase a saying from a later war, once the Americans controlled the price of wine, beer, and meat, the Rhinelanders' "hearts and minds followed." The concordance between the occupier and the occupied was also aided by the fact that large numbers of Germans spoke English and many more dough-boys spoke German than French. As the wartime American Army quickly disbanded, the "American Forces in Germany" was reduced to around sixty-eight hundred men. The occupation formally ended on January 24, 1923, with the Americans turning their sector over to the French Army.[28]

Some of the doughboys' interactions with the Germans went well beyond concerns of trade and Bolshevism. When the Americans first occupied the Rhineland, the AEF GHQ's nonfraternization order should have made is-sues of love, sex, and marriage between the American soldiers and German women a moot point. However, biology did not succumb to mere army or-ders. By the spring of 1919, a rapid increase in pregnant German women, and repeated requests by soldiers to marry them, forced the 3rd Army to make a decision. In this case the army was in a bind. If it did not allow the mar-riages, the army risked alienating the locals and undermining the "dignity of the United States." If the army allowed the soldiers to marry after violat-ing the nonfraternization order, discipline would suffer. In the end, the 3rd Army commander decided that discretion was the better part of valor and allowed the doughboys to marry without threat of punishment. The army feared that the new policy would encourage German women to get pregnant and marry a soldier to gain passage to the United States. In October 1919, the 3rd Army required all soldiers to get permission from the first section of the AEF General Staff before marrying. In certain circumstances, the 3rd Army commander could waive the requirement "provided an investigation proved the former good character of the girl."[29]

The issue of doughboys marrying Europeans had actually arisen soon af-ter the first doughboys arrived in France. The marriage question set off a vigorous debate within the high command over the military, legal, and ethi-cal ramifications of wartime wedlock. Pershing and the AEF's senior lawyers ultimately decided that the doughboys' military status did not change their personal rights to marry. When it came to the process for actually contracting marriage, however, the AEF took the easy way out and defaulted to French law. To obtain a marriage certificate, both parties had to provide proof of their identities, age, and lack of any legal impediments to marriage and the upcoming nuptials had to be publicly posted as banns in the residences of the bride and groom. These requirements placed a burden on the soldiers. The doughboys lacked ready access to birth certificates or other legal proof of their birth and identities and their vagabond existence made the publishing of banns problematic. It was not until four months after the Armistice that the French government, the AEF, and the U.S. State Department all reached an accord to liberalize these legal requirements. The agreement allowed officers of the U.S. Army Judge Advocate General corps to verify the soldier-groom's identity, place of residence, and legal eligibility to wed. Although commanders feared that such liberalizing would lead to an avalanche of marriage requests, their fears were unjustified. Many soldiers saw the cultural gap between the two parties as too great, and relatively few doughboys seemed interested in the prospect of marriage. As one commented, "I would rather take five more years in the army than a war bride." It is interesting to note that while getting married did little to change the male soldier's official status in the army, if a woman serving in the military, Red Cross, or other welfare agencies got married in France, she was immediately discharged and sent back to the States.[30]

Although the AEF generally took a hands-off approach to marriage and treated it as a civil rather than a military matter, it did get involved in certain cases. To keep in the good graces of the French people and to "do the right thing" if a soldier admitted the paternity of a child from a relationship with a French woman and was willing to marry her so "that the wrong would be righted," it was the policy of the AEF "to lend every assistance to the consummation of the marriage." The concern of family members at home and many of the senior officers in the AEF was that many of these pregnant females and war brides were of poor character and morals and had only wed to get the chance for a better life in America. As one officer accused, "In many cases the women involved were designing persons of questionable character who contracted marriage for the purpose of obtaining allotments and ultimately perhaps insurance." To prevent these designing women from reaching the pure shores of the Republic, the AEF issued orders requiring the women to undergo examinations for venereal disease and the soldier's officers had to swear to the bride's "reputable character" before she was allowed passage to the United States.[31]

In the end the doughboys returned home with over five thousand European war brides. Franziska (Francis) Fischer was one of them. Francis was born in Zweibruecken, Germany, on January 9, 1902, and had moved to Diedenhofen (the name the Germans gave Thionville during their occupation of the town from 1871 to 1918) with her family in the early years of the twentieth century. The sixteen-year-old Francis met Adolph Ferdinand Decker soon after the Armistice, when his unit, the 403rd Telephone Battalion, was stationed in Thionville. The twenty-one-year-old Decker was smitten with Francis. Despite their budding relationship the army had other plans for Decker and the youngsters were soon separated by his posting to Verdun in March 1919. As he wrote Francis on March 13, "How I miss Thionville & my good little girl. But there is a day coming when I will be back. It can't be more than a year." Just before leaving for the United States, the lovesick doughboy wrote on May 26, 1919, "There isn't a day goes by that I don't think of you."

After arriving stateside, Adolph returned to Baltimore and began planning for the couple's reunification. On August 2, 1919, he wrote Francis imploring her to "please let me know if you still love me enough to become my *wife*. Please write & let me know, I am very anxious." With the continued economic collapse and political instability in Germany, Decker grew concerned over the safety and well-being of Francis's family. He was particularly concerned about rumors of food shortages. On December 30, 1919, he wrote, "I truly hope you have plenty to live on." He did have good news, however, and two weeks later he informed Francis that he was sending her a voucher for a second-class ticket to the States and assured her that his intention was to marry her on board the ship as soon as it docked so "when you step on the shore you are then an American citizen."

Unfortunately, something in the plan went awry, and on February 8, 1920, Adolph apologized to his beloved that as the United States had not yet made peace with Germany, "it would be folly to make a move" to bring her to the States at the present time. He tried to reassure her that "his attentions were still the same," and pleaded to her to "be good & be careful of the company you mix with." In the following months he wrote that he hoped that a new president would finalize the peace treaty and open the way for their reunion. He also begged Francis not to "get tired of waiting," for "good times are waiting for us both." Decker further admitted his fear that in the face of the mounting delays, "some little German boy will win your love." Throughout 1920 and early 1921, the couple faced a roller coaster of raised and shattered hopes. The Red Scare had led to increased efforts by some politicians and civil groups to restrict immigration, and in December 1920 Decker informed Francis that he had heard that the American government was considering imposing a one-year moratorium on any new immigrants to the United States. Despite all the drama, the star-crossed lovers were ultimately reunited. Franziska Fischer arrived in Boston onboard the SS *Potomac* on June 10, 1921, and shortly thereafter married Adolph Decker. The two eventually settled in Glen Burnie, Maryland, where Decker continued to work for the local telephone company. They spent the next forty-two years together. Adolph died at age sixty-seven in July 1963 and Francis died in August 1985 at age eighty-three.[32]

Despite Pershing's efforts to keep the AEF at a high pitch of combat readiness, it proved impossible to keep the doughboys, and their voting family members back home, from focusing on anything other than demobilization. As previously noted, the AEF GHQ tried to channel the doughboys' post-Armistice energy by creating a robust sports program, by pushing a training regimen, and by crafting a liberal pass and leave program for the doughboys to see France and enjoy the army's recreation centers. In spirit of the Progressive Era, the AEF also sought to uplift the doughboys and set them on the path to a brighter postwar future by establishing a strong education system. On January 13, 1919, Pershing directed the YMCA's Army Educational Commission to assist commanders from the army to the regimental level in establishing post schools to teach modern languages, American and world history, and civics. A month later, in General Orders 30, the GHQ expanded this mandate by increasing the scope of the division schools and by establishing the AEF University in Beaune, France. The AEF further coordinated with the Allies to allow a select group of American veterans to attend civilian universities in France and Britain. In the end, seventy-five hundred doughboys were afforded the opportunity to learn in French universities while another 2,023 attended British schools.[33]

The division schools were organized on an eight-week term and offered vocational-technical courses on automotive repair, electrical wiring, wire and wireless electronic telegraphy, telephone installation, and aircraft repair. The

AEF University worked on an eleven-week term. The students had classes five times a week and took three courses per term. The university's library boasted thirty thousand volumes, all donated from the American Library Association. The university offered 245 different classes in its eleven colleges: agriculture, education, engineering, journalism, law, letters, science, art, business, medicine, and music. Classes on business had the largest enrollment, with an average of 188 students per class. Art, music, and law classes were the next most popular courses with an average of forty-four, forty-one, and thirty-seven students enrolled in those courses. The university also held a cadet college that prepared enlisted men to take the entrance examination to West Point. Some of the 188 cadets in the program completed their studies in time to enter the Military Academy on July 1, 1919. Lastly, the university built a farm school on 250 acres of land near Beaune. Students studying agricultural science learned modern farming techniques and how to care for the farm's one hundred hens, eighty horses and mules, eleven milk cows, and fifty hogs. The university had a staff of 797 and had registered 13,259 students by May 1919. Unfortunately, over sixty thousand students withdrew from their courses before receiving grades. Most of them left because their units were preparing to sail for home.[34]

The doughboys were generally pleased with the AEF's educational opportunities. Many were concerned with finding work upon their return to the States. "While I am over here I might as well make use of it if I can get it," a Marine wrote home in January 1919, and admitted that attending the university "would help me out if I go back to my old profession and will do no harm in any case." The students also welcomed a break from Pershing's training plan and the monotony of army life that the classes offered. Robert Bressler was fortunate to be selected to attend a bookkeeping course after the Armistice. In March 1919, he informed his parents, "I like it pretty good at the school. We have drill for one hour in the morning and then classes for three hours which finishes my recitations for the day. I then have the afternoons for study & prepare lessons for the following day. Do not have any lessons on Saturday but have inspection in the morning and are then finished til Monday." Self-improvement while avoiding long, forced marches in the European winter was an unbeatable combination.[35]

Even those doughboys who could not or would not attend the AEF University often sought less formal opportunities for education and enlightenment. Chaplain Arthur Hicks organized twenty-two courses for the men in his unit, which ranged in subjects from French, algebra, and American history to salesmanship, drawing, and gas engine repair. Donald Mitchell decided against attending university courses in France because he believed that it would slow his return to the States and thus hinder his ability to find a job on his return. That did not stop him and his comrades from indulging in some intellectual pursuits. As they waited to return home, members of his unit gave lectures on topics as varied as Shakespeare, Bible interpretation, fossil remains, French history, prehistoric man, textile fabrics, and the customs and religion of Japan.[36]

Even with diversions such as education and sports, what most of the doughboys wanted after the Armistice was a quick return home. Most soldiers believed that they had accomplished the task that the Republic had given them and now wanted nothing more than to get on with their lives. "I want to get out so bad I am nearly crazy. I am sure I have done my part in this *war* and I think that every boy that crossed over has done the same," a Georgian complained to his parents.

This sentiment was shared by a sergeant in the 91st Division, who wrote his girlfriend,

> Oh boy wait till I get home, believe me I shure will make up for lost time and no fooling it is just 6 months since we arrived in France and it seems like 6 years to me. It was not so bad while the excitement was on but now all the boys think of is when do we get home. I can safely say that I am through roaming and ready to settle down.

One doughboy was so anxious to return to his wife that he joked, "Give me a row boat, one oar and a sail and I will get to the States all right."[37]

What weighed heavily on the minds of many doughboys was their prospects at finding a job upon their return home. In the days before the GI Bill, the returning veterans had scant safety nets to ease their transition back into civilian life. The veterans of the AEF rightly feared that the soldiers who never left the States would be in a better position to snap up fleeting job opportunities than those cooling their heels in Europe while waiting to sail home. In February 1919, a disenchanted doughboy went so far as to note in *Stars and Stripes* that the veterans of the AEF would be at a disadvantage because employers wanted "clever fellows that had enough sense to stay home," rather than those who went to France with nothing to show for it than overseas stripes. This fear certainly caused Cornelius Freely much anxiety. In January 1919 he confided to his girlfriend, "I am not sorry one bit that I came over here as I got quite an experience, but I must say now that the war is over why I am anxious to get home as quickly as possible as I feel that I am now wasting my time and good money, while staying over here." A month later, after being informed that his unit would not sail home until June or July 1919, he lamented, "Why when we get home the people will have become tired of seeing soldiers, and I suppose all the good jobs will be taken."[38]

There was one job readily available for those seeking opportunities. Faced with a rapidly demobilizing force and the need for troops to serve in Germany, the AEF encouraged its veterans to enlist in the Regulars for duty in the Army of Occupation. The army played upon the veterans' fear of a bleak postwar job market and printed recruiting materials touting the benefits of a career in the service. One pamphlet promised, "You don't have to worry about chow, clothes or a good bed *in peace* times. And a sensible soldier never has to be in debt and can always have his *own* money in his pocket." Some men took the army up on the offer because of the promise of a steady job, because of the fact that they found military life appealing, or because they believed that their opportunities in postwar America would be limited. Alonzo LaVanture was in the latter category. As his mother was dead and he believed that he "practically had no home," he convinced his commander to reassign him to Germany as an MP. When the war ended, John Miholick, who had enlisted underage in April 1917, found himself too uneducated and unskilled to make a go at civilian life. When the army offered him technical training as an automechanic if he reenlisted, he jumped at the opportunity. He remained in the Army until 1925, when he took a civilian job working in the navy's petroleum supply system at Pearl Harbor. He retired from that job after twenty-one years of service and lived to see his son become a lieutenant colonel in the Air Force. Although some doughboys opted to remain in the army, most had had their fill of the military. Many would have agreed with the sentiment of a veteran who wrote home in March 1919, "I wouldn't be a soldier anymore for $1000 a month."[39]

As with so many things in army life, boredom and the absence of any meaningful communications from their superiors meant that rumors were rife among those waiting to sail home. In early April 1919, a 3rd Division soldier wrote to a friend that he was not sure when he would return to the

States. The current rumor circulating in his battalion at the time was that the army was sending ten divisions to Russia and that his might be one of them. This possibility was far from comforting to him, as he noted, "It is so cold there that when you piss it puts an icicle on your stem." The Marine George McLaughlin endured similar anxieties. As he told his mother, "Just at present it looks like we are stuck in this camp for a while although all kinds of rumors are flying about our going home, to Germany, Russia and every other nook and corner of the Earth." "I wish something definite would be given," he grumbled, but "that is a wish that will never come true for a private in this army."[40]

Fortunately, most of the rumors that fueled the doughboys' fears were unfounded. The trip back home, however, was almost as trying for the troops as the trip over. Most soldiers left France through the port of Brest after having passed through the embarkation camp at Pontanézen Barracks. Pontanézen was a depressing site where the constant tramping of boots had turned the entire location into a muddy quagmire. The camp's mud was so infamous that the shoulder patch worn by its personnel was a duckboard symbolizing the wooden pathways that had to be used to travel through the barracks. Discipline in the embarkation camps was tough and rumors abounded about the numerous pitfalls that could delay the forthcoming departure. One doughboy recalled, "Everyone said that getting assigned to a transport depended on good behavior. There were stories of outfits being kept two months at Brest because they straggled when they marched, or were shy the proper number of tent pegs per man. We believed everything we heard." A rumor spread that one regiment was yanked from the ship taking them home because one of its members had yelled, "Who won the war?" to the dockside MPs. The men of the 1st Gas Regiment were likewise told that "any questionable remarks as to the M.P.'s or Service of Supply men would be radically dealt with and that the authorities of the said downtrodden Service of Supply would take measures to keep the offenders in Brest for an indefinite time." As the combat troops generally held both MPs and SOS soldiers in low regard, these rumors were bound to raise their ire.[41]

Getting ready for sailing also brought a slew of medical and equipment inspections. These inspections, generally done by men who had spent the war far from the front, often irked returning combat veterans. They were also irritated by the cattle-like treatment they received at the facilities. It all started with bathing and delousing, conducted in an efficient assembly-line manner that would have made Henry Ford smile:

> We took off all our clothes and threw them away. Then we filed into a sort of steam chamber where soapy water fell on us from the ceiling. In the room beyond we were painted all over with some white disinfectant by men with large whitewash brushes. Then we progressed to a shower room, after which we were given a towel and told to use them. At the door of the next department the towels were taken away from us and we were given a complete new set of clothes, with no regard for our different sizes.

The army feared the spread of any disease to the United States from the returning troops and constantly monitored the waiting doughboys for sickness and lice. A reappearance of cooties on any soldier meant that everyone in the unit returned to the bath for delousing. The troops were also inspected for venereal disease and anyone found with those maladies was sent to the Pontanézen segregation camp for treatment. This, of course, delayed their return home.[42]

Both the folks at home and the doughboys themselves clamored for a speedy return to the United States. The army and navy responded as well as could be expected to the monumental task of shipping the troops back home. Soon after the Armistice, the British and French withdrew their ships from troop-carrying duties. To cover these losses and meet the demand to return the troops as rapidly as possible, the Transport Service expanded the carrying capacity of its fleet by constructing more berths, galleys, and washrooms in its existing ships. Furthermore, the Army converted fifty-three cargo ships to carry troops, and in December 1918, the navy assigned thirteen battleships and seven armored cruisers the mission of transporting the doughboys to America. The Peace Commission also gave the Americans nine German passenger liners for the duty. The return of the AEF peaked in June 1919 when the fleet reached 142 ships and 314,167 soldiers landed in the States.[43]

For the most part, the doughboys' return trip to America was uneventful. The lack of a U-Boat threat meant that no time was wasted awaiting convoy orders or zigzagging across the Atlantic. By the spring of 1919, the average round trip for a troop transport from France was down to twenty-five days. The rapid passage home was welcomed by the troops. The ships taking them home were even more crowded than those that had carried them to France. The navy ships assigned to the mission were particularly tight. Battleships carried around eleven hundred soldiers while the cruisers carried 1,750 in addition to their normal crews. Fortunately, by the time that most doughboys sailed home the influenza epidemic had run its course. Although the ships were crowded and the food monotonous and unappealing, few doughboys complained about the voyage. Perhaps it was easier for the soldiers to accept these irritations when the prize before them was hearth and home.[44]

And then there was America. Until April 1919, when the Transportation Service opened receiving stations at Boston, Charleston, and Philadelphia, most doughboys returned to the two major posts that had sent them to Europe: New York and Newport News. Many of those sailing into New York shared the thrill felt by Captain Carroll Swan:

> Sailing up New York Harbor, I stood on the forward deck . . . The old Statue of Liberty, at last, was a reality right in front of us. Steamers and tugs everywhere were making a noisy demonstration. People were waving from building and docks: a picture we had all dreamed of a thousand times. It was a wonderful and exciting scene. After a whole year away at war, I was again gazing upon my own native land.

After the slow and impatient process of disembarkation from the ship, the arriving doughboys were hustled away to the port receiving camps to wait for their baggage to be unloaded and for transportation to be arranged to carry them to their demobilization stations.[45]

At the receiving camps the soldiers had their first opportunity to reintegrate back into society. This could be a disorienting process, especially for those who had served the longest overseas. George Browne was a case in point. He had sailed for France with the 42nd Division in October 1917 and was fortunate to be in one of the first groups of soldiers to return home in January 1919. The day after landing in Newport, Browne wrote his fiancée,

> I'm so glad to be back and there's so many things to see and do that I hardly know what to do first. The thing that struck me first when we got on the streets was to hear the children speak English. I couldn't make it seem natural at first. Then everything is so nice and clean, the civilians so well dressed. I know nothing about the prices of things but just the fact that everything is so plentiful over here. All one has to do is look into the

shop windows and he'd know he was in America. Big apples and oranges, anything like that . . . I just began to live again when I passed down the streets here.

Just as the new arrivals were losing their sea legs and adjusting to their environment, the army added to their bewilderment by quickly moving them on to their demobilization camps. These camps were generally located at the posts where the soldiers' units were mobilized and trained.[46] For the thousands of men who were anxious to get on with their lives, waiting to be officially discharged at the demobilization camps was one of the more irksome experiences in their military lives. The demobilization process was far from smooth or uniform. Much to the chagrin of the AEF veterans, those serving in the States at the time of the Armistice were generally discharged rather quickly. Those arriving from Europe, however, faced wait times of several weeks, or even months, before receiving their discharge papers. Luther Grover was pleased that he had been granted a seventy-two-hour pass to return home and looked forward to his unit's victory parade in Boston but admitted that he was terribly restless and ready to return to civilian life. He complained to his sister in April 1919, "I want to get started to work at something for I have done enough hanging around in this army for the last six months." He was far from being alone in this sentiment. Some soldiers resorted to contacting their congressmen or other powerful connections to speed up their demobilization process. Reflecting the belief of many of his comrades, one soldier groused, "The only way you can get a discharge from this army is to get some party with a pull in the states to start the ball rolling, otherwise you will have to wait until you are mustered out." Corporal H. W. Carver was so intent on getting a discharge from Camp Travis, Texas, that he sent a letter to his wife that included a passage that she was to copy verbatim to him in her next letter. This dictated letter outlined the family's dire economic straights and the poor state of the wife's health and was intended to give Carver the ammunition he needed to sway his chain of command to release him from the service.[47]

Many returning doughboys would have sympathized with the tribulations of Elmer Lewis as he impatiently awaited discharge. His unit, the 361st Infantry, landed in New York in late March 1919 and had taken a long train ride across the continent to its demobilization station at Camp Lewis, Washington. He was anxious to be reunited with his girlfriend, Goldie Little, but bad luck dogged his steps. On April 30, 1919, he wrote her,

> Well honey this damn hay wire outfit is out of luck again as usual. We are in for a 14 day quarantine for measles . . . I don't suppose I will get home to you till the middle of May. One of the boys in our company has them so the doctors think, but we don't know for sure yet. Maybe I will be over soldiering any way if they don't put all the guards in camp around us. The boys are about ready to turn Bolshevik if they don't find out he has them . . . I think that it is just a big frame up to keep some of us here to police up the camp till all the division is discharged.

A week later he groused, "I cannot come home this week and we have been raising Hail Columbia around here but so far we cannot get any satisfaction off anyone . . . the time simply drags here. I shure wish that the days would go by so I could get out of this army and get home where I can be my own boss." Like many in the demobilization camps, for a time Elmer even considered going AWOL to visit Goldie, but the number of unauthorized soldiers leaving the camp had become such a problem that the officers had cracked down. He worried that if he was caught being AWOL it would delay his ultimate discharge even further. "I would like to take all the Majors and shave tails," he railed against those who delayed his departure, "and fix them like the way the Indians used to torture their captives."[48]

The slow disintegration of units during demobilization was a bittersweet process. On the one hand, soldiers like Lewis were happy to regain the freedoms of civilian life, but on the other, the discharges led to the breakup of buddies and primary groups that had been welded together through the hardships of war. For officers, demobilization meant the dissolving of organizations that they had painstakingly built and led through the hardest of times. The officers were often the last of their units' personnel to be discharged, for they were required by the army to settle all of their units' bookkeeping. When asked by his mother when he would return home, Lieutenant Dewitt McIntyre could only reply, "To-morrow I will discharge 150 of my men, and the next day the remainder of them. All of our officers who are not responsible for property are going to move down to Louisville to Camp Taylor to-morrow. The rest of us I believe will be here for a while until we settle up all of our accounts. I had about $200,000 worth of property to my account." As McIntyre well knew, to the very end, the army bureaucracy had to be served.[49]

At the demobilization camps the soldiers were given some limited assistance to prepare them to return to civilian life. They were given the opportunity to continue their War Risk Insurance policy at rates that were much lower than the civilian market. For example, a twenty-five-year-old veteran would have a monthly premium of 66 cents for every thousand dollars of coverage. The troops were further offered a host of brochures and advice outlining the government's obligations to, and programs for, the returning veteran. Veterans who were disabled in the line of duty were entitled to compensation. This compensation varied depending on the severity of the injury. If a soldier had lost his eyesight or was bedridden, he would receive $100 per month plus a payment from the War Risk Insurance Bureau if he had taken out a policy prior to the injury. Disabled veterans were also entitled to free artificial limbs and vocational training. A disabled doughboy who was single and undergoing his instruction under the Federal Board of Vocational Training also received a stipend of $65 a month.[50]

Doughboys without disabilities found the government to be somewhat less generous. Reflecting the prevailing views of the purpose of the federal government of the time, the veterans were told to expect not a handout from the government but only the opportunity to help themselves out. Upon discharge a doughboy with an honorable service record was given a $60 bonus and a payment of five cents per mile to cover the cost of a train ticket and incidentals to return the man to the place that he had been inducted or to his home. The soldier was also allowed to retain one complete set of his uniform, plus a raincoat and an overcoat if he was discharged during the cold months. Upon leaving the service, the man was to wear a red discharge stripe on his left sleeve to indicate his new status and to avoid further hassle from military authorities. Veterans of the AEF were allowed to retain their helmets and gasmasks as mementos of their overseas service. For some, these few items were the only stitch of clothing to their names. Soon after being discharged in the States, one veteran wrote a friend, "I went broke last week and had to go to work . . . I haven't got any clothes at all [and am] wearing russet shoes the army blouse & overcoat and I was so cold today in my legs I guess I'll wear the uniform to work."[51]

Each demobilization camp had representatives from the United States Employment Service and the United States Civil Service Commission to offer advice and some degree of assistance in finding a job or furthering the man's education. The only promise that the federal government made the veteran when it came to employment was that it would give him preference in obtaining an open civil service job if he was qualified for the position. The Department of the Interior's Reclamation Service offered returning doughboys the possibility of owning their own homestead or farm if they agreed to assist the government in the recovery of overlogged and marginal plots of land. The department envisioned the creation of soldier farming settlements on the restored and newly profitable lands. The veteran-colonist would be paid by the government to drain swamps, build dams and canals, and remove stumps from the land. From these wages, the government expected the veteran to pay for his homestead and the stock and farming implements that it provided for the endeavor. In the end, few doughboys took the offer or made a go of this scheme.[52]

The doughboys' expectations of what they would receive for their service and what their place would be in postwar America varied greatly. Some returned with the belief that their military service and sacrifices had entitled them to be the new vanguard that would shape the future of the Republic. A few weeks after the Armistice one of the men wrote his father,

> I don't believe yet that the people of America have awoke to the fullest extent to the situation. Very little do the fathers and mothers know of what their loved ones have gone through many of them would hold up their hands in horror if they could see some of the houses and pig pens that we called home, but for the ones that volunteer their services, I have the highest admiration and when we are all back in the good old U.S.A. there will be a class of men numbering about 2½ million, who will move the country with what they say and do, so look out for this gang will be the hard-boiled A.E.F., the men who have given up everything and who will have to start life all over again, men who have forgotten how to talk and use their manners before ladies, these men in the years to come will be the ruling power of America.

He was not the only doughboy to return home with new attitudes and aspirations. The historian Nancy MacLean noted that "once having experienced an alternative to white southern life," African American soldiers across the rural South "would never be the same—nor would the communities they returned to." In fact, 70 percent of the plantation owners in Clarke County, Georgia, reported that large numbers of black veterans left their employment soon after returning from the war. The ambitions of many, if not most, white and black doughboys were much more restrained. In the winter of 1919, the Morale Branch asked post and unit morale officers to survey the troops awaiting discharge on their opinions of the army, their time in the service, and their future expectations. Chaplain Earle Stigers reported in March 1919 that at Camp Funston "the men believe they should be provided with work but there does not seem to be any marked tendency to expect 'coddling' because of military service rendered."[53]

Although a discussion of the veteran's life after the service is beyond the scope of this work, it should be noted that the transformation from being a soldier to a civilian was often rocky. The doughboys may not have expected "coddling," but large numbers of the veterans who responded to the U.S. Army Military History Institute's survey in the 1970s and 1980s remained dissatisfied with the lack of assistance that the federal government had given them during this period of transition. William Nemec bitterly recalled, "The government just kicked us out with no job in sight & no way to make a living." He considered his service a "detriment" that forced him to sacrifice his former life while leaving him ill prepared to reenter civil society. Many doughboy-veterans compared the scant assistance that they had received upon their discharge to the lavish benefits that the grateful nation bestowed on the following GI generation. Over seventy years after the war, Edgar Hastings still angrily noted, "Compared to veterans in recent wars, I think World War I veterans have been greatly short-changed in benefits."[54]

As they returned home, the majority of doughboys believed that their contribution had won the war, or they at least maintained that the Americans had been one of the most important factors in the Allied victory. This is not to say that some of the veterans were not cognizant of the cost of the nation's unpreparedness for the war or were uncritical of the army's performance. In a survey of returning AEF officers conducted by the Morale Branch, a captain groused,

> What did the Army do? It gathered men into camps . . . and ship them to New York. England furnished ships. In the great majority of the men were thrown to the front with half the necessary equipment and poorly trained. But the higher officers knew that the men had grit and that there was plenty more coming—"So what the hell"—let them die. Only those who do not know, talk about the accomplishments of the Army.

Another merely maintained, "We did not win the war. We simply were balancing power—as the supreme military nation of the world. Our accomplishments were not military feats but feats of transportation and money."[55]

After studying thousands of surveys that Great War veterans filled out for their home states in 1919, Edward Gutiérrez concluded that the doughboys were quite proud of their military service and were not mentally and emotionally shattered by the horrors that they endured. He rightly maintains that the image of a vast postwar "Lost Generation" of cynical veterans disillusioned by the pointlessness of the war was largely a product of novelists, many of whom had never got within earshot of the fighting. In fact, as noted before, scores of soldiers returned home with a new or renewed faith in American exceptionalism. Long after the war, one veteran unapologetically stated, "Those who fought & were in foreign countries appreciate our form of government. The more something costs you, the more effort you put into something, the more you value it." This is not to say that the soldiers were not touched by the war. In fact while the conflict was still raging, Albert Robinson recorded in his journal, "One must admit that war does bring out something in a man . . . [He] becomes refined or consumed. It makes him or breaks him." Some were also at a loss in trying to explain to the folks back home what they had gone through. Shortly after his return home, Earl Seaton's aunt invited a number of people to her house to have Earl tell everyone about his war experiences. Seaton later mused, "You cannot tell people who have not been there how it was and I don't think I tried. I should have told what was going on. Maybe I could have told a few things." Perhaps most doughboys would have agreed with the sentiments of the artilleryman Walter Bedell. Soon after the Armistice he wrote his father, "Altogether Pa this sure was some experience and I wouldn't take anything for it but I'm damned if I want it over again."[56]

At some point, all returning doughboys had their final parting of the ways with the military. Paul Maxwell returned home to Clarksburg, West Virginia, on December 14, 1918, after having been away for fourteen months. After leaving the train depot he hopped on a trolley that would carry him home. He was immediately aware of the peculiarity of the situation and the contending senses of what was new and what was familiar. One of the first things he noticed was that "on the street car the conductor was a stranger; one time I had known them all, but rolling up and down hill and around familiar curves assured me we were on the right course." When he finally spied his house, he recalled, "I realize I am home at last." At the same time, however, he could not help thinking, "I am out of the army but I have a feeling, it will be a long time before the army is out of me." Like his fellow Pershing's Crusaders, he reached home and the time had come to shed his armor and sword, yet the memory of the crusade would linger for the rest of his days.[57]

NOTES

CHAPTER 1. PERSHING'S CRUSADERS

1. Letter from Capt. Herman Ulmer to Col. W. M. Whitman, dated November 30, 1918, Whitman Papers, 325th IN, 82nd Div, MHIWWIS.
2. This point has also recently been made by Edward A. Gutiérrez in his study of surveys taken by American soldiers shortly after the war. Edward A. Gutiérrez, *Doughboys on the Great War* (Lawrence: University Press of Kansas, 2014), 33–38.

CHAPTER 2. "I WANT YOU FOR THE U.S. ARMY"

1. United States Department of War, *War Department Annual Report* (Washington, DC: Government Printing Office, 1916), 242; Leonard Ayres, *The War With Germany: A Statistical Summary* (Washington, DC: Government Printing Office, 1919), 16–21.
2. Gerald F. Linderman, *Embattled Courage* (New York: Free Press, 1987), 8–12, 17–19, 35–36, 83–84.
3. Reid Mitchell, "Soldiering, Manhood, and Coming of Age: A Northern Volunteer," in *Divided Houses: Gender and the Civil War*, ed. Catherine Clinton and Nina Silber (New York: Oxford University Press, 1992), 44.
4. Bell Irvin Wiley, *The Life of Johnny Reb* (New York: Doubleday, 1971), 16–19; originally published by Bobbs-Merrill in 1943.
5. Bell Irvin Wiley, *The Life of Billy Yank* (Baton Rouge: Louisiana State University Press, 1978), 39–40; Reid Mitchell, *The Vacant Chair* (New York: Oxford University Press, 1993), 154–155; Linderman, *Embattled Courage*, 80–82.
6. James M. McPherson, *For Cause and Comrades* (New York: Oxford University Press, 1997), 12.
7. Samuel Stouffer et al., *The American Soldier*, vol. 2, *Combat and Its Aftermath* (Princeton: Princeton University Press, 1949), 107–111, 137–140, 150–151.
8. S. L. A. Marshall, *Men against Fire* (Glouchester, MA: Peter Smith, 1978), 138–156, 161–162.
9. Elmer Stovall, 5th Cav; Richard McBride, 328th IN, 82nd Div, memoir, "Passing in Review: Memories of World War I," both in MHIWWIS.
10. Leroy Bicknell, 9th MGB, 3rd Div; Walter Eichenlaub, Field Hospital 7, 3rd Div; Robert L. Girton, 314 EN, 89 Div, all in MHIWWIS.
11. Martin Hogan, *The Shamrock Battalion in the Great War*, ed. James J. Cooke (Columbia: University of Missouri Press, 2007), 16.
12. Quoted in Edward J. Reneham, Jr., *The Lion's Pride* (New York: Oxford University

Press, 1998), 25. For Roosevelt's influence on the doughboys, see Laurence Stall-ings, *The Doughboys* (New York: Harper & Row, 1963), 117–118; Henry Berry, *Make the Kaiser Dance* (New York: Doubleday, 1978), 133–135, 263n; H. W. Brands, *TR: The Last Romantic* (New York: Basic Books, 1997), 752–753, 812–815.

13. John W. Chambers, *To Raise an Army* (New York: Free Press, 1987), 134–140.
14. Provost Marshal General, *Second Report of the Provost Marshal General to the Secretary of the Army on the Operations of the Selective Service System to December 20, 1918* (Washington, DC: Government Printing Office, 1919), 6, 222–226.
15. Paul Landis, 76th FA, 3rd Div; Edgar Hastings, Field Hospital 326, 82nd Div; George Williams, Quartermaster Corps, all in MHIWWIS.
16. F. L. Miller, unpublished memoir, "The War to End All Wars," 2–3, Emory.
17. Donald Kyler, 16th IN, 1st Div; Francis W. Moore, 103rd IN, 26th Div, both in MHIWWIS.
18. Glendon L. Armstrong, 101st MGB, 26th Div; Arthur W. Hutchinson, 16th IN, 1st Div; Elmer Stovall; Harry House, 325th IN, 82nd Div, all in MHIWWIS.
19. Chambers, *Raise an Army*, 196–198; Alonzo LaVanture, 111 IN, 28th Div; Irving Jacobs, 1st Div; Ralph Williams, 2nd EN, 2nd Div, all in MHIWWIS.
20. *Stars and Stripes*, August 2, 1918, 1.
21. Warren Jackson, *His Time in Hell* (Novato: Presidio Press, 2001), 4; Anders Peter-son, 6th Marines, 2nd Div; Rollie Waggoner, 6th Marines, 2nd Div; Letter from Lloyd Short, 6th Marines to "Dear Father," dated April 21, 1918; Letter from Lloyd Short, to "Dear Aunt," dated May 15, 1918, all from MHIWWIS.
22. Letters from Richard Atkinson to his mother from March 1916 to January 12, 1918, author's collection; John E. Witlock, 16th IN, 1st Div, MHIWWIS.
23. Lionel Harmison, 23rd IN, 2nd Div; John Miholick, 23rd IN, 2nd Div; Gilbert E. Motz, 307th Tank Bn, all in MHIWWIS.
24. Horatio Rogers, *World War I through My Sights* (San Rafael: Presidio Press, 1976), 1–3.
25. M. O. Leuck, 314 Ammunition Train, 89th Div; Lloyd Kidwell, 341 FA, 89th Div; Elmer Virkler, 129th IN, 33nd Div, all in MHIWWIS; "Memorandum for the Chief of Staff from BG Joseph Kuhn, Chief of the War College Division, Sub-ject: Appointment of Provisional Second Lieutenants in the Regular Army, dated 23 April 1917," in NARA, RG 165, "Letters, Memorandum, Reports, etc. of the Citizens Training Camps, Officers' Training Camps, Central Officers' Training Schools, and Student Army Training Corps," NARA Microfilm File 9226, Roll 261.
26. Emerson G. Taylor, *New England in France 1917–1919: A History of the Twenty-Sixth Division* (Boston: Houghton Mifflin, 1920), 23; Colby L. McIntyre, *The Old Man of the 103rd: The Biography of Frank M. Hume* (Houlton, ME: Aroostock Print Shop, 1940), 66–67.
27. Duncan Kemerer, 111th IN, 28th Div, manuscript "My Memories as a Soldier in World War I," MHIWWIS.
28. S.M.C., "The Present Problem," *Infantry Journal* 6, no. 2 (September 1909): 250,

255; Charles R. Wilson, *Baptized in Blood: The Religion of the Lost Cause, 1865–1920* (Athens: University of Georgia Press, 1980), 171. The view that war was an antidote for the ills of society and a means of demonstrating manhood was not limited to the United States. This theme was also prevalent in prewar European society. See Joe Lunn, "Male Identity and Martial Codes of Honor: A Comparison of the War Memoirs of Robert Graves, Ernst Junger, and Kande Kamara," *Journal of Military History* 69, no. 3 (July 2005): 713–735.

29. Mervyn Burke, HQ Troop, 1st Div, MHIWWIS; Stouffer, et al., 131–135.

30. John Stringfellow, *Hell No!* (Boston: Meador, 1936), 55.

31. Letters from Ernest McKeighan, 110th EN, 35th Div, to his wife, dated August 31, 1917, and September 6, 1917, NWWIM.

32. Letter from Karl O'Brien to "Dear Father & Mother," dated June 2, 1918; Letter from George O'Brien, 121st FA, 32nd Div, to his mother, dated February 1, 1918, both in MHIWWIS.

33. Letter from George O'Brien to his mother, dated November 18, 1917, MHIWWIS; Letter from June B. Smith, 130th FA, 35th Div to his mother, dated April 23, 1917, from the family collection of Dave Hinkley, Lees Summit, MO. Copy in author's possession.

34. William E. Hocking, *Morale and Its Enemies* (New Haven: Yale University Press, 1918), 153; Letter from Al Fraas to his sister dated May 24, 1918, NWWIM.

35. Howard Supple, 137th IN, 35th Div; Seaven Rice, 1st EN, 1 Div, both in MHIWWIS; Letter from Pvt. Paul Rhodes, to Helen Naito, dated December 27, 1917, author's collection.

36. Frederick F. Seidel, Quartermaster Corps; Glenn L. Denton, 355th IN, 89 Div, Frank L. DeVane, 115th MGB, 30th Div, all in MHIWWIS.

37. Anonymous (Bob Casey), *The Cannoneers Have Hairy Ears* (New York: J. H. Sears, 1927), x; William L. Langer, *Gas and Flame in World War I* (New York: Knopf, 1965), xviii–xix; "Report of the Second Conference on Control of Morale," in NARA, RG 165, Records of the Army War College Historical Section, Records of the Morale Branch, Box 131, NM-84, Entry 310, File 7–36.

38. Fred Sasse, *Rookie Days of a Soldier* (St. Paul: W. G. Greene, 1924), 77.

39. *Literary Digest* 49, no. 11 (September 12, 1914): 441–445, 449–460, and 464; "American Sympathies in the War," *Literary Digest* 49, no. 20 (November 14, 1914): 939–941 and 974–978.

40. Clarence L. Mahan, manuscript, "Hoosier Doughboy with the First Division," MHIWWIS.

41. Letter from Charles Clement to "Dear Mother," dated April 21, 1918. The letter is in the private collection of Ben Byrnes. Copy in the author's collection; Frank Merrill, 6th Marines, 2 Div; Philip Foster, 356th IN, 89 Div, both in MHIWWIS.

42. Letter from Milton Sweningsen, 138th IN, 35th Div, to his mother, dated July 4, 1918; William Roper, 130th MGB, 35 Div; Edgar Hastings, 307th Sanitary Train, 82nd Div, all in MHIWWIS.

43. Quoted in Hocking, *Morale and Its Enemies*, 34; "Report of the Second Conference on Control of Morale," NARA, RG 165, Entry 310, Box 131, File 7–36.

44. Samuel Black, "Non-Military Activities at Camp Gordon," dated September 13, 1918, NARA, RG 165, Entry 377, Box 5; Reports of Camp Devens intelligence officer, dated March 11, 1918, and August 26, 1918, NARA, RG 165, Entry 377, Box 3; Report from Acting 91st Div Intelligence Officer to Chief Military Intelligence Branch, dated March 4, 1918, NARA, RG 165, Entry 377, Box 9.

45. Report of Camp Grant Morale Office entitled "A Study in Morale," receipt date January 30, 1919, NARA, RG 165 Entry 377, Box 6.

46. Stringfellow, *Hell No*, 199; *Second Report of the Provost Marshal*, 2, 31, 223–228.

47. *Second Report of the Provost Marshal*, 6.

48. Ayres, *War with Germany*, 17; *Second Report of the Provost Marshal*, 147–149.

49. *Second Report of the Provost Marshal*, 2, 75–81, 226–228.

50. Ibid., 51, 113–114.

51. *Second Report of the Provost Marshal*, 108–122; Arthur Barbeau and Florette Henri, *The Unknown Soldiers* (Philadelphia: Temple University Press, 1974), 35–36; José Ramíez, *To The Line of Fire* (College Station: Texas A&M University Press, 2009), 24–27; David M. Kennedy, *Over Here* (New York: Oxford University Press, 1980), 156–163; Chambers, *Raise an Army*, 224–228.

52. Chambers, *Raise an Army*, 211–213; *Second Report of the Provost Marshal*, 199–207.

53. Dell Wilson, 4th IN, 3rd Div, MHIWWIS; Letter from Lillian McCarley to May Peters, dated November 22, 1917, author's collection.

54. Letters from Private Lunie McCarley, 110th IN, 28th Div, to May Peters (sister) September 1917–February 1919, author's collection.

55. Letter from Benson Oakley to Helen Chadwick, postdated August 9, 1917, author's collection; Paul Maxwell, Camp Lee, 314th FA, 79th Div, memoir "The Diary of a Dud," MHIWWIS; Letter from C. P. Stowers to "Friend Harry," dated July 24, 1917, author's collection.

56. Memorandum to 83rd Div G2 from "J.E.P." dated September 7, 1918, NARA, RG 120, Entry 195, (one box).

57. Report of Acting 83rd Division Intelligence Officer, dated March 25, 1918, NARA, RG 165, Entry 377, Box 14.

58. *Second Report of the Provost Marshal*, 158; Sgt. Richard McBride, 325th IN, 82nd Div, unpublished manuscript, MHIWWIS; Report of Intelligence Officer, Camp Jackson, dated September 23, 1918, NARA, RG 165, Entry 377, Box 7; Letter from James M. Miller to "Mama and Rest," dated August 6, 1917, author's collection.

59. Report of Intelligence Officer, 86th Div, dated March 11, 1918, NARA, RG 165, Entry 377, Box 6; Report of Camp Devens intelligence officer, dated September 17, 1918, NARA, RG 165, Entry 377, Box 3.

60. Memorandums to 83rd Div G2 from "J.E.P.," dated September 12, 1918, and October 15, 1918, NARA, RG 120, Entry 195, (one box).

61. Reports of Camp Gordon intelligence officer, dated July 22, 1918, NARA, RG 165, Entry 377, Box 5.

62. *Verick's the American Weekly* 6, no. 24 (July 18, 1918): 395–397.

63. File of Capt. Felix R. Campuzano, NARA, RG 120, Entry 541, Box 2300; Memorandum from Assistant Chief of Staff, G2, AEF GHQ to Commanding Officer, Mechanical Repair Shop 302, subject: First Lieutenant Samuel G. Scherk, dated May 9, 1918, in NARA, RG 120, Entry 186, Box 6218.

64. *Verick's American Weekly* 6, no. 24 (July 18, 1918): 395–397.

65. Memorandum to 83rd Div G2 from "C.V.L." dated October 31, 1918, NARA, RG 120, Entry 195, (one box); *Second Report of the Provost Marshal*, 86.

66. Knud Olsen, 325th IN, 82nd Div, MHIWWIS.

67. George Lokides, 326th IN, 82nd Div; Elmer Jacobson, 326th IN, 82nd Div, both in MHIWWIS; *Second Report of the Provost Marshal*, 101–107; Report of Camp Dodge intelligence officer, dated August 2, NARA, RG 165, Entry 377, Box 4; Letter from Reginald Thomson, to Lillian Cottrell, from Camp Sherman, OH, dated June 20, 1918, NWWIM.

68. Quoted in Chad L. Williams, *Torchbearers of Democracy* (Chapel Hill: University of North Carolina Press, 2010), 43; Edward Jackson, 372nd IN, 93rd Div, MHIWWIS; José de la Luz Sáenz, *The World War I Diary of José de la Luz Sáenz*, ed. and trans. Emilo Zamora (College Station: Texas A&M Press, 2014), 60, 82.

69. *Second Report of the Provost Marshal*, 57–62.

70. Ibid.

71. Report of Camp Gordon intelligence officer, dated June 17, 1918, NARA, RG 165, Entry 377, Box 5; Reports of Camp Devens intelligence officer, dated August 27, 1918, and September 6, 1918, NARA, RG 165, Entry 377, Box 3.

72. Report of Camp Custer intelligence officer, dated May 18, 1918, NARA, RG 165, Entry 377, Box 1; Reports of Camp Gordon intelligence officer, dated September 30, 1918, and October 7, 1918, NARA, RG 165, Entry 377, Box 5; Chambers, *Raise an Army*, 216.

73. Quoted in Chambers, *Raise an Army*, 216; Byron Farwell, *Over There* (New York: Norton, 1999), 53.

74. Irving Crump, *Conscript 2989: Experiences of a Drafted Man* (New York: Dodd, Meade, 1918), 71; Report of Camp Custer intelligence officer, dated May 18, 1918, NARA, RG 165, Entry 377, Box 1; "Proposed questionnaire for discharged men" by Schuyer Garth, undated, NARA, RG 165, Entry 377, Box 5; Report of Asst. Intelligence Officer, 91st Div, dated May 1, 1918, NARA, RG 165, Entry 377, Box 9; Meirion and Susie Harries, *The Last Days of Innocence* (New York: Random House, 1997), 133.

75. Letter from George O'Brien, 121st FA, 32nd Div, to his mother, dated February 1, 1918, MHIWWIS.

CHAPTER 3. "OH! HOW I HATE TO GET UP IN THE MORNING"

1. Irving Crump, *Conscript 2989: Experiences of a Drafted Man* (New York: Dodd, Meade, 1918), 12.

2. Paul Maxwell, Camp Lee, 314th FA, 79th Div, memoir "The Diary of a Dud," MHIWWIS; Crump, *Conscript*, 6.

3. U.S. Army Medical Department, *The Medical Department of the United States Army in the World War*, vol. 15, pt. 1, *Anthropology* (Washington, DC: Government Printing Office, 1921), 64–65.

4. Ibid., 46, 296–298.

5. Ibid., 34–36, 46, 299.

6. United States Department of Commerce, *Statistical Abstract of the United States for 1916* (Washington, DC: Government Printing Office, 1917), 51; David M. Kennedy, *Over Here: The First World War and American Society* (New York: Oxford University Press, 1980), 24, 157; John W. Chambers, *To Raise an Army* (New York: Free Press, 1987), 89–89; Maj. Granville Fortesque, "Training the New Armies of Liberty," *National Geographic* 32, nos. 5 and 6 (November-December 1917): 433–434.

7. NARA, RG 120, Records of the AEF, G5 Schools—Army Candidate Schools, Box 1634, File 319.1, "Vocational Qualifications of Men."

8. Fred Sasse, *Rookie Days of a Soldier* (St. Paul: W. G. Greene, 1924), 11; Maxwell, "Diary."

9. Provost Marshal General, *Second Report of the Provost Marshal General to the Secretary of the Army on the Operations of the Selective Service System to December 20, 1918* (Washington, DC: Government Printing Office, 1919), 238.

10. Letter from Floyd Sosey, 160th IN, to Mrs. J. C. Sosey (mother), dated June 20, 1918, author's collection; Letter from Walter Shaw to his mother, dated June 9, 1917, NWWIM.

11. Crump, *Conscript*, 2.

12. Sasse, *Rookie*, 16; Crump, *Conscript*, 6–7.

13. Letter from Henry Schulz, 309th IN, to Edward Schulz (brother), dated November 22, 1917, author's collection.

14. "Training the New Armies of Liberty," *National Geographic Magazine* 32, nos. 5 and 6 (November-December 1917): 435; William E. Hocking, *Morale and Its Enemies* (New Haven: Yale University Press, 1918), 105; John W. Castles, unprinted manuscript "War Diary of John W. Castles," entry for June 18, 1917, Castles Papers, USMA.

15. Maxwell, "Diary," 7–12; Lyman Varney, 3rd Bn Machine Gun Training Center, Camp Hancock, MHIWWIS; Letter from Dewitt McIntyre to Mrs. G. W. McIntyre, dated June 16, 1917; Letter from Pvt. Cornelius Freely, to Mae Murphy, dated June 15, 1918. Both from author's collection.

16. *Second Report of the Provost Marshal*, 152–154; William J. Robinson, *Forging the Sword: The Camp Devens Story* (Concord, NH: Rumford Press, 1920), 27; Intelligence Officer, Camp Gordon, "Weekly Report, General Information, Week Ending July 22, 1918," NARA, RG 165, Entry 377, Correspondence Relating to Morale at Army Installations 1917–1920, Box 5.

17. Sasse, *Rookie*, 21; Letter from Walter Shaw to his mother, dated April 17, 1917, NWWIM.

18. Letter from Dewitt McIntyre to Mrs. G. W. McIntyre, dated June 16, 1917, author's collection; Lyman Varney; Maxwell, "Diary"; Horatio Rogers, *World War I through My Sights* (San Rafael: Presidio Press, 1976), 114.

19. U.S. Army Medical Department, *The Medical Department of the United States Army in the World War*, vol. 7, *Training* (Washington, DC: Government Printing Office, 1927), 418; Letter from James M. Miller, A Co., 10th EN to "Mama and Rest," undated circa July 1917, author's collection; Sasse, *Rookie*, 35.

20. Robert M. Yerkes, "Psychological Examining in the United States Army," in *Memoirs of the National Academy of Sciences*, vol. 15 (Washington, DC: Government Printing Office, 1921), 7–12.

21. Clarence Yoakum and Robert Yerkes, *Army Mental Tests* (New York: Henry Holt, 1920), 17.

22. Yoakum and Yerkes, *Mental Tests*, 12; Robert M. Yerkes, "Psychological Examining in the United States Army," in *Memoirs of the National Academy of Sciences*, vol. 15 (Washington, DC: Government Printing Office, 1921), 488–493, 678–680, 696–699, 743–744.

23. Yerkes, "Psychological Examining," 531–532, 703–708, 732–744, 764–766, 785–790; Arthur Barbeau and Florette Henri, *The Unknown Soldiers: Black American Troops in World War I* (Philadelphia: Temple University Press, 1974), 46–48.

24. Yoakum and Yerkes, *Mental Tests*, 17; Yerkes, "Psychological Examining," 505–522, 779.

25. Yoakum and Yerkes, *Mental Tests*, 207–211, 218–219; Yerkes, "Psychological Examining," 79; Edward Coffman, *The War to End All Wars* (Madison: University of Wisconsin Press, 1986), 59–61.

26. Sasse, *Rookie*, 49–50; Edgemont W. Ruschke, ed., *Lieuie VI: Being the Chronicle of the Battle of Camp Lee as Fought by the Deathless Sixth Battalion, Central Officers' Training School, Camp Lee, Virginia* (Petersburg: Privately published, 1919), 53; Machine Gun Officers' Training School, *Four Months of Sand* (Augusta, GA: Phoenix Printing, 1918), 37.

27. The National Army Camps were Devens, MA; Upton, NY; Dix, NJ; Meade, MD; Lee, VA; Jackson, SC; Gordon, GA; Sherman, OH; Taylor, KY; Custer, MI; Grant, IL; Pike, AK; Dodge, IA; Funston, KS; Travis, TX; and Lewis, WA. National Guard Camps were Greene, NC; Wadsworth, SC; Sevier, SC; Hancock, GA; Wheeler, GA; McClellan, AL; Sheridan, AL; Shelby, MS; Beauregard, LA; Logan, TX; MacArthur, TX; Bowie, TX; Doniphan, OK; Cody, NM; Kearney, CA; and Fremont, CA.

28. Fortesque, "Training," 427–428.

29. Sasse, *Rookie*, 205–209; Fortesque, "Training," 427–428.

30. Sasse, *Rookie*, 205–209.

31. Letters from Dewitt McIntyre to Mrs. G. W. McIntyre, dated August 25 and

September 10, 1917 (author's collection); H. A. Honaker, AEF North Russia and 142 MGB, MHIWWIS.

32. Crump, *Conscript*, 15–16; Walter J. Aamoth, Officers' Training Schools, Camp Pike, MHIWWIS; Charles Camp, *History of the 305th Field Artillery* (Garden City, NY: Country Life Press, 1919), 21–22.

33. Letter from William McCrea to Lieutenant Edgar O'Neal, dated June 17, 1918; Letter from Bernard Bockemuehl to Miss E. A. Bockemuehl, dated March 27 and April 4, 1918; Letter from Pete Scheck to "Dear Sister," dated July 7, 1918; Letter from Floyd Sosey, to Mrs. J. C. Sosey (mother), dated November 3 and December 11, 1917, all from author's collection.

34. Letter from June B. Smith to his mother, dated September 10, 1917, from the family collection of Dave Hinkley, Lees Summit, MO, copy in author's possession. Letters from Frank Fraas to his mother, dated October 7 and 26, 1917, NWWIM.

35. Letter from Floyd Sosey, 160th IN, to Mrs. J. C. Sosey (mother), dated November 3, 1917, and December 3, 1917, author's collection.

36. Letter from Floyd Sosey, to Mrs. J. C. Sosey (mother), dated November 3, 1917, and December 3, 1917; Letter from Mike Dowling to "Dear Folks," dated January 13, 1918, both from author's collection.

37. Maj. Charles R. Tips, "Selecting and Training Military Leaders," *Infantry Journal* 15, no. 7 (January 1919): 541.

38. James A. Moss, *Officer's Manual* (Menasha: George Banta, 1917), 185.

39. Warren Jackson, *His Time in Hell* (Novato: Presidio Press, 2001), 8–9.

40. Jackson, *Time in Hell*, 11; Letter from June B. Smith to his mother, dated November 27, 1917.

41. Letter from Henry Schulz, 309th IN, to Edward Schulz (brother), dated October 9, 1917; Letter from Lewis Dengler to his brother, Robert, dated May 22, 1918; Letter from Mike Scheck, to "Dear Sister," August 30, 1918, all from author's collection.

42. Letter from June B. Smith to his mother, dated January 3, 1918; Letter to Andrew Magnus from "Bunny" Brown (female friend), dated November 21, 1918; Letter from Mike Scheck to "Dear Sister," August 30, 1918, both from author's collection.

43. James A. Moss, *What Sammy's Doing* (Menasha: George Banta, 1917), 141.

44. Letters from Ira Wilkenson to "Dear Lillie," dated October 13, 1917, UGA; Letter from Mike Scheck to "Dear Sister," August 1918, author's collection; Letter from Paul F. Andrews, Co G, 308th IN, 77th Div to his aunt, dated March 13, 1918, NWWIM.

45. Letter from Fay Neff to Adam Keichler (brother-in-law), dated May 12, 1918; Letter from Joe Scheck to "Dear Bert," dated June 15, 1918; Letter from Dewitt McIntyre to Mrs. G. W. McIntyre, dated September 10, 1917; Letter to Andrew Magnus from "Bunny" Brown, dated October 15, 1918, all from author's collection.

46. Letter from George Hetrich to Robert Dengler, postdated July 10, 1918; Letter from Mike Scheck to "Dear Sister," August 1918, both in author's collection.

47. Letter from Cornelius Freely to Mae Murphy, dated June 14, 1918, author's collection; Letter from George O'Brien, 121st FA, 32nd Div, to his mother, dated November 25, 1917, MHIWWIS.

48. Letter from James M. Miller to "Mama and Rest," July 29, 1917, author's collection; Letter from June Smith to his mother, dated October 27, 1917.

49. Sasse, *Rookie*, 127–129.

50. Letter from June B. Smith to his mother, dated November 12, 1917; Letter from Lloyd Short, 6th Marines to "Dear Father," dated April 21, 1918, MHIWWIS.

51. T. P. Smith, "Confidential Report on the Zone at Camp Funston," NARA, RG 165 Records of the General Staff, Entry 377, Box 5, Camp Funston file.

52. Letter home from Raymond Stanbeck, 6th Marines, 2nd Div, dated December 3, 1917, MHIWWIS; Letter from James M. Miller to "Mama and Rest," dated August 6, 1917, author's collection.

53. Letter from Billy Brennan to William Berry, dated April 21, 1918; Letters from Dewitt McIntyre to Mrs. G. W. McIntyre (mother), dated September 11 and November 11, 1917, all from author's collection.

54. Letter from Floyd Sosey to Mrs. J. C. Sosey (mother), dated November 3, 1917, author's collection; Sasse, *Rookie*, 127–129.

55. Sasse, *Rookie*, 215–216.

56. Harvey L. Harris, *The War as I Saw It* (St. Paul: Pogo Press, 1998), 91; U.S. Department of Labor, *Department of Labor Report 991: 100 Years of U.S. Consumer Spending* (Washington, DC: Government Printing Office, 2006), 9–13.

57. U.S. Department of Labor, *100 Years of U.S. Consumer Spending*, 10.

58. Undated pamphlet, *Our Boys in Khaki* (n.d: n.p. [circa 1918]), 21; Chicago Daily News, *The Chicago Daily News War Book for American Soldiers, Sailors and Marines* (Chicago: Chicago Daily News Company, 1918), 133; Grand Magasins aux Galeries Lafayette, *Paris for Englishmen and for Americans* (Paris: Ehrmann Publicité, n.d. [circa 1918]), 13–14.

59. Sasse, *Rookie*, 165–166.

60. War Department, *Annual Report of the Secretary of War, 1919*, vol. 1 (Washington, DC: Government Printing Office, 1920), 536; Letters home from Raymond Stanbeck, 6th Marines, 2nd Div, dated October 24 and December 3, 1917, MHIWWIS.

61. U.S. Department of War, *Special Regulations No. 72: Allotments, Family Allowances, Compensation, and Insurance* (Washington, DC: Government Printing Office, 1918), 26–28.

62. Letter from Henry Schulz to Emily Schulz (sister), dated January 10, 1918; Letter from Paul Rhodes to Helen Naito, dated June 6, 1918, both from author's collection; Letters home from Raymond Stanbeck, 6th Marines, 2nd Div, dated October 24 and December 3, 1917, MHIWWIS.

63. Letter from George O'Brien to his mother, dated January 20, 1917 (most likely 1918), MHIWWIS; Letter from Wallace Mansfield, 56th Inf, 7th Div, to Mrs. F. M.

Mansfield (mother), dated March 11, 1918; Letter from Bernard Bockemuehl to Mrs M. Bockemuehl, dated June 26, 1918, both from author's collection.

64. George Browne, *An American Soldier in World War I*, ed. David L. Snead (Lincoln: University of Nebraska Press, 2006), 31; Letter from Eugene Laudon, 2nd IN to his mother, dated November 4, 1918; Letter from Ed Guiss to Mrs Fanny Dohrman (sister), dated July 4, 1918, both from author's collection.

CHAPTER 4. LEARNING "THE SAVAGE GAME"

1. Letter from Ed Guiss to Mrs. Fanny Dohrman (sister), dated September 16, 1918, author's collection; John W. Nell, *The Lost Battalion: A Private's Story* (San Antonio: Historical Publishing Network, 2001), 5.

2. Congressional Committee on Military Affairs, *To Increase the Efficiency of the Military Establishment of the United States*, 64th Cong., 1st Sess., January 27, 1916, 264; Granville Fortesque, "Training the New Armies of Liberty," *National Geographic* 32, nos. 5–6 (November–December 1917): 433.

3. War Department, *Infantry Training* (Washington, DC: Government Printing Office, 1917), 5–12, 20–29.

4. Ibid., 20–23.

5. Letter from Pvt. Oscar Strange to Sarah Book, dated November 19, 1917, author's collection; Irving Berlin, "Oh! How I Hate to Get Up in the Morning," 1918.

6. "Replies to Officers' Questionnaires" from Morale Branch of the War College and War Plans Division to the Chief of Staff, dated November 5, 1919, NARA, RG 165, Entry 378, Box 6 (hereafter cited as Morale Branch Officers' Survey), 77. I would like to thank James "Ty" Seidule for providing me a copy of this report.

7. War Department, *Manual of Physical Training* (Washington, DC: Government Printing Office, 1914).

8. George Browne, *An American Soldier in World War I*, ed. David L. Snead (Lincoln: University of Nebraska Press, 2006), 30; Intelligence Officer, Camp Jackson, SC, "Weekly Information Report," dated October 21, 1918, NARA, RG 165, Entry 377, Box 7.

9. Browne, *American Soldier*, 30; Fred Sasse, *Rookie Days of a Soldier* (St. Paul: W. G. Greene, 1924), 122–123; Irving Crump, *Conscript 2989: Experiences of a Drafted Man* (New York: Dodd, Meade, 1918), 59–60.

10. War Department, *Manual for Noncommissioned Officers and Privates of Infantry* (Washington, DC: Government Printing Office, 1917), 181–182; Sasse, *Rookie*, 92–94.

11. AEF GHQ, "Program of Training for the 1st Division, A.E.F.," October 6, 1917, in *World War Records, First Division*, vol. 20, *Training First Division* (Washington, DC: Army War College, 1930), n.p.

12. Sasse, *Rookie*, 71; War Department, *Small Arms Firing Manual, 1913, Corrected to April, 13, 1917* (Washington, DC: Government Printing Office, 1917), 78–80, 185–186.

13. 328th Infantry Historical Committee, *History of the Three Hundred and Twenty-Eighth Infantry Regiment* (N.p., 1922), 7–8; Benedict Crowell, *American Munitions, 1917–1918* (Washington, DC: Government Printing Office, 1919), 184; Lonnie J. White, *Panthers to Arrowheads: The 36th Division in World War I* (Austin, TX: Presidial Press, 1984), 55–56; Christian A. Bach and Henry N. Hall, *The Fourth Division: Its Services and Achievements in the World War* (New York: Country Life Press, 1920), 21, 27.

14. Leslie J. Martin, 16th IN, 1st Div, manuscript "The Story of My Life," MHIWWIS; Letter from Lewis Dengler to his brother, Robert, dated May 22, 1918, author's collection.

15. *Three Hundred and Twenty-Eighth Infantry Regiment*, 7–8; Crump, *Conscript*, 87–90; *Manual of Physical Training*, 133–171.

16. Letter from Pvt. Oscar Strange, 130th Infantry to Sarah Book, dated November 19, 1917, author's collection; Letter home from Raymond Stanbeck, 6th Marines, 2nd Div, dated December 22, 1917, MHIWWIS.

17. Warren Jackson, *His Time in Hell* (Novato: Presidio Press, 2001), 11; Letter from Henry Schulz to Edward Schulz (brother), dated December 2, 1917, author's collection; Letter from Lloyd Short, 6th Marines to "Dear Sis," dated May 12, 1918; Letter home from Raymond Stanbeck, dated December 28, 1917, both in MHIWWIS.

18. "Summary of the Reports of the French Advisory Mission," dated February 16, 1918, in NARA, RG 165, Entry 310, Box 208; Crowell, *Munitions*, 61.

19. Lonnie J. White, *The 90th Division in World War I* (Manhattan, KS: Sunflower University Press, 1996), 40; White, *Panthers to Arrowheads*, 55–56; *The Battery Book: A History of Battery "A," 306th F.A.* (New York: DeVinne Press, 1921), 21.

20. G. Edward Buxton, Jr., ed., *Official History of the 82nd Division American Expeditionary Forces* (Indianapolis: Bobbs-Merrill, 1919), 4; White, *Panthers to Arrowheads*, 55–56; "Summary of the Reports of the French Advisory Mission," dated February 16, 1918.

21. George Marshall, *The Papers of George Catlett Marshall*, vol. 1, *The Soldierly Spirit: December 1880–June 1939*, ed. Larry I. Bland and Sharon Ritenour (Baltimore: Johns Hopkins University Press, 1981), 102; Charles Dienst et al., *They're From Kansas: History of the 353rd Infantry Regiment, 89th Division, National Army* (Wichita: Eagle Press, 1921), 3–4; Letter from Harry Callison to "Dear Folks," dated October 20, 1917, author's collection; George English, Jr., *History of the 89th Division, U.S.A.* (Denver: Smith-Brooks, 1920), 21; *The Battery Book*, 18.

22. Edward Coffman, *The War to End All Wars* (Madison: University of Wisconsin Press, 1968), 57; W. A. Sirmon, *That's War* (Atlanta: Linmon, 1929), 29; Report of Acting Intelligence Officer, 83rd Div, dated April 1, 1918, NARA, RG 165, Entry 377, Box 14; Richard Faulkner, *School of Hard Knocks* (College Station: Texas A&M Press, 2012), 126–129.

23. Lucian Truscott, Jr., *The Twilight of the Cavalry: Life in the Old Army, 1917–1941*

(Lawrence: University Press of Kansas, 1989), 19; Robert S. Sutliffe, *Seventy-First New York in the World War* (New York: Seventy-First Regiment Association, 1922), 41; James W. Rainey, "Ambivalent Warfare: The Tactical Doctrine of the AEF in World War I," *Parameters* 13, no. 3 (September 1983): 34–46; Timothy K. Nenninger, "Tactical Dysfunction in the AEF, 1917–1918," *Military Affairs* 51, no. 4 (October 1987): 177–181.

24. Sutliffe, *Seventy-First New York*, 47; Richard McBride, 325th IN, 82nd Div, manuscript; Letter written by Milton E. Bernet, 89th Div, to "Sue," dated July 26, 1917, both in MHIWWIS; Chester Baker, *Doughboy's Diary* (Shippensburg: Burd Street Press, 1998), 11.

25. Alan D. Graff, *Blood in the Argonne* (Norman: University of Oklahoma Press, 2005), 41; Browne, *American Soldier*, 28–29; Frank Graves, 28th IN, 1st Div, MHIWWIS.

26. Crowell, *Munitions*, 412–428; Archibald Hart, *Company K of Yesterday* (New York: Vantage Press, 1969), 37; Duncan Kemerer, 111th IN, 28th Div, manuscript "My Memories as a Soldier in World War I," MHIWWIS.

27. Charles Heller, "Chemical Warfare in World War I: The American Experience, 1917–1918," *Leavenworth Papers No. 10* (Leavenworth: Combat Studies Institute, Sept 1984), 38–44; "General Information Report, Week Ending September 16th, 1918," Intelligence Officer, Camp Gordon, NARA, RG 165, Entry 377, Box 5; William Robinson, *Forging the Sword: The Story of Camp Devens* (Concord, NH: Rumford Press, 1920), 68–69.

28. Letter from P. Benson Oakley to Helen Oakley postmarked March 26, 1918, author's collection; Carol R. Byerly, *The Fever of War: The Influenza Epidemic in the U.S. Army during World War I* (New York: New York University Press, 2005), 8–9.

29. Report from the Acting Intelligence Officer, 83rd Division to Chief, Military Intelligence Section, Subject: "General Information," dated February 28, 1918, NARA, RG 165 Records of the General Staff, Entry 377, Correspondence Related to Morale at Army Installations, Box 14, Camp Sherman file; Bach, 23–24.

30. Intelligence Officer, Auxiliary Units, Camp Devens, "Weekly Report of General Information," dated July 23, 1918, NARA, RG 165, Entry 377, Box 3; War Department, *Annual Report for 1919*, vol. 1, pt.1 (Washington, DC: Government Printing Office, 1919), 652–653.

31. Fred Takes, 325th IN, 82nd Div, memoir, "World War I, Co A., 325th INF, 82nd Div"; Edmund Grossman, 139th IN, 35th Div; Harty Siegfried, 1st EN, 1st Div, all in MHIWWIS.

CHAPTER 5. OF "CANNED WILLIE," "SLUM," AND HARD BREAD

1. David M. Kennedy, *Over Here* (New York: Oxford University Press, 1980), 117–123.

2. John C. Fisher and Carol Fisher, *Food in the American Military: A History* (Jefferson: McFarland, 2011), 119–120.

3. James A. Moss, *What Sammy's Doing* (Menasha: George Banta, 1917), 35–36.

4. Clarence L. Mahan, manuscript, "Hoosier Doughboy with the First Division"; Letters from Pvt. Milton Sweningsen, 138th IN, 35th Div, to his mother, dated August 2 and November 3, 1918, both in MHIWWIS.

5. War Department, *Manual for Army Cooks* (Washington, DC: Government Printing Office, 1916), 40; Grenville Fortesque, "Training the New Armies of Liberty," *National Geographic* 32, nos. 5 and 6 (November–December 1917), 428; Moss, *Sammy*, 36; Paul Maxwell, Camp Lee, 314th FA, 79th Div, memoir "The Diary of a Dud"; Frank Faulkner, 23rd IN, 2nd Div, manuscript "Written from Cochem Germany while with the American Occupation 1/2/19," both in MHIWWIS.

6. Reports of Camp Gordon intelligence officer, dated July 8, 1918, NARA, RG 165, Entry 377, Box 5.

7. Letter from George O'Brien, 121st FA, 32nd Div, to his mother, dated October 28, 1917, MHIWWIS; Letter from Bernard Bockemuehl, to Mrs. M. Bockemuehl (mother), dated March 27, 1918, author's collection.

8. Fred Sasse, *Rookie Days of a Soldier* (St. Paul, MN: W. G. Green, 1924), 54–56; Richard McBride, 328th IN, 82nd Div, memoir, "Passing in Review: Memories of World War I," MHIWWIS.

9. Letter from Frank Fraas, 129th F, 35th Div, to his mother, dated November 30, 1917, Gold Star Mothers Paper, NWWIM; Sasse, *Rookie*, 182–183.

10. Elmer Straub, *A Sergeants Diary in the World War*, Indiana Historical Collections, vol. 10 (Indianapolis: Indiana Historical Commission, 1923), 21, 247–248; Letter from George McLaughlin, 13th Marine Regt, to Mrs. L. H. McLaughlin (mother), dated December 29, 1918; Letter from Howard Andrews, to Mrs. Frank Andrews (mother), dated December 27, 1918, both from author's collection.

11. Fisher and Fisher, *Food*, 124; *Stars and Stripes*, "Varieties of Slum," April 5, 1918, 4; Albert M. Ettinger, *A Doughboy in the Fighting 69th* (Shippensburg: White Mane, 1992), 28.

12. *Stars and Stripes*, March 1, 1918, 7; Herman Dacus, 28th IN, 1st Div, MHIWWIS.

13. McBride, "Passing in Review"; Fred Takes, 325th IN, 82nd Div, diary entries for May 15, May 27, June 1, June 16, June 17, June 21, and June 25, in manuscript entitled "World War I Co A, 325th Inf. 82nd Div" both in MHIWWIS; Mitchell A. Yockelson, *Borrowed Soldiers: Americans under British Command, 1918* (Norman: University of Oklahoma Press, 2008), 61; Maj. W. H. Wells, "Personal Experiences of a Machine Gun Platoon Commander, October 17th–20th 1918," DRL.

14. AEF General Orders 18, July 28, 1918; AEF General Orders 26, August 28, 1917; AEF General Orders 11, January 17, 1918; AEF General Orders 19, January 31, 1918; AEF General Orders 176, October 11, 1918.

15. Letter from Francis J. Byrne to "Little Sweetheart," dated June 19, 1919, author's collection.

16. Ettinger, *Fighting 69th*, 28.

17. Leslie Langille, *Men of the Rainbow* (Hamond, IN: W. B. Coakley, 1933), 158;

Warren Jackson, *His Time in Hell* (Novato: Presidio Press, 2001), 46; Tom Carroll, 16th IN, 1st Div, manuscript, "Tom Carroll's Diary," MHIWWIS.

18. Thomas H. Barber, *Along the Road* (New York: Dodd, Mead, 1924), 71–72, 83; "Notes Made by the Inspector General A.E.F. during the Active Operations from 12 September 1918 to 11 November 1918," NARA, RG 120, Entry 588, Box 116; Major Merritt Olmstead, "A Critical Analysis of Troop Leading within the 5th Division during the Second Phase of the Meuse-Argonne Offensive," CARL.

19. Wilbert Stambaugh, 1st Div; Thurmond Baccus, 307th Field Signal Bn, manuscript, both in MHIWWIS.

20. U.S. Army Center of Military History, *The United States Army in the World War*, vol. 15, *Report of the Commander, SOS* (Washington, DC: Government Printing Office, 1988), 95; Sanitary Reports for Sept 1918 for 77th Div and November 1918 for 92nd Div, NARA, RG 120, Entry 2113, Box 5209; Memorandum from Lt. Col. Henry Beeuwkes to 1st Army Forward Office, Inspector General, dated October 10, 1918, NARA, RG 120, Entry 590, Box 1; Mahan, "Hoosier Doughboy," MHIWWIS.

21. Jackson, *Time in Hell*, 65; Charles Minder, *This Man's War* (New York: Pevensey Press, 1931), 329.

22. Franz A. Koehler, "Special Rations for the Armed Forces, 1946–53," QMC Historical Studies, series 2, no. 6 (Washington, DC: Historical Branch, Office of the Quartermaster General, 1958), 12–16.

23. Ibid.

24. *Stars and Stripes*, June 28, 1918, 18, 2; Letter from Fay Neff, 310th IN, to Miss A. W. Keichler (sister), dated December 5, 1918, author's collection.

25. Benedict Crowell, *America's Munitions, 1917–1918* (Washington, DC: Government Printing Office, 1919), 437.

26. Jackson, *Time in Hell*, 9; Letter from James Miller, to Mrs. James Miller (mother), dated February 5, 1918, author's collection; Wilbert Stambaugh, 1st Div, MHIWWIS.

27. Crowell, *Munitions*, 444; Koehler, "Special Rations," 12–16; I would like to thank Charles Pautler for allowing me to examine an original unopened emergency ration from his collection.

28. Monthly sanitary reports from HQ Base section 5, Cherbourg, dated October 1918 and Evacuation Hospital 14, dated September 1918, NARA, RG 120, Entry 2113, boxes 5205 and 5207; S. A. Honaker, AEF North Russia and 142nd MGB, manuscript "Memoirs of the World War"; Duncan Kemerer, 111th IN, 28th Div, manuscript "My Memories as a Soldier in World War I," both in MHIWWIS.

29. *Historical Report of the Chief Engineer*, AEF (Washington, DC: Government Printing Office, 1919), 60–63; Monthly sanitary report from the 82nd Division, dated October 1918, NARA, RG 120, Entry 2113, Box 5207; Captain Ben Chastaine,

Story of the 36th (Oklahoma City: Harlow, 1920), 134; Wardlaw Miles, *History of the 308th Infantry* (New York: G. P. Putnam's Sons, 1927), 132.

30. Jackson, *Time in Hell*, 97; Carl E. Haterius, *Reminiscences of the 137th Infantry* (Topeka: Carne, 1919), 153; Baccus, MHIWWIS; Memorandum from, Forward Office, Inspector General's Department, 1st Army to Inspector General AEF, Subject: "Combined Reports on 91st Division" dated October 16–19, 1918, NARA, RG 120, Entry 590, Box 1.

31. Henry Thorn, *History of the 313th Infantry* (New York: Wynkoop, Hallenbeck Crawford, 1920), 33, 35; John McDaniels, 126th IN, 32nd Div, "A Tanglefoot's Diary" Entries for October 11–16, 1918, MHIWWIS; Horace Baker, *Argonne Days* (Columbia: University of Missouri Press, 2007), 79.

32. "Replies to Officers' Questionnaires" from Morale Branch of the War College and War Plans Division to the Chief of Staff, dated November 5, 1919, in NARA, RG 165, NM 84, Entry 378, Box 6 (hereafter cited as Morale Branch Officers' Survey); Minder, *This Man's War*, 289–290; Sanitary Report, 26th Division for September 18–30, 1918, and Sanitary Report from Clermont-en-Argonne, for October 1918, dated November 10, 1918, NARA, RG 120, Entry 2113, Box 5207.

33. Carroll, "Diary," MHIWWIS; John W. Castles, "War Diary of John W. Castles," 54–55, USMA.

34. Jackson, *Time in Hell*, 113; Horatio Rogers, *World War I through My Sights* (San Rafael: Presidio Press, 1976), 211; *Stars and Stripes*, September 27, 1918, 3.

35. Donald Kyler, 16th IN, 1st Div, MHIWWIS; Henry Bandholtz, *History of the Provost Marshal General's Department, American Expeditionary Forces* (Chaumont, France: AEF Provost Marshal, 1919), 2.

36. Baker, *Argonne Days*, 39; Barber, *Along the Road*, 71–72, 83.

37. Reports of 82nd Division Inspector General from October 6 to 18, 1918, in NARA, RG 120, Entry 590, Box 1; Takes, MHIWWIS.

38. Diary of Gilbert Max, 307th IN, 77th Div, entry for October 27 and November 8, 1918, NWWIM; Sanitary Report for November 1918, 1st Div, NARA, RG 120, Entry 2113, Box 5209; "Notes Made by the Inspector General, AEF during the Active Operations from 12 September 1918 to 11 November 1918," in NARA, RG 120, Entry 588, Box 116.

39. Morale Branch Officers' Survey; Sanitary Report for November 1918. Army School Area, Langres, NARA, RG 120, Entry 2113, Box 5209; U.S. Army Center of Military History, *The United States Army in the World War*, vol. 15, *Report of the Commander, SOS* (Washington, DC: Government Printing Office, 1988), 95.

40. Takes, diary entry for June 25, MHIWWIS; Ettinger, *Fighting 69th*, 24, 28; Letter from Lt. Dewitt McIntyre to Mrs G. W. McIntyre (mother), undated, author's collection.

41. Letter from Wallace Mansfield to Mrs. F.M. Mansfield (mother), dated May 30, 1919, author's collection.

CHAPTER 6. OF "TIN HATS," "LITTLE TANKS," AND ENTRENCHING TOOLS

1. *General Information for Military Passengers Sailing on Commercial Lines,* undated, circa mid-1917, in William Haselton 18th IN and Div Staff, 1st Div, MHIWWIS.

2. Walter Wolf, 129th IN, 33rd Div, MHIWWIS; AEF GHQ General Orders 122, July 26, 1918.

3. *Stars and Stripes,* May 31, 1918, and June 7, 1918.

4. Seaven Rice, 1st EN, 1st Div; Elmer Stovall, 5th Cav, both in MHIWWIS; "Replies to Officers' Questionnaires" from Morale Branch of the War College and War Plans Division to the Chief of Staff, dated November 5, 1919, in NARA, RG 165, NM 84, Entry 378, Box 6.

5. Wilbert Stambaugh, 1st Div; Frank Merrill, 6th Marines, 2nd Div, both in MHIWWIS.

6. Letter from Henry Schulz, 309th IN, to Edward Schulz (brother), dated October 9, 1917, author's collection; Stovall, MHIWWIS.

7. Arthur Hanson, 6th Marines, 2nd Div, MHIWWIS.

8. Irving Crump, *Conscript 2989: Experiences of a Drafted Man* (New York: Dodd, Meade, 1918), 51–53; Fred Sasse, *Rookie Days of a Soldier* (St Paul, MN: W. G. Green, 1924), 39–40; Lyman Varney, 3rd Bn, Machine Gun Training Center, Camp Hancock, MHIWWIS.

9. *Stars and Stripes,* May 31, 1918; Sanitary Report, 90th Div, dated November 1918, NARA, RG 120, Entry 2113, Box 5208; "Notes Made by the Inspector General A.E.F. during the Active Operations from 12 September 1918 to 11 November 1918," NARA, RG 120, Entry 588, Box 116; Letter from Walter Shaw to his mother, dated January 6, 1918, NWWIM.

10. *Stars and Stripes,* September 6, 1918.

11. *Stars and Stripes,* September 13, 1918; AEF GHQ General Orders 7, January 9, 1918; John W. Castles, "War Diary of John W. Castles," 56, Castles Papers, USMA.

12. AEF GHQ General Orders 182, October 19, 1918; Martin Blumenson, *The Patton Papers,* vol. 1 (Boston: Houghton Mifflin, 1972), 399; War Department Circular No. 85, February 19, 1919, which stated, "The Sam Browne or Liberty Belt is not authorized in this country and will not be worn. This belt is the distinguishing mark of the commissioned officer abroad, but there is no necessity for its introduction into the United States."

13. Pete Scheck to "Dear Sister," undated, author's collection; Letter from George O'Brien, 121st FA, 32nd Div, to his mother, dated May 20, 1918, MHIWWIS; *Stars and Stripes,* August 2, 1918.

14. Ernest Sherwin, 326th IN, 82nd Div; Letter from Elmer Jones, 325th IN, 82nd Div, to "Dear Jen," dated October 12, 1918, both in MHIWWIS; Jonathan Lighter, "The Slang of the American Expeditionary Forces in Europe 1917–1919," *American Speech* 47, nos. 1–2 (Spring-Summer 1972).

15. Sasse, *Rookie,* 39–40; Letter from Henry Schulz, 309th IN, to August Schulz (father), dated October 10, 1917, author's collection; George H. English, Jr., *History*

of the 89th Division, U.S.A (Denver: Smith-Brooks, 1920), 27; Reports of the 91st Division Morale Officer, March 4, March 11, March 23, April 1, and May 18, 1918, NARA, RG 165, Entry 377, Box 9.

16. War Department, *The Medical Department of the United States Army in the World War,* vol. 15, pt. 1, *Anthropology* (Washington, DC: Government Printing Office, 1921), 273; Sasse, *Rookie,* 39–40; Letter from Fred Neff, 347th IN, 87th Div, to Miss A. W. Keichler (sister), dated August 9, 1918, author's collection; Richard McBride, 328th IN, 82nd Div, memoir, "Passing in Review: Memories of World War I," MHIWWIS; Crump, *Conscript,* 27.

17. Letter from Harry Callison to "Dear Folks" undated but marked "Tuesday night," circa October 1917, author's collection; Crump, *Conscript,* 25, 77.

18. Letter from Benson Oakley to Newton and Lomis, Props, Star Clothing House, Norwich, New York, dated September 8, 1918; Letter from Francis Loughram to Beau and Daisy Loughram, dated July 25, 1918, both from author's collection.

19. AEF GHQ General Orders 23, August 20, 1917; *Stars and Stripes,* June 21, 1918, 4.

20. Anonymous (Bob Casey), *The Cannoneers Have Hairy Ears* (New York: J. H. Sears, 1927), 190; Thurmond Baccus, 307th Field Signal Bn, unpublished manuscript, USMHI Survey; Sanitary Reports for November 1918 for 90thDiv, 1st Div, and 36th Div, NARA, RG 120, Entry 2113, Boxes 5208 and 5209.

21. "Notes Made by the Inspector General A.E.F. during the Active Operations from 12 September 1918 to 11 November 1918," in NARA, RG 120, Entry 588, Box 116; Sanitary Report for November 1918 for 81st Div and letter from 81st Div Quartermaster to Division Commander, dated December 10, 1918, NARA, RG 120, Entry 2113, Box 5209.

22. Morale Branch Officers' Survey; Warren Jackson, *His Time in Hell* (Novato: Presidio Press, 2001), 208; Burt A. Richardson, manuscript, "Episodes in the Great War," dated July 1926, 71, Emory; Sanitary Report for November 1918, 1st Pursuit Group, NARA, RG 120, Entry 2113, Box 5209.

23. Sasse, *Rookie,* 104–105.

24. Charles Minder, *This Man's War* (New York: Pevensey Press, 1931), 38–39; Letter from Milton Sweningsen, 138th IN, 35th Div, to his mother, dated July 2, 1918, in MHIWWIS.

25. AEF GHQ, *Equipment Manuals for Service in Europe,* series A, no. 1, *Infantry Regiments* (Chaumont: AEF AG Printing Section, 1918), 60–62.

26. *Stars and Stripes,* July 26, 1918; Minder, *This Man's War,* 230; William Graham, *Hell's Observer* (Canal Winchester: Badgley, 2012), 85.

27. Jackson, *Time in Hell,* 46, 77, 90–94.

28. AEF GHQ, *Equipment Manuals for Service in Europe,* 60–62.

29. Letter from James Dalgren, 10th FA, to Adelaide Bowden, December 22, 1917, Emory; Morale Branch Officers' Survey.

30. C. L. Crane, "The Great War: 1917–1918–1919." Entries for July 30, 1918, in unpublished diary in the possession of Dr. Conrad Crane of the Army War College. A

copy of the diary is in the possession of the author; Herman Dacus, 28th IN, 1st Div, MHIWWIS.

31. L. V. Jacks, *Service Record by an Artilleryman* (New York: Charles Scribner's Sons, 1928), 21, 89–93.

CHAPTER 7. BE IT EVER SO HUMBLE

1. Letter from James Miller to Mrs. James Miller (mother), dated February 5, 1918, author's collection; Sanitary Report for October 1918 for 324th Labor Bn, and November 1918 for the 2nd Detachment, Co C, 321st Labor Bn, NARA, RG 120, Entry 2113, Box 5207 and 5209.

2. Sanitary Report for October 1918 for Mobile Hospital No. 1 and No. 2, NARA, RG 120, Entry 2113, Box 5204.

3. Letter dated December 22, 1917, in Raymond Stanbeck, 6th Marines, 2nd Div, MHIWWIS.

4. Knud Olsen, 325 Infantry, 82nd Div, MHIWWIS.

5. Horatio Rogers, *World War I through My Sights* (San Rafael: Presidio Press, 1976), 32–35; Letter from Francis J. Byrne to "Dear Ed," dated February 23, 1918, author's collection.

6. Sanitary Reports for October 1918 for Base Section 5 and for Camp Victor Hugo, both in NARA, RG 120, Entry 2113, Box 5204; Sanitary Report for November 1918 for Camp Pontanezen, NARA, RG 120, Entry 2113, Box 5209.

7. Sanitary Reports for October and November 1918, 1st Pursuit Group, NARA, RG 120, Entry 2113, Box 5207 and 5209.

8. Charles Minder, *This Man's War* (New York: Pevensey Press, 1931), 40–41.

9. Craig Gibson, *Behind the Front: British Soldiers and French Civilians, 1914–1918* (Cambridge: Cambridge University Press, 2014), 90–91, 109–146; AEF GHQ General Orders 18, January 31, 1918.

10. Letters home from Benjamin Heath, HQ, 82nd Div, dated July 7 and 23 and October 20, 1918, MHIWWIS; AEF GHQ General Orders 18.

11. AEF GHQ General Orders 43, March 22, 1918; Lee J. Levinger, *A Jewish Chaplain in France* (New York: MacMillian, 1922), 65.

12. Richard McBride, 328th IN, 82nd Div, memoir, "Passing in Review," MHIWWIS.

13. *Stars and Stripes*, December 27, 1918; AEF GHQ General Orders 218, November 28, 1918; U.S. Army Center of Military History, *United States Army in the World War, 1917–1919*, vol. 11, *American Occupation of Germany* (Washington, DC: Government Printing Office, 1991), 203–204, 215; Carl Noble, quoted in James Hallas, *Doughboy War* (Boulder: Lynne Rienner, 2000), 314, 316–332; José de la Luz Sáenz, *The World War I Diary of José de la Luz Sáenz*, ed. and trans. Emilo Zamora (College Station: Texas A&M Press, 2014), 316–317.

14. Memorandum from Headquarters 2 Bde, 1 Div, dated May 18, 1918, *World War Records, First Division*, vol. 13, *Operations Reports* (Washington, DC: Army War College, 1930), n.p.

NOTES TO PAGES 155–163   [653]

15. Army War College, *Manual for Commanders of Infantry Platoons* (Washington, DC: Government Printing Office, 1917), 247–255.
16. Charles MacArthur, *War Bugs* (New York: Doubleday, Doran, 1929), 57; Leslie J. Martin, 16th IN, 1st Div manuscript "The Story of My Life," in MHIWWIS; Letter from Luther Grover to Etta Hawk (sister), dated April 17, 1918, author's collection.
17. Warren Jackson, *His Time in Hell* (Novato: Presidio Press, 2001), 52.
18. Letter from James Dalgren to Adelaide Bowden, October 16, 1917, Emory.
19. Sanitary Report for October 1918 for 3rd Div, NARA, RG 120, Entry 2113, Box 5204.
20. Henri Barbusse, *Under Fire* (London: J. M. Dent & Sons, 1926), 17; Diary of Capt. Clarence Minick, 361st IN, 91st Div, entry for September 28, 1918, NWWIM; *The Service Record: Atlanta's Military Weekly*, June 5, 1919, 57; Joe Romedahl, 129th IN, 33nd Div, MHIWWIS; Letter from Richard Atkinson to Mrs. G. B. Atkinson (mother), from France, dated August 22, 1918, author's collection.
21. Clarence L. Mahan, manuscript, "Hoosier Doughboy with the First Division," MHIWWIS; Letter from June B. Smith to his mother, dated October 7, 1918, from France, from the family collection of Dave Hinkley, copy in author's possession; Letter from Franklin Schall to "Dear Bro & Family," dated October 15, 1918, NWWIM.

CHAPTER 8. "GOOD-BYE BROADWAY, HELLO FRANCE"

1. Letter from Harry Callison to "Dear Mother" postmarked April 5, 1918; Letter from Ed Guiss to Fanny Dohrman (sister), dated September 16, 1918; Letters from James M. Miller to "Mama and Rest," dated August 20 and September 7, 1917, all from author's collection.
2. Letter from George Hetrich to Robert Dengler, postdated July 10, 1918; Letter from Bernard Bockemuehl to George Bockemuehl, dated May 22, 1918; Letter from Wallace Mansfield to F. M. Mansfield (mother), dated October 12, 1918, all from author's collection.
3. Horatio Rogers, *World War I through My Sights* (San Rafael: Presidio Press, 1976), 12; Kerr Rainsford, *From Upton to the Meuse with the Three Hundred and Seventh Infantry* (New York: D. Appleton, 1920), 6–7; Letter from Ed Guiss to Fanny Dohrman, dated August 19, 1918, author's collection.
4. Letter from Bernard Bockemueh to Mrs. M. Bockemuehl, dated June 5, 1918; Letter from Mike Scheck to "Dear Sister," dated September 9, 1918; Letter from James Myers to Robert Dengler, dated July 9, 1918, all from author's collection.
5. David Shanks, *As They Passed through the Port* (Washington, DC: W. F. Roberts, 1927), dedication, 43.
6. William Triplet, *A Youth in the Meuse Argonne* (Columbia: University of Missouri Press, 2000), 28; Shanks, *As They Passed*, 166.
7. Letter from Floyd Sosey to Mrs. J. C. Sosey, dated June 25, 1918, author's collection; "General Information for Military Passengers Sailing on Commercial

Lines," undated circa mid-1917, William Haselton 18th IN and Div Staff, 1st Div, MHIWWIS.

8. Christian Bach and Henry Hall, *The Fourth Division: It's Services and Achievements in the World War* (New York: Country Life Press, 1920), 38; Letter from Harry Callison to "Dear folks" undated, author's collection; W. A. Sirmon, *That's War* (Atlanta: Linmon, 1929), 65–66.

9. Albert Ettinger, *A Doughboy with the Fighting 69th* (Shippensburg: White Mane, 1992), 15; Shanks, *As They Passed*, 126–127.

10. Sirmon, *That's War*, 68–69; Shanks, *As They Passed*, 84–89, 104–116, 110.

11. Triplet, *Youth in The Meuse Argonne*, 30–31.

12. Rogers, *Through My Sights*, 15.

13. Vice Admiral Albert Cleaves, *A History of the Transport Service* (New York: George H. Doran, 1921), 25–26, 91, 256–250; Sirmon, *That's War*, 70–81.

14. Shanks, *As They Passed*, 153; Cleaves, *Transport Service*, 88–95; Charles MacDonald, *War Bugs* (New York: Doubleday Doran, 1929), 3.

15. Letter from Russell to "Dear Dad," dated November 23, 1918, author's collection; Rogers, *Through My Sights*, 21; Raymond S. Tompkins, *The Story of the Rainbow Division* (New York: Boni & Liveright, 1919), 18; Beaumont Buck 1917 Diary, entry for June 14, USACM.

16. Clyde L. Eddy, address given before the Historical Section of the American Pharmaceutical Association, Washington, DC, 1920, USMA; War Department, *The Medical Department of the United States Army in the World War*, vol. 6, *Sanitation* (Washington, DC: Government Printing Office, 1926), 424.

17. Letter from Dewitt McIntyre to "Dear folks at home," undated, author's collection; Harvey L. Harris, *The War as I Saw It: 1918 Letters of a Tank Corps Lieutenant* (Saint Paul: Pogo Press, 1998), 3–7; B. A. Colonna, ed., *The History of Company B, 311th Infantry in the World War* (Freehold, NJ: Transcript Printing House, 1922), 14.

18. Tom Carroll, 16th IN, 1st Div, manuscript, "Tom Carroll's Diary," MHIWWIS; Beaumont Buck 1917 Diary, entry for June 19, 1917.

19. Beaumont Buck 1917 Diary, entries for June 12–13, 1917; Leslie Martin, 16th IN, 1st Div, manuscript "The Story of My Life," MHIWWIS.

20. Letter from Russell to "Dear Dad," dated November 23, 1918, author's collection; Triplet, *Youth in the Meuse Argonne*, 33–34; Charles Minder, *This Man's War* (New York: Pevensey Press, 1931), 9–11, 17; Beaumont Buck 1917 Diary, entry for June 19.

21. Beaumont Buck 1917 Diary, entry for 22–23 June; Triplet, *Youth in the Meuse Argonne*, 33–35.

22. Warren Jackson, *His Time in Hell* (Novato: Presidio Press, 2001), 21; Rogers, *Through My Sights*, 19–20; Letter from Walter Shaw to his mother, dated July 5, 1917, NWWIM.

23. Shanks, *As They Passed*, 84–86; Cleaves, *Transport Service*, 187.

24. Letters from James M. Miller to "Mama and Rest," from transport ship, undated,

circa early September 1917 and from Halifax, Nova Scotia, dated September 18, 1917, author's collection; Mervyn Burke, HQ Troop, 1st Div, MHIWWIS; Minder, *This Man's War*, 16.

25. Evan A. Edwards, *From Doniphan to Verdun* (Lawrence: World Company, 1920), 22; Minder, *This Man's War*, 9–10; Mike Scheck to "Dear Sister," dated August 16, 1918, author's collection.

26. William F. Clarke, *Over There with O'Ryan's Roughnecks* (Seattle: Superior Publishing, 1966), 31.

27. Beaumont Buck 1917 Diary, entry for June 26 and 28; Triplet, *Youth in the Meuse Argonne*, 32–33.

28. Burke.

29. Bach and Hall, *Fourth Division*, 42–45; Cleaves, *Transport Service*, 195–201.

30. ————, *20th Engineers, France, 1917, 1918, 1919* (Portland: Dimm & Sons, 1919), n.p.

31. *20th Engineers, France*; www.islayinfo.com/loss-troopship-tuscania-islay.html.

32. www.islayinfo.com/lord_robertson_islay_troopships.html.

33. Byron Farwell, *Over There* (New York: Norton, 1999), 85; Cleaves, *Transport Service*, 190–191.

34. Morale reports to the G2, 83rd Division, dated October 8, October 15, and October 21, 1918, in NARA, RG 120, Entry 195, Box 1; *Medical Department of The United States Army in the World War*, vol. 6, *Sanitation* (Washington, DC: Government Printing Office, 1926), 424–426; Cleaves, *Transport Service*, 190–191.

CHAPTER 9. "THE FRENCH THEY HAVE THEIR CUSTOMS RARE, PARLEZ-VOUS"

1. Cornelius Chandler, 320 FA, 82 Div, MHIWWIS.

2. Crane Brinton, *The Americans and the French* (Cambridge, MA: Harvard University Press, 1968), 67–71; United States Department of Commerce, *Statistical Abstract of the United States for 1916* (Washington, DC: Government Printing Office, 1917), 56; Henry Blumenthal, *Illusions and Reality in Franco-American Diplomacy* (Baton Rouge: Louisiana State University Press, 1986), 7; Samuel Clemens (Mark Twain), *Innocents Abroad* (Hartford, CT: American Publishing, 1869), 126, 137; Jean-Baptiste Duroselle, *France and the United States: From the Beginnings to the Present*, trans. Dereck Coltman (Chicago: University of Chicago Press, 1978), 80–82; Finley Peter Dunne, *Mr. Dooley in Peace and in War* (Boston: Small Maynard, 1898), 257.

3. Wythe Williams, *Passed By the Censor* (New York: E. P. Dutton, 1916), 190; Elizabeth Brett White, *American Opinion of France* (New York: Alfred A. Knopf, 1927), 273; W. A. Sirmon, *That's War* (Atlanta: Linmon, 1929), 89.

4. Raymond Corkery, 102 FA, 26 Div; Eugene Knoke, 362 IN, 91 Div, both in MHIWWIS; Levi E. Hemrick, *Once A Marine* (New York: Carlton Press, 1968), 5; Charles MacArthur, *War Bugs* (New York: Doubleday, Doran, 1929), 11; *Stars and Stripes*, February 22, 1918.

5. Sirmon, *That's War*, 89; Hemrick, *Once A Marine*, 50.
6. "Report on the 1st Army," AEF Paris Base Censor to AEF Chief G-2-D, dated January 13, 1919, NARA, RG 120, Entry 226, Box 6108.
7. John J. Pershing, *My Experiences in the World War*, 2 vols. (New York: Frederick A. Stokes, 1931), 1:58–59; Grendon Armstrong, 101 MGB, 26 Div, Antonio Voyer, 103 FA, 26 Div, both in MHIWWIS.
8. Donald G. Mitchell, Jr., journal entry for August 21, 1918, UGA; Letter from De-witt McIntyre to "Dear folks at home," from France, undated; Letter from Fay Neff to A. W. Keichler, dated August 24, 1918, both from author's collection.
9. "Report on the 1st Army," AEF Paris Base Censor.
10. Letter from D. S. Martin to Lucy Sapoch, dated August 9, 1919, author's collection; August Knohloch to Frieda Knohloch, April 20, 1919, in NARA, RG 120, Entry 226, Box 6109, "Translations of German Prisoners of War Mail," Folder 1; "Report of Chief Liaison Officer on Conditions in Occupied Territory," dated February 3, 1919, in C. H. Goddard, "A Study of Franco American Relations during World War I," Historical Section Army War College, dated July 1942, USAMHI.
11. Eugene Knoke, 362 IN, 91 Div, MHIWWIS; Hunter Liggett, *The AEF: Ten Years Ago in France* (New York: Dodd, Meade, 1927), 244–245.
12. Letters from Walter Shaw to his mother, dated October 19 and November 26, 1917, NWWIM; Thurmond Baccus was surprised that "women worked very hard in the fields and did most any work a man did." Thurmond Baccus, 307th Field Signal Bn, unpublished manuscript in MHIWWIS.
13. Albert Ettinger, *A Doughboy with the Fighting 69th* (Shippensburg: White Mane Publishing, 1992), 32; James G. Harbord, *Leaves from a War Diary* (New York: Dodd, Meade, 1925), 47; Earl Seaton, 16 IN, 1 Div, and Gustaf Hallberg, 101 MP, 26 Div, both in MHIWWIS.
14. John W. Castles, "War Diary of John W. Castles," 34, USMA; Edward Hungerford, *With the Doughboy in France* (New York: MacMillan, 1920), 26.
15. Letter from S. D. Lyon, HQ Regt, 1st Army, to Mrs. S. P. Lyon, dated April 21, 1918, in Samuel and Stuart Lyon Papers, USAMHI ACC188-W-1030–124. Similar comments are made in the February 16 and 17, 1918, entries in the Alphonse Bloemer Diary, UGA.
16. Letters from Elmer Lewis to Goldie Little, dated July 27, 1918, August 31, 1918, and February 27, 1919, author's collection.
17. Lee J. Levinger, *A Jewish Chaplain in France* (New York: Macmillan, 1921), 71; "Report on the 1st Army," AEF Paris Base Censor.
18. Letter from Walter Shaw to his mother, dated June 18, 1917, NWWIM; Elmer Straub, *A Sergeants Diary in the World War*, Indiana Historical Collections, vol. 10 (Indianapolis: Indiana Historical Commission, 1923), 59; Letter from Ira Wilkenson to "Dear Sister," dated April 26, 1918, UGA; Letter from George McLaughlin to Mrs. L. H. McLaughlin (mother), dated September 27, 1918, author's collection.

19. James Luby, ed., *One Who Gave His Life: War Letters of Quincy Sharpe Mills* (New York: G. P. Putnam's Sons, 1923), 313; Sirmon, *That's War*, 185–186; Donald G. Mitchell, Jr., journal entry for August 21, 1918, and letter to "Dearest Mama, Dad and all the family," dated June 25, 1918.

20. James A. Murrin, *With the 112th in France* (Philadelphia: J. B. Lippincott, 1919), 98; William H. Amerine, *Alabama's Own in France* (New York: Eaton and Gettinger, 1919), 80.

21. Hemrick, *Once A Marine*, 50; Henry Berry, *Make the Kaiser Dance* (New York: Doubleday, 1978), 300–301; Christopher Gordon, 101 MGB, 26 Div, MHIWWIS.

22. Frank A. Holden, *War Memories* (Athens, GA: n.p., 1922), 190; Donald Chase, 103 IN, 26 Div, MHIWWIS; Levinger, *Jewish Chaplain*, 112.

23. William L. Langer, *Gas and Flame in World War I* (New York: Alfred A. Knopf, 1965), 12; Holden, *War Memories*, 41; Horatio Rogers, *World War I through My Sights* (San Rafael: Presidio Press, 1976), 44; Straub, *Sergeants Diary*, 286; Marian Baldwin, *Canteening Overseas 1917–1919* (New York: MacMillan, 1926), 50.

24. Leonard Ayres, *The War with Germany: A Statistical Summary* (Washington, DC: Government Printing Office, 1919), 59–62; *Stars and Stripes*, November 1, 1918, and May 2, 1919; Murrin, *With the 112th*, 234; Edward Helming, 120 IN, 30 Div; William Couch, 308 MP Co, both in MHIWWIS; "Report on the 1st Army," AEF Paris Base Censor, January 13, 1919.

25. MacArthur, *War Bugs*, 12–13, 27; Edwin P. Arpin, "A Wisconsinite in World War I: Reminiscences of Edwin P. Arpin, Jr," ed. Ira Berlin, *Wisconsin Magazine of History*, Winter 1967–1968, 19; Levinger, *Jewish Chaplain*, 57; Langer, *Gas and Flame*, 13; Berry, *Kaiser Dance*, 346; Robert Smith, 120 IN, 30 Div; Charles Mechura, 101 EN, 26 Div; Harold McKinnon, Quartermaster Corps; Harvey Fullerton, 316 Supply Train, 91 Div, all in MHIWWIS; AEF GHQ Bulletin 83; "Report on the 1st Army," AEF Paris Base Censor.

26. "Report on the 1st Army," AEF Paris Base Censor; *Stars and Stripes*, January 10, 1919.

27. Letter from Mon. Perrin, Greffier de la Justice de Paix du Canton de Pont-a-Mousson to President of the Council, Minister of War, Subject: "Conduct of Americans Stationed at Pont-a-Mousson," undated, circa March 1919, NARA, RG 120, Entry 918, Box 82.

28. *Stars and Stripes*, February 7, 1919, May 2, 1919; Arpin, "A Wisconsinite," 19; Hemrick, *Once A Marine*, 51–59; Straub, *Sergeants Diary*, 165, 278; "Report on the 1st Army," AEF Paris Base Censor, and "Examination of Mail, 79th Division," Regimental Department Censor Bureau to Chief, Office of the Base Censor, dated April 21, 1919, NARA, RG 120, Entry 226, Box 6108; Clair Kenamore, *From Vauquois Hill to Exermont* (St. Louis: Guard Publishing, 1919), 40.

29. Letter from Ira Wilkenson to "Dear Sister," dated April 26, 1918; *Stars and Stripes*, July 12, 1918.

30. Levinger, *Jewish Chaplain*, 18, 193; Letter from Paul F. Andrews to his aunt dated

May 5, 1918, from France, NWWIM; George C. Marshall, *Memories of My Service in the World War, 1917–1918* (New York: Houghton Mifflin, 1976), 12.

31. *Stars and Stripes*, April 19, 1918; Letter from Luther Grover to Etta Hawk (sister), dated September 22, 1918, author's collection; "Report on the 1st Army," AEF Paris Base Censor.

32. *Stars and Stripes*, March 22, March 29, April 5, and November 8, 1918, and January 17 and June 13, 1919; Sirmon, *That's War*, 98; AEF GHQ General Order 139, October 28, 1918.

33. Letter from Maj. John H. O'Connor to Commandant, Army School of the Line, dated August 26, 1918, and Letter from Lt. Col. Jas. Taylor to Brig. Gen. H. A. Smith, dated July 30, 1918, in NARA, RG 120, Records of the AEF, G5 Schools, Army Candidate School, Box 1623, File 250.1; *Stars and Stripes*, October 11, 1918.

34. Levinger, *Jewish Chaplain*, 65; Letter from Dewitt McIntyre to Mrs. G. W. McIntyre, dated July 8, 1918, author's collection.

35. C. L. Crane, "The Great War: 1917–1918–1919." Entries for April 7–10, 1918, in unpublished diary in the possession of Dr. Conrad Crane of the Army War College. A copy of the diary is in the possession of the author; Clarence L. Mahan, manuscript, "Hoosier Doughboy with the First Division," MHIWWIS; Letter from George Tucker to E. K. Tomlinson, dated March 25, 1919, author's collection.

36. Bradford Perkins, *The Great Rapprochement* (New York: Antheneum, 1969), 4; Hans-Jürgen Schroder, ed., *Confrontation and Cooperation: Germany and the United States in the Era of World War I* (Oxford: Berg, 1993), 14–15; H. C. Allen, *Great Britain and the United States* (New York: Archon Books, 1969), 163–166; David Dimbley and David Reynolds, *An Ocean Apart* (New York: Random House, 1988), 52–53.

37. Charles Minder, *This Man's War* (New York: Pevensey Press, 1931), 26.

38. Lt. Col. Calvin H. Goddard, "Relations between the American Expeditionary Forces and the British Expeditionary Forces: 1917–1920," USAMHI; Knud Olsen, 325 IN, 82 Div; John Switzer, 103 MGB, 26 Div, both in MHIWWIS; *Stars and Stripes*, May 16, 1919; Sirmon, *That's War*, 84; Murrin, *With the 112th*, 80; Harbord, *Leaves*, 38–40.

39. Liggett, *The AEF*, 4; Michael O'Brien, *The Idea of the American South, 1920–1941* (Baltimore: Johns Hopkins University Press, 1979), 185–186; Luby, *One Who Gave*, 313.

40. Levinger, *Jewish Chaplain*, 192; "Answers to Proposed Questionnaire for Discharged Men" by George Ravencamp, "Proposed Questionnaire for Discharged Men" by Schuyer Garth, undated, NARA, RG 165, Entry 377, Box 5, Camp Funston file; Roland Graves, 104 IN, 26 Div, Hugh Hook, 353 IN, 89 Div, Felix Stastny, 346 FA, 91 Div, all in MHIWWIS. In a random sample of the 121 veterans who responded to the question "Since the World War I era was a great national experience, did you learn anything about America and Americans?," 74 (62 percent) wrote that the United States and or the American people were the greatest in

the world and another 15 (12 percent) noted that they learned more about their country or gained a greater appreciation for America.

41. Monroe Mason and Arthur Furr, *The American Negro Soldier with the Red Hand in France* (Boston: Cornhill, 1920), 40; *The Messenger* 2, no. 10 (October 1919): 27.

42. *Stars and Stripes*, December 16, 1918; *Crisis* 18, no. 2 (June 1919): 65; Addie Hunton and Kathryn Johnson, *Two Colored Women with the American Expeditionary Forces* (New York: Brooklyn Eagle Press, 1920), 102; Arthur E. Barbeau and Florette Henri, *The Unknown Soldiers: Black American Troops in World War I* (Philadelphia: Temple University Press, 1974), 106.

43. *Crisis* 18, no. 1 (May 1919): 17–21; Hunton and Johnston, *Two Colored Women*, 190.

44. *Crisis* 18, no. 2 (June 1919): 16–18, 71. DuBois obtained a copy of the memo while investigating the conditions of black soldiers in France in December 1918. The identity of the AEF officer who requested the French to issue the memo remains a mystery. No one in the AEF GHQ claimed responsibility for the memo or denied its authenticity. While much of the document's history is obscure, actions taken against blacks in the AEF point to a wide acceptance and high-level approval of the opinions expressed in the memo. When the contents of the memo were revealed to the French National Assembly in July 1919, the delegates were outraged and passed legislation apologizing for the incident and condemning racial prejudice.

45. Hunton and Johnson, *Two Colored Women*, 103, 182–184; *Crisis* 18, no. 2 (June 1919): 87; and *Crisis* 19, no. 5 (March 1920): 260–261.

46. Hunton and Johnson, *Two Colored Women*, 79; Mason and Furr, *Negro Soldier*, 76; Bertram Lawrence, 349 FA, 92 Div, MHIWWIS; William S. Braddan, *Under Fire with the 370th Infantry* (Chicago: self-published, n.d.), 107.

47. *The Messenger* 2, no. 5 (May–June 1919); and *The Messenger* 2, no. 7 (July 1919): 25; Robert Stevens, 803 PIO IN; Virgil Ragsdale, 349 MG BN, 92 Div, both in MHIWWIS.

48. *The Messenger* 2, no. 10 (October 1919): 27; and *The Messenger* 2, no. 11 (December 1919): 20; Braddan, *Under Fire*, 53; Henry Craven, 367 IN, 92 Div, MHIWWIS.

CHAPTER 10. OF TRENCH GUNS, SHO-SHOS, AND TRENCH KNIVES

1. George Johnson and Hans B. Lockhoven, *International Armament*, vol. 1 (Cologne, Germany: International Small Arms Publishers, 1965), 406–407; Letter from Reginald Thomson to Lillian Cottrell, dated July 29, 1918, NWWIM.

2. Johnson and Lockhoven, *International Armament*, 415; Benedict Crowell, *America's Munitions, 1917–1918* (Washington, DC: Government Printing Office, 1919), 178–186; Bruce Canfield, *U.S. Infantry Weapons of World War I* (Lincoln, RI: Andre Mowbray Publishers, 2000), 83.

3. Canfield, *Infantry Weapon*, 83; Capt. Benhamin Hensley, "Operations of Company F, 34th Infantry in the Puvenelle Sector October 1–November 11, 1918," DRL.

4. Chester Baker, *Doughboy's Diary* (Shippensburg, PA: Burd Street Press, 1998),

49; Christian A. Bach and Henry N. Hall, *The Fourth Division: Its Services and Achievements in the World War* (New York: Country Life Press, 1920), 48.

5. "Notes Made by the Inspector General, A.E.F. during the Active Operations from 12 September 1918 to 11 November 1918," NARA, RG 120, Entry 588, Box 116; Inspector 5th Army Corps to Inspector General AEF, Subject: "Extract Report of Division Inspector 91st Division," dated October 5, 1918, NARA, RG 120, Entry 590, Box 1.

6. Captain Charles Crawford, *Weapons and Munitions of War*, pt. 1, *Infantry Weapons* (Fort Leavenworth: Staff College Press, 1907), 8–11; War Department, *Infantry Drill Regulations, corrected to December 31, 1917* (Washington, DC: Government Printing Office, 1917), 104.

7. Laurence Stallings, *The Doughboys* (New York: Harper & Row, 1963), 335–338.

8. *Infantry Drill Regulations, April 15, 1917*, 116–117; AEF GHQ, "Program of Training for the 1st Division, A.E.F.," October 6, 1917, in *World War Records, First Division*, vol. 20, *Training First Division* (Washington, DC: Army War College, 1930), n.p.

9. U.S. Army Medical Department, *The Medical Department of the United States Army in the World War*, vol. 15, *Statistics*, pt. 2, *Medical and Casualty Statistics* (Washington, DC: Government Printing Office, 1925), 1,019.

10. Crowell, *Munitions*, 228; Canfield, *Infantry Weapons*, 26–32; U.S. Army Center for Military History, *United States Army in the World War*, vol. 1, *Organization of the American Expeditionary Forces* (Washington, DC: Government Printing Office, 1988), 347.

11. Jeffery T. Sammons and John H. Morrow, Jr., *Harlem's Rattlers and the Great War* (Lawrence: University Press of Kansas, 2014), 265–275.

12. Canfield, *Infantry Weapons*, 135–138.

13. Edwin Engleman, Camp Dodge, 163rd Depot Brigade, MHIWWIS.

14. Crowell, *Munitions*, 169.

15. Maj. Zeba L. Drollinger, "Operations of the Machine Gun Units of the Sixth Brigade Near Château Thierry July 1–21 1918," DRL.

16. Walter Wolf, 129th IN, 33rd Div, MHIWWIS.

17. Canfield, *Infantry Weapons*, 211–215.

18. Capt. Welcome P. Waltz, "Operations of C Company, 3rd Machine Gun Battalion at Cantigny"; Capt. Albert B. Helsley, "Operations of the Machine Gun Company, 16th Infantry (1st Division) during the Second Phase of the Meuse Argonne Offensive"; Maj. Charles W. Yuill, "Operations of Co. B, 3rd MGB in the Aisne-Marne Offensive," all in DRL.

19. Ray N. Johnson, *Heaven, Hell, or Hoboken* (Cleveland: O. S. Hubbell, 1919), 101–102; 2nd Lt. Malcolm Helms, 5th MGB, 2nd Div, MHIWWIS; Charles M. DePuy, *A Machine Gunner's Notes, France 1918* (Pittsburgh: Reed and Witting, 1920), 79.

20. Charles Minder, *This Man's War* (New York: Pevensey Press, 1931), 90–94; Maj. M. S. Eddy, "Machine Gun Company, 39th Infantry (4th Division) in the Aisne-Marne Offensive," DRL: General Headquarters American Expeditionary Force,

Report of Officers Convened by Special Orders No.98, GHQ AEF 09 April 1919, An-nex S, 9.

21. Maj. C. A. Dravo, "Machine Guns: The Offensive in Open Warfare," *Infantry Jour-nal* 17, no. 4 (October 1920): 323–325; Joseph D. Lawrence, *Fighting Soldier* (Boul-der: Colorado Associated University Press, 1985), 87; Capt. A. M. Patch, "Machine Gun Organization," *Infantry Journal* 17, no. 2 (August 1920): 145; Helsley, "Ma-chine Gun Company"; "Notes Made by the Inspector General A.E.F., during the Active Operations from 12th September 1918 to 11th November 1918"; Lewis Board, Annexes H, S, and X.

22. Canfield, *Infantry Weapons*, 147–152, 154; Gerard Demaison and Yves Buffetaut, *Honor Bound: The Chauchat Machine Rifle* (Ontario: Collector Grade Publica-tions, 1996), xvii, 59–61, 131–145.

23. Dravo, "Machine Guns," 319; Memorandum from Maj. Gen. C. P. Summerall, Commander 1st Division, dated August 25, 1918, in War Department, *World War Records, First Division, A.E.F. Regular*, vol. 2, *Field Orders, First Division June 1, 1918, to Sept. 18, 1918* (Washington, DC: Army War College, 1930), n.p.; Demaison and Buffetaut, *Honor Bound*, 151.

24. Canfield, *Infantry Weapons*, 156–163; Fred Takes, 325th IN, 82nd Div, entry for December 15, 1918,"World War I Co A, 325th Inf. 82nd Div," MHIWWIS.

25. Canfield, *Infantry Weapons*, 247–250, 257–264.

26. Capt. George J. Foster, "Operations of the 37-mm gun platoon, 26th Infantry (1st Division) October 1–12, 1918," DRL; "Report of Operations Argonne Meuse, Of-ficer of the Inspector, 5th Army Corps, Sept. 25–Nov. 11, 18, Extracts of Reports of Div. Inspectors," NARA, RG 120, Entry 588, Box 116; Lewis Board, Appendix H, 6, Appendix X, 9.

27. Helms; Letter dated April 23,1919, from Raymond Stanbeck, 6th Marines, 2nd Div, both in MHIWWIS.

28. Canfield, *Infantry Weapons*, 238–240; Crowell, *Munitions*, 208; Earl Seaton, 16th IN, 1st Div, memoir, "I Joined the Regulars," MHIWWIS.

29. *U.S. Army in the World War*, vol. 1, *Organization*, 344; AEF GHQ, *Equipment Manuals for Service in Europe*, Series A, No. 1, *Infantry Regiments* (Chaumont: AEF AG Printing Section, May 1918), 60–68.

30. John Parker, "Simplifying the Organization and Tactics of Infantry," *Infantry Journal* 16, no. 7 (January 1920): 567.

CHAPTER 11. "OH, THE ARMY, THE ARMY, THE DEMOCRATIC ARMY, . . .
THE JEWS, THE WOPS, THE DUTCH AND IRISH COPS"

1. Alexander T. Hussey and Raymond M. Flynn, *The History of Company E, 308th Infantry, 1917–1919* (New York: Knickerbocker Press, 1919), 5.

2. David M. Kennedy, *Over Here: The First World War and American Society* (New York: Oxford University Press, 1980), 24, 157; Richard McBride, 328th IN, 82nd Div, memoir, "Passing in Review: Memories of World War I," MHIWWIS.

3. Nancy Gentile Ford, *Americans All: Foreign Born Soldiers in World War I* (College Station: Texas A&M Press, 2001), 3–15, 67–68, 118–119.

4. "Foreign Speaking American Soldiers and Foreign Speaking American Officers," Commander, Camp Dodge to Director of Military Intelligence, dated September 11, 1918, NARA, RG 165, Entry 377, Box 4; "Questions regarding Morale," from Camp Devens Auxiliary Units Intelligence Officer, to Chief Morale Section, dated July 20, 1918, NARA, RG 165, Entry 377, Box 3.

5. Edward G. Buxton, ed., *Official History of the 82nd Division* (Indianapolis: Bobbs-Merrill, 1919), 2; Weekly report from Camp Gordon Intelligence Officer to Chief Military Intelligence Branch, dated July 22, 1918, NARA, RG 165, Entry 377, Box 5; "Questionnaire on Morale Items," from Camp Hancock Intelligence Officer to Chief Morale Section, dated August 19, 1918, NARA, RG 165, Entry 377, Box 6.

6. Ira Greenhut, 307 Ammunition Train, 82nd Div, MHIWWIS.

7. Report from Intelligence Officer, Camp Devens, MA, to Chief, Military Morale Section, Subject: "Questions regarding Morale," dated July 20, 1918, and September 9, 1918, NARA, RG 165, Entry 377, Box 3; Memorandum for Captain Perkins from Foreign-Speaking Soldier Sub-Section, dated September 10, 1918, NARA, RG 165, Entry 377, Box 5, Camp Gordon file; Memorandum from Chief, Military Morale Section, to Intelligence Officer, Camp Dix, New Jersey, Subject: Anonymous Letter of Complaint, dated September 6, 1918, NARA, RG 165, Entry 377, Box 3; Richard Slotkin, *Lost Battalions: The Great War and the Crisis of American Nationality* (New York: Henry Holt, 2005), 92.

8. Report from Intelligence Officer, Camp Devens, MA, to Chief, Military Morale Section, Subject: "Questions regarding Morale," dated September 9, 1918, and Report from Ascanio Di Rago, Camp Devens, MA, to Chief, Military Intelligence Section, Subject: "Report and Suggestions," dated August 10, 1918, NARA, RG 165, Entry 377, Box 3.

9. Ford, *Americans All*, 123.

10. Henry Berry, *Make the Kaiser Dance* (New York: Doubleday, 1978), 323; Slotkin, *Lost Battalions*, 105–106.

11. Charles Minder, *This Man's War* (New York: Pevensey Press, 1931), 140.

12. Thomas A. Britten, *American Indians in World War I: At War and at Home* (Albuquerque: University Of New Mexico Press, 1997), 51–58.

13. Susan Krouse, *North American Indians in the Great War* (Lincoln: University of Nebraska Press, 2007), 28–29, 33; Britten, *American Indians*, 176–181.

14. Krouse, *Indians in the Great War*, 22–23, 64–67, 118–120; Britten, *American Indians*, 64–65.

15. Britten, *American Indians*, 37–50.

16. Ibid., 78–83, 99–104; Krouse, *Indians in the Great War*, 22–23, 64–67, 118–120.

17. Matt Mathews, *The U.S. Army on the Mexican Border: A Historical Perspective* (Fort Leavenworth: Combat Studies Institute, 2007), 62–66; José A. Ramírez, *To*

the Line of Fire: Mexican Texans and the World War (College Station: Texas A&M Press, 2009), 8–15.

18. Ramírez, *Line of Fire*, 75, 80–81, 90.

19. José de la Luz Sáenz, *The World War I Diary of José de la Luz Sáenz*, ed. and trans. Emilo Zamora (College Station: Texas A&M Press, 2014), 72, 87–89, 97.

20. Ibid., 422, 424.

21. Chad Williams, *Torchbearers of Democracy: African American Soldiers in the World War I Era* (Chapel Hill: University of North Carolina Press, 2010), 17; Garna L. Christian, *Black Soldiers In Jim Crow Texas, 1899–1917* (College Station: Texas A&M Press, 1995), 153–172.

22. *The Crisis* 14, no. 1 (May 1917): 8; *The Crisis* 14, no. 2 (June 1917): 59–60; *The Crisis* 14, no. 5 (September 1917): 216; *The Crisis* 16, no. 3 (July 1918): 111; *Messenger* 1, no. 11 (November 1917): 31–34.

23. Williams, *Torchbearers*, 68–72; Slotkin, *Lost Battalions*, 261–262.

24. Williams, *Torchbearers*, 66.

25. "Complaint from Colored Y.M.C.A. Secretary, Camp Jackson, S.C." from Camp Jackson Morale Officer to Chief Morale Branch, dated November 9, 1918, NARA, RG 165, Entry 377, Box 7.

26. Addie Hunton and Kathryn Johnson, *Two Colored Women with the American Expeditionary Forces* (New York: Brooklyn Eagle Press, 1920), 46–47; Williams, *Torchbearers*, 86–92.

27. Memorandum from Chief, Morale Branch to Morale Officer, Camp Gordon, GA, Subject: Letters of complaint from colored soldiers, Camp Gordon, dated November 27, 1918, and Memorandum from Emmett J. Scott to Chief, Military Morale Branch, dated December 13, 1918, both in NARA, RG 165, Entry 377, Box 3; Williams, *Torchbearers*, 115; Hunton and Johnston, *Two Colored Women*, 20–38; Arthur E. Barbeau and Florette Henri, *The Unknown Soldiers: Black American Troops in World War I* (Philadelphia: Temple University Press, 1974), 99.

28. Barbeau and Henri, *Unknown Soldiers*, 65–66, 78–80; Monroe Mason and Arthur Furr, *The American Negro Soldier with the Red Hand in France* (Boston: Cornhill, 1920), 19–20; Edward M. Coffman, *The War to End All Wars* (Madison: University of Wisconsin Press, 1968), 70–72; Emmett J. Scott to Chief, Military Morale Branch, dated December 13, 1918, NARA, RG 165, Entry 377, Box 3; Memorandum from Intelligence Officer, Camp Pike, AR, to Director of Military Intelligence, Subject: Questionnaire concerning Colored Troops, dated November 6, 1918, NARA, RG 165, Entry 377, Box 12; John W. Castles, "War Diary of John W. Castles," 6–7, USMA.

29. O. E. McKaine, "The Buffaloes: A First-Class Colored Fighting Unit," *Outlook* 119 (May 22, 1918), 412; Memorandum from Intelligence Officer, Camp Pike, AR, to Director of Military Intelligence, Subject: Questionnaire concerning Colored Troops, dated November 6, 1918, NARA, RG 165, Entry 377, Box 12; Warner A.

Ross, *My Colored Battalion* (Chicago: self-published, 1920), 1–26; Arthur W. Little, *From Harlem to the Rhine* (New York: Covici Friede, 1936), 351–352; Letter from Reginald Thomson to Lillian Cottrell, dated August 18, 1918, NWWIM; Report of Camp Pike Intelligence Officer to Chief, dated February 25, 1918, NARA, RG 165, Entry 377, Box 12.

30. Robert L. Bullard, *Personalities and Reminiscences of the War* (New York: Doubleday, Page, 1925), 294; Case file of 1st Lt. Julius Rogovin, 350 FA, 92nd Div, NARA, RG 120, Entry 541, Box 2312; John Stringfellow, *Hell No!* (Boston: Meador, 1936), 245–247.

31. Robert H. Ferrell, *Unjustly Dishonored: An African American Division in World War I* (Columbia: University of Missouri Press, 2011), 31–41, 89–106.

32. Williams, *Torchbearers*, 44–46; Gerald Patton, *War and Race: The Black Officer in the American Military, 1915–1941* (Westport, CN: Greenwood Press, 1981), 86–87, 91.

33. William S. Bradden, *Under Fire with the 370th Infantry* (Chicago: self-published, n.d), 71–72; Lt. Rayford Logan Blois Case File, NARA, RG 120, Entry 541, Box 2305; Patton, *War and Race*, 80–87, 183–185.

34. Richard Faulkner, "The School of Hard Knocks: Combat Leadership in the American Expeditionary Forces," PhD diss., Kansas State University, 2008, appendix A and B.

35. Letter from Earl Salle, 13th Regiment, Camp Jackson, SC, to "Dear mamma, papa, sister and brother," dated October 23, 1917, MHIWWIS; W. A. Sirmon, *That's War* (Atlanta: Linmon, 1929), 68; Williams, *Torchbearers*, 87.

36. Herbert Aptheker, *A Documentary History of the Negro People in the United States*, vol. 3, *From the N.A.A.C.P. to the New Deal* (New York: Citadel Press, 1993), 203–206.

37. Williams, *Torchbearers*, 108–111.

38. Charles H. Williams, *Sidelights on Negro Soldiers* (Boston: B. J. Brimmer, 1923), 138–141; Chad Williams, *Torchbearers*, 80; "Report of Negro Morale in and about Newport News" from Maj. C. B. Perkins to Chief, Morale Branch, dated December 31, 1918, NARA, RG 165, Entry 377, Box 12.

39. Barbeau and Henri, *Unknown Soldiers*, 93–97.

40. Charles H. Williams, *Sidelights*, 14; Letter to Emmett Scott from unknown writer, dated December 9, 1918, NARA, RG 165, Entry 377, Box 7; Barbeau and Henri, *Unknown Soldiers*, 99.

41. "Report of Negro Morale in and about Newport News"; Bradden, *Under Fire*, 44.

42. Letter from James Miller to Mrs. James Miller (mother), dated March 14, 1918, author's collection; Edwin P. Arpin, "A Wisconsinite in World War I: Reminiscences of Edwin P. Arpin, Jr," ed. Ira Berlin, *Wisconsin Magazine of History*, Autumn 1967, 18.

43. Hunton and Johnston, *Two Colored Women*, 98–104; Little, *From Harlem to the Rhine*, 351–352; Williams, *Sidelights*, 148; *Crisis* 18, no. 2 (June 1919): 65.

44. Williams, *Sidelights*, 155; Barbeau and Henri, *Unknown Soldiers*, 99–100; Williams, *Torchbearers*, 113.

45. Bradden, *Under Fire*, 107.

46. William Graham, *Hell's Observer* (Canal Winchester: Badgley, 2012), 210–214.

CHAPTER 12. THE NINETY-DAY WONDERS AND SAM BROWNES

1. Leonard Ayres, *The War with Germany: A Statistical Summary* (Washington, DC: Government Printing Office, 1919), 16–21; United States Department of War, *War Department Annual Report* (Washington, DC: Government Printing Office, 1916), 242.

2. José de la Luz Sáenz, *The World War I Diary of José de la Luz Sáenz*, ed. and trans. Emilo Zamora (College Station: Texas A&M Press, 2014), 105.

3. Richard Faulkner, *The School of Hard Knocks: Combat Leadership in the American Expeditionary Forces* (College Station: Texas A&M Press, 2012), 28–33.

4. War Department, *Special Regulations No. 49: Training Camps for Reserve Officers and Candidates for Appointment as Such, May 15–August 11, 1917* (Washington, DC: Government Printing Office, May 5, 1917), 11–13, 22–23; Faulkner, *Hard Knocks*, 81–83.

5. Faulkner, *Hard Knocks*, 38–57, 74–90; Hugh L. Scott, *Some Memories of a Soldier* (New York: Century, 1928), 556.

6. F. L. Miller, manuscript "The War to End All Wars," 3, Emory; "Replies to Officers' Questionnaires" from Morale Branch of the War College and War Plans Division to the Chief of Staff, dated November 5, 1919, NARA, RG 165, NM 84, Entry 378, Box 6 (hereafter cited as Morale Branch Officers' Survey), 52.

7. Morale Branch Officers' Survey; Faulkner, *Hard Knocks*, 33–35, 69–72, 77–78, 93–97.

8. Faulkner, *Hard Knocks*, 14–19, 119–121.

9. Maj. Charles R. Tips, "Selecting and Training Military Leaders," *Infantry Journal* 15, no. 7 (January 1919): 541; Maj. J. C. Wise, "Organization and Initial Training of a Company," *Infantry Journal* 14, no. 3 (September 1917): 201–210.

10. John W. Nell, *The Lost Battalion: A Private's Story* (San Antonio: Historical Publishing Network, 2001), 5; Memorandum to Adjutant General, from Col. H. O. Williams, Subject: Report on inspection of troops at Camp Sherman, Ohio, dated July 31, 1918, NARA, RG 165, Entry 310, Box 185-A NM-84, "Camp Macarthur, Texas, Infantry Training Center"; Charles Campbell, Evacuation Ambulance Company #1, MHIWWIS; Lt. Col. Jennings C. Wise, "The Soldier's Life in Battle," *Infantry Journal* 16, no. 11 (May 1920): 930.

11. Campbell, MHIWWIS; John S. Stringfellow, *Hell! No!* (Boston: Meador, 1936), 35; John L. Barkley, *No Hard Feelings!* (New York: Cosmopolitan, 1930), 23.

12. Morale Branch Officers Survey, 69; D. B. Gallagher, *The Battle of Bolts and Nuts in the Sector of Cognac Hill* (Fort Worth: Gallagher-Crosby, 1931), 13; Maj. Thomas Swann, "The Top-Sergeant," *Infantry Journal* 15, no. 12 (June 1919): 952.

13. French Military Mission, "Improvements in the Condition and Instruction of Non-Commissioned Officers," dated January 10, 1918, in NARA, RG 165, Entry 310, Box 208, NM-84, "Reports of Activities of Advisory Mission"; Morale Branch Officers Survey, 68–69.

14. Hervey Allen, *Towards the Flame* (New York: Farrar & Rienhart, 1926), 7; Charles Miller, *The Customs of the Service Also Some Suggestions and Advise* (Fort Leavenworth: Army Service School Press, 1917), 28–29; Albert Ettinger, *A Doughboy with the Fighting 69th* (Shippensburg: White Mane, 1992), 147.

15. US Army Center of Military History, *The U.S. Army in the World War*, vol. 3, *Training* (Washington, DC: Government Printing Office, 1988), 208–209, 221–222; GHQ AEF, *Report of Officers Convened by Special Orders No.98, GHQ AEF 09 April 1919*, Appendix P, 16 (Hereafter cited as the Lewis Board).

16. Oral History Transcript of the interview of John G. Oechsner by Com. Sgt. Maj. Erwin H. Koehler on January 19, 1982, Noncommissioned Officer Oral History Program, USAMHI; Letter from P. Benson Oakley to Helen Oakley postmarked April 26, 1918, author's collection; Maj. C. A. Bach, "Leadership," *Infantry Journal* 14, no. 8 (February 1918): 607–608.

17. Morale Branch officer survey, 34; W. A. Sirmon, *That's War* (Atlanta: Linmon, 1929), 21; Edward M. Coffman, *The War to End All Wars* (Madison: University of Wisconsin Press, 1968), 57.

18. Allen, *Towards the Flame*, 90; B. A. Colonna, *The History of Company B, 311th Infantry in the World War* (Freehold, NJ: Transcript Printing House, 1922), 12–13; Maj. Albert Gray, Blois Case Files, NARA, RG 120, Entry 541, Box 2299; Capt. Charles M. Harrington, Blois case files, Box 2299; Major Merritt Olmstead, "A Critical Analysis of Troop Leading within the 5th Division during the Second Phase of the Meuse-Argonne Offensive," CARL.

19. Stanley J. Herzog, *Helmets* (Stamford, CT: Bell Press, 1930), 81; Barkley, *No Hard Feelings!*, 232–232; Horace Baker, *Argonne Days in World War I* (Columbia: University of Missouri Press, 2007), 120.

20. Chester Baker, *Doughboy's Diary* (Shippensburg, PA: Burd Street Press, 1998), 59; War Veteran's Association, *History of Company "E," 107th Infantry* (New York: privately published, 1920), 101.

21. Leslie Baker, *The Company History: The Story of Company B, 106th Machine Gun Battalion* (New York: privately printed, 1920), 58, 60, 63; Hugh L. Hook, 353rd IN, 89th Div, MHIWWIS.

22. Joseph D. Lawrence, *Fighting Soldier* (Boulder: Colorado Associated University Press, 1985), 88, 102, 114–115; Horace Baker, *Argonne Days*, 73, 78; Charles MacArthur, *War Bugs* (New York: Doubleday, Doran, 1929), 203–204.

23. Ayres, *War with Germany*, 121; Unpublished diary of Brigadier General Beaumont Buck, entry for May 28–30, 1918, USACM; Henry Thorn, *History of 313th U.S. Infantry* (New York: Wynkoop Hallenbeck Crawford, 1920), 36, 40.

24. L. V. Jacks, *Service Record by an Artilleryman* (New York: Charles Scribner's Sons, 1928), 211–212.

25. *A History of the Three Hundred and Twelfth Infantry* (New York: privately published, 1919), 73; Memorandum from Forward Office, Inspector General's Department, 1st Army, Subject: Inspection 5th Division October 22, 1918, dated October 22, 1918, NARA, RG 120, Entry 590, Box 8; Milton B. Sweningsen, 138th IN, 35th Div, memoirs MHIWWIS, 2.

26. Charles Minder, *This Man's War* (New York: Pevensey Press, 1931), 108; Colonna, *311th Infantry*, 44.

27. William Graham, *Hell's Observer* (Canal Winchester, OH: Badgley, 2012), 44, 60, 98; Lawrence, *Fighting Soldier*, 114–115; Morale Branch officers survey, 25.

28. Charles Strikell, 5th FA, 1st Div; Letter from Lloyd Short, 6th Marines to "Dear Father," dated May 12, 1918, both in MHIWWIS.

29. Morale Branch officers survey, 19–20, 26–34, 61.

30. Report of Raymond B. Fosdick to Secretary of War Newton Baker, Subject: Report to the Secretary of War on the Relation of Officers and Men in the AEF, dated April 17, 1919, in NARA, RG 165, Entry 376, Box 18.

31. Report from Deputy Chief of Staff, SOS, to Commanding General SOS, titled *The Reclassification System of the A.E.F. (Blois)*, dated May 15, 1919, in NARA, RG 120, Entry 465, Box 2257, "Reclassification System Combat Officers' Depot," 1–6, 22–21.

32. Report from Commanding General, Combat Officers' Depot, to the Adjutant General, AEF, subject: "Re-Classification of Officers," dated May 22, 1919, in NARA, RG 120, Entry 465, Box 2254, File "The Reclassification System at Gondrecourt," 6; Harvey L. Harris, *The War as I Saw It: 1918 Letters of a Tank Corps Lieutenant* (Saint Paul: Pogo Press, 1998), 57; Richard Faulkner, "'Gone Blooey' Pershing's System for Addressing Officer Incompetency and Inefficiency," *Army History* 95 (Spring 2015): 7–25.

33. Wendell Westover, *Suicide Battalions* (New York: G. P. Putnam's Sons, 1929), 60; Sirmon, *That's War*, 66.

34. Westover, *Suicide Battalions*, v; Miller, "The War," 4; Emerson G. Taylor, *New England in France, 1917–1919: A History of the Twenty-Sixth Division* (Boston: Houghton Mifflin, 1920), 23; Colby L. McIntyre, *The Old Man of the 103rd: The Biography of Frank M. Hume* (Houlton, ME: Aroostock Print Shop, 1940), 57, 66–67.

CHAPTER 13. AFTER ENGLAND FAILED

1. Clair Kenamore, *From Vauquois Hill to Exermont* (St Louis: Guard Publishing, 1919), 33.

2. Henry Sheahan, *A Volunteer Poilu* (New York: Atlantic Monthly, 1916), 166–167; Arthur G. Empey, *Over the Top* (New York: G. P. Putnam's Sons, 1917), v.

3. "Memorandum for the Chief of Staff from Brig. Gen. H. P. McCain, Army Adjutant General, Subject: Foreign officers as instructors at Officers' Training Camps, dated 16 April 1917," NARA, RG 165, Microfilm File 9226, Roll 261.

4. George H. English, Jr., *History of the 89th Division, U.S.A.* (Denver: Smith-Brooks, 1920), 34–35; Charles Dienst et al., *They're From Kansas: History of the 353rd*

Infantry Regiment, 89th Division, National Army (Wichita: Eagle Press, 1921), 13; Frederick L. Huidenkopfer, The History of the 33rd Division A.E.F. (Springfield: Illinois State Historical Library, 1921), 7.

5. Gerald F. Jacobson, History of the 107th Infantry U.S.A. (New York: De Vinne Press, 1920), 13; Henry Thorn, History of 313th U.S. Infantry (New York: Wynkoop Hallenbeck Crawford, 1920), 13.

6. "Memorandum for the Chief of Staff from Col William Johnston, General Staff Corps, Subject: Foreign Officers as Instructors at Officers' Training Camps, Dissent of Colonel W. H. Johnston, General Staff, dated 27 April 1917," NARA, RG 165, Microfilm File 9226, Roll 261; Hugh L. Scott, Some Memories of a Soldier (New York: Century, 1928), 313–314.

7. Hunter Liggett, The AEF (New York: Dodd, Mead, 1927), 25; James G. Harbord, Leaves from a War Diary (New York: Dodd, Meade, 1925), 206–207; Final Report of Gen. John J. Pershing, War Department Annual Report of 1918, vol. 1, 561; John J. Pershing, My Experiences in the World War (New York: Frederick Stokes, 1931), 1:88, 150–154; Memorandum from AEF G-5 to AEF Chief of Staff, dated July 4, 1918, in Timberman-Fiske Papers, USAMHI.

8. "Extracts from the Report of Major De Reviers, Chief of the Atlanta Sub-District (French Military Mission) for the Two Weeks from March 1st to March 15th," Report of General Claudon on his visit to Fort Oglethorpe, GA, March 4–6, 1918, and Report from Col. James Martin, Acting Chief of French Advisory Mission, to Col. J. Bradley, Acting Director of Training Committee, Subject: Report of Instruction, dated April 18, 1918, NARA, RG 165, Entry 310, Box 208.

9. Lt. Col. Calvin H. Goddard, "Franco-American Relations," part 2 of "Relations between the American Expeditionary Forces and the British Expeditionary Forces: 1917–1920," Army War College Historical Section, June 1942, USAMHI, Appendix 7; B. A. Colonna, ed., The History of Company B, 311th Infantry in the World War (Freehold, NJ: Transcript Printing House, 1922), 19; Albert M. Ettinger, A Doughboy with the Fighting 69th (Shippensburg, PA: White Mane, 1992), 80–81.

10. Goddard, "Franco-American Relations," 10; Frank Sibley, With the Yankee Division in France (Boston: Little, Brown, 1919), 48–49; Anonymous, Wine, Women and War: A Diary of Disillusionment (New York: J. H. Sears, 1926), 14.

11. James A. Murrin, With the 112th in France (Philadelphia: J. B. Lippencott, 1919), 101; W. A. Sirmon, That's War (Atlanta: Linmon, 1929), 101–106; Evan A. Edwards, From Doniphan to Verdun: The Official History of the 140th Infantry (Lawrence: World Company, 1920), 29; Goddard, "Franco-American Relations," Appendix 7.

12. "Report of Training in the American Expeditionary Forces," from AEF G-5 to AEF Chief of Staff AEF, dated July 4, 1918, 29; Timberman-Fiske Papers, USAMHI; Memorandum from Headquarters Army Schools, American E. F. to Directors, Army School of the Line, Army Infantry Specialists' School, and Army Candidates' School, dated August 30, 1918, NARA, RG 120, Records of the AEF, G5 Schools, Army Candidate School, Box 1639, File 325.16 "British Instructors"; U.S.

Army in the World War, vol. 14, *Reports*, 303–304, 403; Donald Smythe, *Pershing: General of the Armies* (Bloomington: Indiana University Press, 1986), 170; Pershing, *My Experiences*, vol. 1, 152–153, and vol. 2, 114–115.

13. Robert R. McCormick, *The Army of 1918* (New York: Harcourt, Brace and Howe, 1920), 67–69; Mark E. Grotelueschen, *The AEF Way of War* (New York: Cambridge University Press, 2007), 36–38, 343–352.

14. Pablo Garcia, 356 IN, 89 Div, MHIWWIS; Lee Kennett, "The A.E.F. through French Eyes," *Military Review* 52, no. 11 (November 1972): 6; *The U.S. Army in the World War*, vol. 3, *Training and Use of American Units with the British and French*, 292–295.

15. Ashby Williams, *Experiences of the Great War* (Roanoke: Stone Printing, 1919), 16–19; Kenamore, *From Vauquois*, 32–33; "Classification Camp Report," dated September 11, 1918, to Maj. Charles Gentsch, G-2, 83rd Division, NARA, RG 120, Entry 195, Box 1.

16. William L. Langer, *Gas and Flame in World War I* (New York: Knopf, 1965), xxi; David Dimbley and David Reynolds, *An Ocean Apart* (New York: Random House, 1988), 52–53: H. C. Allen, *Great Britain and the United States* (New York: Archon Books, 1969), 163–166; Bradford Perkins, *The Great Rapprochement* (New York: Antheneum, 1969), 78–84.

17. Colonna, *311th Infantry*, 30–31; Goddard, "Relations between the American Expeditionary Forces and the British Expeditionary Forces," 12; Williams, *Experiences*, 16–19; F. L. Miller, memoir, "The War to End All Wars," 5, Emory.

18. Miller, "The War," 5; Cornelius Chandler, 320 FA, 82 Div, MHIWWIS.

19. Williams, *Experiences*, 19.

20. Colonna, *311th Infantry*, 17; Leslie Baker, *The Story of Company B, 106th Machine Gun Battalion, 27th Division, U.S.A.* (New York: unit published, 1920), 30.

21. "Classification Camp Report," dated October 21, 1918, to Maj. Charles Gentsch, G-2, 83rd Division, NARA, RG 120, Entry 195, Box 1; Knud Olsen, 325th IN, 82nd Div, MHIWWIS.

22. Dienst, *They're From Kansas*, 24–25; Joseph Lawrence *Fighting Soldier* (Boulder: Colorado Associated University Press, 1985), 21, 143; Henry Berry, *Make the Kaiser Dance* (New York: Doubleday, 1978), 345–346.

23. Thurmond Baccus, 307th Field Signal Bn, manuscript; Frank Edman, 316 EN, 91 Div, both in MHIWWIS; William S. Triplet, *A Youth in the Meuse Argonne* (Columbia: University of Missouri Press, 2000), 47; Baker, *Story of Company B*, 30; Sirmon, *That's War*, 108; "Notes on Training and Discipline," Acting Inspector General, II Corps, dated October 19, 1918, NARA, RG 120, Entry 588, Box 108.

24. Frederick Sidel, QMC; Francis Moore, 103 IN, 26 Div, both in MHIWWIS; Lawrence, *Fighting Soldier*, 20–23; Goddard, "Franco-American Relations," 12; Ashby Williams observed, "To most American officers this seemed an utter waste of time to have tea and toast in the middle of the afternoon." Williams, *Experiences*, 17–18.

25. James Luby, ed., *One Who Gave His Life: War Letters of Quincy Sharpe Mills* (New York: G. P. Putnam's Sons, 1923), 405; Harbord, *Leaves*, 156–157; Williams, *Experiences*, 16–17. Despite his soldiers' dislike of the Brits, the officer admitted, "the few English combat troops that I encountered seemed a fairly decent bunch." Colonna, *311th Infantry*, 30–31.

26. Lee J. Levinger, *A Jewish Chaplain in France* (New York: Macmillan, 1921), 41, 168–169; George Palmer, 102 IN, 26 Div, MHIWWIS; Sgt. David A. Pyle, unpublished manuscript, Patton Museum of Cavalry and Armor (since moved to Fort Benning, GA). Goddard observed, "Americans appear to have fraternized most readily with Scottish and Australians, less quickly with the English ... In the end they found themselves on better terms with the Australians than did the soldiers from the British Isles." Goddard, "Franco-American Relations," 10.

27. Letter from Milton Sweningsen to his mother, dated June 23, 1918, MHIWWIS; Charles MacArthur, *War Bugs* (New York: Doubleday, Doran, 1929), 37; William Brown, *The Adventures of an American Doughboy* (Tacoma: Smith-Kinney, 1919), 30.

28. "Classification Camp Report," dated October 3, 1918, to Maj. Charles Gentsch, G-2, 83rd Division, NARA, RG 120, Entry 195, Box 1.

29. Ettinger, *Fighting 69th*, 64–65, 126–127; L. V. Jacks, *Service Record by an Artilleryman* (New York: Charles Scribner's Sons, 1928), 140–143; Everett Hawley, 18 IN, 1 Div, MHIWWIS.

30. Edward S. Johnston, "A Study of the Nature of United States Infantry Tactics for Open Warfare on July 18, 1918, and of Their Points of Difference as Contrasted with the United States Army Tactics Taught in 1914," CARL, Appendix IV, 2–4; John W. Castles, "War Diary of John W. Castles," 19, and letter dated April 4, 1918, Castles Papers, USMA; "Classification Camp Report," dated October 3, 1918, to Maj. Charles Gentsch, G-2, 83rd Division, NARA, RG 120, Entry 195, Box 1.

31. Kenamore, *From Vauquois*, 45.

32. Charles B. Holt, *Heroes of the Argonne* (Kansas City: Franklin Hudson Publishing, 1919), 41; Levi E. Hemrick, *Once A Marine* (New York: Carlton Press, 1968), 73; Berry, *Kaiser Dance*, 131.

33. Elmer Straub, *A Sergeants Diary in the World War*, Indiana Historical Collections, vol. 10 (Indianapolis: Indiana Historical Commission, 1923), 43, 118; Paul Seelig, 18 IN, 1 Div, MHIWWIS; Leslie Langille, *Men of the Rainbow* (Hamond, IN: W. B. Coakley, 1933), 66.

34. Triplet, *Youth*, 96; MacArthur, *War Bugs*, 38, 88.

35. Goddard, "Franco-American Relations," 17; Warren Jackson, *His Time in Hell* (Novato: Presidio Press, 2001), 86–87; "Classification Camp Report," dated October 22, 1918, to Maj. Charles Gentsch, G-2, 83rd Division, NARA, RG 120, Entry 195, Box 1.

36. Paul Schmidt, *Co. C, 127th Infantry in the World War* (Sheboygan: Press Publishing, 1919), 139–140; Harbord, *Leaves*, 302; Hemrick, *Once A Marine*, 142, 164; Goddard, "Franco-American Relations," Appendix 2.

37. "Classification Camp Report," dated September 23, 1918, to Maj. Charles Gentsch, G-2, 83rd Division, NARA, RG 120, Entry 195, Box 1; Goddard, "Franco-American Relations," 2, Appendixes 4, 5, and 6; Hervey Allen, *Towards the Flame* (New York: Grosset and Dunlap, 1926), 269–273.

38. Goddard, "Franco-American Relations," 2, Appendixes 4 and 5.

39. Allen, *Towards the Flame*, 6; Philip Foster, 356 IN, 89 Div, MHIWWIS.

CHAPTER 14. HARSH SCHOOLMASTERS, DEVIOUS HUNS, AND
DEJECTED PRISONERS

1. E. Alexander Powell, *Fighting in Flanders* (Toronto: McClelland, Goodale and Stewart, 1915), 91; Charles V. Genthe, *American War Narratives* (New York: David Lewis, 1969), 38–39; *Literary Digest*, September 12, 1914, 441–445, 449–460.

2. Richard Harding Davis, *With the Allies* (New York: Charles Scribner's Sons, 1915), vii–x, 29–30; Arnold Bennett, *Over There* (New York: George H. Doran, 1915), 40, 17; Edward E. Hunt, *War Bread* (New York: Henry Holt, 1916), 107.

3. James D. Squires, *British Propaganda at Home and in the United States from 1914 to 1917* (Cambridge, MA: Harvard University Press, 1935), 45–48; M. L. Sanders and Philip M. Taylor, *British Propaganda during the First World War* (London: MacMillan Press, 1982), 167–186; Celia M. Kingsbury, *For Home and Country: World War I Propaganda on the Home Front* (Lincoln: University of Nebraska Press, 2010), 218–261.

4. James Luby, ed., *One Who Gave All: War Letters of Quincy Sharpe Mills* (New York: G. P. Putnam's Sons, 1923), 346, 412; Letter from George O'Brien to his mother, dated October 3, 1918, MHIWWIS.

5. B. A. Colonna, ed., *The History of Company B, 311th Infantry in the World War* (Freehold, NJ: Transcript Printing House, 1922), 16; Anonymous (Bob Casey), *The Cannoneers Have Hairy Ears* (New York: J. H. Sears, 1927), 137–138.

6. Journal of Sgt. Albert Robinson, entry for July 25, 1918, NWWIM; Letter from Lt. Aldridge to Col. W. M. Whitman, dated January 1, 1919, Whitman Papers, 325th IN, 82nd Div; Walter Wolf, 129th IN, 33rd Div, both in MHIWWIS.

7. Robert R. McCormick, *The Army of 1918* (New York: Harcourt, Brace and Howe, 1920), 71–72; Knud Olsen, 325th IN, 82nd Div, MHIWWIS.

8. Robert C. Walton, ed., *Over There: European Reaction to Americans in World War I* (Itasca, IL: F.E. Peacock, 1971), 196; Report from the 102nd Regt. to the 63rd IN Bde, NARA, RG 165, German Miscellaneous File, Box 200; Ernst Otto, *The Battle at Blanc Mont* (Annapolis: United States Naval Institute, 1930), 79, 112–113, 119, 165, 192–194; "Experiences with the American Method of Combat," 111th IN Regiment, dated October 26, 1918; "Experiences from Last Action," German 1st Battalion 170th Infantry Regiment, dated October 20, 1918; Group Argonne, report dated October 10, 1918; Report of 1st Guard Infantry Division, September 30, 1918; 5th Guards Division Battle Diary entry for October 4, 1918; Report of the 3rd Bn 150th Infantry, dated October 5, 1918; Report of the 2nd Bn 150th Infantry, dated October 14, 1918, all in, War Department, *World War Records, First Division, A.E.F.*

Regular, vol. 4, *German Documents: Meuse-Argonne* (Washington, DC: Army War College, 1930), n.p.; "Candid Comments on the American Soldier of 1917–1918 and Kindred Topics by the Germans," AEF GHQ Intelligence Section, Chaumont, France, 1919, 6–14, USAMHI.

9. "Operations of the Base Censors Office," dated January 13, 1919, NARA, RG 120, Entry 226, Box 6107; Memorandum from Base Censor, AEF to Chief, Prisoner of War Mail Section, entitled "Propaganda Letters," dated December 6, 1918, NARA, RG 120, Entry 226, Box 6108.

10. Diary of Pvt. Gilbert Max, 307th IN, 77th Div, entry for September 30, 1918, NWWIM; Warren Jackson, *His Time in Hell* (Novato: Presidio Press, 2001), 202.

11. "Casualties during Operations"; "My Experiences in the Argonne Drive," from Sgt. F. J. Hawke, dated December 16, 1918; "Experiences in the Argonne," from 1st Sgt. John H. Grove, dated December 17, 1918, in Whitman Papers.

12. William Graham, *Hell's Observer* (Canal Winchester: Badgley, 2012), 8; William Brown, *The Adventures of an American Doughboy* (Tacoma: Smitth-Kinney, 1919), 28–30.

13. Journal of Sgt. Albert Robinson, NWWIM; Hervey Allen, *Towards the Flame* (New York: Grosset and Dunlap, 1926), 182–183.

14. Diary of William Phillips, entry for September 29, 1918, NWWIM; Letter from Harry Callison to "My Dear Mother," dated October 16, 1918, author's collection; Graham, *Hell's Observer*, 104; for examples of German treachery from the pages of *Stars and Stripes*, see "Yanks Learn From German Methods," June 28, 1918, 2; and "Kamerad," August 2, 1918, 1.

15. L. V. Jacks, *Service Record by an Artilleryman* (New York: Charles Scribner's Sons, 1928), 238; Pvt. Frank William Graves, 28th IN, 1st Div, MHIWWIS; POW Rudolf Gordun to Prof. Gordun, undated, in NARA, RG 120, Entry 226, Box 6109, Folder 1.

16. Inspector General, 5th Army Corps, "Report of Operations Argonne-Meuse, September 26–November 11, Extracts of Reports of Div. Inspectors"; "Notes Made by the Inspector General, AEF during the Active Operations from September 12, 1918, to November 11, 1918," both in NARA, RG 120, Entry 588, Box 116; Inspector General, 26th Division, "Points Noted during Operations of September 12th, 13th and 14th," dated September 30, 1918, NARA, RG 120, Entry 588, Box 108.

17. Inspector General, 82nd Division, "Daily Report of Past 24 Hours," dated October 15, 1918, NARA, RG 120, Entry 796, Box 3; "Memorandum for Inspector 5th Army Corps," from 89th Division Inspector General, dated October 18, 1918, NARA, RG 120, Entry 590, Box 1; Inspector General, 5th Army Corps "Report of Operations Argonne-Meuse, September 26–November 11, Extracts of Reports of Div. Inspectors," NARA, RG 120, Entry 588, Box 116; Brown, *Adventures*, 46; Pfc. Thurmond Baccus, 307th Field Signal Bn, unpublished manuscript, USMHI Survey.

18. Hans Passin to Paul Passin, December 24, 1918, NARA, RG 120, Entry 226, Box 6109, "Translations of German Prisoners of War Mail," Folder 2; Otto Teubel to

Otto Teubel, dated January 8, 1919; Lt. Alfred Willman to Frederick Feist, February 20, 1919, both in NARA, RG 120, Entry 226, Box 6109, Folder 1.

19. Lt. F. Clausen to Thomas Clausen, dated January 12, 1919; Paul Lucas to Lydia Schepasky, February 23, 1919, both in NARA, RG 120, Entry 226, Box 6109, Folder 1; Lt. Joseph Zahn to Anton Zahn, March 7, 1919; Undated and unascribed translation of POW letter, both in NARA, RG 120, Entry 226, Box 6109, Folder 2.

20. T. Strebe to POW Bernard Hasenhorst, dated December 28, 1918; Ed Harrison to Kurt Harrison, March 2, 1919, both in NARA, RG 120, Entry 226, Box 6109, Folder 1; Hans Zierke to Kurt Zierke, December 11, 1918, in NARA, RG 120, Entry 226, Box 6109, Folder 2; Paul Schmidt, *Co. C, 127th Infantry in the World War* (Sheboygan: Press Publishing, 1919), 144.

21. Carl Schneider to Elly Frolich, January 5, 1919; Carl Lips to Mrs. Meininger, undated, both in NARA, RG 120, Entry 226, Box 6109, Folder 1; P. W. Schuberth to P. Schuberth, February 5, 1919; Paul Waldo to Agnes Waldo, February 16, 1919, both in NARA, RG 120, Entry 226, Box 6109, "Translations of German Prisoners of War Mail," Folder 2, POW, in NARA, RG 120, Entry 226, Box 6109, Folder 2.

22. Richard Obersigner to "Dear Wife and Children" undated; Undated and unascribed letter translation, both in NARA, RG 120, Entry 226, Box 6109, Folder 2; Ernst Haina to Anna Hoss, undated, in NARA, RG 120, Entry 226, Box 6109, Folder 1.

23. Richard B. Speed, III, *Prisoners, Diplomats and the Great War* (New York: Greenwood Press, 1990), 123–138; Lt. I. R. Fredrich, undated letter, NARA, RG 120, Entry 226, Box 6109, Folder 2; Lt. F. Clausen to Thomas Clausen, dated January 12, 1919, NARA, RG 120, Entry 226, Box 6109, Folder 1.

24. P. W. Schuberth to P. Schuberth, February 5, 1919, NARA, RG 120, Entry 226, Box 6109, Folder 2; Walter Mattes to Helene Pruss, March 16, 1919, NARA, RG 120, Entry 226, Box 6109, Folder 1.

25. Ernst Pardolk to Grete Druckhamer, March 21, 1919, NARA, RG 120, Entry 226, Box 6109, Folder 1; Lt. D. R. Klopter to Richard Klopter, February 6, 1919, NARA, RG 120, Entry 226, Box 6109, Folder 2.

26. Paul Weigelt to Henrich Weigelt, dated January 15, 1919, in NARA, RG 120, Entry 226, Box 6109, Folder 1; Speed, *Prisoners*, 130–133.

27. Speed, *Prisoners*, 133.

CHAPTER 15. TRAINING AND TRENCHES IN FRANCE

1. Tom Carroll, 16th IN, 1st Div, "Tom Carroll's Diary," MHIWWIS.

2. John J. Pershing, *My Experiences in the World War*, vol. 1 (New York: Frederick Stokes, 1931), 91.

3. Ibid., 1:154; U.S. Army Center of Military History, *The U.S. Army in the World War*, vol. 3, *Training and Use of American Units with the British and French* (Washington, DC: Government Printing Office, 1988), 36, 59–64; AEF GHQ, "Program of Training for the 1st Division, A.E.F.," October 6, 1917, *World War Records, First*

Division, vol. 20, *Training First Division* (Washington, DC: Army War College, 1930), n.p.; AEF GHQ, "Program of Training for the 2nd Division," in NARA, RG 120, G5–Army Candidate School, Box 1637, File 350.

4. Leslie Martin, 16th IN, 1st Div, "The Story of My Life"; "Tom Carroll's Diary," both in MHIWWIS.

5. Raymond S. Tompkins, *The Story of the Rainbow Division* (New York: Boni & Liveright, 1919), 23–26; John H. Taber, *The Story of the 168th Infantry*, vol. 1 (Iowa City: State Historical Society of Iowa, 1925), 44–58; Martin Hogan, *The Shamrock Battalion in the Great War* (Columbia: University of Missouri Press, 2007), 28–32; Alison Reppy, *Rainbow Memories* (Executive Committee, First Battalion, 166th Infantry, 1919), 9–10.

6. Hogan, *Shamrock*, 32; Taber, *168th Infantry*, 51, 57.

7. James G. Harbord, *Leaves from a War Diary* (New York: Dodd, Meade, 1925), 134–135; Lt. Col. Calvin H. Goddard, "Relations between the American Expeditionary Forces and the British Expeditionary Forces, 1917–1920," Army War College Historical Section, June 1942, USAMHI, part 1, 10–12; James A. Murrin, *With the 112th Infantry in France: A Doughboy's Story of the War* (Philadelphia: J. B. Lippencott, 1919), 101.

8. Chester Baker, *Doughboy's Diary* (Shippensburg, PA: Burd Street Press, 1998), 49; Christian A. Bach and Henry N. Hall, *The Fourth Division: Its Services and Achievements in the World War* (New York: Country Life Press, 1920), 48; Edward G. Buxton, ed., *Official History of the 82nd Division* (Indianapolis: Bobbs-Merrill, 1919), 12.

9. Charles M. Clement, ed., *Pennsylvania in the World War: An Illustrated History of the Twenty-Eighth Division*, vol. 2 (Pittsburgh: States Publication Society, 1921), 570; Baker, *Doughboy's Diary*, 49; H. G. Proctor, *The Iron Division in the World War* (Philadelphia: John C. Winston, 1919), 26.

10. Joseph Sanborn, *The 131st Infantry in the World War* (Chicago: privately printed, 1919), 29–35.

11. Charles Dienst et al., *They're from Kansas: History of the 353rd Infantry Regiment, 89th Division, National Army* (Wichita: Eagle Press, 1921), 33–35; Three Hundred and Forth Engineer Regiment, *The Official History of the Three Hundred and Forth Engineer Regiment* (Lancaster, PA: Steinman & Foltz, 1920), 59.

12. Diary of Captain Clarence Minick, NWWIM.

13. *The U.S. Army in the World War*, 3:162; Henry Berry, *Make the Kaiser Dance* (New York: Doubleday, 1978), 363; Charles Minder, *This Man's War* (New York: Pevensey Press, 1931), 90–94, 125, 154–164.

14. Letter from Dewitt McIntyre to "Dear folks at home," undated, author's collection.

15. James M. Howard, *The Autobiography of a Regiment: A History of the 304th Field Artillery in the World War* (New York: unit published, 1920), 58–64; Diary of Leland O. Linman, B Battery, 129th Field Artillery, 35th Div, NWWIM.

16. Taber, *168th Infantry*, 72; George H. English, Jr., *History of the 89th Division, U.S.A.* (Denver: Smith-Brooks, 1920), 56.

17. Journal of Sgt. Albert Robinson; Letter from Ira Wilkenson to "Dear Sister," dated May 25, 1918, UGA; Richard McBride, 325th IN, 82nd Div, manuscript, MHIWWIS; W. A. Sirmon, *That's War* (Atlanta: Linmon, 1929), 163, 176–180; William S. Triplet, *A Youth in the Meuse-Argonne* (Columbia: University of Missouri Press, 2000), 95.

18. Charles B. Hoyt, *Heroes of the Argonne* (Kansas City: Franklin Hudson, 1919), 51; Robert Alexander, *Memories of the World War, 1917–1918* (New York: MacMillan, 1931), 16–18, 112.

19. Triplet, *Youth*, 95; John Cutchins and George Stewart, *History of the 29th Division, 1917–1919* (Philadelphia: MacCalla, 1921), 106; Emerson G. Taylor, *New England in France 1917–1919: A History of the Twenty-Sixth Division* (Boston: Houghton Mifflin, 1920), 122–131; Taber, *168th Infantry*, 101.

20. Taber, *168th Infantry*, 73; Paul W. Schmidt, *Co. C, 127th Infantry in the World War* (Sheboygan, WI: Press Publishing, 1919), 20.

21. Duncan Kemerer, 111th IN, 28th Div, manuscript "My Memories as a Soldier in World War I," MHIWWIS; Frank B. Tiebout, *A History of the 305th Infantry* (New York: Wynkoop Hallenbeck Crawford, 1919), 74.

22. Taber, *168th Infantry*, 81; Journal of Sgt. Albert Robinson; John W. Castles, manuscript "War Diary of John W. Castles," 23–25, 32, Castles Papers, USMA.

23. Castles, "War Diary," 23–25, 32; Cpl. Frank Faulkner, 23rd IN, 2nd Div, manuscript, MHIWWIS; Triplet, *Youth*, 98–99; Frank A. Holden, *War Memories* (Athens, GA: Athens Book Company, 1922), 71–73.

24. Letter from Edward Hardin to "Dearest Mamma," dated August 5, 1918, Lower Cape Fear Historical Society, Wilmington, NC.

25. "Diary of the 82nd Division," by 1st Sgt. Charles Fagner, Whitman Papers, 325th IN, 82nd Div, MHIWWIS.

26. Warren Jackson, *His Time in Hell* (Novato: Presidio Press, 2001), 66–68.

27. Richard S. Faulkner, "A Georgian in the Argonne: Seeking Redemption on Corney Ridge," *Georgia Historical Quarterly* 95, no. 1 (Spring 2011): 21–41.

28. "Tom Carroll's Diary"; Journal of Sgt. Albert Robinson; Cutchins and Stewart, *29th Division*, 113–121.

29. Letter from Albert Dahinden to Mrs. E. K. Tomlinson, dated May 17, 1918, author's collection.

30. Letter from Edward Hardin to "Dearest Mamma," dated August 1, 1918, Lower Cape Fear Historical Society, Wilmington, NC; Letter from Pvt. Paul F. Andrews to his uncle, dated July 18, 1918, NWWIM.

31. AEF GHQ, *Equipment Manuals for Service in Europe*, series A, no. 1, *Infantry Regiments* (Chaumont: AEF AG Printing Section, May 1918), 55–58.

32. William Graham, *Hell's Observer* (Canal Winchester: Badgley, 2012), 123; Charles MacArthur, *War Bugs* (New York: Doubleday, Doran, 1929), 57; James Luby, ed., *One Who Gave All: War Letters of Quincy Sharpe Mills* (New York: G. P. Putnam's Sons, 1923), 368.

33. Evan A. Edwards, *From Doniphan to Verdun: The Official History of the 140th*

Infantry (Lawrence: World Company, 1920), 41; Thurmond Baccus, 307th Field Signal Bn, manuscript, MHIWWIS.

34. Hoyt, *Heroes*, 51; Edwards, *From Doniphan to Verdun*, 42; Cutchins and Stewart, *29th Division*, 91; Letter from Pvt. Paul F. Andrews, to his aunt, dated June 2, 1918, NWWIM.

35. AEF GHQ, *Report of Officers Convened by Special Orders No.98, GHQ AEF 09 April 1919*, Annex R, 19, Army War College Library; "Replies to Officers' Questionnaires," Morale Branch of the War College, dated November 5, 1919, NARA, RG 165, NM 84, Entry 378, Box 6, 54 (hereafter Morale Branch Survey).

36. Fred Takes, 325th IN, 82nd Div, manuscript, MHIWWIS; Morale Branch Survey, 54; Alexander, *Memories*, 16–18.

37. Report of Infantry Specialist School, Langres, France, dated November 11, 1918; *U.S. Army in the World War*, 14:347; Morale Branch Survey, 54; Emil B. Gansser, *History of the 126th Infantry in the War with Germany* (Grand Rapids: Dean Hicks, 1920), 52–53.

CHAPTER 16. "MOTHER, TAKE DOWN YOUR SERVICE FLAG, YOUR SON'S IN THE S.O.S."

1. Letter from Edward Hardin to "Dearest Mamma," dated February 2, 1919, Lower Cape Fear Historical Society, Wilmington, NC.

2. James G. Harbord, *The American Army in France, 1917–1919* (Boston: Little, Brown, 1936), 400–402.

3. William Haseltine, *The Services of Supply of the American Expeditionary Forces: A Statistical Summary* (Washington, DC: Government Printing Office, 1919), 27, 29, 55; John J. McGrath, *The Other End of the Spear: The Tooth-to-Tail Ratio (T3R) in Modern Military Operations* (Fort Leavenworth, KS: Combat Studies Institute, 2007), 11–16.

4. John J. Niles et al., *The Songs My Mother Never Taught Me* (New York: MacAulay, 1929), 80; Clarence Mahan, "Hoosier Doughboy with the First Division World War One," 1st Div Supply TN, MHIWWIS; Carl Noble, *Jugheads behind the Lines*, ed. Grace Coats (Caldwell, ID: Caxton Printers, 1938), 132–134.

5. *Stars and Stripes*, January 3, 1919, 2; Carty Ranck, *The Doughboys' Book* (Boston: Stratford, 1925), 239.

6. Haseltine, *Services of Supply*, 18, 55, 110, 120, 166; *Stars and Stripes*, November 1, 1918, 6; Perez Simmons, *Twentieth Engineers, France, 1917, 1918, 1919* (Portland, OR: Dimm & Sons, 1919), 23–42.

7. Haseltine, *Services of Supply*, 50; AEF General Orders 33, February 20, 1918; *Stars and Stripes*, April 26, 1918, 1; and *Stars and Stripes*, July 26, 1918, 2.

8. Letter from Reginald Thomson to Lillian Cottrell, dated May 10, 1918, NWWIM; Ranck, *Doughboys' Book*, 215–216, 225–226.

9. *Stars and Stripes*, April 5, 1918, 2; Letter from Benson Oakley to Helen Oakley, dated August 29, 1918, author's collection.

10. Mahan, "Hoosier Doughboy"; Edgar Ferrill, 2nd Ammunition TN, 2nd Div; Donald Alkire, 7th Ambulance Co., 3rd Div, both in MHIWWIS; Quartermaster School, *Operations of the Quartermaster Corps, U.S. Army during the World War,* monograph 9, *Notes on Army, Corps and Division Q.M. Activities in the A.E.F. France* (Philadelphia: Quartermaster School, 1929), 81–95.

11. Letters home from Benjamin Heath, HQ, 82nd Div, dated December 26, 1917, July 23 and October 20, 1918, MHIWWIS.

12. Entry for January 16, 1918, William Haselton diary, 18th IN and Div Staff, 1st Div, MHIWWIS; Letters from Joe Scheck, to "Dear Bert," dated April 20, 1919, and to "Dear Sis," dated April 28, 1919, author's collection.

13. Niles et al., *Songs,* 113; Letter from Edward Miles to Mrs. F. J. Andrews (aunt), dated January 14, 1918, author's collection.

14. Mahan, "Hoosier Doughboy"; Earl Tesca, 15th FA, 2nd Div, "Memoirs of My Experiences in World War I," MHIWWIS.

15. Anonymous (Bob Casey), *The Cannoneers Have Hairy Ears* (New York: J. H. Sears, 1927), 182–183.

16. Benedict Crowell, *America's Munitions, 1917–1918* (Washington, DC: Government Printing Office, 1919), 492–449; William Chaikin, "Quartermaster Supply in the AEF, 1917–1918," www.qmfound.com/supply_aef.htm.

17. General Orders 79, May 27, 1918; General Orders 174, October 9, 1918.

18. Tesca, "Memoirs"; Noble, *Jugheads,* 115–116, 132–134.

19. Letters from George O'Brien, 121st FA, 32nd Div, to his mother, undated circa November 1917 and December 21, 1917, MHIWWIS; Letter from H. W. Carver to his wife, dated December 4, 1918, author's collection.

20. Crowell, *Munitions,* 499–504.

21. *Operations of the Quartermaster Corps, U.S. Army during the World War,* 81–82, 89–95; Mahan, "Hoosier Doughboy."

22. Evan J. Miller, "Diary of a Private in a Base Hospital," and letter to Anna Margaret, dated April 7, 1918, MHIWWIS; Letter from Bernard Bockemuehl to Miss E. A. Bockemuehl (sister), dated September 7, 1918, author's collection.

23. "Replies to Officers Questionnaires" from Morale Branch of the War College and War Plans Division to the Chief of Staff, dated November 5, 1919, NARA, RG 165, NM 84, Entry 378, Box 6, 21; Niles et al., *Songs,* 21, 109–112.

24. B. A. Colonna, ed., *The History of Company B, 311th Infantry in the World War* (Freehold, NJ: Transcript Printing House, 1922), 10; John Stringfellow, *Hell No!* (Boston: Meador, 1936), 163–164.

25. W. A. Sirmon, *That's War* (Atlanta: Linmon, 1929), 193–194; Ashby Williams, *Experiences of the Great War* (Roanoke: Stone Printing, 1919), 60.

26. Hugh Thompson, *Trench Knives and Mustard Gas* (College Station: Texas A&M Press, 2004), 75–76; Jeremiah M. Evarts, *Cantigny: A Corner of the War* (Privately published, 1938), 49–61; Niles et al., *Songs,* 11.

CHAPTER 17. "HOW 'YA GONNA KEEP 'EM DOWN ON THE FARM?"

1. AEF GHQ Bulletin 54, August 7, 1918.
2. Edward M. Coffman, *The Regulars* (Cambridge, MA: Belknap Press of Harvard University Press, 2004), 78–81, 118–119; Nancy K. Bristow, *Making Men Moral* (New York: New York University Press, 1996), 2–6.
3. War Department, *Commission on Training Camp Activities* (Washington, DC: Government Printing Office, October 15, 1917), 3–5.
4. War Department, *Commission on Training Camp Activities*, 25–27; Bristow, *Making Men Moral*, 30–35; Edward M. Coffman, *The War to End All Wars* (Madison: University of Wisconsin Press, 1968), 79–81.
5. Myron Adams, ed., *The Officer's Responsibility for His Men* (Fort Sheridan, IL: locally published, 1917), viii, 46.
6. Selective Service Act of 1917, Pub. L. 65–12, 40 Stat. 76.
7. Mervyn Burke, Headquarters Company, 1st Div; George O'Brien, 121st FA, 32nd Div, both in MHIWWIS; Letter from Henry Schulz to Edward Schulz (brother), dated December 4, 1917, author's collection.
8. Weekly reports of the 91st Div Morale Officer to Chief, Military Intelligence Division, dated March 23, April 1, May 4, May 13, May 18, 1918, NARA, RG 165, Entry 377, Box 9.
9. Richard McBride, 325th IN, 82nd Div, MHIWWIS; Letter dated January 31, 1918, in Raymond Stanbeck, 6th Marines, 2nd Div, MHIWWIS; Case of 1st Lt. Clifford W. Bogan, General Court-Martial Orders No. 45, March 27, 1918; 1st Lt. David S. Carey, Blois Case Files, NARA, RG 120, Entry 541, Box 2291; War Department, *Medical Department of the United States Army in the World War*, vol. 15, *Medical Statistics*, pt. 2, *Medical and Casualty Statistics* (Washington, DC: Government Printing Office, 1925), 576, 670–671.
10. War Department, *War Department Annual Report for 1918* (Washington, DC: Government Printing Office, 1919), 251, 259; War Department, *War Department Annual Report for 1919* (Washington, DC: Government Printing Office, 1920), 694–695, 704–705; Case of Capt. Frank G. Tullidge, General Court-Martial Orders No. 7, January 12, 1918; Case of Capt. Robert G. Igoe, General Court-Martial Orders No. 35, March 7, 1918.
11. AEF GHQ, General Orders 77, December 18, 1918; "Report of the Division of Urology, A.E.F.," dated December 20, 1918, NARA, RG 120, Entry 2117, Box 1; Letter from 1st Lt. C. F. Watson to Leigh Sanford, dated July 2, 1918, Leigh Sanford Correspondence, Emory.
12. Letter from H. C. Mitchell to Leigh Sanford, dated July 30, 1918, Emory; Letter from Walter Shaw to his father dated October 31, 1917, in Water Shaw Papers, NWWIM; William Roper, 130th MGB, 35th Div; Burke, both in MHIWWIS.
13. Knud Olsen, 325th IN, 82nd Div; George O'Brien, 121st FA, 32nd Div, both in MHIWWIS.
14. Report of Arrests, 2nd Army, NARA, RG 120, Entry 918, Box 84; AEF Provost

Marshal, *History of the Provost Marshal General's Department* (Chaumont, France: AEF, April 15, 1919), sec. III-B-2, 7; 2nd Lt. Thomas Hazzard, Blois Case Files, NARA, RG 120, Entry 541, Box 2300; "Report of Conduct of American Officers" from 1st Lt. H. E. Watson to Commandant Army Schools, dated August 2, 1918, NARA, RG 120, G5 Schools, Army Candidate Schools, Box 1623, File 250.1.

15. Letter from Elmer Lewis to Goldie Little, dated August 16, 1918, author's collection; Letter from C. F. Watson to Leigh Sanford, dated July 2, 1918, Leigh Sanford Correspondence, Emory; Harry House, 325th MGB, 82nd Div, MHIWWIS.

16. Charles Minder, *This Man's War* (New York: Pevensey Press, 1931), 104–105; Letter from James Myers, 8th MGB, 3 Div to Robert Dengler, dated April 1, 1919, author's collection.

17. Edmund Grossman, 139th IN, 35th Div, MHIWWIS.

18. War Department, *Annual Report for 1919*, vol. 1, 964, 704; Harvey L. Harris, *The War as I Saw It* (St. Paul: Pogo Press, 1998), 9; Webb Ayres, 2nd Motor Supply Co., 2nd Div, Burke, both in MHIWWIS; Tape and transcripts of oral history by the author of James Lindsey, conducted on April 26, 1996, in Jonesboro, Georgia.

19. Case of 2nd Lt. Thomas M. Lynch, General Court-Martial Orders No. 113, May 29, 1918; Case of 1st Lt. Thomas E. Jones, General Court-Martial Orders No. 23, February 18, 1918; *War Department Annual Report for 1918*, 251, 259; *War Department Annual Report for 1919*, 694–695, 704–705.

20. Charles MacArthur, *War Bugs* (New York: Doubleday, Doran, 1929), 34–35.

21. Ralph Williams, 4th EN, 2nd Div; Wilbert Stambaugh, 1st Div; Charles Holbrook, 1st Div; Frank William Graves, 28th IN, 1st Div, all in MHIWWIS; *Stars and Stripes*, May 2, 1918, 2; Letter from Luther Grover to Etta Hawk (sister), dated September 23, 1918; Letter from Bernard Bockemuehl to Mrs. M. Bockemuehl (mother), dated August 4, 1918, both in author's collection.

22. L. V. Jacks, *Service Record by an Artilleryman* (New York: Charles Scribner's Sons, 1928), 106; Warren Jackson, *His Time in Hell* (Novato: Presidio Press, 2001), 46–47.

23. Letter to Andrew Magnus from "Bunny" Brown (female friend), dated October 24, 1918; Letter from Fred Neff to Miss A. W. Keichler (sister), dated August 9, 1918, both from author's collection; Lyman Varney, 3rd Bn Machine Gun Training Center, Camp Hancock, MHIWWIS.

24. Irving Crump, *Conscript 2989: Experiences of a Drafted Man* (New York: Dodd, Meade, 1918), 54; Frank Sibley, *With the Yankee Division in France* (Boston: Little, Brown, 1919), 170–171; Paul Maxwell, Camp Lee, 314th FA, 79th Div, "The Diary of a Dud," MHIWWIS.

25. Earle Poorbaugh, 26th IN, 1st Div, MHIWWIS.

26. Selective Service Act of 1917, Pub. L. 65–12, 40 Stat. 76.

27. Reports of the 91st Div Morale Officer to Chief, Military Intelligence Division, dated March 4, March 23, April 1, May 1, and May 22, 1918, NARA, RG 165, Entry 377, Box 9; "Proposed eliminations for inefficiency," and memorandum

discussing the case from the AEF Deputy Chief of Staff, LeRoy Eltinge, dated January 2, 1919, NARA, RG 120, Entry 465, Reclassification System Combat Officers' Depot, Box 2254.

28. Earle Poorbaugh, 26th IN, 1st Div; Letters from George O'Brien, 121st FA, 32nd Div, to his mother, dated December 16, 1917, and January 5, 1918, both in MHIWWIS.

29. "Report of the Division of Urology, A.E.F.," dated December 20, 1918, NARA, RG 120, Entry 2117, Box 1; George Walker, *Venereal Disease in the American Expeditionary Forces* (Baltimore: Medical Standard Book, 1922), 101.

30. AEF GHQ General Orders 6, July 2, 1917.

31. Walker, *Venereal Disease*, 46–55, 95.

32. Ibid., 48–49, 84.

33. Letter from Madam Moindroit to "the General Commanding the American Army at Langres," dated April 30, 1918, and Letter from Capt. Henry Young to Commandant, Army Schools, A.E.F., Subject: Venereal Disease in the Army Schools Area," dated July 9, 1918, in NARA, RG 120, Records of the AEF, G5 Schools, Army Candidate School, Box 1650, File 710 "Diseases, Epidemics, Vices."

34. Headquarters Army Tank School, Memorandum No. 3, February 10, 1918, NARA, RG 120, G5 Schools, Army Candidate Schools, Box 1623, File 250.1; Walker, *Venereal Disease*, 68–69.

35. *Commission on Training Camp Activities*, 25–27; Bristow, *Making Men Moral*, 30–35.

36. War Department and American Social Hygiene Association, *Keeping Fit to Fight* (New York: American Social Hygiene Association, circa 1918); AEF GHQ Bulletin 54, August 7, 1918.

37. William Roper, 130th MGB, 35th Div; Edmund Grossman, 139th IN, 35th Div, both in MHIWWIS; Letter from Paul Rhodes to Helen Naito, dated December 27, 1917, author's collection.

38. Earle Poorbaugh, 26th IN, 1st Div, MHIWWIS; Diary of Earl Cave, 58th Bde, 33rd Div, NWWIM; Letter from Robert Mercer to Robert Dengler, dated June 14, 1918, author's collection.

39. Letter from Cornelius Freely to Mae Murphy, dated March 1, 1919, author's collection; Earle Poorbaugh, 26th IN, 1st Div; House, 325th MGB, 82nd Div, both in MHIWWIS; 2nd Lt. Earnest Chase, Blois Case files, Box 2292.

40. Olsen, MHIWWIS; Walker, *Venereal Disease*, 27–31.

41. "Report of the Division of Urology, A.E.F.," dated December 20, 1918.

42. Letter from Benson Oakley to Helen Oakley, dated September 25, 1918, author's collection; Letter from Lt. H. C. Mitchell to Leigh Sanford, dated July 30, 1918; Lee J. Levinger, *A Jewish Chaplain in France* (New York: MacMillan, 1922), 176–177.

43. MacArthur, *War Bugs*, 18, 262; Letter from James Myers to Robert Dengler, dated April 1, 1919; Letter from Benson Oakley to Helen Oakley, dated August 29, 1918, both in author's collection; *Stars and Stripes*, October 25, 1918; Edward Hungerford, *With the Doughboy in France* (New York: MacMillan, 1920), 281;

W. A. Sirmon, *That's War* (Atlanta: Linmon, 1929), 184, 245–246; Henry Berry, *Make the Kaiser Dance* (New York: Doubleday, 1978), 239–240.

44. Berry, *Kaiser Dance*, 7, 410; John W. Thompson, Jr., *Fix Bayonets* (New York: Charles Scribner's Sons, 1927), 68; Albert Ettinger, *A Doughboy with the Fighting 69th* (Shippensburg, PA: White Mane, 1992), 150; Letters from George O'Brien, 121st FA, 32nd Div, to his mother, dated December 16, 1917, and January 5, 1918, MHIWWIS; John J. Niles et al., *The Songs My Mother Never Taught Me* (New York: MacAulay, 1929), 50.

45. Henry McCoy, 105 EN, 30th Div, MHIWWIS; Niles et al., *Songs*, 56–57; Sirmon, *That's War*, 184.

46. Walker, *Venereal Disease*, 101.

47. War Department, *The Medical Department of the United States Army in the World War*, vol. 9, *Communicable and Other Diseases* (Washington, DC: Government Printing Office, 1928), 263–271.

48. Sanitary Reports for the units and months stated in "Sanitary Reports, 1918–1919," NARA, RG 120, Entry 2113, Boxes 5204, 5207, 5208, and 5209.

49. Ibid.

50. Walker, *Venereal Disease*, 21–23, 100–113; Saumur Field Artillery School, Sanitary Report for November 1918, NARA, RG 120, Entry 2113, Box 5209.

51. Levi E. Hemrick, *Once A Marine* (New York: Carlton Press, 1968), 56; Letter from Robert Bressler to "Dear Parents," dated October 25, 1918, author's collection; Letter from Pvt. Paul F. Andrews to his aunt, dated August 25, 1918, NWWIM; James Luby, ed., *One Who Gave All: War Letters of Quincy Sharpe Mills* (New York: G. P. Putnam's Sons, 1923), 381; Robert Glover, 242 MGB, 89th Div; Clarence Goist, 361 IN, 91st Div; Ralph Williams, 4th EN, 2nd Div, all in MHIWWIS.

52. Sirmon, *That's War*, 116; Frank Holden, *War Memories* (Athens: Athens Book Company, 1922), 200–201; José de la Luz Sáenz, *The World War I Diary of José de la Luz Sáenz*, ed. and trans. Emilo Zamora (College Station: Texas A&M Press, 2014), 95; Clarence L. Mahan, 1st Div, "Hoosier Doughboy with the First Division," MHIWWIS.

53. Walker, *Venereal Disease*, 109.

54. Sanitary Reports for the HQ II Corps, November 1918, and for the 27th and 30th Divisions for October and November 1918, NARA, RG 120, Entry 2113, Boxes 5207–5209. In October and November 1918 the 30th Division had forty cases of VD and 475 preventative treatments while during the same period the 27th Division had forty-four infections and 565 who received prophylaxes. Even the II Corps headquarters seemed to enjoy its time with the British. In November the unit had a strength of 615 men and had 421 prophylactic treatments and five cases of VD.

55. Walker, *Venereal Disease*, 82–83, 112.

56. Ibid., 20–24; Sanitary Report for the Savoie Leave Center, November 1918, NARA, RG 120, Entry 2113, Box 5209; Letter from Fay Neff to Adam Keichler (brother-in-law), dated January 29, 1919, author's collection.

57. Walker, *Venereal Disease*, 101–108; Burke; Herman Dacus, 28th IN, 1st Div; George O'Brien, all in MHIWWIS.

58. MacArthur, *War Bugs*, 52; Arthur E. Barbeau and Florette Henri, *The Unknown Soldiers* (Philadelphia: Temple University Press, 1974), 115; *Men of Bronze*, produced by William Miles and Killian Shaw, Pacific Arts Video, 1977; Berry, *Kaiser Dance*, 425.

59. Walker, *Venereal Disease*, 71, 113; Barbeau and Henri, *Unknown Soldiers*, 52–55; Sanitary Reports for Stevedore Division Camp Foreston Creil, November 1918, 324th Labor Bn, October 1918, and 321st Labor Bn, November 1918, NARA, RG 120, Entry 2113, Boxes 5207 and 5209; "Report of the Division of Urology, A.E.F.", dated December 20, 1918, NARA, RG 120, Entry 2117.

60. Walker, *Venereal Disease*, 127–132; James Lindsey oral history.

61. Walker, *Venereal Disease*, 223–231.

62. War Department, *War Department Annual Reports, 1918*, vol. 1, pt. 1 (Washington, DC: Government Printing Office, 1919), 251, 258–260; War Department, *War Department Annual Reports, 1919*, vol. 1, pt.1 (Washington, DC: Government Printing Office, 1920), 694–695, 704–705; War Department, *A Manual for Courts-Martial, Corrected to April 15, 1917* (Washington, DC: Government Printing Office, 1917), 271.

63. Tom Carroll, 16th IN, 1st Div, "Tom Carroll's Diary," MHIWWIS; 2nd Lt. John W. Royer, Blois case files, Box 2313; Maj. L. H. English, Blois case files, Box 2296.

64. Martin Blumenson, *The Patton Papers*, vol. 1 (Boston: Houghton Mifflin, 1972), 429; James Lindsey oral history.

CHAPTER 18. "SKY PILOTS," "HOLY JOES," AND
THE DOUGHBOY'S RELIGION

1. Richard McBride, 325th IN, 82nd Div, manuscript, "Passing in Review," MHIWWIS.

2. Report of Camp Devens intelligence officer, dated October 11, 1918, NARA, RG 165, Entry 377, Box 3, Camp Devens file; Memorandum "Regimental Chaplains" from Senior Chaplain 5th Div to Chaplain's Office, GHQ, dated July 12, 1918, NARA, RG 120, Entry 597, Box 3820.

3. Reports of Senior Chaplains, 36th Div for October 1918; 26th Div for November 8, 1918; 92nd Div for October 1918, NARA, RG 120, Entry 597, Boxes 3821 and 3822.

4. Letter from Roy Burkhart to Jacob Burkhart (cousin), dated March 23, 1919, author's collection.

5. Reports of the chaplains of the 7th Infantry for August 1918; 92nd Div for November 1918; 81st Div for November 1918; 82nd Div for October 1918, NARA, RG 120, Entry 597, Boxes 3820 and 2822.

6. Alvin York, *Sergeant York: His Own Life Story* (Garden City, NY: Doubleday, Doran, 1928), 144–145, 152, 154–155, 168–175, 201–202, 278.

7. Letter from Henry Schulz, to Emily Schulz (sister), dated December 14, 1917, author's collection; Edwin P. Arpin, "A Wisconsinite in World War I: Reminiscences

of Edwin P. Arpin, Jr.," ed. Ira Berlin, *Wisconsin Magazine of History*, Autumn 1967, 136.

8. Thurmond Baccus, 307th Field Signal Bn, unpublished manuscript; Letter from Milton Sweningsen, 138th IN, 35th Div, to his mother, dated October 2, 1918, both in MHIWWIS.

9. York, *Sergeant York*, 202, 278; Letter from Harry Callison to "Dear Mother," dated October 2, 1918, author's collection; Vernon Mossman, 18th IN, 1st Div, MHIWWIS.

10. Letter from Lunie McCarlry to May Peters (sister), dated September 13, 1918, author's collection; Lee J. Levinger, *A Jewish Chaplain in France* (New York: MacMillan, 1922), 155; Reports of 30th Infantry Chaplain on November 3, 1918, and 26th Div Chaplain on October 27, 1918, NARA, RG 120, Entry 597, Boxes 3821 and 3820.

11. Warren Jackson, *His Time in Hell* (Novato: Presidio Press, 2001), 109–110; Charles Minder, *This Man's War* (New York: Pevensey Press, 1931), 331–332; Cornelius Chandler, 320th FA, 82nd Div, MHIWWIS; Reports of 30th Infantry Chaplain, November 3, 1918.

12. Minder, *This Man's War*, 52, 68–69; Richard Schweitzer, *The Cross and the Trench: Religious Faith and Doubt among British and American Great War Soldier* (Westport: Praeger, 2003), 218–220.

13. Letter from Reginald Thomson, 813th Pioneer IN, to Lillian Cottrell, dated January 27, 1918, NWWIM; Letter from Thomas Marshall to Mrs. E. K. Tomlinson, undated, author's collection.

14. Fred Takes, 325th IN, 82nd Div, diary entries for May 19, October 5, and November 16, 1918, manuscript "World War I Co A, 325th Inf. 82nd Div," MHIWWIS.

15. U.S. Army Center of Military History, *The U.S. Army in the World War*, vol. 15, *Reports of the Commander-In-Chief, Staff Sections and Services* (Washington, DC: Government Printing Office, 1991), 419–420.

16. "Examination of Candidates for Appointment as Chaplains in the National Army," dated July 27, 1918; Form letter for chaplaincy recommendations, General Committee on Army and Navy Chaplains, NARA, RG 120, Entry 597, Box 3820; Michael Shay, *Sky Pilots: The Yankee Division Chaplains in World War I* (Columbia: University of Missouri Press, 2014), 2–7.

17. 79th Div Chaplains File, NARA, RG 120, Entry 597, Box 3822.

18. Celestine Bittle, *Soldiering for Cross and Flag* (Milwaukee: Bruce Publishing, 1929), 48–51.

19. Application for chaplaincy for Pvt. Oliver Enselman, NARA, RG 120, Entry 597, Box 3820.

20. *The U.S. Army in the World War*, vol. 15, 421; Reports of Chaplains, 2nd Div for September 19, 1918; 89th Div for October 1918; 92nd Div for October 1918, NARA, RG 120, Entry 597, Boxes 3820 and 3822.

21. Reports of 3rd Div Chaplain, September 2, 1918; 4th Infantry Regiment for August

1918, NARA, RG 120, Entry 597, Box 3820; William Graham, *Hell's Observer* (Canal Winchester: Badgley, 2012), 136–138.

22. AEF Chief of Chaplains, "List of Chaplains in the American A.F.," October 11, 1918, NARA, RG 120, Entry 596, Box 3826.

23. Arthur Hicks, Chaplain Corps, MHIWWIS; Bittle, *Soldiering*, 48–51.

24. Report of Chaplain, 89th Div, October 1918; "Chaplains Eighty Second Division," both in NARA, RG 120, Entry 597, Box 3822.

25. Levinger, *Jewish Chaplain*, 140; Report of 82nd Div Chaplain, September 10, 1918, NARA, RG 120, Entry 597, Box 3822.

26. Graham, *Hell's Observer*, 136–138; Ben B. Lindsey and Harvey O'Higgins, *The Doughboy's Religion* (New York: Harper & Brothers, 1920), 6–13.

27. Letter from 89th Div senior chaplain to Paul Moody, GHQ Chaplains' Office, August 11, 1918, NARA, RG 120, Entry 597, Box 3822; Levinger, *Jewish Chaplain*, 139–140.

28. Report of 37th Div Chaplain, October 6, 1918, NARA, RG 120, Entry 597, Box 3821; Levinger, *Jewish Chaplain*, 110–111, 130–131, 134, 150, 155.

29. Ibid., 8, 17–19, 149–150; Henry Berry, *Make the Kaiser Dance* (New York: Doubleday, 1978), 323; *Stars and Stripes*, May 31, 1918, 4.

30. "The Chaplain"; "The Artillery Chaplain and His Work"; "An Infantry Chaplain's Work"; L. W. Benedict, "Difficulties in Connection with Front Line Work and How to Meet Them," all in NARA, RG 120, Entry 596, Box 3826.

31. M. J. O'Connor, "Infantry Chaplain's Work"; J. J. Halliday, "An Infantry Chaplain's Work," both in NARA, RG 120, Entry 596, Box 3826.

32. Shay, *Sky Pilots*, 62–64.

33. Anonymous (Bob Casey), *The Cannoneers Have Hairy Ears* (New York: J. H. Sears, 1927), 43–45, 270–272; Levinger, *Jewish Chaplain*, 162; Horatio Rogers, *World War I through My Sights* (San Rafael: Presidio Press, 1976), 11.

34. Anonymous, *Cannoneers*, 43–45; Irwin B. March, "We Joined the Army and Saw the World," 8th Field Signal Bn and 4th Sanitary Train, MHIWWIS; Lindsey and O'Higgins, *Doughboy's Religion*, 6–13.

35. Report of 37th Div Chaplain, October 27, 1918, NARA, RG 120, Entry 597, Box 3821; Arthur Hicks, Chaplain Corps, MHIWWIS; Stephen L. Harris, *Duffy's War* (Washington, DC: Potomac Books, 2006), 299–300; Francis P. Duffy, *Father Duffy's Story* (New York: George H. Doran, 1919), 207.

36. Connell Albertine, *The Yankee Doughboy* (Boston: Branden Press, 1968), 125–126; Letter from Arthur Hicks to "Dear Kate," dated February 3, 1919.

37. Gibson Mosher, Chaplain Corps, MHIWWIS; Letter from Roy Burkhart to Jacob Burkhart, dated March 23, 1919, author's collection.

CHAPTER 19. THE LONGEST HOURS

1. Warren Jackson, *His Time in Hell* (Novato: Presidio Press, 2001), 46–47; Charles Minder, *This Man's War* (New York: Pevensey Press, 1931), 42.

2. Dale Wilson, 4th IN, 3rd Div, survey and papers; Tom Carroll, 16th IN, 1st Div, manuscript, "Tom Carroll's Diary," both in MHIWWIS.

3. Horatio Rogers, *World War I through My Sights* (San Rafael: Presidio Press, 1976), 51.

4. Fred Takes, 325th IN, 82nd Div, entry for September 24, 1918, in manuscript entitled "World War I Co A, 325th Inf. 82nd Div," MHIWWIS.

5. Jackson, *Time in Hell*, 136–137; L. V. Jacks, *Service Record by an Artilleryman* (New York: Charles Scribner's Sons, 1928), 21, 89–93.

6. Diary of Capt. Clarence J. Minick, NWWIM.

7. Malcolm Helms, 5th MGB, 2nd Div, manuscript, "My Memories of World War I," in MHIWWIS; Elton Mackin, *Suddenly We Didn't Want to Die* (Novato: Presidio Press, 1993), 91.

8. AEF GHQ, *Equipment Manuals for Service in Europe*, series A, no. 1, *Infantry Regiments* (Chaumont, France: AEF AG Printing Section, May 1918), 60–68; Earle Poorbaugh, 26th IN, 1st Div, MHIWWIS; Charles MacArthur, *War Bugs* (New York: Doubleday, Doran, 1929), 111; Jackson, *Time in Hell*, 165; Jacks, *Service Record*, 21.

9. William L. Langer, *Gas and Flame in World War I* (New York: Knopf, 1965), 31, 39.

10. MacArthur, *War Bugs*, 33; Horace Baker, *Argonne Days in World War I* (Columbia: University of Missouri Press, 2007), 13, 30, 34, 46, 55; Diary of Pvt. Clee B. Baugler, NWWIM.

11. Historical Committee, *The Plattsburger* (New York: Winkoop Hallenbeck Crawford, 1917), 14; Milton E. Bernet, 89 Div, manuscript "The World War as I Saw It," MHIWWIS, 69.

12. Letter from Dewitt McIntyre to Mrs. G. W. McIntyre (mother), from Camp Hancock, GA; Letter from Mike Scheck to "Dear Sister," dated August 30, 1918, both in author's collection; Letter dated May 6, 1917, from Raymond Stanbeck, 6th Marines, 2nd Div, MHIWWIS.

13. Letter from James Miller to Mrs. James Miller (mother), dated March 14, 1918, author's collection; Minder, *This Man's War*, 28, 47; Letter from 1st Sgt. John Grove to Commander, 325th Infantry, dated December 17, 1918, Whitman papers, 325th IN, 82nd Div, MHIWWIS.

14. Letter from Lt. Aldridge to Col. W. M. Whitman, dated January 1, 1919, from Percey le Grand, France, in Whitman Papers, 325th IN, 82nd Div, MHIWWIS.

15. Letter from C. E. Rubendale to Gertrude White, dated December 1, 1918, author's collection; Letter from George O'Brien, 121st FA, 32nd Div, to his mother, dated September 26, 1918; "Machine Gun Company. 325th Infantry," Whitman Papers, 325th IN, 82nd Div, both in MHIWWIS.

16. Jacks, *Service Record*, 21; Letter from Walter Snider to his wife, Jennie, dated October 27, 1918, author's collection; Journal of Sgt. Albert Robinson, NWWIM.

17. Baker, *Argonne Days*, 18, 25.

18. Jackson, *Time in Hell*, 87–88, 103; Thurmond Baccus, 307th Field Signal

Bn; "Machine Gun Company. 325th Infantry," Whitman Papers, both in MHIWWIS.

19. Minder, *This Man's War*, 28, 47, 76–77, 146; Harry House, 325th IN, 82nd Div; Herman Dacus, 28th IN, 1st Div, both in MHIWWIS.

20. The Society of the Fifth Division, *The Official History of the Fifth Division* (Washington, DC: privately published, 1919), 117, 145, 154.

21. Jackson, *Time in Hell*, 160, 197.

22. Letter from John Castles to mother, dated June 26, 1918, in John W. Castles papers, USMA; Mackin, *We Didn't Want to Die*, 228.

23. Letter from June B. Smith to his mother, dated October 7, 1918, from France, from the family collection of Dave Hinkley, Lees Summit, MO, copy in author's possession; Mackin, *We Didn't Want to Die*, 17–19.

CHAPTER 20. THE BIG SHOW

1. Wendell Westover, *Suicide Battalions* (New York: G. P. Putnam's Sons, 1929), 209.

2. Col. E. G. Peyton, "Modern Tactics," *Infantry Journal* 17, no. 2 (August 1920): 120; Charles M. DuPuy, *A Machine Gunner's Notebook* (Pittsburgh: Reed & Witting, 1920), 81.

3. Unpublished 1918 diary of Major General Beaumont Buck, Beaumont Buck Papers, USACM.

4. L. V. Jacks, *Service Record by an Artilleryman* (New York: Charles Scribner's Sons, 1928), 73; Letter from 1st Lt. A. L. Slattery to Col. W. M. Whitman, dated January 15, 1919, and "Machine Gun Company. 325th Infantry," in Whitman Papers, 325th IN, 82nd Div; Earle Poorbaugh, 26th IN, 1st Div, both in MHIWWIS.

5. Capt. Lyman Fraiser, "The Operations of the Third Battalion, 26th Infantry, First Division, in the Second and Third Phases of the Meuse Argonne Offensive," DRL.

6. Buck diary, May 24, May 28–June 3, July 23, 1918; Ernst Otto, *The Battle at Blanc Mont* (Annapolis: United States Naval Institute, 1930), 140–141, 146; Ben Chastaine, *Story of the 36th* (Oklahoma City: Harlow, 1920), 94; Craig Hamilton and Louise Corbin, ed., *Echoes from over There* (New York: Soldier's Publishing, 1919), 205; Fred Takes, 325th IN, 82nd Div, manuscript "World War I Co A, 325th Inf. 82nd Div," MHIWWIS.

7. Diary of Pvt. Willard Thompson, 101st IN, 26 Div, NWWIM; Takes, "World War I."

8. Duncan Kemerer, 111th IN, 28th Div, manuscript "My Memories as a Soldier in World War I," MHIWWIS.

9. Jacks, *Service Record*, 181–182; Burt A. Richardson, 5th Marines, manuscript, "Episodes of the World War," dated July 1925, Emory; Takes, "World War I." That same sound haunted Fred Takes, who later recalled, "There were some men hollering and murmuring all night. They were wounded and didn't get any care."

10. Thurmond Baccus, 307th Field Signal Bn, unpublished manuscript, MHIWWIS; Horatio Rogers, *World War I through My Sights* (San Rafael: Presidio Press, 1976), 233–234.

11. Paul Landis, 76th FA, 3rd Div, written summary of service written on January 15, 1919; Letter from Clarence Hackett, 23rd IN, 2nd Div, to "Dear Mother and all," dated June 16, 1918, both in MHIWWIS; Letter from Walter Shaw to his mother, dated March 11, 1918, NWWIM; Letter from J. M. Miller to Mrs. James Miller (mother), dated March 20, 1918, author's collection.

12. Letters from Fay Neff to Miss A. W. Keichler (sister), dated May 5, 1918, and March 13, 1919; Letter from Frank Town, Evacuation Hospital #8, to Mary Town (sister), dated October 22, 1918, all from author's collection; Charles Minder, *This Man's War* (New York: Pevensey Press, 1931), 170–171.

13. Lee J. Levinger, *A Jewish Chaplain in France* (New York: MacMillan, 1922), 196; Knud Olsen, 325th IN, 82nd Div; Clarence L. Mahan, manuscript, "Hoosier Doughboy with the First Division"; Donald Kyler, 16th IN, 1st Div, all in MHIW-WIS; Edward A. Gutiérrez found similar attitudes toward killing in the responses of the newly returned doughboy veterans. Edward A. Gutiérrez, *Doughboys on the Great War* (Lawrence: University of Kansas Press, 2014), 108–110.

14. Jacks, *Service Record*, 128, 157, 221–222; Olsen, MHIWWIS; Letter from Fay Neff, to Miss A. W. Keichler (sister), dated October 30, 1918, author's collection; Elton Mackin, *Suddenly We Didn't Want to Die* (Novato: Presidio Press, 1993), 191–192.

15. Kyler, MHIWWIS; Letter from Albert Dahinden, to Mrs. E. K. Tomlinson, dated August 2, 1918; Letter from E. F. Satterwhite, 109th IN, to Mrs. R. A. Gerick (sister), dated December 10, 1918, both from author's collection. Satterwhite confessed to his sister, "I thought of you every day and when I was in No Mans land and that little picture that Mary sent me of her and Emily I used to look at just before we went into action and say I wonder if I will ever be able to get back to see them."

16. Rogers, *Through My Sights*, 62–63; Charles MacArthur, *War Bugs* (New York: Doubleday, Doran, 1929), 187; Letter from George O'Brien, 121st FA, 32nd Div, to his mother, dated August 9, 1918, MHIWWIS.

17. Jacks, *Service Record*, 38, 249–250.

18. Letter from Paul F. Andrews to his uncle dated August 18, 1918, NWWIM; Minder, *This Man's War*, 247; Warren Jackson, *His Time in Hell* (Novato: Presidio Press, 2001), 104–106.

19. Letters from Walter Shaw to his family, dated November 21 and 26, 1917, and February 18, May 9, and August 9, 1918, NWWIM.

20. Letter from James Dalgren to Adelaide Bowden, dated November 1, 1918, Emory; Letter from Lloyd Short, 6th Marines to "Dear Sister," dated July 15, 1918, MHIWWIS; Anonymous (Bob Casey), *The Cannoneers Have Hairy Ears* (New York: J. H. Sears, 1927), 192.

21. Letter from Fred Parker to Goldie Little from France, dated November 27, 1918, author's collection; Rogers, *Through My Sights*, 185.

22. Capt. John Stark, "3rd Battalion, 140th Infantry, 35th Division in the Meuse Argonne," DRL; Report by Maj. B. Castle, "The Part Played by Company 'B' and the 1st Battalion, 325th Infantry, in the Meuse Argonne Offensive," Whitman Papers.

23. War Department, *Medical Aspects of Gas Warfare*, vol. 14 of *The Medical*

Department of the United States Army in the World War (Washington, DC: Government Printing Office, 1926), 273; Col. H. L. Gilchrist, *A Comparative Study of World War Casualties from Gas and Other Weapons* (Washington, DC: Government Printing Office, 1928), 16, 23–26; E. W. Spencer, *History of Gas Attacks upon the American Expeditionary Forces during the World War*, pt. 1, vol. 6, CARL, 34–41.

24. John Stringfellow, *Hell No!* (Boston: Meador, 1936), 238–239; Jackson, *Time in Hell*, 55.

25. GHQ AEF, *An Atlas of Gas Poisoning* (France: American Red Cross, 1918), n.p. This is an American reprint of a work of the same title published by the British Army; Army War College, *Memorandum on Gas Poisoning in Warfare with Notes on Its Pathology and Treatment* (Washington, DC: Government Printing Office, 1917), 5–8; War Department, *Medical Aspects of Gas Warfare*, 273–280.

26. Earl Seaton, 16th IN, 1st Div, memoir, "I Joined the Regulars," MHIWWIS; Letters from Walter Shaw to his mother, dated May 9 and 12, 1918, NWWIM.

27. "Notes Made by the Inspector General, A.E.F. During the Active Operations from 12 September 1918 to 11 November 1918," 19–20, NARA, RG 120, Entry 566, Box 116; Consultant in General Medicine for Gas Poisoning, "Report of the Section of Gas Poisoning," dated December 17, 1918, NARA, RG 120, Entry 2117, Box 1; Letter from 1st Lt. A. L. Slattery to Col. W. M. Whitman, dated January 15, 1919, and report entitled "Machine Gun Company. 325th Infantry," Whitman Papers.

28. Jacks, *Service Record*, 148.

29. Letter from Fay Neff to Miss A. W. Keichler (sister), dated December 11, 1918; Letter from Fred Parker to Goldie Little from France, dated November 27, 1918, both from author's collection; Jackson, *Time in Hell*, 54, 117.

30. Letter from George O'Brien, 121st FA, 32nd Div, to his mother, dated December 21, 1917; Maj. Thomas Pierce to "Dear Colonel," dated May 1919, Whitman Papers, both in MHIWWIS; F. L. Miller, memoir, "The War to End All Wars," Emory; Capt. Withers A. Burress, "The Operations of the 23rd Infantry in the Soissons Offensive July 16–25, 1918," DRL; Anonymous, *Cannoneers*, 71.

31. MacArthur, *War Bugs*, 194; Capt. John Taylor, "Impressions and Recollects of the Operations," and Letter from Lt. Rayford Wood to "Dear Colonel Whitman," dated February 1, 1919, both in Whitman Papers. After being strafed by German aircraft, Wood likewise noted, "Lots of opinions were heard as to why *our* planes were not seen at such times."

32. S. L. A. Marshall, *Men against Fire* (Norman: University of Oklahoma Press, 2000), 44; Mackin, *We Didn't Want to Die*, 57, 82; Journal of Sgt. Albert Robinson; Baccus both in NWWIM.

33. Baccus, MHIWWIS; Mackin, *We Didn't Want to Die*, 186.

34. MacArthur, *War Bugs*, 136.

35. Jacks, *Service Record*, 186–187; Report for July 23, 1918, from the German 7th Army War Diary, in War Department, *World War Records, First Division, A.E.F. Regular*,

vol. 2, *German Documents: Aisne-Marne (Soissons)* (Washington, DC: Army War College, 1930), n.p.; Horatio Rogers, *World War I through My Sights* (San Rafael: Presidio Press, 1976), 182.

36. Lecture by Maj. Gen. H. E. Ely, "Battlefield Psychology, Leadership-Morale," delivered to the Army War College, March 27, 1937, USAMHI.

37. Letter from Fred Parker to Goldie Little, dated November 27, 1918, author's collection; Mackin, *We Didn't Want to Die*, 27, 122.

38. Minder, *This Man's War*, 284; Jackson, *Time in Hell*, 104–106; Jacks, *Service Record*, 79–80; Takes, "World War I."

39. John W. Castles, manuscript "War Diary of John W. Castles," 15, USMA; Letter from Lt. Aldridge to Col. W. M. Whitman, dated January 1, 1919, Whitman Papers.

40. Mackin, *We Didn't Want to Die*, 114–115; MacArthur, *War Bugs*, 108.

41. Letter from Capt. Herman Ulmer to Col. W. M. Whitman, dated November 30, 1918, Whitman Papers.

42. Jacks, *Service Record*, 177; Kyler, MHIWWIS; Elmer Virkler, 129th IN, 33nd Div, both in MHIWWIS; Albert Dahinden to Mrs. E. K. Tomlinson, dated August 2, 1918, author's collection. Dahinden confessed, "We are so close to Death most of the time that our experiences are soon forgotten."

43. Levinger, *Jewish Chaplain*, 156; Anonymous, *Cannoneers*, 192.

44. Diary of C. D. Grant, 19th Ambulance Co, 4th Div, NWWIM; Edwin P. Arpin, "A Wisconsinite in World War I: Reminiscences of Edwin P. Arpin, Jr.," ed. Ira Berlin, *Wisconsin Magazine of History*, Autumn 1967, 136.

45. Headquarters, 1st Division, "Report of Self-Inflicted Wounds," dated August 3, 1918, in NARA, RG 120, Entry 588, Box 108; Memorandum from AEF Adjutant General to Commanding General, AEF, Subject: Self-Inflicted Wounds, dated August 8, 1918, in NARA, RG 120, Entry 588, Box 113; Reports of Self-Inflicted Wounds from the following divisions: 1st, 2nd, 3rd, 4th, 6th, 27th, 30th, 33rd, 36th, 39th (5th Depot), 77th, 80th, 85th (4th Depot), 87th, to AEF Inspector General, for August 1918, in NARA, RG 120, Entry 588, Box 108; Report of Lt. Col. V. M. Elmore, Inspector General, 6th Division to the Inspector General, AEF, Subject: Recommendations, dated October 17, 1918, in NARA, RG 120, Entry 588, Box 108.

46. Anonymous, *Cannoneers*, 285; Tom Carroll, 16th IN, 1st Div, manuscript, "Tom Carroll's Diary, Co. F. 16th Inf. A.E.F. WWI," MHIWWIS.

47. Milton B. Sweningsen, 138th IN, 35th Div, unpublished memoir; Letter Lt. Rayford Wood to "Dear Colonel Whitman," dated February 1, 1919, Whitman Papers, both in MHIWWIS; John W. Nell, *The Lost Battalion: A Private's Story* (San Antonio: Historical Publishing Network, 2001), 87–88.

48. Burress, "Operations of the 23rd Infantry"; Jackson, *Time in Hell*, 142; Minder, *This Man's War*, 185.

49. Sweningsen, MHIWWIS; Ray N. Johnson, *Heaven, Hell, or Hoboken* (Cleveland: O. S. Hubbell Printing, 1919), 95; Vernon Nichols, "Our Battle of the Argonne," *Infantry Journal* 15 (September 1919): 189–194.

50. Letter from William Haselton, 18th IN and Div Staff, 1st Div, to "Dear Mother," dated December 19, 1918; Frank Merrill, 6th Marines, 2nd Div, both in MHIWWIS.

51. William Graham, *Hell's Observer* (Canal Winchester: Badgley, 2012), 26; Letter from A. S. White to Adelaide Bowden, dated November 1, 1918, Emory; "Report on the Operations of the 1st Battalion, 325th Infantry, during the Meuse-Argonne Campaign from October 9th to 30th 1918," Whitman Papers; Joe Romedahl, 129th IN, 33nd Div; Letter from Milton Sweningsen, 138th IN, 35th Div, to his mother, dated October 2, 1918, all three from MHIWWIS. Graham wrote, "War is Hell, especially in this country termed Sunny France where it rains eighteen hours out of every 24."

52. Letter from Paul F. Andrews to his mother, dated October 1918, NWWIM; Mackin, *We Didn't Want to Die*, 241.

53. "Boys of Company 'G' 325th Infantry," Whitman Papers; Letter from Paul F. Andrews to his mother, dated October 1918; Diary of Pvt. Gilbert Max, both in NWWIM. The estimates of the caloric value of the doughboy rations came from the calories in modern twelve-ounce cans of corned beef and salmon and from a pound of saltine crackers. While these items are not an exact match to their World War I equivalents, they still offer a rough comparison.

54. Letter from Paul F. Andrews to his mother, dated October 1918, NWWIM.

55. Letter from Francis J. Byrne to "Dear Father" dated June 21, 1919, author's collection; Forward Office, 1st Army Inspector General, "Prevention of Trench Foot," dated October 27, 1918, NARA, RG 120, Entry 590, Box 8; Jackson, *Time in Hell*, 72.

56. Sanitary Report for October 1918 for 26th Div, NARA, RG 120, Entry 2113, Box 5207; War Department, *Annual Report for 1919*, vol. 1, pt. 3, 3374–3376; "Report on the Operations of the 1st battalion, 325th Infantry, during the Meuse-Argonne Campaign from October 9th to 30th 1918."

57. Forward Office, 1st Army Inspector General, "Prevention of Trench Foot."

58. Letter from Paul F. Andrews to his mother, dated October 1918, NWWIM; Baccus, MHIWWIS; Letter from Fay Neff to Mrs. A. Keichler (sister), dated February 22, 1919, author's collection.

59. Baccus, MHIWWIS; Letter from 1st Sgt. John Grove to Commander, 325th Infantry, dated December 17, 1918, Whitman Papers, both in MHIWWIS; Rogers, *Through My Sights*, 217; Minder, *This Man's War*, 126–127.

60. Letter from William Stockton to Kate Blanchard (aunt), dated January 12, 1919, Emory; Letter from Francis J. Byrne to "Dear Father" dated June 21, 1919; Letter from Albert Dahinden to Mrs. E. K. Tomlinson, dated August 2, 1918, both in author's collection; Letter from Milton Sweningsen, 138th IN, 35th Div, to his mother, dated May 18, 1918, MHIWWIS; Buck Diary entry for October 15, 1918.

61. "Report of Inspection," 3rd Division, dated October 15 and 16, 1918, "Report of Inspection," 1st Division, dated October 16, 1918, both in NARA, RG 120, Entry 590, Box 4.

62. "H Company's Activities in the Argonne Meuse Battle," Whitman Papers, MHIWWIS; MacArthur, *War Bugs*, 214.

63. Rogers, *Through My Sights*, 195–196.

64. Takes, "World War I"; Wilbert Stambaugh, 1st Div, both in MHIWWIS; Letter from Francis J. Byrne to "Dear Father," dated June 21, 1919, author's collection.

65. Letter 1st Lt. A. L. Slatterly, to "My Dear Colonel Whitman," dated January 15, 1919, Whitman Papers.

66. MacArthur, *War Bugs*, 119; John L. Barkley, *No Hard Feelings!* (New York: Cosmopolitan, 1930), 232–233; John Cutchins and George Stewart, *History of the 29th Division, 1917–1919* (Philadelphia: MacCalla, 1921), 49–50; Charles Dienst et al., *They're from Kansas: History of the 353rd Infantry Regiment, 89th Division, National Army* (Wichita: Eagle Press, 1921), 261.

CHAPTER 21. "THE CAVALRY, THE ARTILLERY, THE LOUSY ENGINEERS"

1. William Haseltine, *The Services of Supply of the American Expeditionary Forces: A Statistical Summary* (Washington, DC: Government Printing Office, 1919), 50; Leonard Ayers, *The War with Germany: A Statistical Summary* (Washington, DC: Government Printing Office, 1919), 121.

2. Center for Military History, *The United States Army in the World War*, vol. 1, *Organization of the American Expeditionary Forces* (Washington, DC: Government Printing Office, 1988), 334, 353; George Mozley, *Our Miracle Battery* (Lowell, MA: Sullivan Brothers, 1920), 48; "Notes Made by the Inspector General, A.E.F., during the Active Operations from 12 September 1918 to 11 November 1918," NARA, RG 120, Entry 588, Box 116.

3. Horatio Rogers, *World War I through My Sights* (San Rafael: Presidio Press, 1976), 121–123, 225.

4. Earl Tesca, 15th FA, 2nd Div, manuscript, "Memoirs of My Experiences in World War I," MHIWWIS; Henry Berry, *Make the Kaiser Dance* (New York: Doubleday, 1978), 438.

5. Berry, *Kaiser Dance*, 110; Mozley, *Miracle Battery*, 35, 57; Benedict Crowell, *America's Munitions, 1917–1918* (Washington, DC: Government Printing Office, 1919), 430.

6. Rogers, *Through My Sights*, 213, 228–229; Bob Hoffman, *I Remember the Last War* (York, PA: Strength and Health, 1920), 177–178.

7. Anonymous (Bob Casey), *The Cannoneers Have Hairy Ears* (New York: J. H. Sears, 1927), 179.

8. Rogers, *Through My Sights*, 39–40, 160–161; Charles MacArthur, *War Bugs* (New York: Doubleday, Doran, 1929), 69.

9. Rogers, *Through My Sights*, 68–69.

10. Anonymous, *Cannoneers*, 178–179.

11. Rogers, *Through My Sights*, 117–118; Anonymous, *Cannoneers*, 71–81.

12. Anonymous, *Cannoneers*, 198.
13. "Notes Made by the Inspector General, A.E.F., during the Active Operations."
14. Ernest N. Harmon, "The Second Cavalry in the St. Mihiel Offensive, A.E.F., WWI," *Cavalry Journal* 30, no. 124 (July 1921).
15. Frank Mitchell, *Tank Warfare* (Bath, Great Britain: Spa Books, 1987), 257.
16. Dale E. Wilson, *Treat 'Em Rough: The Birth of American Armor, 1917–1920* (Navoto: Presidio Press, 1989), 34.
17. Maj. Rodger Harrison, "301st Tank Battalion in the Offensive Toward Maubeuge September 29–October 23, 1918," DRL.
18. Capt. Thomas C. Brown, "Operations of the Western Detachment 1st Brigade Tank Corps, September 26–October 11 1918," DRL; John W. Castles, manuscript "War Diary of John W. Castles," 36, 53, USMA; Martin Blumenson, *The Patton Papers*, vol. 1 (Boston: Houghton Mifflin, 1972), 589–591.
19. Castles, "War Diary," 46; Harvey L. Harris, *The War as I Saw It* (St. Paul: Pogo Press, 1998), xvi.
20. Harris, *As I Saw It*, 37, 42, 60; Brown, "Operations."
21. L. V. Jacks, *Service Record of an Artilleryman* (New York: Charles Scribner's Sons, 1928), 137; Harris, *As I Saw It*, 131; Harrison, "301st Tank"; Brown, "Operations."
22. Harris, *As I Saw It*, 121–126.
23. Castles, "War Diary," 82–84.
24. Charles H. Williams, *Sidelights on Negro Soldiers* (Boston: B. J. Brimmer, 1923), 155; Chester Davis, *The Story of the First Pioneer Infantry, U.S.A.* (N.p., 1919), 21–34; Paul S. Bliss, *Victory: History of the 805th Pioneer Infantry* (St. Paul, MN: unit published, 1919), 28–36.
25. *The Story of "E" Company, 101st Engineers, 26th Division* (Boston: privately printed, 1919), 48–49; William T. Anderson, "Devil Dogs in Olive Drab: The 2nd Engineers at Belleau Wood," *Army History* 58 (Spring 2003): 20–27.
26. *The Story of "E" Company, 101st Engineers*, 80–87; Bliss, *Victory*, 28–30.
27. Alphonse Bloemer, 1918 Diary, entry for August 9–10 and November 9, 1918, UGA.
28. A. Lincoln Lavine, *Circuits of Victory* (Garden City, NY: Doubleday, Page, 1921), 507–508; Capt. Henry King, "A Critical Analysis of the Employment of Signal Communications by the 1st American Division at Soissons," DRL.
29. Lavine, *Circuits*, 511; Jacks, *Service Record*, 108–111, 280–281.
30. War Department, *War Department Annual Report, 1919* (Washington, DC: Government Printing Office, 1920), 1218–1220, "Report of the Chief of Signal."
31. Crowell, *Munitions*, 581; Ashby Williams, *Experiences of the Great War* (Roanoke: Stone Printing, 1919), 126–127.
32. Robert H. Ferrell, *Five Days in October: The Lost Battalion of World War I* (Columbia: University of Missouri Press, 2005), 25–27, 36; Thomas M. Johnson and Fletcher Pratt, *The Lost Battalion* (Indianapolis: Bobbs-Merrill, 1936), 73–76, 135–137. www.archives.gov/historical-docs/todays-doc/index.html?dod-date=1004 contains a copy of the original message. According to this document, Cher Ami

was released at 3:00 PM, arrived at the loft at 4:05 and reached the message center at 4:22.

33. Elton Mackin, *Suddenly We Didn't Want to Die* (Novato: Presidio Press, 1993), 68–69; Memorandum from Major General C. P. Summerall, Commander 1st Division, dated August 25, 1918, in War Department, *World War Records, First Division, A.E.F. Regular,* vol. 2, *Field Orders, First Division June 1, 1918, to Sept. 18, 1918* (Washington, DC: Army War College, 1930), n.p.

CHAPTER 22. RESTLESS YOUNG MEN WITH GUNS

1. J. Franklin Bell, "Reflections and Suggestions: An Address by General J. Franklin Bell," March 17, 1906, 3, CARL; Lincoln Andrews, *Fundamentals of Military Service* (Philadelphia: J. B. Lippincott, 1916), 37–38; John F. O'Ryan, "The Psychology of Discipline," *Infantry Journal* 10, no. 5 (March-April 1914): 694, 700.

2. This passage was edited from Richard S. Faulkner, "'There Is a Limit to Human Endurance': The Challenges to Morale in the Meuse Argonne Campaign," in *A Companion to the Meuse Argonne Campaign,* ed. Edward G. Lengel (Chichester, UK: Wiley-Blackwell, 2014), 287–291.

3. War Department, *Commission on Training Camp Activities* (Washington, DC: Government Printing Office, October 15, 1917), 3–5.

4. War Department, *Commission on Training Camp Activities,* 3–4; William H. Taft et al., *Service with Fighting Men,* vol. 1 (New York: Association Press, 1922), 383–392; Henry Davidson, *The American Red Cross in the Great War* (New York: MacMillan, 1920), 64–76, 287–292, 347–349; Irving Crump, *Conscript 2989: Experiences of a Drafted Man* (New York: Dodd, Meade, 1918), 54; Letter from Lloyd Short, 6th Marines to "Dear Father," dated April 21, 1918, MHIWWIS.

5. War Department, *Commission on Training Camp Activities,* 17–18; Taft et al., *Service,* 1:334–342, 347–350.

6. www.lewis-mcchord.army.mil/dptms/museum/redshield.htm.

7. AEF GHQ General Orders 26, dated August 28, 1917.

8. AEF GHQ General Orders 33, dated September 6, 1917; "Report of the Investigation of the Y.M.C.A.," NARA, RG 120, Entry 445, Box 3462, Vol. 1, 10–16.

9. "Investigation of the Y.M.C.A.," Vol. 1, 53–54; Vol. 3, 616, 711.

10. Ibid., Vol. 3, 607; Charles MacArthur, *War Bugs* (New York: Doubleday, Doran, 1929), 162; Letter from Harry Callison to "My Dear Brothers" dated January 26, 1919, author's collection.

11. Letter from June B. Smith to his mother, dated December 26, 1918, from the family collection of Dave Hinkley, Lees Summit, Mo. Copy in author's possession; "Investigation of the Y.M.C.A.," Vol. 1, 16–17; Vol. 2, 304–307; Vol. 3; Vol. 6, 148.

12. *Stars and Stripes,* February 8, 1918, 4; Ben B. Lindsey and Harvey O'Higgins, *The Doughboy's Religion* (New York: Harper & Brothers, 1920), 6; "Investigation of the Y.M.C.A.," Vol. 2, 311–312; Vol. 3, 631; Vol. 6, 4, 34, 59, 137.

13. "Investigation of the Y.M.C.A.," Vol. 1, 54–57, 105; Vol. 2, 310.

14. "Investigation of the Y.M.C.A.," Vol. 6, 11, 39–40; Martin Hogan, *The Shamrock Battalion in the Great War* (Columbia: University of Missouri Press, 2007), 75.

15. "Investigation of the Y.M.C.A.," Vol. 3, 614, 713; Vol. 4, 805; Vol. 6, 6–9.

16. Horace Baker, *Argonne Days* (Columbia: University of Missouri Press, 2007), 96; Taft et al., *Service*, 1:158.

17. Letter from Albert Dahinden to Mrs. E. K. Tomlinson, dated May 17, 1918, author's collection. Of his trip, he also noted, "It seemed good to talk to American girls"; *Stars and Stripes*, September 13, 1918, 1; Davidson, *Red Cross*, 134.

18. "Investigation of the Y.M.C.A.," Vol. 1, 79–86.

19. *Stars and Stripes*, March 22, 1918, 7; "Investigation of the Y.M.C.A.," Vol. 1, 86–89.

20. "Investigation of the Y.M.C.A.," Vol. 1, 90–91; Letter from Paul Rhodes to Helen Naito, dated April 11, 1918, author's collection.

21. AEF General Orders 6, dated January 8, 1918; AEF General Orders 38, dated March 9, 1918; Taft et al., *Service*, Vol. 2, 142–150; Letter from Mike Scheck to "Dear Bertha," dated May 1, 1919; Letter from Harold Lane to Charles Lane (father), dated September 17, 1918, both in author's collection.

22. *Stars and Stripes*, June 7, 1918, 5; "Investigation of the Y.M.C.A.," Vol. 1, 137–139; Vol. 6, 21–22; Games Committee, *The Inter-Allied Games* (Paris: n.p., 1919), 30–42, 176a–176e.

23. "Investigation of the Y.M.C.A.," Vol. 6, 65–67.

24. L. V. Jacks, *Service Record by an Artilleryman* (New York: Charles Scribner's Sons, 1928), 286–287.

25. Letter from John Castles to family, dated April 7, 1918, John W. Castles Papers, USMA; Letter from Francis Byrne to Ed Byrne, dated February 23, 1918, author's collection; Alfred E. Cornebise, *The Stars and Stripes: Doughboy Journalism in the World War* (Westport, CT: Greenwood Press, 1984), 3–12.

26. Memorandum from Chief of Press Division to Chief of Intelligence Section, "Announcement of Soldier's Newspapers," dated November 9, 1917; Publication and unit address list from AEF GHQ G.2.D, dated February 5, 1919, both in NARA, RG 120, Entry 222, Box 6111.

27. "Investigation of the Y.M.C.A.," Vol. 6, 101–102; Charles Minder, *This Man's War* (New York: Pevensey Press, 1931), 267; William Graham, *Hell's Observer* (Canal Winchester: Badgley, 2012), 65, 72; Letter from Harry Callison to "Dear Folks," dated August 17, 1918, author's collection.

28. Letter from Francis Byrne to "Dear Mother," dated January 13, 1918, author's collection.

29. *Stars and Stripes*, March 12, 1918, 1; AEF General Orders 166, dated September 30, 1918; Letter from Milton Sweningsen, 138th IN, 35th Div, to his mother, dated October 25, 1918, MHIWWIS.

30. AEF GHQ General Orders 3, dated June 28, 1917; Censorship Card from Otto Seifert Papers, NWWIM.

31. Letter from Luther Grover to Etta Hawk (sister), dated February 22, 1918, author's

collection; Diary of Capt. Clarence Minick, entry for August 16, 1918; Letter from Reginald Thomson to Lillian Cottrell, dated October 12, 1918, both in NWWIM.

32. Letter from Harold Lane to Charles Lane (father), dated October 7, 1917, Letter from Robert Bressler to "Dear Parents," dated October 25, 1918, both from author's collection; Knud Olsen, 325th IN, 82nd Div, MHIWWIS.

33. *Stars and Stripes*, September 6, 1918, 3; William Haseltine, *The Services of Supply of the American Expeditionary Forces: A Statistical Summary* (Washington, DC: Government Printing Office, 1919), 218.

34. Letter from Pete Scheck to "Dear Sister," dated March 5, 1919; Letter from Paul Rhodes to Helen Naito, dated January 31, 1918; Letter from E. F. Satterwhite to Mrs. R. A. Gerick (sister), dated December 10, 1918; Letter from Dean S. Martin, to Lucy Sapoch, dated August 9, 1919, all from author's collection.

35. Letter from Francis J. Byrne to "Dear Mother," dated January 13, 1918; Letter from George McLaughlin to Mrs. L. H. McLaughlin (mother), dated September 27, 1918; Letter from Patrick McDermott to Nana Thompson, dated August 8, 1918, all from author's collection. McDermont wrote, "I guess you had began to think that I had left the earth but I am still here and well . . . I guess that I haven't written since I arrived over here well one don't have much time for one thing. I would like to write more than I do only for that and sometimes writing paper is just about as scarce as hen teeth."

36. Diary of Capt. Clarence Minick, entry for October 22, 1918, NWWIM; Letter from George O'Brien, 121st FA, 32nd Div, to his mother, dated January 9, 1918, MHIWWIS; Letter from Byron Hunter to his mother, dated November 26, 1918, author's collection.

37. Letters from Paul Rhodes to Helen Naito, dated March 12, 1918, and April 11, 1918; Letter from Luther Grover, to Etta Hawk (sister), dated October 6, 1918, both from author's collection; Letters from Ira Wilkenson to "Dear Sister," dated April 30 and May 13, 1918, UGA.

38. Frank Graves, 28th IN, 1st Div, MHIWWIS; Letter from Fay Neff to Mrs. A. Keichler (sister), dated February 19, 1919; Letter from Benson Oakley to Helen Oakley, dated November 4, 1918, both from author's collection.

39. Letters from Elmer Lewis to Goldie Little, dated June 21, 1918; June 27, 1918; August 6, 1918; August 25, 1918; January 17, 1919; February 23, 1919; and February 27, 1919, author's collection.

40. Lee J. Levinger, *A Jewish Chaplain in France* (New York: MacMillan, 1922), 172; for an example of making excuses for failure, see Charles B. Holt, *Heroes of the Argonne* (Kansas City: Franklin Hudson, 1919), 128–133.

41. Journal of Sgt. Albert Robinson, NWWIM.

42. Letter from June B. Smith, 130th FA, 35th Div to his mother, dated October 27, 1917; Letter from James M. Miller to "Mama and Rest," undated circa July 1917, author's collection.

43. Jacks, *Service Record,* 302; Letter from Francis J. Byrne to "Dearest Mother," dated October 16, 1918, author's collection.

44. Letters home from Raymond Stanbeck, 6th Marines, 2nd Div, dated February 1 and February 11, 1919, MHIWWIS; MacArthur, *War Bugs,* 4, 75–76.

45. George Mozley, *Our Miracle Battery* (Lowell, MA: Sullivan Brothers, 1920), 50; Letter from George O'Brien to his mother, dated February 7, 1919, MHIWWIS.

46. AEF GO 26, February 11, 1918; Letter from Harold Lane to Charles Lane (father) dated June 19, 1918, author's collection.

47. Mozley, *Miracle Battery,* 35; *Stars and Stripes,* February 9, 1918, 3; June 14, 1918, 1; May 16, 1919, 1; MacArthur, *War Bugs,* 87–88; Olsen, MHIWWIS.

48. "Hearings before a Subcommittee of the Committee on Military Affairs on S. 64 A Bill to Establish Military Justice," 66th Cong., 1st Sess.

49. U.S. Army Center of Military History, War, *Order of Battle of the United States Land Forces in the World War: American Expeditionary Forces,* vol. 2, *Divisions* (Washington, DC: Government Printing Office, 1988), 383–385; Report from Intelligence Officer, 86th Division to Chief, Military Intelligence Section, Subject: "Summary of General Information, March 11th, 1918," NARA, RG 165, Entry 377, Box 6.

50. Report from intelligence officer, Camp Funston, KS, to chief, Military Intelligence Section, Subject: "Morale at Camp Funston, Kansas," dated July 19, 1918, NARA, RG 165, Entry 377, Box 5; George English, Jr., *History of the 89th Division, U.S.A.* (Denver: Smith-Brooks, 1920), 37–38; Charles Dienst et al., *They're from Kansas: History of the 353rd Infantry Regiment, 89th Division, National Army* (Wichita: Eagle Press, 1921), 2–3; Kerr Rainsford, *From Upton to the Meuse with the Three Hundred and Seventh Infantry* (New York: D. Appleton, 1920), 16.

51. AEF GHQ, *Report of Officers Convened by Special Orders No. 98, GHQ AEF 09 April 1919,* Annex R, 19, Army War College Library; U.S. Army Center of Military History, *U.S. Army in the World War,* vol. 14, *Reports* (Washington, DC: Government Printing Office, 1988), 347; "Replies to Officers' Questionnaires" from Morale Branch of the War College and War Plans Division to the Chief of Staff, dated November 5, 1919, in NARA, RG 165, Entry 378, Box 6.

52. Telegram from AEF GHQ to Commanding General, 29th Division, dated September 18, 1918, in NARA, RG 120, G5 Schools–Army Candidates School, Box 1625, File 300.4; AEF GHQ Special Orders No. 304, October 31, 1918; Gerald F. Jacobson, *History of the 107th Infantry U.S.A.* (New York: De Vinne Press, 1920), 40; Wardlaw Miles, *History of the 308th Infantry* (New York: G. P. Putnam's Sons, 1927), 67–68.

53. Letter from Francis Byrne to "Dearest Mother," dated October 16, 1918, author's collection; Letter from June B. Smith to his mother, dated September 15, 1918.

54. Duncan M. Kemerer, 111th IN, 28th Div, MHIWWIS; Craig Hamilton and Louise Corbin, ed., *Echoes from over There* (New York: Soldier's Publishing, 1919), 105;

Letter from George O'Brien, 121st FA, 32nd Div to his mother, dated January 29, 1919, MHIWWIS.

55. Edgar Fell, *History of the Seventh Division, 1917–1919* (Philadelphia: Seventh Division Officer's Association, 1927), 43. A similar fate befell the 36th Division, see Ben Chastaine, *Story of the 36th* (Oklahoma City: Harlow, 1920), 47–48; John Stringfellow, *Hell No!* (Boston: Meador, 1936), 300.

56. Hugh Thompson, *Trench Knives and Mustard Gas* (College Station: Texas A&M Press, 2004), 160; Testimony of Lt. Col. Eugene H. Houghton in Report of Capt. Albert Rich, Asst. Inspector General, 1st Army to Inspector General, 1st Army, Subject: "77th Division Cutting Off of Seven Companies and One Machine Gun Company, October 3rd, 1918," dated October 8, 1918, in NARA, RG 120, Entry 590, Box 1.

57. Reports from field agents to 83rd Division for the following dates, August 12, 1918, September 7, 1918, September 16, 1918, October 3, 1918, October 29, 1918, November 1, 1918, NARA, RG 120, Entry 195 (one box); Memorandum for the Chief, Training and Instruction Branch, "Inspection Visit to Various Camps," dated October 2, 1918, NARA, RG 165, Entry 310, Box 185, "Camp MacArthur, Texas, Infantry Training Center."

58. *Stars and Stripes*, November 1, 1918, 4; John D. McDaniels, 126th IN, 32nd Div, entry for August 28, 1918, in unpublished manuscript, "A Tanglefoot's Diary," MHIWWIS; Thomas M. Johnson, *Without Censor* (Indianapolis: Bobbs-Merrill, 1927), 315–316.

59. Entries for September 20, 1918, and October 25, 1918, in "A Tenderfoot's Diary," MHIWWIS; Elton Mackin, *Suddenly We Didn't Want to Die* (Novato: Presidio Press, 1993), 39, 70.

60. "Notes Made by the Inspector General A.E.F., during the Active Operations from 12th September 1918 to 11th November 1918," in NARA, RG 120, Entry 588, Box 116; Testimony of Lt. Col. Eugene H. Houghton in Report of Capt. Inspector General, 1st Army, Subject: "77th Division cutting off of seven companies," NARA, RG 120, Entry 590, Box 1.

61. Milton B. Sweningsen, 138th IN, 35th Div, unpublished memoir, MHIWWIS, 5–6, 13.

62. Hunter Liggett, *AEF: Ten Years Ago in France* (New York: Dodd, Meade, 1927), 207; Robert L. Bullard, *Personalities and Reminiscences of the War* (New York: Doubleday, Page, 1925), 251.

63. Memorandum from Ltc. J. C. McIlroy, Advance Section GHQ Inspector General Office to Lt. Col. R. G. Peck, Inspector I Corps, Subject: Stragglers, dated November 10, 1918, in NARA, RG 120, Entry 590, Box 8; "Notes Made by the Inspector General A.E.F., during the Active Operations from 12th September 1918 to 11th November 1918," in NARA, RG 120, Entry 588, Box 116; Brigadier General Henry H. Bandholtz, *History of the Provost Marshal General's Department*,

American Expeditionary Forces (Chaumont, France: AEF Provost Marshal, April 15, 1919), 6.

64. "Report of Operations Argonne Meuse, Officer of the Inspector, 5th Army Corps, Sept. 25–Nov. 11, Extracts of Reports of Div. Inspectors," in NARA, RG 120, Entry 588, Box 116; Report of Inspector, 32nd Division, dated October 14, 1918, in NARA, RG 120, Entry 590, Box 2; Lecture delivered by Col. A. W. Foreman on January 27, 1919, at Fifth Army Corps Headquarters, Subject: "Administration and Supply of the 5th Army Corps during the St. Mihiel Offensive and Meuse-Argonne Offensive 1918," in Lectures: [Operations of the First Army] First Army Staff, CARL; Reports of stragglers apprehended on October 28–31 and November 1, 1918, by Company A, 313th MP, Assistant Provost Marshal, Souilly, France, A Company, 117th MP, B, C, and D Companies, 1st Army MP Bn, and H Troop, 2nd Cavalry, in NARA, RG 120, Entry 865, Box 269; "Memorandum to Corps Provost Marshals and Division A.P.Ms" from 2nd Army Provost Marshal, dated November 9, 1918, in NARA, RG 120, Entry 55, Box 83.

65. For a more complete discussion of the AEF's straggler problem, see Richard S. Faulkner, "Disappearing Doughboys: The American Expeditionary Forces Straggler Crisis in the Meuse Argonne," *Army History* 83 (Spring 2012): 6–25.

66. Jacks, *Service Record*, 171.

67. German propaganda leaflet in Special Collection, Emory, "WWI Misc," Box 1, Item 1; Jacks, *Service Record*, 221.

68. War Department, *A Manual for Courts-Martial, Corrected to April 15, 1917* (Washington, DC: Government Printing Office, 1917), 5–14, 21–23, 151–169; AEF GHQ, Bulletin 45, dated July 9, 1918; War Department, *War Department Annual Reports, 1919*, vol. 1, pt. 1 (Washington, DC: Government Printing Office, 1920), 262, 692, 694–695, 704–705.

69. Fred Sasse, *Rookie Days of a Soldier* (St. Paul: W. G. Greene, 1924), 178–179; Letters dated October 24 and December 18, 1917, from Raymond Stanbeck, 6th Marines, 2nd Div, MHIWWIS; Letter from Luther Grover to Etta Hawk (sister), dated January 22, 1918, author's collection; Warren Jackson, *His Time in Hell* (Novato: Presidio Press, 2001), 34–35.

70. Paul E. Maxwell, Camp Lee, 314th FA, unpublished manuscript, MHIWWIS, 25–26.

71. AEF GHQ General Order 56, April 13, 1918; AEF GHQ General Order 78, May 25, 1918.

72. War Department, *War Department Annual Reports, 1919*, vol. 1, pt. 1, 692, 694–695, 704–705; Leonard Ayres, *The War with Germany: A Statistical Summary* (Washington, DC: Government Printing Office, 1919), 16.

73. War Department, *Manual for Courts-Martial*, 254; War Department, *War Department Annual Reports, 1919*, vol. 1, pt. 1, 694–695, 699, 704–705.

74. War Department, *War Department Annual Reports, 1919*, vol. 1, pt. 1, 674. The wartime death sentences were for the following crimes: murder (53), disobeying

orders (25), desertion (23), rape (20), misbehavior in front of the enemy (11), assault with intent to rape or kill (5), sleeping on post (4), rape and murder (3), and spying (1).

75. General Courts-Martial No. 92 and No. 93, both dated 10 May 1918; Court-Martial No. 121, dated July 3, 1918.

76. "Hearings before a Special Committee on Charges of Alleged Executions without Trail in France," ordered published by 67th Cong., 4th Sess. (Washington, DC: Government Printing Office, 1923), iii–xvi, 74–76, 93–94, 182–191; General Court-Martial Orders No. 45, dated March 27, 1918; "Negro Soldiers Are Executed," *El Paso Herald*, April 5, 1918, 4; Beaumont Buck diary entry for October 21, 1917, in Beaumont Buck Diaries, USACM. Of the remaining three soldiers executed in the AEF, one white soldier was convicted of murder and another for rape. Private Frank Cadue, of Co. E, 26th Infantry, who may have been a Native American, was executed for raping and murdering a seven-year-old girl at Givrauval, France.

77. Report of Acting Intelligence Officer, 29th Div, dated March 11, 1918, NARA, RG 165 Records of the General Staff, Entry 377, Correspondence Related to Morale at Army Installations, Box 10, Camp McClellan file; War Department, *War Department Annual Reports, 1919*, vol. 1, pt. 1, 694–695, 704–705.

78. "Hearings before a Subcommittee of the Committee on Military Affairs on S. 64 A Bill to Establish Military Justice," 66th Cong., 1st Sess. (Washington, DC: Government Printing Office, 1919), 28–41; War Department, *Military Justice during the War: A Letter from the Judge Adjutant General to the Secretary of War* (Washington, DC: Government Printing Office, 1919), 10–25, 32–35; War Department, *Proceedings and Report of Special War Department Board on Courts-Martial and Their Procedure* (Washington, DC: Government Printing Office, 1919), 4–20. This was also known as the Kernan Board after its chairman, Maj. Gen. Francis Kearnan.

79. "Hearings . . . to Establish Military Justice," 299–300; Vincent Gianatasio, 111th IN, 28th Div, MHIWWIS; "Replies to Officers' Questionnaires" from Morale Branch of the War College and War Plans Division to the Chief of Staff, dated November 5, 1919, in NARA, RG 165, NM 84, Entry 378, Box 6; War Department, *War Department Annual Report for 1918*, 235–239; War Department, *War Department Annual Report for 1919*, 671–672, 677.

80. "Hearings . . . to Establish Military Justice," 19–21; Morale Branch Officers' Survey; Draft Special Regulations titled "Central Officers' Training Schools for Candidates for Commission in the Infantry, Field Artillery, and Machine Gun Units," NARA, RG 165, Entry 310, Box 201.

81. "Hearings . . . to Establish Military Justice," 299–300; George Loukides, 326th IN, 82nd Div, MHIWWIS.

82. Letter from Floyd Sosey to Mrs. J. C. Sosey (mother), dated June 11, 1918, author's collection; Levinger, *Jewish Chaplain*, 199; Donald Kyler, 16th IN, 1st Div, MHIWWIS.

83. "Hearings . . . on Charges of Alleged Executions without Trial in France," iii–xvi, 74–76, 93–94, 182–191.

84. Martin Blumenson, *The Patton Papers*, vol. 1 (Boston: Houghton Mifflin, 1972), 616; Capt. Albert B. Helsley, "Operations of the Machine Gun Company, 16th Infantry (1st Division) during the Second Phase of the Meuse Argonne Offensive," DRL.

85. Alonzo LaVanture, 111 IN, 28th Div; Benjamin Dexter, 320th MGB, 82nd Div, both in MHIWWIS.

86. Bandholtz, *History of the Provost Marshal General*, pt. 1, 1–16; pt. 5a, 282–288.

87. Morale Branch Officer's Survey; *Stars and Stripes*, December 20, 1918, 4; MacArthur, *War Bugs*, 119.

88. "Weekly Morale Update," from Asst. Chief of Staff, G2, American Embarkation Center to Asst. Chief of Staff, G2b, 2nd Section, GHQ AEF, dated May 12, 1919, NARA, RG 120, Entry 195, one box.

89. "Hearings . . . on Charges of Alleged Executions without Trial in France," 9; "War Expenditures: Hearings before Subcommittee No. 3 (Foreign Expenditures) of the Select Committee on Expenditures in the War Department," House of Representatives, 66th Cong., 1st and 2nd Sess., Serial 4, Parts 1–25, Vol. 1 (Washington, DC: Government Printing Office, 1920), 657–678, 942–945.

CHAPTER 23. CC PILLS, GOING WEST, AND THE HEN-FLEW-END-WAYS

1. George Clymer et al., *The History of U.S. Army Base Hospital No. 6* (Boston: Thomas Todd, 1924), 65.

2. Irving Crump, *Conscript 2989: Experiences of a Drafted Man* (New York: Dodd, Meade, 1918), 105; Fred Sasse, *Rookie Days of a Soldier* (St. Paul: W. G. Greene, 1924), 89; Charles Minder, *This Man's War* (New York: Pevensey Press, 1931), 249–250; Knud Olsen, 325 IN, 82nd Div; and Fred Takes, 325th IN, 82nd Div, manuscript "World War I Co A, 325th IN 82nd Div," both in MHIWWIS.

3. Letters from William Stout, dated July 6, 1920, and from Jerome McGinn, dated December 26, 1919, to Maj. Martin Tinker, author's collection.

4. Letter from Frank Fraas to his sister, dated December 8, 1917, NWWIM; Minder, *This Man's War*, 207.

5. U.S. Army Medical Department, *The Medical Department of the United States Army in the World War*, vol. 15, *Statistics*, pt. 2 (Washington, DC: Government Printing Office, 1925), 86, 1183. These numbers included "native troops" in Hawaii, the Philippines, and Puerto Rico. Hereafter volumes from *The Medical Department of the United States Army in the World War* will be referred to as *MDWW* and the volume number. The percentage of combat deaths was derived from using an estimate of two million men in the AEF.

6. *MDWW*, vol. 15, *Statistics*, pt. 2, 1019, 1028, 1183; *MDWW*, vol. 11, *General Surgery*, pt. 1, 50, 60, 64.

7. C. Alphonso Smith, *New Words Self Defined* (New York: Doubleday, Page, 1920), 18–19.

8. Horatio Rogers, *World War I through My Sights* (San Rafael: Presidio Press, 1976), 233–234.

9. Letter from Elmer Lewis to Goldie Little, dated January 17, 1919, author's collection; John Stringfellow, *Hell No!* (Boston: Meador, 1936), 324–325.

10. *MDWW*, vol. 11, *General Surgery*, pt. 1, 86–93; *MDWW*, vol. 8, *Field Operations*, 128–135; Maj. F. A. Blesse, "A Comparison of the German and American Systems of Evacuation," CGSCSRP, 1932, CARL; Edwin P. Arpin, "A Wisconsinite in World War I: Reminiscences of Edwin P. Arpin, Jr," ed. Ira Berlin, *Wisconsin Magazine of History*, Winter 1967–68, 135, 138; Frederick Pottle, *Stretchers: The Story of a Hospital Unit on the Western Front* (New Haven: Yale University Press, 1929), 105.

11. Warren Jackson, *His Time in Hell* (Novato: Presidio Press, 2001), 145; "Observations Made on September 27th, 1918," 79th Division Inspector, NARA, RG 120, Entry 588, Box 108; Thurmond Baccus, 307th Field Signal Bn; Anders Peterson, 6th Marines, 2nd Div, both in MHIWWIS.

12. "Observations Made on the 1st Day of Battle, September 26th, 1918," 79th Division Inspector, NARA, RG 120, Entry 588, Box 108; "Daily Report of Past 24 Hours" from 82nd Division Inspector General, dated October 12, 1918, NARA, RG 120, Entry 796, Box 3; Jackson, *Time in Hell*, 145; AEF GHQ, "Notes on Recent Operations 3," dated October 12, 1918, 21.

13. *MDWW*, vol. 11, *General Surgery*, pt. 1, 98–99.

14. "Notes Made by the Inspector General, A.E.F., during the Active Operation from 12th September 1918 to 11th November 1918," 18; "Report of Operations Argonne-Meuse, Office of the Inspector, 5th Army Corps, Sept. 26–Nov. 11, Extracts of Reports of Div. Inspectors," 6, both in NARA, RG 120, Entry 588, Box 116; *MDWW*, vol. 8, 141–142; Irwin B. March, manuscript, "We Joined the Army and Saw the World," 8th Field Signal Bn and 4th Sanitary Train; Russell Warner, 2nd EN, 2nd Div manuscript, "Outline of Experiences," both in MHIWWIS.

15. Letter from Charles P. Darby to his mother, dated April 3, 1918 (1919), NWWIM.

16. F. L. Miller, unpublished memoir, "The War to End All Wars," 9–14, Emory; Arpin, "A Wisconsinite," 138.

17. *MDWW*, vol. 7, *Training*, 143–147; *MDWW*, vol. 11, *General Surgery*, pt. 1, 103–107.

18. *MDWW*, vol. 11, *General Surgery*, pt. 1, 103–104; William Graham, *Hell's Observer* (Canal Winchester: Badgley, 2012), 120; Takes, entry for October 3, 1918, in manuscript "World War I Co A, 325th Inf. 82nd Div," MHIWWIS.

19. Olsen, MHIWWIS.

20. *MDWW*, vol. 7, *Training*, 160–168, 174, 184–186; Letter from C. A. Reifschneider to Randolph Wilson, dated November 3, 1918, Randolph Wilson Papers, Emory; Walter Bachman, *Souvenir Roster and History of Evacuation Hospital No. 15* (Unit published, 1919), 26–27. Seven additional evacuation hospitals arrived in France after the Armistice.

21. Maj. Gen. W. C. Gorgas, *Inspection of Medical Services with the American Expeditionary Forces* (Washington, DC: Government Printing Office, 1919), 7–8, 34–38. Five of the AEF's base hospitals and four of its camp hospitals were in Britain. For

the work of the army's plastic surgeons, see section 2, chapter 3, in *MDWW*, vol. 12, pt. 2, *Surgery*.

22. Clymer et al., *Base Hospital No. 6*, 16–18.

23. War Diary of Base Hospital No. 52, copy in author's possession; Clymer, *Hospital No. 6*, 228.

24. Miller, "The War," 14–19; Gorgas, *Inspection of Medical Services*, 10–11.

25. Warner, "Outline of Experiences," MHIWWIS.

26. Dorothy Schneider and Carl Schneider, *Into the Breach: American Women Overseas in World War I* (New York: Viking, 1991), 287–289; Clymer, *Hospital No. 6*, 55–57; Gorgas, *Inspection of Medical Services*, 5.

27. Warner, "Outline of Experiences," MHIWWIS.

28. Letters from Milton Sweningsen, 138th IN, 35th Div, to his mother, dated October 16 and 23, 1918, MHIWWIS; *MDWW*, vol. 11, *General Surgery*, pt. 1, 60.

29. Lt. (Dr.) Thomas Richmond Papers, NWWIM.

30. *MDWW*, vol. 10, *Neuropsychiatry*, 2–3.

31. *MDWW*, vol. 10, *Neuropsychiatry*, 153; Lt. Col. John Rhein, "History of Advanced Formations," NARA, RG 120, Entry 2117, Box 1, 3.

32. Lord Moran, *Anatomy of Courage* (London: Constable, 1945), xvi, 11, 61–65; Samuel Stouffer et al., *The American Soldier*, vol. 2, *Combat and Its Aftermath* (Princeton: Princeton University Press, 1949), 286.

33. *MDWW*, vol. 10, *Neuropsychiatry*, 333; L. V. Jacks, *Service Record by an Artilleryman* (New York: Charles Scribner's Sons, 1928), 75.

34. Duncan Kemerer, 111th IN, 28th Div, manuscript "My Memories as a Soldier in World War I," MHIWWIS.

35. *MDWW*, vol. 10, *Neuropsychiatry*, 153, 231–232, 306–310; Rhein, "Advanced Formations," 3, 23; Clymer, *Hospital No. 6*, 78–83.

36. Clymer, *Hospital No. 6*, 80–85; Gorgas, *Inspection of Medical Services*, 16–17.

37. Rhein, "Advanced Formations," 10, 15, 33–34, 39; Ben Shephard, *A War of Nerves: Soldiers and Psychiatrists in the Twentieth Century* (Cambridge, MA: Harvard University Press, 2001), 122–132, 153–160.

38. *MDWW*, vol. 9, *Communicable and Other Diseases*, 67–69.

39. Clymer, *Hospital No. 6*, 65, 108; Carol R. Byerly, *Fever of War: The Influenza Epidemic in the U.S. Army during World War I* (New York: New York University Press, 2005), 14–25, 35–37.

40. Letter from Albert Carmoody to "Dear Grandma," dated October 8, 1918, from Camp Funston, KS; Letter from George Hetrich to Robert Dengler, postdated October 17, 1918, both from author's collection.

41. Paul Maxwell, Camp Lee, 314th FA, 79th Div, memoir "The Diary of a Dud," MHIWWIS.

42. *MDWW*, vol. 15, *Statistics*, pt. 2, 1028, 1183; William Haseltine, *The Services of Supply of the American Expeditionary Forces: A Statistical Summary* (Washington, DC: Government Printing Office, 1919), 43; Minder, *This Man's War*, 192–193.

43. Letter from George Tucker to Mrs. E. K. Tomlinson, dated April 17, 1919, author's collection; Elton Mackin, *Suddenly We Didn't Want to Die* (Novato: Presidio Press, 1993), 103–105; Jackson, *Time in Hell*, 143.

44. Graham, *Hell's Observer*, 200; Charles MacArthur, *War Bugs* (New York: Doubleday, Doran, 1929), 179–180.

45. First Army Forward Office, Inspector General's Department, "Investigation of Stragglers in 82nd Division," dated October 18, 1919, NARA, RG 120, Entry, 590, Box, 8; "Notes Made by the Inspector General, A.E.F., during the Active Operation from 12th September 1918 to 11th November 1918," 23; U.S. Army Quartermaster Corps, *Extracts from Historical Report of the Chief Quartermaster, A.E.F., France*, monograph 2 of *Operations of the Quartermaster Corps, U.S. Army during the World War* (Philadelphia: Quartermaster School, June 15, 1929), 95.

46. Lee J. Levinger, *A Jewish Chaplain in France* (New York: MacMillan, 1922), 51; Reports of the chaplains of the 8th MGB and 30th Infantry, both dated October 27, 1918, NARA, RG 120, Entry 597, Box 3820.

47. *Extracts from Historical Report*, 108; "List of Personal Effects Found on Person SGT. James B. Newcomer," signed by 1st. Lt. N. W. Eden, dated September 22, 1918, Entry 675, MHIWWIS.

48. *Extracts from Historical Report*, 104–105; Anonymous (Bob Casey), *The Cannoneers Have Hairy Ears* (New York: J. H. Sears, 1927), 35–36.

49. Cablegram in Lloyd Short, 6th Marines, MHIWWIS; *Extracts from Historical Report*, 93.

50. Letter from Thomas F. Darey, Jr., to John Shaw (Walter Shaw's father), dated January 2, 1919; Letter from Capt. Charles Greenwood to Mrs. Henry Andrews, dated January 21, 1919, both in NWWIM.

51. Celestine Bittle, *Soldiering for Cross and Flag* (Milwaukee: Bruce Publishing, 1929), 121–122.

52. Letter from Pete Scheck to "Dear Sister," dated April 27, 1919; Letter from Robert Bressler to "Dear Parents," dated December 14, 1918, both in author's collection; Kemerer, "My Memories."

53. *Extracts from Historical Report*, 96–102; Letter from Reginald Thomson to Lillian Cottrell, dated June 8, 1919, NWWIM; Lisa Budreau, *Bodies of War* (New York: New York University Press, 2010), 80; www.abmc.gov/sites/default/files/publications/Commemorative%20Sites%20Booklet.

54. Lt. Col. V. M. Elmore "Recommendations" to AEF Inspector General, dated October 17, 1918, NARA, RG 120, Entry 588, Box 108; *Extracts from Historical Report*, 102–111.

CHAPTER 24. "AND WE'LL ALL GO BACK 'CAUSE IT'S OVER, OVER HERE"

1. Letters from Walter Snider to his wife, Jennie, dated September 19 and October 6, 1918, author's collection.

2. F. L. Miller, memoir, "The War to End All Wars," 12, Emory.

3. George Dongarra, 2nd Ammunition Train, 2nd Div, MHIWWIS; Statement of Capt. Joseph H. W. Hinkson, 311th MGB, dated November 5, 1918, and Confidential Memorandum from Lt. Col. C. M. Dowell to Chief of Staff, 26th Division, dated November 7, 1918, NARA, RG 120, Entry 540, Box 2273, Gondracourt Reclassification Depot, Investigation of Brig. Gen. Charles Cole; Memorandum from Commanding General, 1st Army to Commander in Chief AEF, Subject: Recommendations regarding 26th Division, dated November 7, 1918, NARA, RG 120, Entry 540, Box 227; "Brief History of the Case of Major General Clarence R. Edwards," in NARA, RG 120, Entry 464, Box 2267, "Personal Files of Brigadier General R. C. Davis."

4. Letter from John Little to Mrs. Hanna, dated February 17, 1919, in Maj. Mark Hanna Papers, NWWIM.

5. Diary of C. D. Grant, entry for November 10, 1918, NWWIM; William Graves, 28th IN, 1st Div, MHIWWIS; Anonymous (Bob Casey), *The Cannoneers Have Hairy Ears* (New York: J. H. Sears, 1927), 328–239.

6. Grant, diary entry for November 11, 1918; Frank William Graves, 28th IN, 1st Div, MHIWWIS; Anonymous, *Cannoneers*, 329–330.

7. William Graves; Letter from Fay Neff to Miss A. W. Keichler (sister), dated December 11, 1918; Letter from Paul Rhodes to Helen Naito, dated January 31, 1919, both in author's collection.

8. Letter from George McLaughlin to Mrs. L. H. McLaughlin (mother), dated November 12, 1918; Letter from Harold Lane to Charles Lane (father), dated November 13, 1918, both in author's collection.

9. Letter from Reginald Thomson to Lillian Cottrell, dated November 20, 1918, NWWIM; L. V. Jacks, *Service Record by an Artilleryman* (New York: Charles Scribner's Sons, 1928), 128. Jacks, for one, found war to be "incessant excitement and endless thrills."

10. Scott Stephenson, *The Final Battle* (Cambridge: Cambridge University Press, 2009), 153–157; "Daily Report of Inspector General, 2nd Army," dated November 12 and 13, 1918, NARA, RG 120, Entry 903, Box 101; "Miscellaneous," report from IV Corps Inspector General, dated November 12, 1918, NARA, RG 120, Entry 590, Box 4.

11. Edwin P. Arpin, "A Wisconsinite in World War I: Reminiscences of Edwin P. Arpin, Jr.," ed. Ira Berlin, *Wisconsin Magazine of History*, Winter 1967–1968, 219–220.

12. Horatio Rogers, *World War I through My Sights* (San Rafael: Presidio Press, 1976), 212; Letter from Luther Grover to Etta Hawk (sister), dated September 22, 1918, and an undated hometown newspaper clipping describing the souvenirs he sent home, author's collection.

13. Discharge letter from Maj. Gen. Leonard Wood to Sgt. Ferdinand Isern, dated January 13, 1919; Letter from Charles Mitchell to Mrs. E. K. Tomlinson, dated August 19, 1918; Letters from Oliver Van Camp to his mother, dated April 24, July 18, July 22, and August 11, 1918, all from author's collection; David Shanks, *As They Passed through the Port* (Washington, DC: W. F. Roberts, 1927), 48.

14. Hershie Mowrey, 16th Recruit Company, MHIWWIS.

15. Letter from Fay Neff to Adam Keichler (brother-in-law), dated January 29, 1919; Pete Scheck to "Dear Sister," dated March 5, 1919, both from author's collection; Letter from June B. Smith to his mother, dated November 26, 1918, from the family collection of Dave Hinkley, copy in author's possession.

16. William Haseltine, *The Services of Supply of the American Expeditionary Forces: A Statistical Summary* (Washington, DC: Government Printing Office, 1919), 43; Edward Lengel, *Thunder and Flame* (Lawrence: University Press of Kansas, 2015), 40–41; "The 325th Infantry in Its Meuse Argonne Operations, October 10–31 1918," Whitman Papers, 325th IN, 82nd Div, MHIWWIS; Henry Berry, *Make the Kaiser Dance* (New York: Doubleday, 1978), 348–349.

17. "Statements Made by Soldiers Returning from Germany," Whitman Papers; Gerald Jacobson, *History of the 107th Infantry* (New York: unit published, 1920), 271–273.

18. Carl Dennett, *Prisoners of the Great War* (Boston: Houghton Mifflin, 1919), 28–33, 41, 71; *Stars and Stripes*, December 6, 1918, 6.

19. Dennett, *Prisoners*, 48–53, 56, 228–229.

20. AEF GHQ General Orders 207, dated November 16, 1918; Letter from Harry Callison to "My Dear Mother," dated March 2, 1919, author's collection.

21. AEF GHQ General Order No. 218, dated November 28, 1918.

22. Albert Ettinger, *A Doughboy with the Fighting 69th* (Shippensburg: White Mane, 1992), 201; Henry T. Allen, *The Rhineland Occupation* (Indianapolis: Bobbs-Merrill, 1927), 71; Charles Hill, 364th IN, 91st Div, MHIWWIS.

23. Elmer F. Straub, *A Sergeant's Diary*, vol. 10, *Indiana Historical Collections* (Indianapolis: Indiana Historical Commission, 1923), 234–238; Letter from Frank Town to Mary Town (sister), dated January 5, 1919, author's collection; Charles Holbrook, 1st Div; Edward Cave, 356th IN, 89th Div; John Fromke, 347th FA, 91st Div, all in MHIWWIS.

24. "Report of Chief Liaison Officer on Conditions in Occupied Territory," dated February 3, 1919, in C. H. Goddard, "A Study of Franco American Relations during World War I," dated July 1942, USAMHI; Eugene Knoke, 362nd IN, 91st Div; Thomas Cooper, 328th IN, 82nd Div; Frederick Wehmeyer, 342nd MGB, 89th Div, all in MHIWWIS; Elizabeth Brett White, *American Opinion of France* (New York: Alfred A. Knopf, 1927), 285.

25. *Amaroc News*, May 16, 1919; William H. Amerine, *Alabama's Own in France* (New York: Eaton and Gettinger, 1919), 225–227, 331–332; *Stars and Stripes*, February 7, 1919.

26. Alfred E. Cornebise, *The Amaroc News* (Carbondale: Southern Illinois University Press, 1981), 17–23, 178–183, 192.

27. Memorandum from Base Censor, AEF to Chief, Prisoner of War Mail Section, entitled "Propaganda Letters," dated December 6, 1918, and undated memorandum entitled "Correspondence of Prisoners of War," in NARA, RG 120, Entry 226, Box 6108, File "Prisoners of War Section"; Letters from Alfred Refisch to POW

Joseph Refish, dated December 27, 1918; B. Jacobs to Benjamin Fawbs, dated January 9, 1919; Family Allerodder to POW Franze Grelter, all in Box 6109, "Translations of German Prisoners of War Mail," Folders 1 and 2.

28. Anna Fink to Nikolaus Poelhen, dated December 8, 1918, in NARA, RG 120, Entry 226, Box 6109, Folder 2; "Candid Comments on the American Soldier of 1917–1918 and Kindred Topics by the Germans," AEF GHQ Intelligence Section, Chaumont, France, 1919, 32–35, 47–49, USAMHI; Letter from Donald Mitchell to "Dear Mama," dated February 24, 1919, UGA.

29. Center of Military History, *The United States Army in the World War*, vol. 11, *Army Occupation of Germany* (Washington, DC: Government Printing Office, 1988), 205–206.

30. Albert B. Kellogg, "Marriages of Soldiers," Army War College Historical Section Study #6, July 1942, USAMHI, 1–6; Susan Zeiger, *Entangling Alliances: Foreign War Brides and American Soldiers in the Twentieth Century* (New York: New York University Press, 2010), 32–36; *Stars and Stripes*, March 1, 1918, 3; AEF GHQ Bulletin 26, dated March 29, 1919; Straub, *Sergeant's Diary*, 329.

31. Kellogg, "Marriages," 5–8; Zeiger, *Entangling Alliances*, 42–45.

32. Correspondence of Adolph Decker to Francis Fischer from March 1919 to April 1921 from author's collection; 1920 and 1940 U.S. Census for Baltimore Ward 1; Maryland in the World War 1917–1919: Military and Service Records; World War I Draft Registration Cards, 1917–1918; Boston Passenger and Crew Lists, 1820–1943, all accessed from Ancestry.com; Zeigler, *Entangling Alliances*, 13.

33. AEF GHQ General Orders 9, dated January 13, 1919; AEF GHQ General Orders 30, dated February 13, 1919.

34. HQ AEF University, Bulletin 91, pt. 1 and pt. 2 (Beaune, France: AEF University, May 16, 1919); Alfred Cornebise, *Soldier-Scholars: Higher Education in the AEF* (Philadelphia: American Philosophical Society, 1997), 130, 138.

35. Letter from George McLaughlin to Mrs. L. H. McLaughlin (mother), dated January 11, 1919; Letter from Robert Bressler, dated March 23, 1919, both from author's collection.

36. Arthur Hicks, Chaplain Corps, MHIWWIS; Letters from Donald G. Mitchell, Jr., to "Dear Dad," dated January 23, 1919, and January 31, 1919, UGA.

37. Letter from Joseph Haynes Waters to "Dear Parents," dated January 25, 1919, UGA; Letter from Elmer Lewis to Goldie Little, dated January 17, 1919; Letter from Benson Oakley to Helen Oakley, dated November 3, 1918, both from author's collection.

38. *Stars and Stripes*, February 28, 1919, 3; Letters from Cornelius Freely to Mae Murphy, dated January 31 and March 1, 1919, author's collection.

39. Pamphlet "I'll Tell the World," printed by the U.S. Army, 1919; Alonzo LaVanture, 111 IN, 28th Div; John Miholick, 23rd IN, 2nd Div, both in MHIWWIS; Letter from Harry Callison to "My Dear Mother" dated March 2, 1919, author's collection.

40. Letter from James Myers, 8th MGB, 3 Div to Robert Dengler, dated April 1, 1919; Letter from George McLaughlin to Mrs. L. H. McLaughlin (mother), dated December 29, 1918, both from author's collection.

41. Rogers, *Through My Sights*, 264–265; William L. Langer, *Gas and Flame in World War I* (New York: Knopf, 1965), 106.

42. Rogers, *Through My Sights*, 264.

43. Vice Admiral Albert Cleaves, *A History of the Transport Service* (New York: George H. Doran, 1921), 92–99, 250–253.

44. Ibid., 92–99.

45. Carroll Swan, *My Company* (Boston: Houghton Mifflin, 1918), 236.

46. George Browne, *An American Soldier in World War I* (Lincoln: University of Nebraska Press, 2006), 148.

47. Letter from Luther Grover to Etta Hawk, dated April 15, 1919; Letter from Cornelius Freely to Mae Murphy, dated March 1, 1919; Letter from H. W. Carver to his wife, dated January 7, 1919, all from author's collection.

48. Letters from Elmer Lewis to Goldie Little, from Camp Lewis, WA, dated April 30 and May 8, 1919, author's collection. The demobilization camps saw major spikes in AWOL rates. James Mott noted that many soldiers at Camp Pike, Arkansas, "simply skipped out," and so many had been brought in for being AWOL that the post's guard houses were full. Letter from James Mott to Pearl Lansworth, dated December 2, 1918, author's collection.

49. Letter from Dewitt McIntyre to Mrs G. W. McIntyre, from Camp Knox, KY, dated February 4, 1919, author's collection.

50. William Meloney, *Where Do We Go from Here?* (War Camp Community Service), 7–14, 43–45.

51. Ibid., 6, 15, 28; Letter to Andrew Magnus from "Buck Private Neull," dated March 10, 1919, author's collection.

52. Department of the Interior, pamphlet *Hey, There! Do You Want a Home on a Farm?* (Washington, DC: Government Printing Office, 1919).

53. Letter from Russell to "Dear Dad" from Sampigny, France, dated November 23, 1918, author's collection; Nancy MacLean, *Behind the Mask of Chivalry: The Making of the Second Ku Klux Klan* (New York: Oxford University Press, 1994), 28–29; Earle Stigers, "Questionnaire regarding Mental Attitudes of Soldiers," dated March 31, 1919, NARA, RG 165, Entry 377, Box 5, Camp Funston file.

54. William Nemec, 139th IN, 35nd Div; Edgar Hastings, 326th Field Hospital; Merton Seward, 129th IN, 33nd Div, all in MHIWWIS.

55. "Replies to Officers' Questionnaires" from Morale Branch of the War College and War Plans Division to the Chief of Staff, dated November 5, 1919, NARA, RG 165, NM 84, Entry 378, Box 6.

56. Edward Gutiérrez, *Doughboys on the Great War: How American Soldiers Viewed Their Military Experience* (Lawrence: University Press of Kansas, 2014), 15, 55–60, 172–176; Journal of Sgt. Albert Robinson, NWWIM; Frank Graves, 28th IN, 1st

Div; Earl Seaton, 16th IN, 1st Div, manuscript, "I Joined the Regulars"; Letter from Walter Bedell, 320th FA, 82nd Div to "Dear Dad," dated November 24, 1918, all from MHIWWIS.

57. Paul Maxwell, Camp Lee, 314th FA, 79th Div, "The Diary of a Dud," MHIWWIS.

ARCHIVAL AND UNPUBLISHED PRIMARY SOURCES

C. L. Crane. "The Great War: 1917–1918–1919." Unpublished diary in the possession of Dr. Conrad Crane, Army War College, Carlisle Barracks, PA.

June B. Smith, 130th FA, 35th Div letters, from the family collection of Dave Hinkley, Lees Summit, MO

Combined Arms Research Library, Special Collections, Fort Leavenworth, KS

J. Franklin Bell. "Reflections and Suggestions: An Address by General J. Franklin Bell." March 17, 1906.

Maj. F. A. Blesse. "A Comparison of the German and American Systems of Evacuation." CGSCSRP, 1932.

Allen M. Burdett. "A Critical Analysis of the Operations of the American II Corps from September 20 to October 2, 1918." CGSCSRP, 1934.

T. M. Chambliss. "A Study of the Operations of the 30th Infantry, 3rd Division in the Second Battle of the Marne on July 15th 1918." CGSCSRP, 1930.

George Cornish. "The Twenty-Sixth Infantry (U.S.) in the Meuse-Argonne Offensive." CGSCSRP, 1931.

Captain Charles Crawford. *Weapons and Munitions of War*, part 1, *Infantry Weapons.* Fort Leavenworth: Staff College Press, 1907.

J. C. Dickman. "General Service and Staff College Lectures Number Ten: Modern Improvements in Fire Arms and Their Tactical Effects." Fort Leavenworth: General Service and Staff College Press, September 26, 1903.

Captain Henry E. Eames. *The Rifle in War.* Fort Leavenworth: Staff College Press, 1908.

Frank Emery. "What Should Be the Plan of Education for Officers of the Army." CGSCSRP, 1934.

Capt. J. O. Green. "Operations of 3rd Battalion, 23rd Infantry from 30 May to 12 July 1918." CGSCSRP, 1931.

Edward S. Johnston. "A Study of the Nature of United States Infantry Tactics for Open Warfare on July 18, 1918, and of Their Points of Difference as Contrasted with the United States Army Tactics Taught in 1914." CGSCSRP, 1931.

Merritt Olmstead. "A Critical Analysis of Troop Leading within the 5th Division during the Second Phase of the Meuse-Argonne Offensive." CGSCSRP, 1933.

Edward Rehman. "An Analysis of Casualties in the 3rd Division in the Second Battle of the Marne July 15–20, 1918." CGSCSRP, 1930.

E. W. Spencer. *History of Gas Attacks upon the American Expeditionary Forces during the World War.* 1928.

W. P. Waltz. "Personal Experiences of a Machine Gun Officer at Cantigny, 28th–30th May." CGSCSRP, 1933.

Joseph J. Koch Papers

"Lecture Delivered by Colonel A. W. Foreman on 27 January 1919 at Fifth Army Corps Headquarters, Subject: 'Administration and Supply of the 5th Army Corps during the St. Mihiel Offensive and Meuse-Argonne Offensive 1918,'" in Lectures: [Operations of the First Army]/First Army Staff.

"Lecture Delivered by Colonel Willey Howell, on 6 January 1919 to the Assembled General Officers and Chiefs of Staff of the First American Army, Subject: 'The Second Section, G.S., First American Army in the St. Mihiel and Meuse-Argonne Operations.'" In Lectures: [Operations of the First Army]/First Army Staff.

"Lecture Delivered by Major General Alexander, 77th Division, on 3 February 1919, Subject: 'Operations of the Division, 26th of September to the 11th of November.'" In Lectures: [Operations of the First Army]/First Army Staff.

"Lecture Delivered by Major General George B. Duncan, Commanding 82nd Division, on 3 February 1919, Subject: 'General Missions of the 82nd Division in the Argonne-Meuse Offensive.'" In Lectures: [Operations of the First Army]/First Army Staff.

"Lecture Presented by LTC Troup Miller on 20 January 1919 at Fifth Army Corps Headquarters, Subject: 'Plan of communication, supply and evacuation, 1st Corps, for St. Mihiel Offensive and Meuse-Argonne Offensive.'" In Lectures: [Operations of the First Army]/First Army Staff.

Donovan Research Library, Infantry School Student Papers, Fort Benning, GA

Capt. Thomas C. Brown. "Operations of the Western Detachment 1st Brigade Tank Corps, September 26–October 11 1918."

Capt. Withers A. Burress. "The Operations of the 23rd Infantry in the Soissons Offensive July 16–25, 1918."

Maj. Zeba L. Drollinger. "Operations of the Machine Gun Units of the Sixth Brigade near Château Thierry July 1–21 1918."

Maj. M. S. Eddy. "Machine Gun Company, 39th Infantry (4th Division) in the Aisne-Marne Offensive."

Capt. George J. Foster. "Operations of the 37-mm gun platoon, 26th Infantry (1st Division) October 1–12, 1918."

Capt. Lyman Fraiser. "The Operations of the Third Battalion, 26th Infantry, First Division, in the Second and Third Phases of the Meuse Argonne Offensive."

Maj. Rodger Harrison. "301st Tank Battalion in the Offensive toward Maubeuge September 29–October 23, 1918."

Capt. Benhamin Hensley. "Operations of Company F, 34th Infantry in the Puvenelle Sector October 1–November 11, 1918."

Capt. Henry King. "A Critical Analysis of the Employment of Signal Communications by the 1st American Division at Soissons."

Capt. John Stark. "3rd Battalion, 140th Infantry, 35th Division in the Meuse Argonne."

Capt. Welcome P. Waltz. "Operations of C Company, 3rd Machine Gun Battalion at Cantigny."

Maj. W. H. Wells. "Personal Experiences of a Machine Gun Platoon Commander, October 17th–20th 1918."

Maj. Charles W. Yuill. "Operations of Co. B, 3rd MG BN in the Aisne-Marne Offensive."

Hargrett Rare Book and Manuscript Collection of the University of Georgia
Diary of Alphonse Bloemer
Journal and correspondence of Donald G. Mitchell, Jr.
Justus Erwin Owens Papers
Joseph Haynes Waters Papers
Ira Wilkenson Papers

Lower Cape Fear Historical Society, Wilmington, NC
Edward Hardin, 115th MGB, 29th Div, Papers

National World War I Museum and Liberty Memorial Archives, Kansas City, MO
Paul F. Andrews Papers
Diary of Private Clee B. Baugler
Diary of Earl Cave
Charles P. Darby Papers
Frank Fraas Papers
Diary of C. D. Grant
Journal of John L. Hackley
Mark Hanna Papers
Gold Star Mothers Papers
Diary of Leland O. Linman
Diary of Gilbert Max
Earnest F. McKeignan Papers
Diary of Captain Clarence J. Minick
Diary of Sergeant Thomas W. Morrow
Diary of Sergeant William R. Phillips
Thomas Richmond Papers
Journal of Sergeant Albert E. Robinson
Franklin Schall Papers
Otto Seifert Papers
Walter Shaw Papers
Diary of Pvt. Willard Thompson
Reginald Thomson Papers

National Archives and Record Administration Archives II, College Park, MD
National Archives, Records Groups 120, Records of the American Expeditionary Forces
Correspondence Relating to American Officers Suspected of Pro-German Sympathies
Personal Files of Brigadier General R. C. Davis
Records of the Chief Censor

Records of the Chief of Chaplains and Chaplain's Office
Records of the Chief Surgeon and Sanitary Officer reports
Records of the Combat Officers' Depot
Records of the Gondracourt Reclassification Depot
Records of the Inspector General
Records of the Judge Advocate General
Records of the Provost Marshal
Records of Reclassified Officers National Army and National Guard, Blois
Records of the 2nd Army, "Report of the Investigation of the Y.M.C.A."
Reports Related to the Morale of American Troops, 1917–1919

National Archives, Records Group 153
"Record of the Trial by General Courts-Martial of Captain Charles G. Clement, 328th
    Infantry." July 15, 1918, U.S., Box 5977, Docket no. 120515

National Archives, Records Group 165, Records of the War Department General Staff
Letters, Memorandums, reports, etc. of the Citizen Training Camps, Officers' Train-
    ing Camps, Central Officer's Training Schools and Student Army Training Corps
Reports of the Morale Branch of the War College and War Plans Division
Reports of Morale at Army Installations
Reports of Army War College Historical Branch, G5 Schools

Robert W. Woodruff Library Special Collections, Emory University
Adelaide Bowen Papers
James DePass Papers
Lee Dunbar Papers
Francis L. Miller Papers
Burt A. Richardson Papers
Leigh Sanford Papers
William T. Stockton Papers
Dr. Randolph Winslow Papers

U.S. Army Cavalry Museum Archives, Fort Riley, KS
Unpublished diary of Major General Beaumont Buck, Beaumont Buck Papers

U.S. Army Military History Institute, Carlisle Barracks, PA
"Candid Comments on the American Soldier of 1917–1918 and Kindred Topics by the
    Germans." AEF GHQ Intelligence Section, Chaumont, France, 1919.
H. E. Ely. Lecture. "Battlefield Psychology, Leadership-Morale." Delivered to the
    Army War College, March 27, 1937.
Harold Fiske. "Report of Training in the American Expeditionary Forces." Timber-
    man-Fiske Papers, USAMHI.
General Headquarters American Expeditionary Force. *Report of Officers Convened by
    Special Orders No .98, GHQ AEF 09 April 1919,*9–10. The Lewis Board.
Calvin H. Goddard. *Relations between the American and British Expeditionary Forces.*
    Washington, DC: United States Army War College Historical Section, June 1942.

———. "A Study of Franco American Relations during World War I." Historical Section Army War College, dated July 1942.

Robert C. Humber. "Absences and Desertions during the First World War." Washington, DC: United States Army War College Historical Section, (1942), USAMHI AWC Report 36.

Albert B. Kellogg. "Marriages of Soldiers," Army War College Historical Section Study 6, July 1942.

M. G. Spinks. "Major Problems of the Inspector General, AEF, and Their Solutions." Transcript of Lecture Presented to Army War College, October 9, 1933.

United States Army Military History Institute World War I Veteran Survey. This resource contains not only the veterans' answers to the survey questions mailed by the USAMHI but also a number of unpublished letters, diaries, and manuscripts that the veterans returned with their surveys. The following files were cited in this work:

Walter Aamoth, Officers' Training Schools, Camp Pike
Charles Adams, 5th IN, MD National Guard, Mexican Border
Donald Alkire, 7th Ambulance Co, 3rd Div
Glendon Armstrong, 101st MGB, 26th Div
Webb Ayres, 2nd Motor Supply Co, 2nd Div
Thurmond Baccus, 307th Field Signal Bn
Walter Bedell, 320th FA, 82nd Div
Milton Bernet, 89th Div
Leroy Bicknell, 9th MGB, 3rd Div
Ernesto Bisogno, 328th IN, 82nd Div
Mervyn Burke, Headquarters Troops, 1st Div
John Burton, Camp Jackson, 156th Depot Bde
Charles Campbell, Evacuation Ambulance Company #1
Tom Carroll, 16th IN, 1st Div
Edward Cave, 356th IN, 89th Div
Cornelius Chandler, 320th FA, 82nd Div
Donald Chase, 103rd IN, 26nd Div
Edward Chayes, Officers' Training Schools, Camp Johnston
Thomas Cooper, 328th IN, 82nd Div
Raymond Corkery, 102nd FA, 26th Div
William Couch, 308th MP Co
Henry Craven, 367th IN, 92nd Div
Pandelis Cristo, 327th IN, 82nd Div
Herman Dacus, 28th IN, 1st Div
Glenn Denton, 355th IN, 89th Div
Frank DeVane, 115th MGB, 30th Div
Benjamin Dexter, 320th MGB, 82nd Div
George Dongarra, 2nd Ammunition Train, 2nd Div

Frank Edman, 316th EN, 91st Div
Walter Eichenlaub, Field Hospital 7, 3rd Div
Edwin Engleman, Camp Dodge, 163rd Depot Brigade
Frank Faulkner, 23rd IN, 2nd Div
Edgar Ferrill, 2nd Ammunition Train, 2nd Div
Charles Flacker, 112th IN, 28th Div
Berch Ford, 16th IN, 1st Div
Philip Foster, 356th IN, 89th Div
John Fromke, 347th FA, 91st Div
Harvey Fullerton, 316th Supply Train, 91st Div
Pablo Garcia, 356th IN, 89th Div
Vincent Gianatasio, 111th IN, 28th Div
Robert Girton, 314th EN, 89th Div
Clarence Goist, 361st IN, 91st Div
Christopher Gordon, 101st MGB, 26th Div
Frank Graves, 28th IN, 1st Div
Roland Graves, 104th IN, 26th Div
Ira Greenhut, 307th Ammunition Train, 82nd Div
Edmund Grossman, 139th IN, 35th Div
Fendell Hagen, 140th INF, 35th Div
Gustaf Hallberg, 101st MP, 26th Div
Arthur Hanson, 6th Marines, 2nd Div
Lionel Harmison, 23rd IN, 2nd Div
Arthur Harter, Camp Hancock, 1st Provisional Regt
William Haselton, 18th IN and Div Staff, 1st Div
Edgar Hastings, Field Hospital 326, 82nd Div
Everett Hawley, 18th IN, 1st Div
Benjamin Heath, 328th IN, 82nd Div
Edward Helming, 120th IN, 30th Div
Malcolm Helms, 5th MGB, 2nd Div
Arthur Hicks, Chaplin Corps
Charles Holbrook, 1st Div
H. A. Honaker, AEF North Russia and 142nd MGB
Hugh Hook, 353rd IN, 89th Div
Claude Hopkins, Camp Gordon, File
Harry House, 320th MGB, 82nd Div
Arthur Hutchinson, 16th IN, 1st Div
Edward Jackson, 372nd IN, 93rd Div
Irving Jacobs, 1st Div
Elmer Jacobson, 326th IN, 82nd Div
Elmer Jones, 325th IN, 82nd Div
Duncan Kemerer, 111th IN, 28th Div

Lloyd Kidwell, 341 FA, 89th Div
Henry King, 23rd IN, 2nd Div
Eugene Knoke, 362th IN, 91st Div
Donald Kyler, 16th IN, 1st Div
Paul Landis, 76th FA, 3rd Div
Alonzo LaVenture, 111th IN, 28th Div
Bertram Lawrence, 349th FA, 92nd Div
M. O. Leuck, 314th AM Train, 89th Div
George Loukides, 326th IN, 82nd Div
Clarence Mahan, 1st Div
Irwin B. March, 8th Field Signal Bn and 4th Sanitary Train
Leslie Martin, 16th IN, 1st Div
Paul Maxwell, Camp Lee, 314th FA, 79th Div
Richard McBride, 325th IN, 82nd Div
Henry McCoy, 105th EN, 30th Div
John McDaniels, 126th IN, 32nd Div. This file contains the unpublished manu-
    script "A Tanglefoot's Diary" complied by 1st Sgt. Harold C. Woehl.
William McKinley Briggs, Camp Zachary Taylor, KY, 159th Depot Brigade
Harold McKinnon, Quartermaster Corps
Charles Mechura, 101st EN, 26th Div
Frank Merrill, 6th Marines, 2nd Div
John Miholick, 23rd IN, 2nd Div
Francis Moore, 103rd IN, 26th Div
Gibson Mosher, Chaplain Corps
Vernon Mossman, 18th IN, 1st Div
Gilbert Motz, 307th Tank Bn
William Nemec, 139th IN, 35nd Div
George O'Brien, 121st FA, 32nd Div
Anders Peterson, 6th Marines, 2nd Div
Virgil Ragsdale, 349th MGB, 92nd Div
Seaven Rice, 1st EN, 1st Div
Joe Romedahl, 129th IN, 33nd Div
William Roper, 130th MGB, 35th Div
Earl Salle, 13th Regiment, Camp Jackson, SC
Earl Seaton, 16th IN, 1st Div
Paul Seelig, 18thIN, 1st Div
Frederick Seidel, Quartermaster Corps
Merton Seward, 129th IN, 33nd Div
Frederick Shaw, 18th IN, 1st Div
Ernest Sherwin, 326th IN, 82nd Div
Lloyd Short, 6th Marines, 2nd Div
Harty Siegfried, 1st EN, 1st Div

Robert Smith, 120th IN, 30th Div
Wilbert Stambaugh, 2nd Field Signal Battalion, 1st Div
Felix Stastny, 346th FA, 91st Div
Robert Stevens, 803rd PIO IN
Elmer Stovall, 1st Ammunition Train, 1st Div
Charles Strikell, 5th FA, 1st Div
Howard Supple, 137th IN, 35th Div
Milton Sweningsen, 138th IN, 35th Div
John Switzer, 103rd MG Bn, 26th Div
Fred Takes, 325th IN, 82nd Div
Earl Tesca, 15th FA, 2nd Div
Lyman Varney, 3rd Bn Machine Gun Training Center, Camp Hancock, GA
Elmer Virkler, 129th IN, 33nd Div
Antonio Voyer, 103rd FA, 26th Div
Rollie Waggoner, 6th Marines, 2nd Div
Russell Warner, 2nd EN, 2nd Div
Jonas Warrell, 103rd Ammunition Train, 28th Div
Frederick Wehmeyer, 342nd MGB, 89th Div
Walter Whitman, 325th IN, 82nd Div
George Williams, Quartermaster Corps
Ralph Williams, 2nd EN, 2nd Div
Dell Wilson, 4th IN, 3rd Div
John Witlock, 16th IN, 1st Div
Walter Wolf, 129th IN, 33rd Div

Samuel and Stuart Lyon Papers
Oral History Transcript of the interview of John G. Oechsner by CSM Erwin H. Koehler on January 19, 1982, Noncommissioned Officer Oral History Program.
Transcript of Interview of General John E. Hull by Lt. Col. James W. Wurman on October 1973 in Washington, DC, in USAMHI Oral History Collection.

U.S. Military Academy Library Special Collections, West Point, NY
Unprinted diary and manuscript in the John W. Castles Papers
Clyde L. Eddy. Address given before the Historical Section of the American Pharmaceutical Association, Washington, DC, 1920.
Captain John H. Horton Papers
Unprinted manuscript in the Julian L. Schley Papers

Author's Personal Collection of World War I Letters and Document
Oral history interview of James Lindsey, conducted on April 26, 1996, in Jonesboro, GA

Letter collections
Knox Alexander
Howard Andrews, Base Hospital 11
Richard Atkinson, 324th MGB, 83rd Div
Bernard Bockemuehl, Hospital Train #39
Billy Brennan
Robert Bressler, 316th IN, 79th Div
Francis J. Byrne, 3rd MGB, 1st Div
Harry Callison
Albert Carmoody
H. W. Carver
Adolph Decker, 403rd Telephone Bn
Lewis Dengler
Mike Dowling
Cornelius Freely, 321st IN, 81st Div
Luther Grover, 103rd FA, 26th Div
Ed Guiss, 135th IN, 34th Div
George Hetrich, Camp Sherman Base Hospital
Byron Hunter
Harold Lane, 1st Engineer Searchlight Depot
Eugene Laudon, 2nd IN
Elmer Lewis, 361st IN, 91st Div
Francis Loughram
Andrew Magnus
Wallace Mansfield, 56th IN, 7th Div
D. S. Martin
Lunie McCarley, 110th IN, 28th Div
William McCrea
Patrick McDermott, 126th IN, 32nd Div
Dewitt McIntyre, 107th FA, 28th Div
George McLaughlin, 13th Marine Regt
James M. Miller, 10th EN
James Myers, 8th MGB, 3rd Div
Fay Neff, 310th IN, 78th Div
Fred Neff, 347th IN, 87th Div
P. Benson Oakley, 39th Provisional Ordnance Co
Paul Rhodes, 103rd IN, 26th Div
C. E. Rubendale, 115th EN, 40th Div
E. F. Satterwhite, 109th IN, 28th Div
Pete Scheck, 1st Automotive Shop Regt
Henry Schulz, 309th IN, 78th Div

Walter Snider, 36th Div
Floyd Sosey, 160th IN, 40th Div
C. P. Stowers
Oscar Strange, 130th IN, 33rd Div
Martin Tinker, Medical Corps
Frank Town, Evacuation Hospital #8
George Tucker, 304th Sanitary Train
Oliver Van Camp

PRIMARY SOURCE PERIODICAL ARTICLES

"American Sympathies in the War." *Literary Digest* 49, no. 20 (November 14, 1914).

Arps, George F. "Science as Applied to the Selection of Noncommissioned Officers." *Infantry Journal* 15, no. 7 (January 1919).

Bach, C. A. "Leadership." *Infantry Journal* 14, no. 8 (February 1918).

Baltzell, George. "The Proper Training of an Infantry Company." *Infantry Journal* 5, no. 5 (March 1909).

Bigelow, John. "Comments and Criticism" of "The Moral Training of the Soldier." *Journal of the Military Service Institution* 32 (1903).

Bisogno, Ernesto. "The Life and Death of Charles Clement." *American Legion Magazine*, March 1938, 50–51.

Brenner, Leo. "The American 'Million Army.'" *Infantry Journal* 13, no. 5 (February 1917).

Briggs, Allan L. "Training in Morale." *Infantry Journal* 14, no. 4 (October 1917).

Bullard, Robert L. "The Military Study of Men." *Infantry Journal* 8, no. 3 (November-December 1911).

Chester, James. "Comment and Criticism on Moral Preparation of the Soldier." *Journal of the United Service Institution of the United States* 32 (1913).

Clarke, J. L. J. "Infantry in the Attack." *Infantry Journal* 14, no. 11 (May 1918).

———. "Notes on Infantry Work on Western Front." *Infantry Journal* 14, no. 11 (May 1918).

Colson, W. N., and A. B. Nutt. "The Failure of the Ninety-Second Division." *The Messenger*, September 1919.

Crisis 14, no. 1 (May 1918); 14, no. 2 (June 1917); 14, no. 5 (September 1917): 216; 16, no. 3 (July 1918); 18, no. 1 (May 1919); 18, no. 2 (June 1919): 87; 19, no. 5 (March 1920).

Dravo, C. A. "Machine Guns: The Offensive in Open Warfare." *Infantry Journal* 17, no. 4 (October 1920).

Editorial Staff. "The Products of the Training Camps." *Infantry Journal* 14, no. 1 (July 1917).

———. "Reserve Officers' Training Camps." *Infantry Journal* 14, no. 6 (December 1917).

———. "The Spirit of Training." *Infantry Journal* 14, no. 7 (January 1918).

Ellis, O. O. "Hints for Service at Training Camps." *Infantry Journal* 13, no. 6 (March 1917).

Fortesque, Granville. "Training the New Armies of Liberty." *National Geographic* 32, nos. 5–6 (November-December 1917).

Gruber, E. L. "Employment of Field Artillery with Infantry." *Infantry Journal* 15, no. 12 (June 1919).

Harmon, Ernest. "The Second Cavalry in the St. Mihiel Offensive, A.E.F., WWI." *Cavalry Journal* 30, no. 124 (July 1921).

Hitchcock, C. H. "A Letter to a Training Camp Student." *Infantry Journal* 14, no. 1 (July 1917).

Hocking, William E., "Fundamentals of Military Psychology." *Infantry Journal* 14, no. 10 (April 1918).

Hughes, W. N. "A Practical Plan for Infantry Training." *Infantry Journal* 14, no. 1 (July 1917).

Literary Digest 49, no. 11 (September 12, 1914); 49, no. 20 (November 14, 1914).

McKaine, O. E. "The Buffaloes: A First-Class Colored Fighting Unit." *Outlook* 119 (May 22, 1918).

Messenger 1, no. 11 (November 1917); 2, no. 5 (May-June 1919); 2, no. 7 (July 1919); 2, no. 10 (October 1919).

Nichols, Vernon. "Our Battle of the Argonne." *Infantry Journal* 15 (September 1919).

O'Ryan, John F. "The Psychology of Discipline." *Infantry Journal* 10, no. 5 (March-April 1914).

Parker, John. "Simplifying the Organization and Tactics of Infantry." *Infantry Journal* 16, no. 7 (January 1920).

Patch, A. M. "Machine Gun Organization." *Infantry Journal* 17, no. 2 (August 1920).

Peyton, E. G. "Modern Tactics." *Infantry Journal* 17, no. 2 (August 1920).

Richards, John. "Some Experiences with Colored Soldiers." *Atlantic Monthly*, August 1919.

Service Record: Atlanta's Military Weekly, June 5, 1919.

S.M.C. "The Present Problem." *Infantry Journal* 6, no. 2 (September 1909).

Stars and Stripes, February 8, 1918, to June 13, 1919.

Swann, Thomas. "The Top-Sergeant." *Infantry Journal* 15, no. 12 (June 1919).

Tips, Charles R. "Selecting and Training Military Leaders." *Infantry Journal* 15, no. 7 (January 1919).

"Training Negro Officers." *Literary Digest* 55 (July 21, 1917).

Wharton, James B. "A Battalion in Action." *Infantry Journal* 16, no. 6 (December 1919).

Wise, Jennings C. "Organization and Initial Training of a Company." *Infantry Journal* 14, no. 3 (September 1917).

———. "The Soldier's Life in Battle." *Infantry Journal* 16, no. 11 (May 1920).

Verick's The American Weekly 6, no. 24 (July 18, 1918).

PUBLISHED PRIMARY SOURCES

Adams, Myron, ed. *The Officer's Responsibility for His Men*. Fort Sheridan: locally published, 1917.

Adjutant General's Office. *The Personnel System of the United States Army.* Vol. 1, *History of the Personnel System.* Washington, DC: Government Printing Office, 1919.
———. *The Personnel System of the United States Army.* Vol. 2, *The Personnel Manual.* Washington, DC: Government Printing Office, 1919.
Albertine, Connell. *The Yankee Doughboy.* Boston: Branden Press, 1968.
Alexander, Robert, *Memories of the World War.* New York: MacMillan, 1931.
Allen, Henry T. *The Rhineland Occupation.* Indianapolis: Bobbs-Merrill, 1927.
Allen, Hervey. *Towards the Flame.* New York: Grosset and Dunlap, 1934.
American Expeditionary Forces University. Bulletin 91, part 1 and part 2. Beaune, France: AEF University, May 16, 1919.
Amerine, William H. *Alabama's Own in France.* New York: Eaton and Gettinger, 1919.
Andrews, Lincoln C. *Fundamentals of Military Service.* Philadelphia: J. B. Lippincott, 1916.
———. *Leadership and Military Training.* Philadelphia: J. B. Lippincott, 1918.
———. *Military Manpower.* New York: E. P. Dutton, 1920.
Anonymous (Bob Casey). *The Cannoneers Have Hairy Ears.* New York: J. H. Sears, 1927.
Anonymous. *Wine, Women, and War: A Diary of Disillusionment.* New York: J. H. Sears, (1926).
Armstrong, F. C. *The Story of the Sixteenth Infantry in France.* Frankfurt: Martin Flock, 1919.
Army War College. *Lectures on Discipline and Training by Colonel Applin of the British General Staff and Hints to Young Officers by a British Officer.* Washington, DC: War College Press, February 1918.
———. *Manual for Commanders of Infantry Platoons.* Washington, DC: Government Printing Office, 1917.
———. *Notes on Recent Operations, No. 3.* Washington, DC: Government Printing Office, 1917.
———. *World War Records, First Division A.E.F. (Regular).* 25 Vols. Washington, DC: Army War College, 1930.
———. *World War Records, Second Division A.E.F. (Regular).* 10 Vols. Washington, DC: Army War College, 1924.
Ayers, Leonard. *The War with Germany: A Statistical Summary.* Washington, DC: Government Printing Office, 1919.
Azan, Paul. *The War of Positions.* Cambridge, MA: Harvard University Press, 1917.
Bach, Christian A., and Henry N. Hall. *The Fourth Division: Its Services and Achievements in the World War.* New York: Country Life Press, 1920.
Bachman, Walter. *Souvenir Roster and History of Evacuation Hospital No. 15.* Unit published, 1919.
Baker, Chester E. *Doughboy's War.* Shippensburg: Burd Street Press, 1998.
Baker, Horace. *Argonne Days in World War I.* Columbia: University of Missouri Press, 2007.

Baker, Leslie. *The Company History: The Story of Company B, 106th Machine Gun Battalion.* New York: privately printed, 1920.

Baldwin, Marian. *Canteening Overseas 1917–1919.* New York: MacMillan, 1926.

Bandholtz, Henry H. *History of the Provost Marshal General's Department, American Expeditionary Forces.* Chaumont, France: AEF Provost Marshal, April 15, 1919.

Barber, Thomas H. *Along the Road.* New York: Dodd, Mead, 1924.

Barbusse, Henri. *Under Fire.* London: J. M. Dent & Sons, 1926.

Barkley, John L. *No Hard Feelings!* New York: Cosmopolitan, 1930.

The Battery Book: A History of Battery "A," 306th F. A. New York: DeVinne Press, 1921.

Bennett, Arnold, *Over There.* New York: George H. Doran, 1915.

Berlin, Ira, ed. "A Wisconsinite in World War I: Reminiscences of Edwin P. Arpin, Jr." *Wisconsin Magazine of History,* serialized in Vol. 51, Numbers 1–3 (Autumn-Spring 1962).

Bittle, Celestine. *Soldiering for Cross and Flag.* Milwaukee: Bruce Publishing, 1929.

Bliss, Paul. *Victory: History of the 805th Pioneer Infantry.* St. Paul: unit published, 1919.

Bradden, William S. *Under Fire with the 370th Infantry (8th I.N.G.) A.E.F.* Chicago: privately Published, n.d.

Brown, William. *The Adventures of an American Doughboy.* Tacoma: Smith-Kenney, 1919.

Browne, George. *An American Soldier in World War I.* Edited by David L. Snead. Lincoln: University of Nebraska Press, 2006.

Buck, Beaumont. *Memories of Peace and War.* San Antonio: Naylor, 1935.

Bullard, Robert L. *Personalities and Reminiscences of the War.* New York: Doubleday, Page, 1925.

Buxton, G. Edward, ed. *Official History of the 82nd Division.* Indianapolis: Bobbs-Merrill, 1919.

Camp, Charles W. *History of the 305th Field Artillery.* New York: Country Life Press, 1919.

Camp MacArthur Central Infantry Officers Training Camp. *Farewell Book CIOTS, 1918.* Camp MacArthur, TX, (1918).

Chastaine, Ben. *Story of the 36th.* Oklahoma City: Harlow, 1920.

Chicago Daily News. *The Chicago Daily News War Book for American Soldiers, Sailors and Marines.* Chicago: Chicago Daily News Company, 1918.

Clarke, William F. *Over There With O'Ryan's Roughnecks.* Seattle: Superior, 1966.

Cleaves, Albert. *A History of the Transport Service.* New York: George H. Doran, 1921.

Clemens, Samuel (Mark Twain). *Innocents Abroad.* Hartford: American Publishing, 1869.

Clement, Charles M., ed. *Pennsylvania in the World War: An Illustrated History of the Twenty-Eighth Division.* 2 Vols. Pittsburgh: States Publication Society, 1921.

Clymer, George, et al. *The History of U.S. Army Base Hospital No. 6.* Boston: Thomas Todd, 1924.

Colona, B. A., ed. *The History of Company B, 311th Infantry in the World War*. Freehold, NJ: Transcript Printing House, 1922.

Company C, 328th Infantry. *History of Company "C" 328th Infantry*. Privately published, 1919.

Crowell, Benedict. *American Munitions, 1917–1918*. Washington, DC: Government Printing Office, 1919.

Crump, Irving. *Conscript 2989: Experiences of a Drafted Man*. New York: Dodd, Meade, 1918.

Cutchins, John, and George Stewart, *History of the 29th Division, 1917–1919*. Philadelphia: MacCalla, 1921.

Davidson, Henry. *The American Red Cross in the Great War*. New York: MacMillan, 1920.

Davis, Chester. *The Story of the First Pioneer Infantry, U.S.A.* N.p., 1919.

Davis, Richard Harding. *With the Allies*. New York: Charles Scribner's Sons, 1915.

Deckard, Percy. *List of Officers Who Served with the 371st Infantry and Headquarters 186th Infantry Brigade during the World War*. Allegany: Allegany Citizen, 1929.

Dennett, Carl. *Prisoners of the Great War*. Boston: Houghton Mifflin, 1919.

Department of the Interior. "Hey, There! Do You Want a Home on a Farm?" Pamphlet. Washington, DC: Government Printing Office, 1919.

Dickinson, John. *The Building of an Army*. New York: Century, 1922.

Dienst, Charles, et al. *They're From Kansas: History of the 353rd Infantry Regiment, 89th Division, National Army*. Wichita: Eagle Press, 1921.

Dittmar, Gus. *They Were First*. Austin: Steck-Warlick, 1969.

Duffy, Francis P. *Father Duffy's Story*. New York: George H. Doran, 1919.

Dunne, Finley Peter. *Mr. Dooley in Peace and in War*. Boston: Small Maynard, 1898.

DuPuy, Charles M. *A Machine Gunner's Notebook*. Pittsburgh: Reed & Witting, 1920.

Edwards, Evan A. *From Doniphan to Verdun: The Official History of the 140th Infantry*. Lawrence: World Company, 1920.

Eighth Company, Central Officers' Training School, Camp Lee, Virginia. *Take His Name*. Richmond: Garrett and Massie, 1918.

Eisenhower, Dwight D. *At Ease: Stories I Tell to Friends*. New York: Doubleday, 1967.

———. *Eisenhower: The Prewar Diaries and Selected Papers, 1905–1941*. Edited by Daniel D. Holt. Baltimore: Johns Hopkins University Press, 1998.

Empey, Arthur. *Over the Top*. New York: G. P. Putnam's Sons, 1917.

English, George H., Jr. *History of the 89th Division, U.S.A.* Denver: Smith-Brooks, 1920.

Ettinger, Albert M. *A Doughboy with the Fighting 69th*. Shippensburg: White Mane, 1992.

Evarts, Jeremiah M. *Cantigny: A Corner of the War*. Privately published, 1938.

Fell, Edgar. *History of the Seventh Division, 1917–1919*. Philadelphia: Seventh Division Officer's Association, 1927.

Fort Devens OTC Yearbook Committee. *The Pick: 3rd O.T.C. Ft Devens, MA*. Boston: George H. Dean, 1918.

Fort Sheridan Association. *The History and Achievements of the Fort Sheridan Officers' Training Camps*. Chicago: Hawkins & Loomis, 1920.

Gallagher, D. B. *The Battle of Bolts and Nuts in the Sector of Cognac Hill*. Fort Worth: Gallagher-Crosby Company, 1931.

Games Committee. *The Inter-Allied Games*. Paris: n.p., 1919.

Gansser, Emil B. *History of the 126th Infantry in the War With Germany*. Grand Rapids: Dean Hicks, 1920.

General Headquarters, AEF. *An Atlas of Gas Poisoning*. France: American Red Cross, 1918.

———. *Combat Instructions*. Chaumont, France: AEF GHQ, September 5, 1918.

———. *Equipment Manuals for Service in Europe*, Series A, No. 1, *Infantry Regiments*. Chaumont, France: AEF AG Printing Section, May 1918.

———. *Historical Report of the Chief Engineer, AEF*. Washington, DC: Government Printing Office, 1919.

———. *Manual of the Chief of Platoon of Infantry*. Paris: Imprimerie Nationale, August 1917.

———. *Notes on Recent Operations, No. 1*. Chaumont, France: AEF GHQ, August 7, 1918.

———. *Notes on Recent Operations, No. 2*. Chaumont, France: AEF GHQ, September 8, 1918.

———. *Notes on Recent Operations, No. 3*. Chaumont, France: AEF GHQ, October 12, 1918.

———. *Report of Superior Board on Organization and Tactics*. Chaumont, France: AEF GHQ, 1919.

———. *Supplement to Instruction for the Offensive Combat of Small Units*. Nancy, France: Berger-Levarault, April 1918.

Gorgas, W. C. *Inspection of Medical Services with the American Expeditionary Forces*. Washington, DC: Government Printing Office, 1919.

Graham, William. *Hell's Observer*. Canal Winchester: Badgley, 2012.

Grand Magasins aux Galeries Lafayette. *Paris for Englishmen and for Americans*. Paris: Ehrmann Publicité, n.d. (circa 1918).

Hamilton, Craig, and Louise Corbin, eds. *Echoes From Over There*. New York: Soldier's Publishing, 1919.

Harbord, James G. *The American Army in France, 1917–1919*. Boston: Little, Brown, 1936.

———. *Leaves from a War Diary*. New York: Dodd, Meade, 1925.

Harris, Harvey L. *The War as I Saw It: 1918 Letters of a Tank Corps Lieutenant*. Saint Paul: Pogo Press, 1998.

Hart, Archibald. *Company K of Yesterday*. New York: Vantage Press, 1969.

Haseltine, William. *The Services of Supply of the American Expeditionary Forces: A Statistical Summary.* Washington, DC: Government Printing Office, 1919.

Haterius, Carl E. *Reminiscences of the 137th Infantry.* Topeka: Carne, 1919.

Havlin, Arthur C. *The History of Company A, 102nd Machine Gun Battalion, Twenty-Sixth Division.* Boston: privately printed, 1928.

Hemrick, Levi. *Once A Marine.* New York: Carlton Press, 1968.

Herzog, Stanley J. *Helmets.* Stamford, CT: Bell Press, 1930.

Historical Committee. *The Plattsburger.* New York: Winkoop Hallenbeck Crawford, 1917.

History of Company "C" 328th Infantry. New York: Hunter Collins, n.d.

History of the 305th Field Artillery. Garden City, NY: Country Life Press, 1919.

History of the Three Hundred and Twelfth Infantry. New York: privately published, 1919.

Hockings, William E. *Morale and Its Enemies.* New Haven: Yale University Press, 1918.

Hoffman, Bob. *I Remember the Last War.* York, PA: Strength and Health, 1920.

Hogan, Martin. *The Shamrock Battalion in the Great War.* Columbia: University of Missouri Press, 2007.

Holden, Frank A. *War Memories.* Athens: Athens Book Company, 1922.

Holt, Charles B. *Heroes of the Argonne.* Kansas City: Franklin Hudson, 1919.

Howard, James M. *The Autobiography of a Regiment.* New York: privately printed, 1920.

Huidenkopfer, Frederick L. *The History of the 33rd Division A.E.F.* Springfield: Illinois State Historical Library, 1921.

Hungerford, Edward. *With the Doughboy in France.* New York: Macmillan, 1920.

Hunt, Edward E. *War Bread.* New York: Henry Holt, 1916.

Hunton, Addie, and Kathryn M. Johnson. *Two Colored Women with the American Expeditionary Forces.* Brooklyn: Brooklyn Eagle Press, 1920.

Hussey, Alexander T., and Raymond M. Flynn. *The History of Company E, 308th Infantry 1917–1919.* New York: Knickerbocker Press, 1919.

Jacks, L. V. *Service Record by an Artilleryman.* New York: Charles Scribner's Sons, 1928.

Jackson, Warren. *His Time in Hell.* Novato: Presidio Press, 2001.

Jacobson, Gerald F. *History of the 107th Infantry U.S.A.* New York: De Vinne Press, 1920.

Joel, Arthur H. *Under the Lorraine Cross.* East Lansing: privately published, 1921.

Johnson, Ray N. *Heaven, Hell, or Hoboken.* Cleveland: O. S. Hubbell, 1919.

Johnson, Thomas M. *Without Censor.* Indianapolis: Bobbs-Merrill, 1927.

Joint War History Commissions of Michigan and Wisconsin. *The 32nd Division in the World War.* Madison: Wisconsin Printing Company, 1920.

Judy, Will. *A Soldier's Diary.* Chicago: Judy Publishing, 1930.

Kenamore, Clair. *From Vauquois Hill to Exermont.* St Louis: Guard Publishing, 1919.

Kilbourne, Charles, ed. *The National Service Library.* Vol. 1, *Universal Military Training*, by Major General Leonard Wood. New York: F. P. Collier and Son, 1917.

————, ed. *The National Service Library.* Vol. 3, *Principles of Training,* by Major Frank R. McCoy. New York: F. P. Collier and Son, 1917.

————, ed. *The National Service Library.* Vol. 4, *Rudiments of Drill-Mobile Army Troops,* by Capt. William T. Carpenter. New York: F. P. Collier and Son, 1917.

Langer, William L. *Gas and Flame in World War I.* New York: Alfred E. Knopf, 1965.

Langille, Leslie. *Men of the Rainbow.* Hamond, IN: W. B. Coakley, 1933.

Lavine, Lincoln. *Circuits of Victory.* Garden City, NY: Doubleday, Page, 1921.

Lawrence, Joseph D. *Fighting Soldier.* Boulder: Colorado Associated University Press, 1985.

Levinger, Lee J. *A Jewish Chaplain in France.* New York: Macmillan, 1921.

Liggett, Hunter. *The AEF: Ten Years Ago in France.* New York: Dodd, Meade, 1927.

Lindsey, Ben B., and Harvey O'Higgins. *The Doughboy's Religion.* New York: Harper & Brothers, 1920.

Little, Arthur W. *From Harlem to the Rhine.* New York: CoviciFriede, 1936.

Luby, James, ed. *One Who Gave His Life: War Letters of Quincy Sharpe Mills.* New York: G. P. Putnam's Sons, 1923.

Lyon, C. C. *Experience of a Recruit in the United States Army.* Washington, DC: Government Printing Office, 1916.

MacArthur, Charles. *War Bugs.* New York: Doubleday, Doran, 1929.

Machine Gun Officers' Training School. *Four Months of Sand.* Augusta, GA: Phoenix Printing, 1918.

MacIntyre, W. Irwin. *Colored Soldiers.* Macon: J. W. Burke, 1923.

Mackin, Elton E. *Suddenly We Didn't Want to Die.* Novato: Presidio Press, 1993.

Malstrom, George M. *The 131st Infantry in the World War.* Chicago: privately published, 1919.

March, Peyton. *The Nation at War.* New York: Doubleday, Doran, 1932.

Marshall, George C. *Memories of My Service in the World War, 1917–1918.* New York: Houghton Mifflin, 1976.

————. *The Papers of George Catlett Marshall.* Vol. 1, *The Soldierly Spirit, December 1880–June 1939.* Edited by Larry Bland. Baltimore: Johns Hopkins University Press, 1981.

Mason, Monroe, and Arthur Furr. *The American Negro Soldier with the Red Hand in France.* Boston: Cornhill, 1920.

Maverick, Maury. *A Maverick American.* New York: CoviciFriede, 1937.

McArthur, John C. *What A Company Officer Should Know.* New York: Harvey Press, 1918.

McCormick, Robert R. *The Army of 1918.* New York: Harcourt, Brace, and Howe, 1920.

McIntyre, Colby L. *The Old Man of the 103rd: The Biography of Frank M. Hume.* Houlton, ME: Aroostock Print Shop, 1940.

Meloney, William. *Where Do We Go From Here.* War Camp Community Service, 1919.

Miles, L. Wardlaw. *History of the 308th Infantry.* New York: G. P. Putnam's Sons, 1927.

Miller, Charles. *The Customs of the Service Also Some Suggestions and Advise.* Fort Leavenworth: Army Service School Press, 1917.

Minder, Charles. *This Man's War.* New York: Pevensey Press, 1931.

Mitchell, Frank. *Tank Warfare.* Bath, Great Britain: Spa Books, 1987.

Morehead, Robert. *The Story of the 139th Field Artillery, American Expeditionary Forces.* Indianapolis: Bobbs-Merrill, 1920.

Moss, James A. *The Noncommissioned Officer's Manual.* Menasha, WI: George Banta, 1917.

———. *Officer's Manual.* Menasha: George Banta, 1917.

———. *What Sammy's Doing.* Menasha: George Banta, 1917.

Mozley, George. *Our Miracle Battery.* Lowell, MA: Sullivan Brothers, 1920.

Murphy, Elmer, and Robert S. Thomas. *The Thirtieth Division in the World War.* Lepanto, AK: Old Hickory, 1936.

Murrin, James A. *With the 112th in France.* Philadelphia: J. B. Lippencott, 1919.

Nell, John W. *The Lost Battalion: A Private's Story.* San Antonio: Historical Publishing Network, 2001.

Niles, John J., et al. *The Songs My Mother Never Taught Me.* New York: MacAulay, 1929.

91st Division Publication Committee. *The Story of the 91st Division.* San Francisco: H. S. Crocker, 1919.

Noble, Carl. *Jugheads behind the Lines.* Edited by Grace Coats. Caldwell, ID: Caxton Printers, 1938.

Otto, Ernst. *The Battle at Blanc Mont.* Annapolis: United States Naval Institute, 1930.

Our Boys in Khaki. N.p., n.d (circa 1918).

Parker, James. *The Old Army: Memories, 1872–1918.* New York: Stackpole Books, 2003.

Peixotto, Ernest. *The American Front.* New York: Charles Scribner's Sons, 1919.

Pershing, John J. *My Experiences in the World War.* 2 vols. New York: Frederick Stokes, 1931.

Pollard, James E. *The Forty-Seventh Infantry, a History, 1917–1918–1919.* Saginaw: Press of Seeman & Peters, 1919.

Pottle, Frederick. *Stretchers: The Story of a Hospital Unit on the Western Front.* New Haven: Yale University Press, 1929.

Powell, E. Alexander. *Fighting in Flanders.* Toronto: McClelland, Goodale and Stewart, 1915.

Pratt, Walter M. *Tin Soldiers: The Organized Militia and What It Really Is.* Boston: Gorham Press, 1912.

Proctor, H. G. *The Iron Division in the World War.* Philadelphia: John C. Winston, 1919.

Provost Marshal General. *Second Report of the Provost Marshal General to the Secretary of the Army on the Operations of the Selective Service System to December 20, 1918.* Washington, DC: Government Printing Office, 1919.

Rainsford, Kerr. *From Upton to the Meuse with the Three Hundred and Seventh Infantry.* New York: D. Appleton, 1920.

Reppy, Alison. *Rainbow Memories.* Executive Committee, First Battalion, 166th Infantry, 1919.

Robinson, William J. *Forging the Sword: The Camp Devens Story.* Concord, NH: Rumford Press, 1920.

Rodney, George B. *As a Cavalryman Remembers.* Caldwell, ID: Caxton Printers, 1944.

Rogers, Horatio. *World War I through My Sights.* San Rafael: Presidio Press, 1975.

Ross, Warner A. *My Colored Battalion.* Chicago: self-published, 1920.

Ruschke, Edgemont W., ed. *Lieuie VI: Being the Chronicle of the Battle of Camp Lee as Fought by the Deathless Sixth Battalion, Central Officers' Training School, Camp Lee, Virginia.* Petersburg: privately published, 1919.

Sáenz, José de la Luz. *The World War I Diary of José de la Luz Sáenz.* Edited and translated by Emilo Zamora. College Station: Texas A&M Press, 2014.

Sanborn, Joseph. *The 131st Infantry in the World War.* Chicago: privately printed, 1919.

Sasse, Fred. *Rookie Days of a Soldier.* St. Paul: W. G. Greene, 1924.

Schmidt, Paul. *Co. C, 127th Infantry in the World War.* Sheboygan: Press Publishing Company, 1919.

Scott, Emmett J. *Scott's Official History of the American Negro in the World War.* New York: n.p., 1919.

Scott, Huge L. *Some Memories of a Soldier.* New York: Century, 1928.

Shanks, David C. *As They Passed through the Port.* Washington, DC: W. F. Roberts, 1927.

———. *Management of the American Soldier.* New York: Thomas Ryan, (1917).

Sheahan, Henry. *A Volunteer Poilu.* New York: Atlantic Monthly, 1916.

Sibley, Frank. *With the Yankee Division in France.* Boston: Little, Brown, 1919.

Simmons, Perez. *Twentieth Engineers, France, 1917, 1918, 1919.* Portland, OR: Dimm & Sons, 1919.

Sirmon, W.A. *That's War.* Atlanta: Linmon, 1929.

Smith, C. Alphonso. *New Words Self Defined.* New York: Doubleday, Page, 1920.

Society of the Fifth Division. *The Official History of the Fifth Division.* Washington, DC: privately published, 1919.

Spears, Francis, et al., eds. *Damitall: Twentieth Company, Central Officers' Training Camp, Camp Gordon, Georgia.* Atlanta: privately published, 1918.

Stewart, Worth P. *The History of Company "K" 117th Infantry in the Great War.* Privately published, 1919.

Stimson, Henry L. *On Active Service in Peace and War.* New York: Harper & Brothers, 1948.

Story of "E" Company 101st Engineers 26th Division. Boston: privately published, 1919.

Strab, Elmer F. *A Sergeant's Diary.* Indiana History Collections 10. Indianapolis: Indiana History Commission, 1923.

Stringfellow, John S. *Hell! No!* Boston: Meador, 1936.

Sutherland, S. J. *The Reserve Officers' Handbook.* Boston: Houghton Mifflin, 1917.

Sutliffe, Robert S. *Seventy-First New York in the World War.* New York: Seventy-First Regiment Association, 1922.

Swan, Carroll J. *My Company.* New York: Houghton Mifflin, 1918.

Taft, William H., et al. *Service with Fighting Men.* Vol. 1. New York: Association Press, 1922.

Taylor, Emerson G. *New England in France 1917–1919: A History of the Twenty-Sixth Division.* Boston: Houghton Mifflin, 1920.

Thompson, Huge. *Trench Knives and Mustard Gas.* College Station: Texas A&M Press, 2004.

Thorn, Henry. *History of 313th U. S. Infantry.* New York: Wynkoop Hallenbeck Crawford, 1920.

328th Infantry Historical Committee. *History of the Three Hundred and Twenty-Eighth Infantry Regiment.* Self-published, 1922.

Tiebout, Frank B. *A History of the 305th Infantry.* New York: Wynkoop Hallenbeck Crawford, 1919.

Tompkins, Raymond S. *The Story of the Rainbow Division.* New York: Boni & Liveright, 1919.

Triplet, William S. *A Youth in the Meuse-Argonne.* Columbia: University of Missouri Press, 2000.

Truscott, Lucian K., Jr., *The Twilight of the Cavalry: Life in the Old Army, 1917–1942.* Lawrence: University Press of Kansas, 1989.

20th Engineers, France, 1917, 1918, 1919. Portland: Dimm & Sons, 1919.

United States Army Center of Military History. *Order of Battle of the United States Land Forces in the World War: American Expeditionary Forces.* 2 Vols. Washington, DC: Government Printing Office, 1988.

———. *The United States in the World War.* 17 vols. Washington, DC: United States Army Center of Military History, 1988–1992.

United States Army Medical Department. *The Medical Department of the United States Army in the World War.* 15 vol. Washington, DC: Government Printing Office, 1921–1929.

United States Army Quartermaster Corps. *Operations of the Quartermaster Corps, U.S. Army during the World War.* Monograph 2, *Extracts from Historical Report of the Chief Quartermaster, A.E.F., France.* Philadelphia: Quartermaster School, June 15, 1929.

United States Congress, Congressional Committee on Military Affairs. *Hearings before a Special Committee on Charges of Alleged Executions without Trail in France.* 67th Cong., 4th Sess., 1923.

———. *Hearings before a Subcommittee of the Committee on Military Affairs on S. 64 A Bill to Establish Military Justice.* 66th Cong., 1st Sess., 1919.

———. *To Increase the Efficiency of the Military Establishment of the United States.* 64th Cong., 1st Sess., January 27, 1916.

———. *War Expenditures: Hearings before Subcommittee No. 3 (Foreign Expenditures) of the Select Committee on Expenditures in the War Department.* 66th Cong., 1st and 2nd Sess., Serial 4, Parts 1–25, Vol. 1, 1920.

United States Department of Commerce. *Statistical Abstract of the United States for 1916*. Washington, DC: Government Printing Office, 1917.

United States Department of War. *The Army as a Life Occupation for Enlisted Men.* Washington, DC: War Department, 1907.

———. *Commission on Training Camp Activities.* Washington, DC: Government Printing Office, October 15, 1917.

———. *Document No. 656: Infantry Training.* Washington, DC: Government Printing Office, 1917.

———. *Field Service Pocket Book.* Washington, DC: Government Printing Office, 1917.

———. *Field Service Regulations of the United States Army, with Corrections to May 21, 1913.* Washington, DC: Government Printing Office, 1913.

———. *Instructions for the Training of Platoons for Offensive Action.* Washington, DC: Government Printing Office, 1917.

———. *Instructions on the Offensive Conduct of Small Units.* Washington, DC: Government Printing Office, 1918.

———. *Manual for Army Cooks.* Washington, DC: Government Printing Office, 1916.

———. *A Manual for Courts-Martial, Corrected to April 15, 1917.* Washington, DC: Government Printing Office, 1917.

———. *Manual for Noncommissioned Officers and Privates of Infantry.* Washington, DC: Government Printing Office, 1917.

———. *Manual of Physical Training.* Washington, DC: Government Printing Office, 1914.

———. *Memorandum on Gas Poisoning in Warfare with Notes on Its Pathology and Treatment.* Washington, DC: Government Printing Office, 1917.

———. *Military Justice during the War: A Letter from the Judge Adjutant General to the Secretary of War.* Washington, DC: Government Printing Office, 1919.

———. *The National Defense Act Approved June 3, 1916, with Updates to June 1924.* Washington, DC: Government Printing Office, 1924.

———. *Notes on Infantry Cavalry and Field Artillery.* Washington, DC: Government Printing Office, 1917.

———. *Proceedings and Report of Special War Department Board on Courts-Martial and Their Procedure.* Washington, DC: Government Printing Office, 1919.

———. *Report of the Acting Chief of the Militia Bureau, 1916.* Washington, DC: Government Printing Office, 1916.

———. *Small Arms Firing Manual, 1913, Corrected to April, 13, 1917.* Washington, DC: Government Printing Office, 1917.

———. *Soldier's Hand Book, Revised 1913.* Washington, DC: Government Printing Office, 1913.

———. *Special Regulations No. 49: Training Camps for Reserve Officers and Candidates for Appointment As Such, May 15–August 11, 1917.* Washington, DC: Government Printing Office, May 5, 1917.

————. *Special Regulations No. 72: Allotments, Family Allowances, Compensation, and Insurance.* Washington, DC: Government Printing Office, 1918.

————. *Training Circular No. 12: Combined Training of a Division.* Washington, DC: Government Printing Office, October 10, 1918.

————. *United States Army Regulations, 1913, with Corrections to April 15, 1917.* Washington, DC: Government Printing Office, 1917.

————. *War Department Annual Report.* Washington, DC: Government Printing Office, 1914–1921.

U.S. National Guard Bureau. *Report on Mobilization of the Organized Militia and National Guard of the United States 1916.* Washington, DC: Government Printing Office, 1916.

Viereck, George, ed. *As They Saw Us: Foch, Ludendorff and Other Leaders Write Our War History.* New York: Doubleday, Doran, 1929.

Walker, George. *Venereal Disease in the American Expeditionary Forces.* Baltimore: Medical Standard Book, 1922.

Walters, Raymond, et al. *F.A.C.O.T.S.: The Story of the Field Artillery Central Officers' Training School, Camp Zachary Taylor, Kentucky.* New York: Knickerbocker Press, 1919.

Ward, Frank H., ed. *Camp Sherman Souvenir.* Cincinnati: Lambertson, 1918.

War Department and American Social Hygiene Association. *Keeping Fit to Fight.* New York: American Social Hygiene Association, circa 1918.

War Diary of Base Hospital No. 52. Unit published, 1919.

War Veteran's Association. *History of Company "E," 107th Infantry.* New York: privately published, 1920.

Westover, Wendell. *Suicide Battalions.* New York: G. P. Putnam's Sons, 1929.

White, Elizabeth Brett. *American Opinion of France.* New York: Alfred A. Knopf, 1927.

Wilhelm, Carl, et al. *Pass in Review: The Book of the Fourth Officers' Training School, Camp Dodge, Iowa, 1918.* Camp Dodge: privately published, 1918.

Williams, Ashby. *Experiences of the Great War.* Roanoke: Stone Printing, 1919.

Williams, Charles. *Sidelights on Negro Soldiers.* Boston: B. J. Brimmer, 1923.

Williams, Wythe. *Passed By the Censor.* New York: E. P. Dutton, 1916.

Wright, William. *Meuse-Argonne Diary: A Division Commander in World War.* Columbia: University of Missouri Press, 2004.

Yerkes, Robert M. "Psychological Examining in the United States Army." In *Memoirs of the National Academy of Sciences*, vol. 15. Washington, DC: Government Printing Office, 1921.

Yoakum, Clarence, and Robert Yerkes. *Army Mental Tests.* New York: Henry Holt, 1920.

York, Alvin C. *Sergeant York: His Own Life Story and War Diary.* Edited by Tom Skeyhill. New York: Doubleday, Doran, 1928.

SECONDARY SOURCES

Allen, H. C. *Great Britain and the United States.* New York: Archon Books, 1969.

American Battle Monuments Commission. *American Armies and Battlefields in Europe.* Washington, DC: Government Printing Office, 1938.

Anderson, Maxwell, and Lawrence Stallings. *What Price Glory?* (1924). In *Twenty-Five Best Plays of the Modern American Theatre,* edited by John Gassner. New York: Crown, 1952.

Anderson, William. "Devil Dogs in Olive Drab: The 2nd Engineers at Belleau Wood." *Army History* 58 (Spring 2003).

Aptheker, Herbert. *A Documentary History of the Negro People in the United States.* Vol. 3, *From the N.A.A.C.P. to the New Deal.* New York: Citadel Press, 1993.

Armstrong, David. *Bullets and Bureaucrats: The Machine Gun and the United States Army.* Westport, CT: Greenwood Press, 1982.

Ashworth, Tony. *Trench Warfare, 1914–1918: The Live and Let Live System.* London: Macmillan, 1980.

Barbeau, Arthur F., and Florette Henri, *The Unknown Soldiers: Black American Troops in World War I.* Philadelphia: Temple University Press, 1974.

Baynes, John. *Morale: A Study of Men and Courage: The Second Scottish Rifles at the Battle of Neuve Chappelle, 1915.* New York: Frederick A. Praeger, 1967.

Berry, Henry. *Make the Kaiser Dance.* New York: Doubleday, 1978.

Blumenson, Martin. *The Patton Papers.* 2 Vols. Boston: Houghton Mifflin, 1972.

Blumenthal, Henry. *Illusions and Reality in Franco-American Diplomacy.* Baton Rouge: Louisiana State University Press, 1986.

Braim, Paul F. *The Test of Battle.* 2nd ed. Shippensburg: White Mane, 1998.

Brands, H. W. *TR: The Last Romantic.* New York: Basic Books, 1997.

Brinton, Crane. *The Americans and the French.* Cambridge, MA: Harvard University Press, 1968.

Bristow, Nancy K. *Making Men Moral: Social Engineering during the Great War.* New York: New York University Press, 1996.

Britten, Thomas A. *American Indians in World War I: At War and at Home.* Albuquerque: University of New Mexico Press, 1997.

Bruce, Robert. *A Fraternity in Arms: America & France in the Great War.* Lawrence: University Press of Kansas, 2003.

Budreau, Lisa. *Bodies of War.* New York: New York University Press, 2010.

Byerly, Carol R. *The Fever of War: The Influenza Epidemic in the U.S. Army during World War I.* New York: New York University Press, 2005.

Canfield, Bruce. *U.S. Infantry Weapons of the First World War.* Lincoln, RI: Andrew Mowbray, 2000.

Chaikin, William. "Quartermaster Supply in the AEF, 1917–1918." www.qmfound. com/supply_aef.htm.

Chambers, John W. *To Raise an Army.* New York: Free Press, 1987.

Christian, Garna L. *Black Soldiers in Jim Crow Texas, 1899–1917*. College Station: Texas A&M Press, 1995.

Clifford, John G. *The Citizen Soldiers*. Lexington: University of Kentucky Press, 1972.

Cochran, Rexmond C. *Gas Warfare in World War I*. Washington, DC: U.S. Army Chemical Corps Historical Office, 1957.

Coffman, Edward M. *The Hilt of the Sword: The Career of Peyton C. March*. Madison: University of Wisconsin Press, 1966.

———. *The Old Army*. New York: Oxford University Press, 1986.

———. *The Regulars: The American Army, 1898–1941*. Cambridge: Belknap Press of Harvard University Press, 2004.

———. *The War to End All Wars*. Madison: University of Wisconsin Press, 1968.

Cooke, James J. *Pershing and His Generals*. Westport, CT: Praeger, 1997.

Cooper, Jerry. *The Rise of the National Guard: The Evolution of the American Militia, 1865–1920*. Lincoln: University of Nebraska Press, 1997.

Cornebise, Alfred. *The Amaroc News*. Carbondale: Southern Illinois University Press, 1981.

———. *Soldier-Scholars: Higher Education in the AEF*. Philadelphia: American Philosophical Society, 1997.

———. *The Stars and Stripes: Doughboy Journalism in the World War*. Westport, CT: Greenwood Press, 1984.

Davis, Henry B. *Generals in Khaki*. Raleigh, NC: Pentland Press, 1998.

Demaison, Gerard, and Yves Buffetaut. *Honor Bound: The Chauchat Machine Rifle*. Ontario: Collector Grade Publications, 1996.

Dimbley, David, and David Reynolds. *An Ocean Apart*. New York: Random House, 1988.

Duroselle, Jean-Baptiste. *France and the United States: From the Beginnings to the Present*. Translated by Dereck Coltman. Chicago: University of Chicago Press, 1978.

Farwell, Byron. *Over There: The United States in the Great War, 1917–1918*. New York: W. W. Norton, 1999.

Faulkner, Richard S. "Disappearing Doughboys: The American Expeditionary Forces Straggler Crisis in the Meuse Argonne." *Army History* 83 (Spring 2012).

———. "A Georgian in the Argonne: Seeking Redemption on Corney Ridge." *Georgia Historical Quarterly* 95, no. 1 (Spring 2011).

———. "'Gone Blooey' Pershing's System for Addressing Officer Incompetency and Inefficiency." *Army History* 95 (Spring 2015).

———. "Our Patriotic Duty at Home and Abroad: The University of Georgia in World War I." *Georgia Historical Quarterly* 79, no. 4 (Winter 1995).

———. *The School of Hard Knocks: Combat Leadership in the American Expeditionary Forces*. College Station: Texas A&M Press, 2012.

———. "Up in the Argonne: The Tragedy of Lieutenant Justus Owens and the 82nd

Division in the First World War." *Georgia Historical Quarterly* 80, no. 2 (Summer 1996).

Ferrell, Robert H. *America's Deadliest Battle: Meuse-Argonne, 1918.* Lawrence: University Press of Kansas, 2007.

———. *Collapse in the Meuse-Argonne: The Failure of the Missouri-Kansas Division.* Columbia: University of Missouri Press, 2004.

———. *Five Days in October: The Lost Battalion of World War I.* Columbia: University of Missouri Press, 2005.

———. *Unjustly Dishonored: An African American Division in World War I.* Columbia: University of Missouri Press, 2011.

Finnegan, John P. *Against the Specter of a Dragon: The Campaign for Military Preparedness.* Westport, CT: Greenwood Press, 1974.

Fisher, Ernest, Jr. *Guardians of the Republic: A History of the Noncommisioned Officer Corps of the U.S. Army.* New York: Ballantine, 1994.

Fisher, John C., and Carol Fisher. *Food in the American Military: A History.* Jefferson: McFarland, 2011.

Foner, Jack. *The United States Soldier between Two Wars.* New York: Humanities Press, 1970.

Ford, Nancy Gentile. *Americans All: Foreign Born Soldiers in World War I.* College Station: Texas A&M Press, 2001.

Genthe, Charles V. *American War Narratives, 1917–1918.* New York: David Lewis, 1969.

Gibson, Craig. *Behind the Front: British Soldiers and French Civilians, 1914–1918.* Cambridge: Cambridge University Press, 2014.

Gilchrist, H. L. *A Comparative Study of World War Casualties from Gas and Other Weapons.* Washington, DC: Government Printing Office, 1928.

Graff, Alan D. *Blood in the Argonne.* Norman: University of Oklahoma Press, 2005.

Grotelueschen, Mark E. *The AEF Way of War.* New York: Cambridge University Press, 2007.

———. *Doctrine under Fire: American Artillery Employment in World War I.* Westport, CT: Greenwood Press, 2001.

Gutiérrez, Edward A. *Doughboys on the Great War.* Lawrence: University Press of Kansas, 2014.

Hallas, James. *Doughboy War.* Boulder: Lynne Rienner, 2000.

———. *Squandered Victory: The American First Army at St. Mihiel.* Westport, CT: Praeger, 1995.

Hamburger, Kenneth E. *CMH Publication 24–1: Learning Lessons in the American Expeditionary Forces.* Washington, DC: Government Printing Office, 1997.

Harries, Meirion, and Susie Harries. *The Last Days of Innocence: America At War, 1917–1918.* New York: Random House, 1997.

Harris, Stephen L. *Duffy's War.* Washington, DC: Brassey's, 2006.

———. *Duty, Honor, Privilege.* Washington, DC: Brassey's, 2001.

Heller, Charles. *Leavenworth Papers No. 10, Chemical Warfare in World War I: The American Experience, 1917–1918*. Fort Leavenworth: Combat Studies Institute, 1984.

Henderson, William H. *Cohesion: The Human Element in Combat*. Washington, DC: National Defense University Press, 1985.

Howard, Michael. "Men against Fire: The Doctrine of the Offensive in 1914." In *Makers of Modern Strategy*, edited by Peter Paret. Princeton: Princeton University Press, 1986.

Infantry Journal. *Infantry in Battle*. Washington, DC: Infantry Journal, 1939.

James, D. Clayton. *The Years of MacArthur*. Vol. 1, *1880–1941*. Boston: Houghton Mifflin, 1970.

Johnson, Douglas V., and Rolfe L. Hillman. *Soissons 1918*. Austin: Texas A&M Press, 1999.

Johnson, George, and Hans B. Lockhoven. *International Armament*. Vol. 1. Cologne, Germany: International Small Arms Publishers, 1965.

Johnson, Thomas M., and Fletcher Pratt. *The Lost Battalion*. Indianapolis: Bobbs-Merrill, 1936.

Keene, Jennifer D. *Doughboys, the Great War, and the Remaking Of America*. Baltimore: Johns Hopkins University Press, 2001.

Kennedy, David M. *Over Here*. New York: Oxford University Press, 1980.

Kennett, Lee. "The AEF through French Eyes." *Military Review* 52, no. 11 (November 1972).

Kingsbury, Celia M. *For Home and Country: World War I Propaganda on the Home Front*. Lincoln: University of Nebraska Press, 2010.

Koehler, Franz A. *Special Rations for the Armed Forces, 1946–53*. QMC Historical Studies, series 2, no. 6. Washington, DC: Historical Branch, Office of the Quartermaster General, 1958.

Krouse, Susan. *North American Indians in the Great War*. Lincoln: University of Nebraska Press, 2007.

Lengle, Edward G. *A Companion to the Meuse Argonne Campaign*. Chichester, UK: Wiley-Blackwell, 2014.

———. *Thunder and Flames*. Lawrence: University Press of Kansas, 2015.

———. *To Conquer Hell*. New York: Henry Holt, 2008.

Lenney, John J. *Rankers*. New York: Greenberg, 1950.

Lerwill, Leonard L., ed. *The Personnel Replacement System in the United States Army*. Washington, DC: Government Printing Office, 1954.

Lighter, Jonathan. "The Slang of the American Expeditionary Forces in Europe, 1917–1919." *American Speech* 47, nos. 1/2 (Spring-Summer 1972).

Linderman, Gerald F. *Embattled Courage*. New York: Free Press, 1987.

Lunn, Joe. "Male Identity and Martial Codes of Honor: A Comparison of the War Memoirs of Robert Graves, Ernst Junger, and Kande Kamara." *Journal of Military History* 69, no. 3 (July 2005).

Lupfer, Timothy. *The Dynamics of Doctrine: The Changes in German Tactical Doctrine during the First World War.* Fort Leavenworth: Combat Studies Institute, 1981.

MacLean, Nancy, *Behind the Mask of Chivalry: The Making of the Second Ku Klux Klan.* New York: Oxford University Press, 1994.

Mahon, John K. *History of the National Guard and Militia.* New York: MacMillan, 1983.

Marshall, S. L. A. *Men against Fire.* Glouchester, MA: Peter Smith, 1978.

Mathews, Matt. *The U.S. Army on the Mexican Border: A Historical Perspective.* Fort Leavenworth: Combat Studies Institute, 2007.

McGrath, John J. *The Other End of the Spear: The Tooth-to-Tail Ratio (T3R) in Modern Military Operations.* Fort Leavenworth: Combat Studies Institute, 2007.

McPherson, James M. *For Cause and Comrades.* New York: Oxford University Press, 1997.

Meigs, Mark. *Optimism at Armageddon: Voices of American Participants in the First World War.* New York: Palgrave MacMillan, 1997.

Men of Bronze. Produced by William Miles and Killian Shaw. Pacific Arts Video.

Miller, Nathan. *Theodore Roosevelt: A Life.* New York: William Morrow, 1992.

Millett, Allan R. *The General: Robert L. Bullard and Officership in the United States Army, 1881–1925.* Westport, CT: Greenwood Press, 1975.

Millett, Allan R., and Williamson Murray, eds. *Military Effectiveness.* Vol. 1, *The First World War.* Boston: Allen and Unwin, 1988.

Mitchell, Reid. "Soldiering, Manhood, and Coming of Age: A Northern Volunteer." In *Divided Houses: Gender and the Civil War,* edited by Catherine Clinton and Nina Silber. New York: Oxford University Press, 1992.

———. *The Vacant Chair.* New York: Oxford University Press, 1993.

Lord Moran (Charles Wilson). *Anatomy of Courage.* London: Constable, 1945.

Murray, Williamson, and MacGregor Knox, eds. *The Dynamics of Military Revolution.* New York: Cambridge University Press, 2001.

Neiberg, Michael S. *Making Citizen Soldiers: ROTC and the Ideology of American Military Service.* Cambridge, MA: Harvard University Press, 2000.

Nell, John W. *The Lost Battalion: A Private's Story.* San Antonio: Historical Publishing Network, 2001.

Nenninger, Timothy K. "The Army Enters the Twentieth Century." In *Against All Enemies,* edited by Kenneth Hagen and William Roberts. Westport, CT: Greenwood, 1986.

———. "John J. Pershing and the Relief for Cause in the American Expeditionary Forces, 1917–1918." *Army History,* Spring 2005, 20–32.

———. "Tactical Dysfunction in the AEF, 1917–1918." *Military Review* 51 (October 1987).

Nosworthy, Brent. *The Bloody Crucible of Courage: Fighting Methods and Combat Experience in the Civil War.* New York: Carroll & Graf, 2003.

O'Brien, Michael. *The Idea of the American South, 1920–1941.* Baltimore: Johns Hopkins University Press, 1979.

Owen, Peter. *To the Limits of Endurance: A Battalion of Marines in the Great War.* College Station: Texas A&M University Press, 2007.

Painter, Nell. *Standing at Armageddon.* New York: W. W. Norton, 1987.

Patton, Gerald W. *War and Race: The Black Officer in the American Military, 1915–1941.* Westport, CT: Greenwood Press, 1981.

Pearlman, Michael. *To Make Democracy Safe for America: Patricians and Preparedness in the Progressive Era.* Urbana: University of Illinois Press, 1984.

Perkins, Bradford. *The Great Rapprochement.* New York: Antheneum, 1969.

Pouge, Forrest. *George Marshall: Education of a General, 1880–1939.* New York: Viking, 1963.

———. *George Marshall: Ordeal and Hope, 1939–1942.* New York: Viking, 1963.

Rainey, James W. "Ambivalent Warfare: The Tactical Doctrine of the AEF in World War I." *Parameters* 13 (September 1983).

———. "The Questionable Training of the AEF in World War I." *Parameters* 22, no. 4 (Winter 1992–1993).

Ramíez, José. *To The Line of Fire.* College Station: Texas A&M University Press, 2009.

Reneham, Edward J. *The Lion's Pride.* New York: Oxford University Press, 1998.

Rickey, Don. *Forty Miles and Day on Beans and Hay.* Norman: University of Oklahoma Press, 1963.

Sammons, Jeffery T., and John H. Morrow, Jr. *Harlem's Rattlers and the Great War.* Lawrence: University Press of Kansas, 2014.

Sanders, M. L., and Philip M. Taylor. *British Propaganda during the First World War.* London: MacMillan, 1982.

Schneider, Dorothy, and Carl J. Schneider. *Into the Breach: American Women Overseas in World War I.* New York: Viking, 1991.

Scholz, Hermine. *Special Bibliography 20.* Vol. 1, *World War I Manuscripts: The World War I Survey.* Carlisle Barracks: U.S. Army Military History Institute, 1986.

Schroder, Hans-Jürgen, ed. *Confrontation and Cooperation: Germany and the United States in the Era of World War I.* Oxford: Berg, 1993.

Schweitzer, Richard, *The Cross and the Trench: Religious Faith and Doubt among British and American Great War Soldiers.* Westport: Praeger, 2003.

Seidule, James T. "Morale in the AEF." PhD diss., Ohio State University, 1997.

Shay, Michael. *A Grateful Heart: The History of a World War I Field Hospital.* Westport, CT: Greenwood Press, 2002.

———. *Sky Pilots: The Yankee Division Chaplains in World War I.* Columbia: University of Missouri Press, 2014.

Shephard, Ben. *A War of Nerves: Soldiers and Psychiatrists in the Twentieth Century.* Cambridge, MA: Harvard University Press, 2001.

Shils, Edward, and Morris Janowitz. "Cohesion and Disintegration in the Wehrmacht in World War II." *Public Opinion Quarterly* 12, no. 2 (Summer 1948).

Slotkin, Richard. *Lost Battalions.* New York: Henry Holt, 2005.

Smith, Leonard V. *Between Mutiny and Obedience: The Case of the French Fifth Infantry Division during World War I.* Princeton: Princeton University Press, 1994.

Smythe, Donald. *Pershing: General of the Armies.* Bloomington: Indiana University Press, 1986.

Speed, Richard B. *Prisoners, Diplomats and the Great War.* New York: Greenwood Press, 1990.

Squires, James D. *British Propaganda at Home and in the United States, 1914–1917.* Cambridge, MA: Harvard University Press, 1935.

Stallings, Laurence. *The Doughboys.* New York: Harper & Row, 1963.

Stephenson, Scott. *The Final Battle.* Cambridge: Cambridge University Press, 2009.

Stouffer, Samuel, et al. *The American Soldier.* Vol. 2, *Combat and Its Aftermath.* Princeton: Princeton University Press, 1949.

Thomas, Lowell. *Woodfill of the Regulars.* Garden City, NY: Doubleday, Doran, 1929.

Trask, David. *The AEF and Coalition Warmaking, 1917–1918.* Lawrence: University Press of Kansas, 1993.

United States Department of Commerce, Bureau of the Census. *Historical Statistics of the United States Colonial Times to 1970.* Part 1. Washington, DC: Government Printing Office, 1975.

U.S. Department of Labor. *Department of Labor Report 991: 100 Years of U.S. Consumer Spending.* Washington, DC: Government Printing Office, May 2006.

Vandiver, Frank. *Black Jack: The Life and Times of John J. Pershing.* College Station: Texas A&M Press, 1977.

Walton, Robert, ed. *Over There: European Reaction to Americans in World War I.* Itasca, IL: F. E. Peacock, 1971.

White, Lonnie J. *The 90th Division in World War I.* Manhattan, KS: Sunflower University Press, 1996.

———. *Panthers to Arrowheads: The 36th Division in World War I.* Austin: Presidial Press, 1982.

Whitehorn, Joseph. *The Inspectors General of the United States Army, 1903–1939.* Washington, DC: Government Printing Office, 1998.

Wiengartner, Steven, ed. *Cantigny at Seventy-Five: A Professional Discussion.* Wheaton, IL: Robert R. McCormick Tribune Foundation, 1993.

Wiley, Bell Irvin. *The Life of Billy Yank.* Baton Rouge: Louisiana State University Press, 1978.

———. *The Life of Johnny Reb.* 1943; New York: Doubleday, 1971.

Williams, Chad L. *Torchbearers of Democracy.* Chapel Hill: University of North Carolina Press, 2010.

Wilson, Charles R. *Baptized in Blood: The Religion of the Lost Cause, 1865–1920.* Athens: University of Georgia Press, 1980.

Wilson, Dale. *Treat 'Em Rough.* Novoto: Presidio Press, 1989.

Winter, Dennis. *Death's Men.* London: Penguin, 1978.

Yockelson, Mitchell A. *Borrowed Soldiers: Americans under British Command, 1918.* Norman: University of Oklahoma Press, 2008.

Zeiger, Susan. *Entangling Alliances: Foreign War Brides and American Soldiers in the Twentieth Century.* New York: New York University Press, 2010.

INDEX